Flower of the Desert

SUNY series in Contemporary Italian Philosophy
Silvia Benso and Brian Schroeder, editors

Flower of the Desert

Giacomo Leopardi's Poetic Ontology

Antonio Negri

Translated by Timothy S. Murphy

SUNY
PRESS

Original Italian publications, *Lenta Ginestra: Saggio su Leopardi*
© 1987 SugarCo, © 2001 Mimesis

Published by State University of New York Press, Albany

© 2015 State University of New York

For information, contact State University of New York Press, Albany, NY
www.sunypress.edu

Production, Eileen Nizer
Marketing, Anne M. Valentine

Library of Congress Cataloging-in-Publication Data

Negri, Antonio, 1933-
   [Lenta ginestra. English]
   Flower of the desert : Giacomo Leopardi's poetic ontology / Antonio Negri; translated by Timothy S. Murphy.
      pages cm. – (SUNY series in contemporary Italian philosophy)
   Includes bibliographical references and index.
   ISBN 978-1-4384-5847-2 (hardcover : alk. paper)
   ISBN 978-1-4384-5848-9 (e-book)
   1. Leopardi, Giacomo, 1798–1837–Philosophy. I. Murphy, Timothy S., 1964- translator. II. Title. III. Title: Giacomo Leopardi's poetic ontology.

PQ4710.N3913 2015
851'.7—dc23   2014045876

10 9 8 7 6 5 4 3 2 1

For Nina

❦

Contents

❦

Translator's Note and Acknowledgements

Throughout this book, Antonio Negri cites Giacomo Leopardi's works from the Sansoni edition assembled by Walter Binni and Enrico Ghidetti, *Tutte le opere* (Florence, 1976), in two volumes. Volume 2 contains the *Zibaldone* and volume 1 contains all Leopardi's other works. References to those volumes in the notes are abbreviated *TO I* and *TO II*, followed by page numbers. In addition, Negri cites Leopardi's *Canti* in the critical edition by Emilio Peruzzi (Milan: Rizzoli, 1981); references to this edition in the notes are abbreviated as Peruzzi, followed by page numbers.

Since no uniform English edition of Leopardi's works yet exists, this translation draws upon the following versions of individual works (and often modifies them in order to conform more closely to the details of Negri's interpretations):

- *The Canti*, translated by J.G. Nichols (Manchester: Carcanet, 1994) and abbreviated as Nichols.

- *The Letters of Giacomo Leopardi 1817–1837*, selected and translated by Prue Shaw (Leeds: Northern Universities Press, 1998) and abbreviated as Shaw; many of Leopardi's letters are not included in Shaw's translation and the notes reflect this.

- *The Moral Essays (Operette morali)*, translated by Patrick Creagh (New York: Columbia University Press, 1983) and abbreviated as Creagh.

- *Pensieri*, translated by W.S. Di Piero (Baton Rouge: Louisiana State University Press, 1981) and abbreviated as Di Piero.

- *The War of the Mice and the Crabs (Paralipomeni della Batracomiomachia)*, translated by Ernesto G. Caserta (Chapel Hill: North Carolina Studies in the Romance Languages and Literatures, 1976) and abbreviated as Caserta.

- *Zibaldone*, edited by Michael Caesar and Franco D'Intino (New York: Farrar Straus Giroux, 2013) and abbreviated as Caesar/D'Intino. According to the conventions of Italian Leopardi scholarship, all references to the *Zibaldone* begin with the page numbers to Leopardi's original manuscript, followed by the page numbers of *TO II* and Caesar/D'Intino.

Like all my translations, this one has taken a long time to complete, but the delay allowed me to benefit from the help of many friendly and capable people. First of all I would like to thank Toni Negri for his encouragement and support of this project and many others over the past twenty-four years. Linda Austin, Dan Cottom, Michael Hardt, and Martin Wallen read drafts of this translation, and their keen eyes saved me from many errors and embarrassments. I also owe a debt to the translators of the French edition of *Lenta ginestra*, Nathalie Gailius and Giorgio Passerone, whose work helped me to clarify Negri's syntax in numerous places. Silvia Benso and Brian Schroeder, the editors of SUNY Press's Contemporary Italian Philosophy series, remained enthusiastic about this book throughout the editorial and production processes; and Andrew Kenyon, the philosophy acquisitions editor, has been extraordinarily flexible and patient. As always, Juliana made sure that I had an ideal working environment (and that I kept at it even when the magnitude of the project daunted me), while Daisy and Emma made sure none of my reference books blew off my desk. Don't blame any of them for whatever errors or embarrassments remain.

The present translation of "The European Leopardi" was originally published in *Genre: Forms of Discourse and Culture* 33:1 (Spring 2000), pp.13–26. It is reprinted here, in revised form, by permission of the University of Oklahoma.

Translator's Introduction

Leopardi and Us

When Antonio Negri was arrested in 1979 on spurious, politically motivated charges of masterminding the kidnapping and assassination of former Italian prime minister Aldo Moro and of "armed insurrection against the powers of the state," his double career as a distinguished university professor and an intransigent political militant effectively came to an end. Although the University of Padua reluctantly kept him on the payroll for several years thereafter (at less than a third of his salary, which went to his family), and although the participants in *Autonomia operaia* [Workers' Autonomy] and other militant groups continued to look to him for analysis and inspiration, his years of shuttling back and forth between the lecture hall and the factory gates were over. He was cut off from his comrades as well as his colleagues and students, despite the fact that many of them had been imprisoned along with him on similar charges. As his own pretrial period of detention stretched from weeks to months to years, and as the political movements in which he had participated were systematically decimated by state repression, he came to the sobering realization that his work and, indeed, his very life would need a new foundation. He sought that new foundation in the study of three disparate figures who had been important to him since youth. The first of these was Baruch Spinoza, to whom Negri dedicated his first year's work while in prison; the result of that work is his celebrated book *The Savage Anomaly: The Power of Spinoza's Ethics and Politics* (1980, translated into English in 1991). The third was Job, from the Old Testament, whom Negri reads against the grain in *The Labor of Job* (1990, translated into English in 2009). The second was Giacomo Leopardi, whose materialist ontology Negri celebrates in *Lenta ginestra* (1987), the English translation of which you now hold in your hands.

Taken together, these three books constitute Negri's credo, his attempt to construct a new conceptual and affective basis for thought and militancy in the wake of his prison experience. In explicating Spinoza's radically immanent "second foundation" in the *Ethics*, Negri begins to construct his own second foundation, and he demonstrates its tremendous critical power by heretically confronting one of the central texts of orthodox Christianity, Job, in order to appropriate it as a parable of immanence, human labor, and resistance to hierarchical authority. Between those books lies *Flower of the Desert: Giacomo Leopardi's Poetic Ontology*, which is in many ways the most challenging and personal of the three.[1] It is by far the longest—at over 180,000 words, it is only a few pages shorter than Negri's longest solo work, *Insurgencies: Constituent Power and the Modern State* (1992)—and it focuses on a writer who is best known as a poet and philologist, not as a metaphysician or political philosopher. Although Negri had rarely referred to Leopardi in his previous writings, the entry in his prison diary for March 26, 1983 explains his renewed fascination:

> I spend the day studying. I am reading Leopardi. I have been working on him for a while now and he fascinates me. There are curious analogies between our personal situations—imprisonment in Recanati and the omnipresent wretchedness of the Italian provinces; also between our historical situations—the defeat of the revolution, the disaggregation and the lack in Italy of any centre of cultural production; and at the level of our metaphysical crisis—in solitude only the poetic voice makes it possible to live an ethical tragedy that is so fully under way; and all this constitutes itself into a desire for flight—this is the continuous dimension of Leopardi's poetry.[2]

A few months later, upon fleeing to France after being elected to the Italian parliament and released from prison, he contemplates publishing an edition of Leopardi's writings.[3] That project never came to fruition, but the study begun in prison grew into a massive, passionate vindication of Leopardi's revolutionary materialism as well as an announcement of Negri's own re-commitment to radical thought that appeared in the midst of the flurry of intellectual activity that defined Negri's years of Parisian exile.

Twenty-five years later, Negri would reiterate and clarify the analogies between Leopardi and himself, describing *Flower of the Desert* as

> an attempt to understand what the hell one can do when one feels so completely defeated, what ontological forces might be able to break through such a stifling, regressive, reactionary crisis—much like the one we were going through in the 1980s. I wanted to clarify what the crisis of the revolutionary project had meant for Leopardi and what it

meant for us in the 1980s. The revolution haunted Leopardi: his whole
life and his entire thought were marked indelibly by that event and by
the attempt to understand it. Leopardi is someone who never stopped
asking himself: What happened? All his works echo with that question.
In this sense, the book on Leopardi does not constitute a deviation in my
work: all my historiographical works. . .share the same concern, namely,
to assess the significance of the reply one gives to crisis, to evaluate how
one acts in the face of total defeat. All the works that I began in jail, as
well as most works that I wrote right after my time in jail, are works
of this type, namely, works that are trying hard to find out what comes
after defeat, how not to be defeated by defeat.[4]

    One important strategy that emerges from those works, including *Flower
of the Desert*, is the forging of new conceptual and political alliances to
replace those lost in the defeat. The three books of Negri's new foundation
mark the start of his systematic engagement with contemporary French
philosophy, especially the work of Michel Foucault, Gilles Deleuze, and
Félix Guattari. In his preface to *The Labor of Job*, Negri refers to this
process of transition as "washing my clothes in the Seine," which entails
"'incarnating' French theory in Italian practice and, consequently, excavating the subversive content of practice from within the theoretical ontology
of freedom" articulated by the French thinkers.[5] The books manifest this
project of excavation with varying degrees of directness—for example,
The Savage Anomaly explicitly acknowledges its debt to Deleuze's work on
Spinoza when Negri writes, "without Deleuze's work, my work would have
been impossible,"[6] while *The Labor of Job* concludes by abstractly endorsing
Foucault, Deleuze, and Guattari as theorists of subjectivity within modernity
in opposition to Jürgen Habermas.[7] *Flower of the Desert* carries out the
project of excavation and alliance-building in a very different way—by
identifying and analyzing a specifically Italian genealogy for the critique
of modernity in the figure of Giacomo Leopardi.
    Although Leopardi, who was born in 1798 and died in 1837, is a widely
studied and beloved figure in the history of Italian literature—similar in
stature to Petrarch, Ariosto, Tasso, and Manzoni, if not Dante—he is virtually unknown in the English-speaking world, despite the repeated efforts
of many translators over nearly two centuries. His *Canti* virtually define
Romantic poetry in Italy, but he also wrote bitter satirical dialogues (the
Operette morali), pessimistic aphorisms (the *Pensieri*), and incisive critical
essays on Romantic poetry, Italian morality, and other controversial topics of
his day. Perhaps his most astonishing work, however, is the 4,500-page manuscript of philological notes, draft arguments, philosophical musings, and

socio-political observations that he called the *Zibaldone*, which provides day-by-day documentation of Leopardi's intellectual and aesthetic development and ranges far beyond the formal and thematic limits of the works published in his lifetime.[8] The closest parallel to this work that would be familiar to English-speaking readers is probably Nietzsche's *Nachlass*, the immense collection of unpublished notes and drafts that formed the basis for the volume *The Will to Power*, which is currently being translated into English from the authoritative edition of Giorgio Colli and Mazzino Montinari. Indeed, in *Flower of the Desert*, Negri explicitly interprets Leopardi as a "precursor to Nietzsche"[9] by historicizing Leopardi's work between the aftermath of the French Revolution and the emergence of the nationalist movement for Italian unification, which historians call the *Risorgimento*.

Negri's reading is not strictly historicist, however, because it discovers in the relationship between Leopardi's classical philology and his post-Kantian philosophy an element that can only be called "untimely" in the Nietzschean sense: "I do not know what meaning classical studies could have for our time if they were not untimely—that is to say, acting counter to our time and thereby acting on our time and, let us hope, for the benefit of a time to come."[10] Untimeliness allows thinkers critical of their own time to step out of that time and address our time and other times to come concretely and effectively. More than anything else, Leopardi's untimeliness makes him a direct precursor to Nietzsche (as the latter acknowledged) and, as I have argued at length elsewhere,[11] allows him to function in Negri's work the way that Nietzsche functions in the work of Foucault, Deleuze, and Guattari. That is to say, it allows him to function as a direct precursor, as a thinker and stylist who attacks both Hegelian dialectics and scientific positivism in the name of a creative materialism of the body, the affects, and the imagination, and thereby offers profound lessons for anyone pursuing a comparable project today. Like Nietzsche, Leopardi constitutes an alternative to modernity within modernity, a force of rupture and recomposition—a uniquely Italian one—who is as relevant now as he was in the nineteenth century. Thus with *Flower of the Desert*, Negri does not simply adopt and apply the French thinkers' genealogy of modernity; he supplements and enriches it with the singularity of Italian Romantic poetry.

In analyzing Leopardi, Negri characteristically deploys a variant of the biographical-materialist method that he developed in his earlier studies in the history of philosophy.[12] He moves freely among the disparate sources, genres, and consequences of Leopardi's writing at every stage, situating them against the backdrop of the Napoleonic restoration that followed the French Revolution and the spectrum of reactionary, liberal, and progressive political projects that proliferated throughout that period in Italy and across

Europe. He explicates Leopardi's growing resistance to transcendental idealism—with its emphasis on legislative reason's power to resolve antagonisms into abstract syntheses—and his slow development of a sophisticated poetic materialism focused on the constructive power of the imagination and its "true illusions." Pierre Macherey has argued that much of the force of Negri's reading of Spinoza comes from the way in which Negri identifies with Spinoza and "becom[es] a sort of double of Spinoza whenever he writes about him."[13] A similar identification marks Negri's readings of Marx, Lenin, and Leopardi as well. The method of identification allows Negri to bring Leopardi's struggles to life, to reactivate his untimeliness, and reveal him as our contemporary. As with his readings of Spinoza, Marx, and Lenin, this identification with Leopardi allows Negri to go beyond the letter of his subject's incomplete or inconsistent texts and extrapolate lines of argument and even conclusions that exceed the available evidence (see the opening section of chapter 5).[14] In his political writings of the 1960s and 1970s, Negri called this logic of extrapolation "the method of the tendency," and grounded it in Marx's analysis of the process of capitalist subsumption of prior modes of production.[15] In his most recent writings on Empire, the multitude, and the common, that method permits him and Michael Hardt to distinguish emergent, growing forms of social control and contestation from residual or declining ones. In the case of *Flower of the Desert*, Negri's willingness to go beyond the documentary evidence in order to reveal a European, materialist, collectivist, revolutionary Leopardi may have contributed to the chilly reception the book received among Italian scholars of Leopardi's work who have tended to present the poet as a provincial, unworldly, individualistic, proto-liberal, or proto-progressive figure.[16] Perhaps in an effort to demonstrate his familiarity with the tradition of Leopardi studies and thereby forestall the dismissal of his work as that of a non-specialist, Negri has laden his text with extensive references to that tradition—the notes make up more than a quarter of the book's overall bulk, far more than in any other of his books. If that was his intent, we must acknowledge that it did not work. *Flower of the Desert* has not been a major influence on the development of Leopardi studies in Italy over the past quarter century, but it is an important step in the development of Negri's own philosophy. The book's historical analysis of Romanticism as the prefiguration, in a period of formal subsumption, of the characteristics of postmodernism that derive from the real subsumption of society by capital, led directly to the elaboration of the theory of Empire as the political constitution of the postmodern period. Likewise, the book's articulation of a materialist ontology—focused on the capacity of poetry to construct new being at the edge of existing being—constitutes the first formulation of the challenging and sophisticated ontology that Negri theorizes (in Wittgensteinian numbered propositions) in "Kairòs, Alma Venus, Multitudo," written during his second sojourn in prison at the end of the last century.[17]

But its value as a precursor to more recent and familiar arguments should not obscure the singular value of *Flower of the Desert* itself. First of all, it stands as Negri's only extended work of literary theory and criticism, although the claims it makes about literature are dependent upon and hence subordinate to its metaphysical and political claims. Second, in aiming to reclaim Leopardi for materialist philosophy and revolutionary politics, it both renews the older tradition of Leopardi studies undertaken by internationally influential philosophers such as Benedetto Croce and Cesare Luporini, and at the same time refutes that tradition's idealist and conservative orthodoxies. Third, it brings the Spinozian second foundation of Negri's thought into the post-Kantian era and strengthens it to confront the present with its own untimely power. The strength and passion of that ongoing confrontation with the present are evident on every page of *Flower of the Desert*, so perhaps it is not unreasonable to hope that the appearance of this book in English, along with the recent publication of the *Zibaldone* in English translation, might finally persuade English-speaking readers to engage with and appreciate Leopardi's works as those works have always deserved.

Notes

1. The original Italian title, *Lenta ginestra*, literally "gentle broom," is an allusion to the last stanza of Leopardi's poetic testament, *La ginestra, o il fiore del deserto* [*The Broom, or The Flower of the Desert*], which Negri explicates in the final chapter. For the English edition the title was changed, with Negri's approval, because most English readers would recognize neither the allusion to Leopardi's poem nor the botanical meaning of "broom."

2. Antonio Negri, *Diary of an Escape*, trans. Ed Emery (Cambridge: Polity Press, 2010), p. 25. References in *Letters 10* and *15* of *Pipeline: Letters from Prison*, trans. Ed Emery (Cambridge: Polity Press, 2014) indicate that Negri had been working on Leopardi since at least January 1982. For a more detailed chronology of Negri's prison experience from 1979 to 1983, see my introduction to *Pipeline*.

3. Ibid., p. 232.

4. Negri responding to Cesare Casarino in *In Praise of the Common: A Conversation on Philosophy and Politics* (Minneapolis: University of Minnesota Press, 2008), pp. 169–70.

5. Negri, *The Labor of Job*, trans. Matteo Mandarini (Durham: Duke University Press, 2009), pp. xxii–xxiii.

6. Negri, *The Savage Anomaly*, trans. Michael Hardt (Minneapolis: University of Minnesota Press, 1991), p. 267n4.

7. Negri, *The Labor of Job*, op. cit., p. 107.

8. All the works mentioned are available in the English translations cited in the Translator's Note and Acknowledgements and/or in the endnotes to the translation itself. With the publication of Michael Caesar and Franco D'Intino's English edition of the *Zibaldone* in 2013, for the very first time all of Leopardi's major works are available to English-speaking readers.

9. Negri, *The Labor of Job*, op. cit., p. xviii.

10. Friedrich Nietzsche, *Untimely Meditations*, trans. R.J. Hollingdale (Cambridge: Cambridge University Press, 1983), p. 60.

11. See T.S. Murphy, *Antonio Negri: Modernity and the Multitude* (Cambridge: Polity Press, 2012), pp. 133–46.

12. See Matteo Mandarini and Alberto Toscano, "Antonio Negri and the Antimonies of Bourgeois Thought," translators' introduction to Negri, *Political Descartes: Reason, Ideology and the Bourgeois Project* (New York: Verso, 2007), pp. 1–4.

13. Pierre Macherey, "Negri's Untimely Spinoza," trans. T.S. Murphy, in *Genre: Forms of Discourse and Culture* 46:2 (summer 2013), p. 146.

14. See also Negri, "*Reliqua desiderantur*: a conjecture for a definition of the concept of democracy in the final Spinoza," in *Subversive Spinoza: (Un) Contemporary Variations*, trans. T.S. Murphy et al. (Manchester: Manchester University Press, 2004), pp. 28–58; *Marx Beyond Marx: Lessons on the Grundrisse*, trans. Harry Cleaver et al. (Brooklyn: Autonomedia, 1991); and *Factory of Strategy: 33 Lessons on Lenin*, trans. Arianna Bove (New York: Columbia University Press, 2014).

15. See Negri, *Books for Burning: Between Civil War and Democracy in 1970s Italy*, trans. T.S. Murphy et al. (New York: Verso, 2005), pp. 27–29.

16. English-speaking Leopardi scholars have tended to follow the lead of their Italian colleagues; but a few, such as Giovanni Carsaniga, have anticipated aspects of Negri's argument by denouncing the "long and painstaking process of obscuring the revolutionary contents of Leopardi's thought, of denying the philosophical validity of his speculation, of reducing him to the status of a mere lyrical poet (even if the greatest lyrical poet of the age), of misrepresenting his convictions. . . . [This] neutralization was to continue for over a century after his death." (Carsaniga, *Leopardi: The Unheeded Voice* [Edinburgh: Edinburgh University Press, 1977], p. 121).

17. Negri, "Kairòs, Alma Venus, Multitudo," in *Time for Revolution*, trans. Matteo Mandarini (New York: Continuum, 2003). For a more thorough and detailed account of Negri's imprisonment, trial, release, and exile, see my introduction to *Books for Burning*, op. cit., pp. x–xxviii.

Preface to the French Translation (2006)

Is it possible to develop a discourse that would be simultaneously philosophical, poetic, and political about an author of Leopardi's stature? Is it possible to engage in a reading that would make the paradoxical encounter between philological and philosophical critique into the line of a political interpretation of the poet Leopardi? Such is the objective pursued in this book.

This book was born in unusual circumstances. I began to reread Leopardi (a favorite author during my adolescence) in prison. This reading compelled me, not merely ironically, to confront an analogous situation of theoretical solitude and political defeat. At the same time as I was reading Leopardi, I was also reading the Book of Job. Yet neither of these texts drove me to pessimistic conclusions regarding solitude and defeat. Why? The Book of Job, that formidable mixture of myth and theology, is traversed by an immanent urgency and a perception of eternity that shattered every catastrophist and/or eschatological determination: in pain and solitude, Job 'saw' and thus reappropriated his God. In the enormous *Zibaldone* wherein he expressed his thought, occasionally interrupted and illuminated by prodigious poetic set pieces, Leopardi constructed a philosophical and political discourse that is entirely open to time-to-come [*l'à-venir*]. Wherever pain and solitude become the real conditions of life, it is possible to open up a space of hope, to invent an active disutopia, and glimpse a constitutive praxis of a new world: in this way, Leopardi reappropriated his God. This reading of Leopardi helped me resist. But is it true, is it adequate to the reality in which his poetry moved?

Upon my release from prison, at the beginning of a long exile in France and in the midst of the crisis that touched all of us in the middle of the eighties, I had the opportunity to confront this intuition of reading with a study of the extensive critical literature produced about Leopardi. It was a matter of passing through it without becoming its prisoner. The non-academic situation in which this research had developed helped me bring this labor to its conclusion. This passage was shaped not only by a political

passion in the process of being reborn, in the sadness of the historical condition of that era (the eighties), but also by a confidence in the possibility of
overturning the interpretations proposed by the positivist and/or idealist
schools of the 'consumptive poet' by means of an answer to a series of
questions posed to me by the present. As Auerbach taught us for literature,
and Deleuze for philosophy, only an interrogation brought to bear on the
present opens up a schema of interpretation capable of traversing the reality
of *poiesis*—be it poetic or philosophical—without dissipating its historical
quality but rather recapturing it, in the will to make the truth, constructive power [*puissance*]. The attempt seems to have succeeded: discovering
Leopardi's truth presupposed restoring him to the present. And in fact,
Leopardi himself prompted this restoration.

First of all, I discovered his rupture with Italian literary and philosophical
tradition, contested here (in the first phase of his thought and poetry) from
a resolutely materialist point of view. The Enlightenment came to Italy
belatedly but powerfully [*puissamment*], no longer characterized by a
reformist wave derived from the eighteenth century, but with the force of a
materialist and revolutionary riposte to the crisis of the French Revolution.
In the second place, I found in Leopardi a progressive reconciliation with
Romantic thought, not in the mode of repetition but that of surmounting
[*dépassement*]—in any case, of displacement: the history and problematics
of an Italian rebirth and the necessity of reassembling a cultural centrality
for the country were not developed in dialectical terms but opened onto the
horizon of a constitutive practice. This superiority of praxis, this active hope
shattered any possibility of mediation with the past. Leopardi's so-called
pessimism constituted a realist terrain without flourishes or illusions. The
criticism (the part of it that runs from Nietzsche to Luporini) knew how to
grasp the crucial rupture of the dialectic that he carried out. But this was
not enough.

This rupture, this surmounting of the dialectic, opens—under the
impulse of praxis—onto the experience of the imagination, an imagination
that constructs new worlds. In reinterpreting the Enlightenment thinkers
and passing beyond the dialectic, Leopardi's materialism offered a mobile
horizon, an alternative to the modern at the heart of the crisis of the modern.
As always, they tried to silence this incredibly powerful voice. Croce called
him the "hunch-backed poet," just as Hegel had characterized Spinoza as
the "consumptive philosopher." A strange comparison? Not so if we imagine
that just as Spinoza undertook it at the moment of emergence of the modern
age, so Leopardi, at the start of its decline, articulated an 'other' hypothesis
of modernity and the imagination of a life freed from the wretchedness of
domination, one capable of love.

That is the reason this research helped me. In rereading Leopardi during the eighties, the years of the worst restoration after the crisis of 1968 and as we were plunging into the crisis of real socialism, this reading allowed me to reconstruct the stages of a philosophical and political discourse that proposed a project of transformation, beyond every illusion but with the capacity to imagine a new subjectivity and new heavens. I do not believe that this experience was mine alone or that it was a matter of individual experience. It is certainly singular, but by virtue of this singularity it is multiple. It involves not only Leopardi's experience, but refers to all periods of crisis in modernity: it concerns the Italian situation as well as the French, the European as well as the American. Leopardi's discourse is extremely potent [*puissant*]. In *The Broom*, his last great poem, Leopardi clearly expresses the project of "making the multitude," the conception of a resistance to domination in the form of a movement of recomposition of singularities. It is not merely a matter of folding poetry into ethics but of inventing new figures of freedom. Today this is our task.

For all these reasons, I view the appearance of this book in French as excellent news. I thank the friends who have undertaken, with much perseverance, to translate this difficult book. I hope that their effort will help everyone advance toward the imagination of a collective emergence from crisis and solitude.

Antonio Negri
2006

❧

Preface to the First Edition

The European Leopardi

Discussing the 1850s in his article "L'Italia fuori d'Italia [Italy outside Italy]," Franco Venturi remarks that "[t]hose were the years in which Leopardi became the symbol of Italian poetry and, in some sense, of the whole country, of an Italy cut off from its past by a historical void."[1] Sainte-Beuve had already spoken of this in 1844.[2] On the other side of the Channel, in a long text dedicated to Leopardi in March 1850, Gladstone listed among the sources of the "pathetic interest" aroused by the poet, "the misfortunes of his country, both its political and social, and its religious misfortunes." For the English politician, "the blindness of the Christian faith" that Leopardi manifested all through his life became the most painful and highest expression of the adverse destiny that struck the poet as well as his homeland.[3] In 1855, a Russian émigré, friend of Herzen, and survivor of 1848, Nicolai Ivanovich Sazonov, affirmed in the columns of the *Atheneum français* that Leopardi was "one of Italy's great poets and one of the most original thinkers that the history of philosophy offers us." Of course, "consecration by popular acclaim" had not yet come to crown his fame. But Italy was by this time mature enough to understand him and, ultimately, to appropriate him. "The Italy that accomplished the national rehabilitation [*restauration*] of science and thought, that lovingly studies its great philosopher Giordano Bruno, will not forget to raise a noble monument in its Pantheon to one of its most worthy children."[4] In the same period, Leopardi's works were translated, and he became widely known in Germany.[5]

If by the middle of the century Leopardi was well-known in Europe as the symbol of the past grandeur of Italy and its ruin, and as a sign of and a demand for its revival [*risorgimento*], this could happen on one condition: that Leopardi's thought showed a profound consonance with European thought. Leopardi was an 'Italian case,' but that case could be understood because it expressed a homogeneous passage at the European level. This has too often been forgotten by those critics who are tied to a very provincial conception of the *Risorgimento* and to a reductive national literary tradition and theory. And yet even if one remains on a strictly aesthetic terrain, it is difficult not to see that there are very potent analogies linking Leopardi's poetry to the transformative dynamics of nineteenth-century poetics—characterized in Europe by an enormous force of innovation, on an extraordinary poetic market, from Hölderlin to Rimbaud, from Romanticism to the constructivism of the century's end. All this is even more striking if we examine the problem from a philosophical point of view: we can indeed affirm, without risk of exaggeration, that in the figure of Leopardi and him alone, the Italian revival reaches the level of European metaphysics. Italian thought was cut off from European developments at the beginning of the seventeenth century: the execution of Giordano Bruno and the condemnation of Galileo represent this moment of crisis and separation. Time was withdrawn from thought and poetry.

Seventeenth-century repression isolated Italy from the political and cultural accord of Europe. Italy became a geographical notion, its cultural traditions petrified; absence of passion defined the tone of civil life. Leopardi's thought and poetry immediately make us live in another dimension: they restore time—the metaphysical time of poetry and the time of a political alternative; they make us draw a deep breath of imagination, transgression, revival. The memory of catastrophe is taken up here as a central theme in the long-lasting recollection of the Renaissance crisis—in short, as the experience of the defeat of the Enlightenment, Jacobinism, and the revolution. Confronting these historical crossroads and raising them to the level of the European sensibility of the century, accomplishing within this sensibility a process of recomposition of historical memory and its liberation toward a universal horizon: all this is what Leopardi achieves. Leopardi is thus a European case, first of all because, not content with representing Italian wretchedness at the European level, he demonstrates, from Italy, the recomposition of a culture at the European level—in any case he displays the will, the tension, and the passion that were to come. Culture rediscovers time as its own proper dimension.

Hegel writes, "It is said that everything *arises* and *passes away* in time . . . time itself is this *becoming*, arising, and passing away, it is the *abstraction* which has *being*, the Cronos which engenders all and destroys that to which it gives birth,"[6] and "the spirit of a particular people . . . is in time. . . . [I]t has, in short, a history of its own. But as a limited spirit its independence is something secondary; it passes into universal world history, the events of which exhibit the dialectic of the particular national spirits—the judgment of the world."[7] Thus in Europe, it was the dialectic that proposed time to thought as its own proper dimension. The dialectic, however, before becoming the encyclopedia of absolute spirit, was Encyclopedism, the Enlightenment, political revolution. The historical forms of the dialectic appeared before its theoretical figure. Time was imposed upon thought by practice. And this is the reason the consciousness of time—and of its crisis, of negativity, of becoming, and the rupture of becoming—could be emancipated from dialectical philosophy. The dialectical problem did not conclude in the resolving figure that philosophy and power [*potere*] raised to hegemony in the nineteenth century. And one can even say that the modern was born only when the hegemony of the dialectic was ruptured, and time was liberated from the controlling net in which German absolute idealism or the new French positivist theologies had enclosed it. The function of rupture seems to be assigned to poetry: Hölderlin intensifies this effort at the very moment the dialectical system arises, while Rimbaud dissolves every prison of time in his lyric heights. Leopardi, too, exists within this free temporal sensibility of the modern. He anticipates it, reconstructs its practical genesis, and brings its theoretical consciousness almost to maturity—all *in vitro*, in the distance between the province and the metropolis, in the separation from a "center" that he feels forming and moving always farther "toward the north." But suddenly and unexpectedly, by one of those strange relations of causality, that heteronomy of situations and ends that history has taught us to appreciate, his distant perception of the central philosophical problem, his appropriation of the temporal dimension as the axis of modern thought becomes an extraordinary critical terrain. It is not enough to reach the level at which one can grasp the fact that the dialectic restores time to thought, that Europe has experienced and is now living the real dialectic of liberation—its crisis and negativity but also the hope and the tension of recovery—that capitalism constructs new social structures. Along with the consciousness of the present, the critique of the future must be experienced. Time constrains thought to this mutability [*mobilità*]. Now, on the horizon of time, the solitary place from which Leopardi begins to regard the world opens a vast space for him. Before and after are seen and critiqued—while the present suffers in the tension imposed by this critique. Freedom and liberalism, economic initiative and capitalism, technological development and modernization: all this is not enough; he must know the ends, and he must understand that this new reality, far from stupefying us, imposes critique upon us. Time is thus taken up into philosophy as criticized [*criticato*] time. Leopardi's separation from/ in the European cultural cycle of the nineteenth century is the privileged position of critique. And if, as we have indicated and as we see better in the course of our work, Leopardi is assuredly not the only one to develop this critique in the period preceding the revolutions of mid-century, during the European *Vormärz*—if other currents of thought from Schopenhauer and the Hegelian left to Nietzsche and Burckhardt were and will be present on this terrain—nevertheless Leopardi's distance, arising from a faraway Italian culture that took the measure of the crisis several centuries before, creates a transgressive effect, a radicality of judgment, and a tension of the project that make Leopardi's historical situation extraordinary. Leopardi is born at the level of European metaphysics: moreover, the path that leads him there and the violence of this relation exalt as exceptional the critical function of which he is the interpreter.

Thus, the European Leopardi. His memory is European and the time that he grasps is that which governs the whole historical cycle of the Enlightenment, the revolution, and the restoration. The intersection of several living currents of thought gives rise to the originality of Leopardi's approach—first of all a materialist approach, because it is on this terrain that the consciousness of time refuses to sanctify the present and hence becomes critical. If the dialectic placed time at the center of thought, the critique of time could only be anti-dialectical, materialist. This is the second paradox that Leopardi immediately displays—thereby manifesting the radicality of his approach to the European metaphysical thematic as well as the force of his critique. Along with the limited but convergent lessons of direct historical experience, three lines of thought come together to constitute Leopardi's materialism.

First of all, there is the sensualism and materialism of the Enlightenment, in the full complexity of dimensions and scenarios that they develop—from the empiricist-philosophical attitude to linguistic constructivism, from physical atomism to the metaphysical imagination. Second, there is the Italian philosophical and poetic tradition: the Renaissance humanist tradition that saw humankind constructing history and history, for better and for worse, made significant by human action. In Leopardi this humanist ontology continually encounters and clashes with Enlightenment materialism. The form in which materialism and humanism confront each other, therefore, is tragic. A very strong antagonism runs through this encounter. This is a moment of the highest theoretical originality in Leopardi's thought. Here all the stakes become clear. And just as in the then-most-recent historical experience, the revolution exchanged claims of right for terror, cosmopolitanism for the revival of national sentiment, and universalism for humanism, so in historical memory the dialectic of time reveals the ontological emergence of difference. The synthesis of past and present, a synthesis that reconciliatory thought defines as dialectical, is not possible in Leopardi. The relationship to Enlightenment materialism unbalances the dialectical design and shatters its ontology. The sense of the determination is not forced to rely on the perspective of sublation [*superamento*]. In Hegel, on the other hand, the dialectic is an absolute and, as Eugenio Garin notes,

> temporality is burned out: the relationship between before and after is reduced to a pure link of premise to conclusion, the future is completely preconstituted and loses all unpredictability, while the present is emptied

of all multiplicity, choice and freedom. . . . [I]n sum, if history is this
mutability of temporal life, in Hegel history is burned out.[8]

In Leopardi therefore life and consciousness and poetry are given as
openings of experience to always-new determinations, openings of the intelligence to the continuous process of imagination. The infinite is never actual
[*attuale*]; nor is it ever concluded. And even if it were, for example in the
form of nothingness [*nulla*], human passions would shatter its solidity. Pain
and desire are opposed to "solid nothingness"—they demand no absoluteness against "*progress to infinity . . . a contradiction* which is not resolved
but is always only enunciated as *present*," against "the perpetual repetition
of one and the same content, one and the same tedious *alternation* of this
finite and infinite."[9] No, there is no demand for absoluteness. However, the
infinite remains infinite in Leopardi—an infinity of the determinations
and essences of the imaginary. The dialectic thus does not achieve closure.
Leopardi experiences the genesis of the contemporary problematic, or rather
he grasps the problem of classical German philosophy in its genesis. He
proposes constructive alternatives to transcendental subjectivity, under the
rubrics of naturalism and materialism. He defines transcendental constructiveness in order to subject it to the clash with an irreducible real. He sees
the transcendental imagination deployed in an incomplete manner—and
nurtures in this incompleteness his materialist hope. In other words, Leopardi
considered in advance all the aporias, difficulties, and crises of the dialectic
in the immediacy of their appearance, in their necessity: such is the terrain
on which his thought is put to the test. Critique thus yields to materialism. In
consequence, materialism is raised to the level of critique. This relationship
between the humanist tradition and Enlightenment materialism is deployed in
a critical or post-critical form. There is no way to bring to closure the crisis
produced by the revolution; or rather there is only one way, and that is to
grasp, beyond any sort of synthesis, exactly what it is that the revolution, its
developments and variants proposed to us in a vision that is as disenchanted
as it is potent. This means grasping the world that was constructed during
the revolution and that still struggles today in crisis, the transcendental of a
defeated revolution, as the only given reality—but it is not one to be enjoyed;
rather it is an intolerable one. The imagination thus traverses this world,
accepts its conditions and weight—and when it detaches itself from the world
and rises up, it is always within the determinations of this real: and yet
with what force! Memory is a prison that is traversed and broken—hence
the possibility of constructing everything. The poet walks in the dark, but
he does walk nonetheless. This is the reason Leopardi's materialism is not
ancient materialism, having no rigidity of metaphysical specifications: it is

instead a materialism that clashes directly with the dialectic and opposes to it a material, poetic, and social relationship as the key to the interpretation and transformation of the world. The sense of true being functions to continuously discriminate the real—it plays a role a bit like that of irony in Schlegel, so to speak: but it does so only when, in the latter, irony is not a way of relativizing the present in relation to the past but rather a way of completing the same operation in relation to being, to hope, to action. "Irony is the clear consciousness of eternal agility, of the infinite plenitude of chaos." In this sense, Schlegel goes on to write, "Romantic poetry is a universal progressive poetry."[10] Leopardi is progressive only in this sense—on the path opened up on the ontological terrain by the light of a disenchanted and potent reason, he discriminates and poetically recomposes the figures of true being.

Poetry is situated at the same level of reflective thought. It forms one body with thought, because only poetry can advance the knowledge [*conoscenza*] of being and organize so vigorously such a series of materialist ruptures. Poetry is the form in which materialism exalts the critical dimension that constitutes it. If it is impossible to imagine Leopardi outside of his poetry, this is because his poetry contains a knowledge [*sapere*], a complex of knowledges, a theoretical key for the construction of the world. Words and things are brought together in a poetic relation; they are rediscovered and reproduced, the totality of their dimensions determined through a constitutive process that is increasingly revealed as a veritable hermeneutic of being: poetry speaks being because it is the keystone of being, the form adequate to a dynamic and constitutive content—all this within materiality, within the world of determinations, of the 'this.' At each moment, Leopardi's poetry is like a cruise along a rocky ocean shore: the determinations, the many forms of 'this' succeed one another like reefs and shoals. Nevertheless, there is a possible trap here, and that is the possibility that poetry, in the midst of this triumph of determination, will choose to sink into the indifference of itself as production. To speak like Heidegger, if poetry "according to its innermost will . . . is metaphysical" since it is "the essential way in which beings are made to be beings,"[11] where will the determinations end up? At the very moment when critical materialism becomes radical by expressing itself as a poem, it resigns itself to flux and loses itself on an ungraspable horizon. The path that once seemed so linear now becomes confused. And yet this is the point at which Leopardi succeeds in one of the most original and complex operations of modern and contemporary philosophy: if being as such is poetic, if there is no being other than poetic being, this does not mean a loss of determinations but a discovery of differences. It is a displacement of the terrain of determination of the world of knowledge [*conoscenza*] to the ethical horizon. This choice is not Kantian, and even less is it Schopenhauerian, because even though it is displaced, the horizon remains that of the ethical determination, the 'this' of the ethical subject. Leopardi develops a veritable 'metaphysics of morals' based on this onto-logical apprehension and difficulty. He sees that ethical action constitutes the conditions of human production and reproduction, social duration and intersubjective communication, as well as the worlds of virtue and politics. But at the same time, he sees that ethical action discriminates, chooses, and separates. Life against death, joy against pain; and even if we do not succeed in making this difference that we suffer and seize in practice triumph on the terrain of history, nevertheless poetry continually reaffirms conflict, antagonism, and rupture without respite. "'There are no more Manicheans in the world,' said Candide. 'Well, here I am,' said Martin."[12]

On the basis of this critical situation, we can grasp a third characteristic of Leopardi, who has already been defined as a European and as a materi-alist poet: contemporaneity [*attualità*]. Leopardi's experience traces a totally specific path. This path leads him, across the sensualist universe, from a critique of nature to the elaboration of the concept of 'second nature.' This concept of second nature is a notion that is no longer current in contem-porary thought. We are not interested in knowing if this concept, and the universe of representation and communication that fills it, was elaborated by the philosophers of Ideology or by the Romantic poets—beyond this specific question, we are interested in grasping the general scope of this image. The world has become artificial, but this artificiality does not take away any of the world's reality. The determinations of communication cover the whole space of human interactions and grant it its only possible sense. Leopardi experiences and describes this passage—from nature to second nature—as a passage from signification to sense, from things to words, and he understands how this passage completely invests being, redefines and redetermines it. Leopardi frequents this second nature, the world of the psyche, of knowledge [*sapere*], and politics, whose dialects he translates and whose spirit he penetrates. Poetic forms multiply—Leopardi's making [*fare*] assumes an extreme mutability, by turns ironic, joyous, sarcastic, and cruel: a whole encyclopedia of the poetic spirit. The artificial universe is artfully displayed. Linguistic facts become ontological games. Here, poetry constructs a world. The materialist metaphysics of morals begins to dance. Levity and indifference continually exchange roles, but the artificiality does not take away any of the dense worldliness [*mondanità*] of the scene. This illusion is effective. The lyric Machiavelli's grand strategy begins to come forward in the definition of the scene. For this dignity, this contemporaneity, and this enormous constructiveness that participate in the metaphysical power [*potenza*] of the second nature leave things in an extremely critical situation. The world is continually being constructed but does not manage to offer proof of its own reality—a sense is imposed on the world, but we do not succeed in understanding its signification; and the seduction that connects us to this changing horizon takes away none of the perversion of the absence of value. A great historical passage is represented in this poetic scene—it describes the absorption of society by capital, that innovative catastrophe that the nineteenth century lives through to the end: it is not simply the capitalist revolution but the formation of the hegemony of capital. Leopardi's contemporaneity, therefore, consists in this: he was the first to perceive, at the level of poetry and in accordance with the rhythm of the structural gradations of the metaphysical game, this passage in the submission of society to capitalist artificiality—a powerful [*possente*] artificiality, one that is artificial solely because it is the fruit of art and not of nature, but is potent like a second nature. Leopardi describes the genesis of this process, grasps it in its formal dimension, criticizes it, and moreover follows its fantastical schemata and dynamics.

Today we are living the reality of this submission, and not just its formal dimension or possibility—the subsumption of society by capital makes up our everyday experience of the solidity of command and the impossibility of transcending it—and for this reason we feel all the more the force of Leopardi's approach. That long century that separates us from Leopardi has been a period of progressive submission of society to capital—it displays the maximum expression of unhappiness and destruction. Poetry has anticipated the real, and the real has confirmed poetry. Leopardi is contemporary [*attuale*] because he offers a critique of the process as well as an initial understanding of it. That is to say, this indifferent and compact world that he sees being constructed, which is sensed but not signifying, is what he wants to shatter. He wants to, and must, destroy all the dynamics that come to compose this figure. The event of critique is carried out when it is freed from the determinations of metaphysical subjection and made to bring forward, within these determinations, a new proposal—metaphysics must be founded on ethics. And there is no reason to reject and deride this required operation by calling it "foundationalist." For Leopardi does not want a foundation—the foundation is the ontological whole in which he is immersed; it is the game of ever-renewed natural determinations, this suffocating, demeaning material of domination. Against the foundation rise up the ethical act, the critical event, the poetic strategy. There is no foundation; there is only an incomplete, dynamic, and dramatic relation that aims to make itself a subject. Or rather, that post-critical materialism of which we have already spoken becomes an ethical subject here. It refuses to be swept away in the indifference of second nature, or in the totality of non-signifying dimensions that constitute it. It seeks being. Ontology rouses itself from artificiality. It seeks itself as subject. Again we find antagonism, Manicheanism, the poet's cry of revolt. In the force of his critical appraisal of our world, we understand the contemporaneity of Leopardi's poetry.

To this European Leopardi a desolately provincial Italian criticism responds. If Leopardi is in fact the poet of revival, he is not the poet of the *Risorgimento*, that fortuitous as well as wicked alliance of profit and rent handed down to us by history. Heroes and epigones of this *Risorgimento* felt at once Leopardi's difference: and at once, therefore, we have an interpretation that, when it encounters Leopardi—an inevitable clash—tends to limit his impact. The ethical subject of Leopardi's poetry is thus flattened onto the individual subject, and the poet's sad life is distorted into a symbol of his poetry and his metaphysics: from having a "strangled life" to being an "idyllic poet." Nor, on the other hand, have those who are opposed to this interpretation given a better characterization of the figure of Leopardi: picking up the standard that the bourgeoisie let drop and raising it toward a radiant horizon, they have transformed Leopardi into an apologist for a false sense of progress. From this point of view, Leopardi's protest is no longer a revolt against the senselessness of this process of development and the individual unhappiness that results from it, but against the historical incompleteness of this development, itself also strangled. A moralist Leopardi, a progressive Leopardi: this too is a disguise Leopardi does not want to adopt, because his thought and his poetry are revolution, pure and simple. There is no memory to defend, nor any continuity to impose.

His poetry is born of rupture. Rupture defines, characterizes, and sums up his poetic approach, a rupture that is above all interruption, transgression, violence—rupture in the strict sense. This rip [*strappo*] marks Leopardi's poetic will [*volere*], a rip that the classical elegance of his labors icily spreads throughout the poetic process. This act of contrariness [*eversione*] is essential and determinate: at this crux, dialectical synthesis and overcoming are eliminated, seen as phantasms, as simple ideal possibilities. The secret and the miracle of Leopardi's poetry consist in this as well: in knowing [*saper*] how to keep alive the violence of the approach as a radical characterization of poetic development. This is in the first place; then the discourse broadens. With respect to history, poetry displaces knowledge [*conoscenza*] and situates it on a new ontological level. Whatever is extrinsic, superficial, or artificial is then traversed and reconstructed by the poetic reading. This displacement ends in ethics: in fact, poetics, breaking through the superficiality of being, projects a veritable human constitution of the world. By participating in this constitutive flux, Leopardi's poetry poses the highest alternative to any conspiracy intended to resolve the historical process dialectically. Leopardi dislocates the real all the way to a horizon on which the world is constructed. And the relation between the gentle [*lento*] ontological movement of being and the power [*potenza*] of poetic inspiration, between the act of rupture and that of constitution, thus becomes central: between the "gentle broom [*lenta ginestra*]" and "*Begeisterung* [inspiration]." This relationship is the foundation, a completely open and tragic, precarious and constitutive foundation, and yet one defined by hope. It is a movement that sometimes seems to be pendular, but that in any case is never dialectical, because the segments of this rhythm seem to be broken up in the advances of poetic production. Poetry and metaphysics coincide, in Leopardi, with this course of being. Here poetics is so internal to ontology that the mechanisms of self-valorization manifest themselves as a natural flux: not simply a first or a second nature, but rather a third, a fourth, an *n*th nature that is consolidated from successive ruptures and hope and that comes to be determined for that 'historical animal' that is human consciousness. Thus, there is a revolutionary Leopardi—an experience of revolution that, going beyond the *Risorgimento*, situates itself within European experience, within materialist experience, within the contemporaneity of a process that liberates the whole human being. A radical, revolutionary, and collective humanism organizes Leopardi's poetry and its process: a humanism that destroys all hypocritical fables of the limits of freedom and massive progress, a humanism constituted by an antagonistic foundation and an infinite desire that produces a materialist project of solidarity.

Thus, what constitutes the contemporaneity of Leopardi's poetry is right in front of us. We must try to free it from the museum exhibit where it now lies, complacently catalogued as the result of a long labor of neutralization. We must return to the critical event, to action, to the ethical project that animates it; we must recognize its philosophical grandeur that serves as a radical alternative to the dialectical bourgeois culture of the last century. Leopardi should be celebrated in this critical work because he forced the truth of the world to the point of discovering its dynamic and vital, collective and constitutive dimension. As Giorgio Colli reminds us,

> He was able to do this because he was a man of action, like every authentic philosopher. Telling the truth was his action, a tremendously heroic action bound up with the very destiny of humankind. While his scornful and crystalline words preclude any sweetness, he offers others the chance to know [*conoscere*] life by leaping into the icy waters of a healthy reason that will shake them out of the torpor of modern narcotics. Young people already love Leopardi the poet; they will now have to honor him as a philosopher.[13]

❧

Chapter 1

The Catastrophe of Memory

··

Time of the Dialectic

September 1818: *To Italy*, Leopardi's first great canzone. A "civil Petrarchan canzone," according to the critics, that "among other things takes up the themes of a certain eloquent lyricism, that of the Scriptures, of Chiabrera, from Filicaia to Monti. . . ." Strange commentary, and for me the first lines of the canzone already raise a host of other problems.

> My native land! I see the walls, the arches,
> The columns, and the statues, and the lone
> Ancestral towers;
> But I do not see the glory. (ll.1–4)[1]

A sharp disjunction appears: "But I do not see the glory." Is this "not seeing" a symptom of the poet's internal malaise [*malessere*] or the revelation of an objective rupture of the historical horizon? In any case, Leopardi is declaring a critical situation: memory clashes with the present, and its movement is discontinuous. Is this the originary condition of Leopardi's poetry? Perhaps. The sense of the canto certainly rests on this disjunction and on the rupture thus revealed. Can we say as much about Leopardi's entire early poetic production? I believe it is useful to undertake an inquiry from this perspective, for beyond the rhetorical question, I suspect that an important problem is foreshadowed here. We set out from the proposition that the relationship with memory is also a relationship with language and with a certain public. Yet since the poet's relationship with that public, with the aristocratic and cultivated elite that corresponds to his own universe of expressive values, is mediated by memory—in this precise case, the tradition of classical culture and its revolutionary Jacobin translation (memory serving as the basis of universal understanding and the means of common research)—this is the sphere in which the young poet will stake his claim to glory, in the repetition of the rite and in the renewal of the event. Indeed, here he raises the problem of verifying his own language and his anxiety to communicate. "But I do not see the glory" is a strong, contagious declaration that suggests that the crisis of memory is inseparable from the poet's current condition, the condition of his public and civil society. Whether it can open up to redemption or must close down in wretchedness is the theme that is being debated here.[2]

The first lines of the canzone *To Italy* open up a vast scenario, without which our line of questioning could not be proposed with such intensity. For it is in this disjunction that the specificity of the young Leopardi's sensibility lies and begins to manifest itself. This specificity that we aim to interrogate is far from simple. It involves grasping Leopardi at the heart of the European cultural problematic, at the heart of its breadth and its crisis.[3] Yet during the preceding thirty years and well beyond Recanati, the flux of historical memory was disorganized, and the sequences allowing a translation of current events into classical terms no longer appeared to be homogeneous.[4] Crisis of the public? No doubt, but the stakes were more profound and substantial. In Europe between 1789 and 1815, memory went mad. In the theater of the public sphere [*Öffentlichkeit*], revolution and reaction had exchanged masks: the Jacobin was found to be a despot, and Brutus was made out to be Caesar. On the side of reaction, or simply restoration, the mutations were no less radical nor any less paradoxical and confused. The resistance to revolution, rooted in the old traditional and religious values, had ended up, in an unforeseen fashion, producing or upholding claims of individual and national autonomy; religious restoration flirted ambiguously with a robust sense of freedom of conscience and the cult of patriotic traditions with the birth of modern nationalist sentiment.[5] But all this was in an indistinct and confused manner. The collective imaginary was subjected to a great epochal tension. Relayed by the unequivocal reports and virulent denunciations of unease that, beyond and through De Maistre and Chateaubriand, De Staël and Benjamin Constant, arrived in the newspapers and libraries of European cultivated society and in particular—with the speed of the telegraph—of Italian society, the crisis and the attempts to resolve it explicitly pose the problem of the continuity of values and of historical memory. The essential point concerns the translatability, in the continuity of classical memory, of the terms "reason," "progress," "enlightenment," and "freedom": the homology is broken, the alternatives are innumerable, and no synthesis is foreseeable.

A new climate is in the process of emerging, but in a hazy atmosphere, without reference points and without solid condensations of new values. In the old materialist jargon, these new tendencies would be said to be more noticeable to the sense of smell than to touch, perceptible in the weak sense rather than the strong sense. Therefore the tension is not transformation; it does not have the power [*potenza*] for that. It is low profile, as regards the French influences. The influence of the new German culture—gentler, certainly deeper—is still almost imperceptible in Italy. Although the first translations of Lessing, Kant, Goethe, and Schiller are at least beginning to appear in the catalogs, minor authors are widely distributed. These do not offer decisive determinations, but rather introduce, beyond German soil as well, a climate—Romanticism—that, at first glance, appears marked by an indistinct program and a sort of postmodern sensibility (which from the start is perhaps, as Leopardi denounced it a decade later, a pernicious "new creed"). What common point is there in this set of influences? Indisputably, it is the reaction to the age of Enlightenment. In more concrete terms, the banalization of the recent past of revolutionary transformation in the most worldly and moderate currents of restoration; in all of them, the destruction of the hegemonic determination of classical memory as revolutionary projection; lastly, the invention of a new model of memory and, in the extremist currents of political reaction, its exaltation as the indistinct, profound power [*potenza*] of the continuity of history. Where did this movement lead? We are at a central point here. Only an absence of opposition to this ideological redefinition of memory would have permitted the political restoration, the bald-faced reaction, to take on the appearances of hegemony. It was not so. The rupture of memory, its reactionary innovation, did not gain the upper hand.

Resistance is at least as strong as reaction, and the play of equal and opposite forces prolongs the critical state. There are some who suffer the disaster of memory yet nevertheless refuse to renounce it. There are those who dream of reconstructing the new dimensions of values and the Enlightenment. In fact, whatever the modes of configuration of the new ideology, a great transformation of minds is confirmed. No reaction, however blind, no restoration, however intelligent, could get it right—although eclipsed, the revolution lived. The form of discontinuity of memory, more important than the contents of restoration that tried to filter through it, thus became, in an equivocal manner, the central element. The manner is equivocal precisely because the form of discontinuity could no longer become the hegemonic horizon. Indifference wins. So we have a reactionary springtime—but one that reproduced itself under the sign of negativity, of the low profile, the impossibility of subjectively assuming the objective catastrophe of historical memory. In short, nothing succeeded in breaking the impotent and vicious conjunction of the sense of catastrophe of a revolutionary era and the attempt at restoration of a dehistoricized memory.[6] The young Leopardi's demand for glory is measured against this climate of confusion and lassitude into which these divergent alternatives plunged Europe.

For it is precisely in the tiresome atmosphere of that reactionary season that the canto *To Italy* also takes shape. Let us attempt to compare it with Petrarch's canzone; the shock corresponds to what, in the same epoch, Leopardi describes so well in the *Zibaldone*: the clash of origins and repetition, of the heroic and the rhetorical, the living and the dead.[7] And yet, in emphasizing the discontinuity of memory with respect to the ideological form that they want to impose on it, Leopardi's canzone achieves moments of great poetry.

> Sooner shall stars, uprooted from the sky,
> Hiss as they plunge extinguished in the deep,
> Than will memory and our love for you
> Be lost or extinguished. (ll.121–24)[8]

The irreducibility of historical experience is opposed to the ideological transformation of memory. It has a natural power [*potenza*]—how could the rhetorical and the ideological, even diluted in nature, compel it to produce them? The elegy is the articulation of the catastrophe of memory.

> While on Antela's hill, where by their dying
> The sacred band withdrew themselves from death,
> Simonides went up
> And gazed upon the sky the sea the earth.
>
>
> And with his cheeks streaming with floods of tears,
> With his breast panting, and his foot uncertain,
> He took in hand his lyre. (ll.77–83)[9]

This, therefore, is a mode of liberation of the true from the atrocious events of historical memory! Even when we are oppressed by historical memory, poetry in its immediacy can rejoin and sing the true. Is this, therefore, the sense of the discontinuity we are proposing? Perhaps. In fact, Leopardi experiences a difficult and common condition, that of the prisoner of a culture that, in contrast to the recent revolutionary past, wants an interpreter of ancient forms and reactionary contents—without being subjugated. But what is this residue of freedom good for? Aggravated by philosophical studies carried out with a ferocious determination to the point of saturation, his condition is constructed within a sad horizon. The moments of poetry do not resolve that condition: they illuminate it. Whatever its connotations—low profile, indifference—memory remains a prisoner. At twenty, Leopardi experiences himself as memory.

> And then it was the bitter recollection
> Took root inside my breast, and closed my heart
> To every other voice, to every image.
> And a long sorrow searched my troubled breast,
> As happens when Olympus rains without distraction
> And melancholy washes all the fields. (*First Love*, ll.61–66)[10]

Certainly his is the normal condition of the intellectual at the beginning of the nineteenth century. This heavy, absurd content, this dense, indistinct memory weighs on everyone, and it can be grasped only in the confusion of its elements. In this historical concretization of memory, the world is experienced in images of unhappiness: "Even the love of glory was no longer/Heard in my breast" (*First Love*, ll.73–74).[11] The objective situation redoubles the subjective condition. Glory—that is to say, the transfiguration of memory into passion, the hope of its future collective efficacy—stays quiet. Hence memory is not practicable, nor can glory be. This explains how the two great civil canzoni of this period do not attain a high poetic figure.[12] Both are cut from the fabric of memory that does not allow any clear design to appear. The confusion of the contents of memory jumbles the discourse, which never stops seeking a substitute for the development of the poetic intention in the act of heroic will, in invective, or in parallel fashion in psychological, elegiac, and naturalistic withdrawal.

> To arms, to arms: I'll fight
> Alone, and fall face forward, I alone.
> And may my blood, O heaven,
> Become a fire to inspire Italians. (*To Italy*, ll.37–40)[13]

Here we have rhetoric, with a deaf, almost Ossianesque naturalism as complement.

> The boreal desert places of their sorrow
> Were witnesses as were the hissing woods.
> They came to such a pass
> Abandoned corpses no one came to bury,

Scattered across a horrid sea of snow,
Were torn by savage beasts. (*On the Proposed Monument*, ll.154–59)[14]

Some political themes are clearly evoked in these two canti, notably a ran-corous anti-Napoleonic attitude combined with a sincere pity for the Italians who fell during the retreat from Russia. But these themes are developed without any real coherence. They do not support the work of clarification and, at best, play a contrapuntal role with respect to the rhetorical emotion of the canti. The historical question emerges nevertheless: "Why were we born into a time of such perversity?" (*On the Proposed Monument*, l.120).[15] But this question finds no answer here. Vanishing into the confusion of memory, these civil canzoni contain passages that the ironic genius of the *Batracomiomachia* could appropriate in order to attribute them to crabs or mice.[16] And the fact that these canzoni, upon their publication in 1819, had been welcomed, as Giordani testifies, with enthusiasm and described as "miracles" does nothing to modify this judgment. This "electric fire" remains a matter of eloquence and does not become lyrical. The moral invec-tive and the classical sound do not succeed in disturbing the indifference of memory or in giving life back to the past; they constitute at best a tribute to the past, the basis for a monument and not for hope.

The indistinctness of memory petrifies the past; that is to say, it estab-lishes the impossibility of traversing it, of making discriminations within it, of articulating it. It blocks and fetishizes the past. In other poetic works of the same period, these perverse effects immediately become evident. In the two fragments *The ray of daylight*[17] and *Still walking up and down outside this door*[18] the naturalistic outburst annihilates the recollection, and the "I" is confused with the storm. The irruption of natural elements ("O precious clouds, O sky, O earth, O trees")[19] is transformed into an inventory of meteorological lamentations. The storm, the artificial representation of which exaggerates the drama of memory and exasperates its motif (the departure of the beloved), does not form a Giorgionesque tableau of chiar-oscuro, planes, and contrasting expressive determinations. Everything falls flat. "Silence all round, and she had turned to stone" (*The ray of daylight*, l.76).[20] The single dramatic development of these compositions—"Serene and happy hours, how soon you vanished!/Nothing down here that pleases ever lasts,/Or even makes a pause, except hope only" (*The ray of daylight*, ll.25–27)[21]—is suddenly, forcibly overwhelmed by the naturalistic image. The natural catastrophe is not an atmosphere, a process, nor an occasion for human counterpoint. It is stone. The argumentative profusion and stylistic care of *First Love* do not modify the harshness and the difficulties that mark this first Leopardian poetic condition; but, on the contrary, they allow them to be better understood. The insistence here on the concept of "imago" ("that wholly pure/and shining imago I have kept inside me" and "in my thought still breathes the lovely imago" [*First Love*, ll.88, 101, and passim])[22] does not alter the canto's elementary tones of naturalism. The intimate intermingling of sensations—of sight, of hearing, of the nocturnal tremors of the soul—does not abolish the indistinct and otherwise predicable connection with the states of nature. It is more an ecological than a lyrical condition, more an immersion in indifference than an impassioned tension: the dramatic character of the dialogue is annulled in cold description. On the other hand, the imago, isolating itself and offering almost the illusion of a lyrical tension, presents itself there to be seized, though only slightly. Not even this succeeds, and the imago does not manage to shape the canto, which is also static, repetitive, and stony. If it sometimes has the glitter of crystal, it also has its geometrical coldness. The imago is stylized memory, perhaps the effective symbol of the determinations of Leopardi's memory, of memory as density of closed states of mind, nature, and history. The more this density takes shape and accumulates, the more it demands an articulation, and the more the lack of a secure poetic methodology manifests itself. The development of a poetics of the imago fixes rather than sets in motion the ensemble of heroic, naturalistic, and psychological contents of the poetic will. The imago is the reductive form of a confused memory.

If our inquiry were confined to these first of Leopardi's compositions, we could style ourselves Croceans and note the substantial failure of the poetry. But the genesis contains the paradigm of development—it is in this sense, then, that we can emphasize how aware Leopardi is of the limits of his poetic making [*fare*], his making truth [*fare verità*].[23] Consequently he strains against these limits. We will see in the letters and the *Zibaldone* (which he began to compose at that time) how violently and systematically the limits are transformed into obstacles to surmount. Leopardi knows how to begin. Genius appears as a vocation. These compositions are only an outline, but one dense with problems. These compositions constitute the problem, give it shape, offer it to us to analyze, offer it to Leopardi to solve. The poetic difficulties do not eliminate the will to art [*Kunstwollen*]. Let us make the point for the first time. Despite everything, we are faced with a marvelous apparition of poetic genius, and we are also faced with a first, vague but decisive problematization of memory. The fact that it is presented here as "stony" or as a "monument" does not prevent the poetic labor from taking the measure of this world with this vast intentionality. On the basis of this first block of problems, we must therefore see how Leopardi proceeds, how he develops the problem of memory, and how, through this singular intersection of poetry and culture (congealed in memory and its crisis), he succeeds in opening up a new possibility for poetic creation.

There is a first series of elements to take into account. The theme of memory, however obtained, is posited at the center of the poetic making, permitting the emergence of time, its concept and its problem.[24] Through memory, time becomes poetic material. If memory here presents itself as stone, it remains nonetheless a temporal constitution—a time without hope, a time of petrification, but time nevertheless. This indication seems to me to be worthy of insistence: whatever the definition of memory in these first verses by Leopardi, and despite the indistinctness that characterizes them, this centering of the discourse in itself brings about one of the great innovations that Leopardi's thought both experiences and produces. Time is posited as the argument and the exclusive fabric of poetry. And this time is also posited as a category that transcends every immediately psychological given: that is to say, it is posited more as the form than as the content of poetry. This functional complexity, evident in the civil poetry, appears equally clearly in the elegiac poetry, the naturalism of which, by means that are still experimental (in this very early poetics), has the effect of detaching the psychological elements from the form, expelling them from the poetic web [trama], and exhausting them. It is not by chance that the subject of The ray of daylight, the "I" of the first draft, becomes "the lady" in the definitive version.[25] Nor is it by chance that in the civil canzoni a certain refining of the subject beyond any purely psychological characterization takes place through the insistent forms of eloquence; that is, by means of an argumentative and dialectically structural figure. The fact is that time, woven and shaped by this advance of Leopardi into the world, is immediately ontological time—that is, the dynamic and transformative dimension of being—being in its entirety. The historical time of memory is immediately ontological time. Thus the static and paralyzing density of memory and its crisis that appear to the young Leopardi as the dimension of poetic creation illuminates his thought beyond every possible or effective perverse effect and plunges it into temporality. From here on we must be able to grasp this position and see how the different scansions of the poetry derive from this centrality of time. The discovery of the time of memory as ontological time unleashes numerous variants that lead poetry onto a properly practical terrain. The first of these variations or scansions is that which constitutes, in ethical thought, the temporal dimension of Leopardi's poetry and his search.

Before digging deeper into the latter motif and trying to understand how ethics is capable of organizing poetics and thereby transforming the ontology of time, let us try to understand the fundamental importance of Leopardi's accession to an ontology of time, which consists in the fact that it permits the poet to immerse himself in the lively course of a European problematic. Let us repeat: memory is the fabric of poetry, but memory is time or, more precisely, it is time problematized. Monument or "stone": in any case the time that constitutes it cannot be arrested, for it is vital matter, duration, and continuity. At the European level, in the crisis of revolutionary development in the fallout from the Napoleonic disaster, memory represents the critical element—and the element of innovation—since time increasingly makes itself evident as the web of memory. Submitting to a corrupted memory means being constrained to problematize time. The crisis of memory, the confirmation of the impotence and indifference of its concept, delivers us over to (or rather hurls us) into the ontological dimension of time. By placing the problem of memory and time at the center of his properly poetic advance, Leopardi inserts himself into a European process. His poetry at once has this impulse.

During those same decades, Hegel accomplishes the same operation: time becomes the center of the philosophical scene.[26] The metaphysics of time, whether philosophical or poetic, becomes the thread of the search for the true. Thus for Hegel, the discovery and exaltation of the centrality of the concept of time also derives from the crisis and the problematization of memory. He aims to liberate the spirit of the past and make what has been consumed in time become the property of substance, a process by which spirit frees itself in time; and "reminiscence" is nothing other than the sleep of a true, otherwise absolute movement, a "Bacchanalian revel."[27] This function of the restoration of time to the philosophical scene at the basis of the dialectical invention must not be attributed to Hegel alone. Indeed, the entire genesis of grand German idealism and the philosophy of the era can be found in the effort of the critique of memory and the discovery of the ontological function of time. Starting in 1796, among Hegel, Schelling, and Hölderlin, the problem is posed;[28] the crisis of memory is apprehended and resolved in the distinction between the mechanicism of nature and the freedom of the true—an aesthetic philosophy, a mythology of reason, in order to relight the flame in the deconsecrated temple of metaphysics. A new time, a utopia, and an ethics.[29] All this constitutes an articulation that deserves a moment's pause; and it is also good to recall at this point that the presence of and the alternative proposed by Hölderlin to this imbroglio of problems will become, for those of us who study Leopardi, very important in what follows of our inquiry. For the moment, it suffices to conclude this theme by recalling that Leopardi's operation, aimed from the heart of memory and its crisis toward an ontological dimension of time as the basis for poetic making, has a great force of innovation. We soon see how Leopardi's labor is not situated solely within a European problematic but also represents a decisive alternative to it.

Let us return to the points whose development was set aside in order to follow the track of the European dimension. We have indicated how the theme of time opens up to an ontological characterization of poetic making. Let us add that in Leopardi, the ontology of time is immediately ethical, which means that the time in which we are immersed is the time of making. Over and against the crisis of memory, which constitutes the condition of Leopardi's first poetic creation, the potentiality of time is the horizon of innovation of the making—certainly not a technical, mechanical making but instead an action to which we are destined and which represents the very problem of the foundation and significance of living. Anticipating the moment of a deeper discussion, we can emphasize here the absurdity and complete vacuity (if it is not simply bad faith) of all the oppositions between one Leopardi, the lofty lyric poet, and another Leopardi, the mediocre civil philosopher.[30] Leopardi's poetry is fully civil because it is, in its totality, a metaphysical questioning of the significance of action. So we follow our course. We have already seen that the question "Why were we born into a time of such perversity?" remains for the moment without an answer. But this does not prevent us from remarking that just as this question situates the canto at a temporal limit, it also confronts it with a transcendental ethics. The question has no answer, but it is certain that the answer, if there were one, could only be practical. And already, in the absence of any perspective, consciousness reacts practically: "For grief without disdain by now is stupid" (*On the Proposed Monument*, l.14).[31] The remark is all the more valid with regard to the canzone *To Italy*.

And there is much more proof of the validity of this assertion. For example, let us read the *Essay on the Popular Errors of the Ancients*[32] (1815) and the *Principle for a Recasting of the Essay*[33] (1817). Among the many interesting motifs, there is one that I consider essential both to the definition of the philosophy of the essay and to the demonstration (or at very least to a first illustration) of my thesis. It seems to me in fact that the immense mass of philological labor, intended to clarify the 'pseudodoxia' of the ancients, indicates less a moralistic-pedagogical intention than, as the *Principle for a Recasting of the Essay* demonstrates, a practically determined metaphysical intention. The world of illusion, Leopardi tells us, is terribly effective, concrete, and potent. The deception of reason is a reality. "A large part of truth, which the philosophers have had to establish, would be useless if error did not exist; another part of it remains useless by reason of the many errors that still persist" (*Essay*, 770). That being the case, how do we demystify it? The philosophy of the Enlightenment sets truth in opposition to deception, which presupposes a reality principle with which to compare the work of critique. But where is this reality principle? In some Platonic region? No, the reality principle of demystification consists in critique itself, in the critical labor. "Inasmuch as errors are enemies that are vanquished as soon as they are discovered, and minor errors are discovered only when we look for them" (*Principle*, 908). A new illusion? Perhaps, but it is an illusion that forms one body with the positive ethics of time, that is measured against the material difficulties determined by time, the life of illusions, and the effectiveness of their power [*potere*]. The moralistic component, scornful and pedagogical, here becomes inessential.

What is central, on the contrary, is the ethical fabric of the critical function.[34] Ethics is the force that controls and even organizes the ontological dimensions of time: time of demystification, time of critical labor, and time of truth. From this perspective, the very insistence with which this pedagogical inclination is expressed has a function that is not solely negative. It sometimes appears, precisely because it is subordinated to the critical labor, as a minor form—incomplete, in certain respects unconscious, undesired, and yet necessary—of Leopardi's warning about the crisis of memory and its progress on the terrain of the ontology of ethics. If ethics is rendered banal in pedagogy, the latter nevertheless demonstrates the urgency of the former. We are able to make analogous remarks regarding the function of irony in Leopardi in what follows: pedagogy and irony are, in his poetic making, the younger sisters of prophecy and sarcasm, of metaphysical lucidity and historical realism. In this very early Leopardi, the pedagogical tone is the still coarse form of the mediation between the perception of the ethical dimension of ontological time and the attempt to make this dimension live within historical time. This is a practical mediation that intends to confer distinction and sense on a historical memory that is now without signification. If the sinking of memory into crisis restores to us the dimension of time, the positioning of ethics seeks to define the sense of time and confer a dialectical distinction upon the development of historical time and historical memory.

This, therefore, is the time of the dialectic. German philosophy in that period is preoccupied, as we have already indicated, with elaborating the grand scenario in which everything will be at stake, positively or negatively, in the centuries that follow. The reconquest of time by philosophical thought constitutes the central point of this veritable innovation, in the strong sense, of the European metaphysical paradigm, a common fabric to which our Leopardi belongs up to this point. But in him the concept of time adopts a singular figure that renders it not merely irreducible but an alternative to the founding and definition of the dialectical project. Before showing this alternative in action, we define the other particular characteristics of the temporal category in Leopardi. Different elements come into play here, elements already perceptible in that very first poetic period.

Concerning the characterization of Leopardi's conception of time, two elements, which form one body with his youthful work and with the solitary and artisanal aspects of the construction of his genius, are primary. To begin with, one finds a philological conception of time: the long, palpable time of classical philology. To assert here that the philological tradition emerging from Vico (and that ontological dimension of time that governs the particular form of his 'historicism') constitutes a first chromosome could seem an exaggeration. But nevertheless it is so. At the end of the Enlightenment, the renewal of historical-philological studies (not only in Italy but above all there) is for Leopardi a kind of privileged terrain of culture: a culture that, through philology, opens up to life. Study of the *Zibaldone* demonstrates this, but the exceptional range of his youthful philological studies already provides the proof.[35] Leopardi could have been an Italian Niebuhr. If he was not, it is because the dimension of historical time immediately became a critical conception and was developed within an ontological perspective. When I refer to ontological time, I am also referring to physical time: a specific conception of physical time is indeed the other element that Leopardi immediately draws from the tradition. A second chromosome.

This is the conception of time that we already find in the *History of Astronomy from its Origins to the Year 1811*,[36] written during his earliest youth, and in the *Dissertation on the Origin and Early Progress of Astronomy*.[37] It matters little that these are purely, indeed massively, works of compilation. What is fundamental, on the contrary, is the manner in which the young Leopardi never ceases, in the course of this labor, to transform himself from classical philologist into modern *philosophe*: physics, the great astronomical measurements, and scientific naturalism are inherent in his work—and perhaps even more in his mind than in his work. This balance between philological activity and naturalistic application is, nevertheless, not strange. Indeed, physical philosophy historically constitutes one of the fundamental terms of the construction of the historical and philological spirit.[38] Galileo is as important as Descartes in Leopardi's history of astronomy, and both are as valid as the most ancient figures, from Ptolemy to Copernicus; this current of thought is integrated into the unity of a knowledge [*sapere*] that becomes human to the extent that knowledges [*conoscenze*] are unified beyond any distinction of disciplines. This thought is absolutely secular, not because it refuses theological totalitarianism, but because it effectively opposes itself to a theoretical totalitarianism of the opposite sign. On the side of the historical dimensions, the concept of time takes on the physical figure that is its own. Here too Leopardi follows the spirit of his age. It is not by chance that Herder, to take one example, is situated at the genesis of modern historicism alongside the philologist Winckelmann and the philosopher Hegel.[39] The naturalism of the Enlightenment and Romantic historicism do not come to occupy different pigeonholes of an idealist dialectic of history, but together they experience the genesis of a new ontological conceptualization of human time. Paradoxically, this is equally true of the early texts by other authors of classical idealism—certainly in Schelling and even in Hegel. Who could doubt it after a simple glance at Schelling's first notes on natural philosophy or Hegel's *Jenenser Realphilosophie*, and after having attempted to understand the metaphysical intensity and conceptual complexity of the "ether" and to confront the use Hölderlin made of it?[40]

Two further elements contribute to the singular determination of the concept of time and therefore to Leopardi's intervention regarding the dialectic, regarding the time of the dialectic. These two elements appear in the poetic pages that we have already begun to read. Indeed, despite the abstract character of the transcription in terms of the imago or of a furious and impotent voluntarism, it is obvious that the concept of time is presented, as much in the elegies as in the civil canti of this earliest period, as a fluid movement of consciousness, of an absolute consciousness. I mean that psychological, internal time is analyzed with the aim only of making it flow back into the dimension of objective being. It is taken up only for structural purposes. The operation can certainly miscarry, the abstract can win, and the canto beat a retreat; but this in no way reduces the demand to show states of consciousness as concrete structures, *Sachsverhalten*, "states of things." From this perspective, the verses from *To Italy* ("Sooner shall stars, uprooted from the sky,/Hiss as they plunge extinguished in the deep") or from *The ray of daylight* ("Nothing down here that pleases ever lasts,/Or even makes a pause, except hope only") take on a different meaning from that which was previously indicated. They present a consolidated figure of ontological time, filtered by consciousness but not enclosed within it. They present a time that comprehends everything and that is open to the sequence: nature-being-humankind, objectivity-metaphysical structure-action. In short, they present a structural time. Such is the third characteristic of the concept of time in Leopardi. But let us pursue and grasp a new element.

The ontological dimension presents itself forcibly, as power [*potenza*], every time that consciousness collides with present history. The fact that the confrontation remains unresolved does not tell us much. The ethical determination of the collision tells us little more. This fourth definition of the relationship to ontological time is (taking everything into account) perhaps the most important. Indeed, it rivals the determination of historical time, memory and its indistinctness. The dramatic character of the confrontation makes possible the catastrophe of memory. The experience of historical time does not withstand that of ontological time. However, to the extent that ontological time is revealed as ethical activity, all the elements that characterize it are led back to unity. The lack of awareness of this youthful phase does not detract from the importance of the ethical founding: this will appear right away.

Here we come back to the essential point. This time is that of the dialectic, which means that the first problem is that of historical memory, the dialectic constituting an attempt to establish discriminations in its indistinctness. But in order to discriminate, it must commit itself. Yet during those years that inaugurate the nineteenth century, revolution and reaction sleep under the same blanket. It is not a game—although everything exchanges roles. The dialectic is entangled in this imbroglio of the real. And Leopardi is affected by the confusion; as a provincial he is immersed in it. In *To the Italians: An Oration on the Liberation of Piceno*,[41] hatred for the tyrant cannot be distinguished from an exaltation of preservation accompanied by a certain demagogy. Nevertheless, the attitudes on display in this oration are not reactionary; they are only retrograde conservative banalities. In effect, beyond the rhetorical tones and exhortations, the oscillation between anti-French nationalism and ideal nationalism in imitation of the ancients is resolved in an ethical key. Despite everything, the oration moves onto a realistic terrain, and the anti-French resentment does not eliminate the specificity of the problems that belong to the Italian illusion. The ferocious judgment on the Napoleonic experience does not ooze hatred; it only pledges to resolve the fallout the experience will have for Italy. The lassitude of memory and the denunciation of the historical present are traversed by the will to act adequately. The discriminating action of memory is realistic, or at least it tries to be. The engagement is positive, and the radicalism of the position taken is ultimately less ideological than practical. This is the essential point. This time of the dialectic is that of discrimination of the real in which we are immersed, following in the tracks of a concept and a method that articulate its time and forms. Yet classical idealism tries to construct a logical key for the reading of time and to reformulate ontology in terms of a logic of time. It withdraws the time of freedom and imposes the being of logic. It is not worthwhile to trace the long history of this new logical overdetermination of being here. Elsewhere we have already done an analysis of its *Krisis* and what follows from its perverse effects.[42] Faced with the same problem, Leopardi begins to travel a different path. Still in confusion, immersed in the inextricable complexity of the problem, he tries to avoid regarding the situation from the hypostatic level of an eventual solution, but instead to grasp it by the middle, with an intention to resolve it determined by ethics (with a will that is not logical but ethical). It is an ethical path. How deep into the genesis of modern metaphysical thought does Leopardi's choice take us! *"Eine Ethik"*: again we find an identity with the program of the earliest German idealism, the program that Schelling and Hegel betray through dialectical logic, but that is preserved by Hölderlin.[43] And so what of Leopardi?

In Leopardi's comportment is something that makes him a singular character for the era: the insistent Jacobinism of his expressions.[44] This singularity is not explained by his exemplary positions on nascent Italian nationalism, nor by the grandiloquent form of his heroic voluntarism: both of these determinations are broadly present in the culture of the era. Nor is it explained by the fact that in the lyrics and orations of this period (with or without Giordani's solicitation: we see soon enough), he dons classical costumes in the triumph of Plutarchian reminiscences. In reality, the application of the classical model permits stylistic and ideological variants that are much wider in range than a simple travesty behind some masks of Brutus.[45] On the contrary, the Jacobin characterization is theoretical: it unfolds from the assumption of the primacy of practice and from the will as capacity for learned representation and construction of the true. Here the reality principle of Jacobinism manifests itself: the true as need for action, as hypothesis of transformation. It could be objected that the model of Enlightenment and Jacobinism is antiquated. This is true for France, but it is not true for Italy, where a significant cultural delay (in relation to the eighteenth-century maturity of the Enlightenment revolution) manifests itself. Paradoxically, the effects of this revolutionary process arrive together with the counterrevolution in Italy as in Germany (by different means).[46] One could also object that the picture we are sketching risks becoming confused under the weight of these determinations. Indeed, it tends, through singular intersections and slips, to superimpose the Enlightenment and idealism and to obscure any distinctions. It is not our fault if this time (but it happens often) the traditional hermeneutic categories quite obviously don't correspond to reality. In all Leopardi's writings between 1815 and 1820, that is to say on the verge of the explosion of his mature poetic and metaphysical activity, this accumulation of diverse influences and different problematic strata is perfectly verifiable. But in his work, on all terrains, the movement of the Jacobin theoretical instance is also fully verifiable. The sense of the practical struggle against illusion, against the theological and mythical deceptions of astronomy, and against the mystifications of common knowledge [*sapere*] is Jacobin. Even more than the heroic fervor, the will to truth is Jacobin. So too is the literary proposition that Leopardi explicitly announces during this period in the *Letter to the Compilers of the*

Italian Library[47] and the *Letter in Response to That of Madame the Baroness de Staël*.[48] Leopardi reacts against overwhelming imitation; that is to say, against Madame de Staël's proposal to dip the Italian pen into the Seine or the Rhine. On the contrary, the dignity of the classical tradition can be transmuted into that of Italian literature—since the Italian language is the one that has the most affinity with Greek and Latin, it is the most natural, indeed the only natural one. The revolution is making itself an empire, the empire of the Seine and the Rhine, and becoming complexity, confusion, and domination. Italian literature, therefore, opposes itself to domination as well as to the imperial eclecticism of Madame de Staël, or more precisely, it has the power [*potenza*] to oppose itself because its language is natural, living, organizing the nation, and in short, more true. What ingenuity, what strength! The historical lag of Italian thought in relation to French thought is not experienced as a disadvantage. On the contrary, this difference plays out positively since it permits the revolution to be understood as an alternative experience to the historically effective conclusion of its unfolding, and thus as an experience that is adequate to the proposition of a new theme of transformation. Here we witness an incessant, wearying excavation. The linguistic thematic remains inconclusive, just as do all the other themes, but instead poses and opens up problems. The entire development of Leopardi's thought tends toward their solution.[49]

Conversely, Hegel frees himself rapidly from Jacobinism. Like Madame de Staël, he classifies the reaction as the conclusion of the revolution and absolute spirit as *Aufhebung*—the realization and overcoming of the subjective will. He sees the dialectic working and logic leading Jacobin anxiety and utopia back to 'Reason.' The dialectic shatters the confusion of historical time, intervenes in the catastrophe of memory, and with Hegel, reorders everything. The initial cultural and political lag with respect to the French situation is also marked for the German philosopher. But he resolves the difference by means of a sublime overdetermination, under the sign of reason, of the totality of development. The historical delay allows Hegel to conceive philosophy as the "owl of Minerva" that explores, reorganizes, and sanctifies historical effectiveness. The confusion and deception of memory become the logic of history.[50]

Leopardi's delay in relation to the French Revolution has a completely different meaning. The defeat of the revolution, the confusion of memory, the tower of Babel of significations of historical time reveal the absence of conclusion of the event and the absence of solution to a problem. Of course, the historical delay imposes a displacement of viewpoint, a dislocation onto the metaphysical terrain—for Leopardi as already for Hegel. But in Leopardi this translation of the event leaves the problem open and indicates, within the time of the dialectic, not a logical solution but an ethical opening. The historical delay in relation to the central current of European thought here reveals an extraordinary wisdom: a return to the origins of the Enlightenment in order to avoid falling prey to defeat. The continuity of reference therefore becomes discontinuity with respect to the historical course of the European intellectual adventure. And it is at this point that Leopardi's experience intersects that of Hölderlin. Within the time of the dialectic, confronted with the necessity of discriminating in the chaos of memory, they both refuse the logical solution and the idealist foundation of science. Hölderlin refuses Hegel. Leopardi, as the *Zibaldone* repeatedly confirms for us,[51] has an intuition of the metaphysical miracle that develops in Germany. He is unfamiliar, nevertheless, with the theoretical conclusions drawn there and thus can confront it only at the level of that real history that German metaphysics interprets. This confrontation comes to bear not on representations but on facts. And here Leopardi rejects the dialectical conclusions for he knows the real problem that the dialectic itself reflects. The revolution cannot be cancelled, cannot be surmounted, and cannot be subsumed. Like Hölderlin, Leopardi grasps the discontinuity of memory and the irreducibility of the revolution-event. Rupture is the natural element of the development of mind towards the true and of poetic making. Like Hölderlin, Leopardi seeks in the classics a profound origin from which it would be possible to bring forth both the sense of life and the transformation of history at the same time—an ontological foundation for a practical making. For us, accentuating and insisting upon the manifest differences between the poetics of the two great authors are of no interest here. Whereas in Hölderlin, poetry renews myth, Leopardi deploys mythology as the content of practical experience, and to Hölderlin's fantastic he opposes the suffering of the true. While for the German poet the Jacobin determination radically expresses the verticality of the poetic universe, for the Italian writer, poetics leads to a multidirectional horizon of metaphysical knowledge [*conoscenza*]. We are not interested in the respective specificity of the forms through which the two poets determine and describe the rupture of ontology and history and thereby confront it—forms that are singular and different. The only fact that interests us here is the fact that both establish the impossibility of establishing a foundation beyond the rupture.

Such is the time of the dialectic. Thus from the beginning, Leopardi travels a path of mediation between ontological time and historical time, which wants not logic but practice. He also develops, at a certain distance from and yet within the mysterious community of a European problem and metaphysical project, the practical outline of the first systematic fragment of classical idealism. But a dialectic without a logic to direct it, a mediation that can root itself only in the ontology of ethics, an ever-revolutionized foundation—do these things deserve the name or epithet of dialectic?

Experimenting with the Infinite

Everything that we have said up to now constitutes a hypothesis or more precisely, signs or traces of a tendency and a possible future. Only that. Thus it is necessary to take our relationship with Leopardi to a deeper level and grasp, in a symptomatic context, the singularity of his path. We must see how, during the brief period of his metaphysical initiation between 1817 and 1819, he poses the dialectical problem and at the cost of what suffering he explores its field, thereby succeeding in solving it through the definition of an ethical alternative.

We can begin with a reading of the letters to Pietro Giordani, dated 21 March and 30 April 1817.[52] In the first, which constitutes a kind of literary program, the confrontation with memory is immediate, objective. The denunciation of the wretchedness of Recanati is articulated in the denunciation of the state of Italian letters; the personal motif is transfigured and incarnated in a situation of objective crisis. The questioning of the present thus weaves the fabric of a response which, drawing on reference materials, establishes a strong logical contrast; namely, that the excellence of the literary tradition and the wealth of the history of the language are opposed to the current poverty of Italian letters. To rediscover life against the dead present, one must turn to the classics. This is the path of glory: "I have a huge, perhaps immoderate and insolent, desire for glory."

In the second letter, the tone changes radically. The themes at the heart of the rhetorical contrast between wretchedness and glory, which are outlined in a rather academic and yet strongly programmatic manner, are fortified by the accent placed on interiority. The alternatives and indistinctness of memory are revisited in personal, almost confessional terms. Passion opens up a dialectical context. Once again the recurrent theme, almost an obsession, is always Recanati, its wretchedness and the wretchedness of current memory. But presently the dialectical gaze and suffering, as they react and rise toward liberation, potently excavate interiority, a non-psychological interiority, the psychological states here becoming representations of the world. The letter thus manifests the relationship between a violent, passionate, pathetic *lamentatio* on Recanati and the description of the poetic vocation—its genesis, its development. In this relationship, nature and history become a kind of springboard for glory, traversing despair, sickness, the creeping, damp sense of death—right up to the moment of the catastrophe marked by the contradiction to which the poet is prey, between "barbarous melancholy" and "sweet melancholy," between the "study that kills" and the "violent longing to compose," which creates a state of mind between abandon and despair, to the point that one feels "carried away." Carried away from Recanati. Flight is poetic movement. The necessity of flight is the immanent result of the poetic experience. Away, away from wretchedness, away from study, away from Recanati, away from memory. Away, as only poetic rupture could bring it about.

Pride, the desire for glory, becomes flight. The practical model opposes the rhetorical model. Poetry is this experience of being carried away from oneself, this heroism which has nothing of the aristocratic virtue prescribed by tradition and customs, and which, on the contrary, is no more than ontological displacement. Infinite. The dialectical context is thus posited: a positive and wretched existence and, on the other hand, protest, the negative that creates. Recanati is posited as the condition of an operation of surmounting. Heroism is this act of positing and surmounting, the constitution of the catastrophic dimension of critique—an innovation, something strongly constructive, Fichtean.[53] Thought is pushed toward the infinite that the heroic desires and wants to understand. This is the way that the problem is introduced.

But let us look more closely at this path towards the infinite. It takes shape on the basis of two fundamental elements: the relationship with memory and the necessity of expressing its surmounting in classical, poetic, effective forms. Let us consider in the first place the relationship with memory. Leopardi insinuates himself into it through an elementary act of reflection on existence. Recanati is the monstrous mirror of the nightmare of memory, of an unlivable historical time that manifests the effective impossibility of existence, its potential annihilation. This gives rise to great suffering. Indeed, from the beginning, the question of knowing what memory is receives no answer—the question is not commensurate with the answer, nor unrealistic in its claim, nor wretched in its resentment. It is instead a question charged with expectation, the defenseless revelation of an ingenuous feeling, true ethical and metaphysical innocence. The horror that characterizes the climate of the answer is thus not due to prejudicial idiosyncrasies nor to a literary game. It is merely the objective result of the fact that a candid question obtains a treacherous answer. The violence of the conclusion is unbounded and yet, paradoxically, it remains commensurate with the disposition, with the openness of the questioning. Leopardi wishes to construct knowledge [*sapere*] through "intercourse with scholars." "Intercourse with scholars is not merely useful to me, but necessary for me, and I will seek in each of my studies to profit from the instruction that I will receive from them."[54] How could a more innocent request be imagined? This request for scholarly intercourse expresses the will to participate in the society of scholars. This intercourse is in no way episodic, but corresponds to a vocation, to a constitutive experience: it is the hope of participating in the foundation of a new intellectual community. Yet to the same extent that this relationship of participation in memory is demanded, to the same extent that Leopardi suggests to his tormented humanity the hope of a socially important collaboration, the limits of the request and the obstacles to the hope become evident. Memory is not community but rather it is wretchedness, separation, confusion. The letters provide ever more proof of this. The confidence in an active recuperation of memory through the participation in the society of scholars vanishes within a few years.

Pietro Giordani, with his benevolence and his Paduan bonhomie, seeks a mediation internal to historical memory and civil society, thereby pursuing the reformist experiment of certain intellectual strata of the Enlightenment. He proposes this mediation to Leopardi in the form of a project for reconstructing classical, patriotic, and modern eloquence. According to Giordani, tradition, both present and future, can be inserted into a linear process of the modernization of civil society.[55] Leopardi adopts Giordani's proposition, but only with the aim of testing and exhausting it. He notes that "your capacity to take possession of history is highly exceptional,"[56] but nevertheless memory cannot be put into practice; there is no possibility of using this political faculty.[57] "I'll only say that the more I read the Latins and Greeks, the smaller our own writers become, even those of the best centuries, and I see that not just our eloquence, but our philosophy, and our prose—in every respect, inside and out—must be created. A large field."[58] The radicalism of this declaration must not be underestimated. Italy does not have eloquence, or prose, or philosophy. And to paraphrase Hegel, a country without metaphysics, a temple without a shrine,[59] is a society without human community, without a community of ends, and it expresses this deficiency. Whoever seeks the infinite runs up against this vacuity of the real. Reshaping it is impossible. Memory is empty.

But it constitutes a prison, "this prison of ours."[60] The very young Leopardi's perception is that of the effectiveness of deception. It matters little that reality is mystified: it is no less real for that. Consequently, only a practical condition can escape the weight of the deception. Only escape frees one from prison. But in real terms, how does one construct a dialectic of flight, of surmounting? Reading Leopardi's correspondence during these years allows us to follow his increasingly extreme search for a solution: the desire for suicide, withdrawal from the family, and the great psychological ruptures. The almost unbelievable fact that emerges from this development is that this is not simply a matter of flight, of physical and psychological withdrawal but, on the contrary, the construction of a structure. The form and meaning of the flight are identified with each other and are architectonically structured in an act that Leopardi intends to be promethean. The 1819 attempt to flee is the single properly dialectical project of Leopardi's life experience and cultural experience, an attempt to eliminate memory by transvaluing it. The flight is an *Aufhebung*; it is negation and overcoming, an Alfierian act.[61] At that point the situation is intolerable: "Seven years of mad and most desperate study," and "melancholy as its eternal and inseparable companion."[62] But the poet is always animated by the hope of flight, a flight imagined as rupture of the present and invention of the future, as construction of conditions adequate to the realization of that heroic vocation described above. The discussion with Giordani, to which the most important letters of 1818 are dedicated,[63] gradually becomes a pretext. Flight is organized in dream and reorganizes the real in desire. It does not appear there as a foreseen event but as a motor of the soul and a utopia of the mind. Desire is real, but is no less allusive and contradictory! And indeed, Leopardi prepares for flight as a dialectical construction, as critical destruction of the past, and as its promethean reconstruction, all of which inclines his mind to a radical act of separation. The project aims too high, and the quest for truth is too ambitious. Giordani attempts a reasonable mediation; he attempts to calm the crisis, to introduce elements of moderation, which Leopardi seems to accept. But suddenly he wants to be the poetic interpreter of this historical event and introduces into the operation a radicalism that contains an irrepressible potentiality for destruction. The idea of flight becomes not an act to accomplish but the symbol of rupture with the time of mediation, with the dialectical proposition. It is an unforeseeable but irresistible movement, the declaration of the catastrophe of memory and therefore of the impossibility of dialectizing it. The organization of the flight from Recanati is curious: an *idée fixe* fills his thoughts but is only applied in caricatural form to a concrete departure. Poor Count Monaldo is perfectly correct when he regards his son's efforts with derision.[64] But the grandeur of this first poetic and metaphysical passage of Leopardi's lies precisely in this logistical impotence and in the concomitant outburst of negative thought with respect to any mediation with the real.

Thus we must very attentively analyze this year 1819, when the poet's anti-dialectical choice was made—a choice paradoxically linked to the hope of the dialectic, to the experimentation of the project, but at the same time exposed, we might say offered to the blow, to the definitive crisis of this dream of reason. But the more the desire for flight increases, the more strained the dialectically thought mediation becomes. Of course it does, in a transitory, provisory way during the—brief—period of preparations for flight. But that moment, although contradictory, constitutes the real passage. The dialectic appears here as the key to a cultural mission. We have already seen how the problem of the recasting [rifondazione] of philosophy and political eloquence is more and more fully deployed in a creative task.[65]

In the letters of 1819, this motif returns insistently. To Giordani: the necessity for a new Italian ideology to match the times.[66] To Monti: the necessity for a new Italian literature.[67] It is urgent that Italy return to the popular imagination and metaphysics. "It is not surprising that Italy has no lyric, as it has no eloquence."[68] In reality, this idea, this body of dream thoughts, does not hold up at all. As soon as the project encounters the smallest necessities of preparation for flight, Leopardi proceeds onto the terrain of lamentations: he moans, proclaims his illness, and contemplates suicide—or, on the contrary, in parallel fashion, discovers a taste for invective and finds consonance in the apologetic, rebellious prose of Lorenzino de Medici.[69] Faced with real difficulties, the glorious illusion, the aesthetic of liberation, either turns back or becomes rhetoric once again. But this is necessary. Flight is not at stake, but rather its characterization is; that is, in this case, experimenting with the dialectic—flight as constructive element, as determination of a future possibility, as project for a new culture. The disproportion does not spring from the logistical failure of the flight; it is, on the contrary, the failure that springs from the intensity and complexity of the significations that it overturns. The preparation for flight is punctilious, not in its logistical aspect, but from the ideological point of view; and it touches on the fundamental themes of a new eloquence, a new prose, a new politics. Hölderlin called it a new "popular mythology." He went mad over it. Leopardi fails at it without going mad.

Thus, at the end of July 1819, the flight does not succeed. Let us read the two letters— ironically preserved and addressed to his brother Carlo and his father, Monaldo—which Leopardi left at the moment of departure.[70] To his brother, he wrote of illness, boredom, the idea of suicide as motives for flight. To his father, on the contrary, he penned a bitter, aggravated, ill-tempered letter. Far from the painful serenity of Kafka's *Letter to His Father*, Leopardi's expresses anger, almost fury, an excess of harshness.[71] The language of despair and contempt grows stronger; the employment of adjectives is refined and pushed to the verge of a kind of filial cruelty. The explanation of the failure of the flight is given in a further letter, from August 1819:[72] here the father is made responsible for the failure. But "I do not regret it, and I have not changed. I have desisted from my plan for now." Despite everything, he is resolved to depart—and despairing. He offers unbelievably bitter reflections: "I have no great opinion of myself: yet a person who, having loved virtue from birth, gives himself in desperation to sin will always seem remarkable to me." These are words, nothing but words, since the failure of flight is desired. Indeed, it is impossible because the dialectical project is unrealizable. Leopardi rises from this defeat. "I no longer hope for anything" and "I live and I do not live," he writes to Giordani.[73] In fact, this is the birthplace of Leopardi's metaphysics. I do not believe that poetic creation—or creation in general—demands extreme suffering; that kind of stereotype seems to me false in certain respects and cruel in others. But it is certain that suffering reveals the disproportion of an act that is incommensurate with the project and which therefore self-destructs. And this is all the more true if the experience is theoretical, its visualization and its material insistence being then merely abstract. Leopardi moves into abstraction. He does not flee. His attempt to flee is limited to the destruction of a theoretical possibility. But what range this dramatization has: the possibility of the mediation of life with memory, of creative thought with tradition—dialectical mediation. The immense emotion of the flight and its failure puts the seal of destruction on the dialectical possibility. The infinite cannot be attained.

The idyll entitled *The Infinite* describes the new situation[74] and marks the full stop at the conclusion of the dialectical experiment. In the extreme tension of the lyric we find the history of an intellectual adventure and the definition of its result. In lines 1 to 3 Leopardi establishes the situation of departure from metaphysical thought—its positing and its limitation. Memory, the insertion into the tradition and the persistence in living are given in the form of seeing. "This hedgerow" is the immediate limit of knowledge [*sapere*], excluding the "extreme horizon." In the form of seeing, lyrical activity and metaphysical activity meet and identify with one another. As for life, it is a horizon, a physical dimension considered in the indefinite progression of the horizon, in visual analogy with the concept of time. Its limitation is grasped as an exclusion, as spatial as it is temporal—exclusion of the extreme, of the profound, of totality. The problem arises on this limit that is thus characterized as naturalistically as it is metaphysically. The metaphysical process is set in motion in lines 4 to 8: "gazing," "fashioning in my thought," and traversing "endless spaces," "more-than-human silences," and "the deepest peace and quiet." Leopardi demands of himself a heroic transcendence, a promethean act: thought, the "dear imagining," rules the aesthetic penetration of the infinite, as schemas of reason launched into the depths, projected onto the extreme horizon. The process of metaphysical apprehension is a being within [*un essere dentro*], and also an action within, being. The temporal dimension of this apprehension of being is quite strong. It is in fact the only flight attempted by Leopardi. And it does not succeed: "so much that almost/My heart fills up with fear."[75] The analogy with a shipwreck in deep water in Descartes's *Meditations* and the recollection of the encounter with theological truth in St. Augustine's *Confessions* resonate here as leitmotifs; and these motifs return to conclude the idyll. Gazing, fashioning in thought, constitutes a fundamental phenomenological operation: a being within being. The metaphysical emotion of "filling with fear" gives way to the stupefying admiration that leads to the cognitive adventure and to this bathing, this being bathed in being. Here the exclusion of the "extreme horizon" and the limit of knowledge [*sapere*] are interiorized. Here the promethean projection is blocked. And at the very instant it is blocked, it posits, from within this set of articulations of being, the conditions of the dialectic.

The true dialectical experiment is carried out, therefore, in lines 8 to 13, in the figure of a double comparison: in the first place we have "that infinite silence" and "this voice" and in the second place we have "the eternal,/And the dead seasons" and "the present one/Alive, and all the sound of it."[76] If the alternating content of the comparisons between voice and silence, between life and death, is a ritual one in the dialectical procedure (like those between nothingness and the "I," between nature and mind), the level of the opposition totally avoids ritual. It foresees no hierarchy and admits no positive-negative articulation. "And as I hear/The wind rustle among the leaves":[77] the comparison develops, on a single plane, in the windy interstices of being—a being that refuses overcomings and overdeterminations, since it rejects the classifications or reductions of ontological determination and never includes the dissolution of the "this." The logical and poetic imbalance provoked in lines 8 to 13, in comparison with the dialectical steps and the acquisition of dialectical conditions operating in lines 1 to 8, is prodigious. It is the masterstroke of the idyll, its cognitive, innovative, catastrophic *Blitz*. So if in lines 7 and 8 "almost/My heart fills up with fear," and now, in lines 13 to 15, "in this immensity, my thought is drowned,"[78] then this immensity is that of the irresolvable comparison, the impossible dialectic. Immersion in being does away with every possibility of mediation. "And sweet is my sinking in this sea"—*in* "this immensity," *in* the determinations of being, *in* the infinite contingencies. The final metaphysical paradox and the stupefying poetic result of *The Infinite* consist in the definition of the insolubility of the problem of the infinite, in the insistence on determination as the ultimate horizon of knowledge [*sapere*]. Exaltation of the finite: that is where sweetness lies.

Leopardi's metaphysical initiation is thus focused on two introductory points: the defeat of heroism and the impossibility of the dialectic, or at least of a dialectic that resolves the experience of the infinite. Of course our analysis to this point has not solved other problems in the genesis of Leopardi's thought, which we have to consider later on. But for the moment, we are satisfied with establishing these few certainties bearing on this period of initiation, or rather of transition in Leopardi's thought and poetic making. Thus Leopardi's relationship with the prison of memory comes to an end, critically speaking, over the theme of flight and the infinite: the transition to another, more mature theoretical position is thereby set up. But it is still worthwhile to recall that this passing beyond, marked by such dramatic accents, corresponds not only to a biographical and psychological event (besides, in Leopardi psychological events are always transcribed into the grandeur of the poetic image and, above all, situated in the regions of metaphysics) but also to an acceleration in the discussion of a new cultural problematic, whether internal (which the beginning of the writing of the *Zibaldone* in those years demonstrates) or generically political-historical (which the polemic concerning Romanticism that opens up at that time and that we soon analyze confirms). I mean that the dimension in which Leopardi, with *The Infinite*, imposes a forced takeover on his own problematic is in no way provisory. The themes of the transition can be varied, and we will be turning next to their complexity. At present it is a matter of understanding how the acquisitions of this period of transition are definitive, in the sense that, with *The Infinite*, the general tone of Leopardi's attitude toward the world changes.

Let us take up again the reading of the idyll. What in it reveals the irreversibility of Leopardi's passage? We have already evoked one fundamental element, the sense of the finite arising in contrast to the nullification—in comparison—of the concept of dialectical infinity. We have also insisted on the temporal dimension that the various analogical elements introduce into the definition of the finite and into the perspective of being that unfolds from it. Now we must, in the first place, clarify the ethical dimension of the emergence of the finite. The interpreters of *The Infinite* have recalled many times the importance of the remarks in the *Zibaldone* that are contemporary with it.[79] At least one of those reflections is doubtless particularly interesting for us, with regard to the point of view that we have adopted; that is to say, in reference to the ethical definition of the finite. Here it is:

> One proof among a thousand of how purely physical systems influence intellectual and metaphysical ones is the system of Copernicus. For the thinker, the Copernican system completely changes the idea of nature and man conceived and thought of as natural in the old, so-called Ptolemaic system. It reveals a plurality of worlds, shows that man is not a unique being, in the same way as the position, movement and

destiny of the world is not unique, and opens up an immense field of
thoughts about the infinity of creatures that, according to all the laws
of analogy, must live on other planets that are entirely analogous to our
own, and those planets which, though we cannot see them, may also
move around other suns, namely the stars. It diminishes the idea of man,
and elevates it, uncovers new mysteries about creation, the destiny of
nature, the essence of things, our being, the omnipotence of the creator,
the purposes of created things, etc., etc.[80]

A Kantian motif, a new apology for the Copernican revolution in philosophy
and culture. The ethical dignity of the finite is posited from the viewpoint
of knowledge [*conoscenza*]. The construction of new mysteries opens up
new dimensions and new ethical desires.[81] But there is still more in *The
Infinite*: an exaltation—in the active terms of the dialectical couple, of
the comparison (in the "voice" and in the "present season alive," in its
"sound")—of the ethical mobility of the subject. The fall of the heroic
element, of prometheanism and the rhetorical forms that expressed it, does
not annul the catastrophic sense of the emergence of the subject, of life, of
expressive possibility. Its insertion into a comparative dimension in order
thereafter to place it within the complexity of being mobilizes the poetic and
ethical sense of human creativity. The Copernican revolution is a work that
simultaneously "diminishes and elevates the idea of man." All this is present
in Leopardi. But what is present above all is the transference of the human
adventure onto the adventure of being. The ethical operation—typical of
Kantianism—here immediately becomes a drama in being, ethical action
in being. Its function is not hermeneutic but ontological. Its structure is not
allusive but ethically constitutive. The voice is the "sound of life." Ethics is
life and constitution of being.

Throughout *The Infinite*, then, an important complementary problem
is posed, that of the sense of the determination. The beginnings of German
dialectical thought are totally dominated by the necessity of reducing the passive aspects of determination (*Bestimmtheit*: given, abstract determination,
or determinateness) to the active moments of determination (*Bestimmung*:
restless determination). Activity must dominate passivity,[82] whereas here,
Leopardian determination is the set of active and passive aspects. In *The
Infinite*, the constant reappearance of the determinative preposition "this"
("this deserted hill," "this hedgerow," "these leaves," "this voice," "this
immensity," "this sea") is an index of the metaphysical horizon of determination. Being is taken, or we are taken by being in its entirety. Determination
belongs to all being. It is not an affectation of particularity. It is an attribute of the universal. Thus "filling with fear," "foundering," and "falling

into ruin" represent, in relation to the frequent usage of the determinative preposition, a corrective, an extension into the apprehension of the real. This grasping, this physical apprehension of being, this exceptional ontological corporeality, is the characteristic and irreversible element of Leopardi's transition to a mature philosophy and to a universal poetic conception of the world beyond the dialectic. Of course, an objection is immediately raised. In this fundamental equivalence of determinations of being, doesn't the sense of ethics risk being annulled? No, it is accentuated and in non-equivocal terms for ethics is precisely neither discrimination nor hierarchy of being but rather its constitution: we are within being, inside being, as actors in its continuous creation. The infinite is not a perspective of possession or domination but a cognitive path. The finite is founding; it is an ethical opening.[83]

We might say that Leopardi thereby renews the Kantian critical intuition at the level of ethical being and add that here he discovers and grasps the center of the logical mystification of the dialectical problem, in the sense that he refuses to characterize the ethical indefinite in terms of the logical (or mystical or ideological) infinite. But asserting that would be tantamount to rushing precipitately over these significations that are still only intuitions and that the history of philosophy, culture, and politics elaborates later, through complex events. I am unhappy with such an allusive method. It seems sufficient to stop at this threshold and grasp the potential vigor of Leopardi's theoretical expression in its dawning power [*potenza*]. This poetry that is entirely ontological will soon be converted into a metaphysics of materialism. For the moment it exists in a transitional phase that is somewhat conclusive. We have already underscored the points on the basis of which the elimination of the elements of the initial cultural climate is carried out: the heroic ideology and the dialectical temptation. Now it is a matter of characterizing (and here solely of indicating) the elements that will produce the future.

The first is undoubtedly this particular relationship of the finite and the infinite, immersed in the ethical solution. It is a motive element. The ideological concept of the infinite, to the extent that it is connected to the concept of the absolute, is totally destroyed, or rather it is disarticulated, decomposed. Finitude becomes the realistic basis of the discourse. The ethical solution in which the experiment unfolds assures the liberation of the lyrical intuition. Indeed, poetic enthusiasm is linked with this ontological perspective as the expressive form of an adequate content—for good, in Leopardi's lyrical experience. The pages most charged with his pessimism are governed by this poetic—lyrical and ontological—enthusiasm. This is the way (the second element of a possible poetic future) the confines, the territorial dimensions, and geological profiles of Leopardi's horizon will be configured. This horizon is traced by the path between the finite and the infinite—a horizon constituted of lines that set out from finitude, a flat, ontologically superficial horizon, not because the events are trivial but because the ontological substrate offers them all equally to view on the surface. Numerous interpretations stress the elements of sensualist philosophy that form the material from which the inspiration for *The Infinite* would be drawn.[84] I doubt this and, quite frankly, I even doubt that Leopardi was ever a sensualist. The use of certain philosophical modules does not guarantee the label of origin. If the poetic joy of the senses is present in *The Infinite*, it is the effect of a great pulsation of the ontological universe. The miniaturism of the sensualist artisan does not suit Leopardi. His world is a horizon. Beyond the hedgerow of this extraordinary poetic invention extends the interminable flatness of the ontological horizon, on which determinate historical and physical concretions, their systems and their passions, continually appear. This, and nothing else, is Leopardi's horizon. Sensualism aims, pictorially, to reconstruct the world on the basis of points, an infinity of points; it is an impressionism that plays over minutia; whereas in Leopardi, the ontological horizon is constituted of ethical lines on which gigantic passions accumulate. It is a cubist horizon.

Against this backdrop, the experiment of *The Infinite* projects a third element: the structuralist disposition of Leopardi's poetic and metaphysical intention. We have already noted how a structuralist tension is implicit in classicism—so that the heroic determination becomes promethean within a logic of global reconstruction of the world. When the heroic instance encounters the crisis, the sense of the structuring of the world nonetheless remains, and this sense is tested and organized against the solidity and complexity of the ontological apparatus [*dispositivo*]. The classical physicality, not merely of the image but of the whole poetic project, as characterization of the metaphysical imagination; the development of the thought between series and correspondences of objects and passions: in Leopardi, all this will become a fundamental key for the reading and expression of the world. This also organizes the poet's sense of freedom. Against the physicality of prison, the physicality of liberation is present in him. Prison and liberation are both serial sequences, representations of totality. The prison from which Leopardi wants to be freed is that of memory, historical time, contemporary literature: actual liberation, or the founding of a new proposition of liberation, will have to have the same capacity to structure itself globally—a capacity equivalent to that which is recognized in the enemy. The finite tends toward the infinite, through determination, in a sequence of connections that form the global structure of being, of the ontological horizon.[85]

Finally, but not in last place, is a fourth element of the future. The ontological horizon is experienced from within. Its scansions, its determinations are evaluated at the level of life. Totality, the concept, never precedes determination, passion. Here is the essential point: it is the sense of the transformation, or if you like (and we do), the sense of the catastrophe. Lines 8 and 9 of *The Infinite*, "And as I hear/The wind rustle among the leaves," are the moment of innovation. Leopardi experiences an ontology of wind. Such is his sense of being. This conception of a wind that pervades being is, moreover, that of ancient atomism; nevertheless, the flavor of Leopardi's innovation cannot be rendered by ancient tradition. It proceeds from the restlessness of the ethical actor within being. The poetic *Blitz* follows the articulation of passion, which is nourished on true being. For "sweet is my sinking in this sea."[86]

The Critical Question

What is Leopardi's situation at the end of this first youthful experimentation with memory and poetic liberation? He experienced a dramatic encounter with the indistinctness of cultural references, he tried to take their measure and critique them—and he seems to have succeeded in that critique. Now therefore he begins to construct a new theoretical condition. What are the contents and determinations of this perspective? We are calling the problem implicit in this questioning the "critical question." It is a matter of understanding the framework within which Leopardi's metaphysical intention develops, the framework in which and from which arise his most creative poetic intuitions. This basis of Leopardi's thought is what we are calling "the critical question": it is a sphere, precisely the terrain of intentionality; that is to say, of a continuous movement, posited and not resolved, incessantly pursued over the whole arc of his activity. The critical question is continually reopened—how to get out of the crisis of the thought of the absolute and the infinite, how to keep open the possibility of the finite without ending up in the dialectic. The problem thus posed is extremely radical. Therefore, the critical question can never be resolved once Leopardi breaks *ab imo et principio* with every determination of memory and historical time, with the cultural and philosophical fabric of his time. In this time, which is that of the dialectic, this initial caesura conversely describes the original opening of Leopardi's search. The world does not change because poetry can sing it better. The determinations of being remain unchanged. And if the dialectic is applied to them, because it is the methodology that is homologous to this problematic horizon, Leopardi denies this homology: he considers these determinations of being, the very ones to which some people surreptitiously apply the dialectic of resolution, as a world of scission, of the catastrophe of memory and the tragedy of ethics.

From this viewpoint, Leopardi is a modern philosopher, for his thought is born from crisis. Leopardi's critical question, his metaphysical intention selects this bifurcation as the most general tendency of the century. Of course dialectical thought too rapidly ends up in crisis. But what the dialectic suffers in the time of its development, Leopardi takes up in the very brief period of his poetic propaedeutic. He moves out of the crisis of dialectical thought. He detaches himself, although by small steps, from the intensity of theoretical and poetic emotion he experienced in contact with it. The dialectical flight from being ends, and the ethical path within being begins. Leopardi's maturity is entirely constructed on the weft woven by the dialectic, but in negative form, going beyond it: critical question, critical intention, ethical opening of the finite onto being.

It is therefore not surprising that the tone would be that of disenchantment above all. This disenchantment is due to the intensity of the tragedy experienced. But it is, despite everything, an inconsequential result of what happened around *The Infinite*. The poet proceeds by small steps. He does not develop the critical question, but he formalizes it, unfolds it. He invests the critical question in those fields of thought on which the crisis had developed before reaching the catastrophic moment of poetry and metaphysics—that Cartesian poetics of the "I think therefore I am" that constitutes *The Infinite*: I think, I suffer, so therefore I am a finite substance, a finite determination.[87]

Two idylls immediately follow *The Infinite*: *To the Moon*[88] and *Hear Me, Melissus*.[89] In the first idyll, the Cartesian aspect of the crisis of *The Infinite*, the separation of the "I" from the indifference of nature and history, from the universe of memory, is revisited and deepened. The metaphysical initiation appears as the entry into the age of majority—"It was a year ago": a year has passed and Leopardi explicitly announces it in order to indicate the passage from the "time of youth" to maturity. The content of the passage is the inversion of the relationship between hope and memory.

> What enormous pleasure
> In time of youth, when hope has such great distance
> To travel still and memory so little. (*To the Moon*, ll.12–14)[90]

This is an inversion that is above all a separation: during youth, memory and hope are indeed confused in heroism, while now memory is deployed without any key, rhetorical, heroic, or dialectical, that makes it comprehensible. And hope, for its part, is alone, diminished by this solitude, relegated to the sphere of disenchantment and finitude. A year has been spent: pain persists and is always just as devastating.

My life was full
Of anguish then: and is, nor has it changed,
O moon of my delight. (ll.8–10)[91]

But critique accompanies the pain and imagination affirms, in disenchantment, the function of the "I."

Yet I enjoy
Remembrance, and the reckoning of the age
My sorrow grows to. (ll.10–12)[92]

In this idyll there is nothing consolatory. There is the very noble and nevertheless slight declaration of the rupture of indistinctness, the conquest
of the viewpoint of the finite "I." This is not because there is an answer
to the critical question. On the contrary, the tragic condition of ethics is
accentuated. This condition does not call for solutions, for all the solutions
presuppose the surmounting and annihilation of finitude, pain, life.

   The discourse of the poetic fragment *Hear Me, Melissus* is even more
explicit, in part because it is more pedagogical and less lyrically wrenching.
The repetition of the drama of separation, of the rupture of the hope for the
infinite, here acquires the lightness of tone of paradox.

Hear me, Melissus: I will tell a dream
I had this night; it comes back into mind
Seeing the moon once more. Well, I was standing
Before the window which gives on the meadow,
Looking up in the sky; and all at once
The moon broke loose; and as it seemed to me
The nearer that it came as it fell down
The bigger it grew; until at last it landed
Right in the middle of the meadow; it was
Big as a bucket every bit, and as
For sparks it spewed a cloud of them, which hissed
As loudly as a live coal when you plunge it
In water and put it out. (ll.1–13)[93]

And what appears in the sky?

[L]ooking at the sky, I saw a sort
Of glimmer left, a scar, or socket rather
It could have been torn from. (ll.17–19)[94]

The finesse of the tale, the lyrical delicacy of the dialogue between Alcetas and Melissus, does not in any way detract from the philosophical depth.[95] We are in a Berkeleyan situation: if the "I" detaches itself from memory, affirms its separation, will it succeed in carrying out, in this crisis, a cognitive overturning in relation to nature and history? Is the "I," in its dream and in its separation, capable of reconstructing a horizon of life? Can a thought that detaches itself from the universality of the logical foundation of the world and from the construction of the totality pursue the adventure of psychological idealism and succeed at it? The answer is negative. Solipsism, the illusion of the creation of the world by the individual, is impossible. The relationship no longer has a dialectical solution. Determination can neither be created nor denied. Once the world of representation has been left behind, no ladder can be thrown down. No, Alcetas, the moon is not a falling star.

> There are so many stars
> That little harm were done if one or other
> Should fall, with thousands left. But there is only
> This one moon in the sky, and nobody
> Has ever seen it fall, except in dreams. (ll.24–28)[96]

The affirmation of the "I" is thus the realistic affirmation of the finite "I." The relationship to the moon, to its solitude and its determinability, cannot be suppressed; and here determination, physical consistency, and the solitude of the poet are opposed. "But there is only/This one moon in the sky."[97] Here again, the lightness with which the critical question is posed and articulated does not detract from the depth, a depth that is in no way psychological—the return of pain—but rather philosophical. The philosophical question, in its splendid lyrical form, never gives way to banality. The problem is weighty—the weight of a moon that falls on the meadow. The crisis, in the form of lightness, unfolds. All the protagonists appear on the stage, in the reality of their determination and their finitude. But this philosophical and poetic passage, concerning the crisis of 1819, is of great importance not only because it again proposes all the terms of the critical question but because it extends its range, expands the question, and makes it mobile, multiple. If the dialectic is inconceivable as the resolving form of determinateness and yet the terms of a dialectical problematic remain, and the finitudes are opposed to one another without encountering *Aufhebungen*, then what, on the negative edge of this situation, are the flows, passages, and relations as well as the terms of existence that must be known? Of course, no logical sequence, no linearity is available on this horizon of being. On the contrary, here we come to know ruptures, crises, suffering; but all that is given in being, on an ontological basis that this emergence contains and puts into relation. Moreover, the context of the dialectic, this dialectic that does not resolve, is global, structurally complex, and precisely adjusted to the surface of the world and to its multiple appearances. The dialectic as resolving operation is measured and vanquished in the context of memory— the constitutive memory of nature and mind. So what are the flows that pass not only between finite subjects but between regions of this universe: cultural, psychological, and physical regions? In its lightness, the critical question is not only dense but also progressive. It is not merely intense but also transversal. The critical catastrophe takes place at the high point of the lyric: now it seeks the permeability of the whole fabric of memory, history, and nature. We seem to see Leopardi struggling through this passage, while, from the depth of a lyrical emotion that leads knowledge [*conoscenza*] to the verge of the infinite, he turns his attention—not in disillusion, but with the prudence of one who cannot revive the extremity of pain—to the accumulation of his own experience in order to verify it, to submit it to the riddle of the critical question: the critical intention in the totality of the ethical tragedy of his universe.

It is not by chance, then, that this very young poet, solitary and marginal, intervenes at the highest level of the ongoing cultural discussion. The fact that the composition of *Discourse of an Italian on Romantic Poetry*[98] precedes that of *The Infinite* does not prevent both of them from inhering in the same problematic. Thus this discourse demonstrates, from a methodological point of view, the validity of a critical approach constructed and developed on the basis of thematic structures: the structural sequences gather together diverse times and styles in their development, and the connection does not prevent an eventual relative discontinuity of passages.[99] Now what is the operation that Leopardi accomplishes in the *Discourse*? It is a catastrophic operation, total and decisive, with respect to the contents of memory. We must keep in mind the structure of the *Discourse* and not allow ourselves to be deceived by references to the themes of the dialogue with Giordani, which one can read there. For in opposition to what must have been Leopardi's position—consistent with these themes; that is to say, the claims on behalf of classical poetry—a radically original intention is expressed here. First of all, we see once again an inversion of the terms of the debate, then their displacement and, finally, the metaphysical innovation. Let us follow these operations.

In the first place, Leopardi defines the alternatives of the debate, the "contrary opinions" that confront each other, thereby isolating two series: the first, "nature-imitation-modern-feeling" and the second, "history-fantasy-classic-sense." Each of these terms is opposed to its counterpart in the other series. Classicism and Romanticism are opposed as structures taken in their entirety. But what sense can this abstract opposition have? Unless classicism becomes a stupid and servile repetition and Romanticism a simple taste for the extraordinary, claiming a rigid opposition makes these two tendencies into shams. In reality, quite banally, both thematize different components of the tradition of poetic making and are opposed only abstractly. "Nature against history," or vice versa? "Imitation or fantasy"? But what sense can these oppositions have? Where does one term end and the other begin? Concrete poetic making experiences positively not this alternative but rather the conjunction of the polarity. "Nature does not reveal herself, but remains hidden,"[100] and only the fantasy of the natural and the historical forms of life in common will know how to reveal it to the poet. But on the other hand, poetry does not exist without an inclination toward nature, toward the fundamental, toward the primitive. History and reason cannot replace poetic intention: "as much as the empire of reason will expand, and in proportion as illusions are unnerved and increasingly rare, so much will greatness in men, thought and deed become scarce."[101] Leopardi's argument is deployed without pause; it encompasses and alternates the themes and viewpoints—of course not in rhetorical terms, nor in order to evade the knot of the question. On the contrary, it is here that the overturning of the general cultural thematic is carried out: the problem is not posed from the viewpoint of the poet but from the viewpoint of the public—of poetry as cultural object. The inversion of [Ludovico di] Breme's thematics, of those of the Romantics and their interlocutors and adversaries, is thus produced by imposing the primacy of the public's viewpoint on and against aesthetic purity.[102] The pretext of the purely aesthetic thematic does not replace the making of poetry, and that making is enjoyment on the terrain of culture. The strength of the nationalist dimension aids in the demonstration. The *Discourse* is that "of an Italian"; and the last pages are a heroic, impassioned appeal to the young for the renewal of culture and for the liberation of the nation. Could there be a more apt terrain for signifying the cultural objectivity of making and enjoying poetry? On the other hand, as Leopardi suggests, what difference is there between these new Romantic authors and those who belong to the final stage of the culture of the Enlightenment? Are not the political claims of this Romantic generation, at least some of them, inscribed in a lineage that runs from Parini to Alfieri? And conversely, did not the pedagogy of the Enlightenment demand that poetic culture measure itself against and nourish itself on history? The inversion of the terms of the debate, their continuous, repeated, paradoxical overturning (according to which Romanticism ends up being classical and vice versa) determines the position of the final passage of the discourse, the displacement of the problem. Leopardi asks what relation there is between subjectivity and objectivity in poetry, between desire and lyrical expression, between imagination and truth. Poetry is a cultural phenomenon. All the series can be eliminated or exchanged, but this mixture of forms of expression nevertheless remains subordinated to truth. Only truth, true illusion, makes poetry. Posing the problem of truth constitutes the initial variant of Leopardi's displacement. It is therefore useless to "practice poetry with the intellect." Neither the abstract nor the extraordinary, neither rarity nor psychological reduction makes poetry, but instead the plenitude of the senses and reason make it. This constitutes a refusal and inversion of the terms of the debate, therefore displacement. Truth.

The problem is what routes lead toward truth. Where does it reside? Yet again, an Enlightenment proposition. In this *Discourse*, where Leopardi traverses the entirety of his own cultural memory, the more mature variant of the complex displacement of the debate appears, the first of the catastrophic assertions of the discourse: truth is lived, penetrated being, "a truth which is so true that it has no need to be said." This is an epistemologically materialist position; in any case, it is an anti-dialectical one. Truth consists in determination and the finite. Such is its place. The rupture of the cultural mediation of the debate, which intervenes after the formidable inversion of all the terms, and thus the banalization of the aesthetic problem, here unites with the renewal of the Enlightenment theme of the relation between poetry and truth: materialism; the anti-dialectical determination of the finite. The true is the made [*fatto*]; it is the finite. But here, following the first anti-dialectical rupture, a second rupture marks an advance insofar as it is not merely critical but also contains a proposition. "The Romantics believe that excellence in imitation should be evaluated according to its distance from or proximity to truth, to the extent that, while looking for the truth, they almost forget imitation, since truth cannot be the imitation of itself."[103] The true can only be the creation of itself. The finite world, the crisis of the infinite, the despairing sense of the impossibility of the dialectical solution: they all come to light here. The inversion, banalization, and critique of Romantic aesthetics are displaced onto the terrain of the true, of a material and finite true. And there is nothing anemic or mechanical about this materialism. It is the very terrain of life. Finitude does not dissipate into the absolute; on the contrary, it insists on itself but thereby breaks in advance the order of life. Truth is apophantic; thus it is mythical. We are witness to a new inversion of discourse in which Leopardi mocks his own classicist friends. Truth is the myth that breaks with the order of the intellect, of the series, of psychological reduction, that grasps and expresses the miracle of reason. Poetry is the highest form of rational expression.[104]

This sequence from the *Discourse of an Italian on Romantic Poetry* expresses the redundancy of the metaphysics of *The Infinite* on the cultural terrain: demystification of the Romantic problematic, inversion of its terms, displacement of the poetic problem onto the terrain of truth, mythology of reason as unique philosophical opening, all within insoluble dialectical apparatuses and conditions. In short, it is the mythology of finite reason, the transcendental illusion against the transcendental dialectic. But a second aspect of this fundamental passage also interests us. This regards the relationship between myth and materialism. Indeed, in the displacement of the problematic and the linkage with truth, this is the moment when, in my view, Leopardi carries out a decisive operation on the terrain and materials of memory. Leopardi does not limit himself here to freeing the irreducibly debated terms of memory through an act of historical knowledge [*conoscenza*] and a philosophical intuition that recognizes in the relationship between the Enlightenment and Romanticism a continuity to be globally criticized. This critique is of a historical order: the continuity of the Enlightenment and Romanticism seems extremely clear in Italy—even more so than in other European cultures. But this historical continuity nourishes the most perfidious poisons of intellectualism and a destructive determination![105] We must free ourselves from it. But what are the consequences of such a liberating operation?

Here another critical passage is implied, which consists in forsaking Enlightenment or Romantic intellectualism, recognizing their indifference, and placing ourselves on the terrain of material truth. But if we affirm materialism as the only determination that constitutes an alternative to the idealist totality of memory, then materialism must appear as creativity, as the dynamic of form, as the possibility of myth. The idea that materialism would be capable of myth is Leopardi's great intuition. As soon as we begin to study the *Zibaldone*, we see the intensity with which materialism and the mythology of reason are articulated.[106] For the moment, let us recall that the more any philosophy of empiricism deepens the materialist determinations, the more it is driven to construct a creative sphere of the mind: the "moral sentiment" of Hume and Adam Smith, the *Gefühl* of Hamann, "passion" in Helvetius,[107] and already the *clinamen* of Epicurus and Lucretius.[108] How present and potent is this latter tradition in Leopardi! Thus it begins to become obvious that Leopardi's crisis and the catastrophe of memory do not merely determine the principal elements of framing within which lyric and thought develop; they intervene equally with regard to the form of thought. The catastrophe is not merely a condition but an epistemological key to Leopardi's materialism—a key that, moreover, permits the ethical characterization of his labor in the activation of the critical spirit and lyrical thought. But we examine this point later.

We are at present in a position to understand the singular figure that so-called classicism assumes in Leopardi. We have just recalled the fact that a simple contrast with Romantic poetics cannot suffice to define it. On the other hand, it is enough to take into account the complex figure of Jacobin heroism in order to stop doubting the falsity of a number of oppositions that characterize literary historiography. In direct terms, Goethe and Hölderlin have, through the experience of a sublime poetics, done justice to these presumed oppositions by potently experiencing their specificity and annihilating them in a single continuous labor. Leopardi belongs to the same current. As in Goethe, and above all as in Hölderlin, classicism in Leopardi becomes a kind of grand dispensary where one experiments with the relationship between materialism and mythology, between memory and catastrophe. Already on display in the "letter to Breme"—and it is agreeable to be led there by Xenophanes, as previously by Simonides in *To Italy* (both participate, in different ways, in a genealogy of the gods)[109]—in the canzone *To Angelo Mai* this is perfectly explicit.[110] The motif materialism/mythology or memory/catastrophe is worked out exhaustively here. The themes of the canto addressed to the discoverer of the Ciceronian text *Of the Republic* are three in number: the wretchedness of Italian history, the pain suffered when one confronts it, and the song of the poets and heroes that allows us to be reborn from this wretchedness. These are three singularly connected themes that reappear as constantly renewed entreaties in an impetuous and uneven poetic flux. This classical hymn is perhaps Leopardi's most Romantic—if we must hold on to the classifications and use those exhausted stereotypes. Yet for him the wretchedness of Italian history is not a matter for contemplation. It is rather the material condition in which we move and which the canto records: "this dead era, overshadowed/By such a cloud of boredom?" (ll.4–5).[111] The poet is totally caught:

I, I am destroyed,
Unsheltered from distress, because for me
The future is obscure, and what I glimpse
Always makes hope appear
A dream and foolish fable. (*To Angelo Mai*, ll.34–38)[112]

This wretchedness and pain are the symptoms of a general situation, as subjectively moving as it is objectively heavy. Wretchedness is historical, in the full meaning of the word: an "honourless unclean/Rabble" succeeds the kingdom of heroes.

idleness surrounds
Your monumental tombs; we are become
Patterns of baseness to all future time. (ll.39–40, 43–45)[113]

Memory is immersed in baseness and inactivity, in the mindless leveling
out of the sense of life. Talents are spent insofar as the heroes are dead.
Pain constitutes the first, the only, the elementary refusal. It is memory's
sole product. It does not live on the surface; it belongs to deep history, to
the exploits of so many heroes (the canto enumerates them, from Columbus
to Tasso and Alfieri), rendered mute and tragically neglected by historical
time. Pain forms part of memory. It is one of the elements of its dialectic,
but it is also and above all the sign that this dialectic and memory cannot
be concluded and cannot be surmounted. Pain is a dialectical material.
Nevertheless it is here that catastrophe is inserted—in the positive and
negative sense, with one side the crushing of hope and the other side the
positive limit of pain. Their contemporaneity restores, constructs, indicates
the moment of catastrophe.

Alas! Italian song is born
From grief. And yet the pain of our afflictions
Weighs down and hurts us less
Than the tedium where we drown. Oh you were blessed:
Weeping was life for you! Our swaddling bands
Were bound for us by boredom; motionless
By the cradle, on the tomb, sits nothingness. (ll.69–75)[114]

After this puissant introduction, the rest of the canto traces the metaphysical dimensions of the situation: a historical, materialist metaphysics that
articulates the moment of memory with that of catastrophe, the development
of being towards nothingness, and the necessity of breaking its rigidity—in
the canto, in the "dear imaginings," by means of this "marvelous power
[*poter*]." It is a historical metaphysics that, above the miserable panorama of
the present, raises the voices of rebels, of Torquato and Vittorio, to the level
of myth and thus transforms the heroic illusion into the lyrical emergence
of catastrophe. This is a catastrophe that is also political: this aspect never
ceases to recur, from the first to the last lines, from the hatred of the "rabble"
at the start to the denunciation of the "rising of the crowd" at the conclusion, this invective being always associated with the one directed in parallel
fashion against the tyrant. So once again no more than a paragraph on the
catastrophe of memory is presented to us *sub specie politicae*. These political declarations emerge onto a lyrical and metaphysical terrain, the spirit

and letter of the discourse being lyrical and metaphysical—Leopardi is no more reactionary here than Nietzsche could be, than any being whatsoever who considers truth to be only catastrophe. Such is the situation into which the canto *To Angelo Mai* plunges us. The exclamation "all things are alike; by our discoveries/Only nothingness grows" (ll.99–100)[115] is therefore, from a certain point of view, not in contradiction with the filial invocation.

> Oh famous discoverer,
> Go on, rouse the dead
> Now, since the living sleep; arm the exhausted
> Tongues of early heroes; so that this age
> Of mud may come to lust for life at last
> And rise to noble deeds, or sink abashed. (ll.175–80)[116]

There is no contradiction. It is the simple affirmation of the insoluble coexistence of memory and catastrophe, the elementary givens of the dialectical crisis. Living this determinate contradiction constitutes the ethical and poetic possibility.

This is the point where Leopardi's greatness begins, in the fact of experiencing the crisis of dialectical thought at its origin. Some decades ago, in an unforgettable study, Karl Löwith retraced the vicissitudes of the dialectic among Goethe, Kierkegaard, and Nietzsche,[117] indicating at the same time the critical point of the dialectical conception of history and the moment of its discovery and dramatization: the dialectical insolubility of the finite. In French culture, at the beginning of the sixties, Deleuze's rereading of Nietzsche[118] followed the same path and recovered the anti-dialectical flavor of philosophy by relying on the irreducibility of metaphysical contingency and ethical power [*potenza*]. We must return to the Nietzsche-Leopardi nexus and see how, in the discourse on tragedy and the genealogy of divinity and morality, their paths often simply overlap—as if a mysterious and common destiny existed for true classical philology. In the immediate moment, we wish to linger not over this singular analogy but over another theme in the young Leopardi we are studying. That is the gathering up, as in a short story, of an event in the crisis of the dialectic whose trajectory spans a century. It is the profound articulation of the intuition of the finite, of the metaphysical conception of contingency, and the ethical conception of power [*potenza*]. The idealist dialectic, the fact that it falls into the destructiveness of a totalitarian sentiment, is experienced by Leopardi in contact with the origin, with the arising of a problem that he nonetheless confronts: the crisis of memory, the crisis of historical time.[119] Leopardi therefore anticipates a fundamental critical nexus in philosophical development, the thought of crisis.

But this Leopardian anticipation, precisely because it experiences and traverses the world of memory, is characterized by another singularity. In effect, if on the one hand it is posited as anticipatory consciousness directed against the dialectical project, in other aspects it is the conclusive consciousness of a development that is equally destructive, that of the *Dialektik der Aufklärung* [dialectic of Enlightenment].

Studying the *Zibaldone* permits us to retrace, so to speak, a negative history of Enlightenment thought, from Montesquieu to Novalis,[120] a tableau of great historiographical breadth and prodigious critical meticulousness. A scene unfolds there in which one sees Enlightenment thought come to an end in the same crisis, over the same necessity for resistance and protest of the finite and the concrete against the abstract and the infinite of the intellect. Two histories are superimposed—one of the development of the Enlightenment and the other of dialectical idealism—the dialectic supporting both. Leopardi, who experiences the intersection of these two events, criticizes both. He is opposed at once to a dialectic that he sees concluding in the defeat of the historical time of life and to a new dialectic that he sees sanctifying this defeat of reason. Leopardi's historical position acquires, as a result of this situation between these two worlds, a very great significance.[121] Two characteristics of his thought follow directly from this.

The first, which we could call spatial, refers to the intensity and definition of the relationship to the physicality of the world that it describes. The second is temporal and corresponds to a conception of time that is developed between the critique of the past and the anticipation of the future, forming one body with the conception of being. The first concerns the Enlightenment. The importance of Montesquieu's teaching in Leopardi's work is well known and we see it throughout the pages of the *Zibaldone*. Yet in Montesquieu, the nature-history continuity represents a fundamental element that constitutes the sphere of communication (the theory of political forms), ethical feeling, and constitutional prefiguring.[122] Leopardi always maintains the density of the relationship between history and nature, which in technical terms is structural. He makes this materialist contribution to the critique of the dialectic of nineteenth-century idealist thought, drawing it from the philosophy of the Enlightenment. On the other hand, there is the conception of time, a pervasive, thick, historically dense time. This is the historically determined time that the events, dimensions, and jolts of the unfolding of the Great Revolution have taught us to consider and that German idealism posits at the center of metaphysics.[123] In his own way Leopardi takes up this nineteenth-century conception of time and makes it react with Enlightenment philosophy. The difficulties of a historical apprehension of Leopardi's thought often follow from this exercise and can be resolved only by the discovery of the inversions of signification that he carries out. In this dimension, when the two dialectical scenarios, that of the Enlightenment and that of classical idealism, are superimposed, the concept of crisis emerges with exceptional force; for Leopardi makes space and time, nature and history, Enlightenment and idealism react.

A third, complementary characteristic of Leopardi's thought follows from this. It is in no way a progressivist thought, though not because, on the basis of its historical position, between the conclusion of a defeated past and the refusal of a future that it seems to and does repeat, it cannot be the same dialectic. It is not a progressivist thought because it is not a historicist thought. Luporini, Binni, and others[124] have sometimes forgotten, while they were leading a proud and justified battle against formalism, the rigidity of the nexus between historicism and progressivism. Leopardi is not progressivist because his anti-dialectical thought makes history react only with itself. Leopardi's attitude is that of catastrophe, a catastrophe rooted in a solid, constructive materialism, but one that is neither linear nor progressive. The catastrophe of memory and historical time is the fundamental moment within which Leopardi's thought is situated and on the basis of which its essential motifs are formed. Let us add that the materialism-catastrophe nexus can in no case be interpreted as a reactionary form, not because the concept of reaction would be, after the fashion of the concept of progress, deprived of meaning with reference to Leopardi's lyric and its partial contents, but because the catastrophic nexus discovered and organized by materialism is opposed to every restorative practice, to the repetition of historical time, to the stereotyped resistance of the past. Catastrophe is against reaction. Nevertheless, it cannot be progressivist because there is no thought of time governing the real. There is only human insurrection, the insurrection of the finite that shatters reality and makes it new! The catastrophe of historical memory thus preserves, in Leopardi, the sense of a radical enmity in relation to memory: it is the boredom that leads to nothingness, as the canzone *To Angelo Mai* teaches. The catastrophe of memory is accompanied by a subjective—and metaphysically guaranteed—refusal.

Let us conclude. What we have said so far could perhaps lead to a final qualification that is central to Leopardi's thought concerning the positioning of the critical question. This last qualification, aside from the fact that it is situated within the set of factors already described, imposes a direction that determines all of them. Clashing with the catastrophe of memory, it turns toward the interiority of being. It follows and interweaves the dimensions of space and time, nature and history, and constitutes them together. The interiority of the lyric, of the voice, in crisis: is that the true, catastrophic meaning of Leopardi's thought? Yes, but only if we understand it from the other side, as a constitutive direction. The critical question, by means of a twisting of the very concept, thus unites the critical intuition with the catastrophic constitution. It is the form in which the theme of truth is presented, proposed for the first time in completed terms at the conclusion of the events in *The Infinite*. The catastrophe of memory reaches an extreme limit—historical time can be regained only through a constitutive operation. It is not difficult now to understand the ethical determination of the expected development. The critical question is the field of ethics. Let us examine again the canto *To Angelo Mai*. This thought—which the contempt of the present leads to pain, which through pain rediscovers a horizon of past boredom and the nothingness of the future, which rebels against this condition, which curses, incites, and raises itself up in imagining; this thought that nevertheless does not want the imaginary to reproduce nothingness, in the clear reflection of this risk, that instead wants material rupture and transcendence—this thought is ethical thought. It is, in the highest and most materialist sense, constitutive thought. The critical question in Leopardi is, by means of ethics, a constitutive question. After the experiment of *The Infinite*, the problem is posed in disenchantment, a disenchantment that does not lose its metaphysical density. The pain is too strong.

Chapter 2

The Web of Sense

···

Solid Nothingness

After the crisis of *The Infinite*, Leopardi's thought expands [*distende*], in the sense that the personal crisis is reflected in the conditions of existence in their entirety. He writes to Leandro Trissino: "I will not say that the tears really belong to me, but that they are a necessity of the times and fortune."[1] This objective reflection relieves the "appalling torment of life" at Recanati. "My intellect is weary of chains imposed from within the family and from outside."[2] Leopardi needs to free himself from them, and this liberation is simultaneously supported and produced by an extension of thematics, by their broader projection onto the world. The search for friendship in the letters to Brighenti, the quest for aristocratic esteem and literary recognition in the letters to Trissino are, of course, accompanied by a deepening of despairing themes, a renewed suffering linked to ethical tragedy; but this deepening and suffering are now given within a fully metaphysical dimension. Since the crescendo of a metaphysics of negative reason, discernible in the letters to Pietro Giordani between November 1819 and June 1820, has a constructive tone, it is the promotion of the critical question instead of, or rather beyond, the desperate experimenting with the crisis. It is this beyond, its construction, that we must follow here.

19 November 1819:

I am so stupefied by the nothingness which surrounds me that I do not know how I have the strength to pick up the pen to reply to your letter of the first. If at this moment I were to go mad, I think my madness would be to sit forever with my eyes staring, my mouth open, my hands between my knees, without laughing or crying or moving except when forced to from the place where I happened to be. I no longer have the energy to conceive any desire, not even for death, not because I have any fear at all of death, but I no longer see any difference between death and this life of mine, where not even pain comes to comfort me anymore. This is the first time that tedium not only weighs on me and wearies me, but it torments me and tears me like a terrible pain; and I am so terrified by the futility of all things, and by the condition of men when all passions have died, as they are spent in my soul, that I go out of my mind, thinking that my desperation too is nothing.[3]

This letter to Pietro Giordani marks the passage to a sensibility of a metaphysical order in the correspondence. Its radicality consists in the displacement of all the themes, particularly the theme of suicide, which evolves from suicide for love of heroism or for hatred of prison to the point of the metaphysical distention [*distensione*] and destruction of the very idea of suicide. These themes are deployed in the letter of 17 December. The personal condition ("So do not be distressed on my account, for where there is no hope there is no place for anxiety; rather love me serenely as someone not destined for anything at all, but on the contrary sure that his life is already over. And I shall love you with all the warmth left to this frozen and shivering soul")[4] is reflected in and at the same time detached from "this terrifying desert of the world." Subjectivity is thrown into the world, and within that finitude it experiences a tragic dimension that belongs both to consciousness and to the world. "This universal truth, that everything is nothingness" explodes in the letter of 6 March 1820,[5] which is as good as a canto: "seeing a clear sky and bright moonlight [. . .] I set to yelling like a madman [. . .] I felt an icy fear, not being able to understand how life can be endured." Only in "everything is nothingness" does this metallic madness find relief, expanding in disdain for those "wretched would-be philosophers who take comfort in the boundless increase in reason, and think that human happiness consists in knowing the truth, when there is no other truth than nothingness." It finds relief in the hope for a lyrical invention that would know how to face the unending period of human wretchedness, the wretchedness of the citizen and of literary tradition[6]—in the cognition [*cognizione*] of pain. It finds relief finally ("desperate as I am, I still take on the role of comforter"[7]) in the acceptance of the metaphysical truth that nothingness constitutes the exclusive terrain on which life can be granted: "I believe no man on earth in any circumstance should ever despair of the return of illusions, because they do not come from art or reason, but from nature." "What is barbarity if not the state in which nature no longer has power over men? I do not consider illusions to be insubstantial, but as things which in some way have substance."

Begun in the metaphysical expansion [*distensione*] in the form of the critical question, this set of letters therefore concludes with the focus on a fundamental ontological element: illusions, "things which in some way have substance." In what does this substantial character consist? It is difficult to define this at the present stage of research, but we can begin to approach the sense of this breakthrough in the reality of negative reason. The crisis of memory, a tragedy and catastrophe in being, left a world deprived of sense, deprived of support in being. This deprivation takes the form of nothingness. Reason concludes its cognitive process in nothingness. Negative in all its effects, reason is not for all that any less real. Moving in nothingness—that is to say, in illusion—reason discovers a foundation that is not absolute or infinite but relative and finite. This foundation is illusion itself. The foundation is nothing more than the lack of foundation. Nevertheless, the world is the second nature[8] formed by the set of illusions. It is in this sense that illusions represent, and are, something substantial. This discovery is presented in the letters with great modesty, almost timidly. The discussion proceeds by bits and pieces, defines no project, and appears as an appendix to the lyrical work or as a document of the personal situation and its upheaval. The problem here does not consist in measuring the degree of reality of this world of illusion, this reality of negative reason. We merely know that it is the sole, exclusive terrain on which thought and lyric can be carried out, the only possible sphere for life. We know its fragile and yet irreducible materiality.

But this very first introduction to metaphysics contains more. Not only is the fabric of the critical question taking shape here—since it and it alone can be characterized as real—but the sense of the constitutive intention is also being determined. In this reality that negative reason negatively determines, in this world of illusion, life is an active force. Immersed in nothingness, it continually returns to reality as critical intention and lyrical experience. Clashing with the lack of sense that characterizes it and with the theoretical defeat that founds it, life takes on vigor and complexity. It is totally useless to insist that the critical intention equals in strength and intensity the ethical intention that marks Leopardi's much later experience. Moreover, that would mean carrying out the reading in the equivocal situation of rationally anticipating an element that is only presaged here. But it is indisputable that, in revealing itself as metaphysics, the critical and ethical intention traverses reality in a manner that a contemporary phenomenologist would call "functional"—a creative mode, in other words "noematic," constructive of the object of the cognitive relation.[9] The world of illusions thus becomes a second nature—and a civil second nature, a new public sphere [*Öffentlichkeit*][10] is also postulated, if only in *Letter 146*, and an ethical second nature is posited (if only in *Letter 156*) as a feeling of serenity and an activity of consolation. In the confrontations of critique, even in the most catastrophic moments, Leopardi does not know how to posit himself if not as an ethically intentional and active subject.

Here I would like to open a brief parenthesis. We find ourselves, I repeat, in the earliest stage of Leopardi's metaphysics, a stage defined only by hints. It remains no less the case that the definitions of the terrain and the intention henceforth constitute solid elements of his metaphysical methodology. I ask myself from where was Leopardi able to derive this methodological tonality, outside of his own experience. Was he not able to perceive certain elements in the sphere of the critique of memory and tradition that would enable this foundation? Indeed, it seems to me that in the pages of Leopardi's correspondence, above all in the letters to Giordani, we must single out a line that he considered to be already pedagogically and ethically corrupted in Enlightenment culture, but that was nevertheless rooted, in uncorrupted form, in the highest moments of civil and literary experience in Italian history. In the incomplete dialectic between the definition of the world as real illusion and the lyrical and ethical intention to retrace it, this theoretical and literary tension makes the materialism of Machiavelli, Ariosto, Giordano Bruno, and Galileo insurmountable. This is a line that is always minoritarian, not in terms of poetic and civil power [*potenza*] but in terms of political efficacy, and yet always present and always antagonistic to the other line, embodied in the historical splendors of Platonism, Petrarchism, mannerism, and idealism.

Reading the *Zibaldone* brings to light Leopardi's ambiguous position in relation to the literary tradition, his inability to discern univocal and opposed blocs, not for lack of critical will but through excess of lyrical tension: "Now why so many/Such revivals [*risorgimenti*]?" (*To Angelo Mai*, ll.8–9).[11] A question without answer. That said, it remains the case that the memory (this time not critical but renewing, precise, deep and subtle) of the realistic and ethical materialism of a fundamental current of Italian literature can be recognized in Leopardi's approach.[12] This is a materialism that makes the modes of illusion the sole terrain on which to grasp life and that makes the ethical intervention the only form in which space can take on a sense and humanity can achieve dignity. Emphasizing the continuity and independence of this partisan and minoritarian thought, so aggressive and free, is even more important than any apologetic dialectical history of a universal, flat, impartial, national thought. And this leads us to recognize in Leopardi's metaphysical labor a radicalism, not merely concerning the philosophical intuition but also on the plane of historical antagonism, which is truly exceptional. "Now why so many/Such revivals?" Because the materialist explanation and the ethical will are always revolutionary, and the revolution is the myth necessary for a disenchanted capacity for truth: negative reason.

The *Zibaldone* is born on this terrain.[13] At this point I cannot cover it all, but far from being a gigantic muddle of thousands of scattered intuitions, the *Zibaldone* is an impressive effort to constitute the world of illusion, a gigantic accumulation and sedimentation of states of consciousness, a constantly repeated game for bringing the entirety of the aspects of life to a structural unity and leading the ethical determinations of being to an operational expression. The method of the *Zibaldone* consists in identifying and constructing objects, and its objects are the real. We know what the point of departure is: "It seems absurd and yet it is absolutely true that, since reality is nothingness, there is no other reality or other substance in the world but illusions."[14] But how is the reality of illusions formed? This first "absurd" conclusion, already expressed in the correspondence from the years 1819 and 1820, is only an introduction to metaphysics, the identification of a terrain. This terrain must now be cleared, the world of illusion spun into a genealogy, and the material contents, production, and web of true illusion discovered. The critical question is thus fully posed. The terms of an impossible dialectic must be submitted to a theoretical alternative: if not the dialectic, what constructs the world? What weaves the phenomenological fabric of illusion and attributes to it the truth of the real? What web of the cognitive faculty and the finite states of the real is constituted in the truth of the world? The metaphysical introduction here requires deepening. The first pages of the *Zibaldone*, the scattered notes made between 1817 and the end of 1819, contain a kind of summary of the problems that this deepening makes necessary. Here we try to retrace the first emblematic steps of Leopardi's path.

They consist in a sort of recapitulation of points already seen throughout the correspondence, the first canti and the first discorsi, a summary that confines itself to defining a metaphysical terrain, while indicating the internal channels of flow. Diverse threads of interest are broached: historical-literary, stylistic, philological-linguistic, philosophical-aesthetic, metaphysical, poetic notes. . . . Their intermingling is constructive, as it allows our investigation (and Leopardi's) to set out in any direction. But we begin with the question of the corruption of Italian letters. This is an old question, long without an answer and still unresolved. In effect, what interests Leopardi is not so much the corruption of letters as the corruption of morals. The fact that letters are the expression of morals is not doubted, but this does not constitute a specific answer. The question concerning letters and their corruption is a pretext. Leopardi is interested in aesthetics only as a metaphysician. Therefore morals are corrupt as a result of the triumph of reason. The critique of historical memory is the critique of a reason and a philosophy that, developing around "mutual commerce between peoples" and the birth of industry, posits in reason, along with the civilizing process, "this love of the lights of reason."[15] But "reason is the enemy of all greatness: [. . .] It is nature, therefore, that presses great men to great actions. But reason pulls them back: and so reason is often the enemy of nature, and nature is great and reason is small."[16] If reason here is the cause of corruption, it is because it is an instrumental, individualistic conception. "[R]eason, by making us naturally inclined to pursue our own advantage, and removing the illusions that bind us to one another, dissolves society absolutely and turns people to savagery."[17] The superiority of nature over reason and of the immediate aesthetic of illusions over the transcendental analytic of reason follows from this. Could a reason that is the handmaid of nature exist? "Reason is a light; nature seeks to be illuminated by reason, and not burned."[18] The enemy of barbarism is not reason but nature. Reason burns nature, setting in motion a mechanism of devastation that cannot be checked. The negative dialectic of Enlightenment is a destructive dialectic.[19]

What is to be done on this devastated terrain? How can a web of the sense of life be reconstructed? By recourse to immediacy. This appeal to immediacy, although it later becomes a thematic element, is first of all the indication of a method.[20] On the terrain of method, immediacy is two things: "imitation" of nature and "identification [*immedesimazione*]" in illusion. It is in no way the construction of a utopia of naturalistic fetishes, but rather a critical function, an operational foundation. Not an ounce of Romanticism or barbaric ingenuousness is to be found in these pages. Imitation is the labor of imitating nature but also "the endless study of the Classics." Identification consists in drawing from nature, from the second nature of illusion, the strength to react to the destruction produced by instrumental reason. Identification is "wonder,"[21] a vendetta, the first vendetta of natural wonder directed against the stereotypical admiration of rationalism as the foundation of philosophical activity. Philosophy is living in the real—a totally intra-mundane metaphysics.

Nevertheless the methodical reaffirmation, although strengthened, does not go beyond itself, whereas on the contrary, the negative foundation wills a constitutive web of sense. Following nature then? Nature is certainly a foundation,[22] but the theme is generic. Would not natural or historical religion, or religious feeling, have to specify the sense of natural and ethical living?[23] The question, which is not free of ambiguity, appears nevertheless as purely rhetorical, like a bored, weary, passionless, reminiscent homage.

In philosophy, devotion is stupid. Must we then opt for a natural ethics of the will, for a constructive attitude that would be the heroic reprise of a non-rational overdetermination of nature?[24] No, here the neoclassical and Jacobin theme is definitively exhausted and has lost all ability to act as foundation. Prometheanism is now impotent. And then? How astonishing and how Cartesian is the discovery that the answer is contained in the question, in the methodical process itself!

> The most solid pleasure in this life is the vain pleasure of illusions. I consider illusions to be in a certain sense real, since they are essential ingredients in the system of human nature, and given by nature to all men, so that it is not right to scorn them as being the dreams of a single man, but better to regard them as a real part of man and willed by nature, without which our life would be the most miserable and barbarous thing, etc. Hence they are necessary and form a substantial part of the composition and order of things.[25]

Thus only the capacity to produce illusions is constitutive of nature. Natural illusion is the true force that constitutes second nature—that is to say, society and history.[26]

With this the problem reaches a properly philosophical substrate and the fundamental question is not long in imposing itself: what is illusion? It is the web that, in immediacy, posits sense—a sense that immediately becomes productive imagination and that as such is tested in the web of events and states of reality. The demonstration rests on different themes, all borrowed from the armory of Enlightenment sensualism:[27] psychological analyses, variations on the problem of the preservation of life, and by analogy, on the problem of suicide; homologies between animal life and human life, hierarchized according to the functional complexity of sensibility; evaluations of the complexity of organization of the elements of sensory life; problems of society seen from the viewpoint of sensualist philosophy.[28] Sense is thus the web of true illusion. The imagination positions itself on the crest between sense and the states of reality. But what is the motive force that dynamizes sense and orients it toward reality? The principles of organization of sense are love and hate[29]—an antagonistic organization that we rediscover in the immediate phenomenology of consciousness, so that at the very moment when these dynamic determinations of love and hate set existence into motion, they bring about unhappiness [*infelicità*]. Illusion, although true, remains illusion. Existence is unhappiness. "Oh infinite vanity of truth!"[30] Illusion, although dynamic and constructive, is nothingness. "I was frightened to find myself in the midst of nothingness, a nothing myself. I felt as if I were suffocating, thinking and feeling that all is nothing, solid nothingness."[31] "Solid nothingness" or the web of being, nature, and life. It is "solid," this nothingness, and therefore neither simply a Heraclitean flux nor the seismic depth of Empedocles, but rather a density [*spessore*] traversed by an inertia that stabilizes and fixes the perpetual movement of sensations. Movement is stabilized and illusion becomes reality. Inertia expands like a black thread into the phenomenology of sensations and stitches them together in the solidity of real appearance.[32]

We have indicated, at the beginning of this reading, that the first hundred pages of the *Zibaldone* could be considered as a summary of the metaphysical themes that Leopardi develops later. Now we must recognize that this summary of sensualist philosophy is rather rudimentary. But the ingenuousness and coarseness of the approach in no way invalidate its importance. What in fact happens in those pages? A first trace of the solution to the critical problem emerges. And in fact, let us repeat, we find ourselves faced not merely with a central passage of Leopardi's thought but with a meaningful philosophical marker of the era.

Leopardi fully appreciates the negative conclusion of the dialectic of Enlightenment in all its fecundity. In this context, reason can no longer be expressed except as negativity. This is opposed to the idealist dialectic which takes up Enlightenment thought and, already in Kant, elaborates a transcendental analytic of reason intended to form the basis for an ideal solution to the problem of knowledge [*conoscenza*] and ethical action. Reason is thus relegitimated in the mediation between sensibility, historical time, and existence on the one hand, and transformation, the ideal and absolute time on the other. The analytic is this schema of possibility. Judgment here is synthetic a priori, unifying sense and materiality in the project of an instrumental, dialectically constructive reason. Clumsily but effectively, Leopardi rejects this pretense of reason. His theory of sense is developed in a historically mature problematic—at the height of the times—and if his youthful and provincial expression is clumsy, it remains no less potent and significant at the level where it is situated, that of the transcendental aesthetic. His aesthetic (in other words, the analysis of the forms of constitution of immediacy), contrary to Kant's pretense, intends to root itself in and delimit itself by means of empirical reality. Leopardi's aesthetic refuses the mediation of an analytic a priori. The acceptance of this analytic would mean assuming a positive signification, the ascendancy of the philosophy of Enlightenment—reason as interpreter of sense. Whereas on the contrary it is a matter of reaching, by means of a purely sensory, negative reason of essences, the kingdom of worldly complexity, the total horizon of the world. Such is the line along which Leopardi's research unfolds. The real takes shape along the thread of sensory immediacy; it is an emergence of illusion, not mediated by the domination of reason. Reason itself is only sense that is developed and articulated in reality. This correspondence of sense and reason is true illusion. Sense is constitutive of reality, of the unique, though also illusory, tragic reality that we experience. The sensualist effort of the first phase of the *Zibaldone* is perhaps clumsy, but it already assumes full responsibility for the critical problem. Leopardi weaves a signifying web between the oppositions of the real, a web of sense that determines as positive the limits of reason.[33]

Here we rejoin the great metaphysical struggles of the modern age, not merely the one that in Leopardi arises principally between materialism and idealism, but also—and the opening pages of the *Zibaldone* bear witness to it—the struggle that spans the Enlightenment era between naturalistic sensualism and idealist sensualism.[34] The opposition again thrown into high relief by Leopardi is the one that pits Montesquieu against Rousseau. Leopardi perceives the latter as a singular man, a strange genius.[35] It is a superficial vision, since the Rousseau problem is much vaster: it is the problem of an idealist conception of sensibility and thus of the possibility of inscribing the political and social illusion in the sphere of transcendentality. Is not the general will the very example of a prodigious dialectical mechanism for the obliteration of the finite and the fiction of the absolute[36]—exactly what Leopardi denounces from the start as the model of mystification? On the other hand, Montesquieu weaves a naturalistic web, carrying out a materialist dilution of sensualism, from the theory of taste to the theme of the corruption of empires, between aesthetics and history, sociology and political science.[37] In Montesquieu the critical intention is constructed through an apparatus of naturalistic continuity that makes physicality into the precondition for a scientific typology of empire, takes sensibility as a web of concepts and ethical action as the differentiated foundation of regimes, and so on. These are two sensualist horizons, but Rousseau's ends up in transcendentalism while Montesquieu's is materialist. Rousseau opens onto idealism, whereas Montesquieu marks the genesis, in the harsh metaphysical empiricism of the seventeenth century, of a properly scientific method. Leopardi sides with Montesquieu, whose materialist sensualism elaborates a useful schema for linking the aesthetics of immediacy and imagination while defining a method capable of maintaining in itself and transferring to different degrees of knowledge [*conoscenza*] the solidity of true illusion. If Leopardi is not aware of the full thematics of the ongoing metaphysical struggle, he experiences it by positioning himself instinctively, between presuppositions and consequences, on the side of materialism, of those currents of constructive, scientific materialism that brought honor to the thought of the seventeenth century and since then have managed, with difficulty, to constitute a potent hidden tradition.

But we have seen no more than a first short stretch of the *Zibaldone*'s path. We can pursue it by seeing how this theoretical basis develops in the pages written between 1820 and 1821,[38] and above all in 1820.[39] The first observation is that, up to 1820, the theory of the constitutive power [*potere*] of sense, asserted with such force, is not merely clumsily articulated, not merely subjected to the burden of numerous extraneous ideological motifs, but it is also limited in itself by the extreme precariousness of the definition of the relationship between the phenomenological order and the ontological order. If in the sphere of the problems that shape the critical question, the choice of field is absolutely correct, this strong affirmation of the necessity for an intra-mundane metaphysics is not accompanied by an adequate critical development. "A house hanging in the air suspended by ropes from a star."[40] Two attempts to tie phenomenology and ontology more tightly together were sketched here, one consisting in making the antagonistic love-hate pair the basic rule of ontological dynamism, the other in presupposing an inertial norm that stabilizes the real. Leopardi is aware of the fragility of these propositions. "He put on a pair of glasses made from half the meridian with the two polar circles."[41] This is the reason, throughout the *Zibaldone* entries for 1820, he continually raises, sometimes tiresomely (at least for the reader), the problem of the relationship between these two orders, in a sort of reflex response that, if it corresponds (above all in the first months of 1820) to a moment of great theoretical intensity, ends up with no conclusive result. The corpus of short notes from 1820 could thus be defined as a short treatise on methodical doubt, without thereby underestimating the function that critical doubt fulfills in the preparation for the concluding phase of the metaphysical approach in the writings of 1821. That year 1820 is thus a period of transition that poses the problem of the relationship between phenomenology and ontology without managing to resolve it but clears a good part of the field with a view to bringing the critical question to a conclusion.

In 1820 everything begins again from the critique of instrumental reason, in other words corrupting reason. The refrain is well known: "*Nature is not material, as reason is*"; "*reason is the most material of all the faculties we possess.*"[42] But the theme of corrupting reason develops above all as a critical theme valid first of all as a criterion of the methodical dissolution of the cultural stereotypes to which we are subject. In these pages, the polemical objectives are the culture of Enlightenment, particularly its political wings, and Christianity. The critique of the former carries out a paradoxical overturning of the heroic theme, turning one of the most perfect products of Enlightenment Jacobinism against the culture of Enlightenment. This had already happened, in part, in the first canti, but here Leopardi seems no longer fully to savor the baroque arguments. Anyway, heroism remains nature against reason, against the "materialism of reason."

The materialism of reason must be understood as the series of perverse effects and treacherous sequences set in motion by a philosophy that, resting simply on reason, has broken every link between humankind and nature and produced barbarism. Love of country is thus transformed into nationalist egotism, which is itself propagated, as a private conception, to individuals. The demand for freedom becomes aggressive and justifies the new tyranny, which it settles upon its subjects as ignorance. The feeling for one's country once again becomes love of faction, and morality dissolves. Chimeras and childishness take the place of generosity, and superstition takes the place of love, and so on.[43] It would be pointless to emphasize the fact that, without a doubt, the weight of the tradition of political skepticism is still evident here, and perhaps other echoes of the thought of the Politicians[44] and the "aphoristic politics" that were so widespread throughout the Italian provinces (*Monaldo docet and docebit!*)—rather than a precise knowledge [*conoscenza*] of the political thought of the Enlightenment era. It would be pointless because the movement of Leopardi's thought tends less to illustrate the history of ideas than to refine critically his own philosophical proposition. "[R]eason is often the source of barbarism (indeed is barbarous in itself) and an excess of reason always is. Nature never is, because in the end nothing is barbarous apart from what is contrary to nature, so that nature and barbarism are opposites, and nature cannot be barbarous in essence."[45] "There is no other remedy for the ills of modern philosophy than forgetting, and material pasture for the illusions to feed on."[46]

But Christianity is not one of these real illusions. It too has nullified the power [*potere*] of nature and proposed to humankind an image of perfectibility, which has the same effects as Enlightenment reason. It too takes nature and its power away from humankind.[47] It would serve no purpose, in order to evaluate this settling of accounts with Christianity, to recall the doubts, uncertain judgments, argumentative comings and goings present in these pages, just as it would serve no purpose to emphasize the peremptory declaration that "my system . . . agrees with Christianity." This claim is fallacious when we find ourselves in a speculative framework that denies all theology, admits the corruption of reason but not of nature, refuses all perfectibility and, above all, the idea of redemption.[48] "The mutual enmity of reason and nature"[49] thus involves every mediation that is thought. (Perhaps this is the moment to recall the analogies between the young Hegel's *Spirit*

of Christianity and the proceedings of Leopardi's thought, in an era when
both were young and before their paths diverged. Indeed, the enormous
differences between the two conceptions of the classical do not obscure the
identity of the problem and the common profound distrust of abstract mediation. And in this framework of significations, cannot the term "alienation"
be retained to give shape to Leopardi's conception of false illusion?)[50]

This, then, is how widely the critical function in the *Zibaldone* entries
for the year 1820 expands. However, little advance is made in the deepening
of the true, central problem, that of determining the relationship between
a phenomenology and an ontology of states of consciousness. The critique,
however valid it may be, can at most only unfold the phenomenology into a
logic—it does not succeed in rooting it in being. Something new nonetheless appears in this passage of critique, in its logical development; and a
relationship between the horizontal connections of phenomenology and logic
and the vertical deepening of the critical moment toward the region of being
gradually opens up. The novelty consists in a different appreciation of the
dialectic, otherwise inexhaustible, of reason and nature. Must nature be illuminated by reason? Perhaps, but without being corrupted thereby. It surely
involves a dialectical struggle, but above all it is suffering. The dialectic is
cruel because it cannot be brought to an end. It traverses humankind with
inexhaustible violence. Here then is the point: from out of this insoluble
dialectic, this continual and mutual enmity between reason and nature,
compassion and suffering emerge like a "miracle of nature."[51] The miracle
here consists in the fact that the radical dualism of nature and reason is
ruptured on the side of materialism. Suffering shows us a reason that enters
into nature, a "reason within," a "corporeal reason." Let us pause at this
point. It does not yet represent a developed ontological terrain. Ontology is
still only a horizon. But a very strong tension starts here, a tendency toward
being, the birth of a question within the hybrid, incomplete web of nature
and reason.

Certain variables allow us immediately to measure the deepening of
the critical experience toward ontology. First variable: the polemic against
the moderns (the Romantics?) and the philosophers refers to the extent to
which they lack the "infinite emotion" of ontological cognition.[52] The second
variable (or indication) concerns pain and pleasure, their dialectic, but above
all the ontological importance of the cognition of pain in a psychological and
phenomenological deepening that opens fully onto the abyss of ontology.[53]
Third indication: the perception of the infinite, not a mystical infinite—this
concept is unknown to Leopardi—but an infinite that is absolute cognition
of pain in the comparison between nature and reason and in the impossibility
of a solution to the tragedy that opposes them. The pain of the infinite is thus

also its cognitive pleasure. The tension of the phenomenology of interiority toward ontology thus becomes extreme.[54]

What can be said about this very beautiful passage? It involves an important passage from the philosophical point of view to the extent that the concept of the infinite is validated as a comparison, a dialectic, but with an implicit refusal to logically develop the dimension of comparison and with a tension to find instead its translation into the articulation of being. All this happens without nullifying the terms of the comparison: objectivity is maintained in the wealth of its phenomenological forms, and subjectivity is preserved in the exceptional intensity of the cognition of pain and the perception of the comparison. Leopardi's discovery of the infinite[55] recalls that of Augustine, but as it would be revived by the most modern experience of the corporeality of consciousness. The Kantian transcendental ego is here resolved in the cognition of pain. The foundation of knowledge [conoscenza] does not exclude ethics; on the contrary, it takes ethics into account as an element of the relationship between the theory of sense and the theory of reason.[56] The answer given by this passage to the question posed by action on the logical and gnoseological level is the negation of all teleology. Confronted with the pretenses of reason (as with the alienating ones of religion), the critical definitions here find their foundation, not in terms of a crude sensualism but through the inexhaustible deepening of a strict dialectic of the cognition of pain and the perception of the infinite. It is a dialectic that does not conclude, that mocks reason, and that nature leaves unsatisfied. Thus it is on the ontological level that the critical function is founded, and it is confirmed by the quality of that level. Indeed, the infinite horizon of being requires neither the abnegation of the subject nor the negation of the real, but rather a comparison that preserves all the elements of their individuality, their finitude, and leads them not to a null relationship but to the nothingness of every hegemonic and mystifying rationality, whether transcendent or transcendental.

What, then, is illusion? There it is, irresistibly raising us to the crest of ontology. Illusion is a "very vigorous root" of life, and humankind lives on nothing else.[57] Illusion is thus the infinite context in which the always-unconcluded dialectics of pleasure and pain, nature and reason are established. Illusion is this point of mathematical infinity that we assume as a limit. It is the progress of knowledge [conoscenza] in this infinitely open field. The theory of the cognition of pain runs sometimes parallel, sometimes interwoven, sometimes identified with the theory of illusion.[58] It is the sign of the non-conclusion of the path toward being, or the non-conclusion of the path of being. There is no perfectibility that can be attained by reason, even intersecting with nature. In this nevertheless necessary encounter, illusion

forms the only possibility of life. And that will remain valid as long as we
are able to reconstruct the concept of a power [*potenza*] that pervades being
and that, through a making that is totally internal to being, knows how to
raise itself from the aesthetic and the phenomenological condition to the
productive imagination and ultimately to the point where pain can become
voice and liberation. Is it possible to encounter Leopardi on this problematic?
Of course. It comes out; it appears and disappears. In the many pages of the
Zibaldone from this era, it is no more than a symptom that does not succeed
in becoming concrete.[59] It presents itself as an entanglement of profound
themes and planes—in such a way that the discourse returns voluntarily, as
to a resting place, to the critique of culture, and there concludes again. We
find ourselves in effect at the margins of a period, of a program. Hence it is
a matter of moving forward, but the difficulties are obvious.

This advance will not be denied us by Leopardi's *Zibaldone* entries for
1821. But because he must run a long race, Leopardi begins by reorganizing
his tools and redefining his horizons. The *Zibaldone* of 1821 can be divided
into two parts that correspond more or less to the two halves of the year.
During the first half he accomplishes the work of clarification that concludes
with the definitive elaboration of a transcendental aesthetic, a theory of the
web of sense; whereas during the second half, the theory of the phenomenological constitution of reality expands into a veritable theoretical dislocation,
thanks to a work of productive imagination of great efficacy and sublime
ontological grasp. We will follow these two phases of elaboration separately.

The first six months of 1821. To begin, almost to force a process of conceptual extension, a first reflection: "Neither the faculty of knowledge, nor
that of love, nor even that of the imagination is capable of the infinite, or
of conceiving things infinitely, but only of the indefinite and of conceiving
indefinitely. Something delights us,"[60] but it does not satisfy us, nor does
it fulfill the conditions of knowledge [*conoscenza*]. Instead, it distances
us or simply carries us away from what seems to be the only important
problem: constructing a subjectivity that, through imagination, establishes
the conditions of determinate existence, validated by critique, of a world.[61]
Sense tries to expand over and unify the determinations, but as a result of
its indefinite character, does not succeed in its task. We are thus faced with a
formal condition of the process that critically blocks us on the path between
phenomenology and ontology and in the attempt to constitute the subject
on the model of sense. Yet here the paradox of the infinite—as has already
been noted—is given only with higher technical-philosophical perfection.

On the other hand, is it possible to trace a linear route between phenomenology and ontology in the framework of the determinations of negative
reason and on the paradoxical terrain in which Leopardi is already firmly

anchored? The question might seem purely rhetorical. But is it not strange to see Leopardi pursuing myths and again seeking alternative routes that he knows are impracticable? He tries and tries again. If we feel pain at the crushing weight of the indefinite and our inability to attain the plenitude of the infinite, does this not follow from the hegemony of reason? In this case, if we strip ourselves bare and regain a childlike imagination, would the infinite—and in it the foundation of the subject—be possible for us?[62] But the theory of childlike imagination does not succeed. An imagination organized in this way is of course possible. The poetic voice bears witness to it. But it constitutes an exception to the normal condition of humanity. This immediate reality quickly dissolves and the indefinite of sensations, intuitions, and imaginations reappears, spreading its confusion over the historical time of life. In short, this elementary Viconian conception, this theory of psychological ages—which appears frequently in Leopardi—lasts here only for the space of an instant. Nevertheless, suffering remains, and negative thought does not suppress it. The desire for an intensive infinite and its formal conditions continues to gnaw at thought, in the most unforeseen forms. And the great variation of themes, the coexistence, even in the same day's work, of so many different arguments serves to demonstrate the pressing character of the theoretical problem and Leopardi's extreme inventiveness, his ability to present it according to multiple scenarios, other contrasting frameworks, and scenes. For example, *ex abrupto*, a question arises: what is a good government? And what could the solution to the problem of the bad infinite be if it is not the surmounting of the dimension of the indefinite?[63] What seems a somersault is not one.

The continuity of political thematics in the *Zibaldone* is now familiar to us. Here, however, from the habitual political phenomenology (and its implicit conclusions: nature makes people sociable and departing from nature makes them barbarous, so the theory of government is the theory of dominion over barbarism: therefore, long live the monarchy!)[64] and the development of political pessimism that follows from it arises a truly radical question. And this is a question that poses, without ingenuousness, the problem of the relationship between good government and historical development, between historical conditions and the conditions of the civilizing process: can the indefinite, situated as it is between nature and reason and posited at a certain level of development, positively resolve itself in social life? Can the indefinite of the multitude restore unity to the practice of the concepts of country and freedom? In this form, the political question is only a variant of the fundamental problem of the formal constitution of a subject between phenomenology and ontology, and in this sense it interests us.[65]

In trying to reach a solution to the crisis and to pain, Leopardi constructs an immense conceptual net that allows him to gather together the variations of the theme of the subject and take hold of them. Let us return to the political question. Once again it is answered negatively. Once again Leopardi does not manage to shake off a skepticism and a political pessimism that are not without elements derived from a vulgar reactionary rhetoric:[66] the necessity of a division of society into categories and levels, slavery being one of them; the problem of political freedom is an abstraction, and national thought is a practice of subjection of other peoples, etc., etc.[67] The historical schema once more devolves into extreme terms: the civilizing process corresponds to a process of barbarization; evolution is really destruction of virtue, unmasking the lovely fables told by the Enlightenment; "civilization, science, etc., and impotence are inseparable companions"; cosmopolitanism is the tedious mystification of egoism.[68] Nevertheless, this pessimist phenomenology does not manage to satisfy the conditions posited by the philosophical problem, and this dissatisfaction continually reintroduces the nostalgia for the infinite: there must have been a moment when multitude, country, and nation were one and the same thing and were "great virtue."[69] Ah, "if princes were to revive illusion!"[70] In short, Leopardi cannot and does not want to free himself from the demand for an intensive infinite capable of restoring, beyond the catastrophe of memory and the impossibility of a dialectical resolution to the vicissitudes of history, an ontological rooting of life. In these pages he again takes up the definition, already mentioned, of the Copernican revolution as the opening up of hope and the assertion of equality by resizing the images of the human and the infinite.[71] And there is one very strange, singularly calm page: present time can be considered

> to be the era of revival from barbarism. A revival beginning in Europe through the French Revolution, a revival that was weak and very imperfect because it derived not from nature but from reason, indeed from philosophy, which is a very weak, false, sorry, unenduring principle of civilization. And yet it is a kind of revival [. . .] I do not go so far as to say life, but a certain palpitation, a certain distant impression of vitality.[72]

"And that is how the present time may be regarded as an era featuring a new (though weak) revival of civilization."[73] So why this contradictory articulation of themes and these new hopes? There is only one answer: across these multiple fields of inquiry—the theory of childlike imagination as well as, at the opposite extreme, the theory of political forms—Leopardi seeks the solution to a structural and metaphysically based problem without ever discovering a moment of founding stability. Allusions, hopes, occasionally 'weak' forms of solution, but the problem remains.

Yet this process of research, so contorted, muddled, and confused, these thematic polarizations, these untiring approximations are nevertheless anything but useless. The problems are not solved in their singularity, but the development of the investigation constructs a terrain, a sphere, in which the solution to the problem of sense can be situated. We indicated from the start of our reading of the *Zibaldone* that Leopardi's method is constitutive of its object. A thousand routes are taken with the aim of establishing this conceptual net through which the passage from the phenomenology of states of consciousness to the constructive ontology of sense could be apprehended. Certain determinations are already given at this intermediary stage of research: the complexity of the terms of the discourse, the basic dialectical situation, nature and history, nature and reason. They are aspects that have long been on the table in the analysis, but here reprised, reanalyzed, resituated.

Two new elements are added. First of all, the framework is temporal; in other words, the framework of true illusion within the conceptual network that begins to distinguish it has become dynamic, projected toward the future. "Human pleasure . . . can be said to lie always in the future, to be only in the future, to consist purely in the future."[74] There is more. The vital tension is gradually sketched as future tension. The infinite, although still unresolved, is not merely a spatial tension but above all a temporal tension. Imagination from the subjective point of view and illusion from the objective point of view are inserted into this tension. All this evokes a kind of Spinozian *conatus*. Of course there is unhappiness that results from this unrealized absolute, but there is nevertheless movement, the opening to dynamic being, to power [*potenza*].[75] "'The present,' says Pascal, 'is never our goal; the past and the present are our means: the future alone is our object: thus we do not live but hope to live.'"[76] And further: "The memory of pleasure may be likened to hope and it produces more or less the same effects."[77] The search for pleasure unfolds into a dynamic that presupposes and awaits time; the non-resolution of the problem of the infinite bends to the dimension of the temporal indefinite, not for external reasons but because that is the law of this region of being. Any true phenomenology can be a theory only of the composition of space and the constitution of time.[78]

A second element is added to this temporal and dynamic determination of the conceptual network proposed by Leopardi. It involves—he explicitly announces it—systematic effort. The system is simultaneously a structure of relations and a foundation, a viewpoint, an option of rooting, the latter being rigorously materialist: "Our mind is incapable not only of knowing but

even of conceiving of anything beyond the bounds of matter."[79] Within the
sphere of this strict materialism, Leopardi makes the structure of relations
the "systematic principle," in the literal sense, of the theory of sense and
its sequences,[80] the system of sense resting on "a machine that is very vast
and composed of countless different parts"[81] that it will be necessary and
possible to traverse—a kind of overturned "theodicy."[82]

Are we now, thanks to these acquisitions, in a position to confront the
heart of the critical question? Perhaps. In reality, such a series of theoretical elements is capable of bringing to maturity—in botanical terms—the
systematic fruit. Everything tends toward a conclusion—except Leopardi.
Whereas we are expecting him to set to work on the subject, here on the
contrary we are faced with what seems to be a detour in the analysis; in
other words we find ourselves faced with a systematic precipitate of the
materials of linguistic analysis and the theory of language. Now if one keeps
in mind the enormous quantity of linguistic material, this prodigious crafts-
manship of language that characterizes the *Zibaldone* (particularly in 1821,
the pages dedicated to these questions form the clear majority), it should
not be surprising that precisely this activity of the linguist, philologist, or
phonologist is always situated on a subaltern terrain, forming a minor part
of Leopardi's activity in view of the philosophical and systematic preten-
sions that are so clearly marked during this period. We are in fact faced
with one of those unforeseen moments of sudden theoretical innovation of
which we have already seen that Leopardi is capable, a moment in which
the solution to the problem does not deny its genesis but bears the marks
of a leap forward, of originality, and a new productivity. Thus, he asks
himself, will not the constitution within the linguistic sphere of the web of
sense, the ontological site of states of consciousness, and the definition of
the subject preserve the conditions of analysis while allowing the solution
to the problem to be effectively projected? The *Zibaldone* entries for 1821
offer us a kind of "short treatise on language," the articulations of which go
in precisely this direction.[83]

Leopardi begins with some considerations on the threat facing the Italian
language (in imitation of the French language) of falling into dryness,
expressive timidity, and poverty.[84] These considerations are interspersed
with a long reflection on the sixteenth century: "The sixteenth century is
the one and only true golden age, of both our language and our literature."[85]
In that era, the language was being constructed richly and in expressive
felicity, and it developed a popular function. That era knew the corporeal
language of prose.[86] Consequently we must oppose the barbarization of
language. We can do so, and language can do so, because it is a historical
power [*potenza*] of imagination and congealed naturalness. Thus it is not for

language to measure up to humankind; but on the contrary, it is for human-kind to measure up to language. The entirety of Leopardi's apparatus for restoring natural and imaginative humankind against reason and barbarism is developed here within the question of language.[87]

Language can reveal life, present us with happiness, and elevate human-kind.[88] Inasmuch as it constitutes the universe of communication, language therefore constitutes an eminently human universe. The arguments on this score proliferate, and they not only constitute concepts and thoughts forged by theory, but they continually appear and reappear within this gigantic philological labor that Leopardi accomplishes in this period. Language thus becomes the central object of analysis. It allows him to reach a conclusive definition of this phenomenological universe in which nature and history are intermingled, in which national space and historical time are superim-posed. Language is the essence of society at the very same moment that it is the expression of nature.[89] The formal web of a metaphysics of sense can thus be traced over the vital web of language. This is a passage of decisive importance. On the one hand it appears historically as the conclusive ele-ment of the great tradition that sprang from Vico; but on the other hand, it innovates on the theoretical plane. This definition of language contains not a historicist dimension or a merely naturalistic horizon, but rather a metaphysical conception of humankind as expressive essence, of society as a communicative ensemble, and thus of language as a constitutive power [potenza]. The contradictions to which the nature-history relationship gives rise are all taken into account on the linguistic horizon as they were on the experimental terrain, but here they are resolved, because the form is able to accommodate the phenomenological given. The solution to the problem of the transcendental aesthetic, that of providing an ontological content to the modes of phenomenological emergence, is in this way and at this level made accessible—with the power [potenza] that this synthesis, this operation of ontological fulfillment, gets from the fact that Leopardi's argument situates itself on the plane of sense, the terrain of materialism.[90]

The force of theoretical anticipation of Leopardi's perspective must not be underestimated. It raises problems that have become familiar to us only today, in an era in which the critical question has finally lost the stigmata of its Kantian and idealist origin and presents itself on the terrain of the theory of communication, its historical genesis and intersubjective functioning. Communication is a universe, the sole, unique, human universe.[91] Where can we find a more impressive definition of that "solid nothingness," which Leopardi uses to characterize his own fundamental metaphysical percep-tion, than in this advent of the universe of communication as the exclusive substrate of thought?

We are now entering the second period of the *Zibaldone* of 1821, the analysis of the writings from the second half of the year. It seems to me that in these pages, Leopardi tries to formalize what he had constructed and carry this linguistic discovery further into the sequences of the theory of sense. In other words, Leopardi here reaches the highest definition of the subject, to the extent that the definition of the subject signifies the solution to the critical question. We are setting out again from language, from the general communicative and ethical essence that it represents. Let us reread its constitutive fable: primordial language is the beginning; a society grows as it shapes its power of speech; the progressive formation of languages shapes the differences among peoples; the invention of writing, early and obscure incunabula of society, takes its first steps; etymologies and synonyms follow as anthropological keys to reading; alphabets result.[92] Language is thus a creative system. But this creativity of language consists of rules of development, internal dynamisms that must be identified. The subject is not absent from the structure; it is on the contrary required by the structure.

But what subject? Certainly not the subject offered by tradition and religion, nor that proposed by ideology. Let us wipe the slate clean of tradition and ideology. Everything on this terrain is relative and the ontology is ungraspable. By pushing us toward depth, the ideological tradition pushes us into nothingness, a vain, ungraspable nothingness, like all its concepts. The exemplification is as always lengthy, meticulous, sometimes driven to fury by the anxiety to destroy these hollow fetishes.[93] The attack is directed in the first place against Platonic idealism and the doctrine of ideas. The theme is that of the demystification of ideology, a theme that is taken to the point of demonstrating the nothingness of ideas:[94] illusions whose foundation is nothingness and whose matrix is utilitarianism—a "science" engendered by fear, egoism, the principle of utility. The human condition is completely dominated by these false illusions and this false science. Have we had to wait all these centuries to discover it? Is that the progress of the Enlightenment? And "me, poor intelligence, without aid," I have to accept it. No, this philosophy that produces illusions must be rejected. We must turn to nature, to human completeness. But on this terrain of the search for a vital rooting that will transform our experience into a heroic ability to live the real, new fetishes arise: religion and particularly Christianity.[95] A theory of egoism and baseness, key to the destruction of nature and generosity, abstract figure of a potent alienation, adversary of the concreteness of life: such is Christianity.

The anti-Christian polemic shows no reservations and no doubts now that the metaphysical dimensions on the basis of which it proceeds have been clarified. These are thoroughly, even arrogantly materialist dimensions: "Nothing preexists things. Neither forms, nor ideas, neither necessity nor a reason for being, and being thus or thus, etc. . . . . *Everything* is posterior to *existence*." "The infinite possibility that constitutes the essence of God, is necessity."[96] Thus we experience a totally positive ontology that leaves no place for ideology, in whatever way one interprets it. Our sole ontology, for better and for worse, is that of speaking, communicating. Here negative thought reveals all its splendor. But once again the question is posed: what subject, what dynamic, what life of this sole human horizon? It is quite true that "the principle of things, and of God himself, is nothingness," but it is also true that this nothingness is "solid," that the world is everything that exists, that human completeness exists within these conditions. So how does one reconstruct the web of life on the basis of this existence, which is indisputably our own, on the basis of this sensibility and corporeality that situate us in the world, on the *tabula rasa* of science, and in the plenitude of society and language? The question is pressing. It has dogged us since the *Zibaldone* of 1820: all the movements, all the alternatives up to now have merely sought to enlarge the field of the question, to specify the conceptual network, to establish—by means of intense labor—a terrain. We are nearing the answer.

Or answers. The first, the classic sensualist response, is familiar to us. Leopardi proposed it several times without bringing the argument to a conclusion and then displacing the field of investigation. He tests it more forcefully now. The negative philosophical breakthrough of the second half of 1821 imposes this on him. Thus with almost peaceful continuity, his thought fortifies and consolidates itself on a sensualist basis. The sensualist emphasis of the proposition aiming to solve the critical question comes to the fore. We are in a situation like Condillac's.[97] By means of sense, we must depict our subject and constitute it. The themes and sequences are indicated: sense, habituation, composition/association, simplicity/complexity, memory, sign, expression, plasticity of empirical consciousness (childhood), etc., etc. "In short, everything in man is habituation."[98] Against reason, which is "a bad source, poisonous to life"[99] and causes death, we are seeking the genealogy of vital creativity in the dynamic of sense. Leopardi takes up the theme of habituation—and the linear history of the construction of the subject that it proposes—from all angles, under great tension. This is an extremely strong theme in his work.[100] The linearity of the theme is evident not solely from the viewpoint of the construction of the subject—the accent here is placed on the possibility of making the law of habituation a general physical law: "The force of *general* habituation."[101] The linear generalization of a constructive theory of sense is an experiment that Leopardi carries out in its entirety. In these pages of the *Zibaldone*, he seems to repeat experiments that were customary in the Parisian salons of the preceding century. In effect we see him unfold this philology of the senses and describe the

mechanisms of acquisition of any faculty in general.[102] Here we are, among
the possibilities of nature that the senses and only the senses determine,
secreting memory, feeling, and sensing as objects of a specific analysis.[103]
Poor plague carrier, perhaps philosophy is something else! But he doesn't
stop there. As does Condorcet's sensualism, Leopardi's sensualism intends
to devour history, to determine sensualist genealogies that are adequate
not only for the statue (the pedagogical simulacrum of sensualism) but for
the *multitudo*—which, thank heaven, will always remain external to every
monumental homology. "For habituation is everything, both in peoples and
in individuals."[104] After so much invective against the Enlightenment era,
where can we find a more straightforward exaltation of the Enlightenment
and a sort of gloomy dedication to exaggerating its most caricatural image
if not in these pages of the *Zibaldone*? It reaches the point of quantifying
the general law of habituation: just like the law of gravity, habituation thus
finds a geometrical multiplier.[105]

Yet the sensualist response does not stop there. Initially faced with the
problem of the articulation of the ontological fabric, we spoke of multiple answers. That was inexact: the conclusive answer in this part of the
Zibaldone is instead an articulation within sensualism. It is different from
sensualism, but has solid points of anchorage there. It provides an answer
and a foundation of great theoretical force, internal to sensualism. Leaving
aside the most resolutely mechanical aspects of this theory, what is revealed
to us as its theoretical base? Without doubt an extremely strong constitutive
tension. Read from this point of view, habituation is not an organic growth,
the concretion of atomic elements, but rather the theory of a constitutive
accumulation, a structural process. The quantitative moment itself, which
certainly seems paradoxical in its claim to level the different aspects of
life, seems much less so if we consider it as the expression of an organizing
and ordering intention of the subject. From this viewpoint, it is interesting
to note how many of the relativistic impulses of Leopardi's discourse are
ultimately more reliant on a certain tradition of moral and literary cynicism
than they are on sensualist theory:[106] indeed, the latter can be relativistic
from the phenomenological or gnoseological viewpoint but not from the
ontological viewpoint. In sensualism there is an absolute, classical measure,
such as the synthesis of spontaneity and solidity, or the law of the finite.[107]
Furthermore, precisely within this implicit dialectic, the theory of sensualism presents an internal aspect of cognitive and organizational "activity"
that produces an element that is irreducible to mechanism.[108]

Therefore, alongside the elements of a lethargic and linear sensualism,
we see this other element in Leopardi. It comes out fresh, articulated in the
context of Leopardi's philosophical, ethical, and lyrical experience in an

original way that, on other occasions, has allowed us to speak of a movement of innovation. Therefore we must consider this "sense" in an intensive
way, with true passion. What are we looking for? We are looking for a
means that provides us with a coherent discourse uniting reason, nature,
and history. The history of philosophy has shown us how all possible philosophical interpretations—above all the rationalist ones—could not bear the
weight of this nexus. Sense is the immediate experience that gives us this
awareness, that organizes internal nature; not because sensualism would
trace unbelievable geometries but rather because sense in itself is nature,
spontaneity, a dimension of life. The world is illusion? So be it. But sense
is hope. All sensible motion, even despair, lives in and on hope.[109] It is that
future opening that we have considered, that open time. It is desire.[110] How
is subjectivity configured in this world that we have led to its image, to the
exclusive universe of language and communication? The subject is desire
that solidifies and reclaims ontological reasons from this nothingness. Here
sense is absolute. The structure has a subject, and the process is full of this
ontological reference. Nothingness is solid.

> It could be said (but it's a question of names) that my system does not
> destroy the absolute, but rather multiplies it. That is, it destroys what
> is considered absolute, and makes absolute what is termed relative. It
> destroys the abstract and *antecedent* idea of good and evil, of true and
> false, of perfect and imperfect independent of all that is. But it makes
> all possible beings absolutely perfect, that is, perfect in themselves,
> having the cause of their perfection in themselves and in this, that they
> exist thus, and are made thus, a perfection independent of any extrinsic
> cause or necessity, and of any pre-existence. Thus all relative perfections
> become absolute, and absolutes, instead of vanishing, multiply, in such a
> way that they can be both diverse and contrary to one another. Whereas
> hitherto contrariety has been supposed impossible in everything that
> was absolutely denied or affirmed, everything that was reckoned to
> be absolutely and independently good or bad, with contrariety, and its
> possibility, being restricted to relatives, and their ideas.[111]

What can be said about this prodigious thought? Sense has become a transcendental element of subjectivation—but in a materialist universe and only
for this universe. The materialist radicality does not deprive the subject of
its absoluteness but rather reclaims it. Time becomes concrete here as power
[*potenza*] and constructive function. Negative thought, having settled its
score with idealist philosophy and every ideology, is ultimately measured
in reconstruction.

Here we are at the last knot of the discourse. Sense, thus finally founded, is nothing other than the long-sought nexus between transcendental aesthetic and transcendental imagination. It constructs true illusions. Leopardi dedicates many pages to it. What is imagination?[112] It is possibility that is realized, habituation that innovates; it is enthusiasm, feeling, heroism. It is illusion that becomes active; it is the renewal of knowledge [*conoscenza*], a new relationship between representations and states of the real. It is poetry. The imagination is the struggle of nature and reason that thereby produces reality; it is time that condenses toward the future, and it is also "honor," that is collective identification. It is a collective inflammation; it is lyric—it is sense that moves forward. After this enthusiastic determination, a series of technical and philosophical definitions follow. In synchronic terms, imagination is the prolongation of sense.[113] In diachronic terms, imagination is the movement that develops between states of consciousness and states of nature and history, comparable to the thermodynamic passage between cold and heat—it is Leopardi who says this, not me or Prigogine.[114]

Next comes a dialectical hypothesis of the definition of imagination. It is action, the intention of life and the rupture of dead inertia.[115] This dynamism of the imagination depends on the fact that it experiences not only the continuity of nature and reason but above all, their contrast. In this open and insoluble struggle, the imagination grasps the very source of its own dynamism.[116] Everywhere in these pages, then, the imagination is defined as power [*potenza*]: it is no longer a dialectical dynamism but one that is directly ontological. It is defined as an "innovative faculty," the "source of reason as well as feeling"—energy, vigor, force, projection.[117] To this a collective, sociological definition of the imagination is added: it is the faculty capable of organizing collective feelings and actions.[118] It is not worthwhile here (but we return to the matter) to follow the various, multiple, repeated thoughts, imbued with relativism, or rather with political skepticism that are erected almost defensively in the face of the positive opening of the imagination that is produced here[119]; or to emphasize the drastic character claimed by these judgments, since this renewal of the concept of collective imagination as possibility of uniting *multitudo* and hope, history and truth, has an extreme, catastrophic force. Utopia? Perhaps. It is undeniable that these texts also propose a utopian definition of the imagination, situated in relation to the golden age, to that forceful image degraded and destroyed by reason that the imagination intends to (can?) restore as truth.[120] Take heed: this final definition is in no way preliminary, some sort of confirmation or consolation from the land of fable—it is on the contrary a lyrical figure of the absolute destiny of the imagination, the indication of the necessity for it to regain absoluteness. The myth confirms and founds the power [*potenza*] of negative reason after having been its product.[121]

Myth: the imagination as conclusion of the course of negative thought; the web of sense rediscovered by the laborious work of an analysis that follows the rhythm of a corporeal sensibility. Here imagination and myth are reasoning, a structural activity. Myth is certainly other, and imagination is certainly creative; but if we put ourselves back into the materiality of the process from which all these events have arisen, we can add that here, imagination and myth also and above all play a role in stabilizing the system. In other words, this linguistic and communicative horizon, discovered and established during this period, finds itself, by means of this creative activity, linked to an ontological foundation. It is the imagination that discovers it. Of course, this relationship is ambiguous.

At this stage of the *Zibaldone*, imagination and myth are first of all nature, whereas the linguistic and communicative universe is a second nature. How can they be put in contact? How can this universe be articulated? How can creative joy in existence be established once again? Be that as it may, it is certain that here, nature is integrated into the imagination. It is thus, and only thus, that the conditions for the passage from the phenomenology of consciousness to ontology, from a transcendental aesthetic to a dialectic of true illusion take shape. Why? The universal reason of movement resides solely in the process.

Pain and Desire

The complexity of the path taken by Leopardi in the pages that we have just read leaves one stunned. Beyond the elements that we have brought to light, beyond the traces that we have followed, the *Zibaldone* of 1821 elaborates a framework of the life of the mind and an attempt to solve the critical question that has no cause to envy Hegel's *Phenomenology*. Leopardi is, at an equivalent level of metaphysical complexity, an anti-Hegel. The fact that the timorous, provincial, and servile Italian culture of the nineteenth and twentieth centuries did not reveal this constitutes a historical disaster. But could it have been otherwise? A culture faithful to the crown and the altar can only remain mute in the face of the subversion of being. And Leopardi, at the antipodes from the restorationist Hegel, is a subversive of being. The key to subversion is pain. It follows from the affirmation of an upside-down being, the tension of myth, the desire to realize an unexhausted negativity. Let us now look into the devastating flashes of Leopardi's critique and into the articulations of its development in this period.

The course of our reading in the *Zibaldone* of 1822[122] and in the correspondence of that period[123] seems at first to disappoint our expectation of seeing those earlier potentialities express themselves. In fact, the

Zibaldone left us in the great sea of the linguistic universe, within a natural and positive structure.[124] This structure carried out a simultaneous determination of the properly linguistic conditions and consequently the cultural, political, and civil conditions of every later development.[125] Their nexus is continuous—and now cold. As for the more dynamic concepts such as the infinite, that veritable war machine of Leopardi's lyrical and metaphysical thought, either they do not appear in the foreground or they are gathered up under purely formal and stylistic rubrics.[126] A great dead calm seems to descend upon this sea, washing over everything. The concepts constructed earlier, now outside the rhythm of construction, outside the enthusiasm for the adherence to the problematic and constructive mechanism, fall silent and seem to fold up in fatigue.

> It is not possible to be great except by thinking and working against reason, and to the extent that one thinks and works against reason, and has the strength to overcome one's own reflectiveness, or let it be overcome by enthusiasm, which always and in every case encounters reason as an obstacle, and a mortal enemy, and a deadly, chilling virtue.[127]

The *Zibaldone* entries written in Recanati in 1822 are completely squashed onto this horizon of dead calm. The properly philosophical points, the problems of sensualism, are reread in purely pessimistic terms.[128] The web of sense, so laboriously constructed and pursued with so much enthusiasm, now cools down; and the horizon of sense displays, instead of the myth of innovation, a panorama of uniformity and tedium.[129] As for social considerations, a blind and deaf custom dominates the relations between people, and no one escapes this asphyxiating condition.[130] Only a maximum imbalance could break open this dead surface, deprived of all life and conviviality. Not the imbalance of innovation, but only that of equally blind and deaf chance. This is illustrated by a fable: the invention of glass. Well, every invention at base is as fragile as glass. Only an apology for chance is able to introduce a weak gust of wind into this dead calm, this flattening of the horizon.[131] Here we are, then, within this new psychological perception of metaphysical malaise, trying to understand it. From the inside? Along the thread of biography? Let us try. "I've almost forgotten poetry, because I can see but I don't feel anything anymore," writes Leopardi in 1820.[132] And a little later: "I am tolerably well in body. My mind, after very long and very fierce resistance, is finally tamed, and obedient to fate."[133] Then he seems completely indifferent: he seeks work outside Recanati, any situation whatsoever, even a lowly one ("a lowly position—but what is lower than my life?").[134] In the following letters, and above all those of 1822, this malaise, this indifference, boredom, the search for any practical outcome whatsoever, even a base one (why not become a priest? Go to the Vatican, into that "den of superstition, ignorance and vice"? No, that would perhaps be too much. But there is no passion in his refusal to be an abbot. At root the church is a purgatory in the hell that is life)—thus the practical dimension completely overwhelms Leopardi's life.

If we seek to understand the metaphysical malaise that is expressed during this period, then we cannot follow the biographical route. At this moment personal misfortune appears more as an effect than as a cause. The dead calm is objective. Other pages of the *Zibaldone* from 1822 emphasize the motifs that we have considered as keys to the construction of the web of sense, of the signification of the real. The polemic against finalism and teleology is pursued, however (and here, for the first time, irony becomes a tool of metaphysical polemic).[135] There is an extreme radicalization of the judgment against Christianity—it feeds on the hatred of existence (these pages are worthy of the Hegelian left).[136] But none of these motifs allows us to glimpse the shocks of a metaphysical innovation, the possibility of which the preceding theoretical development had constructed. On the contrary, just as in an irresistible calm, thought closes down, folds back destructively on itself. Abstract ideas of suicide appear like icy flashes in a situation as desperate as it is indifferent.[137] Psychology is unable to explain the calm. There is only one way to do so: go back over the motifs of the crisis underlying the philosophical argument of the 1821 *Zibaldone* entries. That slow construction of a universe of illusion, that "solid nothingness," that structure of language answered the critical question concerning the solution to the crisis of memory: they restored communication. Communication was produced on the basis of sense; it represented its web. But what was its signification? The subject situated itself within this universe of sense and the senses. But what was its position? Was indifference, from which critique was liberated by the construction of a unitary web of sense, really dissolved? Or was it merely shifted, displaced? What does humankind signify in this reconstructed world? What is humankind in second nature? This new problematic arises from the mental calm of 1822, at the very moment when the storms of existence seem to be appeased and the crisis of metaphysics, having been dislocated, seems to be pacified. As for the final rupture of the universe of second nature, where nature and reason seemed to be newly conjoined—a rupture provoked by imagination and myth—it is not enough to determine the signification of a new universe, one whose sense appears to be purely formal. The problem did not consist in the definition of a possible dynamic key to the system of second nature; the problem was to break the new indifference, to say where, in which direction to break off, and toward what to move. The web of sense having been constructed, the sense of this web must be identified.

Leopardi's wanderings begin here, on the lyrical plane, before the departure for Rome, between 1820 and 1822, contemporaneous with the development of the *Zibaldone*. This temporal gap between the mental wanderings and the departure from Recanati is surmounted by the anticipatory force of lyrical thought over philosophical thought. The wanderings begin within the new universe that he had constructed but where he did not succeed in living. The disorientation that is the precondition for these wanderings is the result of a situation that can be characterized as intellectual apathy—not because the philosophical and especially the lyrical labor go less well, but precisely because this labor is erratic, experimental, without a crucial objective—a labor so different from that in which we have seen Leopardi engaged up to now. Is it perhaps a vague complacency regarding the crisis that he is undergoing, a respite that the passions of the soul seem to have found? No, it is only a certain lassitude, a momentary feeling of disproportion between his own theoretical strength and this continual forward movement of the problems of metaphysics, something like the awareness of his actual impotence to grasp and embrace them. To wander is to detach oneself from the center, to roam, to follow a dream, to experiment with forms that are perhaps inessential but are satisfying to the intellectual curiosity along the path being traveled, in a phase of metaphysical lassitude. This experimenting is primarily lyrical.

The Evening of the Holiday[138] constitutes a kind of poetic summary. In this situation of relative theoretical tranquility, of the repose of the most acute passions,

> The night is mild and clear without a wind,
> And silent over the roofs and down in gardens
> The moonlight pauses, and distantly reveals
> In all serenity each height. (ll. 1–4)[139]

Here Leopardi can regroup his customary themes, compare them, try new paths, in a dialectic of elements that develops dramatic positions from which he tries to extract and describe a common web. The elements of this dialectic are the following: the confrontation of the motifs of a poetry of intimacy with a renewal of the heroic canto; spurts of desperate philosophy extended into naturalistic images; the production of myth and the composition of landscape. The stylistic and formal effort is absolute, and it is tested precisely in the assembly of the different elements of the lyrical discourse, but he does not bring the poetic states to a satisfactory synthesis. Through this reanalysis and retracing of its intuition, the theoretical consciousness of the web of sense achieves neither an internal balance of feeling nor a strident expressive imbalance.

> And now this festival
> Is gone, and hard upon its festive heels
> The common day must tread; time steals away
> All human circumstance. Now where's the noise
> Of all those ancient peoples? Where's the shout
> Of our great forebears, the imperium
> Of that great Rome, the arms, the constant clash
> That spread from Rome all over land and sea? (ll.30–37)[140]

Here we have a beautiful example of synthesis sought but not realized. Despite this difficulty, the experimentation in this canto (as in others that we examine) achieves a formally important result: constituting the canto into a structurally liquid, fluid whole. Although the elements do not melt into the articulation of the canto, they nevertheless extend throughout its complexity. What this moment of experimentation offers us is the construction of a kind of background, a vivid scenario in which the static character of the most obvious oppositions is dissolved. Beyond "ancient nature the omnipotent" (l.13), beyond the great chiaroscuro of the heroic opposition of the first canti, here a melodic fabric is constructed, a comprehensive form: "A song I chanced to hear along the paths/Dying into the distance bit by bit" (ll.44–45).[141] Analogous comments could be made regarding *The Dream*.[142] But here, the dramatic form of the canto manages to consolidate itself in a physicality that articulates the dialogic relationship. Leopardi seems to cling to this passionate, material, sensuous determination of the web of sense that is so characteristic of his thought during this period. In *The Dream*, the assembly and counterpoint not only of the great stereotypes of the imaginary but also of dolorous and amorous voices, are physically defined. Some verses, notably the most resolutely sensual, can seem exaggeratedly expressive:

> Now while
> I cover [your hand] with kisses, and I hold it—
> Trembling the while in my distress and pleasure—
> Against my panting breast, my face is burning,
> My body too, my voice sticks in my throat,
> And everything I look at seems to sway.
> Then, both her eyes with such great tenderness

Fixed on my eyes, Do you forget already,
She said, that I have been despoiled of charm?
It is in vain you shake, unhappy man,
And burn in love. This is my last goodbye. (*The Dream*, ll.81–91)[143]

The exaggeration typical of adolescence and inexperience in no way detracts
from the delicacy and sweetness of so many other passages, so many other
physical approaches in this dream that, in a prodigious poetic movement,
Leopardi makes real "in the uncertain ray/Of the sun's light" (ll.98–99).[144]
No withdrawal: here too he seeks, as a matter of priority, this new dimension of fluency and sensuous complicity of all the terms of the discourse,
seemingly reclaimed by the audible harmony. But this is no longer the moon,
it is the morning sun; it is no longer transparency, it is light that materially
underpins the circularity of the dialogue. The same stylistic exercise is
found in *The Solitary Life*[145] and the same desire to extend the horizon and
the gaze.

From time to time I sit in solitude
Upon the sloping border of a lake,
A lake engarlanded with silent growth.
Therein, with noonday wheeling through the sky,
The sun is able to reflect his face,
No blade of grass or leaf bends in the wind,
And not one surface wrinkle, one cicada
Clicking, one feather lifted on the bough,
Or fluttering butterfly, or voice or motion,
Nearby or distant, can be heard or seen.
The deepest stillness dominates those banks;
Almost I lose myself and all the world,
I stay so still; it really seems my limbs
Are now so loose and slack no sense or spirit
Can move them more, their immemorial stillness
Merged in that place and in its silences. (*The Solitary Life*, ll.23–38)[146]

The fact that this canto is undoubtedly the least successful of the three
(up to the disastrous poetic collapse of lines 70 and following) is of less
interest to us here. It is more important to emphasize the continuity of the
search. The fact that an overabundance of Romantic elements (in the sense
that Leopardi gives to this poetics) covers up a kind of lyrical discontent,
that the metaphor maladroitly brushes up against the limits of hyperbole
and the cognition of pain is diluted in an overly diffuse landscape-painting

tonality is all well and good. But this does not detract from the importance of the attempt at formal synthesis that Leopardi makes. He tries to situate the poetry on that terrain of unified sense that his philosophical labor had constructed. If the poetic effects are absent, this lack follows from the limit of the metaphysical discourse; it is the sign of that limit.[147] But this search is nonetheless tremendously important. Its fundamental characteristic is expressed in a vital movement that makes the complexity of perception, reflection, and expression systematic, pulsating, and circular. It situates itself creatively within the totality of being. To each innovation of the central intuition thus corresponds the displacement of all the complementary elements. The mutation of the paradigm unfolds on the terrain of the broadest articulation of the complexity and invests it completely.[148] In Leopardi this process is sometimes paradoxical because the totality of the development of the ideal paradigm is situated among forms—philosophical and lyrical, rational and natural—that are often superficially defined as contradictory. Beyond the apparent contradiction a sort of flow of truth operates, and the paradox of the formal situation serves only to dramatize, and thereby exalt, the inspired force of the expressive synthesis. The lyrical experiments of 1820 to 1821 are a significant example of this progression of Leopardi's world of life, in all its complexity, qualities, and crisis. The movement is this global displacement that we are analyzing.

Let us sum up its terms: the insoluble character of the dialectic that results from the fact that its material basis, the truth of determinations, does not allow ideal solutions; the deepening of this materiality and an effort to construct a web of significant senses; the impact of a new indifference that second nature or the universe of communication seems to interpret. We are experimenting with the dynamics and articulations of this new fabric of the imagination while constructing it. The first experiments are lyrical, and they do not succeed. In effect, they establish a new framework for the whole, forge stylistic tools of formal synthesis at the level of second nature, but still do not succeed in breaking its rigidity. And this concerns not only poetry: all aspects of life are constrained to this rigidity. The constructive but nonetheless critical condition of the metaphysical landscape does not lead to a dynamic opening. The crisis is certainly not dramatic; it is dead calm—humid, heavy, enveloping, paralyzing. But it is expected. Leopardi experiences it as such, experimenting, perhaps feeling himself nearing the resolving event—all this without hope, in total lucidity.

Another terrain of verification and experimentation is nevertheless proposed to us—that of historical and civil debate. It is proposed to us rather brusquely and immediately. Perhaps this spontaneity of reference rests on the principle of communicating vessels: the metaphysical experience, the lyrical experience, and the historical-civil experience in Leopardi maintain such a relationship; and to the blockage of one corresponds the emergence of the other. What are the effects on this terrain of this very strong metaphysical innovation in the *Zibaldone* of 1821? At first glance, the answer is easy: the same horizon of dead calm, which the correspondence amply demonstrates—a respite for the spirit. The pedagogical inspiration and a certain propensity for irony begin to crop up ("I am getting used to laughing"). The project of the *Operette morali* (*Moral Essays*) is explicitly mentioned.[149] Let us ask once again: how can we grasp the metaphysical displacement on the terrain of civil philosophy and in reference to the definition of second nature? There is something new in this passage, and it consists in the rupture of the relationship with tradition. Up to now, the crisis of historical memory had never been refused; instead it corresponded to the attempt at a new articulation. The whole relationship with Giordani is based on this project of critically restoring classicism, on the attempt to make it into a discriminating criterion of the tradition and a reformist project of civil philosophy. This schema presupposes a dialectical web, but that was definitively rejected in favor of the web of sense. Hence we have a complete, radical modification of Leopardi's project involving civil philosophy.

> it is futile to build if we don't begin from the foundation. Whoever wants to do some good for Italy will first of all have to show her a philo-sophical language; without that I think she will never have a modern literature of her own, and without a modern literature of her own, she will never ever be a nation. Thus the effect I chiefly wish to achieve is that Italian writers can be philosophers, inventive and in tune with their times, which is as much as to say writers and not copyists, and so they ought not to be barbarians where language is concerned, but Italians.[150]

Beginning with the foundation of language in order to construct the nation: what more modern image of political making is there? What deeper (and ceaselessly reasserted) rupture with a reformist conception of tradition and the *Risorgimento*—a conception that will know the splendors of the "national-popular"—can there be?[151] Giordani could not subscribe to this displacement of the critical consideration. In that same letter, Leopardi wrote to him: "For a long time you have been as it were the measure and the form of my life." That time has passed, just as any possibility of connecting the web of the dialectic and the web of sense, the reform of tradition and the new foundation, has passed. That said, the new terrain of civil philosophy nonetheless remains inaccessible for now. The displacement is realized, but its significance does not go beyond the stage of sentiment and the declaration of intent. The new metaphysical discourse governs a new level of political philosophy, but it also subjects it to relative impotence for the moment. The web of sense is still unable to perceive the sense, the direction of the web. The new politics and the new literature, for which a potent foundation is imagined, do not succeed in articulating themselves, except in terms of genre—in this instance, on a horizontal dimension ("Countless genres of writing are partially or totally lacking among Italians, but the principal ones, the most fruitful and even the most necessary, are in my view the philosophical, dramatic and satiric genres"),[152] never a vertical one, around a thematic of literary genres and not political values. Of course, this choice is important: in a man of letters like Leopardi, the theme of genres (above all in the metaphysical density of this period) is a study in philosophical *Darstellung*, a figure filled with contents that are certainly not exclusively literary.[153] This is confirmed for us by reiterated commentaries on Galileo's scientific prose, in which the accent placed on the elegance of his writing is immediately representative of a vindication for sensualist philosophy and an apology for truth.[154] Yet these days of peace, this relative solidity of the framework, are not free of a certain disorientation, an imprecision of intention that brings us back to the indetermination of the structure. Despite a substantial enlargement of the framework, the philosophical-civil experiments, like the lyrical experiments, are marked by lack and an air of expectation.

This expectation cannot last. This stability was always precarious. The system of communication must open up. The ontological problem— necessarily—does not delay in manifesting its urgency. Like the human mind, the system is, in effect, always open.

> The human mind is always deceived in its hopes and always deceivable, always disappointed by hope itself and always capable of being so, not only open to but possessed by hope in the very act of ultimate desperation, the very act of suicide. Hope is like self-love, from which it is directly derived. Because of the essence and nature of the animal, neither hope nor self-love can ever desert him as long as he lives, that is, feels his existence.[155]

And we understand why. Because the systematic web is sensuous, because "everything is animated by the contrast and everything languishes with- out it": all stability is indifference and only movement pulses with life, so that every conclusion is a rupture of the imagination, of hope. Every moment is catastrophic. And "resigned desperation, which is the last step of the sensitive man," comes to this catastrophe, perhaps so that a greater

misfortune can take hold of him. The "new suffering in that case is like
a cautery which restores some feeling, some span of life to numbed bodies."[156] We could follow for page after page this affirmation of a dialectic
of surfaces, which is like the rising of the wind after the great dead calm.
But this affirmation remains linked to the horizontal, systematic characterization of the metaphysical framework; that is, to the definition of
its constant balance rather than to its deepening, to any advance in the
solution of the problem. What is once again required here is what Leopardi
described around a year earlier as his own experience of the discovery of
philosophizing.

> In its poetic career, my spirit has followed the same course as the human
> spirit in general. At the beginning, my strength lay in fantasy. [. . .]
> I had not yet meditated on things, and as for philosophy, I had only
> the merest glimmer. [. . .] my condition then was exactly the same as
> the ancients'. [. . .] The total transformation that took place in me, my
> passing from ancient to modern, happened, you might say, in the space
> of a single year, that is, in 1819, when, deprived of my sight and the
> constant distraction of reading, I began to feel my unhappiness in a
> much bleaker way, I began to abandon hope, to reflect deeply on things,
> [. . .] to become a professional philosopher (instead of the poet I was
> before), to feel the incontrovertible unhappiness of the world, rather
> than knowing about it.[157]

Once again, therefore, it involves a deepening that rejoins the path of the
moderns, that breaks the relative indifference of the great intervening displacement whose movements it reorients vertically by rerooting them in
the ethical nature of ontology. Experiencing the unhappiness of the world
rather than simply knowing about it: such is the model onto which philosophy opens, and its opening necessarily assumes this direction which
is precisely its highest dignity. This passage takes place in a set of canti
composed between autumn 1821 and summer 1822. We can still speak of
experimenting here—of the continuation of that experimenting that gave
birth to *The Evening of the Holiday, The Dream*, and *The Solitary Life*,
which is confirmed for us by the reading of these new canti.[158] But whereas
the preceding experiments involved the integration of a formal framework
and tried to fashion a system from the web of sense, here they become
metaphysical and seek to deepen or discover the logical sense and ethical
signification of this web, this universe. With difficulty but continuously,
second nature intends to open up incontestably ontological perspectives.
The negative follows the thread of absoluteness.

First of all, two canzoni: *For the Wedding of his Sister Paolina*[159] and *Ode to a Victor in the Games*.[160] A veritable shaping of the crisis of sense develops here. The thematic framework of both canti is that of historical devolution, of cultural decadence that entails the dissolution of morals and the degradation of nature—so much human wretchedness! These terms are quite familiar to us. But to the reflections of the *Zibaldone* something new is added: above all, the very strong rhetorical plasticity of these canti, the poetic visualization and sensitization of the historical condition. Leopardi's language seems to shape itself to the goal pursued and to take up once again syntactic and semantic forms previously considered outmoded. The rhetorical form forges an adequate language. It carries along with it the old cultural, pedagogical, and moral models and constructs new ones with the aim of establishing a classical horizon that would no longer be heroic or voluntaristic, but rather plastic, sacred. In fact, the crisis of memory is in no way denied or faced with a reminiscence of traditional classicism. On the contrary, memory finds itself fixated in one particular aspect of its development, paralyzed at the height of its growth, and thus projected onto a gigantic screen where the fixity exacerbates the components of crisis and death. Or rather, the horizon of memory is so massively constructed in historical and ideological terms so that its ruinous effects upon philosophy can be overturned. Here the crisis of memory is still directed against the fixity of the system and functions as a chemical solvent for its temporal bases. The most elementary and vital aspects, like the exaltation of procreation and the virtue of youth, end up consigned to the margin of the development of the canti (where they give rise to some splendid images) but in no way constitute points of rupture and hope.

These two canti produce an almost theatrical effect of estrangement. Why? Because only a plastic and totalizing rendering of memory permits the denunciation of second nature as a possible hypostasis, the denunciation of its fixity and the disorientation of values that follows from it—a denunciation that Leopardi turns back against himself and against the present state of his philosophy. For at this point the latter undergoes, within this negative theodicy of memory and this sublime devolution of history—in parallel with the extinction of the most traditional paradigms—an effect of marginalization of the feminine and the heroic.

But this negative labor is not all there is to these two canti. If they can be linked to the canti that follow, in which the philosophical passage toward the ontological sphere is determined, it is because they create one of the necessary conditions for this passage: the forming, in other words the conceptualization, in unitary terms, of the horizon of second nature. Thus a positive labor takes place here, aimed at the general plastic construction of the great philosophical scene. The critique can henceforth develop within this space of great concepts. Memory appears as dead objectivity and as a new system of signs, coherent insofar as their relation is concerned but senseless in relation to the world. The operation of overturning necessitates a dimension in which the process of micro-formation of the web of sense can be repeated. Here the search is oriented, conversely, toward "infinite spaces."

Brutus[161] is the first to rip the fabric of this heightened indifference—with a scream. An immediate movement, a very strong breath of ethics follows the monumental majesty of the preceding canti's poetic flow. Was this paradoxical distance constructed in order to bring about this flip [*ribaltamento*]? Be that as it may, it is constructed: the canto undergoes this harsh negative dialectic. The author, his search, his ethical testimony are in the foreground. This is the reason it is better to speak of the formation of a phenomenology of consciousness than of the dialectic: in this caesura of the practical flow, consciousness does not encounter vague pretexts of ideal continuity but impulses of renewal. It embodies the necessity of ethics and a new epiphany regarding its tragedy. The immediacy of the scream, the force of the ethical testimony, moreover, neither avoids nor dissolves the abstract scene of second nature. In these lines Brutus is a phantasm, not a subject of flesh and bone. The poetic game remains conceptual. And it must remain that way. Strength, in this canto, consists in the mystery—constantly renewed by a philosophy that is itself renewed at this height of the problem—of a necessary, plastic, dramatic detachment from the vicissitudes of the poet and his affirmation of a concrete and immediate truth on a horizon of conceptual essences. Within this reality of the concept and of universal human communication that is cold and senseless, the lyric bears witness to the different, to innovation. The blasphemy is formidable.

> He grieves the gods who enters Tartarus
> By force. (That strength of mind
> Is alien to soft eternal beings.)
> Did gods perhaps arrange our miseries,
> Our bitter chances, our unhappy feelings,
> As drama to delight their hours of ease? (*Brutus*, ll.46–51)[162]

But the ethical guarantee of reality, of the justice of the act, is equally immediate.

> No life of grievous guilt—
> Free in the wood a life of innocence
> Nature ordained for us. (ll.52–54)[163]

The essential thing is that the scream and the imprecation of justice penetrate the spaces of the conceptual universe and, at this level of communication, impose ethical sense, or at least the problem.

> The times
> Change for the worse; we would be made to trust
> To poor posterity
> The honor of high minds and the supreme
> Vengeance for misery. The sable bird
> Wheel on its greedy pinions over me!
> The wild beast crush, the storm
> Carry my corpse away!
> The wind disperse my name and memory. (ll.112–20)[164]

This individual solution is surely not enough to endow the web of sense with ethical force. It is not adequate any more. It is merely desperate. But this desperation that insinuates itself into the horizon of communication rouses it and pervades it completely. The question then begins to shape the problem in a game of universality. How can we significantly articulate the web of sense? What value can be attributed to its power [*potenza*]? What can we ask of or impose upon the Gods?

The canto *To Spring, or Of the Ancient Fables*[165] expands the space of rupture of the world of sense, and in the form of an elementary myth proposes the emergence of ethics. The protest is in no way extraneous: the alternative is internal. It is an elementary myth—that is, an imaginative hypostasis of the concept opposed to that other hypostasis of the web of sense, which is not imaginative but rather conceptual. The fable and the literary myth are directed against a real, the already achieved understanding of which must be transformed.

> May human hearts, buried in suffering,
> Welcome the wished return
> Of that bright age, which misery and the dark
> Torch of the truth destroyed
> Before its time? (*To Spring*, ll.10–14)[166]

To consider the efficacy of this opposition, to ask if it manages to break through the empty solidity of the nothingness of communication or to establish a signifying polarity in the circulation of sense, would be to pose the problem in erroneous terms. All that is nothing. The key to this procedure of Leopardi's is an almost mystical one that aims, by means of the concept

of devolution, to exemplify historical degradation and natural degradation,
identifying the two. Hence the final, skeptical gaze over the canto's own
endeavor to provide a fable of primordial nature and its divinity as effective
alternative.

> I beg you, nature: [. . .]
> Bring the old spark in me once more to birth;
> That is if you still live yourself, and if
> One being does at least—
> Or up in heaven above, or on the earth
> In sunlight, or in chambers of the sea—
> Not pity, no, notice our misery. (ll.88, 90–95)[167]

But the fable of nature does not resolve the sense of the canto. Even here,
in a form that borders on the mystical, the alternative concerns the web of
sense. It constructs a subject—a pure kind of subject that is a voice and that
speaks itself. Spring and its myth are savage subjects in search of a space,
who begin to construct it by force—an incursion of ethical instinct.[168]

Sappho's Last Song[169] appears after the protest and the mystical alternative. Unexpectedly, miraculously, it finds the way, assumes tragedy as such
and imposes it upon the web of sense. "All is mysterious,/Except our suffering" (ll.46–47).[170] The lyric posture is that of suffering. The dimensions of
poetic consideration are folded into the linearity of the subjective position.
The ethical drama is real because it has a subjective referent, which avoids
individualization and never slips to the psychological level. The sphere of
the concept does not deprive the subject of its own characteristics. "And
we shall die" (l.55).[171] This destiny touches us as a part of our being: and
nonetheless love does not bend to necessity.

> You, for whose sake
> Long hopeless love, long faith, and a vain frenzy
> Of unfulfilled desire fasten on me,
> Live happily, if ever on this earth
> A happy mortal lived. (ll.58–62)[172]

What is striking in this canto is the internal shakeup of a world that hereto-
fore seemed fixed. This world of the web of sense is assumed as such, but
pervaded, vivified, by indestructible subjects. If the web is one of death, then
the lyrical voice, suffering, and love are terms of indispensable subjective
identification. The stylistic revolution of this period is accomplished; the
flux of the imaginary is set free. But although this operation of conceptually

transferring the field of application of fantasy can be reductive—permitting only external, substitutive, alternative operations—here the ethical, vital, subjective dimension explodes into the conceptual figure of the whole: an immense metaphysical operation.

There are some who ask philosophy to be pedagogical, logical, and exemplary. Why? Is not this rediscovery by Leopardi of a subject in the web of sense—not the old genealogical subject of sensualism, but a new, universal, and ethical subject—perhaps a philosophical trace of truth? And what can we add to being if not the subjective expression of its truth and its reconstruction in subjective tension, in pain, and in hope? Sappho was unaware of the challenge of her life. But she dares to proclaim the baseness of nature and the Gods. This is neither the anger of *Brutus* nor the pious fable of *To Spring*.

> But unconsidered words
> Are coming from your lips: destined events
> Move by mysterious ways. (*Sappho's Last Song*, ll.44–46)[173]

On the contrary, here it is consciousness that makes itself, without wanting to be divine, without foundering in the abysses of idealist mystification—that makes itself as finite and critical power [*potenza*], without pride and without baseness. The kingdom of sense discovers an ethical subject that suffering organizes and consciousness embodies. "And we shall die," but death is unjust and God is the "blind giver of circumstance." We shall die just as we shall suffer, but the injustice of death and suffering cannot be removed from consciousness. Constructed on the critique of abstract reason, the world of sense has successively become a positive horizon and then an impotent materialism: a customary flip of negative reason. Sappho's indignation rescues us.

After the reading of *Sappho's Last Song*, the gaze wanders and the attention often wavers while perusing the *Hymn to the Patriarchs, or Of the Beginnings of the Human Race*.[174] This is wrong, because without attaining the intensity of the previous canto, the hymn amplifies certain fundamental motifs in it—and if it takes up myth again, along with the clarifying procedure by means of oppositions utilized in *To Spring*, the other hymn composed during this period, this is to better present the dynamic of lyrical development. Thus it is precisely through the synthesis of the intensity of states of consciousness and the reiterated proposition of a lofty mythical inspiration that another pole on the road between the linguistic horizon and the ethical horizon—which constitutes the philosophical objective of the moment—takes shape here. Desire accompanies the pain of existence and the lofty dignity of understanding and resisting it. The subject is no longer merely the residue of elements irreducible to the system of second nature; it is no longer merely the child of pain, but it is also desire, projection.

The concept of the subject consolidates itself and a new, positive alterity grows deeper within the framework of second nature. Myth can thus live on as an ideal alternative embodied in desire, in the progress of historical time and the vicissitudes of its degradation.

> Oh happy,
> All unaware of sin and sad event,
> Deserted earthly seat! (*Hymn to the Patriarchs*, ll.34–36)[175]

It can live not as nostalgia but as critical being, different time, within and against the course of human history—as critique of primitive guilt posited as the basis of the city ("breathless and ailing/Remorse in desperation brings blind mortals/For the first time together and restricts them/To common shelters" [ll.47–50]).[176] It is a critique of servitude—that condition which follows from a forced and guilt-stained foundation of power [*potere*] ("and human life grown weak/Fell prey to slavery, the worst of fates" [ll.55–56]).[177] But it can also live as desire, a realistic desire that has completely internalized the experience of pain and now regards the golden age not as a delightful utopia but as the possibility of hope. The absence of any resignation, the realism in the very proposition of the mystical horizon, as if to exorcise the extreme dilatory function at the very moment when it is reasserted as irrepressible (ll.87–103), gives this hymn an ascetic flavor. Myth is not something that confounds hope but is rather a trace, a harsh, realistic trace offered to hope. Nature is open to this ceaselessly repeated conflict, and though defeated, preserves its hope.

> Still in the boundless Californian woods
> Happy children live on, whose hearts pale care
> Does not draw dry, whose limbs acute disease
> Does not consume; the woodland gives them food,
> The hollowed rock a home, the watered valley
> Gives them refreshment, the dark day of death
> Hangs over them unseen. To stand against
> Our wicked boldness how defenseless are
> Wise nature's realms! The shores the shaded caverns
> The quiet woods invaded and laid waste
> By our unsated zeal! These ravished people

Trained to unprecedented pain, unknown
Desires! Their fleeting happiness stripped naked
And driven out beyond the sunset bar! (ll.104–17)[178]

What an accumulation of complex motifs: an ideal of positive natural right that resists the linearity of an optimistic conception of history and society; a pessimistic conception of reason and civilization, denounced as producers of slavery and death. But "fleeting happiness stripped naked" flees "beyond the sunset bar."

What, then, is the man of second nature? He is pain and desire. He thus breaks this new horizon of indifference constructed by the web of sense. A bridge stretches from this perception of pain and desire to an ontological fabric where values are posited that orient the web of sense. These values are certainly not things but rather states of things that the subject traverses and posits. They are ethical behaviors, dimensions of an ethical time that the subject reveals as so many signs of the activity of being. The definition of a dynamic within second nature in no way weakens the consistency of the web of sense and reintroduces no dialectical hope.

Thus in the canti that we have just read, the artificial complexity of the fabric of second nature and sense is not merely maintained, it is perfected. The "stylistic caesura" that, according to some commentators,[179] marks the lyrical activity of this period represents and is constituted by the attempt to fully adapt the formal movement to this super-real [*surreale*] world constituted by the theory of sense, a super-real world ruled by its own systemic laws and woven of relations that define it—and no less real than this world from which the philosopher-poet, immersed in the confusion of tradition and the wretchedness of memory, has freed himself. Thus it is the only real world, the only truth of the world—but as a horizon, as the overall form of a long-sought displacement of pain and refusal. Once again, after this first genetic emergence of pain and desire, faced with the world organized on the basis of the surmounting of primary dialectical irreducibility—once again, at this new level, pain, refusal, and desire must intervene, with increased strength [*forza potenziata*] gained from the enrichment produced by this progressive metaphysical path. This is the way the stylistic caesura, by adapting the form of the lyric to the world of sense, creates conceptual, universal forms for philosophy, forms that constitute the first new material of its analysis.

Now these conceptual forms too can and must be subjected to critique and made to live in the ontological relation. So much happens. Thus the reductive tensions that produce every systematic figure—above all at this level of abstraction and stylistic perfection—will first be counterbalanced by existential affirmations of protest and resistance, by an abstract claim. Then the reductive tensions will gradually be vanquished and the system surveyed again, in its very abstraction, by consciousness. Finally—without losing any of its perfection of sign or sense—it will be infiltrated by human passions, mobilized by those ontological directional forces that are pain and desire. Leopardi's intense poetic enterprise is all here in this metaphysical exposition (*Darstellung*) of the passages of consciousness on the way to truth and the confrontation of this tension with the states of reality. Pain and desire are passions regrouped under the generic category of relation. In Leopardi, they must be taken up into the ethical category of a materialist metaphysics. That is what confers upon the poetic enterprise, even in its moments of greatest logical and lyrical abstraction, this weight of drama, of ethical tragedy.

The problem raised in this chapter, which corresponds precisely to the series of mutations that we have studied, nevertheless remains unresolved in this period. The possibility of a solution is emerging, however. The irruption of an ethically motivated subjectivity into the world of sense and into its web is indeed very strong. It remains to be seen how the reclaiming of the ontological fabric can benefit this line of subjective unfurling.

Imagining

Subjective does not mean individual experience, *Erlebnis*; nor can lived experience as such resolve the problems of thought. This applies all the more to Leopardi, as we now see. Thus when, in November 1822, the moment nears for the departure from Recanati for Rome (where he stays until May 1823), we feel, without much sense of paradox, that the desire to flee is exhausted. The idea of flight was metaphysically important when Leopardi was confronting the dialectical dimensions of the problem of memory and its crisis. The question now is quite different: it does not involve fleeing but organizing a voyage into being. Rome gives him and can give him nothing. The letters that he sends to his family and friends[180] express a relatively serene expectancy, but in the letters addressed in the same period to his brother Carlo, Leopardi testifies to the unease of relocation and inexperience and the sensation of solitude that had gripped him. In Rome his melancholy persists. "I have lost myself. . . . Love me, for God's sake. I need love, love, love, fire, enthusiasm, life: the world doesn't seem made for me."[181] The people he meets, and of whom he expected so much, appear to him dazed and without generosity. In this situation, Recanati threatens to become a positive recollection.[182] In Rome, literature is non-existent: "Horrors and then more horrors." Antiquarianism rules and culture is mere mercantile trafficking: for these reasons, a world all the more full of prejudices and envy.[183] The denunciation of life in the great cities, in the dissoluteness of morals and thought, recurs. Masses, anomie—we find ourselves alone in the midst of a "dissolute multitude." In Rome, "indifference, that horrible passion, or rather absence of passion."[184] It is the dispassion of indifference. Rome has no other theoretical function than to represent the indifference of the web of sense. If the city is culturally insignificant, politically and civilly Rome is corrupt. The foreigners are better than the Romans: could he not find a post as tutor or Hellenist in the service of some traveling nobleman?[185] The search comes to nothing. Nothing more remains except the possibility of becoming a priest. "I looked around me, and decided I didn't want anything to do with it. . . . [A] long time ago, and before coming here, and much more so since coming, I made up my mind that my life must be as independent as possible, and that my happiness can only consist in doing what suits me."[186] Rome merely raises the problem anew—the problem of a vital orientation called love and freedom that can be guaranteed by truth.

The identification with Tasso becomes important here: "I went to visit Tasso's tomb, and I wept there. This is the first and only *pleasure* I have experienced in Rome."[187]

He goes on:

> You understand the host of feelings that arise from contemplating the contrast between Tasso's greatness and the unpretentiousness of his tomb. But you can't have any idea of another contrast, that is the one felt by an eye accustomed to the boundless grandiosity and vast size of Roman monuments, comparing them to the smallness and bareness of this tomb. One feels a sad and angry consolation thinking that this lack of ostentation is still sufficient to interest and inspire posterity, whereas the most magnificent mausoleums contained in Rome are gazed at with perfect indifference toward the person to whom them were erected, whose name is not even asked, or else is asked not as the name of the person but of the monument. Near Tasso's tomb is the tomb of the poet Guidi, who wanted to lie *prope magnos Torquati cineres*, as the inscription says. He did the wrong thing. I didn't even have a sigh left for him. I could hardly bear to look at his monument, fearing to stifle the sensations I'd felt at Tasso's tomb.[188]

The web of sense is presented here by disproportion, contrast. He feels the problem is coming to maturity and its solution is imminent: here humility is the discriminating element of the "boundless grandiosity" of history—the insistent, humble presence of poetic memory—but also the insistence of humility *tout court*. Hence an opening, superficially unexpected but theoretically motivated:

> Even the street that leads to that spot prepares the spirit for the impres-
> sions of feeling. It is all flanked by houses destined for artisan work, and
> it resounds to the noise of looms and other such implements, and the
> singing of women and laborers busy at their work. In an idle, dissolute,
> disorganized city such as capital cities are, it is a fine thing to contem-
> plate an image of life which is thoughtful, orderly and engaged in useful
> occupations. Even the expressions and the behavior of the people one
> meets in that street have something simpler and more human about them
> than those of other people; and they reveal the habits and the character
> of persons whose life is based on truth and not on falsehood, that is who
> live by hard work and not by intrigue, imposture and deception, as the
> greater part of this populace does.[189]

Passion is pitted against the absence of passion, but this time on the terrain of community: nature against society; an unaltered judgment, despite the political assertions frequent during this period, whose literal form is that of skepticism or at the very least a strong relativism recalling Callicles and Cicero (notably in the few Roman pages of the *Zibaldone*).[190] But these assertions must be placed back in the framework of the motto, "Therefore the original and continuing cause of human unhappiness is society,"[191] which is now more than ever a skeptical declaration only in appearance, while in reality it is an unveiling and critique of existing society and an omen for a revolt of nature.

A progressive Leopardi? Perhaps, in this particular instance, yes—but remaining attentive to the ideological terms and sensitive to the social instances. A wind, or rather a light breeze of liberalism traverses Leopardi's thought at this point: in the polemic against indifference, even the generic vindication of economic freedom seems to bear the sign of the renewal of nature.[192] We seem to be seeing the revival of the concept of the "weak *Risorgimento*," the importance of which we emphasized and which, not by chance, was already linked in those pages to generic but politically meaning-ful considerations concerning economic liberalism (on money[193] and later, similar to here, on commerce[194]). Passion is counterposed to the absence of passion and nature against society.

The return to Recanati finds Leopardi the same as when he left. The framework of his hardships is unaltered. The Roman trip served to enlarge the experiment and consequently deepen the disenchantment. It cannot even be said that the Roman trip represents disillusionment. There is only a certain embarrassment in recognizing that thought had, "in my beautiful Recanati,"[195] acquired a sensibility and themes unsuspected by Roman culture. A gigantic, humiliating disproportion. Indeed, he who descended upon Rome is not an offshoot of the pontifical aristocracy from the provinces—he is a Winckelmann, a Goethe, the vector of a European adventure of thought who finds himself faced with the base commerce in antiquities, a rotten political culture, and Roman prostitution. And he is one who, as in the old heroic canzone, discovers on Tasso's tomb a new incitement to search for truth.

Upon returning to Recanati, Leopardi confides all this to Giordani[196] without regret or disillusion, but with determination and with a sense of vocation that no wandering will ever weaken. Upon his return Leopardi demonstrates a humane maturity strengthened by a theoretically expanded sensibility. His vocation is so firm in its will to systematic construction that it can permit itself two opposed and complementary movements of mind: on the one hand, the reassertion of a deeply rooted historical memory and an ontological link with it;[197] on the other, disenchantment, or rather a disdainful, cynical, or ironic detachment from the wretchedness of the present and its generalized prostitution,[198] a eulogy for the absence of memory. Thus the maturation of Leopardi's independence of judgment seems to be the only important result that follows from the Roman episode. Back in Recanati, from this high observatory, the horizon has now become wider, the hurdle has fallen away, and the vocation contains no traces of resignation, not even hidden ones.

No salvation is thus to be expected from *Erlebnis*, from lived experience, least of all at the level of Leopardi's meditation on the abstractness of second nature, the now-completed revisiting of the web of sense. The intellectual Leopardi is now true, in the sense that he is completely within the discourse. But the problem remains: grafting subjectivity into the web of sense, so that it can give direction to the ontological fabric. This is a problem of redemption. Christianity redeemed the first nature, snatching its indifference and its transferability from the devil. Now, in Leopardi as in Hegel, the problem is that of redeeming time and that worldliness that took shape out of the exhaustion of the theological perspective. Hegelian redemption passes by way of the dialectic. It is a true and proper redemption that confers upon absolute spirit the role of divinity. Leopardi sees the development of the dialectic, which is a real development, end up in a circular and hypostatic schema. The universe of the senses, though charged with material determinations, fails to accommodate and respond to the questions that mind, pain, and desire pose.

Redemption accomplishes two passages in Leopardi. He does not recognize the miraculous Hegelian *Aufhebung* (and we see later how the "*nuovi credenti* [new believers]," already present in the Italian cultural panorama of those days, suggest it to him in native dialects), but instead a process in which an annunciation and a revolution are present, independent of one another. In other words, parodying a Hegelian formula—John the Baptist and Christ. The annunciation consists in the constitution of a real horizon of signification that has its own laws in itself: that is, the constitution of the web of sense. But why think this independent, self-referential construction could be conclusive? And indeed it is not. It is a horizon that justifies itself but produces nothing, that is not nourished by creativity but feeds on itself: such is the web of sense. This constructing produces no future and does not satisfy the inexhaustible character of desire. This horizon must then become constructive. Only this constructiveness is redemptive—a subjectivity that creatively engages the material vicissitudes of determination. Such is the current problem. Leopardi's exclamation that his system completes that of Christianity is therefore true.[199] Paradoxical but true. The idea of redemption is really taken up, but materialized in a secular and blasphemous figure of liberation. The problem is no longer that of demystifying but of producing, of constitution. How does one grasp ontology? All the conditions are given: the redemption of second nature, this abstract world that sense has materially constituted, is the subjective mediation of concrete universality. Like Christ and contrary to Christ.[200]

Let us take another look at the world of the web of sense: leaving aside or behind the suggestions of the Enlightenment and Romanticism, its outline is materially constructed within a genealogy of sensibility, a framework of abstract relations corresponding to the universe of communication, to its formal relations and impotent values.[201] How does one breathe fire, enthusiasm, life into this system? How does one impose a direction, a transformation, an alternative, on this horizon? What is a materialist redemption? If in the system of communication, within the web of sense, subjectivity and objectivity are reciprocally reversible, interchangeable, here their permeable indifference must no longer be granted. Pain and desire, those tensions of a universal and human subjectivity, sabotage the machine. Leopardi's reading of redemption involves grafting the subject into the world of abstraction—and not the repeated negations and sublimations, the Jesuitical mechanism of the *Aufhebung*. All the antagonistic binaries of the metaphysical game are undermined—the aristocratic philosophical tradition loses its colors. A eulogy for the absence of memory. The dialectical stereotype is particularly weakened once Leopardi imposes upon the abstract, inserts into its reality the presence of the subject. Is the abstract the opposite of the concrete? Perhaps, but this is not a certainty. Sometimes the answer is no. Nevertheless, the abstract is certainly not the opposite of concrete subjectivity.[202] The latter absorbs the abstract as its own dimension, as second nature. Christian redemption takes concrete subjects and makes them leap toward the absolute, whereas idealist redemption is mediated by the relationship between negation and overcoming. That kind of redemption is out of the question here.

This materialist redemption is without transcendent or transcendental ends to confront or toward which to tend—it knows only subjects who experience it and determine it, the only ones in a position to construct salvation—love and freedom. Redemption is now confronted with the new conditions of second nature. As long as we fail to understand this, we fail to understand the height of Leopardi's anticipation. The more this world—though in the plenitude of sense—becomes abstract and empties itself of all signification and value, the closer Leopardi's discourse seems to us. How can we rediscover the essential polarities in the indifference of the world? How can we seize an orientation from the ambiguity of the system of second nature? I would tire of tracking the perpetual repetition of this question in Leopardi if not for the ethical charge that it presents. In effect, a stylistic asymmetry exists between Leopardi the person and the thinker: his lyric is metaphysical, but his metaphysics is not immediately lyrical. In his work as in physics, the system of communicating vessels reaches its limits. Nevertheless, we are lucky that the ethical determination balances and regulates the communication of fluids. Hence Leopardi's *Erlebnissen* interest us insofar as they are the most abstract materials at our disposal: ethics as foundation of ontology itself, freedom as foundation of necessity. That means once again giving sense to the web of sensibility, redeeming this second nature that sensibility and its critical and constitutive genealogy have constructed. The ethics of pain and desire is at once the scandal and the motive force of this construction, at this level of abstraction and universality. It is the soul of redemption, its imagining.

To His Lady[203] is the metaphysical exposition that responds to this question. It is a pedagogical manifesto of the materialist path leading from knowledge to redemption. It consists of fifty-five lines divided into five stanzas. Each stanza defines a state of consciousness through a rhythm of continuous searching, which leads from the construction of the abstract back to subjectivity and finally to the indication of the ontological direction of this search. Lines 1 to 11 open the canzone, proposing a high metaphysical tension to desire. The idea of the lady appears, or rather presents itself, offers itself—a carnal, sensual, polymorphous idea. Phantasm of a nocturnal dream, naturalistic apparition, myth of the golden age or hoped-for time to come, she is at once an ideal type and a temporal dimension—a concrete universal, an unappeased, unappeasable tension. All the aspects of memory and the phenomenological relation, the dialectical possibility, thus succeed in taking shape. The intensity is maximal, faced with an idea that presents itself as expansiveness. The web of sense is grasped in the act of deploying itself. The canto opens onto this explosion of the abstract and the ideal. It is a pure and simple apology for the world of sense and the desire that pervades it. Lines 12 to 22 exacerbate the basic situation defined by the first stanza. They transform ideality into transcendence.

> But is there anything on earth
> At all like you? And even if there were
> One like in face, in action, and in voice,
> Her beauty, though alike, would still be less. (*To His Lady*, ll.19–22)[204]

The idea that presented itself as a state of consciousness, as an element of the phenomenology of love and the web of sense, is abstracted: each of the elements experienced in the first approach now tends to be hypostasized, fixed—it is transcendence. Transcendence forms part of the web of sense, results from its movement: the abstract dynamic of the image unfolds in transcendental fixity. The sense of the transcendent is immanent to life. It grows with lived experience, desire, and imagination. This transcendent self-making of desire is the key to its tension toward the real. Only the exacerbation of passion to the point of the ideal allows the materiality of passion to be recovered: the mind extends and realizes itself in this paradoxical passage. Transcendence is the inverted sign of the immanence of passion. It is the internal metamorphosis of passion, and this is the rhythm that the lyric reveals and embodies. Life as the duty of death and desire as poetry are exacerbated along this brief arc in which every experience and every state of consciousness become abstraction. How can the subject possess this abstraction and fill it with feeling, passion, and life? The third stanza answers this question negatively.

The web of sense remains indifferent. The poetic model of this questioning corresponds neither to the *dolce stil novo* nor to Petrarchism. Every possibility of participation, even a degraded one such as participation in the Platonic sense, of the idea in the world is refused.

> But heaven
> Gives no comfort to our suffering,
> And truly mortal life with you would be
> Like that which takes on godhead in the sky. (*To His Lady*, ll.30–32)[205]

The dialectic, which consists precisely in a partial sublimation of illusion and in the recognition of the spiritually creative character of the tension of desire, has no place here. No celestial synthesis takes place. The journey is interrupted, turned back. The ideal of "his" lady appears then as the most concrete universal of existence: it is born within the tension of passion and made absolute on the web of sense. It can therefore return to existence only as absolute, as tragic moment. It is not dialectizable. Heaven and earth remain distinct worlds. The idea does not govern the suffering of the earth. The hypostasis of the ideal, although produced by the development of sense, does not withstand the confrontation with life. This third stanza—the poetic projection of the illusion of a relationship between the idea and the feeling of love—would have made a classical idealist, a Schelling or a Hegel, happy if it had resolved into a synthesis. This is what is so astonishing in Leopardi: he possesses this capacity to experience and revive the time of the dialectic, in very pure terms, in order to negate every project and every possibility of synthesis. Once this synthesis is rejected, how then is the world possible? Only through the subjective traversal of the crisis of values of the great web of sense, and by positing the imagination as the solution—a non-homologizable one—to the need for the dialectic.

Lines 34 to 41 signal this new state of consciousness. Leopardi abandons that youthful error, dialectical hope. An alternative clearly exists, but it is an internal, suffering, desperate, and nevertheless real alternative that governs the awareness of the impossibility of the dialectic and that displaces the terrain of the search for truth. In other words, in the disaster of the dialectic, in the catastrophe of memory, the subjective hypothesis remains valid—not merely valid but productive. Disenchanted, it still operates in the kingdom of the universal. It is imagination.

> Oh could I but preserve,
> Through this dark age and tainted atmosphere,
> Your noble imago, and with it alone,
> Not with the truth, content me as I can. (ll.41–44)[206]

The imago is the insertion of subjectivity into the abstraction of the world of sense; it destroys the haughty suffocating logic of this structural relation and opens it up. But to what? This is where the long labor of Leopardi's problematic ends up, where the leap within the critical thematic that the canto *To His Lady* allows takes place. Dialectical redemption is impossible: we have known it since the experiment of *The Infinite*. The web of sense must be traversed, renewed by the imagination. Its indifference, despite the richness of the sphere of communication that it constructed, must be shattered; and only subjectivity is capable of reclaiming value through the force of imagination. This too we know. But to what end? What is value? If the canto offers no answer, it nevertheless accomplishes a leap forward and marks a lyrical and metaphysical innovation. And anyway, who could give an answer to the question of value? Leaving this question unanswered is now the highest dignity of materialist knowing.

> If you are one of those
> Platonic notions which the eternal mind
> Disdains to cover in a fleshly dress,
> In such ephemeral shape
> To suffer our sad life and its distress;
> Of if another world is where you take shelter,
> One world of countless worlds in whirling gyres,
> While some star close to you, some brighter sun,
> Shines on you, and you breathe a purer air;
> From down here where the years are short and grim
> Accept your unknown lover, in this hymn. (ll.45–55)[207]

There is no answer, but the negation of answering opens up an infinite, indefinitely operative horizon. The subject that emerges from the construction of the transcendental imagination of materialism, irrupting into the crisis of the dialectic, defines a new dimension that is very beautiful and worthy of love. Passion "takes shelter" among the "countless worlds"—in an irreducibly open way.[208] Ideal redemption is impossible, but materialist redemption is accessible—in this abyss to which we are condemned, under this heaven to which we aspire. The metaphysical dimension of materialism explodes. In other words, ontology opens up to free necessity.[209]

The transcendental imagination of materialism unfolds alongside, or rather in contact, in synchrony with the intention that pervaded sensibility and significantly penetrated the existence of the world. As a larva, the imago now emerges from this real. It follows the latter's meanderings, it renews—in reality—the movements of sense, and it reactivates the intellectual and material possibilities. It resists difficulties. Then the larva becomes a butterfly. Sense produces a dream that is more real than the real. It is a "surplus real [*più reale*]" that is sensed, for it answers to the desire that constituted reality and that now constitutes the hyper reality of the imaginary. The developing metaphysical spirit is the larva, seed, spirit of animal life, sensible and sensual.[210] The infinite and inexhaustible space of the thought universe [*universo pensato*] is its place. Ontology is material. The search for depth has discovered infinite spaces. The Platonic ideal is destroyed by being immersed in the reality of experience—but from here on it becomes liquid, projective, ethereal. What the imagination promises us is a series of catastrophes. We follow its tendency without ever exhausting it. Nature, in which we plant the strength of our ideal renewal, is an abstract world, but one made concrete by the imagination. Here, in the infinite spaces of being—no idealization, no hypostasis, only an immense space—an infinite time that we traverse—countless worlds—reconstructed and new times. . . . This lyrical innovation startles the traditional metaphysical experience, which, even in its most recent forms, speaks of being as a thing, a determination. In Leopardi, the irresistible sense of the finite founds a new concept of the infinite and of being. Finite determination is tested in the operative experience of the infinite. Lucretius and ancient materialism stand behind this theoretical will.[211] The idea is destroyed in order to be reconstructed—Leopardi's materialism is not self-limitation but projection. It is a rupture that opens onto future time, armed with weapons of love and desire. It is a radical alternative to the determination of pain, an open, creative alternative, taken to the most essential level of life, there where it encounters death. It is not by chance that, in this period, the disappearance of the idea of suicide is for Leopardi the metaphysical projection of a new life.[212]

I am struggling to do justice to the theoretical force of Leopardi's concept of the imagination. If I compare this concept with classical terminology, from Kant to Heidegger, its signification escapes me, because in Leopardi the imagination is not a cognitive function, or rather it is not only that: it is instead a constitutive function, constitutive of infinite worlds, indefinite times and spaces to experience and traverse. This opening is a value in itself. Being is not a formal power [*potenza*] but a direction of life. To stay in being is to conquer the world in infinite directions. The web of sense can be retraversed in a microscopic manner, opening up a thousand perspectives, a thousand planes of existence as well as the world and interstellar space. Imagination is value, and without it there is no value. Without the larva that breaks open the depth of sense, there is no lived reality. This process of breaking through the real is the direction of the web of sense, its redemption. The passage to ontology through the imagination is the capture of being in order to make it the scenario of human activity. Being's indifference, its density, its coarseness are torn to pieces by hope and the activity of its transformation. This struggle of every moment is posited on the level of being, where living means suffering. Hope and activity are also forms of suffering. But this in no way alters the metaphysical determination; on the contrary, it explains it. The possibility of being is immense—it can extend to the point of chance or to the point of absolute irrationality. Only human experience constructs the determination of the possible within the infinite horizon of countless worlds. We do not expect any grace, participation, or mimesis of the idea in the world. There is only our impoverished nature, one which, through pain and driven by it, knows how to attain prodigious perspectives by working the world. Illusion is not a given; it is a product, a choice.

Faced with Leopardi in this period, we note that the most striking point is the density of his materialism. The ancient cultural references (Epicurus, Lucretius) are only suggestive, and the modern references (the sensualism and materialism of the Enlightenment) are flatly insufficient. Leopardi's materialism is living. It would be more appropriate to evoke Bacon or Galileo (whose fresh materialism Marx celebrates),[213] or even Spinoza's materialism.[214] But all these references, even if they are correct, remain unsatisfactory: they refer to a materialism that still has the insipidness of youth. On the contrary, Leopardi's materialism has a critical aspect. It implies pain and desire, and only an exceptional experience could offer it to constitutive power [*potenza*]. Leopardi asserts a negative solution to the problem of the dialectic, with extraordinary force. Our own historical experience, marked by an unspeakable pain and a still uncompleted and horribly significant drama, confers a definitive character upon Leopardi's anticipation. The "countless worlds" are thus faced with the "solid nothing-ness" in which we live. Only the maximum experience of rupture, only the cognition of pain allows us the freedom of imagination. The imago is not a reflection but a constitution.

Let us return to the reading of Leopardi. We have before us two fragments that were also composed during this period: *From the Greek of Semonides*[215] and *From the Same*.[216] There is nothing much to say about the first text. Traditionally constructed, it develops the theme of human unhappiness for twenty-eight lines. In accordance with a perspective to which we are now accustomed in Leopardi, unhappiness can be seen across the entirety of experience: humankind and nature, divinity and the world. Here this phe-nomenology that we know so well is sculpted, so to speak, into metaphysical material. This is done in twenty-eight lines, and then we have the last five:

> And so, in my opinion,
> A wise man, rescued from the common error,
> Would not agree to suffer,
> Nor give to his affliction
> And to his own distress so much affection. (*From the Greek*, ll.29–33)[217]

The invitation to suicide is explicit. Let us compare this canto straightaway with the following exercise—which corrects it, completes it, and reintegrates it into the discourse.

From the Same takes up again the themes of the preceding fragment, but approaches them with a much lighter step. As a result of the stylistic grace of its approach, the phenomenology of pain does not conclude in the idea of suicide and does not submit itself to the tragic insolubility of sense. The tone that dominates is nevertheless that of an experimenting with the antagonistic elements of human experience: this experimenting constitutes a terrain of truth in itself. Hence the terms of the incitement to suicide are overturned, the theme of unhappiness is transformed into that of illusion, with unhappiness as a given making way for the active determination of living. And the very failure of life remains nonetheless a dignity that forbids any acceptance of death or any incitement to suicide. The references of the internal dialogue are thus overturned: now the old Semonides considers youth as the age of illusion, of course, but of real illusion ("Enjoy, since life is short,/The pleasures hard at hand," *From the Same*, ll.23–24),[218] constitutive hope. The recurring idea of suicide is established on the multiform paradox of emotions and the possibility of being. The argument shifts from dramatic to logical, and logic founders in the ontology of possibility—of youth, nature, and above all passion. Metaphysical logic, that heavy attempt to make the discussion of the values of being immediately founder, here constitutes the ethical paradox. If we manage to read this lyrical fragment born from the idea of suicide without being injured by it—since youth is identified with the constellation of restlessness[219] rather than that of mere unhappiness and the death drive, and its demands make insistent reference to life and true illusion—the entire framework is thereby overturned and resounds as an appeal to the vitality of desire and the submission to ethics.

These two fragments are not without a certain irony. It tinges the gaze when it establishes the imbalance that youth determines in being. Life against death is unripe, as is the ethical opening, to the extent that hope is young and ruddy. We must be attentive to this passage: although ironic— almost inadvertently so—it nevertheless expresses Leopardi's first successful brush with the edge of being. He encounters a new limit on the terrain and time of second nature. In these two fragments, the web of sense is the old one; but contrary to what too easily happens in such cases, it does not conclude rhetorically. It exacerbates youthful restlessness in order to exacerbate the tension to surmount the formal universe of communication and to enfranchise ontology. The edge of being is the limit of hope: something can still arise from there. . . .

In these two canti the imago is thus no longer merely the instrument for the destruction of the constraints of being, as web of sense. For the first time, perhaps timidly but really, the imagination appears as a constitutive force. *To His Lady* is a stylistic and intuitive miracle, whereas here that awareness

of the metaphysical function of the imagination is inscribed in the heart of
the poet's lyrical craft, in his everyday attentiveness, in his labor. And it is
important that the great metaphysical sensation that accompanies the poem
To His Lady is articulated with the perception of the past. Semonides—
already viewed as a poetic master from the first encounter with the dialectic
of time, the first author of ethical voluntarism—is now the one who indicates
the outcome of the web of sense. Semonides, the blind: such is humankind,
in the interchangeability of roles imposed by the web of sense and this
normative universe. Therefore we poor blind ones can free ourselves—and
sing the ambiguous power [*potenza*] of youth no longer in terms of heroism
but instead with cognitive hope. Here the figure of Semonides is a lightning
rod, an alternative pole: all of them lead toward being. The metaphysical
possibility grows tense: its elasticity is now reduced. Semonides speaks
to us of being. The suicide that he proposes to us—today as philosophers,
yesterday as heroes of Marathon—as an ethical solution, far from being the
end, is only the backdrop to an ethical operation. Suicide is not the negation
of being but, if necessary, the verification of an aim, a choice—an act of
freedom. It is a sacrifice for the imagination. But the imagination can avoid
it and speak, live, produce the creative delight of humankind. Imagination is
the force of critical being. Leopardi thus posits the constitution of being by
means of the imagination as an act that intervenes at the limit, on the edge
of being. It does not want the dialectic to usurp the terrain of a constructive
mediation. It wants pain and desire to be, in a linear fashion, as in the
inspiration of Semonides, as in the material rupture of his blind, twisted
wandering, at the root of the valorizing [*dar valore*] of reality. The old man's
knowledge [*sapere*] expresses the restlessness of youth, and disenchantment
and hope join hands. Could this happy conjunction have been imagined if the
critical question had not now become an ontological question and if history
were not entirely thought as an alternative, as the capacity of the subject to
make desperation itself fertile? Thus the passage to ontology is constructed
within the framework of these diverse impulses, these contradictions. The
imagination is tested in the construction of a new, positive imago of the
world. Of course, if you seek to grasp this passage, it escapes you. But the
will to construct it does not escape you, nor does the determinateness of
the occasion, or the complexity of the step forward invented by Leopardi.
Everything must lead to this opening onto being. Leopardi has shown us the
way. Hope must be verifiable.

On the one hand poetry and on the other classical philology: the latter is
fully capable of real and productive imagination. The gigantic philological
labor that Leopardi carried out throughout his life,[220] which the *Zibaldone*
of those years extensively documents, constitutes a passage of particular

importance in this moment of liberation from the difficulties of the web of sense, toward an ontological horizon. The philological breakthrough, above all in the direction of the classical world, allows the articulation of the metaphysical method. Leopardi experiences a particular moment in the development of classical philology—the period that runs from Niebuhr to Nietzsche. At that time philology became the genealogical science of the imagination. During that extraordinary period, the world of antiquarianism, the archaeology of the eighteenth century, is shattered by the genealogical reconstruction of the ancient web of sense. Dionysus succeeds Apollo, and philology itself is made the bearer of an Orphic design.[221] It is a genealogy of gods and values that traverse and organize the ancient world, a grafting of imagination onto that conceptual and historical universe.

By means of classical philology, Leopardi seems to undertake a metaphysical apprenticeship. We have seen the fundamental role that the figure of Semonides, bard and shaman, plays in this phase of philosophical labor. The study of Homer pursued throughout those years plays an equivalent role, the properly philosophical importance of which must be emphasized.[222] Imagination is not transcendence. It is instead the power [*potenza*] that constructs and organizes a conceptual world. This identification of imagination with the world is, above all, what classical philology teaches him. For this reason we can say that the classical breakthrough and the philological labor are decisive for the critical passage of those years. The logical and poetic construction of the canto *To His Lady* would not have arisen with such intensity if it were not underpinned by this practice of the imagination: this unforeseen apparition has a long history. From this viewpoint the work on Homer, although it privileges poetry and the epic, is more important than the more specifically philosophical work that Leopardi carried out without respite on Plato, Gemisthus Pletho, and the neo-Platonists[223]—more important, we mean, for the solution to the problem of the web of sense. This is because the labor involving Homer puts into play a material relation, the production of an imaginary, the poetic reconstruction and enjoyment of a world.

Here we are led back once again to the problem of a materialist theory of the imagination. We discover that in this framework the imagination is not a result, the last element in the series of intellectual faculties that appears when the powers [*potenze*] of the intellect have been exhausted. It is on the contrary a primary faculty, so intimately linked and articulated with sense that their separation can be stated only in hypothetical terms. It cannot be done in the system of reality. In reality, the imagination can have only a separate genesis: but once the function has developed, the imagination ceases to be recognizable in an independent form. It fertilizes the world in its totality. Examined in this light, the classical world functions as a model[224] that in no way occludes the theoretical productivity and originality of the passage accomplished by Leopardi. On the contrary, the strict inherence of imagination in the world as classical philology conceives it determines and projects an extreme materialism of cognitive conception and poetic function—which corresponds exactly to the most specific and irreducible aspects of Leopardi.

At this point, what can be said to conclude this chapter? There is little left to add, except to insist once more on the depth and breadth of the alternative that Leopardi determines in the development of European philosophy in the era of the dialectic. The problem of the dialectic, although confronted, is declared insoluble. So reason is not led back to the absoluteness of spirit but considered as a critical and negative function. The world is rediscovered in those conditions where it had been left by reason. Thus it must be reconstructed by sense. The construction of this terrain is materialistic, a solid, entirely non-dialectical materialism. This universe nevertheless threatens to close up again on this web. In an ambiguous yet potent manner, rupture and opening will be subjected to the action of imagination. This passage aroused the protests and drew the polemical fire of the philosophers of idealism—even his contemporaries—who understood the force of Leopardi's arguments and his anti-dialectical objective, which in effect propose that the imagination pervades, as its own horizon, the interminable concept of the infinite and inscribes human subjectivity there—and does not enclose and mortify it in the absolute as idealism and the dialectic did. In Leopardi as in all critical materialism, the relationship between finite and infinite is a disutopia, one so charged with subjectivity, pain, and hope that the metaphysical framework, opened up to this ontology, acquires a terrific force. Infinite spaces, countless worlds stand before us. And behind us, and within us? Other worlds as well, just as countless. We can explore some of them.

Thus the classical world is not simply the privileged terrain for a study that models the correct method for inserting the imaginary into the world; it is not merely a methodological experience. It is also a substantial historical experience in which the characterizations of thought, ethics, and the mantic take shape—a materialist, pagan, and poetic world. The circularity of all the aspects of Leopardi's experience is now understandable, graspable. It constitutes one of the strongest characteristics of his ontological comportment. Philologist and poet: everything must function as in a system of communicating vessels. Countless worlds that all communicate among themselves: countless worlds, or rather plural times, stratifications of being that arise separately but can be intermingled. Lyric and philosophy communicate on this terrain of the true and productive imagination that classical philology prefigures. On the same terrain, countless different worlds confront and encounter each other—and this strange architecture, irreducible to any conventional center of the intellectual faculties or possible worlds, confers meaning upon our image of the world. The imagination innovates within these universal dimensions the macrocosm as well as the microcosm, between the web of the senses and that of illusions. The passage to ontology, sometimes required, sometimes suffered, is thus given here—in an unexpected but very potent way, by means of a prodigious dilation of sense, by means of a gorgeous explosion of the imagination: the classical prefiguration.[225]

Leopardi thereby situates himself also in relation to the development of Kantian critique. If I add this note, it is not because it seems to me particularly important to respond to the neo-Kantian provocation that regularly arises in the history of philosophy (imposing the mystified problematics of the transcendental), but because the originality of Leopardi's lyrical and metaphysical speculation can in this way be further illuminated. In critical terms, we can assert that Leopardi takes up the problem of a transcendental aesthetic, but far from thinking that the problem of the constitution of the sensible world can be resolved only through the construction of analytical forms of knowledge [conoscenza], he constructs—successfully—a web of sense. Pain and desire construct it, and together determine, with their implacable testimony, with the continuous projection of immediacy onto the stage of philosophy, the impossibility of a transcendental analytic. The analytic is, in the language of idealism, the fixing of the transcendental horizon; it is the subjective expression, independent and metaphysically absolute, of the universality of knowing [conoscere]—the analytic is the secret origin of all idealism. Leopardi denounces the abstraction and mystification of sense in these operations, their powerlessness [impotenza] to recognize value.

Thus Leopardi proceeds on his path of innovation: from the terrain of the aesthetic and the refusal of the analytic, he identifies an immediate function of the constitution of signification: the imagination. Pain and desire, the powers [potenze] of ethical life, once again constitute its horizon. In critical philosophy and idealism, the transcendental imagination fulfills an analogous function, but one that is completely displaced in its metaphysical situation: it allows one to pass from descriptive judgments to constitutive judgments, from essences to determinations, from the conditions of knowing [conoscere] to its transcendental foundation. This function rests on the analytic: the transcendental and mediation appear once more as central elements. The schematism of reason organizes the imagination, whereas in Leopardi, it is the imagination that organizes the schematism of reason.

But this is not enough: imagination has the form of immediacy; it is grounded in the materiality of experience. Matter commands imagination. Imagination follows the material articulations of being. This frank materialism is not impoverished: it clings to the richness of the forms of the world, of constitutive times and spaces.

I will not insist upon the modernity of this Leopardian figure of a material schematism of the imagination and its proximity to us.[226] This path is the opposite of the one that all the forms of transcendentalism have always followed. So let us follow it. The imagination has thus discovered its world, and the web of sense is starting to have a signification. Poetry moves on these horizons, and it is an immediate function of truth. Imagining is the power [*potenza*] of constituting the world, countless worlds. It is a human particle of cosmic power [*potenza*], a larva that knows how to become a very beautiful butterfly. The imagination is the seed of the cosmos.

Chapter 3

Poetics of True Being

....

Metaphysics of Morals

"I no longer seek anything but the truth, which I once so hated and loathed. I take satisfaction in ever more clearly discovering and tangibly feeling the wretchedness of men and things, and in experiencing a cold horror, reflecting on this unhappy and terrible strangeness of life in the universe."[1] Is this a philosophical program? Some have overstressed this passage and similar ones in Leopardi. If at one time the stereotypical conjunction of Leopardi and Schopenhauer served to erase the subversive range of Leopardi's critique,[2] today the style has changed. The new jinx is Leopardi and Kafka:[3] Leopardi the great loser [*vinto*], cosmic pessimism, etc. But nothing is less true. This hunt from citation to citation for the most despairing one from which to draw definitive conclusions is a bad habit. Furthermore, Schopenhauer and Kafka have their own grandeur, and it is hard to see how they could be included in a case study of Leopardi. Indeed, in Leopardi there is no trace of Schopenhauer's progressive phenomenological theology of nothingness, nor of his taste, which is in fact dialectical, for the negation and devolution of reality into figures of evanescence. (In Schopenhauer, for example, one sees "suffering humanity and the suffering animal world, and a world that passes away," so it is no longer enough "to love others like himself, and to do as much for them as for himself, but there arises in him a strong aversion to the inner nature whose expression is his own phenomenon, to the will-to-live, the kernel and essence of that world recognized as full of misery.")[4]

In Leopardi, the real is always beyond discussion and the backdrop of his materialism is irreducible. Leopardi is unlike Kafka: there is no hallucination, no gnoseology inherited from Mach ("in the world of Babel, there is almost an asphyxiation of speech"), nor does Leopardi share Kafka's phenomenalist analytic of the psyche ("a merely apparent end causes real pain").[5] In Leopardi, the psyche is constantly related to the mechanism of sense, and it founds and reconstructs itself materially. Study of "the unhappy and terrible strangeness of life in the universe" therefore does not constitute a program. It is simply the backdrop to the philosophical labor, the long and passionate search for a significance for life on the basis of the material conditions of the constitution of the world. It is true that this philosophical labor often verges upon the abysses of absolute pessimism, and therefore it is also true that Leopardi's sensualism and materialism, despite his nostalgic and stylistic attachment to the tradition of the schools of the Renaissance and the seventeenth century, definitively lack that tradition's serene progressive force. But this is probably where his great originality and modernity lie, his living and innovative contribution to the metaphysics of materialism.

Let me explain further. Precisely during this central phase of his life and work, Leopardi carries out a kind of Copernican revolution in materialism. If Kant's critical revolution consists in establishing a transcendental horizon within which humankind contributes to the construction of the true—or at least to the project of a human true—this sense of relativity being precisely what can found a critically confirmed true, then Leopardi leads an analogous operation, but outside any transcendental horizon, an operation caught in the web of a dialectic of nature and history, totally finite and material, with which humankind, as a finite element of this universe, is confronted. It is only human presence that confers upon or withdraws from the world its signification. Humankind is thrown into this world, and it is through practice, by means of sense and its transfiguration, by means of the progression from sense to the faculty of imagination, that humankind constructs the signification of the world. Now we must add a new element to our consideration of the Copernican revolution in the philosophy of materialism: the inherence of humankind within the material horizon defines the pre-eminence of ethics.

Modern materialism is ethical and humanist or it does not exist. Classical transcendental philosophy, above all Kant's philosophy, posits the absoluteness of ethics so as to illuminate the relativity of knowledge [*conoscenza*], whereas Leopardi's ethics is part of the relativity of the world, subject to the dimensions of finitude; but precisely for that reason it constructs the cognitive horizon. Ethics is the impulse and not the guarantee of knowledge [*conoscenza*]. Ethics confronts and penetrates the mystery of the world; it cannot fail to do so because pain and desire impel it and the imagination organizes it. So what is Leopardi's ontology? It is this labor of ethics, posited at the extreme limits of the imagination, on this web that extends between the subject and the world—a continual vital interrogation and a continual construction of life.

Leopardi is one of the authors of that Copernican revolution of materialism that makes the subject the central element of the world's horizon. From this viewpoint, his thought is not far from and contains a problematic that is analogous to what develops in Marx's critique of transcendental philosophy and in the construction of contemporary revolutionary materialism. This passage renews the history of the metaphysics of materialism. This revolution detaches the idea of matter from the determination of metaphysical inaccessibility in order to make it the sphere of human life, to confront it with history. In these dimensions, sustained by an ethical appreciation of the real, sense and imagination carry on this harsh struggle that is the very form of existence. Thus ontology increasingly qualifies as a metaphysics of ethics, a metaphysics of morals. This discovery of Leopardi's is indisputably anchored in a cultural process, which despite great uncertainties, is being brought to fulfillment in a general way. The relationship Leopardi establishes in this period with Vieusseux and with the constitutive idea of the program of the *Antologia* bears witness to the maturation of these ethical and metaphysical ideas.[6] But in comparison with the dynamics and tendencies of his environment, in relation to the slow maturation of this new philosophy, in Leopardi there is a critical and metaphysical radicalism that is unequalled. If ontology must become a metaphysics of morals—and on this point Leopardi participates in the tendencies of the century—this is because ethics and morals are ontology, deployed materiality, elements of the vast and tragic machine of the universe—and here Leopardi goes beyond the lines defining the timid philosophy of his time and reaches those spaces that belong to the greatest metaphysics.

Thus we have a metaphysics of morals.[7] The *Zibaldone* of 1823 represents a first important draft.[8] The analysis there is entirely situated in this now-revolutionized materialist universe that we have seen arise from the conjunction of second nature and the imagination, since one is internal to the other, and every movement, those of existence as well as those of the innovation of life, develops within this *Umwelt*. Language, as natural and historical horizon, initially serves best to present us with these dimensions of the world. Linguistic and philological labor occupies many, many pages during this period.[9] However, the importance granted to language cannot be reduced even to this immense labor carried out by Leopardi: there is more. It is quite true that these extensive philological jottings often reveal a very modern analytic of language and the intuition of what we can risk calling a *theory of pictures* [English in original], but there is still more.

The identification of this first elementary fabric of the analysis—which takes up again, so to speak, the philosophical investigations of the preceding period—contains a new definition of second nature as power [*potenza*] of collective communication and constitution. The imagination is completely grafted into the universe. Language is the result of the internal productivity of a structural power [*potenza*].[10] Every national language contains structural elements of self-productivity that are expressed according to immanent norms. But this is not enough. Beyond the structural elements, every language is constructed on the basis of the rhythm of civilization of a nation.[11] The historical system of languages is thus doubly open to the dynamic of creativity: on the structural side and on the historical side. Leopardi mobilizes the most modern terms of a philological dialectic of history and structure, of creativity and style, with the aim of constantly bringing the general assertions back to particular analyses.[12]

But what is most important in this analysis (which in some ways also constitutes a tribute [*elogio*] to languages and nationalities—the French language lauded as the language of style and stylistic force, for prose and poetic prose; the German language praised for its conformity, its adaptability, its capacity to imitate the real as the language of science; the classical languages, Greek and Latin, as well as Italian acknowledged as the languages *par excellence* of creativity and poetry)[13] is the fact that linguistic second nature always presents itself as power [*potenza*], a power that conforms to history but also innovates in history and thereby determines characters even as it is subjected to involution and degradation. It is a living power in every way. Let us repeat it: the imagination is grafted into the depths of second nature and consequently becomes collective. This theme of collective imagination, of imagination as historical power [*potenza*], is not discussed enough in studies dedicated to Leopardi.[14] The reason for this is obvious. It is in effect a working hypothesis that radically modifies every interpretation of Leopardi's thought, across the entire range of its multiple perspectives: from formalism to the religious interpretation, from the sentimental and biographical reading to that of progressive politics. The unmentioned presupposition of all these interpretations is the individualism, almost the solipsism of Leopardi's poetic experience. But as we are discovering, the opposite is true: at this moment when he reaches theoretical and poetic maturity, the new basis and the new tone of Leopardi's discourse are those of the collective. Human universality is considered in the articulations that the great national subjectivities, then the groups, and then individual subjects produce according to the schema of linguistic creativity. The transcendental schematism of reason is thus demystified and brought back to this historical, determinate, organic materiality. The grand abstract subject of idealism, the veritable lever of the mystifying translation of the real, is destroyed and referred back to the articulations of autonomous subjectivity and subjective self-configuration. The idea of linguistic communication developed here, beyond the fact that it is posited as the basis of a very modern conception of language, is the parameter of the collective constitution of the world.

At this point it is easy to understand why Leopardi's philological-linguistic labor seems so important to us in the construction of his metaphysics of morals. The linguistic tool is a tool that creates the relationship between this universe in which we are immersed and our activity—the ethical activity of subjects. The elements of metaphysical construction rain down around us one after another, countless, like the sparks from a burning branch. Sparks, "shades [*larve*]" as Leopardi might have said, of a knowledge [*sapere*] that we reconstruct for infinite lives, of a true that, through so much suffering, is constitutive. Leopardi elaborates upon his marvelous rediscovery of language, on the unveiling of this mystery in which nature and history, structure and creativity, play so well together. He tarries, loses himself in a labyrinth of problems, merges different hypotheses, invents.

One of the most curious and yet interesting aspects of these pages[15]—the recollection of which permits us to emphasize the richness of this linguistic wandering—is the interest taken in the genesis of the alphabet. It simultaneously registers his stupor in the face of this collective construction, this prodigious work from the dawn of human civilization, and the experimenting with a strongly structured analytic-genetic method for the analysis of language as natural power [*potenza*].[16] What can we add? Second nature is presented to us, in these first brief linguistic analyses, as already capable of being structured into a metaphysics of morals. Numerous elements—the joining of nature and history, the intermingling of creativity and history, the discovery of collectivity, the decisive definition of the functional and ethical character of language—are thus definitively taken up into the perspective of a deployed metaphysics of morals. On the basis of these premises, revolutionized second nature will now be read within the complex of determinations of the real.[17]

The real or the web of the senses. We are present here at a turn—that is in fact a return—in Leopardi's analysis. The web of the senses too must now be brought to a conscious conjunction with imagination. We have already seen the development of this hypothesis:[18] it is a matter here of consolidating and making operative the intuition and labor so that the tremendous ontological sketch of the linguistic theory can be transformed into a full and complete design. Thus imagination lives within the web of sense. How does it break, redefine, and make new the movement of the senses?

In the year 1823 we must submit to the repetition of numerous themes from 1821, the tiresome and sometimes almost maniacal reprise of typologies of the negative dialectic of pleasure. Just a few examples: negative dialectic of the means for obtaining pleasure, sloth, indolence,[19] boredom;[20] then love and hate, the impossibility of making them coexist and the continual exacerbation of tensions;[21] then sensory illusions,[22] including those of dreams and sleep as repose;[23] and finally childhood with its illusory and tragic hopes.[24] Even languages will be considered one of humankind's miseries, by reason of their diversity and the impossibility of establishing a general determination.[25] Lastly, let us not forget egoism, one of the fundamental keys of negative dialectics; it can be profitable for us, but at what cost, accompanied by what decline in the significance of living![26] And so on, and so on. I am not exaggerating. The fact is that Leopardi repeats himself,[27] demands repetition: is not science itself repetition and boredom? As for pleasure, it "is always past or future, and never present."[28] Only ephemeral things, extending between temporal unrealities, prepare a non-existent pleasure, and we can enjoy only this preparation:[29] thus happiness and enjoyment exist only with the aid of chance and fortune in the ephemeral and the not-yet existent. But is fortune a true aid?[30] In reality desire never reaches its goal[31] and only resignation is pleasure.[32] We could continue, for whole pages, to construct sequences of this sort. They belong to those paradoxical tracks that Leopardi follows from time to time in order to define the radicality of his critique. The "experimental" radicality of his critique: indeed, we must never forget that the *Zibaldone* was not prepared for publication.

This reprise of themes from 1821 concludes in these terms: civilization is the bearer of maladies, the contaminator of humanity and nature.[33] What a beautiful Manzonian conclusion! What an ecological slogan! Respect for the complexity of Leopardi's text must not, therefore, make us forget the extreme coherence of the destructive and nihilist themes of the first phase of his thought.

But on the other hand, it must allow us to grasp the reconstructive themes that predominate [*con prepotenza*] here over the earlier ones and open a space within the structure of the critical discourse. First of all, some hints: of course human wretchedness is immense, but what is the consciousness of this wretchedness? What is the dignity in recognizing the finite? On 12 August 1823, St. Clare's day, Leopardi responds in these terms:

> No one thing shows the greatness and power [*potenza*] of the human
> intellect or the loftiness and nobility of man more than his ability
> [*poter*] to know and to understand fully and feel strongly his own

smallness. When, in considering the multiplicity of worlds, he feels himself to be an infinitesimal part of a globe which itself is a negligible part of one of the infinite number of systems that go to make up the world, and in considering this is astonished by his own smallness, and in feeling it deeply and regarding it intently, virtually blends into nothing, and it is as if he loses himself in the immensity of things, and finds himself as though lost in the incomprehensible vastness of existence, with this single act and thought he gives the greatest possible proof of the nobility and immense capability of his own mind, which, enclosed in such a small and negligible being, has nonetheless managed to know and understand things so superior to his own nature, and to embrace and contain this same intensity of existence and things in his thought. Certainly no other thinking being on this earth ever managed to conceive or imagine it was but a small thing, either in itself or compared to others, even if with respect to its body it is but a billionth part of man, to say nothing of its mind. And in truth, the greater a being is, which man is above all other earthly beings, the more capable it is too of the knowledge [conoscenza] and feeling of its own smallness. Hence such knowledge and feeling, even among men, are greater, and more lively, more common and continuous, fuller, the greater, higher, and more capable are the intellects and minds of the individuals concerned.[34]

Next he celebrates those "described as singular and original"[35] who proudly throw their smallness and weakness—but also their consciousness—into the face of a very potent and vigorous nature. Then he writes some very beautiful pages on unhappiness and time.[36] No, Leopardi does not renounce anything that he has stated up to that point: more humanely, more philosophically, he experiences the content of the negative dialectic of pleasure and its multiple directions while ceaselessly demanding, at the summit of despair and in the midst of nothingness, the reason for the subject and its existence. An almost Pascalian move, with a slight but very sharp difference: here human wretchedness seeks no consolation—on this edge of being that suffering indicates, immersed in a time that flees and destroys, it simply opens itself up again to hope. Is this the imagination, this atheist and materialist ascesis of reason? Is it Pascal's wager realized within the finite? It is in any case a tension that makes things new, just as time never stops offering new days, new possibilities to nature, to history, to consciousness. In these moments of consciousness, in these signs of a discourse open to time and to the verification of hope, Leopardi's sensualism loses every phenomenalist characteristic and every uncertainty. It simply becomes a solid materiality. Philosophy hardens into materialism.

We will have to reconsider the passage from "solid nothingness" to this solid materiality; but for now it is important to emphasize that this transformation is carried out by the imagination, which corresponds here to a kind of Spinozian *cupiditas*. It makes everything it touches real, material and open to the future. Imagination is a kind of full sensory capacity—it brings unhappiness, but it makes existence new.[37] This imaginative desire invests all human faculties, understands them in depth—and above all renews intelligence. The faculty of thinking is incorporated into desiring,[38] but reciprocally, imagination is only nourished by the quantity and quality of pleasure.[39] The power [*potenza*] of the body, the subject and reason thus traverses reality to the point of exalting the absolute time of existence over the vicissitudes of life, to the point of emancipating the imaginative dimension of the mind from the flatness of life.[40] And furthermore, the imagination takes on all the negative powers [*potenze*] of being and transforms them into power [*potenza*]. We see a kind of Newtonian force of attraction set in motion. The traditional theory of *cupiditas* is enriched. Sense, memory, and imitation are swept up in this creative process, in this power [*potenza*] that measures itself against nature and makes it new. Sense, memory, imitation,[41] and habituation.

The theme of habituation introduces a new chapter of the discussion. But before dealing with it, let us try to understand fully the significance of this first of Leopardi's moves on the terrain of sense, within the web of sense. The insertion of subjectivity thus has two effects. The first is the destruction of all naturalism. Sensualism is propelled out of the sphere of naturalism: the senses not only construct but form part of second nature. They stir there and repeat human wretchedness, while proposing the conditions of renewal. But there is more. The web of sense is integrated into that of imagination, of the movement of the subject amid the emergences of nature—consequently, the system of nature is increasingly definable as a practical horizon. Through these logical and metaphysical keys, sensualism ever more fully configures the world as an anthropological, cultural, and historical context. The contrast between the subject and the world is not forgotten; it is simply made ready in the circulation of the imagination deployed in the world of history. That is the second effect of Leopardi's theoretical move in this period.

At this stage, we can go back to the discourse on habituation and consider its definition. This definition does not break with the speculative process developed up to now; it integrates and completes it. "What then is the true human form?"[42] It is obvious that if the dynamic of sense developed in the free form, which we have noted and which gradually integrates the set of human faculties and dimensions of existence, then there could be no absolute or fundamental answers to this question. The answer can follow only from a continual deepening of this complex of relations that constitutes the world. The human form is constituted through a series of accidents and accidental relations—the circumstances present themselves from time to time as passive and/or active—in a global interaction of elements. Freedom does not exclude necessity and vice versa: there is no determinism.[43] We call habituation this framework of relations and its balance: such is this second nature that is constituted in habituation:[44] "Man is able to do and to suffer as much as he has become habituated to do and to suffer (whether the habituation is continuing or whether, however much in the past it may be, its effects still remain, in whole or in part), no more and no less."[45] Analogous positions, of a Spinozian flavor and style, proliferate[46]: we are now moving in a world formed by productive relations. There is no skepticism in this procedure. No ideal value is in a position to judge the free movement of the senses and the processes of formation of the figures of habituation. We are seeing sensualist mediation tend more and more decisively toward a pure materialism. "The limits of matter are the limits of human ideas."[47] That said, the problem of habituation is nonetheless not exhausted so long as the necessity of evaluating the degree of consolidation of the figures of existence within the framework of these dynamic relations remains open. We know Leopardi's final answer to this question: it was proposed during the long process of research running from the crisis of the web of sense to the great opening to the imagination in the canto *To His Lady*.[48] Our intention here is to see how the materialist mediation of all the elements of the dialectic of the senses deepens and, in the figure of habituation, takes on a consistency, which is, so to speak, metaphysical. A kind of general extension of the dialectical figure of the dynamism and its internal balance that guarantees, according to Leopardi, in one of those flashes of extreme poetry that are so frequent in the *Zibaldone*, the "repose" of reason.[49]

It is a repose granted by the perception of the balance that presides over "grand nature" by appeasement in the "grace derived from the extraordinary and from contrast"[50] of every motion of the mind, and by the consideration of the power [*potenza*] of the "miraculous and stupendous work of nature, . . . the machine and mass, as immense as it is most artfully designed, of all the worlds."[51] This is not enough: the thematic of habituation—that is to say, the dialectic of the senses and its figures of balance—is also developed on the terrain of the history of the human species, the dialectic of evolution and cultural production, and with regard to the so-called progress of the human spirit.[52] We have at our disposal, therefore, a concept of habituation that is transformed into a tool for the social, historical, and anthropological sciences, within what is perhaps a slightly crude and rudimentary methodology but nonetheless one that permits us to grasp the complexity of the framework and to prepare, on the basis of this fabric of metaphysical formalization, the passage from the problem of sense to that of signification. And the question is posed anew: "What then is the true human form?" The Copernican, ethical figure of humankind arises from this prodigious scenario. It is entirely subject to this dialectic that extends from the microcosm to the macrocosm, to the relationship of contrast or balance among the elements that confer upon the universe its definitive figure. But at the very moment when it posits itself at the center of this universe, humankind is power [*potenza*], "conformability and supreme organization" in the universe and of the universe: a new passage. Nevertheless, by virtue of this very position, the power [*potenza*] of humankind is revealed along with its complete impotence. Its situation at the center of the universe, at the limit of the microcosm and macrocosm, makes humankind the most mutable and corruptible element, and consequently one that is incapable of being happy. No, "Man is not by nature unhappy." His existence, condemned to an unending tension of power [*potenza*] and *cupiditas*,[53] is the product of his metaphysical situation. And it is certainly not to the vain nostalgia of unbelievable fables that he invites us when, in this great movement of a metaphysics of ethics, Leopardi flirts with the primitive image of humankind: "the child is supremely wise, and the savage of California, who does not know *thinking*."[54] Only the dignity and tragedy of the human species, "naked by nature,"[55] presents itself within the orderly/disorderly immensity of nature, at the center of all possible directions. That is the significance of humankind. That is the ethical determination.

This ethical determination, which in our study of the *Zibaldone* of 1823 we have defined as a turning point by means of the web of sense and the theory of habituation, thus arrives at its conclusion. Here we have reached the end of the road with the awareness of having added a new fundamental element to the ensemble of operational concepts of our metaphysics: in this case, it is a new determination of humankind as historical power [*potenza*]. On this new basis, the uneven path of the web of sense can rejoin the main road of the theory of the imagination—a poetic imagination, but also, and we will see how potently, an ethical imagination. The true begins to show itself. Second nature, revolutionized by this set of powers [*potenze*] accumulated within it, begins to move on its own. It shows its own creativity; it opens forward. The road traveled by Leopardi is now absolutely explicit. The discourse starts out with a polemic against the transcendental analytic of pure reason:

> Whoever examines the nature of things using pure reason, and without
> the help of the imagination or feeling, or without affording either of

them any scope, which is the procedure adopted by many Germans in
philosophy, that is to say, in metaphysics and politics, will certainly be
capable of doing what the meaning of the word *to analyze* involves, that
is, to resolve and undo nature, but they will never be able to recompose
it. [. . .] Nature thus analyzed differs not in the slightest from a corpse.[56]

The power [*potere*] to recompose the real and construct the true must instead
reestablish a direct relationship between the aesthetics of sense and the
dialectic of the imagination. When it dissolved this nexus, German critical
philosophy became impotent. It lost the ability to grasp "the universality
of things," which is "made up of, fashioned and ordered toward a poetic
effect." Only "the imagination and sensibility" allow us to rejoin the path
and reappropriate the riches of the indefinite true,[57] just as they allow us to
materially restore the centrality of humankind in the universe.

While the transcendental analytic of pure reason destroys the effects of
the Copernican revolution, the theory of sensory imagination proposes to
us the inverse: a constructive and self-reflexive path. Self-reflexive above
all: here the imagination can turn once more toward the microcosm of consciousness, discover the constructive procedures that extend among all the
passions with the aim of resolving the unbalanced tension and the wearying,
continuous struggle for the conquest of happiness, for the expansion of *cupiditas*. Every feeling, every passion is capable, in this rhythm, of overturning
itself: boredom can be a desire for happiness, love can be unhappiness—and
if the greatest suppleness can be transformed into rigidity of mind, the
converse is no less possible—life and death can be equally repugnant and
desirable, and so on.[58] "Nothing absolute,"[59] except the spirit that is pure and
simple imagination, the strength to situate itself in relation to the immensity
of the dialectic of the senses and the power [*potenza*] of matter, the ability
to grow through all that, the form of the universe, "spiritual matter."[60] It is
this intimacy of spirit with matter and matter with spirit that makes the path
of sensibility and imagination a constructive project.

At this point the theory of the imagination becomes a constitutive theory,
the possibility of constructing the true, as philosophy and as poetry. Truth
is poetic.[61] The imagination is the great forward rupture of the sensory universe. It constructs another universe and creatively transfers, displaces, situates the first within the second. The rupture of imagination is constructive
because it is within the materiality of the world and totally pervades each
of the world's articulations.

On the basis of this, another Leopardian theoretical movement develops.
By continuing to deepen the productive function of the imagination, and
by doing so in such material terms, the metaphysical dimension gradually

diffuses: the conceptual instrumentation of the imagination and its objects is distributed among the subjective forces that govern it. Conceptual universality speaks through the collective universality of subjects. What the linguistic profile of this section of the *Zibaldone* showed us now takes on a new, denser signification—one conferred on it by the intervening metaphysical operation.

Poetry, above all tragic poetry,[62] shows us the imagination at work as collective power [*potenza*]. Language shows it to us at work: it is precisely that collectivity which is so rooted in singular subjectivities that it impedes the existence of a universal, abstract, conceptual language—which could appear only as a corruption of the collective imagination, of its adherence to the multiple reality that it expresses.[63] A sort of revision of the same analysis of the web of sense follows from this. In effect, the latter is now pervaded in a constructive manner by a collectivity of subjects who move and animate it. Poetics and imagination thus intervene with poietic force into the universe of humankind and transform the terrible passions experienced by individuals: the sense of death and physical pain, the sense of danger, the sensation and feeling of hatred.[64] Collective projection, collective redemption, liberation: fear is thus articulated with hope, and the imagination governs the sense of the future. Desire collectively finds a balance among the immensities that it experiences, and so on.[65] "The imagination always drives us toward what does not fall within reach of our senses"—without dematerializing, therefore, but instead conquering this totality of the life of the true that our common, collective destiny offers us. Hence the denunciation of solitude as abstract and mystifying power [*potenza*].[66] Hence the refusal of all individualist philosophies: the tools of reason are impoverished if they rely upon the individual. The most concentrated reasoning reveals, in the extraordinary intensity of these passages, the pure and simple identity of imagination and life. The triumph of the poetic imagination is the triumph of life. "Continual imagination"[67] in things. All ambivalence fails, poetics redounds upon life and shapes it. Everything is restored to production and to the discriminating ethics of the imagination—in the collective.[68]

The conditions of a metaphysics of morals are now prepared. The analysis must embrace the constructive rhythm of the ethical imagination, the collective imagination, and follow closely not only the ontological reality but also this historicity with which it is confused and which, through the action of the imagination, participates in constituting it. "Nothing absolute": Leopardi continues to insist on this theme[69] that he considers the operational key to the construction of the ethical world and the metaphysics of morals. Nothing absolute, yet this project of construction of a mediation between sensibility and imagination goes by the name of "classicism."

We must be extremely careful regarding the definition of the actual fecundity of the concept of "classic" and "classicism" in Leopardi, which henceforth no longer has much to do with a category of the *Altertumwissenschaft* and even less with the moralizing ideals of Giordani's rhetorical style. Leopardi's classicism refers immediately to the project of a metaphysics of morals; it is a metaphysical concept. How does Leopardi express it? Through a search that follows a strict logic and leads from the not-very-convincing definition of the aesthetic criteria of formal elegance[70] to the posing, in a much more convincing manner, of a grandiose classical model: the *Iliad*.[71] In the work of Dante,[72] the Italian language possesses its own *Iliad*. Italian can in fact govern the classical model since it has at its disposal the power [*potenza*] of an unmatchable tradition. It has a classical nature.[73] For Leopardi, classicism is thus a living body, a power [*potenza*] that materially constitutes itself into collective subjectivity, a metaphysics of the *Risorgimento*. A new renaissance can be produced only on the basis of the richness and breadth, the beauty and the power [*potenza*] of this ancient Italian language and literature; only these can generate a new collective body, an ethical second nature. In this sequence concerning classicism, in the continually established relationship among the Homeric model, Dante's epic poetry and the revival of Italian letters and the Italian nation there is something so strong, so physically forward-looking, that it could end up in a barbarous characterization of the concept of the classic. But it is nothing of the kind: Leopardi's language and thought never allow the resignation of preventive reflection or of a conventional or hypothetical measure ("nothing absolute" is equally valid in this regard) to participate, purely and simply, in the classical sensibility. But it is true that within this metaphysical opening, joy and frenzy begin to appear in the apprehension of being: we will recognize this power [*potenza*] of being deployed in the *Operette morali*. The pages dedicated to the "classic" in the *Zibaldone* of 1823 are thus the prolegomena to a metaphysics of morals, which is awaiting an immediate verification and a deepening of the investigation into the reality of the historical context. The web of sense and the theory of imagination, intermingling on the terrain of language, have constituted a living body, a collective subject that wants to and now must define itself materially.

On the basis of this corporeality of the metaphysical presuppositions we can read, as the first example of the execution of the determinate project of a metaphysics of morals, the *Discourse on the Present State of Italian Morals*.[74] Composed in March 1824, it is not merely chronologically contiguous with the *Zibaldone* of 1823, it completes the latter's design. Indeed, the political pages of the *Zibaldone* from this period provide us with no valid indications: they contain only scattered notes containing the habitual resonances of political skepticism[75] and attempts to reelaborate the theory of climate[76]—pages charged with an undeniable haughty immaturity and that ignorant pretentiousness that one sometimes encounters in Leopardi's political discourse, but never in other regions of being.[77] But this aspect is not exactly what interests us. What we want is to see the metaphysics of revival develop—that or its impossibility. This alternative, of the possibility or impossibility of a revival, is at the basis of Leopardi's discourse, for this renewal or otherwise is a real alternative that belongs to all European peoples. The revolution is dead of consumption. The Enlightenment calmed the passions by means of a progress of reason that has gradually devoured its children. Thus we find ourselves in a static situation, but nevertheless a precarious one. Creation has been blocked by reason, which leaves us in a world of illusion, an illusion so diffuse that it is confused with reality: how can we recognize reality if everything is illusion? The Enlightenment burned nature out. What remains is fragile, tenuous, no more than ashes. What is under the ashes?

Everyone wonders, particularly foreigners: what happened in Italy? What remains of the revolutionary times? The passion and interest underlying these questions go beyond what they deserve, for if it is true that the revolution changed Italian morals to an incredible degree, those changes are bizarre and their dimensions and tendencies are ambiguous. "I will say a few things regarding present morals (dealing with them in general) with the freedom and sincerity that a foreign writer would be able to exercise."[78] At present, "Italy has morals that are notably different from those of other civilized peoples."[79] Tradition having lost all efficacy as a result of the general and profound upheaval brought about by the revolution, in Italy "the preservation of society seems rather the work of chance than of any other reason; and one could rightly marvel that society can exist among individuals who continually detest, undermine, and seek by any means to harm each other."[80]

It is a marvel (pardon us this irony) that, contrary to what all authors since Horace have thought, a social link can still subsist and laws survive in Italy without the support of morals. Italy lives by habit and not by ethics. This second nature is empty—the sensibility is deprived of imagination, and illusion is effective but not true. The other European countries possess and maintain a preservative principle of public morality: "that principle is society itself"[81]—or rather, they have at their disposal a narrow [stretta] "intimate society"[82] that holds them together and itself establishes social values, assures their rationale, the passion and strength to understand, defend, and propagate them. The illusion is true. On this centripetal tension, dominant hegemonic values take shape and act: for the aristocracy there is the principle of glory, while for the bourgeoisie the principle of honor commands and defines actions—the latter a cold yet extremely potent illusion.[83] It is articulated through "public opinion," which is a kind of blood circulation—still an illusion, a web of the senses, "very humble and cold" but nevertheless potent. "Thus it is that, in the nations of which I speak, by producing good taste, society itself produces the main and even the sole guarantee of morals, public as well as private, that can be had today, and it is therefore the immediate cause of its own preservation."[84] (How many and how important are Leopardi's deductions in these pages! The concept of civil society, the concept of "narrow society" and thus of hegemony, of *Öffentlichkeit*, an institutional definition of law and right, etc., etc.,—with the first historical sketch of the principles that govern public morality, a veritable synthesis of sensibility and imagination, as much with regard to their founding [*fondazione*] as to their foundation [*fondamento*]; all this according to a schema that takes into account the link between values and social classes and that gives rise to the process of "sub-jurisdiction [*sub-tribunalizzazione*]" of the ethical referents that leads from the centrality of glory to honor and esteem. Each of these themes is enormously suggestive, and my reader will surely have a fine game of identifying the subsequent long lines of research and researchers that issue forth from one or the other and from this method, from Hegel to Tönnies to Weber, from Simmel to Habermas to Luhmann.[85] Nevertheless, Leopardi's position also constitutes an alternative to all these traditions, at least insofar as they are marked by dialectical thought. Leopardi's thought "without" dialectics in fact views these principles as principles of illusion. What is important is not to follow the development of their logic but to become familiar with them, recognize them, render them paradoxical. Leopardi does not seek a model or an ideal type or a dialectical category. He seeks a determination of the senses and illusion to insert into a mechanism of truth; that is to say, a sensory schema of illusion that, by means of verification and paradox, knows how to develop into the imagination.)

Let us return to our proposition. Italians "are, since the time of the Revolution, with regard to morality, as philosophical, as reasonable and as geometrical as the French or any other nation; indeed the people (the thing is worthy of note) are perhaps more so than those of any other nation."[86] But Italians have no society; they have neither "center" nor "narrow society." Consequently, there is neither an "Italian public"[87] nor an Italian literature: they lack a "determinate Italian taste"[88] and thus any social principle of honor or conviviality. Each Italian is equally honored and dishonored— the sole social virtue is the "absolute diversion"[89] from any production of value. Here the discourse tends implicitly toward extreme limits: the very description of the paradox exacerbates the problem. How can a people live without literature? Why is the real not true? Why is there no philosophy? It may well be noted ironically that if all the European nations "are more philosophical than the Italians from the intellectual point of view, the latter are, in practice, a thousand times more philosophical than the greatest philosopher who can be found in whatever nation mentioned."[90] But this ironic and paradoxical assertion merely allows room to breathe: the framework for the analysis of the efficacy of false illusion, of the muted vigor of a web of sense that is incapable of liberation, soon deepens with a ruthlessness proportionate to the despair.

In Italy, there is no public opinion and no one notices. In Italy, life has no substance, no truth: perhaps it no longer has any elsewhere, but here "not even the appearance is preserved."[91] There is no illusion that, although deceptive, can ground authority. This is the result of a "daily and continuous dissipation without society."[92] Everyone lives by habit, by cold habituation, which feeds neither the passions nor the imagination—there are really no morals, those ethical concretizations of social values and reciprocity, but only habits. All these elements constitute plagues for civil life.[93] Hence the cynicism: "the position I call the most reasonable is that of a full and continual cynicism of the mind, thoughts, character, morals, opinions, words and actions."[94]

Cynicism and laughter: "Italians laugh at life: they laugh much more than any other nation, and with more truth and more intimate conviction of scorn and coldness than any other."[95] Cynicism and laughter characterize all social classes and ground a general disregard, a universal immoral diversion: "one cannot behave thus without having first contracted the habit of disregarding, scorning and being indifferent to oneself."[96] Egoism and misanthropy are the true plagues of this century.[97] Italians are depraved and corrupt. This denunciation is in no way moralistic: the system of cynicism is structural and constitutes the real obstacle to the truth of illusion and the revival of minds. Here the metaphysical theme increases its range—or rather it constitutes itself, and from being critical becomes projective. "I am quite far from imagining that a different and more beautiful world than ours exists in the countries beyond my gaze"[98]—nevertheless, if the present obliges us to be realistic, the imagination of time is wider, more historical and freer. These Italians carry with them a past and a language that have passed through barbarism and renaissance. Medieval barbarism brought with it the reign of guilds, fiefdoms, churches, clans, without society. The Renaissance corresponds to classical antiquity and its renewal: "The revival brought us out of the barbarism of base ages, not out of the ancient state [. . .] In summary, civilization was not born in Europe in the fifteenth century, but reborn."[99]

And now barbarism is returning. A "very strong, very profound, complete, total disillusionment [*disinganno*],"[100] indifference: "coldness is the true ice that comes with great heat."[101] The Enlightenment burned everything out, producing true barbarism. Let us take up nature once again against this "civilization"! Let us take up the power [*potenza*] of the historical time of liberation once again against this barbarism!

The last pages of the *Discourse* are organized according to a strange, paradoxical rhythm. The first paradox concerns antiquity, medieval barbarism, the Renaissance, that is to say a cyclical time that breaks with the historical condition of the renewed barbarism produced by the Enlightenment. The second concerns the theory of climates, definitively abandoned since it is unable to account for the current displacement of the centers of influence of culture and imagination: "It seems that the time of the north has come. Up to now, it was the south that always shone and acted in the world."[102] A spatial paradox follows that of the temporal relation—antiquity, barbarism, renaissance. But what is the nature of these paradoxes? They refer to an extreme and irreducible desire for true illusion, ethical illusion, a superhuman inspiration and ability to transform existence. "After the destruction or weakening of the moral principles founded on conviction—destruction caused by the progress and spread of Enlightenment,"[103] "one no longer finds fanatics of any kind in Italy."[104]

The whole of Leopardi's thought developed in the search for an exaltation of sense, the recovery of the truth of passion, the liberation of imagination. This historical lack of innovation, the absence of any subversion of a cold, icy real and of the ethical testimony of truth, constitutes the first fundamental paradox facing the imagination. Leopardi's metaphysics of morals is founded on that paradox, and its first application seized and described it in a remarkable way. Quite obviously it is not enough to solve the problem of the metaphysics of morals, but it allows him to define the ontological terrain on which this ethical science, this unique and authentic metaphysics of being, can develop.[105] The challenge is to advance the search, to grasp being. The paradoxes at the end of the *Discourse* are only appeals, maneuvers. But they mark the end of a laborious process of maturation for Leopardi's thought: "I no longer seek anything but the truth, which I once so hated and loathed" because its definition was not given in this intersection of the world of sense and the productive imagination, but rather as a light that kindled the surface of the real and forbade visiting it. Now the power [*potenza*] of the sensory and productive imagination is implanted in the surface of being. The echoes of being are contradictory, difficult to grasp, sometimes antagonistic. But the metaphysical will to cross the terrain of ethics, however arduous and uneven it is, is now irreducible and embedded in this horizon. The new nature has already been revolutionized by the imagination. It is now going to undergo an operation of complete conquest and organization.

One last remark. Is there anything in all this that could be understood as referring to Leopardi's progressivism? Not at all, if that progressivism is thought of as distinct from this stand in being and kept so, not in order to dominate it but to follow its uneasy movement, its force of continuous subversion of existence. The transformation is thinkable only in this way— and its sense can be conferred only by the subject who suffers and rebels and by the way the imagination is grafted into being, by the contrasts and antagonisms of this intersection. In truth, very little suggests that Leopardi had anything to do with progress. Rather, he had to do with the disquiet of being. He is contrary [*eversivo*] and not progressive.[106]

The Sense of True Being

The *Operette morali* of 1824 and 1827[107] (we pause later to examine the ones from 1832) represent a kind of lightning rod in the interpretations of the poetry and above all the philosophy of Leopardi. De Sanctis and above all Croce and his school[108] reproached these works for a certain "frigidity," suggesting that the blockage of the author's lyrical activity in this period was transformed into fatigue across the entirety of the poetic field. The density of the materialism in this period obviously inspires a negative judgment among the idealist interpreters, a judgment that simultaneously implicates and eliminates the form and content of the work. Nevertheless, it is true that the compact density of this materialism has worried all commentators to some extent. Thus the very ones who have grasped the synthetic character of the *Operette*, as much on the formal as on the theoretical plane, seem almost to dread the drastic, catastrophic character of the philosophizing. This applies to Gentile, who nevertheless clearly grasps the living unity of the work,[109] to Fubini, who brings out with masterly elegance the character of the intellectual synthesis,[110] and to many others,[111] since they all go along with Luporini's verdict: of course, the *Operette morali* constitute a high poetic synthesis, but this synthesis, in passing from the vivacity of the debate within the *Zibaldone* into the formal completion of the new literary genre, into a prose with pedagogical intent, loses its energy, blurs; and the stylistic exercise does not fully restore the life and articulation of the philosophical discourse to us.[112]

It seems to me that this series of assessments distracts us a little from the true problem, which is not to evaluate the place of the *Operette morali* in Leopardi's evolution (from this viewpoint Binni's generous judgment,[113] which associates the *Operette* as philosophy with the return to lyrical activity of the years 1828 to 1830, also goes astray): even if this question deserves to be posed, the problem first of all is to grasp the high poetic originality and the singular philosophical force of this work taken as a whole, an *ens* of Leopardi's universe. Any comparative judgment, whether literary or historicist, seems to me to presuppose the negation or attenuation of the masterpiece that the *Operette morali* constitutes, of the intensity of its inspiration, its form of exposition, its *Denkens-und-Kunstwollen*. Because the *Operette* is a philosophical work, a correct historical-philosophical methodology must manage to grasp (as always when thought constructs an extraordinarily adequate expressive form) not so much the relation to other possible forms as the resolution of all possible relations in a creative act. This is valid for the Platonic dialogues—why not for the *Operette*? Besides, like the dialogues, it is a work of sublime poetry, which has no cause to envy Leopardi's great lyrics and which displays the same frantic inspiration and the same long and continuous labor.[114]

A poetic work of philosophical prose: "Leopardi, master of prose," as Nietzsche said.[115] In comparison with the inspired jottings of the *Zibaldone*, the unity and stylistic perfection of each of the parts as well as the whole set of *Operette* belonging to the same chronological grouping are complete. Maturity of conception of the world, serenity of philosophical judgment, ironic progression in prose as in fable, and attention to literary form go hand in hand. I do not understand why there is such resistance to considering this materialist canto as an exceptional stylistic document precisely because of the extreme density of its materialist contents.[116] Why should a rigorous materialism impede our poetic pleasure and deprive us of the joy of a truly corporeal style?

For Leopardi, prose has always, that is to say since he began to pose the problem of its status in his epistolary dialogue with Pietro Giordani, been characterized as corporeality. Upon this corporeality, which is opposed to the geometrical spirit and the mannerist emphasis on technique and which is thus a living corporeality, rests the possibility for prose to represent the external mediation of the passions.[117] There is no pedagogism here: prose, and above all that of the *Operette*, in no way constitutes the medium of teaching, but rather the figuration of the life of being in the corporeal forms of external communication. In prose, the "I" is mediated with the world, for in its corporeality, prose is the most adequate tool for expressing the materiality of our worldly relationship. The extremely rigorous affirmations of materialism of the *Zibaldone* in this period are thus translated first of all into style, into the corporeality of prose style. Let us take a thought from the *Zibaldone*, which is quite remarkable for the extreme atheism and materialism that it expresses as well as for the philosophical elegance of the argument. Reading this will allow us to understand how the corpo-reality of the *Operette*'s poetic prose takes shape and to discern in brief outline how materialism is a positive power [*potenza*] in the construction of communication.

> When we say that the soul is spirit, we do not say anything other than that it is not matter, and we actually utter a negation, not an affirmation. Which amounts to saying that *spirit* is a word without an idea, like so many others. But since we have found this word in a grammatically positive form, we think, as we often do, that we have a positive idea of the nature of the soul expressed by that word. In trying to define this spirit, however, we might well accumulate a thousand negations, visible or hidden, drawn from the ideas and property of matter, which are denied to the spirit, but we could not add anything really affirmative to it, or any positive quality, unless it was drawn from the effects of the senses, and therefore from matter in a manner of speaking (thought, sense, etc.) which we freely ascribe exclusively to this spirit. And what I say about the soul I say about other immaterial beings, including the Supreme Being—*Spiritual* amounts to the same as *immaterial*; the latter is grammatically negative, the former ideologically so.[118]

What makes the *Operette* a short treatise on philosophical method is beginning to emerge. Posing in poetic fashion the problem of demystification as a problem contained within the problem of communication in prose, it is really preparing to solve a problem that up to now has been left to the side in the often non-systematic progression of Leopardi's philosophical thought: that of an analytic of reason. We know that this problem cannot be resolved in a transcendental manner. In the same era, referring expressly to Kant's philosophy and emphasizing its metaphysical force, Leopardi once again keeps his distance from the reveries of the transcendental.[119] But the fact of rejecting the transcendental conclusion to the analytic problematic (that is, the transcendental response to the problem of the rational experiment-ing of the scientific knowledge [*conoscenza*] of nature and of the real in general) does not mean abolishing the problem. Leopardi is not pre-critical; he is post-critical. He foresees the disaster of criticism. Leopardi's prose in the *Operette* is a kind of negative analytic of reason and its relation-ship with the science of the real—an analytic method, neither synthetic nor conclusive, relying on the awareness of its own strength and its inherence in the internal mechanism of a real that is as dramatically split as reason is. It is a method that makes almost every single text into an example of regional phenomenology in which the relation *noesis-noema*, subjectivity-reality, imagination-sense is specified in the intensity of diverse experiences, of paradigms of regions of being—with a never-resolved tension and with tremendous capacity to make the clash of phenomenological—and ontological—polarities philosophically paradoxical. Other critics have singled out this splitting of the analytical fabric as the fundamental key to the construction of the *Operette*—and nonetheless made this posing of the problem out to be psychological and a little pathetic: "The unceasing clash and strange amalgamation of two extremes: the youth and the science of their author. Paradox and lunar caprice are their legitimate sons, not wisdom."[120]

But this is not the way this profound analytical key must be envisioned: in the poetic explosion of the *Operette*, it is totally objective; it is the metaphysical *Darstellung* of a rhythm of thought and the enjoyment of its ontological complexity, of the objective density of thought. By means of analysis, the *Operette* construct a world. The great poetic key lies in the crystalline objectivity of the clash between intellectual and metaphysical powers [*potenze*], in the framework of the sublime abstraction and glassy objectivity of the true. Can all this be expressed any better than it is through the dense prosaic split in the linguistic universe, through this new literary genre? The great poetry of the *Operette* is constructed by finding within itself its own origin, to the extent that the state of the metaphysical problem, the analytic will, in other words the awareness of the impossibility of concluding, creates an adequate form. Origin and dynamic go together.

The *Operette* of 1824 and 1827 develop according to an internal curve that is completely conditioned by the nature of the problem considered: a curve that goes from the construction of the abstract analytic universe to its dissolution, from the forgetting of being in the analytic to the desperate reconstruction of the thread of its truth. Through continuous experimentation, the styles bend, adapt, and potently caress or express this movement of reason. These *Operette* are German in the sense of the extraordinary technical adaptability that Leopardi attributes to the language of that people—which takes nothing away from the beauty of his Latin tongue. They are also German in the sense that they take up, with extraordinary consonance, the typical problems of classical German philosophy, critical and post-critical, to which they propose an original solution. A great speculative poetry confronts the European philosophical genius in its entirety. Permitting ourselves a paradox, we can conclude these remarks by observing that the theme of the *Operette* echoes Kant's answer to the question *"What is Enlightenment?"*: but they answer in a diametrically opposite manner.[121]

The *Operette* of 1824 are composed by dint of continuous daily labor from the middle of January to the end of November. Our preceding remarks permit us to read them along a continuous line of development. I do not know whether the project of the *Operette*, which certainly goes back several years,[122] includes the clarification of the stylistic project and the metaphysical web that we here see untangled. If we consider the fragments of 1820 to 1822 that were excluded from the definitive edition,[123] we may doubt it. The effort to define an original semantic fabric has not come to an end, and the search for an adequate relationship between philosophical and anthropological themes, between metaphysics and ethical-political considerations, seems unsatisfactory. But it is certain that the final edition of the *Operette* permits instead a reading concentrated at the highest speculative level: and it is essential, at this stage, to understand if and how the process of fabrication modified the product.

We propose a reading of the *Operette* of 1824, which can be divided summarily into two groups. In the first nine little poems, from "The History of the Human Race" to "The Wager of Prometheus," written between January and May, Leopardi constructs the metaphysical terrain of the discourse. In the eleven that follow from May to November, from "The Dialogue of a Physicist and a Metaphysician" to "The Canticle of the Wild Cock," Leopardi intervenes on this terrain through major experiments in metaphysical rupture. The two dialogues of 1827, "Copernicus" and "The Dialogue of Plotinous and Porphyry," conclude this cycle and offer a new metaphysical tension deployed within the true, within being.

Let us consider the first three essays of the first group: "The History of the Human Race,"[124] "The Dialogue of Hercules and Atlas,"[125] and "The Dialogue of Fashion and Death."[126] With this opening, the horizon of the *Operette*, the project of research, takes shape. The tone is varied and the construction of these three compositions is disparate: the first is a mythological fable, the second a facetious popular dialogue in the form of a myth, and the third a theatrical dialogue marked by lugubrious irony. Nevertheless, only "The Dialogue of Hercules and Atlas" manages to unite that stylistic dryness and that classical lightness that make certain of the most successful *Operette* exemplary. In short, this beginning seems labored. But that is not what interests us. What interests us is the horizon that is constructed here—that is to say, the theme, the problem posed. But it is worthwhile to note that the tiresomeness of the poetic beginning does not prevent the horizon from appearing immediately as a compact problematic receptacle, with a strict, sometimes obsessive rigor. The variations in poetic approach thus constitute an extremely suggestive surreal scene where different forms converge toward the same content.

This single theme is announced by Fashion: "I have put into the world such regulations and morals that life itself, as regards both the body and the soul, is more dead than alive; so that with perfect truth this century might be called the century of death."[127] The problem is thus this abstracted world of life—abstracted because the "lovely shadows [*larve*]"[128] from which humankind drew hope for life have disappeared. It is abstract and deprived of passions and the sounds of glory and ideas: "it's a long time now since the world stopped making any noticeable sound or movement; for my part I had the strongest suspicion that it must be dead, and expected it from day to day to infect me with its stench."[129] The time of life is no longer the course of great desires and passion for ideas—only Love still manages to shake us. It is a time of implacable and silent entropy that the lively and roguish cheerfulness of Hercules cannot manage to loosen, a lugubrious time in which death has spread over the whole surface of life and established morals. While being oppressive and constraining, this world nevertheless remains extremely cold and abstract: the extremity of the description does not detract from its initial, fundamental character. There is no denunciation, no invective: there is only the contrast that follows from the malaise of the abstract, from its oppressiveness and constraint. This paradoxical key dominates the rhythm of the exposition and sometimes programmatically overloads it, opposing the richness of the dream or the vivacity and youth of Hercules to the ineluctable advance of death. And when at last the time of life, which is death, ceases to be considered as a general envelope, as a worn-down and absorbing backdrop, and instead is described in a well-known fashion, on the basis of the slower rhythm of the hopeless decline from youth to old age, this does not negate but instead increases the effect of abstraction—and consequently increases the contrast. Is there an alternative, a way of rearticulating life and love and grasping their place and time? Does a hope of regaining the vigor of a natural and heroic childhood, of snatching the morals of life away from death, exist? These questions are in no way implicit. They too are imposed by contrast. Once again it is the force of abstraction that makes the condition described intolerable, paradoxically inhuman. There is no howl of protest here, even less a hypocritical pedagogy: there is merely the increasingly stylistically accomplished description of a potent abstraction, a theoretical lucidity that aims for the poetic effect. Is this in order to arouse refusal or protest? No. It is only in order to provide the dimensions of the metaphysical framework's truth. When the metaphysical framework is filled out, it will signal the enormous tension accumulated here.

The technique of paradox is developed here in a literarily perfect way because it is experienced in a fully metaphysical way. Then there is the inessential and slightly futile "Announcement of Prizes Offered by the Academy of Sillographers"[130]—which nevertheless begins with the extremely modern paradox of people constituted by machines before concluding with a series of annotations and accents, which are more comic than ironic, relying somewhat on dialect although not unrestrainedly. A certain ethical lull begins to seep from the paradoxical fabric—this inaugurates the second part of the *Operette morali* of this first group. The abstract backdrop of the metaphysical framework is preserved and even extended in this set of texts. It brings to light views and perspectives from a wide range of regions of being in order to reinforce itself, eliminate objections, and intensify the complexity. The different planes are distinguished while nevertheless converging toward the same design.

"The Dialogue of an Imp and a Gnome"[131] is a happy, scintillating dialogue directed against the "human presumptuousness" of science. The fable-like backdrop is that of gnomes who rule over the depths of the earth and imps who are lords of the forests and meadows. Through this fable and beyond it, the gaze is led toward the metaphysical dimension of the two infinites, the microcosm and the macrocosm, toward the inexhaustibility of species and countless cycles. The denunciation is addressed to anthropocentrism as well as to teleology. But this little work is moral and practical and therefore operates within the everydayness of the paradox of a life that is death, all of which demonstrates the madness of humankind, driven by presumptuousness and nourished by perverted knowledge [*conoscenza*], which is made a collaborator in the destruction of humanity and nature.

Two dialogues, "The Dialogue of Malambruno and Farfarello"[132] and "The Dialogue of the Earth and the Moon"[133] again take up the theme of the cognitive unfathomability of the real in order to displace the reflection on the traditional discussion of the insurmountable limits of knowing [*conoscere*] and the problems of moral responsibility that follow from them toward the demystification of the proclaimed goal of knowledge [*conoscenza*], the conquest of happiness. Both develop this negative dialectic of pleasure according to which unhappiness is born of the very quest for happiness ("Therefore, as you necessarily love yourself with the greatest love you are capable of, you necessarily desire your own happiness as intensely as you can; and never being able by a long way to be satisfied in this craving, which is supreme, it follows that you can in no way avoid being unhappy");[134] and such unhappiness is necessary: ("misfortune is common to all the planets in the universe, or at least in the solar system, exactly like roundness and all the other qualities I mentioned, no more and no less").[135] What quality do these arguments that we know from the *Zibaldone* take on once they are situated within the discourse of this work? A sort of icy sadism and a cold Epicureanism are added to the conviction of death: "It therefore follows that, speaking in absolute terms, not living is always better than living."[136] Nevertheless, the stylistic progression uncovers a contrast, like the blazing sun casting deep shadows, which no argument is able to quell.

In "The Dialogue of Malambruno," the Socratic progression of the argument ends up in a kind of mystique of death, of suicide, with any analytic mediation of the discussion having been withdrawn from this will to moral coherence; in "The Dialogue of the Earth and the Moon," the critique of anthropocentrism develops into a pessimistic naturalism that expresses an inspired madness, in the style of Ariosto, of the universe. In other words, paradox pushed to its extreme limits does not annul the terms that constitute it. These are woven and brought together, thanks to an unequalled stylistic effort, and exacerbated by the luminosity of the style. Along with and following the paradoxical definition of the insurmountable limits of an analytic of science and an analytic of morals, a new region of being arises to be explored: "The Dialogue of Nature and a Soul."[137] It is a Romantic dialogue: "Live, and be great and unhappy."[138] The superiority of the spirit is a calamitous and deathly gift—the glory to which the soul aspires procures only a horrifying, monstrous increase in unhappiness. Here the immediacy of Leopardi's confession almost manages to undermine the abstract perfection of the style: we feel pain, and it is not beautiful. But the contradiction that, in this specific case, involves the emergence of subjectivity is controlled at once. The soul asks to be "stripped of the ruinous gifts that make me noble" and to become "like the most stupid and insensitive human spirit."[139] And it adds that "in exchange for immortality, I beg you to hasten my death as much as possible."[140] No idea of history or progress could escape this brilliant illustration of ontological specificity.

"The Wager of Prometheus"[141] arises from a parodic rhythm made possible by detachment, by the supremacy that the game of retaliation between life and death has now acquired. But this parodic beginning, on the pleasant experiences of the gods, is followed by the usual cold argument. Prometheus's wager—that humankind, which he made and provided with fire, is the most perfect nature, the best work of the immortals—is lost. It is lost because the human condition is unhappy, and the contradictions in which humans live are insurmountable; but above all it is because this contradiction becomes absolutely irrational ("human civilization is more the work of chance than of nature")[142] and because the development of civilization is consequently the development of irrationality, the failure of nature, and the cruelty of morals. The myth of Prometheus, which plays a Copernican role in the critical tradition, is here not merely demystified but pushed to the point of the shameful (curious, ironic, always heart-rending) demonstration of the cruelty of human morals and moral barbarism. Thus concludes the framework of regions of being and with it the impossibility of grasping, in each of those regions, the occasion for an analytic mediation. Through a prodigious articulation of philosophical discourse and stylistic intensity, the demonstrations that "life is more dead than alive" have been engraved in the coldest marble, so to speak.

This metaphysical description constitutes the backdrop against which the experiments of the second group of *Operette morali* of 1824 commence. These experiments aim to disturb the perfection of the unhappy world narrated up to this point, to emphasize the contrast that the abstract semantics of the *Operette* paradoxically constructed, brought to a sublime intensity, and must now confront, or rather extend, the tension of which must now be made to explode in the relationship to life, subjectivity, and imagination. This project brings together four dialogues composed in May and June 1824. Their relationship forms a kind of dialectical episode, in the rhetorical and argumentative sense. They are, in order of composition, "The Dialogue of a Physicist and a Metaphysician,"[143] "The Dialogue of Nature and an Icelander,"[144] "The Dialogue of Torquato Tasso and his Guardian Spirit,"[145] and finally, bound to the others by circumstances that are at once chronological and argumentative, "The Dialogue of Timander and Eleander."[146]

In the first of these dialogues, Leopardi, the metaphysician, poses the problem of the rupture of the theoretical schema within which the discourse has developed up to now; that is, the expression of the desire for a time that would not be futile, woven of idleness and tedium, a desire that would fill "those interminable intervals of time in which our being is enduring rather than living"—"life must be vital, that is, truly life; otherwise death incomparably surpasses it in merit."[147] What is a simple prolongation of life such as the "Physicist" wishes worth? Nothing, for "not pure being, but only being happy, is desirable."[148] In what does the happiness of being consist? In the intensity of sensations and passions. It is situated in an "other" time than that of the course of life and its insignificance; it condenses in the potentiality of desire. Hence the extraordinary paradox:

> rather than retarding or interrupting the processes of our bodies so as to prolong life, as Maupertuis proposes, I wish we could accelerate them so as to reduce our lives to the span of certain insects, called ephemera, of whom it is said that the oldest live no longer than a day, and for all that die as great-grandfathers. In which case, I reckon that there would be no room left to us for boredom.[149]

Thus the problem is not this life, this time, irremediably prisoners of the abstract, but an "other" life and time. The abstract, insofar as it is posited as absolute, is opposed to another absolute, an "other" absolute: no longer its weak simulacra—pleasure, glory, all those listed in the *Zibaldone*—but a temporal and vital absolute.

The metaphysical innovation could not be more potent. Out of the recognition of the impossibility of following any line of analytic mediation arises this radical alternative, this total opposition. The word "hope" in Leopardi is characterized by this intensity, this extraordinary tension. (And they speak of "serenity" with regard to this and other ethical dialogues in the *Operette*, pretending that poetry, however progressive it might be, can only consist of serenity! What ideological poverty the literary tradition expresses here!) Of course, this hope can be illusory, as it is in "The Dialogue of Nature and an Icelander." But there is more: the negative dialectic of pleasure develops by denying all hope, emptying the propositions of the metaphysician of their most significant links point by point.

In the "Icelander," to the proposition of the principle of hope there corresponds not only the negation of this principle but also a proposition of solitude, of balance in suffering, and resigned despair. This negative extremity of the dialogue can be stylistically and logically developed through the exaggeration of the image of Nature as a cruel and savage deity, mistress of the "perpetual cycle of production and destruction"; that is, "the life of this universe."[150] The biblical suffering of the Icelander, who nevertheless uninterruptedly repeats his demand for happiness, is destroyed by the philosophical sarcasm of Nature. The violent state of the world is represented by the philosophy of Nature. The search for an "other" life and time clashes with the enormity of the law. The Icelander's invective is no more successful: "who is gladdened or who is benefited by this most unhappy life of the universe, preserved by the injury and death of all those things that go to make it up?"[151] In response, the Icelander will be devoured by two emaciated lions "worn out and wasted by hunger,"[152] like those to be seen in zoos, or bowled over by a sandstorm and in that mausoleum naturally shrunken and mummified. Thus, in the dialectical episode, the violence of nature is opposed to human hope and denies it: the two dialogues are given in that relation. The metaphysical proposition of separation and construction of an "other" time on which hope is formed is simply mocked.

"The Dialogue of Torquato Tasso and his Guardian Spirit" transcribes this passage and subjects all its terms to a more mature philosophical resolution. First of all, the dream of the metaphysician: "O if only I could see my Leonora again!"[153] No, thinking this way is preferable because the true leads back to the difficulty of life, and the dialectic of pleasure is the dialectic of suffering. No, pleasure is only valuable if it is "a speculative thing, not a real one: a desire, not a fact; a feeling that man conceives in thought, but does not experience; or, to put it better, a concept, and not a feeling . . . pleasure is either past or future, but never present."[154] It participates in another dimension of time. On this path of research and the transcription of theoretical experience, the opposition is immediate. It is the Icelander who asks, in so many words: if pleasure belongs to the dream and to another time than the present, does this mean that it is nothingness? "So it appears," answers the familiar spirit and nature. But this nothingness is aggressive; it is a "violent state" laden with violence and boredom, an Aristotelian physics of boredom and pain. The solidity and cold flatness of this despairing universe are represented here: with the same universal penetration that the air has, the violence of nature permeates the world. We might expect lions to appear once again in Tasso's prison: but sarcasm has no more place in this dialogue than invective does.

To the extent that this work does not resolve its rhythm in the clash of these two rhetorical figures, it begins to construct a horizon to rupture the abstract world, and a strong proposition—not ingenuous like that of the metaphysician—emerges that is much more potent than it is constructive. It is true, boredom and pain fill everything. But "by boredom we should understand none other than the pure desire for happiness."[155] As for pain, it is a "remedy against boredom," the most potent remedy of all. This totality of negativity is thus ruptured by a separation that runs through and divides the metaphysical polarity. "Other" hope, "other" time, and "other" life are not opposed abstractly to the world of unhappiness: instead, they traverse it by surmounting it. Boredom, pain, and solitude again acquire a doubling of functions which, in this situation of a dialectic internal to metaphysics, can be separated. In this state of violence, boredom, and pain, the possibility of an alternative—or rather, a constitutive dynamic—is restored. For these elements, which are elements of the real, are separated there but also reaggregated and recomposed.

A constructive power [*potenza*] is outlined: "solitude almost does the office of youth; or at least it rejuvenates the spirit, reinforces the imagination and sets it to work, and renews in the much-tried man the benefits of that primal innocence you long for."[156] Rupture is separation. Rupture traverses the whole and constructs a different line of the productive imagination, contrary to the abstraction of the world. Of course, this constructive dynamic, at the moment it appears fully deployed in the *Operette*, contains within it the habitual relativist counterweights: as the dialogue of the spirit and Tasso concludes, "Thus between the constructions of dream and those of the imagination you will slowly consume away your life, to no other end than to consume it."[157] But it is also sustained, in the proper sense, by a metaphysical method and project.

It is enough, in this regard, to consider "The Dialogue of Timander and Eleander," which rightly follows and completes the preceding ones—not because it enters into the game of the internal dialectic of metaphysical innovation, but because, as befits a conclusion (or rather a preface) to the *Operette*,[158] a reply to possible adversaries, it clarifies the method. In this case it involves less a dialogue than an interview to which Timander subjects Leopardi. The confidence in the imagination as moment of rupture and innovation of the abstract world, outside of the degradation of the Enlightenment and of the natural universe, is here potently [*con potenza*] declared, and all relativist nostalgia is excluded. Truth is poetic: poetic books construct morality. "I say poetic, taking this term in a broad sense; that is, books intended to move the imagination; and I mean no less in prose than in verse."[159] Isolation, the lofty attitude of the imagination, is neither misanthropic nor proud: it is creative. "[I]ncapable of and impervious to hatred," the imagination seeks truth—"intoleran[t] of any kind of simulation or dissimulation," any fiction. Familiar with fate, the imagination does not oppose it except by declaring itself an "other." Mocking the urgency and refusing the conceptual necessity of fate, the imagination's only opposition answers to a Copernican vocation: to be "other." And to construct "other"? The only hope is imagination. The study of the "miserable and frigid truth" does nothing for us. The possibility of the analytic constructing a line of truth is destroyed, for truth is "other"; it is the construction of an alterity. What a strong flavor this "*sapere aude* [dare to know]," too often claimed as the mechanical power [*potenza*] of the *Aufklärung*, has here! Truth, sunk as it is in separation from every "rational or fantastic being," becomes subject. The imagination that separates is the sense of true being.

But what is the power [*potenza*] of the imagination? How can the conditions of an innovative poetics be united with those of a true life? How can this separated imagination traverse making? This problem is at the center of the three *Operette morali* of summer 1834: "Parini, or Concerning Glory,"[160] "The Dialogue of Frederick Ruysch and his Mummies,"[161] and lastly, to a lesser extent, "The Memorable Sayings of Filippo Ottonieri."[162] All three works respond negatively to the questions posed—nevertheless, each in its own way constitutes material for later elaboration concerning these problems that are considered real and current. Parini was "one of the very few Italians" who, with great profundity of thought, posed the problem of making.

And truly, if the principal subject of literature is human life, and the first object of philosophy to guide our actions, there is no doubt that working [*operare*] is as much worthier and more noble than meditation and writing, as the end is more noble than the means, and as affairs and things matter more than words and discourses. Indeed, no mind is created by nature to study; nor is man born to write, but only to make [*fare*].[163]

The subject thus posed, the long text of the essay develops a series of themes that consolidates the projective tension. Nevertheless, the making considered here is literary, a making that is constituted on the depth and continuity of a labor of language and style, as well as on the extension of inspiration and on the unitary appropriation of all the forms of innovative knowledge [*sapere*]. Philosophy, literature, and poetry are forms of the constitutive imagination. And so on. We are familiar with all the terrains that Leopardi surveys through his "Parini." In this essay, perhaps the only one in which a certain pedagogism appears clearly, we find an extremely strong ethical emphasis of the discourse, an ethical emphasis that becomes the very substance of the definition of the subject. Imagination surveys the city of letters and the abstraction of the world on the basis of a subjective substrate. But the central question of an innovative making here becomes weightier as it gets closer to a solution. When Leopardi redefines the theme of glory no longer as heroic myth but as the problem of making in relation to the future, as a bourgeois and economic expectation of the future, this marks a crisis. It is a critical moment in the essay, one that is perhaps disastrous for its development. In fact, this work reveals itself to be a pedagogical work that is defined on the terrain of an impossible pedagogy, since no guarantee can be given to making with respect to the future nor to the quest for glory with respect to the form of its value. The conclusion is vaguely stoic ("our destiny, wheresoever it may lead, is to be followed with a spirit strong and great")[164] and vaguely rhetorical. Nevertheless the forceful assertion of the value of subjectivity as the basis of the productive imagination and its hope remains: if future time and the project to produce it are, above all in our era, "slow to come and measured," "superior and singular spirits" can advance, even rapidly race, over this terrain of the future. This aspect, of little importance in itself, nevertheless confirms Leopardi's ethical adherence, the foreshadowed definition of an ethical progress founded on the labor of subjectivity. "Parini" is a small but substantial step in the process of defining the new elements of metaphysical constitution.

The discourse on the power [*potenza*] of the imagination goes deeper in "The Dialogue of Frederick Ruysch and his Mummies," in a twilight through which "dreadful specters [*larve*]" move, in a magical and lunar confusion between life and death. The tone is pedagogical but the style grotesque: the key to a truth that succeeds in being stated only by means of contorted and unsettled images, that is sought among the shadows, and finally unveils itself. The imagination will surely never manage to grasp the real, poetics will never become the moment of making, nor will subjectivity posit itself in a dramatic but true relation with the real if it is not admitted that death forms part of life—and so should not be feared—and that the different time necessary to the imagination moves in this new space and therefore detaches itself from the common. First theme: is the moment of death, therefore, not particularly painful? Although engaged in a (fictive) polemic with the Epicureans, the response is Epicurean: while we exist, there is no death, and when there is death, we no longer exist. There is no difference, aside from an extreme opposition, which is incommunicable and in any case inconceivable to analytic thought, between life and death. Yet this extreme opposition, this absolute phenomenon, precisely because it is not the object of any participation, is an element of coexistence, a gentle coexistence that involves the soul: "Take it as certain, that the entrance and exit of the soul are equally gentle, soft and easy."[165] Second theme: "Then what is death, if it is not pain? Rather pleasure than otherwise."[166] It is like the coming of sleep, voluptuous and languid. Is this "a last courtesy of death"?[167] No, the same "happens to many people."[168]

The same happens in the imagination that must, if it intends to rejoin reality, submit completely to the weight of death and make that weight its own. If the new time, the alternative to the abstraction of the world, is that of pure vital intensity, then death must be torn away from its specific image and understood, as in a mirror image, solely in the nature of the imagination. Death is very sweet: it is the dream itself. The imagination invests nature and overturns, makes acceptable, maneuverable, a fundamental ethical element, that in which nature shows itself to be in the highest degree hostile toward us. Nature is transfigured and ultimately possessed by this kindly refiguration of death. Is pleasure an imitation of death?[169] Only because death is diluted in life. In reality, the imagination, the singularity takes precedence over nature. The most radical materialism is not the confrontation with nature but the dominion over it. Lyric and imagination are possible and constructive only when, through the phantasms of corrupted nature, they are transformed into the logical power [*potenza*] of construction. "Children" is what Frederick Ruysch calls his dead. Death is a child because it forms part of life. True life includes death. The initial framework of the *Operette*, that of a life that is dead, is completely overturned. The poem begins with the discovery with which the laborious construction of the "Parini" essay concludes.

The song of the dead, which serves as an overture to "The Dialogue of Frederick Ruysch," makes use of the great beauty of the remote past tense for the verbs "to die," "to live," and "to be": "we died," "we lived," "we were." Unbelievable depths open up. The sense of true being is at hand. The fact that mummies present the solution to the relationship with nature, the choice of a function that, by including death, entails the construction of life, is grotesque. Mummies: but didn't the Icelander himself end up a mummy in some museum, perhaps that of Ruysch? A sort of optimism of the intellect confronts and comprehends, in any case grasps the ontological limits of the real. To the extent that it grasps them, it can transform these limits into obstacles to surmount. In the grotesque but serene community of the dead, life, making, and producing seem near to us. Of course this dialogue is only one more experiment, but what incredible force it expresses!

Concerning the long chapters of the "Memorable Sayings of Filippo Ottonieri," there is, on the other hand, little to say. We know why this pastiche of the *Zibaldone*,[170] this collection of moral *excerpta*, was composed in these circumstances before being inserted into the structure of the *Operette*: because the material is ethical, because the ethics is sensualist, because all the paradoxes of sensualism are explored anew. And for all these reasons, these "Memorable Sayings" could just as well not have been assembled here, since the ethical thematic, in the generality of Leopardi's discourse, had progressed much further, and the sensualist fiction had been exhausted. Nevertheless we find here an extraordinary passage in which human pleasures are compared to odors—a desire and a faculty strictly connected to matter and which reveal its indistinct glimmer[171]—a theme whose great poetic force anticipates those canti of Leopardi's that are more strongly marked by the sense of true being. For the rest, it is a matter of pastiche. A lapse in the poetic inspiration and the metaphysical tension? Of course, but we must not exaggerate its importance: it has no effect on the complex of *Operette morali*. This self-declamatory fiction can be considered as a genre apart, that of the declamation or dialogue by means of *excerpta*, a genre that is obsolete from the outset and that is valid only insofar as it completes this encyclopedia of literary genres in prose that the *Operette* is, from the viewpoint of the literary marketplace. As we have said, the obvious and important contradiction raised by the "Memorable Sayings" concerns less the literary plane than the directly metaphysical one. Indeed, if there is a stylistic lapse, this depends upon and follows directly from the fact that after being raised to the intensity of the two preceding dialogues, Leopardi's materialism here once again confuses itself with the process without a subject of sensualism. Despite its literary elegance, this piece bears witness to a theoretical disorientation that seems confirmed by the thirty days necessary for its composition[172]—if one keeps in mind the capacity for work that Leopardi shows in the drafting of other, more complex essays. Materialism and sensualism: the reading of the *Zibaldone* has shown us how the internal instability of the sensualist thematic can only tend toward a surmounting. These *Operette morali* have allowed us to grasp a negative analytic of reason that completely emancipates materialism from sensualism. Thus this relapse does not have a precise explanation. It is a fact that must be attributed more to the character of Leopardi's metaphysical vocation, to the tradition that he experiences than to the metaphysical and stylistic innovation that is in the process of developing. Perhaps this lapse is connected to the fact that the search for new elements of metaphysical construction on the terrain of ethics, of making, in these essays—including the preceding ones, "Parini" and "Ruysch"—has not gone very far. Some prodigious illuminations have again invested the metaphysical fabric. But the fabric of ethics? Isn't it perhaps better to cling to the sensualism that helps us to live than to venture into the impossible enterprise of the reconstruction of ethics? This is a plausible doubt. Is not a pre-critical materialism, in the end, more convenient than a post-critical, metaphysical materialism?

No, it is not. The perspective of total innovation is restored to us in the last essays of the *Operette* from 1824. The theoretical pressure once again explodes with great force. Reason can wander in the region of sense, but not experimental reason, not poetic reason, which verifies its own truth in the transformative, ethical, creative result. From this new point of view, the "Memorable Sayings of Filippo Ottonieri" appears almost as a chiaroscuro, intended to dramatize the passage and philosophically intended to be taken up in order to illustrate the obviousness of the innovation.

"The Dialogue of Christopher Columbus and Pedro Guiterrez"[173] illustrates a new scene. What is it that does not function in our concept of the imagination? And in our conception of ethics that only the imagination constructs? It is the fact that we continue, despite all our efforts, to consider the imagination as an instrumental function, in relation to reason—that consequently we continue to trap the contrast between nature and subjectivity in a closed relationship. We separate reason from imagination, ethics from the world of abstraction, and we are content with carrying out such a separation. But that is not how it is: closing down is not permitted here. Ethical reason and imagination, although separated, are creative entities; nature delimits them but neither encloses them nor relegates them to separation. On the contrary, despite their separation, ethical reason and imagination produce against nature.

> *Guiterrez*: So that you, when it comes down to it, have staked your life, and those of your companions, on no more than a mere speculative opinion?
> *Columbus*: So it is; I cannot deny it.[174]

Of course nature is extremely potent, and Columbus's reason is not happy: "Every voyage is, in my opinion, a leap from the cliff of Leucas."[175] Sometimes boredom reigns, but the dream of glory and navigation itself "for a while keep us free of boredom, render life dear to us":[176] all this runs together skeptically to enhance the climate of mental unhappiness. But it is precisely here that the metaphysical miracle of the *Operette*, its non-dialectical analytic of reason, is realized: when the unhappy consciousness that is reason and sense is posited as constitutive power [*potenza*]. This dialogue is one of rational catastrophe. After so many approximations, negations, subjective frustrations, the tension begins to slacken in the continuity of a style of exaggerated serenity. The objective and dominating monster that we call Reason, Enlightenment, Nature has produced its opposite which, in separation, has begun to construct its world—an independent, autonomous world, nourished on the unbelievable unhappiness brought about by the impossibility of the transcendental and the dialectic. Nature is potent—faced with the act of rational will, with Columbus's optimism of the intellect, it insinuates the doubt and false predictions that are capable of nurturing the rebellion of the crew. But Columbus's rational wager stands. A new Prometheus? No. Here it is not the illusory divinity of passion but the radical unhappiness of the mind that determines the certainty of reason, transforms it into and founds it on will. Pessimism of the intellect and optimism of the will? No, that old and always reactionary distich establishes a separation between reason and will that does not exist in the world—but there is an optimism of poetics that is articulated in making, in constituting, and which, against the backdrop of the impossibility of understanding everything, against the derision that the forces of nature and history determine, establishes the hope of making, ethical knowledge [*sapere*]. This positive catastrophe of rationality is repeated in the concluding essays of the *Operette*, which were composed in autumn 1824: "In Praise of Birds,"[177] "Apocryphal Fragment of Strato of Lampsacus,"[178] and "Canticle of the Wild Cock."[179]

The first of these canti is a formidable natural fresco on which is inscribed the parable of poetic rupture and the constitutive imagination. "Birds are by nature the most joyous creatures in the world."[180] "With every pleasure and every satisfaction they feel, they sing,"[181] but "in these things, a vast part of what we call natural, is nothing of the sort; indeed it is rather artificial."[182] The bird participates in civilization, enters into human second nature. "[B]irds share man's privilege of laughing."[183] How can this first catastrophe of the pure intellect, which sees the imagination dismantling and surveying nature, be explained? Laughter, that strange balance of the human mind wrapped up in endless travails, that ephemeral sort of madness, that rambling and that delirium in tears and drunkenness—laughter, that inconceivable form of hope ("a history of laughter, which I am thinking of making").[184] And yet the bird laughs. "[W]e may infer that [birds] must have enormous force and vivacity, and enormous power of imagination [of a] rich and varied kind, light, changeable and childlike [. . .] birds . . . have a manifest resemblance to children."[185] "I would like, for a little while, to be transformed into a bird, to experience the joy and contentment of their life."[186] The catastrophe of nature is specified in the separation of the subject, in the frenzy of the canto, in the definition of a desire and a hope that traverse first and second nature and free themselves in pure imagination. Let us keep in mind that this concept of laughter has a metaphysical importance.[187] But it is more than metaphysical; it is constructive. It is a power [*potenza*] that represents one of the figures of the imagination and that, pressing it to the point of confrontation, in its independence and autonomy, with the abstract world, nevertheless frees it. Laughter is an act of right [*diritto*], a declaration of freedom.

The "Apocryphal Fragment of Strato of Lampsacus" once again throws us from these heights into the cosmic compactness of unhappiness and nothingness. Leopardi seems almost to produce constant provocations against his own thought and the hope of the imagination. It is a fable of cosmogony: "Concerning the Origin of the World" and "Concerning the End of the World." A little materialist treatise on atomism: one or more forces continually shape and destroy the universe. "[A]n infinity of worlds in the infinite duration of eternity" ends in destruction. A physical-eschatological hypothesis: the world is transformed from a sphere into a disk, then from a disk into a ring before finally falling into fire. The rings of Saturn teach us this. A seventeenth-century atomist could not have said it better. Leopardi equals Gassendi? However,

> [w]ith the dissolution of the planets, the earth, the sun and the stars, but not of their matter, new creatures will be formed from this, divided into new genera and new species, and through the eternal forces of matter new orders of things will be born, and a new world. But concerning the nature of this world and its orders, as indeed of those innumerable others that once were and the infinite others that will be thereafter, we are unable even remotely to conjecture.[188]

And the "Canticle of the Wild Cock" adds: "As that which never was cannot die, therefore out of nothingness sprang the things that are."[189] Out of a natural, human, historical nothingness. "In any kind of mortal creature whatsoever, the greater part of life is a wilting away."[190] "Every corner of the universe hastens indefatigably towards death, with wondrous yearning and celerity. Only the universe itself seems immune from decay and enfeeblement."[191] Unlike its parts? No, "the time will come, when this universe, and nature herself, will be snuffed out. [. . .] there will remain no sign; but a naked silence, and a most lofty calm, will fill the immensity of space. And so this wondrous and terrifying mystery of universal existence, ere ever it be declared or understood, will perish and pass away."[192] Very well, but this destiny is the one that our enemy has ordained, the conclusion to the violence of nature. But the wild cock, like the bird of "In Praise of Birds," laughs. For the imagination has freed itself from all this, and if it can produce the image of inimical nature, it need not submit to it. Destruction, the entropy of the universe: "a poetic and not a philosophical conclusion. In philosophical terms, existence, which had no beginning, will never have an end." This conclusion is poetic and metaphysical. The imagination frees itself. The more deeply we go into the catastrophe of reason, the more it appears as an other possible foundation. The cosmic disaster is the sole foundation of morality. We must have it in mind, possess it—so that freedom and imagination can be granted.

The *Operette* of 1824 carried out the assignment that they were given— to describe a negative analytic of reason—and reached the point at which the conditions, not for a reconstruction of the world, but for the foundation of a constitutive, poetic power [*potenza*] are given. From this point of view, they truly conclude a cycle of Leopardi's thought. Henceforth, and already in the *Operette* of 1827 (which we examine), it will no longer be a matter of writing prolegomena to a possible-impossible knowledge [*conoscenza*], but of producing this knowledge in the given ontological condition. The period that runs from the *Operette* of 1824 to those of 1827 is decisive in Leopardi's life. He sets out on his wanderings from Recanati to Milan and Bologna and back, then to Bologna once again, and then to Florence and Pisa.[193] This exhausting voyage in search of glory and work, oscillating between illnesses and frustrations, can in certain respects appear as disruptive or, worse yet, as destructive. "I am . . . a walking sepulchre."[194] In fact it is the external symbol of the end of an era and proof of a passage in Leopardi's expectations and passions. The most obvious internal sign of this passage, it seems to me, consists in the progressive reduction and then the definitive abandonment of work on the *Zibaldone*. The *Zibaldone* undoubtedly comes to an end for very practical reasons: Leopardi begins to work for a living and much of the material that was freely composed earlier is now integrated into projects related to the literary marketplace. "I have put in order a great number of materials that I possess with an eye toward works to be determined when these materials are sufficient and my health improved."[195]

Later in a delectable letter addressed to Pietro Colletta, he mentions a long series of titles corresponding in part to the works effectively in progress, in part to fantasized works: "You'll laugh at such an abundance of titles; and I laugh at it too, and I see that two lives wouldn't be enough to carry out so many plans. And these are not even a fifth part of the ones I'm leaving out."[196] But beyond all these practical reasons, there are also substantial ones that draw upon the metaphysical project. In other words, the experience of the *Operette* seemed to Leopardi to be positive on the systematic terrain. Where the "system" tends to develop, and having now proven that it cannot do so according to an analytical-deductive line (the illusions of sensualism and of "my system" of 1821!), the search can be organized into broad rubrics that correspond to the phenomenological and ontological regions to be explored: "Memories of my life," "Manual of practical philosophy," "Social Machiavellianism," etc., to which are added the systematic return to the work on Homer, the youthful discourse on the "popular errors of the ancients," and so on.[197] These rubrics are not merely publishing projects but fields for the deepening of a metaphysics of morals. The function of the *Zibaldone*, to be the free hodgepodge of ideas and sensations, the master book for a savage navigation, is fulfilled: the routes are now established and in the definition of a constitutive, poetic power [*potenza*], creatively anchored in being, Leopardi finds a compass.

By following the *Zibaldone* of this period from the inside, we can on the other hand see how it is positively inserted into the ideal process that the *Operette* follow, and therefore, from every point of view, how it produces its own extinction: in the first place, by ceasing to be necessary and submitting to the systematic progression of the *Operette* and then because the latter takes up, at a higher level, the former's most mature conclusions. The *Zibaldone* of 1825 to 1827 (and its final appendix from 1828 to 1829)[198] thus constitutes a kind of unifying link between the *Operette* of 1824 and those of 1827, and does this through its very exhaustion. Here we find first of all a *pars destruens*.

Just as Leopardi himself does during this period, we regroup the arguments under different rubrics. The first is entitled "Against teleology." We are familiar with the fabric of Leopardi's reasoning, but here we find it expressed in an extremely radical form. Teleology is attacked on the experimental plane—for its insensitivity to the suffering of humankind and animals.[199] It is attacked on the moral plane—it is impossible to define the order of the universe morally: even if the universe had an order, that order would not be moral.[200] And finally it is attacked on the properly metaphysical terrain: the sole order of life is chance, which constitutes the sole end of existence: "a supreme and terrible conclusion."[201] But the importance of this attack on teleology lies not so much in the repetition of well-known themes as in the fact that, mixed in with its radicalism, there is an ambiguity, the resistance of which we have already noted regarding sensualism in Leopardi's system. Sensualism, in its inductive and associative mechanism, contains, if not a spark, at least a last glimmer of teleology. This residue must be eliminated.[202]

Hence the second rubric, marking an impressive passage: "On second nature or the world of illusion." Sensibility, notes Leopardi, does not present itself as an immediate movement or appetite that governs knowledge [*conoscenza*] and life; its very emergence is on the contrary mediated by the idea, confused within the horizon of illusion; and it is only within second nature that immediacy is represented, emptied out, and transfigured.[203] Every teleological residue is thus expelled from the sphere of signification—it is non-sense—and the real presents itself as the world of illusions.[204] Every teleological propensity is the anthropomorphic production of illusory needs—it is false, either because its basis is illusory or because its reproduction is fantasized.[205]

Third rubric: "On the dialectic of destruction or nature as violence." If there are no laws internal to the world and if representations are illusions, the horizon of life is not value but war. Nature is therefore an ontological flux of illusions determined by the violence of the contrast between continuous constructions and destructions, by the total lack of final causes, and by the chaos of partial causes, drives, and so on.[206] Yet the violence of nature and the chaos of illusions are unfailingly overturned and represented in the world of life taken in its proper sense, as a historical, political, and social world: these pages are full of impertinent casuistry and indeed genuinely reactionary remarks.[207] But this critical proceeding that is raised to the level of a cynical and destructive poetic game is quite familiar to us now from the pages of the *Operette*. The essential point to emphasize here is the emergence, alongside the well-known rhythm of critique, of a *pars construens*. If the *Zibaldone* is generally frank, representative, those features above all are manifested in these pages. Here a set of minor argumentative rubrics opens up. The first of these arguments concerns "the materialist machine." It has frequently been remarked that the most radically nihilist assertions of Leopardi's thought are found in this period.[208] That is true. Random infinity of the world:[209] "It seems that only what does not exist, the negation of being, nothingness, can be limitless, and that the infinite is substantially the same as nothingness."[210] Then that extraordinary "theory of the spot":

> Everything is evil. That is to say everything that is, is evil; that each
> thing exists is an evil; each thing exists only for an evil end; existence is
> an evil and made for evil; the end of the universe is evil; the order and

the state, the laws, the natural development of the universe are nothing but evil, and they are directed to nothing but evil. There is no other good except non-being; there is nothing good except what is not; things that are not things; all things are bad. All existence; the complex of so many worlds that exist; the universe; is only a spot, a speck in metaphysics. Existence, by its nature and essence and generally, is an imperfection, an irregularity, a monstrosity. But this imperfection is a tiny thing, literally a spot, because all the worlds that exist, however many and however extensive they are, since they are certainly not infinite in number or in size, are consequently infinitely small in comparison with the size the universe might be if it were infinite, and the whole of existence is infinitely small in comparison with the true infinity, so to speak, of nonexistence, of nothingness.[211]

This is a complete overturning of Leibniz's image of the world. This efficacy of nihilist writing continually recurs throughout the pages from this period. The overturning of the concept of the infinite into the concept of nothingness has developed up to now on the basis of the analysis of spatial infinity;[212] now the discourse is applied to the analysis of the concept of time, of eternity, of temporal infinity and nothingness.[213] And here too, the nihilist deductions are rigorous. But why call *pars construens* these pages in which such a ferocious nihilist vigor is set in motion? Because here as in the *Operette*, Leopardi's nihilism functions only as a metaphysical reagent: it dissipates every naturalistic pretension and liberates us from every sensualist induction. It is a truth, the *époché* truth of materialism. "Nothingness does not prevent a thing that is from being, existing, remaining."[214] Only such a radical conception of nothingness allows the purification of every spiritualist residue from the definition of mind and allows it to be made an entirely material essence.[215] "That matter thinks is a fact. It is a fact because we ourselves think; and we do not know, we are not aware of being, we are not capable of knowing or perceiving, anything but matter."[216] Leopardi's nihilism is not a theory but a practice of accepted negation and thus the overthrow of the mysticism that through the practice of negation, hypostasizes a positive infinite. "Anyway, who told you that to be infinite is a perfection?"[217] The materialist machine is on the move and nihilism is its point of ignition. It is true, at the price of much pain—but is not this relationship between the nihilist radicalism of critique and its corporeal materialist inscription the basis of the only possible concept of reason?

Second rubric of constructive propositions: "Mythology of reason." We have no illusions that can be opposed to the illusions of nature, but as soon as this lack is registered as pain, in the knowledge [*conoscenza*] of truth that is always the cause of pain, then we are in a position to construct a new reality.[218] Only pain allows us to withstand the violence of nature, the destructive march that it imposes upon us. Not doubt but pain is the basis of science.[219] Mythology is not an art of dissimulation and hypocrisy, as the moderns sometimes perceive it; it is a weapon of the demystification and reappropriation of the world. Mythology, for the ancients as well as us today, constructs reality against the suffocating weight of the heavens.[220] How everything that was transmitted to us as ordinary and tranquil in the traditional image of Leopardi is overturned! In reality, it is all academic bombast and a projection of the most reactionary of powers [*poteri*] over culture and free knowledge [*sapere*]! Leopardi thus renews this *Mythologie der Vernunft*. The analysis of its terms was the point of departure for this study, and we see it renewed after his thought has traversed the analytic of reason and its mortal direction, freeing us. Here Leopardi restores to us the genesis of classical German philosophy as materialism, poetic making, constructive mythology—as a great metaphysics extracted from idealism.

Third rubric: "Poetics." Mythology is specified in poetics as a metaphysical act that avoids philosophical abstraction ("great philosophers have the most anti-philosophical nature there is"),[221] invents itself in practice,[222] and produces true knowledge [*conoscenza*]. Mythology is the d'Alembert of the "Discours préliminaire" of the *Encyclopédie*: we want knowledge [*conoscenza*], knowledge [*sapere*] of the concrete, and art that contains habit and servitude—we want poetic knowledge [*conoscenza*].[223] Who could ever have believed this vigorous reprise of the Enlightenment would appear in the most nihilistic Leopardi? In truth, "My philosophy not only does not lead to misanthropy, . . ."[224] On the contrary, "I live, therefore I hope."[225] The irreducibility of hope in pain, through the positive mythology of reason, avoids despair, breaks with resignation, makes itself poetic. Poetics means the construction of being, liberated imagination[226]—hope, that is to say seeing, hearing, singing.[227]

Here we are in the midst of the *Operette* of 1827: "Copernicus"[228] and "The Dialogue of Plotinus and Porphyry."[229] Two themes dominate the dialogue "Copernicus": the first concerns the constitutive function of poetry; the second, the materialist sense of the Copernican revolution. The burlesque game is revealed right away in a discourse on knowledge [*sapere*], poetry, and philosophy as activities cooperating in the mutation of humankind. Philosophy and poetry thus fulfill a creative function in that great mutation that is the Copernican revolution, in that transformation of the general conception of humankind. And poetry more than philosophy, although they are from the same family, because indeed, even if "these times are no longer heroic times," poetry finds itself entrusted with the metaphysical vocation of inciting humankind to knowledge [*sapere*] and to life by means of illusions: "while the philosophers dissuade them."[230] The power [*potenza*] that philosophy and poetry are called upon to describe is nevertheless a revolutionary power [*potenza*], because that invention, that wrenching, that displacement of the Earth from the center of the universe implies the end of every anthropomorphic conception and every religious and traditional ideology. Copernicus assures us that a lever will allow us to roll the Earth away from the center of the universe. But the matter is more complex.

> But in substance I wish to say, that this business of ours will not be so purely material, as it appears to be on first sight; and that its effects will not pertain solely to physics: for it will upset the degrees of importance of things, and the hierarchy of beings; it will alter the purposes of creatures; and so doing it will cause a vast upheaval even in metaphysics, indeed in everything that touches the speculative part of knowledge. And it will come about that men, even supposing that they are able and wish to consider things sensibly, will discover themselves to be quite another thing, from what they have been so far, or have imagined themselves to be.[231]

The feeling for the materialist revolution inherent in Copernican thought here is total. An unbelievable materialist and atheist happiness animates the dialogue. The invention of the fable conforms to and cooperates in the success of the critical effect. And all this in no way attenuates but instead accentuates the fundamental complexion of the metaphysical framework: the fact that a corrosive irony runs through those spaces in which the poetic fiction situates the dialogue, in the majesty of countless worlds and times, and so discards the hypotheses of an entropic exhaustion of the Sun and of other rational beings inhabiting the planets, and so on. The creative Copernican alternative, the constructive function of knowledge [*sapere*] is all the more exalted thereby. The more the shadow of nature lengthens, obscures, and prevents recognition, the more the "other," the "different," the human constitution can begin to take shape within this disaster of the analytic of reason.

In "The Dialogue of Plotinus and Porphyry" (the first name refers here to Plato and to the whole spiritualist tradition and the second to Leopardi), the discourse against nature, against the fixity of natural law and the whole series of consequences that follow from it, is reinforced. Suicide is indeed only the apparent subject of the dialogue. Its attention is no longer specifically concentrated on the pessimistic assertions regarding life, which are nevertheless quite numerous and radical. Instead, the center and soul of the dialogue are represented by the contrast between that "second nature . . . governed and directed for the most part by reason"[232] and a "primal nature" that claims to dictate its law to humankind, but is nonetheless only unhappiness. So second nature, despite its artificiality or more precisely because of it, is the only world that is henceforth livable.

> The truth is this, Plotinus. That primal nature of ancient man, and of the savage and uncivilized peoples, is no longer our nature; but habituation and reason have created in us a different nature; which we have, and will have forever, in the place of the first.[233]

Thus it is on the terrain of second nature that it is possible for us to develop our imagination and our hope—and also to refute death. The time that constituted second nature offers it to us in its contradictory dimensions: at least one of them can be constituted in hope. "And however fortunate it may be, the present is always sad and disagreeable: only the future can give delight."[234] The Copernican revolution becomes second nature. In this dimension of the world, human unhappiness has become so great that knowledge [sapere] has become constitutive power [potenza]. In this enormous tension, the sense of true being experiences its free projection: a method that subverts [eversivo] reality, nature, all possible legislation: an outline of a constitution that can be realized only in the future. For if the future is nothingness, that does not prevent it from being, in human hope, in its power [potenza], a Copernican illusion.

Grasping Nothingness

Some insist that materialism conjoined with ethical conduct can entail only a great logical and psychological tension—however, this tension is neither deducible nor definable in advance, and there is no need for it to end up in pessimistic conclusions or despairing results. Indeed, on the ethical terrain materialism also offers solutions of the opposite sign, and above all great examples of the philosophy of mental serenity and practical realism. In these variations in the form of relation between metaphysical materialism and ethical philosophy, the central problem is not so much experiencing the tension as it is dominating it. This is true above all with regard to ancient materialism and its historical tendencies,[235] but it is less true in the case of a materialist position situated on the post-critical terrain. Here, in fact, the relationship of consciousness to the materialist background of the world is not marked by distance, domination, or control, but by participation. On the other hand, the world of materiality, having become second nature, is pervaded by diverse beams of light, by alternatives; and by participating in this second nature, consciousness participates in its mutability. My aim here is not to deny to ancient materialism the possibility of deducing ethics that post-critical materialism has. On the contrary, I am asserting that in post-critical materialism, the impossibility of ethical deduction is extreme and insurmountable, and so—and this is fundamental—the tension in which the relationship between psychic consciousness and metaphysical consciousness, between "I" and world, is established is just as insurmountable. On the terrain of this implacable tension, it is extremely difficult to comprehend a materialist ethics of serenity and realism. When consciousness lives in material being and participates fully in its dramatic existence, mythological and theological *intermundia* are not available. The critical problem, the metaphysical problem, and the ethical problem continually exchange testimonies to the insoluble character of the nothingness in which they participate. But—such is the extraordinary innovation that post-critical materialism constructs—out of this nothingness, in this participation and exchange of the human faculties and natural powers [*potenze*], being can be produced. The tension of consciousness and the world is insurmountable, but it is productive—productive of being. What being? Obviously a being made up of new tensions, new contradictions. Second nature knows much more than first nature did. But that is not the problem. The point that interests us is the fact that, in post-critical materialism, production necessarily becomes the form in which the metaphysical tension between consciousness and world is expressed. The critical moment, excluding dialectical solutions, establishes itself on the ontological horizon: the critical moment is constitutive and the ontology is an ontology of constitution. The world becomes richer and perhaps more unhappy.[236]

In Leopardi, the poetic principle interprets this revolution in the thought of materialism. I must not dwell further upon that circularity of metaphysical analysis, of development of the critical problem, of the rereading of history, of the vindication of the imagination already covered up to this point. Nor is it worthwhile to insist once again on the fact that Leopardi's materialism has all the characteristics of what we are calling a post-critical and at the same time non-dialectical philosophy. On the contrary, what seems to me to require emphasizing, once the general conditions aforementioned have been taken into account, is the constitutive specificity of Leopardi's poetry. This is explicitly proclaimed in the famous letter to Melchiorri of 5 March 1824:

> Dear Peppino. You were not wrong to make a promise on my behalf, because you weren't to know that I wasn't like all the other people who write poetry. But I want you to know that in this and every other respect

I'm quite unlike and very inferior to everybody else. And as far as poetry is concerned, it will be useful for you from now on to understand my nature should a similar occasion ever arise. In my life I've written only a very small number of short poems. In writing them I've never followed anything but an inspiration (or frenzy); when it came on me, in two minutes I formed the outline and plan of the whole composition. When that is done, it is always my habit to wait for another moment to come, and when it does come (which normally happens only a few months later), then I set about composing, but so slowly, that it is not possible for me to finish a poem, even a very short one, in less than two or three weeks. This is my method, and if inspiration does not come of its own accord, it would be easier for water to come from a tree trunk than a single line from my brain. Other people can write poetry whenever they want, but I absolutely do not have this ability, and no matter how much you asked it would be to no avail, not because I did not want to oblige you, but because I could not. I have been asked many other times, and I've found myself in situations similar to this, but I've never written half a line on request, no matter who the person or what the circumstances. Prevail on Mr. Carnevalini to accept these excuses of mine, thanking him for the opinion he reveals of my poetic ability (as false as it is kind), and assuring him that along with all good men I weep from the heart for the death of his worthy brother: I think him very deserving of honor and of tears, and I am delighted that steps are being taken to celebrate and perpetuate his memory. My verses would have rather the opposite effect, but however he in his kindness chooses to judge the matter, it is certain that asking a difficult and unproductive nature like mine for a poem is the same as asking me for a bishopric: the latter I cannot give, and the former I cannot write except by chance.[237]

An inspiration or a frenzy born of chance and articulated through labor. The relations are anything but linear: inspiration and labor, frenzy and chance. But they are constitutive: what this poetry demands is a materialist *surplus*. Discontinuity and constitution are equally true, equally irreducible. Poetry is neither serenity nor the control of the passions, neither an ascetic technique nor a mystical flight: it is the reviving of the contradiction of being by proposing it in its entirety once again, but enriched with other elements. A Dionysiac function? Of course, but liberated by labor from every acritical imbalance. An Apollinian function? Of course, but charged with the tension of the world. Labor saves us from Dionysus, chance preserves us from Apollo—inspiration is the frenzy of a contradictory being. "From Homer onward everything got better, except poetry."[238]

Poetry is the making of being: it is at once the revelation of its discontinuity and the highest moment of its continuous revolutionizing. It comprehends thought and interprets the moment of innovation in thought's march between structure and history, between nature and world. Poetry is imagination that interprets, breaks up, and constitutes the series of being. The point that should be kept in mind is not so much the constitutive signification of this poetic function as it is the materialist dimension of the constitution. Poetic value, its emergence, its irreducibility to other values, is a material novelty of the universe. In its specific characterization, its ontological insistence is equivalent to that of any other object whatsoever that is fashioned, produced *ex novo* by human activity. But in conjunction with this determinate materiality, poetics reaches the limit of the world, metaphysical knowledge [*conoscenza*].[239] Its word is that of the knowledge [*conoscenza*] of the limit of existence and of the continual struggle in which the powers [*potenza*s] of the universe intermingle their existences. The materiality produced by humankind accumulates in being and constantly offers us the measure of constructiveness. In this post-critical philosophy, the tension of mind and matter has been rendered insoluble to the same extent that the mind participates in matter. We are thus traversing the edge of being. Poetry tells us that everything that moves on this limit, as on the edge of destruction, in the absolute randomness of essence, can be made new. The highest paradox of materialist consciousness is the poetic paradox: making in nothingness, giving birth to being from nothingness, in the magic of a creation of objects that contains within itself one single law—the law of constitution and the new, of the only truth that we can speak, in the only mode in which we can speak it.[240]

Let us put ourselves back into Leopardi's situation, at the leading edge [*limite basso*] of the great poetic phase of 1828 to1830. It is in the world of the *Denken* that the conditions for this highest of *Dichten* are constructed.[241] The *Zibaldone* and the *Operette* bear witness to it. The lived experience and wanderings of those years are not particularly inspiring for poetry, and if they are, this is in a dialectical and paradoxical sense. Leopardi indeed participates in a totally common human comedy—looking for work, along with the changes of residence that are connected to it; falling in love and disillusion; friendships, social relations, and some good literary relations. To these must be added the difficult, always unresolved but nevertheless affectionate link with the family and the poor condition of his body. But what turns out to be determinant in Leopardi's transition from a situation of slackening and poetic impotence to this highest period of lyrical production is not so much the social relation experienced by the poet as it is the alternative relationship that thought and the theoretical project establish with the

social. Initially, this relationship is utterly negative, asphyxiating for the will
to poetic rupture and for the ability to understand the metaphysical tension
of the situation—attention is subjugated to the insignificance of the world
and thus inclined to proclaim the impossibility of a poetic writing [*poetare*]
that accepts this privation, this predominance [*prepotenza*] of the interdic-
tions of an inert world. But it is precisely here that refusal explodes, and it
is out of this refusal of the social that the great poetic experience of 1828
to 1830 is born. The refusal is anticipated by the *Denken* and experienced,
with the normal ambiguity in which survival consists, throughout all the
years of wandering—but in the meantime the poetic return unconsciously
accumulates, takes shape, prepares itself. The effect of the social, of the
return to a broad civil relationship by the "hermit of the Apennines,"[242]
is thus paradoxical: social life becomes merely a negative stimulant to the
writing of poetry [*poetare*], and the *Denken* accepts the social into itself
only in order to evaluate it as illusion and nothingness. Leopardi succeeds
in producing a lofty new poetic cycle as a result of the refusal, a refusal that
is in no way anarchic, petty, or momentary; we have already emphasized
its metaphysical importance. I realize how difficult it is to explain all this.
I will try again.

Leopardi's insertion into the world brings him into contact with a wretchedness that repulses him. For a long time he is imprisoned by it, so to
speak, or at very least tangled up in it: the metaphysical point of view does
not manage to confront the real. It is only when the refusal of the world's
wretchedness and banality, the refusal of the arrogance of that appalling
circulation of things that forms the everyday horizon is asserted that the
imagination can tear itself away from habituation and set itself back in
motion according to the rhythm of metaphysical thought. It is not society
that produces Leopardi's poetry; it is Leopardi who, refusing that society
from the highest viewpoint of poetic contrariness [*eversione*], is moved to
constitute a different, other reality.

The poetic epistle of 1826, *To Count Carlo Pepoli*,[243] is absolutely characteristic of this phase. A canto chronologically isolated from the rest of the
oeuvre, it is commonly undervalued when it is not disdainfully rejected as
reactionary.[244] But it is precisely its chronological isolation in relation to the
other canti that makes it especially significant: because chronological isolation certainly does not mean thematic isolation or the rupture of Leopardi's
thought process. Indeed, the poetic epistle allows us to grasp the mediating
term of that relationship between *Denken* and *Dichten*, and between metaphysical vocation and experience of the world that we discussed earlier, and
to confirm its quality. An unbelievably harsh phenomenology of the time of
life and a repugnance for the time of life and its organization: such is the

backdrop of this canto. The critique is conceptual, moving and developing in the sphere of the abstract without, for all that, losing its concrete, courageous cynicism. Just one example: the conception of labor. It passes through diverse but articulated episodes: a denunciation of "incessant" labor—that is, the vital insignificance of the labor of proletarians (ll.12–37); a denunciation of the "sensory" idleness of the rich—that is, the uselessness of filling life with sense (ll.37–53); a declaration of the idle uselessness of life and labor in general:

> All human life,
> Whatever state we live it in, is idle,
> If all of that exertion which pursues
> No worthy end, or cannot realize
> Ever its true intent, is rightly called
> An idle thing. (*To Count Carlo Pepoli*, ll.7–12)[245]

We are far from the exaltation of the Roman artisans' labor in the street that led to Tasso's tomb! Here the workers belong to "the countless race of animals,"[246] certainly not because an aristocratic contempt of proletarians animates Leopardi's words or has settled into his spirit, but because along with a still greater disdain for the idleness of the aristocracy, a new level of social phenomenology is recorded: no longer nature against reason, passion against dispassion, as in the time of the trip to Rome and the visit to Tasso's tomb, but instead the affirmation of a new, insolent, and total unreality of the world, which can be broken up only in an advance with an eye toward moments of total poetic reconstruction. In this phenomenological passage there is a feeling of the complete blockage [*scacco*] of the concepts of social practice, of the sense of history, of the reform of morals. The whole society is a spectacle of idle insignificance, subtle malady, and certain death: a phenomenology of death implacably looms. It is impossible to flee.

> Another, turning to escape the wretched
> Fate of mankind, and spending all his age
> In change of land and weather, seas and hills,
> Runs over the whole globe, and to the limits
> Of space that nature opens up to man
> In all the endless fields of man's endeavor
> His journeys take him. High upon the prow,
> However, sits black care, and so whatever
> The weather or his fate, happiness
> Is called upon in vain, and sadness rules. (ll.78–87)[247]

The feeling of the blockage of social practice must now be shifted to the
level of poetic practice and find an innovative expression adequate to the
intensity of the blockage, to its potential—Leopardi's thought proceeds in
this direction. Nevertheless, here we can grasp only the necessity of this
passage in terms of unease, the drying up of inspiration and nostalgia.
The world having been reduced to indifference, the writing of poetry
[*poetare*] must accompany this reality uneasily but effectively in order
to depict what is appalling, to be true to the world. Writing poetry here
is a cold impulse that is perfectly adapted to the material. The dryness
of the poetic writing [*poetare*] reflects the dryness of the material: the
relationship is oratorical; the poem must reproduce the real. Given these
conditions of unease and blockage, who can still insist that this canto
does not represent an important contribution to the construction of the
poetic horizon for the cycle of 1828 to 1830? A whole series of elements
that have become stereotypical—"sweet deceptions," "delightful images,"
"serene and solitary smile," "the silent moon," "bitter truth," "obscure
fate," "this strange universe"—are used up, so to speak. If they are to be
taken up again, it will be in a different framework that totally modifies
their consistency and their relations. Now the problem is to discover a new
poetic form that knows how to adapt itself to the advance rupture of the
order of the real that is truly and effectively constitutive. Up to this point,
we can conclude, with the coldest irony:

> In questions of this kind I shall consume
> My idle days; for truth, once known, though sad,
> Has its delights. (ll.150–52)[248]

To think, to seek the true, to persist . . .

The continuity of this period is of a metaphysical order. Great poetry
arises from the accomplishment of the philosophical investigation. The
poetic series takes shape as a product of thought. But poetry has an advantage: it transforms the world. As soon as thought joins poetic practice, it
is again constrained to confront the true, a new true. Poetry changes the
definition of the true. It is in Pisa, at the beginning of 1828, that Leopardi
apparently begins to extricate himself from the unease brought on by the
contrast between the conception of the true as second nature and the difficulty, the impotence in speaking it. But already, two years earlier, shortly
after the composition of the epistle *To Count Carlo Pepoli* (if we accept the
biographical notes concerning this period, which seem to me to have little
value), in a letter addressed from Bologna to his brother Carlo, Leopardi
writes of a woman whose friendship

disillusioned me with disillusion, . . . convinced me that there really are pleasures in the world that I had thought impossible, and that I am still capable of lasting illusions, in spite of my longstanding conviction to the contrary; and it has revived my heart, which has been asleep (or rather completely dead) for so many years.[249]

But it is in Pisa too that Leopardi notes in the *Zibaldone*:

The absence of any hope, after my first entry into the world, gradually extinguished almost every desire within me. Now, through changed circumstances, with hope revived, I find myself in the strange situation of having much more hope than desire, and more hopes than desires, etc.[250]

Again, here is a biographical note to be read according to the track and texture of Leopardi's thought and its development. This hope is the attainment of the positive limit of metaphysical thought, where the will to make and to construct develops from the strength of the tensions. The Pisan *Jeu d'esprit*[251] of 1828 reveals this tension, this supreme moment of expression of a poetic will that nevertheless constructs. The "file" of poetic making is missing, Leopardi jokingly suggests at the last of his frequent meetings with truth: "The file is now worn smooth,"[252] the muse replies. The poet insists, recalcitrant: "And I responded: But/Should it not be repaired, if it is worn?" (ll.16–17).[253] "She said: It should be, yes: we have no time" (l.18).[254] Here we are, therefore, no longer amidst the banality of equivocations, the biographical declarations that are always ambivalent, but plunged into the rhythm of what is already great poetry, at the initial revealing of a new poetic cycle, faced with the tension generated between hope and "no time," between metaphysical maturation and its imprecise and laborious opening onto the future. The lightness of this poetic experiment does not deceive us. Also, since the passage has not been overburdened with significant allusions, we can certainly recognize that the many themes coldly and conceptually expressed in the epistle *To Count Pepoli* ripen here in a few words. The file of an adequate general culture and a universally developed poetic school is lacking. From this follows the necessity of rupture, a necessity determined by the development of metaphysical thought. The conceptual hammering of the epistle to Pepoli is revealed here to be a strategic operation, a massive pressure before the breakthrough. It is only by poetically surveying the impossible horizon of true being that true being can be constructed, grasped, and maintained. Modern poetry, new metaphysics. The old tools no longer serve. The file is worn smooth, but there is no time. For Leopardi time and hope are, in this theoretical phase and in the very cautious realism (bordering on pessimism) of its definitions, almost synonyms. In another, perhaps more literal and more habitual context, the assertion "there is no time" could signify "there is no hope." Here, on the contrary, the longing expressed by this "no time" is a declaration of the "presence of hope"— a nervous presence, a malaise that is explicit yet open to poetic labor. It is a longing that nothing justifies from a biographical point of view, that metaphysics alone governs, while imposing poetics as an attempt to resolve the problematic of the unease, as the constitutive tension of new being: the return of craft labor [*lavoro d'officina*] at the very heart of true being.

Although we have scarcely begun to address the leading edge of the great poetic cycle of 1828 to1830, it is difficult to propose a general characterization. Nevertheless, I cannot avoid suspicion with regard to the interpretations that suggest a kind of internal logic linking the canti of this period.[255] Not because these canti cannot be regrouped or do not present remarkable analogies from a stylistic and above all a conceptual point of view, but because in these canti Leopardi's poetics becomes a practice of being, grasps particular senses and the general sense of being in order to transform them. The analogies are subordinate to the innovation; and what is interesting is how Leopardi progressively experiences this deepening toward true being and the sense of its apprehension. This is a path that, to the extent that Leopardi develops a properly metaphysical point of view, is internal to being and could be said to be dominated by being. The important thing in the study of these canti is thus not the search for summary formulas but rather the readiness to follow a project that adapts and becomes, in accordance with the rhythms of a metaphysical injunction to which Leopardi surrenders, a readiness to follow his slow repossession of this dimension, this poetic "ether" of being.

In the form of this surrender, a surrender to the flux of being presented as the flux of remembrance, the construction of a self-consciousness of the rhythm of being is set in motion in *The Revival* [*Il Risorgimento*]:[256] the whole negative dialectic of pleasure and desire is thus re-traversed and its results redefined—the "serene" impotence of the subject and the hegemony of a "gloomy century." How foreign serenity is to the tension and positivity of writing poetry [*poetare*] appears here with definitive force—serenity is the figure of the death of the century and the extinction of virtue, the surface of the surrender to the insensate beat of the particles of life, to vegetative life.

Who is this who arouses
Me from my long dull quiet?
What is this novel vigor?
This which I feel inside?

Images, sweet commotion,
Throbbings, time-honored error—
Is not my heart for ever
To such as you denied? (*Revival*, ll.81–88)[257]

The revival itself appears as an inversion of the sign of being. The heart suddenly emerges from the necessity of death: the question "who?" enacts this inversion of tendencies, this reopening of the tension opposed to serenity. Nevertheless it remains unanswered. The poet relies on a phenomenology of being in which the discovery of revival through remembrance is equally the objective of the most explicit experimenting with death.

I lay insensate, bewildered,
Not even seeking solace;
Dead almost, and forsaken,
My heart sank in despair.
How changed I was! (ll.37–41)[258]

The revival is a surrender to being and consequently to "sweet deceptions" (l.110), to the real world of illusion.

And yet I feel reviving
The obvious deceptions;
My breast is full of wonder
At motions of its own. (ll.145–48)[259]

Why this change, this transformation of the sign of illusion? Why this beautiful wonder? There is no answer. Just as it was constructed in Leopardi's thought, here it is only sensed [*presentita*] and not expressed.

The gentle noble spirit
Receives, I know, no comfort:
Fate, beauty, world, and nature—
All give it up for lost.
But if, poor heart, you live, and
Fate has not won you over,
I will not call her ruthless
Who gave me breath at first. (ll.153–60)[260]

In the form of surrender, the relationship to being reveals an abrupt interval between thinking and writing poetry: here hope is only a simple presentiment, whereas for philosophy it is already an action. But this poetic presentiment runs through being and transforms it in a way that philosophy cannot. The poetic miracle is at work and modifies the very concept of philosophy by making (contrary to secular tradition) logic the abstract science of the "must be," a lunar reality, where poetry is the concreteness—as imperfect and indefinite as you wish, but real—of being. Here, then, the poetic tradition of the philosophical project thus produces a first surprising effect: slipping being into presentiment constitutes a physical, immediate terrain of thought.

To Silvia[261] is evidence of this new passage of the physicality and immediacy of thought as it is filtered through feeling, in the construction of the real. As we said, each canto is now a concrete passage, a new stitch in a fabric, a new gear of a poetic machine that is not preordained but consequent; and each one reorganizes a stratum of being—often the same one that an identical poetic process had just constructed, always bearing in mind the complexity of the components.[262] Nevertheless, in To Silvia this method undergoes a swerve, perhaps a negative one. A repetitive concession to remembrance? No, that is not it. In fact, a gross physicality suffuses these lines, in which the stylistic and poetic theme laid out in The Revival is taken up again and developed.

> Do you remember still,
> Silvia, that moment in your mortal days
> When you, so beautiful,
> With your bright eyes still bent upon the ground,
> Had hardly thought of really going through
> That door with youth beyond? (To Silvia, ll.1–6)[263]

But the absorption of the amorous and lyrical theme into the solemn rhythm of remembrance and its rational control deprives the poet of the necessary freedom. Reason exercises its control over and against physicality, which fails to yield. There is no alternative: nature, time, and feeling are pacified, perhaps under the effect of memory and certainly under the influence of reason—and death and pain are incorporated into a kind of rational compassion. "The moment truth appeared/You shrank away, poor wretch" (ll.60–61).[264] In short, To Silvia follows the suggestion of The Revival—making the reconstruction of the poetic true pass through the filter of feeling: beneath its apparent lightness, the poetry is highly conceptual—but the path is interrupted, so to speak, by an imbalance, by a slip that is at once pathetic and rational. The concept becomes physical, but it does not become metaphysical; it becomes sentimental, but it does not develop the presentiment of a new web of being. Leopardi—having left Pisa and its climate of provincial Romanticism that nevertheless so attracted him[265]— returns again to Recanati and to that "melancholy that by now is not far short of madness,"[266] and there he considerably deepens the problem.

The Solitary Thrush[267] is a robust correction of poetic orientation. Above all it has a dry style from which any concession to Pisan softness is eliminated. The metaphysical tension rends the veils of pathos and appears in its materiality. This canto is in no way consolatory: it is the first realist canto. This realism in the descriptions of nature and peasant life and above all in the depiction of psychological states determines its structure. The tensions that constitute being begin to be grasped as such and are dramatically represented. The sequence is perfect: the vicissitudes of the solitary thrush, perceived through the contrast between the luminous backdrop of the valley and its thoughtful separation; the poet's solitude as analogy.

> When, lonely little bird, you reach the evening
> Of that brief day of life the stars allot you,
> Then you will not regret
> Your way of life; since each least desire
> Of yours is natural.
> But I, should my prayers fail,
> And I must cross the threshold
> Of horrible old age,
> When eyes no longer speak to other eyes,
> When all the world is empty, and the future
> More tedious than the present day, more black,
> How shall I see my desire?
> How shall I see these years? And how they're spent?
> I know I shall repent,
> And often, uncomforted, I shall look back. (ll.45–59)[268]

This conclusion bears witness neither to an assured grip on the possibility of being nor to the imminence of a metaphysical manifestation. But the pallid physicality of *To Silvia* is invigorated and consolidated in an objective imagination. Let us strip the bark from this poetic tree piece by piece! Leopardi keeps trying. Here he achieves, within and through levels of always-irresistible poetic force, a first real density of metaphysical imagery, of the tension between nature and the "I." Of course this realism, the stylistic adjustment comes out cold: the synthesis of remembrance, topical description, and reflection freezes in the pursuit of the density of the image. The solution proposed here for the representation of the tension of being seems to be merely cognitive: the last lines and in particular, "And often, uncomforted, I shall look back" seem almost to send us back into the abstract garden of the poetic epistle to Pepoli. But that is not the case. To the limits, weighty and obvious, of the canto's metaphysical expression corresponds a maturation of the forms of penetration of being. Consolidation of the physicality of the image, accomplished conceptualization, dramatic structure: these elements are extremely important on the stylistic terrain—above all when the style is merely the pulsation of a being that is constructing the figure of its own creation, the practical function of the metaphysical true.

Remembrances[269] again marks a new passage. The pulsation of being begins to become breath—an enlargement and intensification of the progress toward being, which we are following here. The descriptions are enormously rich in these remembrances; the seasons pass, and as with the seasons of nature, so with those of life. The physical imaginary is deepened to the utmost degree. Of course, the disproportion and contradiction between the abstract materialist imaginary at the beginning of the canto ("Beautiful stars of the Bear . . .") and the physical imaginary of the concluding stanzas ("O Nerina . . .") are very strong. The intervening parts that must mediate this expressive passage toward the concretization of the imaginary, from the abstract to the concrete, are constantly folded into an impotent and repetitive reflection on the fleetingness of life. Nevertheless, these limits are not enough to determine a negative course in the canto. There is a crescendo in the discontinuous appearance of being that these canti, taken together and individually, construct and offer to view. Here the metaphysics of being is now completely taken up into that of the imaginary. The negative dialectic of desire and its implacable development are also interrupted by the power [*potenza*] of the imaginary.

> But, whenever
> I think again of you, my ancient hopes,
> And that dear first imagining of mine;
> And then regard this way of living, pointless
> And so distressed, and see that it is death
> Which still remains to me of such great hope;
> I feel my heart contract, and feel that never
> Could I resign me to my destiny. (*Remembrances*, ll.87–94)[270]

The power [*potenza*] of the imago rises again. It no longer emanates from the metaphysical will of the author, but is taken up by a productive mechanism, by an expressive structure with which Leopardi collaborates, laboriously or happily. From *The Revival*, in which the poet surrenders to being, to *To Silvia* and *The Solitary Thrush*, in which being seeks a physical expression in the drama of the world, to *Remembrances*, in which the quest for physicality is now applied to the metaphysical dimensions and in which poetry begins to allude to an ontological argument of the demonstration of being: this first passage of the 1828 to 1830 poetic cycle proves its extraordinary internal vitality, each of these canti expanding upon another; and all are increasingly mature aspects of a fundamental project of exposition, a *Darstellung* of constitutive being.[271]

A short parenthesis before attacking the reading of the last canti of this period, which also mark the end of a whole poetic and metaphysical phase. We have said that the line of speculative development determines the continuity of the poetic line, which the canti that we have just analyzed have shown. Despite an absolute formal individuality, internally they in fact express a homogeneous tension of metaphysical truth—a multiform, discontinuous, and convergent desire that grows ever stronger. However, it is not merely a logical thread but a dense poetic line directed toward the definition of metaphysical truth. In describing this poetic process, the reading emphasized the (exceptional) form of this development of thought rather than its overall dynamic. But it is now necessary to draw attention to an original and specific aspect: the path that we are following is not a philosophical path developed in a poetic form, but it is directly poetic-metaphysical; it is the specific path of a materialist metaphysics that is directly experienced and immediately practiced. Poetry is a subject.[272] Practicing a metaphysics of materialism poetically means assuming that poetry is a creative power [*potenza*]. Creative of what? Of an absolute human imaginary—absolute in the sense that it reveals the truth of our existence. Here Leopardi is a thoroughly materialist critic. He dissolves, in practice, every origin and every horizon of the imaginary because he wills it as thing, as presence, as reality. Life can be grasped only in accordance with the rhythm of the imaginary—in its truth, only in accordance with the rhythm of the production of true illusions. Poetry is an activity of direct metaphysical excavation or expression.[273] These canti undertake a great materialization of the image of life, which is completed in sublime forms in the next and last canti of this cycle. This materialization becomes possible at the very moment when all the false illusions disappear. The content of a poetic metaphysics of the imaginary is the destruction of every origin, every separate dynamic, every hypostasis of the imaginary—every origin that is not the web of the concrete desires of humankind, every genesis that is not a historical genealogy.

One last remark: between these categories—metaphysics and destruction, abstract and concrete—the understanding of the creative effects that properly constitute poetics and its always prodigious simplicity runs the risk of being dispersed. But this separation, between our technically correct language from the viewpoint of materialist philosophy and Leopardi's poetic power [*potenza*], represents the superiority of poetic making to philosophy. Is it merely a matter of the superiority of poetic making? I have the impression that Marx's gloss of Feuerbach (it is time to know the world by transforming it, and only the transformation determines the knowledge [*conoscenza*]) contains a metaphysical reflection to which the power [*potenza*] of Leopardi's poetic making alludes. And not only does it allude to this reflection, but also extends its range. For Leopardi, by developing the phenomenology of materialism, at the very least establishes the definition of one term of the paradox of absolute contingency. He manages to assert, or rather to produce, an image of the world as the product of destruction, as arising from nothingness, immersed in complete irrationality. Theory stops here. Then all it has to do is adhere to the syllogism of true practice, to the paradoxical declaration that wherever everything can be destroyed, everything can be constructed—the apology for a free and constitutive rationality. Leopardi's poetics, at its metaphysical apex, not only alludes to the assertion that once philosophy has accomplished its duty of interpreting the world, the world will now change: it also tells us that it is an infinite reserve of possibilities and that destruction or creation depend upon poetry, upon the imagination, upon *poïesis*, upon the ethical drive of all knowledge [*conoscenza*], upon making; in nothingness.[274]

Two canti, *The Calm After the Storm*[275] and *The Village Saturday*,[276] show us this metaphysical and poetic tension fully developed. The typical image of the village characteristic of landscape painting that opens both poems is only a means to plunge the gaze into grand nature and the wide horizon of history and to establish at the conclusion of both, by means of invective, a metaphysical contrast. This element of landscape is not without interest: naturalistic in the first canto, it becomes historical-sociological in the second; the two canti are complementary. The landscape painting is initially light.

> The storm has passed away:
> I hear birds singing out in joy, the hen,
> Now back upon the road,
> Reiterate her cry. (*Calm*, ll.1–4)[277]

> The country girl is coming from the fields
> Before the sun has set.

Her head is balancing trussed hay, her hand
A bunch of blooms, the rose the violet. (*Village*, ll.1–4[278])

Then it gradually becomes deeper, and seeks to give rise to poetic effects within the descriptions or to make itself the means by which grand nature reveals itself.

Men shuddered in their dread,
Sweating, cold, mute, and pale, seeing en masse
Such powerful enemies:
Lightning, low cloud, and wind. (*Calm*, ll.38–41)[279]

This day of seven is best of all,
So full of hope and joy:
The hours will bring ennui
Tomorrow, and sadness, making everyone
Return in thought to his accustomed toil. (*Village*, ll.38–42)[280]

There is something extremely interesting here: the landscape fulfills the theoretical function of the schema of reason; it is a hypothesis through which the metaphysical backdrop is constructed, what the logicians sometimes call the "third term" in the relationship between concrete and abstract.[281] But all this happens on the poetic terrain and in particular on a poetic terrain that is, in itself, a metaphysical hypothesis. In other words, this extraordinary poetic schematism does not lead the imagination toward unity, does not leave it at rest, but instead leads it to the maximum of metaphysical tension, to definitive rupture. The schema of reason extends over the edge of being, toward nothingness. At the conclusion of *The Calm After the Storm*, the discovery of nature, of being, becomes invective.

O courteous nature, there
Are the gifts you give to us,
These are the true delights
You offer mortals. To be loosed from trouble
We think is happiness.
You scatter troubles with free hand, and sorrow
Comes of its own accord; while as for pleasure,
Whatever by some miracle sometimes
Comes born of pain, is profit. Humankind,
The darling of the gods! And happy, yes,
To have a breathing space,

Some sorrow gone: but blessed
When death, all sorrows done, remakes you sound. (ll.42–54)[282]

The metaphysical sarcasm clashes with the physical powers [*potenze*]. Here the
most profound motifs of the *Operette* resonate. The conclusion of *The Village
Saturday*, although gentler, is no less significant on the metaphysical plane.

Playful boy, full of zest,
Know all that flowering time
Of yours is like the splendor of a day,
That clear, unclouded day
Which tends to come before life's festal prime,
Enjoy it, little boy: a happy state
Is yours, a pleasant lull.
I say no more; but if your festival
Delays, that is no reason to regret. (ll.43–51)[283]

Here, in a historical-psychological fabric, the invective becomes an ironic
challenge to future time, or rather the revelation of the metaphysical contrast
at the temporal level. In these pages, in both these canti, the psychological
tonalities are diluted—the drama is situated at the metaphysical level and
completely organized according to conceptual categories—but this maturation in no way eliminates; on the contrary, it accentuates the sensory,
physical moments of the image and the poetic writing [*poetare*]. All the
threads and problems raised at the beginning of the poetic cycle thus succeed
in condensing. This condensation certainly remains fragile, the unfolding
of thought into poetry is still marked by some conceptual lapses, and it is
still psychologically motivated.

Pleasure is born from pain,
Hollow pleasure, the fruit
Of terror overblown but now, his terror
That he might soon be dead
Who'd hated life before. (*Calm*, ll.32–36)[284]

But as we said, this fragility does not prevent the maturation of the metaphysical framework from taking place with an irresistible progression. The
separation, gap, or interval between thinking and writing poetry progressively closes, but within a creative progression.

  We are still seeking to understand this mystery that is materialist poetics,
constructed in making, defined in the extreme tension of a reality that is

denied as origin and presented as creative surface. But the progression of
elements, which we have seen taking place, from the problematic unease
of the epistle *To Count Pepoli* to this last series, by means of an effort that
consists above all in determining a high physical synthesis of the elements
of abstract rationality, holds little mystery. It is only the revelation of the
polarity of being and poetic subjectivity in a relationship that denies all
pre-existing reality and restores being to us as revolution, radical transformation. The materialist beautiful is constructed on the passage from
metaphysical consciousness to ethical consciousness. And this ethical consciousness has no need of consolations, no need of Platonic ideas or religious
enthusiasms in order to be beautiful. It finds its origin in the nothingness
of existence and the infinity of creation: it is the outcome of this pair, so
extreme as to be logically without signification—but aesthetically beautiful
and ethically traversable. We must not uncover the mystery but experience
it. Leopardi's poetry progresses toward nothingness, toward the infinity of
a transformative practice of being that is the most complete of freedoms.
There is nothing mysterious here—it is merely a true and materialist interpretation of life.

> The wind
> Has plucked me from the beech where I was born.
> It rises once more, and bears me
> In the air from the wood to the fields,
> And from the valley up into the hills.
> I am a wanderer
> For ever: that is all that I can say.
> I go where everything goes,
> I go where by nature's law
> Wanders the leaf of the rose,
> Wanders the leaf of the bay. (*Imitation*, ll.3–13)[285]

The progressiveness of Leopardi's poetry is a metaphysical wind that blows
toward an unknown destiny: the only manifestation of knowledge [*conoscenza*] and the only unveiling is the movement of leaves. To regard it and
to recognize freedom in it is the aesthetic foundation of materialist ethics:
an aesthetics of imitation and an ethics of creation, in being.[286]

Thus we are introduced to the reading of *Night Song of a Wandering
Shepherd of Asia*,[287] one of Leopardi's and modern European poetry's
supreme masterpieces—and the conclusion of the metaphysical argument
of this lyrical cycle. The climate, the atmosphere, the space are immediately
cosmic in dimension. "'Several of them' (of the Khirkiz), says Monsieur

de Meyendorff, 'pass the night sitting on a stone and looking at the moon, and improvising quite sad words to tunes that are no less so.'"[288] The full physicality of the imaginary so sought after by Leopardi is completely realized here. But the immensity, the space through which the shepherd makes his way and in which the moonbeam, the sky, the desert, and the valleys are lost arouses astonishment, wonder, amazement that turns into doubt—the questions are posed not by the subject but by the real itself, by the indifference of subjects in this immense space. The identity of destiny is the identity of the question.

> Tell me, O moon, the use
> Of the shepherd's life to him,
> Of your lives there to you. What is the goal
> Of my brief wandering,
> Of your immortal course? (*Night Song*, ll.16–20)[289]

The great images—the shepherd and his flock—the parable of the "old man, white, infirm" (ll.21–38), and the well-known questioning of the misery of birth and death (ll.39–60) are suffused with a dense physicality that renders any internal articulation impossible: an implacable rhythm poetically documents the intensification of the metaphysical questioning, a questioning that is increasingly difficult to discern. This path through the heavens is a deepening of the search within consciousness itself. Our little shepherd is a great Copernicus. I mean that from the moment when, in the fourth stanza (ll.61–104),[290] the shepherd directly questions the moon, it becomes impossible to distinguish the subject from his interlocutors: the shepherd is the flock, faced with the moon; the moon is the flock, faced with the shepherd. The contrast is no longer between subjects, but between a traditional knowledge [*conoscenza*] that tells us nothing and a sovereign non-knowledge [*non conoscenza*] that constructs the metaphysical question. This great indifference is material, concrete. It deepens further in the fifth stanza of the canto (ll.105–32): the continual repetition of doubt creates an intolerable, psychologically unsustainable tension, a vertigo at the heart of habituation. But through all this, a critical function arises, which is just as pressing and which is abstracted from the indifference of the flock, the moon, nature, and the shepherd. This abstraction is the transcendence of reason faced with nothingness.

> What are these torches for?
> This infinite air, and that profound
> Infinite clear sky? Whatever is the meaning
> Of this great solitude? And what am I? (ll.86–89)[291]

It is a transcendence that can now arm itself with arrogance and sarcasm in the face of nature itself: "But you, for certain,/Young and immortal, know it all" (ll.98–99).[292] It is a transcendence in the face not only of nature but of the totality of the indifference in which we are embedded. This transcendence is that of a reiterated demand for the true, a practice that continues to seek truth, perhaps to rediscover it? In any case, to ceaselessly proclaim, from within the practice of life, its own dignity through the question.

In the final stanza of the canto (ll.133–143), three "perhaps" appear in the space of eleven lines.

> Perhaps if I had wings
> To fly up in the clouds,
> And number all the stars there one by one,
> Or stray, as thunder strays, from peak to peak,
> I would be happier than I am, my flock,
> I would be happier than I am, white moon.
> Or perhaps these thoughts are at fault,
> Failing to understand an alien fate?
> Whether in lair or cradle,
> Perhaps it always is upon
> A day of great ill-omen we are born.[293]

It is this "perhaps," so Latin in the different valences it contains, that revives hope. You say to me: that is not much. But at this level of metaphysical intelligence, it is a huge thing. Thus, to his German translator Bothe, who objected that the last seven lines of the canzone could seem tautological, Leopardi responded that it was not so:[294] "perhaps" hope is born of nothingness. And it is precisely this that interests us: this rousing of a universe conceived in its absoluteness, its total nullity, this possibility of desire and hope, this posing of the metaphysical question on the basis of the nothingness of the world, and thus the nothingness of logical determinations—in other words, solely on the basis of the possibility that it be posed, on its irresistible and "other" power [potenza]. Could we say of this world that it is "other"? Certainly, because it can be acted otherwise. The fact that the nothingness of the determinations of the world has been understood means that a particular act of mind is developed: an act whose determinations of content are null, therefore a grasping of nothingness, a true act of creation from nothingness. That is true being: where no sense is given, every sense is taken, is seized. Leopardi's materialism fully reveals the nature of its post-critical conception of the world in the moment when, reaching the edge of nothingness and therefore denying every origin, it fully rediscovers the sense of being, ethical being. This is an absolute materialism of true illusion, because it is without any illusions. The discourse that develops here is not a subjective one—instead, within this lack of horizon, the subject too can be grasped, just like nothingness and being. They are constructed on this edge of nothingness.

And there is one final aspect that must be kept in mind. With this operation, Leopardi definitively breaks the indifferent web of sense. He imposes on it, against it, a polarity of value—a difference. Poetry is not deployed in the face of nothingness: it is within nothingness; but by that very fact it is affirmed as difference, spoken as affirmation. The anti-dialectical development of Leopardi's thought is complete: it passes through the nihilist overthrow of indifference and affirms itself as an alternative in nothingness. This grasping of nothingness is the radical affirmation of being. Indeed, this materialism is the only possible metaphysics.

Chapter 4

Dialects of Illusion

Irony; or Concerning the Psyche

How does one once again grasp the determination of existence, after having so deepened the analysis of being and having established its primary horizon—its originary nothingness—within an insoluble metaphysical tension? Materialism, this post-critical materialism, must now reconstruct the routes and expressions of the life of being, elaborate phenomenological scenarios within which to determine the passions, and discriminate true illusions from false ones. This is the difficult path that Leopardi travels in experimental terms. It is not that the problem is confused, but that the modes of solution are difficult, and going astray is inevitable on the tortuous terrain of the illusions of the psyche. Indeed, Leopardi's rejection of psychologism, definitively established in the high poetic phase of 1828 to 1830, in no way denies the central importance of a phenomenology of the psyche; and it is a matter now, from this consolidated metaphysical viewpoint, of accounting for it.[1] How? By persevering in the critique and dissolution of the descriptive categories of transcendental thought and seeking to define a corporeal foundation for the illusions of the psyche. Materialism moves in the grand dimension of illusion, determining, articulating, founding the discriminating elements of the real upon corporeal referents. We have seen to what extent Leopardi's poetry was gradually able to become physical, concrete. Here the theoretical problem of the discrimination of true illusions from false ones pushes this engagement forward on a concrete terrain. A strong sense of corporeality, of subjects who are implicated in the passions and are producers of illusions, thus supplants, in Leopardi's imaginary, every prior function of value, whether abstract or weakly characterized. This theoretical route, which is immediately organized at the highest level of poetic production, is not linear, so the problem posed in *The Dominant Thought* does not manage to develop in continuity. Thus in other poetry from this period such as *Love and Death* and *Consalvo*, we witness a kind of swerve, a thematic nervous contraction, whereas in *To Himself* and above all in *Aspasia*, the theme leads to a conclusion; and the power [*potenza*] of bodies becomes the material horizon capable of sustaining the discrimination of true illusions and their practice.[2]

The Dominant Thought[3] is the transcription of a great adult love. It follows a poetic silence of three years and is inscribed in the theoretical horizon that we have described. The poetic physicality of this passion and the extremely solid classicism of these lines reveal first of all the maturity of the theme.

> Powerful, and most kind
> Ruler over the hidden depths of my mind;
> Awe-inspiring, but precious,
> Gift of the gods; dear friend
> Of my most dismal days,
> You, thought, returning so often to my gaze.
>
> Who does not talk about
> The mystery of your being? Who does not know
> Its power? (ll.1–9)[4]

The amorous illusion thus makes possible a corporeal image of the world. Love does not merely illuminate the vanity of the world; it pervades life and identifies its significations. The passions unfold from love, and it alone constructs a signifying web.

> All affections give place
> To that whence you were born.
> Indeed what but that one
> Affection holds dominion over us?
> Ambition, arrogance, hatred, disdain,
> Zeal for honor, to reign—
> What are they but desires
> Compared with this? Only one true affection
> Lives among us: but one
> Great lord eternal fate
> Has given to rule within the human heart.
>
> Life has no value, life can make no sense
> Without this, which to us is everything. (ll.69–81)[5]

Death is opposed to love. The eternal Empedoclean couple is represented as the horizon, and the development of the passions is undertaken in this contrast. But death has ceased to be that implacable background that we have known elsewhere in order to become an antagonistic, opposed force. Life unfolds within a contrast where love asserts itself. Love is tolerating death and counteracting it. It is hope: "to hearts which are not base—/Life seems at times more lovable than death is" (ll.86–87).[6] It is virtue.

> I find it hard to credit
> I have endured so very long without you
> This miserable existence,
> This world which makes no sense;
> And hard to understand
> How others can aspire
> To any but a similar desire.
>
> Never, from when I first
> Learned by experience what life was like,
> Has dread of death had harbor in my breast.
> It seems a joke today—
> That last necessity
> Which this vile world, which sometimes praises it,
> Abhors and trembles at.
> Should danger but approach, I pause awhile
> To contemplate its menace with a smile. (ll.37–52)[7]

The rhythm of the world is accelerated by this intuition, this passion, this intention of an ethical founding—a founding that renders the world neither indifferent nor emptily valid. On the contrary, it ceaselessly discriminates, makes strong oppositions appear there—so that the smile can instantly turn into sarcasm in recalling the lack of virtue of the abyss of death and nothingness that underpins it.

> Always I have despised
> Cowards, and all who are
> Ignoble. But now anything ill-done
> Stings me immediately;
> Now each vile human action
> Arouses me immediately to scorn.
> I feel I am above
> This arrogant age, which feeds on empty hopes,

In love with tittle-tattle, loathing virtue;
And foolish to require
That everything be useful,
Yet fail to see how things get more and more
Useless. I truly scorn
Human opinion; and I trample down
That mixed and fickle lot
Inimical to you and all fine thought. (ll.53–68)[8]

Thus the ethical program ceaselessly expands. In separation, power [*potenza*] nevertheless remains creative and the obstacles and limits that the horizon of death imposes serve only to inspire this constitutive ascesis. Love and life, love and death, then love and virtue, and now love and dream, love and truth. On an ethical basis, the world of cognitive illusions discriminates itself. Perhaps this is the central point of the canto, where the recognition of the amorous, creative illusion constructs the world of truth, or rather approximates it, circumscribes it, reorganizes it.

For you are a dream,
One to adorn the truth, for the most part;
You are, my sweetest thought,
A dream and clear illusion. But you are,
Of all the happy errors,
Divine; because you are so strong and live
That even matched with truth you can endure,
And even seem like truth,
And never vanish till the time of death. (ll.108–16)[9]

All is illusion, but ethical power [*potenza*], the amorous dream can discriminate an illusion and extract it from indifference. The world is a nothingness of signification, but a signification can be conferred upon it by ethical power [*potenza*]. The true is purely and simply the productive imagination with which we are concerned here. The true of existence (and of the nothingness that presides there) is revealed here: there is an "other" true, which we can debate—one that we have constructed on the basis of this grasping of nothingness and this combat against death. The sense of creation certainly does not escape the poet.

And what a world, what novel
Immensity, what paradise that is
To which it seems your singular enchantment

So often raises me!
Where, straying in an unfamiliar light,
I find I can forget
My earthly state and all reality!
Such are, I think, the dreams
Of the immortals. (ll.100–8)[10]

But this is not yet enough, and in the last stanzas of the canto, the delirium of poetic construction, of an imago that is real, breaks loose. The poetic act is ontological—it is first of all ethical, but only insofar as it becomes ontological. The great imago of the final lines is no longer even approximately, even in accordance with the weak rhythm of traditional literary reminiscences, the residue of emanations of Platonism and the *dolce stil novo*. It is the material, corporeal product of a productive imagination that, in a post-critical manner, plants its roots in the fundamental ontological tension, and steals and substitutes its nullifying valence in order to overturn the conditions of nothingness into conditions of creation.

The metaphysical paradox is no less important than the poetic delirium. Thus a total overturning of the metaphysical road that had led us as far as the *Night Song of a Wandering Shepherd of Asia* takes place. Whereas we were formerly led toward nothingness, toward the origin of the ontological tension, here the path turns back, and poetics breaks through the edge, the barrier of being, and liberates its constructive project. Poetry, now ethically based, rediscovers an ontological program. The images attain a maximum of physicality—their more than obvious corporeality overflows. Love triumphs.

From when I saw you first
What feeling did I have where you were not
Its object? And what minute ever passed
Without a thought of you? How often did
Your ever-ruling image
Stay absent from my dreams? Fresh as a dream,
Angelic apparition,
In earthly habitation,
Or on the pathways of the universe!
What do I ask, what do
I hope to see more lovely than your eyes,
Or hope to have more sweet than thought of you? (*The Dominant
Thought*, ll.136–47)[11]

Time and again we have confronted the problem of the productive
imagination in a materialist philosophy. Now we are faced with one of the
purest examples of its movement. However, preoccupied with its metaphysical situation and its place in the set of faculties in our confrontation with
the theme of productive imagination, we have avoided—or neglected—the
specific tonality that materialist thought attributes to it. It is now possible
for us to specify this quality. So what is it? It is constructive, as we have
seen, but above all—and this distinguishes it from the constructivism of
transcendental idealism—it is an activity that unfolds in accordance with
the rhythm of the tensions of being. Logical contrasts, metaphysical chiar-
oscuros, and passions that deepen in the movement of being articulate the
productive imagination of materialism. The overabundance of this activity's
ontological material can lead to vertigo. But perhaps it is precisely here that
another characteristic element emerges: the fact that, in materialism, the
productive imagination participates directly in the advance of knowledge
[conoscenza]. Conjoined with being, participating in its internal dynamism,
imaginative knowledge [conoscenza] is supple, rich, and poetic in principle.
It can become vertigo, yet it is always a relationship, a relation traversed and
described, an accumulation, a path that is followed.

In this case, the relationship has the principal tones of the smile, irony,
then deception or sarcasm—the wrinkles of a relationship that is within
being. No psychologistic variable, no major or minor psychic experience will occupy the foreground: in the order of the real, these would
instead be relegated to the lowest level. Leopardi's metaphysics has no
more regard for the psyche than for the Platonic tradition: with respect to
both, being comes first. But Leopardi's being is nourished by nothingness.
Consequently "relationship with being" means constructive overturning,
radical practice, and thus this relationship is ironic in the strict sense. A
divine irony, a smile that never expresses serenity but at most the languor
that results from admiring an infinitely null universe: an admiration of
nothingness that inspires the construction of being. The practice of being
unfolds and explains the psyche. Indeed, from this viewpoint and in this
phase of his poetic activity, Leopardi is not a Romantic: or rather, he is one
in a very particular way that we have already emphasized—in a contemporary European way. With a single bound he has passed through critical
philosophy, idealism, Romanticism. With a fierce poetics wielded like a
forceps, he has extracted materialism from the dialectic of the psyche and
the dialectic of Enlightenment in order to make it the element of a world
that is at once disenchanted and totally free and open to illusion. Is this
our contemporary poetic world? Indeed, by means of this link we perceive
materialism becoming the poetic form of the present, our actual language;

and we sense Spinoza combined with Nietzsche, Machiavelli and Ariosto with Rimbaud, Hölderlin with Joyce, and others combined with our materialist hope for revolution cast into the future.[12]

On the other hand we recalled that the path is not always linear. *Love and Death*,[13] the composition of which immediately follows that of *The Dominant Thought*, confirms this. Nevertheless, the non-linearity of the path, the impediments and difficulties along it do not mean that the framework will not be enriched. The dense transcription of love as a metaphysical force carried out in the preceding canto now tends to transform itself into a practical incursion into the "sea of being," into the phenomenology of the passions. This is an appropriate aspiration for the program of this period: the ethical qualification of the metaphysical project of discriminating between true illusions and false illusions.

> Love and death were delivered into light
> At the same time by fate.
> There is, in this world here,
> Nothing so fine, nor in the stars up there.
> From one all good is born,
> The greatest pleasure born
> That may be found throughout the sea of being;
> The other takes our pain
> And grief, and wipes them out. (*Love and Death*, ll.1–9)[14]

We witness a metaphysical expansion of the ethical project of the recasting [*rifondazione*] of true action.

> For where you offer aid,
> There courage, Love, is born,
> Or wakens up; and then all humankind
> Is wise in what it does; not, as so often,
> Wise only in the mind. (ll.22–26)[15]

But here the metaphysical intention undergoes an abrupt distortion and, on the web of a poetic autobiography, psychological description takes over.[16] The ontological program is suborned by an officious psychology, by an overabundance of surface, but with strange effects. In its poetic failure, this canto offers us a kind of genetic analysis of writing poetry, *Love and Death* thus constituting an act of poetic theory. Nevertheless, it conveys an enrichment of thought on the jagged path we are following. To love and death as forces inspiring poetry is added fate.

To fervid forceful minds,
Minds that are fortunate,
May one or other of you be given by fate,
Kind lords, and kinder friends
Of the human family,
Nothing at all in this immensity
Resembles, and no power can overcome,
Of all the powers there are, but fate alone. (ll.88–95)[17]

The physicality and corporeality of the poetic images in this period, the attempt to render the genesis of writing poetry cosmogonic, cannot therefore be underestimated even though these powers [*potenze*], bent to autobiography and to the fixity of psychological descriptions, do not succeed in expressing themselves with the poetic efficacy of the *Night Song of a Wandering Shepherd of Asia* and *The Dominant Thought*. The metaphysical question of lines 31 to 33 ("We sense a languorous desire to die./ Who can say how? But such/Is that effect of love which strikes us first"[18]) remains unanswered. In this climate of diffuse psychologism, materialism is tainted. The body loses its corporeality. The final passage to ethics and the invocation of death (ll.96–124) no longer proposes an alternative, for here ethics, in accordance with the rhythm of autobiography, presents itself as resistance and not as articulation of being. It is a psychologically motivated ethics and not an ontological medium. Materialism is tainted with fatigue. A few poetic breakthroughs that give shape to impressive specimens of materialist aesthetics do follow:

. . . nor in the stars up there (l.4)

. . . the sea of being (l.7)

. . . this desert (l.35)

And, presaging a storm because of that
Within his heart, he longs for peace and quiet,
He longs to come to port
Fleeing before desire
Which roars and darkens everything about.

Then, while that awesome power
Envelops everything,
And passion shines like lightning in the heart,

How very many times,
With desperate desire,
You are invoked, Death, by the troubled lover! (ll.40–50)

. . . in this immense universe (1.94)

Of all the powers [*possanza*] there are, but fate alone (1.95)[19]

But materialism nonetheless is tainted in the lengthy ambiguity of a poetry that leaves behind traces of materialist construction without consolidating them into a project. Poetry makes only glancing contact with the center of the recomposition under examination in this period, without producing a qualitative leap between psychology and ontology—that is to say, between the delirium and the metaphysical irony that color the poetic high points of this period. *Love and Death* is an ambiguous canto: it takes up the ontological program, but without managing to realize it; it presses toward the ethical recasting, but remains the prisoner of autobiography and its psychological valences. It is a transitional canto that touches on the problems but does not succeed in enclosing them within the materialist nexus of ontology. The swamp in which ethics and ontology are mired is psychologism, the determination of recollection. The only advantage for knowledge [*conoscenza*] offered by this canto, certainly an important one, is the effort that crossing the swamp implies, the difficulty that it imposes, the psychological shifts necessary to the motion of the poetic process—that is, a description of poetic making and its enormous difficulties.

But why is the terrain of the psyche so dense, so swampy? Along with the force and ontological dignity of the lyric, upon which we have often insisted, and its metaphysical power [*potenza*], we now touch upon another aspect, the fragile one of its highest vocation. Love and death first pervade the lyric and the more they pervade it, the more it touches upon the absoluteness of the function of the true. The lyric is a function of truth and constitution. These functions are collective. Yet the lyric is made by a subject: its individuality is subjected to an enormous effort of anticipation and prefiguration of being. The fragility of the schema of imagination is made manifest in this passage.

Leopardi is without equal in great modern poetry when he drives poetic making beyond the edge of being; breaking with all psychological continuity, even that which leads to the abyss and into the vortex of vertigo, he constructs new being and throws bridges over the void—the material plenitude of illusion. What terrible, intolerable, desperate fragility that path offers us! Here we are faced with a materialist, completely secular Pascal, oscillating between the finitude of human making and the power [*potenza*] of universal ethics, between individual anticipation and collective communication! But we must not lose sight of another aspect: it pertains not to producing and what is related to it, but rather to illusion. Leopardi's era and the cultural stimuli to which it is subject are dialectical. This malady of the spirit cannot be eradicated once and for all. It extends and reproduces itself in subtle ways. And every time Leopardi breaks through to a constructive path, as in this phase, the obstacle arises again, with the psyche for a medium and psychology for a backdrop. Whenever passion is sucked toward the levels of individuality and the dynamic of feelings is led back to or filtered through autobiography, the dialectical illusions reappear without fail.[20] We do not know [*capisce*] how Leopardi understands it—often we get the impression that he suffers it—but a lunge toward corporeality, toward a horizon of absolute metaphysical materiality, always ends up imposing itself. This lunge is not immediate—it is conclusive. It stretches across the concreteness of the poetic elements that construct the metaphysical framework, and it has the latter's same continuity and force. The destruction of dialectical illusions coincides with the surmounting of the sticky fabric of psychology, with the liquidation of the transcendental project that the psyche ambiguously produces. Never has a lyric poet so deepened the psychological passage to truth in order to consume it and regain the ontological fabric of truth.

Consalvo[21] is a canto that seizes, defines, and develops some of these problems and above all some of these difficulties. The fragility of psychological time and of autobiographical vicissitudes is preventatively diagnosed here. The canto opts for an epic-lyric form borrowed from Tasso as a precaution against these possible poetic weaknesses. The epic-lyric rhythm thus allows Leopardi to succeed in rooting the definition of the passions and the feeling of the proximity of death in the terrain of corporeality. The passion conveyed by the narration of Elvira's kiss given to the dying Consalvo has only rare equivalents in Leopardi's poetry.

> Bringing those heavenly features and that mouth—
> Desired so much, and for so many years
> The object of all dreaming and all sighs—
> Closer and closer to his face, so drawn
> And drained of color in his agony,
> She pressed, out of sheer kindness and from all
> Her depth of pity, kiss after kiss upon
> The trembling lips of the enraptured lover. (*Consalvo*, ll.67–74)[22]

Furthermore, the broad terms of the metaphysical tension of this period are represented here with great force and clarity: "This world has two fine things:/And they are love and death" (ll.99–100).[23] These two powers [*potenze*] pervade the canto and at no moment give ground to the facile dialectical solution: the story (for this canto tells a story) ends with the reaffirmation of the impossibility of resolving the drama of life: "before the evening came, his first/Day's happiness was fleeing out of sight" (ll.150–51).[24] That said, the poetic success of the canto remains debatable. If Leopardi avoids the intellectualism of *The Dominant Thought* and the slide into psychologism of *Love and Death*, he does not succeed in giving a conclusive direction to his sketch of the moment: articulating the determinate forms of the apparition of being. The fluidity and tranquility of the amorous dialogue and the approach of death ultimately turn out to be inadequate for the construction of the profound dimension that the phenomenological description of such an event demands. The will to situate being within life, the immensely strong and singular grasp of the two great powers [*potenze*] of being—love and death—seems to want to avoid the vigorous shadow of the tragedy of ethical being. The horizon that was proposed as an alternative solution against the dialectical process seems to vanish. *Consalvo* is an attempt that is simultaneously metaphysical and stylistic, but it is a failed attempt. Corporeality and metaphysical subjectivation do not achieve the required metaphysical synthesis—and that is quite a pity, for as we have seen, rarely have the themes been posited with such clarity and conscientiousness.

I do not believe that those critics who maintain that Leopardi's attempts to deal with his own private affairs in poetic form will inevitably fail are correct.[25] That explanation of failure, of the nervous contraction of these lyrics in the face of the metaphysical program, seems banal to me. The emergence of these limits conveys something more, perhaps the difficulty of occupying the privileged poetic place imposed by the metaphysical development. This difficulty arises not solely from the melancholic repetition of private experiences—other idols than these are at stake in this search and its perpetual vacillating. The difficulty, therefore, is metaphysical. In *Love and Death* and *Consalvo*, it seems first of all that the centrality of the place where poetry is spoken is lost. It is a metaphysical place, an ethical place. Thus it is necessary to impart a turn to the writing of poetry and to the very position of the problem. In effect, no continuous line leads from the affirmation of the originary nothingness of being (and the ethical-metaphysical tension that follows from it) to the analysis of the regions of being.[26] Ever since *Night Song of a Wandering Shepherd of Asia*, Leopardi has certainly been aware of this discontinuity—nor does the program of *The Dominant Thought* deny it. But perhaps it loses its importance faced with the necessity of other passages: progress toward corporeality, the realization of a singular, productive metaphysical articulation. No, the new passage is only possible if the ethical and metaphysical viewpoint that we grasped with such intensity manages to remain principal and foundational within our framework. The last poems renounced this centrality, which we must now restore.

The problem is entirely philosophical. Contemporary post-critical philosophies continually lead us back to it. After having identified the places that belong to the creative tension of being, those philosophies tend to manage the effects in terms of logical linearity, on the terrain of partial ontologies; then, when they experience the difficulties that follow from their methods, they declare the completion of this philosophical task impossible or, in order to preserve it, they impoverish it to the point of making every ontological presupposition unrecognizable—thus rendering the world, and in any case a relationship between humankind and the world, utterly impoverished.[27] Conversely, when faced with obstacles, Leopardi tries again and again to surmount them. Above all he understands that in metaphysics, the ethical revolution constitutes a point of no return. Every region of illusion must be traversed by the full power [*potenza*] of the metaphysical recasting. We cannot leave such an impoverished world intact following the intervention of the critical passage.

> Now you must rest forever,
> My weary heart. The last deception has died,
> I had thought everlasting. (*To Himself*, ll.1–3)[28]

Thus begins the prodigious "torso" that is *To Himself.* No dialectic of deception is therefore possible. The blockage of philosophy, of logic, of logical hope is total, just like the blockage of that logical hope which, by preserving the consciousness of metaphysical tragedy, nevertheless seeks to pervade the whole completely on the basis of ontological differences.

> I feel
> Not hope alone, desire
> For dear deceptions in us has come to fail. (ll.3–5)[29]

Nothing in modern poetry has so completely illustrated the impossibility of a constructive dialectic of deception. The absolute separation must be reaffirmed.

> Nothing is worth
> One beat of yours; nor is it worthy sighs,
> This earth. Bitterness, boredom
> Are all life is; and all the world is mud.
> Lie quietly. Despair
> This final time. (ll.6–12)[30]

This despair is the restoration of the metaphysical place of critique. It is a lucid despair that is opposed to the cruelty of nature, to the nothingness in which it finds its origin.

> Now despise yourself,
> Nature (the brutal power
> That furtively ordains the common harm),
> And this infinite vanity of the whole. (ll.13–16)

This transformation of the despising of nature and "this infinite vanity of the whole" into rage and consciousness restores the ethical place of critique. This prodigious poem carries out a forced takeover, a violent restoration of the place of poetry—that is to say, of the subject who constructs against nothingness, from within nothingness.

Compared with *Love and Death* and *Consalvo, To Himself* marks the extremely painful but strong overturning of that poetic illusion, a brutal reformulation of the metaphysical project. It is an exceptional passage in the form of a poetic syllogism. The despising that nature reserves for us is turned back: the brutal furtive power; its irrationality as well as its lack of ethics is denounced: "the common harm." "Furtive power [*potere*]" is an enemy, a Machiavellian adversary. Furthermore, in the overwhelming personification of the contrast there is an ancient and cosmological resonance ("Fate granted to our kind/Nothing but dying" [ll.12–13])[31] that further accentuates the personification of the antagonism, radicalizes it, and expresses a stronger, more desperate and more constructive contrast than that of heroic confrontation. We unexpectedly find ourselves once again in the most significant metaphysical place. What can be said? How can we fully grasp the force of this recalibration of the subject? We have said it again and again. This movement is imposed by the difficulty of traversing the regions of being, by the swampy attraction that the search endures in this passage. But this causal indication, although correct, tells us little, because the rupture carried out here is of such absolute ethical and poetic value as to escape the network of interpretive relationships. It is a constitutive thought, and that is enough.

Every constitutive thought gives rise to irreversible displacements, and in this case *To Himself* allows Leopardi to take up again, without further ambiguity, the project of leading the psyche back to constitutive ethics. And here one of the absolute masterpieces of Leopardi's poetics springs up: *Aspasia*.[32] This canto raises anew, on the basis of this irreversible displacement, the central problem of this whole poetic cycle, that of the imagination—that is to say, the discrimination of true illusion from false illusion on the basis of the constitutive power [*potere*] of the imagination, of poetic making as sign of truth. All the terms of the problem are present here, and the psychological aspects that had often flattened and confused the theme of truth in the set of illusions are refined and at the same time negated. The presence of more psychological determinations in *Aspasia* than in other canti—vivid renunciations, raging exclamations, biographical recollections—does not mean initial slippages or ambiguous representations. *Aspasia* appears rather as a formidable incitement to the ontological deepening of the discourse. Here love, revenge, jealousy, and rage are categories of the productive imagination. Truth is constructed within this corporeality, within this materiality. In materialism, truth is not external to the imagination, to the poetic act: it is that act's form and the result of the ethical struggle to construct it. Such, therefore, are the first consolidated results of the uncertain and sometime difficult search of this poetic period, of the huge forced takeover of *To Himself*. The displacement is accomplished, and the reading of *Aspasia*, keeping in mind these fundamental metaphysical tonalities of the overall framework, allows us to verify it in all the articulations that it produces.

Lines 1 to 32 form an introduction of incredible corporeality: a sensuous image, perhaps incestuous, of the woman loved of old. Every problem and every difficulty in poetic construction disappears here through the refiguration of the body and its fundamental capacity to support illusions. The approach to the body, previously laborious, is a given here.

So that I never
Find out the perfume of a floral slope,
Or catch the breath of flowers in city streets,
But that I see you as you were that day
When, nestling in the charm of your apartment
Which had the scent of all the freshest blooms
Of spring, and clothed in garments of the color
Of darkest violets, your angel shape
Offered itself to me, your curving thigh
Resting on glossy furs, with all around
Arcane voluptuousness, while you—you so
Accomplished temptress—kept on loosing hot
Resounding kisses down upon your children's
Curved lips, which meant you often had to stretch
Your snowy neck, and with your gentle hand
To press your children, strangers to your motive,
Against your breast, hidden, desired. (*Aspasia*, ll.10–26)[33]

But can the body stand the movement of the imagination? Where does this pain, this terrible physical suffering that is the sign of the disruption of the amorous illusion and of the imagination, begin? When does that relationship with the reality that we call love reach a crisis and wound us?

> And so it was that you
> Drove into my not unprotected side
> Most forcibly that dart, which afterwards
> I carried, howling out with pain, until
> The day the sun had come full circle twice. (ll.28–32)[34]

Thus the amorous illusion calls the body into question. Pain becomes metaphysical just like love, now definitively within that corporeality that defines subjects. The howling (*ululando*) of love and pain in line 31 is one of the most materialist, most Lucretian gerunds in Italian literature. It is the definition of a crisis that, throughout the amorous region of being, grasps the ground of the real and represents the unappeasable demand of truth.[35]

Lines 33 to 60, which correspond to the second stanza of the canto, answer the questions raised. The body cannot stand the dialectic of illusion since it is subjected to the confusion [*scambio*] of the image and the real.

> The wounded mortal
> Must thenceforth live in longing for the child
> Of his own mind, the amorous idea,
> Composed of such Olympian ideals,
> And in its face its habits and its speech
> So like the lady whom the enraptured lover
> Desires and in confusion thinks he loves.
> Now it is that idea, and not this lady,
> Which even in bodily embraces he serves and loves.
> Seeing at length his error and confusion of objects,
> He feels his anger flare; and often blames
> His lady. (ll.37–48)[36]

The confusion of the image and the real brings about the defeat of all imagination that develops only on this terrain. In this confusion—the "confusion of objects"—constructed of bodies, illusion is taken for truth and error is enjoyed. How can he free himself from this circularity of illusion? Prisoner of its corporeality, the poet passes enraged judgments: a fierce anti-feminism, even misogyny is expressed here (see lines 52–53, 58–60). These are not mere affectations but orderly and impotent attempts to escape

from the insignificance of the circulation of illusion, from alienation, from
the untruth of the confusion between reality and imagination. How can
he free himself from all this? The overturning is carried out in the third
stanza (lines 61–88)—the reality principle is restored, and love is over:
"Now that Aspasia whom/I so much loved is dead" (ll.70–71).[37] But suddenly
love arises again; the image reappears in the form of a "precious shade
[*larva*]" (l.73). This nostalgic and painful reminiscence is also the regaining
of a terrain of reality, a possible discrimination of true illusion from false
illusion—and an affirmation of imagination, which makes life lively and
brings pleasure. Nothing is resolved: the imagination does not construct a
happy world, but rather a true world in which illusions are discriminated and
realistically led back to the flavorlessness of truth—that is what imagination
provides. The paradox of the real is posited here with extreme force: in the
real, we need illusions in order to live and to feel pleasure, but we cannot
sublimate them or mediate them; only by leading them back to the real, by
affirming their value of negation, which is indestructible and specific, can
we regain or rather construct our truth. In these lines there is a veritable
epistemological overturning—a conception of the true that is born out of
the defeat of the illusion that reality can be mediated. In clashing with the
real, our imagination discovers the partiality of the affirmation of the true.
Our imagination discriminates the real. A reality principle is thus posited,
that of the amorous imagination that is opposed to illusion.

The final stanza of the canto (ll.89–112) carries us into a new world
dominated by this reality principle of the true imagination. The overturning
of the world of illusion, however much pain it brings with it (truth is a practical operation), leads to a new state of mind. The conquest of the truth of the
human situation is not a superficial condition. Mind recognizes matter, the
truth of fact, and becomes one with it. Tenderly, with a smile,

> The spell
> Was broken, and this yoke; and both at once
> Fell down to earth; and I am glad. However
> Replete with tedium, I am happy—after
> Such servitude, such madness—to embrace
> Good sense and liberty. For, though a life
> Bereft of feeling and of fine illusion
> Is like a winter's night which has no stars,
> It is my comfort, and my compensation
> For man's hard fate, that here upon the grass
> Idle, unmoving, I can contemplate
> The sea the land the sky, and I can smile. (ll.101–12)[38]

This smile is not a wrinkle of the mind; on the contrary it is a profound irony, a harsh and difficult passage through the real. The present contemplation of it, marked by that sense of distance born of the confrontation of its own weakness—which is nonetheless reality, body, irreversible matter—with the whole world, is a very violent act. The smile and the irony do not save us from the infinite vanity of the whole: they make us understand it, make us live within it, in order to know it and to free the poetic imagination, the sense of truth. Mind finds rest in a dimension that is natural and metaphysical, but the intensity of the oppositions with which the vicissitudes of mind are confronted is enormous; that intensity remains intact and nothing can abolish it. Here Leopardi neither laughs at himself nor even smiles: on the contrary, he has set forth a key to understanding by means of the real—an ironic key for a desperately non-signifying world. Does this key permit us to open the doors of the real, to grasp its sense? No, and the problem is not even posed. Does it permit us to accede to the understanding of the regions of separate being and in them to construct an ethical role for subjectivity? In short, is it possible to recast ontology in an ethical key?

As we know, this is the sole theoretical problem posed by Leopardi ever since the *Night Song of a Wandering Shepherd of Asia*. It is obvious that this period provides no positive and global answer. But the lack of a response conveying a large metaphysical opening does not alter the fact that the problem persists, that it is continually reposed, that the possibility of misleading solutions has been eliminated. Lastly, an operative tool has been discovered and tested: the concept of irony.

Irony has a fundamental quality consisting in organizing subjectivity outside of the psychological flux and within a relationship—fragile but real—with the objective determinations of being. Irony is an operation of the transcending [*trascendimento*] of the particularity of the subject and the transfer of the faculty of judgment to the objective level of being. Irony is ethical despair transformed into transcendence and into the objectivity of judgment. It thereby preserves the ethical origin and quality. Hence the judgment that it expresses is not determining but reflective: it is a schema of a rational and ethical project. In other words, and in principle, it is a poetic project. The necessity of making the poetic absolute the basis for the internal articulation of ontology, this ontology of nothingness and tension, is in no way diluted by the passage through irony; on the contrary, it is accentuated by it. The particular dialectic that is established in this period, from *The Dominant Thought* to the negative realization of its project *in Love and Death* and *Consalvo*, from the reemergence of the program in *To Himself* to its positive realization in *Aspasia*, demonstrates the fundamental importance of this poetic moment. If in the great period of 1828 to 1830 metaphysics carried poetics forward, so to speak (assuming that it is possible to distinguish genres in Leopardi's work), in this later period it is poetics that carries metaphysics forward. For grasping the ethical emergence against the backdrop of nothingness and the unresolved tension of being is a poetic act.

The miracle of *To Himself* constitutes the necessary foundation for a regional phenomenology of feeling, of the psyche, and for its logical solution in *Aspasia*, which is possible only on that basis. Every dialect of illusion can be broken up only if one opposes to them the absoluteness of an "other" foundation. Ontology is the science of the rupture of being, one that leads back to a nothingness of signification, against which the poetic foundation of subjective, separate ethics is posited.

We still have to consider certain aspects of this recovered ironic key. It involves first of all understanding how the smile in *Aspasia* relates to the "despair/This final time" of *To Himself*—not from the genetic viewpoint, the viewpoint of the poetic dynamic, but rather from a directly metaphysical viewpoint. What is the smile? What is despair? What is irony? Let us recall: the smile is not a wrinkle of being, but it is its very movement and an objective state of mind. A movement towards what? Why this lightness? Why do despair and this final vital demand subside into that smiling repose? Why does the despising, the rejection of nature, of its terrible hidden powers [*poteri*], end up in such a contrast with this tender act of superior awareness? One possibility is that this serene irony verges upon death, so that the gaze of the survivor corresponds to the extinction of passion ("Died," l.3 of *To Himself*). When the world is once again illuminated, the smile is like the morose glance that the sun casts over the brush with death. Leopardi accustoms us to this weary reappearance of the light after the storm, almost as a confirmation, in the repose of nature, of its abominable destiny. But the smile of *Aspasia* is not the expression of a consciousness that has undergone the vicissitudes of death—or rather, it is, not insofar as it bears the stigmata of that, but insofar as, through death, it has understood that its presence in life does not define existence. That smile bears the mark of fragility; it is as light as a feather or as Pascal's reed: like the feather it has the strength to fly, and like the reed it is supple and firmly rooted. Irony takes the form not of convalescence but of new life: the irony of the mind, the irony of a rejuvenated psyche, of a reconstructed ethical objectivity.

Next, then, we must emphasize that the nature of this smile and this irony is less cognitive than ethical—an ethical nature that does not exclude but rather prepares an act of knowledge [*conoscenza*]. This marks a perfectly clear path: from the poetic act to the state of ethical consciousness, to prepare an act of knowledge [*conoscenza*] to follow. This development is neither secondary nor relative; the succession is necessary. This sequence of cognitive powers [*potenze*] is fundamental for the phenomenology of consciousness that is taking shape: first a poetic act that declares, in the annihilating tension of being, a desperate and radically constructive taking of position, a vital option; then, an ethical moment of evaluation of the surface of the world and the active discrimination of the universe of illusions;[39] lastly, an act of knowledge [*conoscenza*], a knowledge [*sapere*] and its critique. Ethical irony and the smile thus do not appease despair insofar as they divert its finality; on the contrary, they complete it insofar as they integrate the fundamental option—for life, in life, within an inexhaustible horizon where reference points must be selected. Traversing the dialects of illusion is thus an operation of recasting of the viewpoint that succeeds in regaining signification by rooting the sense of the gaze in a desperate, separate being. This path is in no way totalitarian, nor is it simple knowledge [*conoscenza*]. It is a path that becomes knowledge [*conoscenza*] on the basis of the presupposition of a poetic act that creates a viewpoint, rupture, separation, and project, that creates a smiling, ironic, ethical capacity to physically embody this presupposition.

Deception; or Concerning Knowledge

The psyche is light and fragile, but not because the operation of demystifying its dialect was light or fragile. It has led us to the origin of the metaphysical tension of being, revealed the necessary options and established an order in the search for truth that leads from the poetic act to ethical discrimination and finally to knowing [*conoscere*]. Now the search expands, calling into question knowing [*conoscere*] and its dialects. The problem remains unchanged—traversing the determinate regions of being and the world of illusions, seeking the determinations and discriminations of truth for each of them—only the field is modified. But what is the difference between the psyche and knowledge [*sapere*]? What is the quality of the illusions of knowledge [*sapere*] compared with those of the psyche? The difference consists in the universal claim and collective function of knowledge [*sapere*]. The form of truth does not change its value; faced with the relations that the psyche structures, those that knowledge [*sapere*] organizes are transformed and enlarged. Without changing its backdrop, the problem is specified as a question regarding the determinations of collective being, the linguistic universal, cultural knowledge [*sapere*]. Will a reconstruction by means of the illusions of knowledge [*sapere*], a determination of sense in this universe, prove to be possible? And if, in the immediacy in which this universe presents itself, this is impossible, what are the alternatives, the options of truth? How does the absoluteness of the constitutive poetic act confront this world? And how does the ethical option confront it? A thousand and one questions arise. But before we confront these problems explicitly, we must raise a more radical question that might even deny them concreteness.

After the metaphysical affirmation of *Night Song of a Wandering Shepherd of Asia*, can the problem of signification still be posed in relation to culture? Is it not, can it be anything other than, a pure and simple deception? If the illusions of the psyche have led us to grasp a moment in which, by objectifying every psychic faculty, a poetic and ethical comportment becomes possible and a new direction for reason arises from negation, will an analogous operation ever be possible in the face of the deception of knowledge [*sapere*]? On the other hand, will we not witness a sort of gradual loss of power [*depotenziamento*] of the metaphysical question now that consciousness, immersed in poetry and in the singular, separated from the ethical redemption that restores the poetic act to it, confronts the problems of culture and history? In confronting this complex of themes, at the level that Leopardi's thought reaches here, the question's loss of power in this sphere is a given. Indeed, the power [*potenza*] of the founding poetic act is such that the research on culture and history necessarily becomes secondary, not only in the order of research but also in the ontological order of significations. The extent of this loss of power, however, remains to be measured.

The first texts that we consider in studying these themes are the two or three *Operette morali* composed in 1832.[40] Their stylistic characteristics are striking: in them we do not find the poetic hypothesis, the absolute adherence to ethical being and its critical movements that are characteristic of the *Operette* of 1827. The exposition instead grows rigid and the style conveys a painful fixation of themes. According to some interpretations of Leopardi's work, a rising curve links the happy research of the first *Operette* to the perfection of style and thought of those of 1827 before falling back in 1832 to end in blockage and the exhaustion of this vein of ethical thought.[41] Even if we could reconstruct the internal history of a work, separate from the complex problems that surround it, in a continuous development or in relation to the different stages of its composition—and I am not convinced of this—in this case I do not believe this is the best method. The falling curve of the *Operette* of 1832 seems to me to follow decisively from the problematic swerve that intervened with great power [*potenza*] into Leopardi's poetic life: between 1827 and 1832, he composed the *Night Song of a Wandering Shepherd of Asia*. The three *operette* of 1832 (if we include, as we intend to do, the "Fragment on Suicide"[42]) refer to this problematic swerve, to the radical modification of the metaphysical theme and the position of the poet. The "Fragment on Suicide" is a limpid demonstration. It is animated by a vigorous will to demystification, by the sense of a profound and irreversible ethical and historical rupture.

> It is no longer possible to fool or deceive us. Philosophy has made us understand how impossible this forgetting of ourselves, which was once so easy, has now become. Either the imagination will regain its vigor and illusions will again be embodied in an energetic and mutable life, life will become lively again and no longer be deathly, the grandeur and beauty of things will recover their substance, and religion will inspire belief again; or else this world will become a seraglio of the desperate and perhaps also a desert.[43]

The desperate dimension of the problem—which reason brings out not so as to incite suicide but in order to explain the fact that suicides have never been so frequent—echoes the radical conviction of the philosopher: here we are at the limit where death becomes palpable, and only the tangible presence of nothingness can produce a revolution of consciousness. But is a collective escape from this desert, from this "seraglio of the desperate" still possible? The answer is uncertain, in part objectively hopeful and in part pessimistic.

> I know that these remarks will appear to be dreams and follies, just as I know that whoever might have predicted, thirty years ago, the immense revolution of things and opinions of which we have been and are still spectators and participants would have found no one who would deign to scoff at his pompous predictions, etc. In short, the continuation of this life, the unhappiness and nullity of which we have long known, without vivid distractions and without those illusions upon which nature has based our life, is not possible. Nevertheless politics continues to be almost purely mathematical, instead of being philosophical, as if it were inconvenient for philosophy, having destroyed everything, to endeavor to rebuild (even though today this task must constitute its true object, in contrast to times of ignorance), and as if it should never bring great benefit to men, since up to now it has brought them nothing but small benefits and great evils.[44]

To the metaphysical necessity of a way out of this situation is opposed the paucity of means available. One must nevertheless react: "Nature's whole plan for human life falls under the great law of distraction, illusion and forgetting. The weaker this law becomes, the more the world goes to perdition."[45] This last assertion has convinced some that the fragment is from 1820 and should be related to the period in which Leopardi attributed an ingenuous and heroic role to illusion.[46] But examined closely, the important point is not so much the reassertion of the "great law" as it is the necessity of creatively breaking it. And collectively breaking it? If we stick to a literal reading of the "Fragment," we might deduce this. Indeed, the doubt concerning the aptitude of political means for providing an adequate solution to the problem does not exclude the possibility that other collective tools could do so. But we do not believe so, and many other considerations hereafter will confirm this.

For the moment it is enough to recall that the collective is not in any case a continuation of the psyche or a larger, linear definition of the subject. The collective is first of all deception, false illusion; and only a radical reconstruction setting out from ethics, from the "immense revolution of things and opinions," can provide us not only with its concept but with its reality. So then, how can it be reconstructed, and how can the true be discriminated from the false within it? Must we proceed in a continuous manner, or will any continuity whatsoever drive us, as in the regional ontology of the psyche, through growing ambiguities, from theoretical failure to theoretical failure, to the point at which only a radical inversion of the spirit of research will reopen the hope for a foundation of the collective? Perhaps. In any case, these pages do not offer even the most remote hypothesis of a viable way aside from that of a radical recasting.

The ambiguities that were tolerated in the treatment of the dialects of the psyche, however, are not present in the *Operette* of 1832 and the *Pensieri*. Nonetheless, this recognition must not lead us to throw the baby out with the bath water; for if the search among the illusions of culture and history will lead us to denounce the senselessness of every illusion that is not born of the taste for nothingness, the historical and cultural dimension of the ethical upheaval is always implicitly present—even though we are still waiting for the scientific criteria of a correct exposition.

Finally, one last reflection on this argument: as with Leopardi's prior confrontations with the problem of history and culture, here too the theme of time returns to the foreground. In the case of the "Fragment," it is the time of the revolution, of that unresolved past of Leopardi's era. The organic link connecting the historical and cultural themes to time constitutes an "other" to the specificity of the current approach: discriminating the dialects of knowledge [*sapere*] means discriminating time. Does this imply a progressive Leopardi? No, only a Leopardi who, in introducing this theme and rediscovering the definition of time on the very site of the ethical revolution, establishes in materialist fashion a creative figure of time: time as dimension of action, as possibility and as choice. Exactly as it is for ethics.

"Almanacs, new almanacs, new calendars! Want any almanacs, sir?"[47] Thus the "Dialogue of an Almanac-Pedlar and a Passerby" invites us to a reflection on time. Earlier we spoke of a certain loss of power [*depotenziamento*] of the metaphysical question: here is proof of it. The "Dialogue" undertakes a pessimistic banalization of the metaphysical question. Not only does it crawl from one negation of illusion to another, but its pages are filled with a morose humor. Life is perceived not as time that flies, but as unhappy time—the sooner it flies, the better, since no one would want to relive the life that he lived "at any price."

> *Passerby*: What sort of life would you like, then?
> *Pedlar*: A life just as it came, as God gave it, with no strings attached.
> *Passerby*: A life at random, knowing nothing of it beforehand, just as we know nothing about this new year?
> *Pedlar*: That's it.[48]

At this point there is a slight inflection of the discourse. It is introduced by that "life at random," in the sense that this formula expresses the intense expectation of a new time, without any illusion of happiness but with a sense of irony and a smile. "That life which is a fine thing is not the life one knows, but the life one does not know; not the life of the past, but of the future."[49] Is this an ancient materialism that Leopardi expresses here, a sort of cultural reminiscence, an Epicurean conception of time, though with a smile? Perhaps. But wanting to see in this evocation of the future a reopening of the relationship between happiness and chance and, in the sense of the future, a forceful accentuation of freedom and possibility, would be a forced interpretation in any event. There is none of that. There is only a new and more profound insistence on the theme of temporality as the constitutive form of the metaphysical question. It is an element of the construction of a more advanced conception of ethics, but it remains for the moment inoperative in this climate of weakening of the metaphysical theme. Thus the demystification of knowledge [*sapere*] and its illusions proceeds with great intensity, but it does so within a purely negative perspective. Only deception constitutes the basis of knowledge [*sapere*], and the relevant materials for reconstruction elaborated by Leopardi's phenomenology (such as the concept of the collective and the constitutive concept of time) are for the moment set aside. Demystification does not pass through the experience of ontological tension, but descends from it, almost falls from it.

Everything is different in the "Dialogue of Tristan and a Friend," where the mechanism of demonstration is extremely potent. The dialogue begins in "stupefaction, anger and laughter" in the face of the continual negation of human unhappiness that the century produces. Now, convinced by the propaganda that the era spreads about itself, the Enlightenment, and progress, Tristan acknowledges having changed his opinion: "I realized that the unhappiness of man was one of the inveterate errors of the intellect, and that the falsity of this opinion, and the happiness of life, was one of the great discoveries of the nineteenth century."[50] But this change of opinion is only the key to a paradox: the nineteenth century is superior to the preceding centuries ("Most assuredly. All ages have thought this of themselves, even the most barbarous; and thus my own age thinks, and I along with it");[51] in that century the Enlightenment thinkers spread—and human nature affirms—the notion of its own complete perfectibility, and all this despite the decadence of the body and society! "[T]he body is the man," yet

> with us, for a very long time now, education has not deigned to think of the body, a thing altogether too base and abject: it thinks of the spirit: and by its very desire to cultivate the spirit, ruins the body: without realizing that in ruining this, it also in turn ruins the spirit. And even if we could remedy this in education, it could never be done without radically changing the present state of society, finding a remedy that held good for the other aspects of private and public life, which all, by their very nature, conspired together in antiquity to perfect and preserve the body, and today conspire to wreck it. The result is that in comparison with the ancients we are little more than children, and that the ancients in comparison with us can more than ever be said to have been men. I speak thus of individuals compared with individuals, as well as of the masses (to use this very pretty modern term) compared with the masses. And I will add that the ancients were incomparably more manly than us, also in their systems of morals and of metaphysics. In any case, I am not going to be moved by such puny objections, and firmly believe that the human race is constantly gaining ground.[52]

It is strange and singular, then, that in the nineteenth century, the progress of spirit, however unarguable, proceeds despite the decadence of philosophy, science, and knowledge [*sapere*] in general ("except perhaps in Germany, whence learning has not yet been hunted out")[53]—a striking decadence in relation to the ancients.

> *Friend*: In short, to put the whole matter in a word, concerning the nature and destinies of men and things (since now we are not speaking of literature or politics) do you think what the newspapers think?

Tristan: Exactly. I believe in and embrace the profound philosophy of the newspapers, which by murdering literature and all other studies, especially if hard and disagreeable, are the teachers and beacons of the present age. Is this not true?[54]

The irony becomes increasingly bitter as the dialogue proceeds—we are now getting close to the sarcasm that Leopardi soon inflicts upon politics. I therefore accept, Tristan continues, the profound philosophy of the newspapers and the massification of knowledge [*sapere*]—"Leave it all to the masses; though what they are likely to do without individuals, being composed of individuals, I desire and hope to have explained to me by those experts in individuals and masses, who are now shedding enlightenment upon the world"[55]—even if I am convinced that the superficial culture of the nineteenth century will be blotted out by the experience of the next century, that nothing will remain of this "din and confusion" and nothing will resist this flattening of values.

And so it is, that while all the most base consider themselves illustrious, obscurity and nullity of achievement become the common fate both of the base and of the loftiest spirits. But long live statistics! Long live the economic, moral and political sciences, the pocket encyclopedias, the manuals, and the many wonderful creations of our century! And may the nineteenth century live forever! Poor maybe in things, but exceedingly rich and generous in words: which was always a very good sign, as you know. And let us rejoice, that for another sixty-six years, this century will be the only one to speak and to expound its theories.[56]

At this point the sarcasm has become ferocious and the paradox has been laid bare. The interlocutor suggests to Tristan the hypothesis that the century's faults are the effects and pains only of transition. Enough of these reformist inanities [*scempiataggini*], replies Tristan.

All centuries, more or less, have been and will be ages of transition, because human society never stands still, nor will there ever be a century with a state of things likely to last. So that this fine word either does not in the least excuse the nineteenth century, or this excuse is common to all centuries. It remains to enquire, if society continues along the road it is traveling today, where it is likely to end up, that is, if the transition now taking place is from good to better or from bad to worse. Maybe you will tell me that this is a transition par excellence, that is, a rapid passage from one state of civilization to another utterly

different from the one before. In that case I ask your leave to laugh
at this rapid passage, and reply that all transitions ought to be made
slowly; for if one makes them in a rush, after a short while one is back
to where one started, and has to make them all over again, step by step.
It has always happened this way. The reason is, that nature does not go
by leaps and bounds, and that by forcing nature one does not achieve
lasting results. Or else, to put it better, such precipitate transitions are
apparent but not real.[57]

But the friend could have responded, what is reality? That question is not
posed. What is the true? The response underlies the whole dialogue. The
truth is the extreme unhappiness of life and consists in remaining "astonished, stupefied, motionless" in the face of the nothingness of the signification of being, meaning the "deceptions not of the imagination, but of the
intellect," and in having

> the courage to bear the privation of every hope, to gaze intrepidly on the
> desert of life, not to conceal from myself any part of human unhappi-
> ness, and to accept all the consequences of a philosophy that is grievous,
> but true. Which, if it is not useful to any other end, confers on strong
> men the august satisfaction of seeing every mask torn from the veiled
> and mysterious cruelty of human destiny.[58]

Such is the motive force, therefore, that produces this demystification of the
century: a feeling that, faced with the disasters of time, becomes gloomy
and renounces all irony and all paradox in its treatment of this backdrop of
tragedy.

> And moreover I tell you frankly, that I do not submit to my unhappiness,
> or bow my head to destiny, or come to terms with it, as other men do;
> and I dare to long for death. . . . Too ripe am I for death, and it seems
> too absurd and incredible, dead as I am in spirit, and the fable of life
> in every way so utterly concluded in me, that I should have to endure
> another forty or fifty years, the number threatened me by nature. The
> very thought of this makes me shudder.[59]

The incredible lucidity of judgment passed upon the nineteenth century
and upon what is being prepared for us in terms of destruction and
death is sustained by a desperate ethical dignity, by a constitution of
ethics that can be granted only by traversing death and the nothingness
of present life.

Thus, in this "Dialogue of Tristan and a Friend"—the ideal epilogue to the *Operette*—the theoretical question of the signification of knowledge [*sapere*] is pushed to an extreme point, and this same question, in specific conditions, is denied insofar as it is a projection and investigation into the value of a region of being. Nevertheless, despite the proximity of and desire for death, the affirmation of poetic subjectivity is so strong that the entirety of the problem is reinvigorated rather than effaced. The affirmation plumbs the depths of the metaphysical drama: it is there that the reinvigoration must be carried out. The deception of culture and knowledge [*sapere*] is total because this world cannot be the bearer of the reality of life. Once Leopardi sought a signification, a direction for the web of sense, in the sphere of materialist sensualism. Here the critique tends to assert the complete senselessness of every possible cultural web of sense. But at the same time, it promises a profound, radical overturning of viewpoint, and thus the possibility of restoring significations and values. This web of sense that collapsed section by section into senselessness reshapes the catastrophe of historical memory. The "culture of the nineteenth century" is the continuation, the modernization of that catastrophe. Identifying the total internal homology of signifying and destructive values, Leopard opposes the second catastrophe just as he opposed the first. He shudders at this spectacle, but he resists.

In these pages, the force with which the sense of the catastrophe, its heavy objectivity, becomes a line that leads to a reassertion of poetic subjectivity, of the constitutive possibility of poetics, is incredible. The more it expands its contact with death, the more potent the poetic affirmation becomes. "Every pleasant fancy, every thought of the future, which I have, as happens, in my solitude, and with which I pass the time, resides in death."[60] It is neither paradoxical nor lazy for us to find an affirmation in this forceful, determined expression of a desire for death. That would mean drowning the relation in dialectical necessity, in a relationship that sees the "I" rise again from nothingness or from the not-me with necessary logic and an ineluctable consequence. No, it is not that. In Leopardi, the affirmation is determined in a solitary way, as necessity of expression, as production. This is the irreversible sign of a tragic existence that does not know how to become dialectical and vainly hopes, but that is also determination and critique. And it is precisely on this basis—and not by chance—that the reconstruction of the materialist fabric of critique develops. For Leopardi has made the unease of the century and of knowledge [*sapere*] his own in the form of paradox, in the desire for death; but however prefatory, the appropriation is carried out, it develops, and the unease of the century will be verified—and the position of the subject, in its poetic force, perhaps reconstructed.

It will be done so by means of the experience of death, if the century imposes it upon us, but in any case, ethically against this will of the era and its barbarism. Otherwise, Leopardi's theory would only be paradox and laziness, a kind of macabre game played over and against life, a conviction of death. We know that this is not so, that the theory is entirely within life and corresponds to it—even if this astonishes us. "The most unexpected thing for someone who is entering social life, and very often for someone who has grown old there, is to find that the world is as it has been described to him, and as he already knows and believes it to be in theory. Man is stupefied to see in his own case that the general rule is shown to be true."[61]

That is the last note in the *Zibaldone*. Leopardi then begins the assembly of the *Pensieri*.[62] Does it involve a confirmation of the unease of the century? Research into the deception of knowledge [*sapere*] and a justification of its existence and dimension? A new attempt to develop a regional phenomenology of knowledge [*sapere*]? If we stick to the selection of *Pensieri* published posthumously and if we evaluate each of the selections in its frank and immediate signification, all these questions will in fact remain unanswered. Indeed, in large measure the *Pensieri* are drawn from the pages of the *Zibaldone*,[63] though why such a specific selection was made and for what purpose appear obscure at first glance. So the protests of Carlo Leopardi and Giordani, who suspected Ranieri of more or less dubious maneuvers—most notably an undue condensation—when he published the book, appear justified.[64] And the letter that Leopardi addressed to De Sinner, in which he indicates wanting to give the press "an unpublished volume of Thoughts on the character of men and on their conduct in society,"[65] does not help us much to understand the reasons for the selection, unless we situate the *Pensieri* at the programmatic turn and within the phenomenological design that we are describing. Thus our questions become, in the absence of a proof of Leopardi's precise and specific intention, a hypothesis of research to be verified.

At this point we can add a remark that is rather obvious but not devoid of interest. Leopardi considers the *Zibaldone* as the notebook of a lifetime and as a set of materials for reelaboration. In following the development of thought in the *Zibaldone*, we have identified a careful internal logic, which Leopardi maintains from the viewpoint of his life experience; but nothing forbids him from reorganizing these materials (aside from all those that are in tiny pieces) on another register, a more current register determined by the finality of the cultural struggle that the present proclaims.[66] We are thus beginning the reading of the *Pensieri* from the perspective of our hypothesis of research and asking ourselves if they respond to the demand for a phenomenology of the deception of knowledge [*sapere*] and to the project of its specific demystification.

Such seems to me to be the case. The *Pensieri* represent a kind of summary of everything that Leopardi had developed in terms of the critique of knowledge [*sapere*]. The selection of thoughts from the *Zibaldone* and their recasting in this miniature *Zibaldone* that is the *Pensieri* follows a critical internal logic, as if the new thoughts were adapted to this logic, so that the very signification of the pages repeated from the *Zibaldone* finds itself modified when they are situated in the new project. The difference in writing between the two texts, even when the content is identical or analogous, should be noted. The style of the *Pensieri* reflects the new conceptual concatenation, and its so-called coldness results from the negation of a direction in the web of sense and the frank confrontation with the conclusive character of the critique and the metaphysical undertaking. The inversion of the sensualist universe is presupposed by the project of the *Pensieri* and is reflected in its style.

The deception of knowledge is therefore the first point, an essential nucleus to which these *Pensieri* always return. Leopardi forcefully renews psychological realism in the definition he gives of human relationships, of the form of deception within which they develop, and of the knowledge [*sapere*] humankind has of that, to the point of concluding in a Machiavellian conception (in the vulgar sense) of social life. The evolution of the reflections, which is in no way systematic, is marked by multiple variations that are unified by a profound sense of the need to demystify the social relationship. We pass from a vision of the world as "a league of scoundrels against men of generosity, of base men against men of good will"[67] in which the former are constantly the victors (and those who are sincere should beware: "It is an unpardonable crime for humankind, which does not so much hate an evil-doer, or evil itself, as they hate the man who calls evil by its real name. Thus an evil-doer often becomes rich, honored, and powerful, while the man who identifies evil is dragged off to the gallows. For men are willing to suffer almost anything from each other or from heaven itself, so long as *true words* do not touch them"[68]) to a schema of social relationship summed up thus: "The human race, from the individual on up, and even in its smallest units, is split into two camps: those who impose themselves through power [*prepotenza*] and those who submit to it."[69] Seduction and force are allied in imposing injustice and domination,[70] and even the honest person does not escape the seduction of the multitude.[71] Social life consists in "a war of all against all and all against one,"[72] in which only egotism allows the individual to assert himself. Egotism and self-regard, directed against others, will never disappear since society is like a fluid: every molecule, every globule, presses hard against its neighbors above, below, and on all sides, and through these exerts pressure on far-off molecules as well, while being pushed back in the same way; if at any point this active resistance flags, within a split second the entire mass of fluid rushes to that weak spot and fills it immediately with new molecules.[73]

Leopardi sees in the work of Francesco Guicciardini a model for understanding this social world: he is "perhaps the only modern historian who not only knew a lot about men, but whose knowledge of human nature also formed the basis of his historical philosophy. He avoided any political science that could be divorced from the knowledge of man (and therefore mostly illusory)."[74] These are only a few examples of the progression of this research, the cold lucidity and assurance of which define a condition of Leopardi's philosophizing. Nevertheless, this assurance and this irreversibility are based on a framework of metaphysical relations that are themselves fixed, in which the dialectic of illusion immediately finds its ontological contrary. This world without virtue, however, does not succeed and will never succeed in eliminating the power [*potenza*] of virtue. This is the second recurring nucleus in the *Pensieri*, on the basis of which the framework of Leopardi's reflection opens up—that is to say, on the basis of the conflict that imposes the power [*potenza*] of virtue against this Machiavellian figure of society and knowledge [*sapere*]. But if this is the world, the power [*potenza*] of virtue can be only rupture, violent discrimination of this truth that smothers us.

If the same end awaits both the innocent and the guilty, says the Emperor Otho in Tacitus, then it is more manly to die for a good cause. I believe that thoughts of this sort preoccupy certain men who, though of noble mind and born to virtue, will eventually turn wicked once they enter public life. For they will have experienced the ingratitude, injustice, and miserable hatred men show toward their own kind, most of all toward the virtuous. They turn wicked not from depravity, not from the weak man's emulation of others, not from self-interest or excessive desire for means and frivolous profit, nor finally from any impulse to remain free of the general moral disease. Rather, they turn wicked by free choice, to avenge themselves, taking up arms against mankind and exacting measure for measure. The wickedness of such people is all the more profound when it results from their experience with virtue, all the more formidable when joined, however rarely, with strength and greatness of spirit—and it becomes a kind of heroism.[75]

The classical image quickly finds a foundation in the history and psychology of individuals—and here too virtue appears as heroism, as rupture, as a moment that overflows the opaque totality of true deception. It is a heroism that has nothing to do with the crazy will to individual revolt, which, on the contrary, marks a cognitive metamorphosis and a total refusal of the world.

> Finally life takes on a new look; he sees it change from something merely heard about into something seen, from something imagined into something real. And he feels himself at the very center of life, perhaps no happier than before but in a sense more potent, that is to say more capable of making use of himself and others.[76]

It is quite interesting to find here a definition of human power [*potenza*] that is the same one Spinoza established.[77] Nevertheless, this identity has no great significance beyond the fact that both thinkers are militants in the great current of modern materialism. Indeed, although modern, Spinoza's materialism is pre-critical, so its concept of power [*potenza*] goes beyond the dialectic only in a programmatic way. Leopardi's concept of power [*potenza*] is post-critical, and it is posited as one of the poles of an insoluble relationship with being that renders the tension irreversible. Leopardi's power [*potenza*] is against. It is rooted in nothingness.[78] We have already said it: if the world is this set of deceptions that contain truth, virtue can only be rupture, power [*potenza*], and creation of another world. Leopardi expresses this desire with maximum force, posits it as other, and accepts the solitude of that alterity. For metaphysics as well as for poetics, rupture had already become a central yet other element. But the specificity of the problem here consists in establishing a relationship, which is perhaps merely cognitive, between these two worlds. How can virtue be thought in this situation? In the total separation of the two worlds, virtue is inevitably presented as devoid of all content and hence unable to catch the real and make it its own, but continually repels it in a pure act of rupture. Virtue, for being, must be creation. But here it cannot be. In rupture, in expressing the radical violence of rupture and making refusal its foundation, it is reduced to a potentiality, and an empty one at that.

The *Pensieri* verge upon sophism. Faced with the emptiness of a world without virtue, they demand an energetic virtue that breaks with this atrocious horizon. But virtue is devoid of content, and the emptier it is, the more radical it becomes. So then, how can we define this nonexistent relationship? The sophism consists in the fact that the word "virtue" is endowed with a double meaning: in the first place, that of plenitude opposed to the void of life and knowledge [*sapere*], and in the second place, that of a void in contrast to the nauseating but effective life of the real. For Leopardi truth is historical effectiveness, efficacy. But virtue has neither efficacy nor historical consistency, whereas the world, in its putrefaction, does. Why? Here we come to a third set of arguments.

Paradoxically (and it is interesting to observe that here paradox is no longer merely an argumentative weapon but acts to pin down the spirit, so to speak), then, the definition of the emptiness of virtue presses toward an analysis of the phenomenological region of knowledge [sapere]. Why is virtue empty? Leopardi's question is impassioned. The answer is terrible: virtue cannot be filled with content because its solitude is total, because history and knowledge [sapere] have worked frantically to empty it of all content. The insufficiency and the possible sophism of the definition of virtue are ascribed to history.[79] The analysis is further specified, taking up again the titles and rubrics of Leopardi's historical polemic in icy and definitive terms that do not exclude protest or revolt or overturning, but on the contrary take them to extremes, to a point that exceeds the contradiction. But before coming back to the ethical answer and its characteristics, we must determine with precision the articulations of Leopardi's critique.

History, progress, and the Enlightenment have emptied history of virtue. His denunciation adopts diverse tones, from contempt to sarcasm. Contempt, always profound, is addressed to a smug century that does not know how to construct but only how to talk, a century in which the lack of realism combines with a mawkish utopianism, all to cover up the continuing intensification of the commodification of life. Then there are the reformers, Enlightenment and liberal reformism—in the specificity of the Italian historical continuum:[80] "Some centuries presume to remake everything in the arts and other disciplines because they themselves do not know how to make anything."[81] The Enlightenment thinkers and their claim to moralize the world completely: "There's no greater sign of being a poor philosopher and wise man than wanting all of life to be wise and philosophical."[82] That claim to rational conformity has for effect the triumph of the abstract power [potere] of money, which becomes the only common substance among people. "As if men, holding different opinions on everything else, were united only in their respect for money, as if money and nothing else were what constitutes man's essence. Everything indicates that this is what mankind takes as its working assumption, especially in our own time."[83] So long live statistics, industry, and money. "Fine. In the meantime, as industry prospers and proliferates, so do certain other things, such as moral depravity, coldness, egoism, greed, falsehood, mercantile treachery, and all the other most ignoble qualities and passions of civilized men—though virtues are expected."[84]

The sole effect of the dialectic of Enlightenment is the emptying out of every value, the commodification of human relationships, the loss of power [*depotenziamento*] of history. Virtue disappears because the power [*potenza*] of human making, which constitutes the foundation of virtue, disappears. It is true that the dialectic of Enlightenment and its terrible consequences develop in a cultural context that, in western civilization, has known no interruption. The dialectic of Enlightenment would have to be connected to the dialectic of Christianity, the effects of which are no less terrible: Christianity is contempt for the world. That judgment—Christ himself historically establishes the scorn for filling virtue with positive contents—is immediately reinforced by the judgment passed upon the people of antiquity, their love of virtue, history, and the world.

> Jesus Christ was the first to point out clearly to mankind that teacher and celebrator of false virtues; that detractor and persecutor of all true virtues; that enemy of all man's intrinsic and truly unique greatness; that mocker of every noble sentiment it believes true and every gentle affection it thinks intimate; that slave of the strong, tyrant of the weak, hater of the unhappy—which he called "the world," a name preserved in all civilized languages down to the present. This general idea, so obviously true and so dependably useful, did not, I think, occur to anyone before that time.[85]

And furthermore: "The concept of the world-as-enemy-of-the-good is as celebrated in the Gospels and in modern secular writers as it was unknown—or barely known—to ancient writers."[86] This generality of the concept of virtue is emptied out in Christianity just as in the Enlightenment. Christianity constructed an abstract idea of the world alienated from the totality of power [*potenza*] and from ethical creativity. This general schema of alienation forms the basis for the development of the Enlightenment: those heavy negations of ethical power [*potenza*] are dipped in the same ink.

Furthermore, education organizes this historical emptying out of history and the withdrawal of the power [*potenza*] of virtue. "The wisdom passed on, especially in Italy, to those who are educated (who, as we know, are few indeed) is a formal traitorous conspiracy of weakness against strength, age against youth."[87] And this is not only because

> the interest of common tranquility, domestic and public, runs contrary to the pleasures and endeavors of young people; hence even good education, so called, consists largely in tricking students into postponing their own comfort for the sake of others. But even apart from this, our elders are naturally inclined to destroy youth, to erase it entirely, since they

abhor the very sight of it. . . . The fruit of such a malevolent culture, which benefits the cultivator while ruining the plant, is that students, having lived like old men during their growing years, become ridiculous and unhappy in old age because they yearn to live like boys; or else, as happens more often, nature triumphs and the young live "youthfully" in spite of education, rebelling against their teachers. Had these teachers won their pupils' confidence by *encouraging* the use and enjoyment of the gifts of youth, they could then have regulated these gifts and would never have lost that confidence.[88]

The harrowing portrait of historical decadence in which humankind is revealed as the sole producer of its own ruin and of virtue reduced to mere appearance concludes in bitterness: "It has often been said that the faster genuine virtues decline in a state, the faster apparent virtues spring up."[89] But this bitterness, which in the *Pensieri* often stands in for disdain and sarcasm, in no way weakens the force of Leopardi's historical synthesis. As we have emphasized several times, here we rediscover in its entirety the contents of the historical polemic that, from the Enlightenment to Romanticism, from Kant's philosophy to dialectical philosophy, has embodied the European foundation of a critical and reconstructive project. Whether in Lessing or Hölderlin, Rousseau or Schiller, even Kant or Hegel, the theme of religious and capitalist alienation, the nostalgia for the *polis* as desire for the world, and the conception of virtue as ethical power [*potenza*] are absolutely central—as they are in Leopardi. If, in accordance with the internal logic of many of these authors, this harsh denunciation concludes—at least it effectively, historically concludes—with a reconciliation that restores history to metaphysics and restores the old corrupt series in a new hypostasis of corruption, the Hegelian event is exemplary from this point of view. In Leopardi the question instead remains unresolved. History is found to be devoid of metaphysics, and thought and life are devoid of truth. This gap is insurmountable, and these results are the product of a homogeneous force that cannot be redeemed. The only possible alternative is not synthesis but creation. So how can one be virtuous? Only by creating, by bringing about a potent general innovation that invests the world *ab imo* and reconstructs it.

Let us take up the progression of the *Pensieri* once again. In a first phase, corresponding to a first set of thoughts, we witness a reprise of the denunciation of the deception of knowledge [*sapere*]; a second group of interventions insists on the necessity of revivifying virtue, thereby breaking open the opacity of the historical process, while at the same time recognizing that this rupture risks being merely formal, given that—third group of reflections—all of history tends in the direction of an alienation of human essence and virtue. This third set of thoughts returns us to the terrain of the regional phenomenology of knowledge [*sapere*]—at this stage, corresponding to the fourth moment of Leopardi's discourse in the *Pensieri*, the question of what virtue can be attempts to extricate itself from the paralyzing formalism of the initial formulation, tries to respond to the demand for a rupture of instructions and of the positive project. A first attempt to escape from the condition of formalist impotence follows a path that is well known in Leopard's method, but that does not seem to produce great results. We can call this methodological variant the use of paradox in ethics. *Pensiero II* presents the paradox of paternal authority and the son's rebellion: although both are justified, their collision annuls them as such. *Pensiero VI* concerns the paradox of old age and death: "Death is not evil, for it frees man from all ills and takes away his desires along with desire's rewards. Old age is the supreme evil, for it deprives man of all pleasures while allowing his appetites to remain, and it brings with it every possible sorrow. Yet men fear death and desire old age."[90] We could go on citing the ethical paradoxes that litter the *Pensieri*, but this would lead us ineluctably toward a renewal of the discipline of the seventeenth- and eighteenth-century moralists and preachers and to a certain sense of futility. Indeed, nothing here nourishes virtue, the power [*potenza*] of rupture. But there is another route that virtue can take in trying to restore its name and the rupture of a potent project. This is the route of positing paradox not within ethics but in the relationship between ethics and the world—the imagination confronts ethics and seeks to form a material whole with it. Thus life is a great imposture that nature continually nourishes, and only through the imagination can life become "congenial and tolerable."[91] Are these new deceptions, an amplified reproduction of the imposture? Perhaps, but a new terrain in the confrontation between the imagination and truth, humankind and the world is thereby established. This confrontation remains unresolved; the relation between thought and action, even when posed forcefully, is often impassable in ethical terms, and the moral syllogisms are seemingly impossible. Let us note with irony:

> In the present century, black people are believed to be totally different from whites in race and origin, yet totally equal to them with regard to human rights. In the sixteenth century, when blacks were thought to come from the same roots and to be of the same family as whites, it was held, most of all by Spanish theologians, that with regard to rights blacks were by nature and by Divine Will greatly inferior to us. In both centuries, blacks have been bought and sold and made to work in chains under the whip. Such is morality; and such is the extent to which moral beliefs have anything to do with actions.[92]

Nevertheless the problem indeed consists in moving into the reproduction of deception and into the nonlinearity, the extreme relativity, of the relationship between thought and action. How? By pushing this contradiction to the extreme limit, to maximum contradiction, where the act of rupture becomes ethical material. Through an act of great ethical beauty expressed in a literarily refined form, Leopardi overturns for example the concept of boredom, making it no longer a state of weariness and barbarized emptiness of mind but rather a potent condition of a paradoxical knowledge [*conoscenza*] of the world.

> *Noia* [boredom] is in some ways the most sublime of human feelings, though I don't believe it's responsible for bringing about *all* the effects that many philosophers attribute to it. But there is certainly at least one: the inability to be satisfied by any worldly thing or, so to speak, by the entire world. To consider the inestimable amplitude of space, the number of worlds and their astonishing size, then to discover that all this is small and insignificant compared to the capacity of one's own mind; to imagine the infinite number of worlds, the infinite universe, then feel that our mind and aspirations might be even greater than such a universe; to accuse things always of being inadequate and meaningless; to suffer want, emptiness, and hence *noia*—this seems to me the chief sign of the grandeur and nobility of human nature. This is why *noia* is practically unknown to unambitious men and scarcely or not at all known to other animals.[93]

Knowledge [*conoscenza*] founds ethics to the extent that it renders irreversible the determination of rupture, and virtue is the very content of it. From here a series of positive ethical thoughts, a kind of deduction of models of behavior and decision unfolds. It is only a trace, but an important one, for it excavates the negative and the solitude of ethical rupture in order to bring out, not a prescription, but the line of a traversable tendency. Therefore rupture first of all, the denunciation of the cunning hypocrisy that pervades the world, and the refusal of any pacification, any abstract mediation: irony, laughter, and sarcasm are, from this viewpoint, acts of the highest ethicality. "The power of laughter among men is great and terrifying, and no one can consciously protect himself entirely from it. He who has the courage to laugh is master of the world and is not much different from one who is prepared to die."[94]

To laughter is added sarcasm that demonstrates the insoluble character of ethics conducted by means of paradox and horror. *Pensiero XX* is, in this regard, a minor masterpiece of ethical art. And so on. (The pages that we dedicate to political matters permit us to glimpse the vast domain to which the method of sarcasm lays claim, through the intermediaries of irony and invective.) That being said, the fundamental operation that consists in deducing positive conduct from negation and rupture is repeated here. *Pensiero LXIV* evokes the modesty of great men who

> measure themselves not in comparison to other people but to the idea of perfection ever present in their minds, an ideal infinitely clearer and greater than any the common people have, and they also realize how far they are from fulfilling their ideal. The masses, on the other hand, readily and perhaps rightly believe that they have not only realized the idea of perfection they have in mind, but that they have surpassed it.[95]

Pensiero XXXVII recalls that "no human trait is more intolerable in everyday life, nor in fact less tolerated, than intolerance."[96] And so on, all the way up to the great profession of ethical faith and the declaration of the separate foundation of ethics that is *Pensiero LXXXIX*: "He who has little contact with men is seldom a misanthrope. True misanthropes are not found in isolation but among men, for it is practical experience in life, not philosophy, that makes men hate. And if such a man withdraws from society, in withdrawing he gives up his misanthropy."[97] This is a conclusive allegory of the foundation of a possible ethics: the only possible ethics is alternative.

In the deepening of the dialects of the illusion of knowledge [*sapere*] and history we find what appears now to be established as Leopardi's metaphysical conviction: the feeling of an insoluble tension, of a split in being and of the impossibility of traversing the world of illusion if not by insisting on the critique of illusion. However, the feeling of a possible poetic and ethical alternative is just as strong—but only when the originality of virtue as independent ethical power [*potenza*] is fully affirmed. Leopardi's "serenity" in this period is often mentioned—too often, in my view. It seems to me that there is no such thing. There is, on the contrary, a very acute sense of the power [*potenza*] of being as alternative form of destruction, of the subversion of being as it is given. This tension is suffused with a profound suffering. The almost marble-like coldness of the style—which is intended here and achieved—conceals a superhuman tension. If there is a moment that we could describe as Nietzschean in Leopardi's thought,[98] this is it. In the sphere of a regional phenomenology of knowledge [*sapere*], deception is thus sovereign. It is impossible to traverse the world of deception and discover alternatives that are internal to it. It is likewise impossible to identify within it a dynamic that, as in the world of the psyche, gets back [*rinvii*] to the metaphysical ground of the question—precisely from within the analysis.

Here in the world of knowledge [*sapere*], the return [*rinvio*] is external; it is organized immediately as an opposition. Illusion has no dialectic, even a false or unstable dialectic. It is immediately the solidity of deception—a machine of deception, a history of the alienation of human power [*potenza*]. There is no possible internal alternative, no identification of the crisis, no continuity of a minor but effective element with an antagonistic and different spirit: there is only global antagonism. Power [*potenza*] is opposed to knowledge [*sapere*] as one world to another world. Where could serenity be at this stage? The further we advance into the world of illusion, the more that world bears the mark of a progressive loss of its power and its being, of the possibility of redemption—nor could these ever be restored. This loss of power [*depotenziamento*] becomes definitive when we enter into the world of politics. But to this loss of power of objective being corresponds a complementary process of expansion of subjective, poetic and ethical being, an ontological extremism of the subject in relationship with the world, an extremism of power [*potenza*] against the deception of the world.

Sarcasm; or Concerning Politics

It is good to establish right away the frame of reference for the analysis of Leopardi's relationship with the *Risorgimento*, with politics in the proper sense. The political world is not merely the world of illusion, but the world of absolute illusion, of the maximum loss of power [*depotenziamento*] of existence. The entire evolution of Leopardi's regional phenomenology leads up to this point. Every material a priori of politics has been eliminated. It is the world of pure senselessness and vulgarity. If there was irony in relation to the psyche and love, if the cultural fabric and knowledge [*sapere*] possessed a solidity and an efficacy that were paradoxically strengthened by deception (which they precisely represented), political objectivity on the contrary is immediately "other," the other of absolute negativity and dead life. Ethics, presenting itself as rupture, has nothing to do with all this. The *Risorgimento* is reaction; the liberals and the legitimists all take part in this mystified, cruel but ontologically weak objectivity, subject to chance and stupidity, to the emptiest of human passions. Sarcasm alone is the key to a knowledge [*conoscenza*] of politics, an arrogant knowledge [*conoscenza*] that separates itself from a real that it despises and whose extreme characteristics it throws into grotesque relief. It defines an irreducible distance between ethics and politics, between subject and world. Constantly radicalizing itself further, it reaches the level of insult and, in its ferocity, eliminates all possibility of pacification, every "effect of abolition" in the denunciation of "the dissonances of degraded being."[99] This framework will remain stable and firm in the late Leopardi. There is no internal alternative to this evaluation and the relationship between ethics and politics remains insoluble. Unless politics is completely recast in an ontologically pure and radically different sphere, unless politics is rediscovered beyond everything that is real, unless. . . . We must of course return to this possible passage.

Now, however, before analyzing the mature phase of Leopardi's judgment on politics, we must immediately set aside a possible objection or rather a possible explanation of the absolute character of Leopardi's refusal of politics. This consists in referring his thought to an irreducible individualism that would not permit him to appreciate the collective form of social living. We know, the lyric poet is always solitary, and so on! Obviously this is rubbish. Nevertheless, this argument raises a serious problem, which consists in considering insoluble the crisis that occurs between an individualistic and self-referential morality and the rules of behavior vis-à-vis the human community. In particular, the quest for glory and social esteem opens up to the individual a contradictory path and lures him/her into real paradoxes; sometimes, faced with an obstacle or with the senseless circularity of social references, it drives the individual back into solitude, toward the definition of an extreme self-differentiation. But this rejection reverberates through society, or at least through those organized forms of social morality that politics especially embodies.[100] Furthermore, if the discovery of objective moral conflictuality registers the subjective quest for esteem and glory as an element that feeds this same conflictuality, there again the individual withdraws and makes his/her own isolation the desperate basis of his/her own dignity. Individualism flirts with misanthropy in this comedy of ethical morals.[101] These processes, effectively active during phases of profound cultural transformation such as Leopardi's era, phases that are marked by the decline of aristocratic as well as bourgeois virtues, may be discernible in Leopardi's experience. But I do not think so, for several reasons that I will list, but above all, for a reason that seems fundamental to me and that includes all the others: Leopardi refuses to justify his own freedom at the social level or to qualify it faced with the inevitable perversions of politics.

From his point of view, solitude belongs to a different ontological level; it produces poetry that is opposed to the social relation and to the political relationship. Leopardi's analysis of the misdeeds of individualism and the insignificance of the circular sensory web in which it encloses morality, ridding itself of all direction and all dignity, constitutes a preliminary analysis. Nor is a substitutive form of this dialectic of individualism, with its ethical values wallowing in uselessness, possible. Leopardi's juridical and political

skepticism is total: the collective forms of the organization of ethical-political values are just as vain as those of individualism. The often-caricatural
polemic against "statistics"—taken up again in maturity—takes aim at the
illusion of a middling and vulgar self-referentiality of social values.

> In the end I begin to feel nauseated by the arrogant disdain professed
> here for all literature and everything beautiful: especially as I cannot
> get it into my head that the pinnacle of human knowledge is knowing
> about politics and statistics. Indeed, reflecting philosophically on the
> almost perfect uselessness of the studies made from the age of Solon on
> to attain the perfection of civil states and the happiness of nations, I am
> inclined to laugh at this frenzy of political and legislative calculation
> and quibbling; and I humbly ask if the happiness of nations can exist
> without the happiness of individuals. Individuals are condemned to
> unhappiness by nature, not by men and not by chance: and as a consola-
> tion for this inevitable unhappiness I think that the study of beauty, of
> feelings, imagination, illusions, is more effective than anything else.[102]

The individualistic determination and the collective determination are
equivalent in their participation in the world's senselessness (those "very arid
disciplines"). Only the imagination and the power [*potenza*] of the affects
distract from this misery. Poetry is only possible from this perspective of
innovation, from an independent critical place, posited against this horizon.
The social and politics are not rejected from the viewpoint of individualism or the collective, but from the viewpoint of an ontological alternative:
individualism and collectivism have in effect been preventatively expunged
from every theoretical alternative. This aspect, already quite clear in the
last pages of the *Zibaldone*,[103] is even more so in the *Pensieri*. The dejection
of the political world, its lack of ontological reference, includes individualism as well as collectivism. Only a form of poetic charisma, metaphysical
charisma, an alterity that positions itself in total asymmetry with the stream
of historical and social time, can recast the social relationship. Recasting a
signifying communication is possible only on the basis of the refusal of the
entire phenomenology of politics. The paroxysmal character of Leopardi's
anti-dialectical polemic is a sign of the times. This sense of a value that
cannot be recovered in the world of politics but instead is identifiable in
a different, "other" sphere, that creation, labor, free activity, and power
[*potenza*] constitute it—this is a quest that all the authors of the crisis of
the dialectic undertook at that time, everywhere in Europe. I am not in any
way trying to establish filiations for Leopardi; I would not think of it. But
just as I am convinced that the problem of the dialectic, in other words the

comprehension of the world's contradictions on the basis of the rhythm of mediation, was fundamental for the European genesis of Leopardi's thought, I am persuaded that its radically anti-dialectical tension, its full awareness of the crisis of dialectical thought, allies Leopardi's critique of politics and the world with European philosophy in a thousand ways. The concept of the other, the potent and creative alternative that is opposed to the world, is inscribed in the great line of critical philosophy that, from the young Marx to Nietzsche, spans the nineteenth century—which was consequently not merely the century of progress, of new productive dimensions, and, alas, of wars and destruction, but also a century pervaded by a lucid, forceful and painful critique. Leopardi is in the mainstream of that century.[104]

The world of politics is therefore degraded being. No dialectic is applicable to it, and no hope can suffuse it. As firm, as irreducible as this theoretical conviction of Leopardi's is, it is nonetheless not an idée fixe: it is constructed. It is essential to step inside it, along with Leopardi, and consider the profound honesty of his progressive approach to politics; because in fact it is only in this way that we can understand his current refusal as a product of critique. If it is useless to recall once again the great passages, from the web of sense to its demystification, from the experience of the metaphysical catastrophe to the poetic recasting of ontology, we must nevertheless remember that they always had a political side, an aspect and an opening that tended toward the social world. So there is a Leopardian route to politics, from the heroic archaeological nationalism of the earliest canti to the attempts to participate in the (cultural and political) "narrow society" that he made in Milan, Florence, and Pisa. This route can be verified in certain personal decisions, in the deepening of certain friendships, and the adherence to reform programs.

One of the most beautiful of these decisions—by reason of its profound political resonances—is the oft-recalled one of refusing to enter the ecclesiastical profession. We saw the first fundamental determination in this matter at the time of the first trip to Rome: the disillusion occasioned by the Vatican milieu was then accompanied, within a fundamental anti-clericalism, by the definition of an irreducible secular and ethical vocation. In 1826 this decision is repeated: "The very fair considerations you put to me . . . fully convince me of the impossibility of reconciling my present life with the position of a person holding an ecclesiastical benefice."[105] The refusal thus has a positive content: Leopardi wants to be at the service not of religion but of the true, of philosophy. The secular choice is a vocation. Before being linked with the materialism and atheism of a philosophical position, the decision for the secular state is a decision to belong to the world—and one of detachment from the clerical and legitimist domain of politics. In that sense, this choice of the secular state is an introduction to that participation in the *Risorgimento*, which is a specific and certain determination in the young Leopardi. The friendship with Giordani is proof of it. It develops theoretically around the question of prose. Retracing the articulations of this thematic, reexamining the themes, and asking ourselves once again how eloquence, poetry, and prose can be united and produce results, do not matter. One thing is certain: prose is politics, or at least it can be, and it can be a tool of collective construction. Much later, when the affectionate and privileged relationship with Giordani is dissolved, Leopardi still confirms his conviction in a letter to his friend Puccinotti.

> Europe wants solider and truer things than poetry. By cultivating verses and frivolities (I'm speaking here in general) we're doing an express service to our tyrants, because we reduce literature to a game and a pastime—and literature alone could be a starting point for the regeneration of our country.[106]

That would be a secular and active regeneration of the country, for the sake of which Leopardi participates in what I would call the movement of critical editions, translations, and philological renewal. This movement combines philology and love of country and tries to reconstruct a living tradition that would be a moment of political identity and a positive way to approach the past.[107] The great Niebuhr had done so in Germany, and a secular and republican political passion had animated his "prodigious work":[108] "philosophy applied to philology and knowledge of the ancient world."[109] Leopardi considered it a great honor to have met Niebuhr, who himself spares no praise for the young philologist[110] who, amidst immense difficulties, perseveres in his labor with full patriotic faith—for in Italy, philology must be reinvented as well as love of country.[111] So let us continue to follow Leopardi's generous attempt to participate in the world and labor for the cultural and political regeneration of his country.

The *"Prefazione dell'interprete"* to Petrarch's *Rhymes*:[112] poetry is no "more than the science of passions and morals," and the history of a mind and of the country. The *"Manifesto"* for Petrarch's *Rhymes*[113] and the *"Manifesti"* for the editions of Cicero:[114] in the first place, throughout them we find the serenity of a collective task to accomplish, despite the great difficulties, for a renewal of science and common knowledge [*sapere*]. It does not matter that in Petrarch one meets with only a "few (but really very few) poetic beauties," and it does not matter that his Platonism is not merely "a fable" but also hypocrisy[115]—what is essential is to restore the continuity of a tradition and a universe of language and truth.[116] Leopardi explicitly insists on this point in his presentation of the *Crestomazia italiana de' prosatori*:[117] he undertook his selection so that "beauty would not be unaccompanied by important thoughts and things."

In his preface to the *Crestomazia italiana de' poeti*[118] he adds that all his labor aims to construct the "historical cognition of national poetry." However hard the labor, it will be done with faith in a possible reconstruction of minds. The letters to Stella reveal the great intensity of Leopardi's commitment and his ingenuous generosity.[119] In this spirit, as we have seen, he somewhat timidly supports the work of Vieusseux, despite ideological reservations. It is in fact in the movement of the reviews, and in particular in the work of the Florentine review, that the cultural project of the *Risorgimento* reached the greatest maturity and the highest degree of awareness. Leopardi was there, front and center. With Vieusseux he plays a clever yet candid game, each of them loyally enticing his partner onto the terrain of a collaboration. Leopardi at first parries Vieusseux's invitation: "this bad habit of *absence* is in me incorrigible and desperate"[120] and I could not be the "*Heremite des Apennins*" that you wish me to be; but we will meet again and discuss our project "which, in many of its parts, has the honor of not appearing to be of Italian workmanship." The discussion takes place; Leopardi then enters the Florentine circle and participates actively in its project. Once he leaves Florence, wherever he is, he remains in contact with the work of the *Antologia*:[121] "Your journal is already in a position no longer just to *profit* but to *bring honor* to Italy."[122]

The hermit of the Apennines is now in the national movement. His philosophy and melancholy do not prevent him from seeking that continuous mediation of a difficult web of sense and communication, in order to contribute to the collective work of renewal. The provincial, the solitary one, the absent one forces his working hypothesis onto this terrain, wanting a relationship that would begin to realize that narrow society, that initiative aimed at hegemony that constitutes the necessary preamble to any radical political innovation. But there is more: cultural work produces some positive effects.

> Why are you astonished that the French speak of me at Sinagaglia? You do not know that I am a great man; that in Romagna I scored a triumph; that women and children almost fought to see me? No joke.[123]

> Dear Pilla, The portrait is very ugly; nevertheless show it around in Recanati, so the townsfolk can see with their own eyes (the eyes of the body being the only ones they have) that the *Leopardi hunchback* is reckoned to be something in the world, whereas Recanati isn't even known by name.[124]

Dear Pilla, I've formally handed over all my philological manuscripts, etc.
to a German philologist who will have them published in Germany. . . .
You can't think how cheered I am by this development; for a few days
it has taken me back to the ideas of my early youth; and God willing, it
will give life and usefulness to vast labors.[125]

Glory, therefore, and friendship, and the esteem of many Italian, German,
and French intellectuals: "I'm treated with great consideration by Florentine
men of letters, or those settled in Florence."[126] He meets Manzoni.[127] He
regularly and attentively follows the movements of Gioberti, with whom
he tries to make contact.[128] Numerous ambassadors, cultural attachés, and
foreign travelers meet and esteem him. Glory acts as a cognitive mediation
aimed at the objectivity of the cultural and political world.

We have not recalled these passages in order to create a halo of literary chiaroscuro around Leopardi's liquidation of the world of politics. Our
obligation, rather, is to arrive at the clearest possible understanding of that
liquidation. Indeed, the latter is not carried out from a resentful viewpoint
or an experience of defeat. Even if it is incomplete and limited by the immaturity of contemporary Italian history, Leopardi's experience of the cultural
world is in fact a success. Of course, financial difficulties persist and he does
not escape some traditional forms of intellectual misery: the misunderstand-
ings with Manzoni concerning his work[129] are significant in this regard, to
say nothing of the "pestilential" relationship with Tommaseo (to which we
have to return). Nevertheless, this did not deprive the young intellectual
of the chance to participate in the world and in the political setbacks that
this cultural participation included, due to the general backwardness of
political communication. Why does a crisis of this relationship, a crisis of
such theoretical and political import, arise? Why does this ardent will to
knowledge [conoscenza] and participation founder so violently, at the very
moment when knowledge [conoscenza] and participation, responsibility and
authority are increasing?

A first answer to these questions requires turning back to the poetic
context of Leopardi's work. The discourse that condenses in poetic form in
the Night Song of a Wandering Shepherd of Asia marks the point where the
rising momentum of his intention to participate in the world runs out. The
metaphysical growth imposed by this poetic passage must not be underestimated in any case. On that basis the will to knowledge [conoscenza]
folds back on itself, while the components of a refusal of the world, of
this political and cultural world, appear fundamental. It is rather astonishing how the repercussions of the metaphysical experience of the Recanati

winter of 1829 to1830 manifest themselves with a certain elasticity, as if the
weight of the consequences that it entails were immediately avoided and
nevertheless the necessity of experiencing the relationship with the world
imposed its rules. In fact, a slow maturation is required. It is difficult to
discern the exact moment when the metaphysical experience resolves itself,
without further hesitation, into political sarcasm. In the last *Operette*, as
in the *Pensieri* of 1832, the process is complete; but the icy discourse and
the rigidity of the effects do not explain the passage, which is registered in
generic form rather than shown in mobile articulations. We do not grasp
the maturation, the precipitation of the crisis in its actuality. Nevertheless,
the metaphysical tragedy dominates and the ontological discourse is strong.
Leopardi fears the radicality of the impact of his thought upon the real. The
elasticity of repercussions of the philosophy of *Wandering Shepherd* and
the evasion of its consequences reveal neither indecision nor prudence; they
reveal instead the harshness of an extreme impact, of a thought that knows
its distance from the real even if it is true, of a poetry that is illuminated
by the creative instant and that with difficulty transforms itself into ethical
charisma. How human is all this! We are still proceeding, therefore, by
approximations.

From November 1828 to April 1830, Leopardi is in Recanati. The *Night
Song of a Wandering Shepherd of Asia* is the supreme expression of this
period. Then Leopardi leaves. He has decided to have done with this life.
He writes to Giampiero Vieusseux: "My very dear friend, I am resolved,
with the little money that remains from when I was able to work, to set
out on a journey to seek health or to die, and never to return to Recanati
again."[130] He leaves, plunges once again into the polite life of Florence.
This mildness muffles the metaphysical caesura, though not completely.
Metaphysical thought becomes karstic, reappears occasionally on the
surface, and ripens into a dull but effective polemic directed precisely
against that cultural and political world in which mildness, the continuity
of the project, and reform by means of the Enlightenment still constitute
an inescapable horizon. The revolution of 1830 to 1831 is in progress. What
is it? Is it something that the shepherd's glance cast over nothingness can
prefigure? Anyway, "in the absence of French or English reviews, I do not
believe it possible that any of you could even approximately arrive at a
correct idea of the French Revolution, nor of the present state of Europe,
nor of a probable future."[131]

So what comes next? The Provisional Governing Committee of Recanati
names Leopardi to an improbable National Assembly to be held in
Bologna.[132] Almost at the same time, Leopardi writes to his father.

> My dear papa, I very much wished that you could have gone to Rome in
> the present circumstances in order to give the benefit of your enlighten-
> ment to the government, which surely lacks minds capable of doing
> good amidst so many difficulties. But alas, the misfortune of our State
> will be that once more the present moment will pass without bearing
> any fruit.[133]

What confusion! Everything dissolves into a senseless superimposition of
events and propositions. The political and cultural world vacillates over an
incomprehensible event, an unexpected new revolution. Why? Why all these
words that charm the senses but touch neither the heart nor the reason? Why
is the world of representation and communication, a world that eliminates
pleasure and breaks all contact with being, triumphing?

> I don't think you are expecting any news of me. You know that I detest
> politics, because I believe, or rather I see, that individuals are unhappy
> under any form of government; the fault is nature's, which made men
> for unhappiness; and I laugh at the unhappiness of the *masses*, because
> my small brain can't conceive of a happy *mass* made up of individuals
> who are not happy. Much less could I talk to you about literary news,
> because I confess that I'm in great fear of failing to recognize the let-
> ters of the alphabet, from lack of practice in reading and writing. My
> friends are shocked; and they are right to seek glory and to do good for
> mankind; but I who do not presume to do good, and do not aspire to
> glory, am not wrong to spend my day lying on a sofa, without batting
> an eyelid. And I find very sensible the customs of the Turks and other
> Orientals, who are content to sit cross-legged all day long in a daze
> staring this ridiculous existence in the face.[134]

The sarcasm concerning politics is maturing. The revolution of 1830 is
like the others: it repeats their senseless vacuity. But why? Leopardi passes
the winter months of 1831 to 1832 in Rome, that horrible dead city. It is
literarily dead because it is politically dead, as is revealed by the erudite
correspondence with Luigi De Sinner in which Leopardi, as philological
correspondent, passes this terrible judgment upon Rome:

> You are perhaps expecting me to tell you something about Roman phi-
> lology. But my health here has been so bad until now that I cannot give
> you any satisfying news in this connection, as I'm obliged almost always
> to stay at home. It is true that I am often honored by literary visits,
> but they are not at all philological, and in general it can be said that

if here people know a little more Latin than they do in northern Italy, Greek is almost unknown, and philology almost entirely abandoned in favor of archaeology. How successfully archaeology can be cultivated without a thorough knowledge of the classical languages, I leave to your imagination.[135]

The judgment is global. Was not philology in fact a weapon for the defense and construction of patriotic and revolutionary feeling? Is not the lack of philology, its unhappy decline into archaeology, the demonstration of a political crisis? Here perhaps we are getting closer to a karstic reappearance of critique. The accumulation of sensations and reactions presses for an interpretation of the nothingness of politics. Let us repeat, the poetic vein must organize a definitive critical passage. Where are revolution, change, innovation?

This question is repeated intermittently, but remains unanswered. The Roman holiday of winter 1831 to 1832 nevertheless seems decisive. Leopardi returns to Florence, to depart again in September 1833 for Naples, where he leads a quiet, serene life. Ranieri is an affectionate friend. In those years Leopardi's detachment from politics intensifies. In a crescendo, the metaphysical river rises again to the surface with prodigious, uninterrupted, and compact force. In the refuge of relative Neapolitan quiet where the withdrawal from the world becomes a necessity ("I can no longer tolerate this half-barbarous and half-African country where I live in perfect isolation from everything")[136] without however being converted, despite the sarcastic proclamations (he needs "to get away from these scoundrels and buffoons, high class and low, all thieves and buggered rogues who fully deserve the Spaniards and the gallows"),[137] into an effective will to depart (the intentions expressed to De Sinner—"for many reasons and very strong ones, I'm eager to come and end my days in Paris"[138]—do not seem to me on the whole very insistent)—thus in the relative independence of Naples, metaphysics comes to the surface once more. It is interesting to note that the detachment from politics always takes a political form and that the highest polemic of the metaphysical refusal of politics can be given only in political forms. This does not mean that politics is an overdetermined totality, but rather that the life of the mind constitutes a set of communicating vessels, that metaphysics and politics are subject to a common physical law. It is not the clamor of the external forum but rather the folding back and reflection on ourselves that makes it possible for us to understand this. The deeper we go into the solitary analysis of the world, the more we understand its interrelations and the less misanthropic we are. So what is revolution, innovation, transformation? We are familiar with the desperate metaphysical condition, but in practice? What is the *Risorgimento*? Where is it? And if a political elite exists that moves, operates, constructs on this terrain, what is its truth?

This question of the truth of politics becomes central to the extent that, after having experienced and participated in the activity of a political elite that wants to be innovative—namely, the Florentine elite—after having known the clerical swamps of the government of Rome, Leopardi submits these knowledges [*conoscenze*] to a unitary judgment and to the centrality of the metaphysical question. But he also submits his question to the determinations of political contingency. It is a lasting political contingency that extends from the 1830s to the 1840s, in a kind of stringent though confused line of centrist recuperation of the revolutionary movement—such that eclectic mediating positions appear with increasing clarity between liberalism and legitimism; and it was not difficult to recognize the liberal who discovered spiritualism to be his own terrain of culture or the cleric who glimpsed in religion, correctly interpreted, a glimmer of freedom.[139] Does the long shadow of this political trafficking in ideologies prove intolerable to Leopardi? Just as intolerable as the insipidity of Gino Capponi's secular faith and Monaldo Leopardi's sympathy for liberalism—and above all Tommaseo, the most ardent representative of this encyclopedic and dilettante mixture: "that Italian, or rather Dalmatian, ass," "mad beast."[140]

> O ever unfortunate
> Italy . . .
> With pallid cheek
> You await the plague. Tis finally chosen
> To make known in France
> Niccolo Tommaseo.[141]

Here we have an "intellectual power [*potenza*]" that, among so many others, honors the century![142]

The case of Gioberti is different. In him Leopardi always senses a political ability to rethink the background of ideologies, while Gioberti senses in Leopardi a fund of exceptional political intelligence, which will lead him in *Il Gesuita Moderno*[143] to express the following judgment with regard to the *Paralipomena*:

> Are the Italian people trained for great enterprises? Toward the end of
> his life Leopardi wrote a terrible book in which he mocks the desires,
> dreams, and political efforts of Italians with a bitter irony that rends
> the heart, but is justified. All that we have undertaken for half a century
> on the plane of order is so puerile that I would not get angry with

the foreigners who mock us if they were not also more or less tarred with the same brush. How surprising would it be if the Jesuits were to triumph in a nation reduced to such a state of moral weakness?

That moral weakness must be denounced through a resistance unresponsive to the blandishments of a mindless unanimism that keeps the process of the *Risorgimento* linear and is full of reformist hope in its outcome. It is in this sphere of thought and cultural communication that Leopardi reacts so angrily to the voices that call him a "turncoat," a "penitent," or "convert," after attributing to him the widely disseminated and successful tract written by his father, Monaldo Leopardi, *Dialoghetti sulle materie correnti nell'anno 1831.*[144]

Although these dialogues were published anonymously, it was known that the author was a Leopardi and so they were immediately attributed to Giacomo. Right away, in the climate of centrist mediations and "new philosophy," talk of his conversion began. "I don't really understand the need to keep the author concealed. I believe it is certain that today such things please all the governments except the French, but who is afraid of them anymore?"[145] In the meantime, the fame of the booklet continues to grow, as does the presumption of the attribution to Giacomo. He reacts with very harsh denials that he sends to friends and publishes in the newspapers.

I can't take any more of this, I really can't. I don't want to show my face any more with this blot on it, of having produced that dreadful, truly dreadful, evil book. Here they all think it's by me: because the author is Leopardi, my father is quite unknown, I'm known, therefore I'm the author. Even the government is looking askance at me because of those filthy, fanatical, awful dialogues. In Rome I couldn't mention my name any more or have it mentioned anywhere, without hearing someone say: *ah, the author of the Dialoghetti.* It's impossible for me to tell you all the ridicule I've had to suffer because of that book. In Milan they are saying in public that I am the author, that I'm a convert like Monti. In Lucca the book circulates under my name. I'm printing my declaration in all the Italian Journals: it is coming out any time now in the Tuscan ones. I'm sending a much more strongly-worded one to France. But Rome matters a great deal to me.[146]

It is obvious that the violence of this protest proceeds from the refusal to be perceived as a "convert." Leopardi writes to his father that the duke of Modena—who probably knew the truth—"nonetheless says publicly that I am the author, that I have changed my views, that I am a convert, that the

same thing happened to Monti, that that is what decent men do." My dear
father, on the one hand I do not consider myself worthy of usurping your
fame. But on the other hand, "I will not, and ought not, allow it to be said of
me that I am a convert, or that I am like Monti. . . . My honor demanded that
I declare that I have not changed my views at all, and that is what I meant
to do and did . . . in a few journals."[147] In short, the problem is not only
that of being confused with the author of one of the "most bestial writings
in the world,"[148] but above all that of having to undergo the ignominy of
being considered a penitent, a convert. "My feelings toward fate were and
still are those I expressed in *Brutus*."[149] Leopardi is thus driven back from
political contingency to the metaphysical basis of his discourse just as he
had previously been driven back from the latter to the former; and gradually
all the lines are tied together again in defense of his philosophy and the
continuity of his personal coherence, the refusal of a world of falsehood and
grim superficiality—because only in this way can he rediscover a terrain on
which the problem of politics appears as the theme of recasting.

So, still on the terrain of pure political contingency, as a confirmation of
fidelity to himself and the reaffirmation of a truth, in autumn 1835 Leopardi
composes a ferocious satire of the Neapolitan New Believers [*nuovi credenti*].[150] Previously liberals and atheists, they became Catholic spiritualists.
Leopardi's opinions now displease these gentlemen, and they made a lot of
noise in Naples.

> My Ranieri, the papers in which I tried
> To express human life, like Solomon
> From the throne, by calling it bitter and vain
> Displease them. (*Nuovi credenti*, ll.1–4)

But why do the papers displease them? Leopardi avoids answering, pre-
ferring sarcasm aimed at the "new Neapolitan philosophers" and their
wretchedness.

> Naples takes up arms to defend
> Her macaronis; since the macaronis
> Before dying are too heavy. (ll.13–15)

> What do the mullets and the anchovies say? (l.19)

This *introibo* is followed by other, no less elegant definitions, which are
sandwiched between highly polemical jibes. What does Elpidio, a miserable journalist, say? "Already in the habit of gnashing his teeth against

heaven/Until it pleased France" (ll.40–41), this fine gentleman now goes wild "encountering my pain." He is a pure and simple opportunist.

> Seeing
> Other fashions reign, and the winds shift,
> He turns to pity. (ll.41–43)

His personal immorality is universally known, so let us leave him to squawk. As for Creda, who became a legitimist, he is a coward. His friend Galerio is even worse: undeniably chaste [*casto*] in comparison with the preceding character—perhaps castrated [*castrato*]? Leopardi omits to mention the name or pseudonym of the third member of this clan that frequents the parishes, out of pity for a sick person "in whose bones and veins flows mercury and a terrible venom." In short,

> These and many others who were enemies of Christ
> Up to today are offended by my words
> Because I call living arid and sad. (ll.70–72)

The satire, extremely violent, amounts to a veritable invective.

> Calm yourselves, friends, you who do not come in contact
> With any part of human misery
> That does not afflict foolish people. (ll.76–78)

You can believe in a beautiful, well-rounded progress, continuous, spiritual, and joyful, in a peaceful revival,

> You who are brave and strong, to whom life is dear
> And dying is grave; we effeminate ones,
> Who desire death, life embitters us. (ll.100–2)

Leopardi is neither a convert nor a penitent. This series of polemical contingencies, on the contrary, permits him to express in definitive terms his detachment from the world of politics and the maturation of the hope for a radical alternative. Thus it is not by chance that, against this backdrop, between spring and autumn 1835 he undertakes the composition of the *Palinode to the Marchese Gino Capponi*,[151] which constitutes a sarcastic retraction of his own political pessimism and radicalism and which aims to identify the weakness of the political elite of the revival and to indicate a new terrain of struggle. "I was mistaken, Gino; a long time/And very much mistaken."[152] It is an ironic self-criticism so as not to have to recognize the happiness of the times, even though it pervades the stanzas! But enough, all that has changed. Leopardi is now convinced, amidst cigar smoke, cakes, and ices, by the "living daily light/From newspapers."[153]

> I realized, I saw
> How happiness was public, and the pleasures
> Of human destiny. I saw the lofty
> Condition and the worth of earthly things,
> The course of human life all flowers. (*Palinode*, ll.20–24)[154]

So let us sing this "golden century," and let us sing it all together, as all the newspapers wish and even demand:

>   universal love,
> Railways, and very many kinds of trade,
> Steam-power, the printing press, and cholera bind
> Peoples and climes most sundered into one. (ll.42–45)[155]

Progress is thus unstoppable and the revival is its political figure. Nevertheless we cannot avoid a certain number of reflections (ll.55–96): the law of nature continues to be effective in the form of war, while gold is the content and value of progress. How can one reconcile the permanence of these laws with the great prediction of universal progress? In fact, the themes are already in place and the poetic bow is fully bent. The contrast between the ideology of progress and the repetition of the human experience of pain is given. The poem could end here, but it does not, for the problem is not merely that of demonstrating the emptiness of the world of politics, it is also of identifying a new basis for the ethical foundation of politics.

The central part of the canto thus constructs a moment of great sarcastic intensity: if the law of nature and the violence of history continue to operate in the face of an unstoppable, magnificent, and progressive historical evolution, what are we to make of this harsh, implacable contrast? Pardon me, but this is nothing serious; it involves only a slight problem, a relic of a bygone era! This is followed by a fashionable hymn to its force of transformation and refinement of morals (*Palinode*, ll.97–134), in turn followed by a new sarcastic interlude, a hymn to statistics and newspapers (ll.135–53) as the foundation of true knowledge [*conoscenza*]. But these mystifications cannot stand.

> Just as a boy, taking enormous care
> With twigs and bits of paper, in the shape

Of a temple, of a tower, or of a palace
Raises an edifice; and just as soon
As he finds it finished starts to knock it down,
Because to him those twigs and bits of paper
Are needed for another enterprise;
So nature with any work of hers, however
Magnificent to look at, just as soon
As she sees it perfect, starts to break it up,
Having the bits in mind for something else.
It is in the vain hope to keep themselves
Safe from this wicked game, whose raison d'être
Remains obscure for ever, that mere mortals
Use their abilities a million ways
And with such skill; because, for all their efforts,
Brutal nature, like an invincible child,
Indulges her caprice, and without rest
Destroying and creating stays amused. (ll.154–72)[156]

The lines that follow this apology for nature ("invincible child") deepen the demystification (ll.173–207), always in a sarcastic mode, showing how ideologies and stereotypes of community try to deny this single harsh truth. Wherever we do not succeed in being happy individually, we are offered a common happiness! Long live Rousseau![157] Enough, enough of this time that flies, this everydayness deprived of principle, enough of this time of the newspapers (ll.208–26). Enough of these Capponis, Tommaseos, Vieusseuxs, and all those who induce us merely to experience this time and to imagine the *Risorgimento* in this light (ll.227–59). Leopardi opposes to this dispersal and degradation of being a vivacious claim for time and the function of writing poetry.

The *Palinode* concludes with a witticism: his pen smiles sarcastically at the "bearded heroes" of the ephemeral time of politics. Thus the relationship once sought with the world of politics comes to an end, violently tears itself apart. We knew this was to be expected, but traveling this long route was not useless, for it allowed us not only to verify the passion with which Leopardi sought to establish a relationship with politics but above all to see how the definitive rupture is taking positive shape. This *Palinode* is a great thing, a war machine. The internal structure of the canto is the contrast not only in dialogical terms ("me and you"—the dialogue is strongly personalized and marked by a detachment colored by arrogance) but also in terms of opposing images of time, of the poetic function, of the political sense of life. The canto is formed of successive blocks, the order of which follows an argumentative logic, a rhetorical-political thread. The argumentation must convince and must outline the passions in sarcasm in order to demonstrate the possibility of choosing an "other" path and an "other" desire. There is something very potent, a strong transgression, in this *Palinode*!

A great historian of ideas[158] has justly noted that in every civilization there are things at which one cannot laugh: objects and ideas, metaphysical tendencies or horizons that cannot be transgressed. It is striking to note how violently Leopardi attacks precisely the untouchable stereotypes of his era. He laughs at that at which one cannot laugh, in order to indicate an other terrain of foundation, an other time in relation to which values can be given. This identification of time as an other site of the possible, as a site of future thought, and this choice to measure oneself against an ethical alternative to politics are fundamental. Indeed, it is the sense character [*sensatezza*] of power [*potere*] as such that is contested, the senselessness of power [*potere*] that is denounced. Power [*potere*] is an illusion, an effective illusion but now on the march. The sarcasm with which this truth is revealed is an indication of a contrast, of an other that exists and is given: true illusion, illusion that knows how to pronounce itself the truth of existence. A different time, an other time: such is the true *Risorgimento*. How desirable, how really foreseeable, how possible is it? In any case, there is nothing to expect from the contrary agitation of the reviews and the "bearded heroes." If the true and heroism exist, they conspire under a different heaven. *Palinode*, in other words, means retraction, public penitence.

Well then, here is my palinode, which is certainly not penitent, but on the contrary affirms the conviction that my old rationalist, sensualist, materialist thought was and remains good. Only on this other basis is a political making capable of constituting a program and a struggle possible. Only by playing with the "invincible child" can we lead experience back to philosophy and free political thought from politics. We are leading it toward ethics, toward the unique region of pain and imagination where all being is formed.

In emphasizing these conclusions of the *Palinode*, however, I feel as if I have betrayed Leopardi. Indeed, this divide within political life, so massively other than that which the newspapers and current events present, almost gives the impression of a utopian choice. It is thus necessary to specify and above all to keep in mind that Leopardi often amuses himself with utopianism; he has a taste for it and carries to its highest level.

> In this century of so much lawmaking no one has yet thought of making a utopian code of civil and criminal laws, but in due and proper form, such as to serve as a standard of perfection, which should be a model for all other codes, so that their goodness is judged according to the

greater or lesser extent to which they resemble it; such also as to make
it possible, with few changes or additions required purely by the circumstances of place and time, to be adopted by any nation whatsoever,
at least under a given form of government, at least in this century and
by civilized nations, etc.[159]

Thus he imagines a code of political freedom and consequently a juridical
system in conformity with it. It is obvious that this is only a useful intellectual diversion. Leopardi uses utopia as a logical expedient without ever
reducing his thought to it in any sense. Utopia is ambiguous, a dialectical
form.[160] It is a hope, or at very least its true suspicion fertilizes the real.
None of this is present in Leopardi, for whom utopia is at most a working
hypothesis, a totally conventional element, a form of paradox. The other that
Leopardi proposes in the *Palinode* is opposed to politics and false revival:
thus it is not, cannot, and will not be a utopia. Alterity stands on its feet and
not on its head. It is not utopia but ontology. There is really nothing to say;
we can only stand amazed at how strong Leopardi's option is. It is in no way
utopian but consists rather in an alternative foundation and in a tendency
toward true being on the basis of this recasting: not utopia but an experience
of alternative being.[161]

The *Paralipomeni della Batracomiomachia*[162] is an interesting experiment entirely situated within this problematic framework. Leopardi had
tried three times to translate the pseudo-Homeric text;[163] furthermore, he
had gotten involved with the issue of its attribution to Homer.[164] Now he sets
to work again, but only to take up the poem's pseudo-Homeric epic style in
order to make a free reflection with it—a politically free one. The theme is
the Italian political situation after 1831, but with reference to and examples
from the situation of the kingdom of Naples between 1815 and 1821.[165] This
little poem, conceived and drafted at different times in discontinuous forms
(so that the layers and genres are varied and variously composed: mythic-
epic, parodic, and fantastic in the style of Ariosto or Lucian, etc.), is of
extraordinary importance. A free lyric confronts political reality in order to
discriminate between the epic and the sarcastic: the multiplicity of layers and
genres does not detract from the unitary character of the project, which is
maintained during the six to seven years of composition.[166] The poetic vein
is assured and continuous. This is combined with an extraordinary mastery
of political judgment, whether it involves the past or the present. Playing
with different poetic forms, Leopardi renders his own singular political
judgment on existence; indeed, the fact that this judgment is so assured does
not prevent it from being singular. It is an attempt to completely displace
the political perspective. The parodic form that the discourse takes and

through which the choices are specified must not deceive us. In reality, the
search is very beautiful, profound, and highly articulate. The candor of the
poetic phrasing here is bizarre, because up to now the polemic did not really
attain this level of nimble imagination. The sarcasm includes elements of
ponderousness and blockage. The *Palinode* did not avoid this. But here, in
the *Paralipomeni*, there is something different: an innocent narrative and
poetic machine grants freedom, spontaneity, and felicity to political feeling.
As we will see, this felicity is not merely an aspect of the diversion but it is
above all the discovery of a new terrain of poetic imagination. We can identify an extremely rich passage from canto VI to canto VII, or rather within
canto VI, and we will do so. But right now we must note that this rupture
between reconstruction, the development of the web of discourse, and the
moment of free imagination that follows them is in reality the proposal of
a metaphysical leap and a political project. It is not by chance that the most
beautiful things in the *Paralipomeni* are expressed precisely in relation to
this rupture and these passages—in cantos V, VII, and VIII. Our attentive
analysis of the *Paralipomeni* will simply follow their development.

From canto I to the middle of canto VI, Leopardi follows a historical, or
pseudohistorical, web of events.[167] It is the story of the defeat of the mice by
an army of crabs aided by frogs, and how the mice reorganize Topaia [Rat
City, literally burrow] into a constitutional monarchy after this defeat; how
the king of crabs and their general deceive the ambassadors and the king
of Topaia so as to forcibly impose drastic legitimist alternatives; how the
mice seek to defend their constitution verbally only to ultimately undergo
a shameful defeat that compels them to submit once again to an absolutist regime. The first six cantos all move within the demystification of the
world of politics. The very marked sarcastic vein rebels against the world
of politics in its entirety. Even if the polemic is addressed above all to the
legitimists, the liberals are no better. All the mice are concerned by the
poverty and insignificance of their burrow.

The form of the eight-syllable line and the felicity of the poetic phrasing do not allow Leopardi's inspiration to employ the desperate key of
the grotesque here, though the polemic—primarily against legitimism, as
we said—is no less forceful for all that. Legitimism is described from all
angles: as a theory of political equilibrium (canto II, stanzas 30–39),[168] as an
ideology in the strict sense (canto IV, stanzas 44–46),[169] and finally as the
political theory of the phases and system of the European powers [*poteri*]
(canto V, stanzas 1–15).[170] The fact that the argument is often pushed to the
point of paroxysm in no way detracts from its substantial accuracy and the
singular exactitude of the political language. The logical nature of the strong
polemic, the exactitude of the conceptual terms elaborated, the fact that the

sarcasm is objectively based on the disproportion between the tremendous strength of the reactionary army and the imbecilic pettiness of its political and diplomatic capacity, all demonstrate that Leopardi is certainly not a reactionary.[171] Nor is this comportment a matter of chance—in the same period, writing to his "dear papa," Leopardi can note:

> I was very saddened to hear that the legitimists are showing themselves so ungrateful to your pen for all its battling in their cause. I will say saddened, but not surprised: because this is the way men of all parties behave, and because the legitimists (allow me to say it) are not too keen for their cause to be defended with words, given that merely acknowledging that there is someone on the terrestrial globe who calls in question the plenitude of their rights is a thing that goes far beyond the freedom granted to the pens of mortals: besides which they very wisely have a preference (over reasons, which for better or worse can always be answered), for the arguments of the cannon and imprisonment, to which for the moment their opponents have no answer.[172]

If on the one hand the polemic against legitimism is extremely strong, the one against constitutionalism and liberalism is no less ferocious. Here the attack focuses less on the constitution and freedom than on the unruly way the mice enjoy and abuse them. Following the newly refined description of the constitutional monarchy (canto III, stanzas 36–39),[173] comes a polemic that is anti-plebeian (canto IV, stanzas 27–28),[174] but much more concerned with blasting the long-winded vulgarity, the cowardice in war, and the hypocrisy of the political language of liberalism (canto V, stanzas 29–36, 39–43).[175] The defeat of the mice's constitutionalism in the face of the crabs' reactionary legitimism is also and above all the revelation of an asymmetry in the effectiveness of power [*potere*]—between those who make an exaggerated material practice of it and those who believe they can arrange it in a pure and ideal manner. All the author's realist interventions (in political terms) into the course of the narration aim to demonstrate this truth (above all it confronts the evaluations of an "evil-thinker" [canto V, stanzas 24–28],[176] the very type of the Leopardian "political journalist"). The fact nevertheless remains that liberalism is one of the forms of that political time denounced by Leopardi as ontologically disempowered [*depotenziato*]; and it is certain that if the victory of the crabs leads, by means of the legitimist restoration, to a police state and the decline of industry and civil life that follows from it (canto VI, stanzas 1–14),[177] it is not statistics that will be able to save us from ruin. During the crisis, sects and creeds proliferate, attempts to avoid defeat are plotted . . . ultramontane thinking (object of a

new, extremely virulent polemic: here the theme of obscurantism as such is
the order of the day: canto V, stanzas 1–15)[178] on one side and on the other,
secret society thinking [*pensiero carbonaro*]: "Then there was born among
the mice/A madness more worthy of laughter than of pity" (canto VI, stanza
15, ll.1–2, but see also ll.15–17).[179] And so on, and so on.

   Of course, the world is not totally condemned to this wretchedness.
Leopardi intervenes to bring to light gaps that, although in shadow, hold
great riches: witness the hymns to Italy and her past glory and against the
wretchedness of the present in cantos I (stanzas 26–31)[180] and III (stanzas
11–14).[181]. But this element is not decisive. It is a matter of materials—and
this is also valid for the national spirit—that a different and ontologically
"other" virtue could alone revivify. This theoretical truth has an immediate poetic aspect: it demands that the extreme violence of chiaroscuro, of
heroic writing, pervade the sarcastic fabric of the documentation of existence. Canto V is central in this regard. It begins with the long speech of
Boccaferrata [Ironed Mouth] on the principle and practice of legitimism
(stanzas 1–15),[182] followed by the weak confirmation of the Statute by
King Rodipane [Bread Muncher] (stanzas 16–20)[183] and the commentaries
of an "evil-thinker" (stanzas 24–28); in the meantime (stanzas 22–23 and
29–36),[184] the mice prepare for war in a deluge of words whose rhetorical
force is as great as their lack of efficacy.

> You would have heard all the orators
> Thundering war in all the assemblies,
> Leonidas, Themistocles, Cimon,
> Mucius Scaevola, the dictator Fabius,
> Decius, Aristides, Codrus, Scipio,
> And similar heroes of their ancestors
> Often named in the councils and all day long
> Circulating in the mouths of the populace. (canto V, stanza 29)

And the battle is joined.

> The two phalanxes were face to face,
> Already spread out and about to fight,
> When from all over the plain, from all over the mountain
> The mouse people took flight.
> How, I don't know, but neither stream, fountain,
> Cliff nor forest stopped their course.
> They would still be fleeing, I believe, if flight
> Kept fugitives alive so long. (canto V, stanza 42)[185]

The infamy of the flight and the cowardice of the mice's behavior therefore end up showing the true face of the political world. What remains to be said; what can we add? Virtue stands out clearly against the mud of dishonor.

Of them all only Rubatocchi [Chunk-Stealer]
Remained on the deserted field, as straight
As a cypress, motionless, not thinking it allowed
A citizen to seek his safety after the act of his people,
After the disgrace of which that day
Was only the beginning for the mice.

When they turned against him, the enemy
Felt the Herculean power of his arm.
Though hard and thick, the shell
Was not strong enough to save them from it.
Every cleaving blow of that sword, falling,
Broke it, and made the bones creak,
And cut off the claws, and covered the ground
With a half-dead and gelid crowd.

Thus fighting alone against an infinite number
He remained as long as there was light.
When the sun had descended to other shores,
Feeling his mortal body afflicted and weary,
His chest and side wounded and lacerated all over
By very sharp pains, and no longer able to hold up
The shield, on which a horrible and dense mass
Of spears and various arms were nailed,

He threw it far away, where he felt
The enemy the thickest.
Many remained mangled and crushed from it,
Others who had been squashed dirtied the plain.
After he had gathered his last strength,
He never rested his hand from fighting
Until, the veil of night having thickened,
He fell, but the sky did not see his fall. (canto V, stanzas 43–46)[186]

Love, the constancy of feelings and reason, and freedom had already been celebrated in the *Paralipomeni* (canto III, stanzas 24–34)[187] but in an abstract hymn, literarily convoluted and politically equivocal. Whereas here, after Rubatocchi's death, two stanzas explode in which the shock of the hero's death reveals the metaphysical dignity of an other virtue.

> Noble virtue, whenever it perceives you
> My spirit, as at a happy event, rejoices;
> Nor does it believe that you should be scorned
> Even if you are nourished and cultivated in mice.
> Before your beauty, which exceeds all others,
> Whether renowned or hidden it finds you,
> My spirit always bows down; and not only
> When you are true and real,
> But even imagined, it is warmed by you.
>
> Ah! But where are you? Always dreamed of
> Or sham? Did no one ever see you real?
> Or were you indeed extinguished along with the mice,
> And no longer your beauty smiles among us?
> Ah! If you were not vainly depicted with laurels,
> And did not perish with Theseus or Alcides,
> Certainly from then on your smile was
> Each day more rare and less beautiful. (canto V, stanzas 47–48)[188]

A moment of fundamental metaphysical rupture intervenes in Leopardi's political work. The politeness of the ontological exposition of the rupture does not deceive us as to its radicality. The beginning of canto VI marks the end of what we can surely call the first part of the *Paralipomeni*— that of poetic construction around a historical web. At that moment the historical web breaks off, and to its wretchedness and the infamy of its times are opposed virtue and an other time. The historical web will no longer appear from here to the end of the poem, which is unfinished. It is quite likely that the composition experienced a considerable interruption.[189]

From this point to the end, Leopardi plays with other possible poetic and metaphysical scenarios, not so much seeking a new foundation as alluding to it by defining emblematic sites for it. The junction between the historical first part and the decisively mythological second part of the *Paralipomeni* rests on one character: Count Leccafondi (Bottom-Licker). He was presented in canto I as the mice's ambassador in the crabs' military camp (canto I, stanzas 34–43);[190] he reappears during difficult negotiations, and later becomes the Enlightenment-inspired minister of the constitutional king, and for this reason is especially unpopular with Metternich and the crab who represents him. Sent into exile, the count is then caught in a tempest. Lost, he ends up reaching a magical palace and tells its proprietor the tale of the great events he has experienced (canto VI, stanzas 24–25).[191] Leccafondi's interlocutor is quite a singular character: he is no less than a Dedalus (and it matters little whether ancient or modern), who draws the count and us into a different atmosphere, into a different poetic ambiance, be it a mythical-lyrical or even a resolutely metaphysical one.

I insist once again that this rupture does not achieve who knows what ontological revelation: what appears here, in the form of allusions, of more or less clear indications, is only the possibility of an other terrain, the necessity of which has been clearly stated. Led on by Dedalus, Leccafondi interprets the world of history and worldly virtue—as a professional politician he cannot do otherwise—but for the first time he suspects a problem of truth, a truth so other that it could only exist in the underworld of the mice, at the sources of being where the souls of brute beasts lie and the materiality of truth appears with all its force. The total absence of truth from the political world is thus demonstrated in the allusion to a possible recasting—an other, absolutely different recasting, inspired and prompted by the underworld. Leccafondi thus listens to the teachings of Dedalus, that very Leopardian character.[192] A long parenthesis on the conception of death and the souls of brute beasts (canto VII, stanzas 11–16)[193] authorizes and prepares the decision to make a journey into the world of the dead where Leccafondi may be able to find lessons that will heal the political crisis of his people. Thus a materialist atmosphere takes shape that has the same force as certain passages of the *Operette* and the *Zibaldone*, a materialist, atheist and anti-spiritualist atmosphere that works for the constitution of the conditions for the metaphysical rupture demanded by Leopardi for the construction of a new politics.

The play of allusions and projects is accompanied by an intense meta-physical shock. Dedalus and Leccafondi take wing on the great journey to the kingdom of the dead.

> Thus when both had put wings on their backs
> And had tried out and shaken the new load,
> Up over the terraces of the solitary dwelling
> They took the same paths which the birds had for their own.
> Dedalus looked just like a big bird,
> The one beside him just like a bat;
> They flew a vast distance, and saw from high up distant peaks and seas
> and shores. (canto VII, stanza 24)[194]

The description of this journey that corresponds to a moment of great poetic beauty extends to stanza 37. Then the great mountain of the beasts' hell appears (canto VII, stanzas 38–51).[195] Poor Leccafondi, now alone, descends into the underworld of the mice (canto VIII, stanzas 6–20).[196] The description of the dead city Topaia, marked by a profound serenity and a very tender detachment, is truly splendid. Every fable of paradise finally having been eliminated, all hope, like all despair, is related to humankind. Finally reaching Mangiaprosciutti [Ham-Eater] and Rubatocchi, Leccafondi submits his problem to them: the problem of the *Risorgimento* (canto VIII, stanzas 21–23).[197]

> The deceased is not an animal who laughs.
> On the contrary, by eternal law he is denied
> The virtue by which it is given to the living
> When they discern an unusual stupidity
> To relieve with a loud and convulsive act
> An itching of the internal part.
> Therefore, when they heard the count's question,
> Those departed to the other life did not laugh.
>
> For the first time, however,
> A joyous sound spread upward
> Through the perpetual night and from century to century
> Reached the most remote caves as far as the bottom.
> The fates trembled for fear that the laws
> Imposed on the other world had been broken
> And that gloomy Elysium, having heard the count,
> Would not be able to contain its laughter. (canto VIII, stanzas 24–25)[198]

The formidable burst of laughter that breaks loose from Inferno and Elysium when they hear the count speak of the *Risorgimento* marks the conclusion of the critique, the end of the poem, and the indication of a terrain to traverse all at the same time. What follows up to the (draft) end of the poem—stanzas 26–46 of canto VIII[199] contain the counsel given by the good ancestors and see Assaggiatore [Taster] (perhaps Colletta?) finally chosen as guide for a reprise of the political initiative—is neither particularly beautiful nor particularly intense. The poem is finished. It concludes on the decisive indication of a different terrain, that of an ethical recasting of political making. The fabulist displacement of the political web is valid only as an allusion to a new ontological position of the subject, to a new definition of historical time.[200]

The moment has now come to conclude these pages dedicated to sarcasm and to politics. We have demonstrated the initial assertion of a loss of ontological power [*depotenziamento*] of the world of politics by analyzing how Leopardi tries to traverse this terrain and to deepen the ethical alternative to it. In following this path along with him, we have discovered how, beyond the world of politics and its ontological poverty, Leopardi grasps the tension, commensurate with the dimensions of politics, toward a new ontological position. This tension is for the moment posited as a necessity of critique and is evoked only allusively in terms of reality. The only demonstrative ontological argument in its favor at our disposal is the poetry of the *Paralipomeni*, with its tender resonances of alterity. The tenderness of the allusions combines with the transgression of the *Palinode*, thus rooting itself in an absolutely other historical judgment. How difficult it is for many readers to accept Leopardi's absolutely anti-dialectical decision, his constructive overturning of the tragic! They see only "political vacuity," or cynicism pure and simple, or even a reactionary attitude.[201] They refuse to understand the radical coherence with which, since the 1824 text *On the Present State of Italian Morals*,[202] Leopardi sought but did not find a positive mediation with the real, and how the concept of "narrow society," although proposed with such intensity, was gradually emptied of any signification. Nevertheless, the mediation with the real and the subjectivity of this mediation, concrete historicity and "narrow society" remain, and cannot fail to remain, the very concepts of any political phenomenology whatsoever. The fact that we find them negatively defined, that we find them presented as pathological inflections of a disempowered [*depotenziata*] root and a worn-out being—all this means nothing more than that we must break with the logic that led us to such metaphysics and such historical vacuity. Leopardi's political sarcasm unremittingly relegates the political categories of historicity and the subject to emptiness and insignificance, but it does not destroy them; instead it aims to fill them with a new content, a new political and ethical proposition.

Some readers conclude that if this is correct, then Leopardi does not constitute an alternative *to* the *Risorgimento*, but an alternative *within* the *Risorgimento*.[203] I am no more in agreement with these interpreters than I was with those who refuted Leopardi's positive overturning of the tragic— that is to say, not at all. For what characterizes Leopardi's thought is the confrontation with the ethical foundation of history, the rupture of every dialectical attempt at fixation, the opening of a new ontological discourse on the foundation of politics. Leopardi's nihilism is in search of ontology: certainly not a progressive ontology but an other ontology. If we wished to remain trapped in these terrible and obsolete linguistic dimensions, it would be a matter of indifference to call Leopardi "revolutionary"—or could we not in fact, without prejudice to any other conditions, just as well call him "reactionary"? The only thing we surely cannot do is to call him "progressivist" or "unpolitical." In any case we will not we allow ourselves to be confined to these miserable categories, for Leopardi's negation of politics and his metaphysical laughter at the expense of the *Risorgimento* first of all constitute elements, unresolved but very strong, of a question: what is true illusion in politics, in the social, in the creation of values among humankind? So long as we have not answered this question, all politics, before being reactionary or revolutionary, will be absolutely senseless. But we already have at our disposal some elements that define the metaphysical answer to it: notably the concept of power [*potenza*] and now that of the political world, the collective world and the political subject. How can we reach the level of ontological foundation and signifying universality at which all this, by articulating itself, can become productive? Leopardi, the unpolitical, poses this problem, a problem that is an anticipation, a light on the horizon, not only with force but with provocative violence.

❧

Chapter 5

A Lyric Machiavelli

....

The Event of Critique

Only after eliminating every dialect of illusion and grasping the allusion to the other as foundation of being can the problem of the true be raised once again. What is true illusion in this world where being is illusion, though no less material, no less ontologically solid, for all that? What is true illusion in this world where the displacement of the horizons of significa-tion and the creation of ever newer illusions is a ceaseless process, but in which the subject feels its belonging to being no less strongly? Leopardi's poetic discourse is now engaged exclusively on this problematic terrain. This exclusivity is the condition of the generality, the universality of the discourse. It involves rising from negativity to the foundation that will serve as the basis for characterizing what exists. Even if the foundation is negative and alterity contributes to its formation, nevertheless the characterization will be universal. Leopardi's reconstruction, from the poetic act to the quest for the significance of truth for the world, slowly expands over the horizon of universality. Now we must reach the end of the path by taking up again one of the problems that originally set the search in motion—the question of critique—to see how it is resolved or simply resituated at the culmination of Leopardi's metaphysical experience.

In this regard, a first remark must be made. It will complete the analysis of the political universe and the critique of the true within the phenomenol-ogy of that illusion. What definitively reveals this critical experience to us? The fact that the asymmetry, the difference between material progress, the development of knowledge [conoscenza], and the self-realization of nature on the one hand and on the other the discovery of the true and the new foundation of being, is radical. If it is subjected—as always—to these linear sequences, poetry denies itself as possibility of knowledge [*conoscenza*]. In the dimension of politics, in the generality and objectivity of the relationship between subject and historicity, the true as progress and poetry as knowledge [*conoscenza*] are insignificant, non-existent. Poetry, if it wants to exist, must reveal itself otherwise. History is not truth but illusion, and illusion is practical essence. Poetry can give sense to history by presenting itself as an act of the practical constitution of being, not as the servant of the true but as the practical, material producer of the true. In this it constitutes an important ontological activity. Once the sphere in which the true is considered is that of poetic practice, the definition of the true is thereby entirely modified. The emancipation of the true from a passive and naturalistic definition of knowledge [*conoscenza*] is thus the central theme, the positive presupposition of the critical recasting.

A second remark concerning the nature of poetic making follows directly from the first. To the extent that he extracts the definition of the true from the universe of pure reason and links it to that of practice, Leopardi also destroys the miserable little definition of the aesthetic of the beautiful that has haunted us since Baumgarten and the school of Wolff, according to which it is a minor form of knowing [*conoscere*].[1] Again, no: Leopardi's classicism, his conception of the human as a being who has the possibility of developing all his faculties in a sublime creative unity, reacts definitively against these traditions. The poetic beautiful makes no allusion to knowledge [*conoscenza*]; it is no degraded or sublime, material or prophetic form of knowing [*conoscere*]. It is instead the voice of making, the analysis that, from the senses to feelings, from experience to history, stands as a comprehensive material and constitutive force.

Hence a third remark: this poetic and constitutive making that takes the place of knowing [*conoscere*] and incorporates it creatively must be defined through a collective dynamic. The rule of this dynamic is love. Love constitutes the other ontological moment that the metaphysical allusion had glimpsed. It defines the subject who confronts historicity. Thus it is definitely upon love that the answer to the question rests: what is true illusion?[2]

These Leopardian passages, which have immediate consequences, are not easy to follow. For example, the negation of the true, of progress and the *Risorgimento*, and the necessary displacement of the thematic terrain with respect to the lack of signification that these terms display constitute an enormous problem. It would be easy for us to cling, against the progressivist image that some have foolishly wanted to attribute to him, to the conception of an unpolitical Leopardi, or against the equally foolish interpretation of the unpolitical man from Recanati, to show how there is in him a possibility, at very least an allusion, in short an access to a different terrain for ethical and/or political foundation. But this resolves nothing. Indeed, the problem lies elsewhere, and it rings out: what is a politics of love? What is a radically alternative constitution of being that constructs the true and displays it as practical essence? What is the making of poetry? I do not know how to answer these questions, even though they have been clearly defined by the many necessary directions taken in the development of this search and faced with the results to which it has led us. What is a politics of love? The answer appears quite difficult, but we will try to find one by seeing if a positive propaedeutic can be defined in such a way that the same critical function which, in the refusal of the dialectic, allowed us to approach the tragedy of being and thereby outline a hypothesis of construction will now allow us to begin traveling a complete constitutive road. We are trying to see if, before and beyond the fact of being able to define a politics of love, it is not possible to grasp that moment in which critique, having destroyed every possibility of naturalistic and/or mediated knowledge [*conoscenza*] and having highlighted the demand and hope for another terrain, finally becomes positive, constructive power [*potenza*]. This is an essential moment, of prodigious, extreme critical concentration, an event of critique. In the form of poetry, critique begins to emit a constructive proposition of love and, from it, of the world.[3]

The canto *Upon a Bas-Relief on an Ancient Tomb showing a Dead Girl in the Act of Departing and Taking Leave of her Family*[4] is an experimental passage along this new line.

> Where are you going? And who
> Is calling you away
> Far from your dear ones, beautiful damsel? (ll.1–3)[5]

The scenario begins with the departed, with death and the parents' pain: an idyllic scene although tragic, fixed in the rigidity of an implacable historical repetition: "yet he who casts his eye / Upon your destiny must heave a sigh" (ll.25–26).[6] Then we see Leopardi's metaphysical experimentation at work: pity for the death of a young girl becomes a question regarding the nature of the true or the truth of nature. Why does one ever die? Why does death come to youth, take its innocence, cause pain to its loved ones? The concept of a doubly cruel nature—as bearer of death and as bearer of death to the young—occupies the foreground.

> Never to see the light
> Would be the best no doubt. But—being born—
> That time of life when beauty first reveals

Her regal countenance,
And when the world begins
To bow down low to her from very far;
When hopes are bursting out, and long before
Truth has had time to strike her cheerful brow
With lightning of its melancholy beams;
That time, like mist descending into cloud—
Formations on the horizontal line,
To disappear as though she had not been,
And give up for the gloomy
Silence of the grave the days to come—
Although this to our mind
Seems best, the pity strikes
Right to the very heart of humankind. (ll.27–43)[7]

Nature is irrational: only sarcasm can now exalt the "wonder . . . not worth our praise" (l.46).[8]

Mother feared and lamented
By every living creature in the world,
Nature, a wonder but not worth our praise,
Who bring to birth and nourish to be killed,
Nature, if to our harm
We die before due time, why do you let
The guiltless suffer it?
If to our good, why make—
More than all other ills,
For those who leave, those who are living still—
This one departure inconsolable? (ll.44–54)[9]

We are faced here with a concept of nature that is a concept of the catastrophe of the true, the ruin of all rational consistency. The cognition of the true is the cognition of horror. Nature is not merely a harsh mother; it is a logical catastrophe. The world is given to us in the dialectic of its internal senselessness. But here is a new variation of the search: it emerges as an assertion of inexhaustible resistance to the true, nature, death. Love does not accept the catastrophe of nature.

And yet although,
As I firmly believe,
Living is all misfortune,

Dying a favor, who is there who could,
As he by reason should,
Desire for those he loves their final day. (ll.81–86)[10]

The consciousness of the truth of death is rejected by love and by the human community.

How could you make
Us live beneath this curse:
A mortal and his loving must survive
Another's mortal death? (ll.104–7)[11]

The multiplication of death's cruelty and the malignancy of nature thus inspire the constitution of an irreducible, extremely resistant affective fabric—love is the other of nature, the ethical basis for a different knowledge [*conoscenza*]. And if nature "cares / For something, not for us / Or any good or ill we might think ours" (ll.107–9),[12] then from love something other is sought: nature is no longer merely the unavoidable backdrop of existence; it is also an enemy against whose ferocity a kind of community of love, in any case a subject who refuses to submit to that dreadful natural law, is gradually constructed. The shock at the death of the young girl first constitutes itself in a moment of rebellion and denunciation and then takes the form of an act of recasting and hope. It is upon the very substance of this act that our attention must be brought to bear. In fact it involves a poetic act that displaces the concept of truth from the terrain on which it appears as an irrational forced takeover to one on which love displays the positive essence of the refusal of this law. Love indicates a possible community; it reveals itself as hope. Love is refusal; it begins with a refusal—a paradoxical and extremely rich refusal: love takes shape as other, as suffering subjectivity within nature, but from which develops—or at least is sketched—an "other of" nature, a counterposed subjectivity, a different ontological fabric. This process is sketched in the canto *Upon a Bas-Relief on an Ancient Tomb*, no doubt with difficulty—indeed, this canto is rather laborious—but forcefully. Obviously the importance of this passage cannot be exaggerated. I insist upon the fact that we are moving onto an experimental terrain, but it is indisputable that we have embarked on the road the leads to *The Broom* and to the full maturity of the constitutive theme in Leopardi's last poems. Therefore it is essential not to underestimate, without for all that exaggerating, the importance of this passage, in particular the formal element that strikes the eye—taking "formal" in the critical sense; in other words as the subjective force of forming, as the power [*potenza*] of defining and constituting. The critical event consists precisely in totally recasting the viewpoint from which truth is considered, in transforming the ethical resistance to death and to the true into the formal possibility of a new life and a new true, in unfolding refusal into love. It is essential to grasp this dimension: it congeals, so to speak, all the forces and directions participating in the formation of the allusion to "ontological alterity." This formal passage from allusion to efficacy, from possibility to reality, gathers together the results of all the operations of the demystification of the dialects of illusion, of irony as well as deception and sarcasm, and raises what was experienced as a logical alternative and its contents of intellectual critique to the level of practical antagonism. The event of critique thus brings together, in a transversal operation, all the forces that were constituted in the individual phenomenologies of the sensory and spiritual faculties against the power [*potere*] of false illusion—and restores this set of antagonistic forces to the truth of the world.

The canto *On the Likeness of a Beautiful Lady Carved upon her Tomb*[13] constitutes a further verification of what we are saying. If in the preceding canto the cruelty and the paradoxical character of death were externalized in the contradiction between nature and youth on the one hand and between nature and love/community on the other, then the exemplifications—in *On the Likeness* the metaphysical question interrogates the body, concrete individuality, its determinate time—follow the time of beauty and that of its implacable adversary, death. In this framework, the level of the critical question and the phenomenological paradox rises: since in fact death begins to appear immediately as senselessness, and nature can no longer do so, not even through allusion to the true—or rather, it is within nature itself that the contradiction of the essential coexistence of death and the true explodes. There is no paradox: nature is catastrophe. The catastrophe of the relationship between the true and nature is given as a presupposition and this rupture permits an other logic that establishes a distance between the mind and death. This is a cold and effective logic, a richness that can turn against nature the weapons that it wrested from her, putting an end to the long period during which poetry had been restricted to complaint and invective. A vigorous sensuality infuses the first lines of the canto: the figure in the portrait is described in tones that recall *Aspasia*, the body of the beautiful lady takes on a strong physicality, and the portrait is vital, determinate, since the passage from that vitality and sensuality to death is so violent.

> now mud
> And bone; a wretched thing,
> A shameful thing, and hidden by a stone. (*On the Likeness*, ll.17–19)[14]

The reality is double: on one side life and beauty, on the other, death and its "dirty, hateful, base" nature. A geometrical spirit sets to work here to distinguish, separate, explain, and push to the point of paradox the rupture between life and death. The questioning of death expresses an urge that is more logical than poetic.

> So fate brings down to earth
> That semblance which appeared to us a living
> Image of heaven. Insoluble enigma
> Of all our being. The fountainhead today
> Of high wide-ranging thoughts and secret feelings,
> Beauty looms large, and seems—
> As though a radiance cast
> By something superhuman on this waste—
> The sign and certain hope
> Of blessed kingdoms and a golden world,
> A more than mortal fate
> For our so human state:
> Tomorrow at a touch
> It all turns into dirty, hateful, base,
> Which but a while ago
> Had an angelic face;
> And out of mind at once
> The marvelous idea
> Which had its being thence, must disappear. (ll.20–38)[15]

The metaphysical ascension of the catastrophe of nature is thus fully accomplished here. The canto strongly insists on the totally irrational character of this catastrophe. Lines 39 to 49 show precisely how every construction of nature and knowledge [*conoscenza*], thought and the true, is exposed to the vicissitudes of catastrophe. Its principle is clearly defined: you see how the explosion of a simple dissonance can at any moment reduce to nothing what was laboriously constructed by concerted human effort [*concerto umano*], how it can provoke a global rupture and consign the whole system to nothingness! Death drags into nothingness not merely the individual but the whole complex of vital relationships. The irrational is now the source, the sign, the aura of death. However, ruin and catastrophe do not conclude the canto.

> How do we rise—if we
> Are wholly low and frail,

Dust and shadow—to such high sentiment?
And if noble at all,
How is it that our finest reverie
Can be so readily
For such slight reason both aroused and spent? (ll.50–56)[16]

Death takes possession of the whole world, but poetic making does so too. The senselessness of death takes possession of all reason; the dimension and hope of life will be other.

Longings which have no end
And visions mounting high
Are called up in the mind
As the effect of learned harmony. (ll.39–42)[17]

Life is love and concerted human effort; perhaps it is even community, or at least an allusion and path to it. Death is untruth, irrationality of course, but also the enemy.

In this way a poetic and metaphysical situation of great historical importance takes shape, and it is essential for us to insist upon it. Indeed, we are entering into that constellation of thought which, on the European scene, proposes a radical alternative to the development of the dialectic. The original alternative that motivates Leopardi reappears, matured by the complete development of his thought and revealed with extreme thematic clarity. The subjectivation of the antagonism between life and death, between subject and nature, between poetry and knowledge [conoscenza] first of all underscores this same antagonism. The dialectic is no longer a tool recuperable by thought, even hypothetically. Reality is radically, completely split: not rational truth but making, immediate ethics, youth, and beauty are marked as subjective impulses that predominate on the ontological level. Rational truth is the enemy.[18] In other words, if we take up Kant's terminology again, the transcendental aesthetic opposes the analytic—the former does not seek the latter, does not ask it to complete the possible deduction of the subject, but instead recognizes it as a hostile function, as a mystifying net from which it must free itself, or rather avoid. In the critical making of poetry, the transcendental aesthetic reveals the essence of the subject, its opening to the world, the imagination, true illusion, against the analytic prison of logical truth. That power [potenza], that tension of the possible, that impulse toward the world that results in creativity is directly constructed in the immediate transcendental aesthetic of the subject. Poetic making, that making which aims, without mediation, at the constitution of the universal, is the basis for this overthrow of the epistemological foundation of modern metaphysics. Making is the only element of verification of the subject at our disposal. The true can be constituted only in making; it exists subordinate only to making. This accumulation of practical energy to give form to subjectivity, to reveal ontology, is a critical event indeed.

This transcendental definition of subjectivity gives rise, at this stage of research, to another pair of problems. Space and time are the conditions of sensory knowledge [*conoscenza*] in Kant's aesthetic of pure reason. What, in Leopardi's aesthetic of creativity, immediacy, and ethicality, are the conditions of sensory knowledge [*conoscenza*]—or rather, a knowledge that wants to be sensory but in fact traverses sensibility in order to reach the highest levels of productive imagination? The conditions of development of the transcendental aesthetic and the means of its transgression toward the kingdom of the imagination seem to me to remain space and time; but it is precisely in this tension that, as constitutive forms, they must be grasped and seen functioning. The space of the aesthetic subject is an ethical space, a space in which concerted human effort is constituted and with which the bases of a community of values are posited. It is a space of the elementary values of life, power [*potenza*], and love, their development and intersection. The true can be born only within this ethical projection, within the positivity of the construction of a new world, woven by the passions and constituting an alternative to the degradation of the universe we know. A veritable schematism of ethical reason thus develops here. We have seen several rays of it, however tenuous, appear in the canti of this period. Love constitutes the hard core of aesthetic subjectivity, and from it unfolds the ethical pattern of the world.[19] This is equally valid for the other function that is traditionally assumed to reshape the constitutive form of aesthetic consciousness: time.

Time is truly a power [*potenza*] in the texts of this period. In relation to the Kantian and Romantic theory in which space is the static form and time is the dynamic form, in Leopardi—as we have seen, even if this point was not specifically emphasized in our discussion of spatial form—the relationship is overturned. In Leopardi's aesthetic, space is the dynamic of love, while time is the ontological condition, the determination of alterity. Time is on the one hand the most adequate figure, the fiercest expression of nature. Nature's cruelty is deployed in accordance with the rhythm of time, and truth is annulled in time. Time eliminates every claim to truth, to beauty, to life. On the other hand, it is against this dimension of a time that flies that the dimension of a time that constitutes must be determined: the time of the poetic act, the time of ethical making, the time of the critical accumulation of an alternative against the despair of nature. The time that roots us elsewhere is our time, its intensity as the time of life directed against the annihilating temporal variations of progress, of the heavens, of nature. True time locks onto itself and its will to express the power [*potenza*] of a necessary ethical liberation.[20] The schematism of ethical reason, which must also be considered from this point of view, is thus an advance of consciousness among the articulations of ontological time, which makes them more potent and projective and gives them the possibility of vigorously expanding. The ethical time of Leopardi's aesthetic of subjective consciousness is a creative dimension because it is other, radically alternative, and beautiful. The temporality of the imagination, of true illusion, takes flight from ontological consciousness at this point. Time is the means of being, the constitution of the world, the hope that realizes itself—because consciousness is diluted in the world. The set of powers [*potenze*] set in motion on the sensory level by this spatio-temporal articulation of the movement of consciousness is truly extraordinary. But the most important point is to clarify how this schema is anti-dialectical and anti-rationalist in every sense and in every way. It in no way involves negation or overcoming, the realization of some secret finality of nature or being. On the contrary, it involves constructing an antagonism and seeking a constitutive rule for a radical alternative. The forces of mind intersect in the definition of this vital alternative, an alternative that intends to traverse all of being and redefine poetically all its dimensions. The schematism of ethical and poetic reason is constructive and alternative.

In defining this theoretical profile of critique at the highest point of its expression—and insisting on the definition of the sensory power [*potenza*] of the poetic subject, on the dynamic projections of love, and on the ontological profundity of the experience of time—in clarifying the complexity of the schematic process that follows from these premises, in understanding the importance of the ontological intermediary between sensibility and imagination thus posited: in short, in completing this labor, we must admit that here we are going beyond the documentary evidence that Leopardi's thought and poetry actually offers us—though not beyond the set of complex theoretical indications that emanate from his thought and poetry. We see in the next section, in fact, how some of the theoretical tendencies described here are realized at the highest poetic level in *The Broom*. However, here we allow ourselves to dig deeper into a chapter in the history of European metaphysics in the nineteenth century—a chapter that, if it is not directly included in Leopardi's thought, is nevertheless broadly hinted at there. Leopardi the "provincial," the "marginal," expresses in his poetry a central passage of critical, anti-dialectical thought in European philosophy. And it is particularly interesting to grasp its power [*potenza*] in this mature phase of his thought, precisely when, after having criticized in the spirit of negative thought every dialect of worldly illusion, Leopardi begins to travel a constructive path—drawing from a radical ontological alternative the indication of a radical reform of mind. Premature death interrupts the development of this thought, so let us try to schematize, briefly, a chapter in the history of metaphysics.

The dialectic represents philosophy as absolute rationalism and metaphysics as the science of historical effectiveness. The world is unified in a rational destiny. The enormous importance of the dialectic at the beginning of the nineteenth century consists in reorienting modern thought, relieving it of the crisis that follows the French Revolution and the triumph of cosmopolitan and encyclopedic universalism in the Napoleonic era. The dialectic mediates historicity, its absoluteness and differences, into a complex, articulated, mobile unity of rational thought and leads abstractions back to the institutions of knowledge [*sapere*] and power [*potere*]. The function of dialectical thought is politically restorative—even if, in its plasticity, it knows how to make itself the tool of progressive positions. In any event it proceeds by negations, overcomings, and sublimations that lead reality and its abounding life into a realistic and certain framework of control. The horizon of the dialectic is totality; it is administrative; its style is reasonable and paternalistic. We have already recalled how dialectical thought is the legitimate child of Kantianism and how transcendentalism is the cradle from which it is born, through a theoretical operation that selectively accentuates the importance of the transcendental analytic—contrary to the theoretical path that runs from the transcendental aesthetic to the theory of productive imagination. Now we must see how the oppositions are born not so much in the confrontations of its genesis as in the confrontations of the conclusive and projective theoretical framework of the dialectic. And how Leopardi's thought and poetry are opposed not so much to the origin—although this is effectively the case, even concerning the reception of the dialectical problem, and with such vigor, as we have amply shown—as to dialectical thought in its entirety, to the category of totality, and to the mania for restoration of this metaphysical ideology.

In the course of the nineteenth century, a first general alternative line confronting or rather opposed to dialectical thought is organized and articulated, in strongly irrationalist terms, around all the positions that exclude the possibility of a reformulation of the order of sensibility according to a rationalist logic—it being understood that the world of sensibility has no ontological consistency but only phenomenological consistency. From Hamann to Schopenhauer, from the later Schelling to Mach's spiritualism, dialectical logic was subjected to this attack. Since De Sanctis, Leopardi's name has often been associated with that of Schopenhauer and with this anti-dialectical current.[21] But this reconciliation is improper. For if it is true that reasons of a sensory order are opposed in both to the totalizing process of the dialectic, Leopardi never indulges in phenomenalism. In his thought, the reality of the world does not vanish and being is not dissolved. Being is not opposed negatively, but rather positively, ethically, in an alternative mode, to the nothingness of the becoming of nature. And Leopardi can throw back at Schopenhauer the reproach that the latter addressed to the dialectical philosophers: that of having annihilated, through the unity of the foundation, the specificity, the concreteness, the irreducibility of the sensory. Schopenhauer's nothingness results from the paradoxical overthrow of the absoluteness of spirit,[22] whereas Leopardi traverses the nothingness of being in order to regain, in light of it, the reason of critical antagonism.

It is essential to insist upon the depth of the opposition between ontology and phenomenalism. Leopardi's conception of being is anti-dialectical because the dialectic tries to subject the irreducible determinations of sensibility and ethical immediacy to an undifferentiated unity—and in this way to reduce everything to the phenomenon of a deep substrate. But in Leopardi, the sensory exists irreducibly, and it occupies the foreground of the scene. Pain and the immediacy of the refusal do not annihilate the subject; on the contrary, they construct it. Thus Leopardi does not belong to Schopenhauer's line of resistance to dialectical hegemony. If he adheres to the critical impulse in the confrontation with dialectical rationalism, an impulse that pervades the century, he does so in the name of the defense of particularity, of the realism of the passions, and never according to the model of an asceticism of the phenomenon, of the inexistence or, worse yet, the absence of being.

A second alternative line to dialectical thought during the nineteenth century is the one associated with the developments of the school of the Hegelian left. What is subjected to critique here is less dialectical rationalism as such than it is the fact that a particular use of this tool transforms the critique into an apology for natural and historical effectiveness.[23] It is indisputable that in many ways, Leopardi's thought belongs to the demystifying tendencies of the school of the Hegelian left. They have in common a violent critical impulse directly inherited from the revolutionary tradition of the Enlightenment. In all these authors there is an articulation and development of materialist and atheist positions that at times, despite the great distance that separates their situations, makes their critical paths analogous. Nevertheless, essential differences persist. Although the terrain of reference of the Hegelian left is in any case fundamentally defined by a certain historicist humanism, in Leopardi the demystifying tendency is never limited to the terrain of historicism. Its critical route always leads thought towards a metaphysical opening. Thus in this case we could say metaphysics against historicism, just as we have already said ontology against phenomenalism in the relationship between Leopardi and Schopenhauer.

A third alternative line to dialectical thought flows through the nineteenth century, and that is the thought of singularity, of the vindication of the tragic absoluteness of existence. Kierkegaard represents the most lively and most eminent position on this terrain.[24] The existentialist and Leopardian positions share a certain number of theoretical comportments, such as the insistence on being and on the singularity of consciousness, the protest against any operation that aims to manipulate the order of sensibility and the immediate ethical horizon.[25] And yet, beyond this common protest, what a radical difference! It is made more obvious yet by the analysis of what constitutes the hard core of their resemblance. They are both ontological thinkers, characterized by a strong metaphysical fecundity, but one is spiritual and pushes the critique of transcendentality toward the transcendent, while the other is rigorously materialist. Singularity is called "grace" in Kierkegaard and "chance" in Leopardi. We could pursue this, but instead let us sum up.

The three elements common to Leopardi and the anti-dialectical currents of the nineteenth century do not in any way detract from the originality of his philosophy; instead they deepen it. Indeed, Leopardi combines a strong metaphysical predisposition to a materialist ontology with irrationalism, the sense of demystification and the pleasure of singularity. This is the framework within which Leopardi constructs an absolutely original and, to my mind, extremely strong historical and anti-dialectical position. So the absolute rationalism of dialectical thought is not attacked by Leopardi solely insofar as it is a rationalist presumption, an apologetic function, and a totalitarian tendency; it is unhinged because of its inexistence and insignificance faced with the material determinations of existence, of the production and reproduction of humankind, and of being in its entirety. Within this set of complex articulations, Leopardi's protest becomes an autonomous metaphysical position, and the antagonism of true illusion is situated within an ontological horizon.

At this point, then, let us take up our chapter in the history of nineteenth-century philosophy from another angle. We must try to understand if these positions, these tendencies, these philosophies that are opposed to dialectical rationalism are equipped—and if so, to what extent—not only to criticize its effects but also to substitute constructive mechanisms for it; for dialectical rationalism is a thought that is exceptionally and potently [*prepotentemente*] constructive. It realizes the encyclopedic and constructive spirit of the Enlightenment, despite abandoning the latter's ethical and revolutionary ferment. The mystified and false world presented by dialectical idealism is not, for all that, any less efficacious and cruel: it is the world in which we live viewed as a necessary world. The grandeur of dialectical thought consists in having transformed the critique of knowledge [*conoscenza*] and values that, in the era of the Enlightenment, functioned as a war machine into an apologetic machine: now every criterion of selection, verification, and judgment is sacrificed to the mere functional exaltation of the machine and its efficacy. Critique serves as the basis for the project of a pure and simple apology for the real—not a static apology but, on the contrary, the incessant production of effectiveness, a continuous immersion in a reality that is given as such.

How do the anti-rationalist and generally anti-dialectical currents oppose this constructive capacity and its hegemonic thrust? The problem is posed neither by the philosophies of Schopenhauerian inspiration nor by the existentialist currents: the protest sets itself up on the border of being, delights in its own purity, and renounces the struggle. The Hegelian left adopts quite a different critical position in this situation: a subversive and demystifying critique is employed to redefine a productive context on the basis of which a world of truth could be constructed. The productive force defined on this horizon and the ontological autonomy of its foundation often represent a strong and precise alternative to the proposition of the dialectical machine. But how fully does this alternative manage to deploy itself? Furthermore, does not the utopian content that often characterizes these attempts threaten to limit their impact?

In summary, for the Hegelian left, the passage to a constructive project often plays out, in cases where it is detached from historicism, between the vanity of a utopian project and generic, purely critical positions. The power [*potenza*] of the alternative is sometimes suggested, but as Nietzsche judiciously declared with regard to the Hegelian left, it does not succeed in becoming a subject.[26] But it is precisely here that the ontological impulse of Leopardi's thought is set free: in making critique a subject, a separate, open and productive subject. Let us see how that happens. Up to this point we have called the formation of this subjectivity the event of critique, and we have analyzed from various viewpoints how all the critical inflections of Leopardi's thought converge on it. But this is not enough. The critical function is not merely a formal element—the formal element constructs the conditions of subjectivity and its critical power [*potenza*], but it must be actualized. The dynamic of actualization of poetic subjectivity, of the critical event, is the synthesis of Leopardi's entire thought. Thus we are now able to see how the tragic overturning of the moral conflict and the protest against death are articulated with the firmness of the ethical position, and how all this tends to resolve itself into a series of schematic processes of the imaginative constitution of being. Leopardi passes from nothingness, from the denunciation of death, to the affirmation of the necessity of resistance and to the definition of a route of the imagination, so as to produce a subject. This poetic subjectivity is potent. Leopardi has drawn hope from the history of Italian literature and philosophy. There, between Machiavelli and Galileo, he sees one of the privileged places of language and of an adequate thought in which a subjectivity that is up to the task of redeeming the mind had perhaps taken and in any case could take shape.[27] This is still not enough: Leopardi establishes himself, not at all unconsciously, at the level of the European philosophical polemic. He weaves the alternative thread that leads from the documenting of sensibility to the affirmation of the power [*potere*] of imagination, but he does so by including all the contingencies of the critical process and driving them toward the heart of being. Subjectivity is born within this continuous process, within this intentional and phenomeno-logical relation that absorbs subjective knowledge [*sapere*] into the network of the refusals and negations that produce it. It is a constitutive phenomenol-ogy, a reprise of the philosophy of the Enlightenment, of its starting point and its ethical tension, as the critical and productive tool par excellence. The rupture with the dialectic and rationalism corresponds in Leopardi to the attempt to construct subjectivity: a materialist subjectivity, traversed by the determinate conditions of existence that grant it a direction and sustain it. To speak of subjectivity is to speak of action. In Leopardi, poetic action [*agire*] constitutes being. Poetic action is subjectivity that posits being fac-ing itself, not in an idealist way but in a materialist one, by confronting the subject with the conditions of existence and by making concerted effort and relation the conditions of a continually open, continually reinitiated struggle. Leopardi takes up the philosophy of the Enlightenment (and the force of practical discrimination that it contains) in a post-dialectical con-text, just as he takes up criticism from a post-dialectical viewpoint. But he synthesizes the whole into an exemplary and extreme subjectivity that is poetic making, critical making on the margins of nothingness, hence against nothingness.

Leopardi breaks with the development of nineteenth-century European philosophy to the extent that he seizes the constructive force of the dialecti-cal machine in order to overturn its functioning. He does not set it back on its feet (as some claim) but confronts it with being, with nothingness, with the construction of determination. This power [*potenza*] of the negative, in its full power [*potenza*] and autonomy, this flash of self-valorization within the dimensions and in accordance with the rhythms of catastrophe—this is the Leopardi who installs himself in the history of nineteenth-century European philosophy.[28]

Ethics as Foundation

Ethics is overthrow in the face of nothingness; it is action that follows from separation from the dialectic of nothingness, that insists on an other region of being. The theoretical precariousness of this foundation forms part of its nature, as a consequence of its exposure to the whole tragic dynamic of being; but the foundation is not any less real for all that. We have seen how the two canti of winter 1834 to 1835, *Upon a Bas-Relief on an Ancient Tomb* and *On the Likeness of a Beautiful Lady*, allowed Leopardi to posit the premises of a constitutive phenomenology of alterity by constructing against and across the subject-nature, life-death antagonism a series of schemas for the formal reconstruction of the autonomy of the subject. Now we will be able to see this transcendental aesthetic of ethics develop. We will consider the terms "constitutive phenomenology" and "transcendental aesthetic" as interchangeable, since whatever the context evoked (phenomenology or aesthetics),[29] the fundamental element is imagination, the constitutive intention—that is to say, this becoming concrete, dynamic, material of the critical event, its transformation into power [*potenza*]. With that, criticism is effectively driven to catastrophe and its course consequently bifurcates: with the analytic of reason and the dialectical, totalitarian, and absolute solution to its ideal aporias on the one side, and on the other (on Leopardi's side), the tendential passage to the sphere of imagination, to a different world that is antagonistic to the analytic world. To the latter's abstract order and logic is opposed a concrete order of the imaginary and ethical life. The ethical foundation is necessary once the materialist advent of the world reduces the logical universal to a pure hypothetical and practical function of action. The foundation is intensive since universality is, in materialist ethics, intensive—a common notion, certainly, a nominalist *ens*, but also the explosion, the flash of a creative light that humankind recognizes when performing an activity of ethical reflection and thus ontological identification.[30] This activity of recognition happens against the backdrop of nothingness. The only being that we construct is that which we extract from nothingness—and this is equally valid for the being we know [*conosciamo*]. To speak of ethics as foundation, then, is to assert the absence of any absolute foundation, an absence that can be surmounted only when the cognitive will sets to work—and that is indestructible. Only death tests it, but in so doing makes it stand out, for the constructiveness of the mind is exercised tirelessly on and against this limit. It must traverse and absolutely oppose nothingness. There is power [*potenza*] in that opposition—a power [*potenza*] born of no deep and secret origins, which takes shape contextually in the act of opposing. Then this opposition grows; it discovers the potentiality of alternative time in which it is inscribed and the dimensions of the communitarian space onto which it opens. To speak of ethics as foundation is exact, therefore, only if this foundation is considered as a process that is absolutely free of presuppositions, one that is constructed, in the midst of the whole tragedy of being, as the strong and autonomous comprehension of a possible alternative, a possibility to realize. There is no other being than what we produce. All the rest is nature, false illusion, slavery, and death.

During the Neapolitan spring of 1836, in the period of Leopardi's full poetic maturity, these problems are at the center of the two great canti: *The Setting of the Moon* and *The Broom* or *The Flower of the Desert*. Let us pause over the first.[31] Its philosophical opening and poetic success are much less important than what we observe in *The Broom*, but it is useful to consider *The Setting of the Moon* as an essential introduction to the next canto and to the definition of the tragic, antagonistic fabric of Leopardi's critique. This canto is composed of four stanzas that articulate a logical hypothesis on life and death.

> As when in lonely night,
> . . . .
> The moon goes down; and drains the world of color;
> All shadows go, and one
> Obscurity envelops hill and vale;
> The night is left blind . . .
> So our youth disappears;
> So it leaves our mortal years. (*Setting*, ll.1, 12–15, 20–21)[32]

The simile has the force of a classical inscription and thereby exposes the rupture of every unitary conception of nature. It collects true illusion regarding youth in order to oppose it to false illusion, old age, and death.

> Just so they take to flight,
> The shadows and the shapes
> Of the illusions giving such delight,
> And all the distant hopes
> In which we mortal beings put our trust.
> Our life is now at best
> Abandoned and obscure. (ll.22–28)[33]

The asymmetry of the time of life, the difference between the time of youth and that of old age—these divisions are projected onto the vast metaphysical perspectives of Leopardi's writing of poetry. This setting of the moon is equivalent to a descent into the underworld: here it is death, its approach, which illuminates life. The response to the perception of crisis and the consciousness of tragedy is sarcastic; the antagonistic event is forcefully expressed in invective.

> Our lamentable fate
> Would still have seemed too happy
> To those above, if but our youthful prime,
> Where each and any good is fruit of trouble,
> Had been allowed to last a whole lifetime. (ll.34–38)[34]

Thus the ethical foundation of the critique is fully expressed and revealed: death, the flight of time, and the natural fact are the law—one cannot evade them—but consciousness can free one from them. And it is this act of liberation, in the ferocious shadow of the impossibility of experiencing the tragedy of the world, which must be grasped as the ethical foundation. When the beauty of youth has faded away, life remains a widow: death, only death, not the cycles of natural events or the repetition of days and seasons, is granted to humankind. But we possess a superior form of knowledge [*sapere*], and in this situation the critical event, the ethical breach, ontological alterity arises. The canto lacks grace, has a dubious stylistic consistency, and is sometimes even pedagogical. Yet considering this poetic vein as simply a laborious repetition of an experience already consummated in the Recanati *Idylls*[35] does not seem justified to me, for it allows us to grasp an essential critical passage: traversed by catastrophe, the concept of nature splits, leaving us faced with youth and old age; in other words, with a polarity of values, a definitively open alternative. In the early Leopardi, youth is the production and redemption of nature; here it is the constitution of an other time: it is life against death, life against nature. Nature is objectified, not as backdrop, not statically, but in the face of and against the subject. The despair of being breathes it in as the contrast of an antagonistic movement of liberation.

Thus we come to the central point of Leopardi's construction of the metaphysical perspective, where we can reconsider its genesis. In the first place, we have a complete and radical revision of the concept of nature. This is not presented as a unitary essence but immediately as a split: it is one of the masks of the vicissitudes of being, implicated in the catastrophe that constitutes its essence. This passage is extremely important: we recall how much Leopardi worked on the concept of nature and how, in a continuous succession of passages, it was transformed from an internal limit to the web of sense into a harsh, negative, self-subsistent figure, from the pessimistic representation of the *Operette* to the current definition, the fierce, extreme figure of the split. Some of these passages and definitions can certainly be referred to Enlightenment culture.[36] But the importance and intensity of these references and sources take nothing away from the authenticity and innovative force of Leopardi's conceptual and philosophical development, the singular path of which is incredibly modern. It sets us face to face with the concept of nature as a context of alternative values to be discriminated. Nature is something split; thus it is the terrain of a choice to which we are driven, or rather constrained, by the possibility of destruction and death that it nonetheless implies. Tragedy alone nourishes thought and the ethical importance of its approach.

In the second place, before nature stands the image of the subject, which is also constructed in an original way in Leopardi's thought and through his poetics. It too was often confounded with the heroic dimensions and sensualist determinations; then it was gradually reconstructed between the conception of pain and the feeling of nothingness in order to end up in the constitutive passage that we are now beginning to verify: here, between the critical event—that is, the recognition of a cognitive breach, against the nothingness into which the mind threatens to sink—and an ethical act, a constructive breach opens. It is the quest not merely to escape nothingness but to constitute the schema of the ontological imagination on the basis of this separation.

Here we have the third point of Leopardi's reconstruction of a metaphysical perspective. The nature-subject antagonism is dynamic and open because of a double rupture: first on the side of nature, by a series of radical alternatives of value, between positive and negative, life and death, youth and old age; and second on the side of the subject that moves between nothingness and the being of consciousness, seeking life and opposing death. It tries to understand the relationship that ties it to nature in the complexity of the exclusions, alternatives, and ethical choices that this relationship entails. Ontology in Leopardi could not be better described: the laborious selection of a true fabric, in the inconclusiveness of labor on the foundation and the continuous impulse that is subject to the power [potenza] of being. Even though it is in no way progressive, our extraction of existence from nothingness is quite effective; and gently but with great force it unfolds into consciousness, into subjectivity, into world: a metaphysics of constitution.

The Broom or The Flower of the Desert[37] is Leopardi's song of the unfolding of being and of a new definition of the relationship between subject and world. This canto sums up many of his themes and concludes the discourse that leads up to it. Indeed, beyond the important mechanism of self-reference inherent in the body of the canti and in the poetic intentionality that suffuses them, beyond the repetitions and thematic deepenings, The Broom presents the philosophical characteristics of a conclusion. This conclusive character refers less to the genesis of the canto's themes than to the new horizon of truth that is constructed in it. Not that internal references to the preceding poetic development are lacking; they are, on the contrary, abundantly present.[38] It is enough to emphasize the most conspicuous themes.

- the nostalgia for Rome: "that city once the mistress of the world" (l.10)[39]
- the deserts: "O sweetly scented broom, / Denizen of the desert" (ll.6–7[40]); "you send / Your incense-breathing perfume to the sky / And comfort desert places" (ll.35–37)[41]
- the catastrophe of time and nature (ll.45–48, 202–36)
- the anti-progressive and anti-*Risorgimento* sarcasm of the citation of lines 50–51: "*impressive destiny and fated progress,*" that precedes the invective against the "Proud century and stupid" (ll.52–58)
- the justification of the ethical refusal (ll.59–77)[42] and then the immersion in the countless worlds and the metaphysical emotion that follows from it (ll.167–84, etc.)
- the heroic apology for himself (ll.305–6)

These references—the simple enumeration of which plunges us into the continuity of a potent poetic flow and incites the imagination to enjoy this lyrical past—merge here and conclude in a new feeling. It is always a delicate matter to speak of the last song of a poet who will soon disappear from the earth: this canto is a conclusion. The fortuitous and cruel event that is death thus seems, in our fragile interpretation, to point to a rational dimension. There is something like justice in death when it follows such a prodigious poetic explosion. That is not what I mean here, and I willingly leave to the philosophers of the dialectic that macabre humor that would flatten rationality onto the most brutal effectiveness. The conclusion that I find in *The Broom* differs from that of a continuous discourse: it is a leap, an innovation, the creative act of a new metaphysical equilibrium. The undoubted thematic continuity is introduced into a new structure, in which it performs an operation of innovation. A step-by-step analysis of *The Broom* shows this clearly. For now, by way of introduction, we consider the progression of the canto and recognize, in a rapid overview, how continuity and innovation are articulated within the indisputable predominance of the latter.

The Broom is composed of seven long stanzas. The first three stanzas construct and elaborate, in a tremendous crescendo, the philosophical question of the subject of historical transformation. Having been defined as an interrogation into being and confronted with the century and tradition of the Enlightenment, in the third stanza—which clearly represents a highly and forcefully innovative moment in Leopardi's thought—the ontological question is immersed in practice and accepts it as the sole constitutive horizon of the true. This is the novelty, the tone and climate of innovation. The old themes are reprised in the next three stanzas (4 to 6), which serve as contrapuntal exposition: the theme of the infinite and that of memory repel one another, and the theme of human wretchedness is confronted with that of time, its vanity and alternative experience. After the extraordinary theoretical-poetic flight of the first three stanzas, stanzas four to six represent a sort of line of stabilization, a terrain for practical experimentation in the course of which the mind is strengthened. Finally, in the seventh and final stanza, the apology for himself brings the ontological innovation into the canto, the direct expression of subjectivity onto the metaphysical stage of the world. With what prodigious force does the search progress in this canto! With what lyrical maturity are tradition and invention linked, on the formal plane as well, in a continuous and appropriate stylistic counterpoint!

But enough of these formalistic considerations. In order to understand and reach the source of Leopardi's singing here, we must follow the voice that slowly, gradually penetrates being—we must follow the determinations just like the inflections of a voice. The canto opens with a confrontation: the scented, contented broom faced with the desert, with ruin.

> Here, on the barren back
> Of the alarming mountain
> Vesuvius the destroyer
> Embellished by no other tree or flower,
> You spread yourself in solitary tufts,
> O sweetly scented broom,
> Denizen of the desert. (ll.1–7)[43]

Then the recollection of Rome, the image of nature petrified by lava, the memory of the beautiful civilization, the volcano and the sudden destruction.

> Now all around
> Nothing is found but ruin,
> Where you are rooted, gentle flower, and where,
> As pitying other people's harm, you send
> Your incense-breathing perfume to the sky
> And comfort desert places. (ll.32–37)[44]

Nature and history are overwhelmed in the opposition between the ruin of the landscape and the life of the broom. More than any other, the life of the broom is precarious, but it is real, and it is true. On the other hand: nature and history, the terrible debris of ruin, whether under way or possible.

It is not hard to see
Depicted in this place
The impressive destiny
And fated progress of the human race. (ll.48–51)[45]

Sarcasm can tell us the weight of the ruins, faced with any illusion, with any attempt to mystify the real. We know these sarcastic themes and how frequent they are during this period of Leopardi's poetry; the sarcastic violence is now almost pacified, and its function here is not so much innovative as demonstrative. In fact, in the first stanza of *The Broom* (ll.1–51), Leopardi poses a problem that is also a kind of recapitulation of his own philosophical life—hence the development, in the meshes of this lofty lyricism, of an epic ontology. Nature and history—the great figures of ontology—are immediately integrated into a non-linear rhythm, which does not develop by analogous series but rather according to moments of opposition and conflict—logical, moral, and political. Memory too develops by integrating historically opposed elements. In short, the poetic opening is conflict, tragedy. Nature and history are definitively split, and the split is the very structure of the poem. The broom is the subject— Leopardi himself is the one who asks the questions—and Vesuvius is the world in an extreme representation: the fantastic universe and internal world of Leopardi's previous poetry, the sum total of the legacies and debris that weigh on this global experience, a world that must be subjected to analysis, a scene where crisis and the actual polarity of the split accumulate—a world prefigured by what we have been experiencing lyrically and metaphysically.

This first stanza broaches what the rest of the canto demonstrates: in this contrast between subject and history, between psyche and nature, no synthesis is given. Nevertheless, we see a method take shape, a tension, one of continuous interchange between reality and imagination, an attempt to immerse the subject in the world, not in order to resolve the crisis but in order to forge the subject's power [*potenza*]. The first stanza of *The Broom* thus poses in extreme terms the problem of the relationship between the subject and nature/history. The split is consolidated. It is on this terrain that we must understand how the subject can carry out the task of the transcendental imagination: by passing from the suffering of separation to the consciousness of constitution, to the singular joy of that solitary and materially constructive act. But in order to carry out this task it is necessary to historicize, to determine the problem in the specificity of the century and the cultural climate and in the particularity of the debate.

The second stanza (*Broom* ll.52–86) is dedicated to this. Against the illusions of the century, only the true can allow us to revive. The path of the true cannot be abandoned. Revival means holding high the light of truth.

> Here see yourself reflected,
> Proud century and stupid,
> You who have left the way
> Where man's renascent thought had made its mark
> And signaled you to follow, you who take
> Some pride in moving backwards,
> And even call it progress. (ll.52–58)[46]

Here we witness a vindication of the Enlightenment, no more, no less—the Enlightenment in Leopardi's version, as materialist, sensualist, radical philosophy. We cannot demand freedom so long as thought is not free; we—above all intellectuals—cannot flee shamefully from the duty of materialist knowing [*conoscere*].

> You dream of liberty, but also wish
> To enslave that thought by which
> Alone we rose a little
> Above barbarity, by which alone
> We grow in civil living, and which only
> Betters the people's lot.
> So much you loathe the truth
> About the bitter fate, the abysmal place
> Nature allotted us. And that is why
> You turned your coward back upon the light
> Which showed the truth; why, while you flee, you call
> Him base who seeks the light,
> Him only noble who,
> Deceived or else deceiving, mad or wise,
> Exalts the human lot above the skies. (ll.72–86)[47]

The duty of materialism is not resignation, and even less is it mystification: on the contrary, it is the realistic recognition of the mortal condition and the strength to persevere in it, against it, while armed with the true and organized in truth. The physical and metaphysical drama of the broom and Vesuvius is thus referred to the elementary ethical dimension. In this overturning of metaphysics into ethics, this continuous unspooling of an ontological thread that traverses the tragedy of nature and history, we can recognize one of the highest points of Leopardi's philosophy—thus it was not necessary to wait for the contemporary philosophies of crisis in order to see the philosophical horizon united in the experience of ethics. The great ontological movement of the third stanza is thus prepared (ll.87–157), a movement foreseen and in some way already tried out during the Neapolitan period. We mentioned this every time we considered the schematism of ethical reason, its new discovery and recasting, as the fundamental passage of that period.

The subject now tends toward collectivity. Separation constructs and valorizes itself. The limit becomes truth. This is the point of great novelty in *The Broom*, upon which the whole canto condenses and reveals its overall strength. "Stinking pride," stupidity, impiety, and wickedness characterize the desire to resolve in a unitary way, dialectically, the relationship between the subject, history, and nature. We must, on the contrary, set out from separation, knowing it is definitive. Its surmounting is solely material.

> He is a noble being
> Who lifts—he is so bold—
> His mortal eyes against
> The common doom, and with an honest tongue,
> Not sparing of the truth,
> Admits the evil of our destiny,
> Our feeble lowly state;
> Who shows himself to be
> So strong in suffering he does not add
> A brother's angry hate,
> Worse than all other ills,
> To his own misery, by blaming man,
> But fixes guilt where it belongs, on Mother
> Nature: mother because she bears us all,
> Stepmother, though, by virtue of her will.
> She is his enemy. (ll.111–26)[48]

Virtue is born of the recognition of the enemy, of the affirmation of a practice of solidarity that permits her to be vanquished. The ethical community is born, positively, in separation.

> [A]nd since he thinks,
> What is the simple truth,
> Mankind has been united, organized

Against her from the first,
He sees all men as allies of each other,
And he accepts them all
With true love, giving
The prompt assistance he expects from them
In all the varying danger and the troubles
Their common war gives rise to. (ll.126–35)[49]

The necessity of the "common war" poses the conditions of solidarity and, through them, of freedom.[50] Constitutive practice is born of the
limit, in separation. On the basis of the unmystified recognition of rupture,
reconstruction and the force of its projection are continually extended. This
horizon is exclusive, and every other position is a mystification. On the
other hand, on this necessary basis, the nascent community enlarges and
expands in feelings of love. Some would like to hear an echo of Christian
caritas here:[51] in truth, it is quite a strange *caritas* that arranges its war
machines upon these materialist deserts! It surely cannot be a matter of
caritas. At most we can sense a continuity with the Spinozian materialist
conjunction of freedom and necessity, love and community, that is common
to all materialist currents of thought of the eighteenth century.[52] But it seems
to me that, beyond this tendency (see especially lines 147–49, "And when
that terror which / Drew men together first / Against cruel nature in a social
bond," in which a pessimistic interpretation of the social contract is clearly
proposed), there is something more: probably an anguish at the historical
tragedy, at the social war being waged, anguish of an intensity never before
attained by philosophical thought.

Leopardi's concept of love is elaborated against this backdrop, in a violent
conceptual crisis, in accordance with the rhythm of a strong aversion to
death. Love is understood in the sense of community: it is one component
of the latter, just as freedom is another. The collective in Leopardi is constructed not to the detriment of but rather complementary to individuality: love and freedom are thereby organized into the superior feeling of
community—*The Broom*, a civil canto, as has been said again and again.
The entire progressivist interpretation of Leopardi is in fact based on lines
126 to 135.[53] It is true that *The Broom* is a civil canto. But is it a progressivist canto? To my mind, it is only a desperately revolutionary canto. It is
a constricted and irritating, disenchanted and arrogant civil canto and not a
progressivist canto, since death is its substrate. And then there is the other
side: from death life is born; death precedes life, which conquers it, extracts
itself from the enemy nature, from death itself. This is a dualist philosophy,
not a dialectical philosophy. The community, therefore, is opposed to nature

to the point that it is born from that conflict. The community is the collective subject that is constructed within the horizon of war. To succeed in basing a perspective of reconstruction on crisis, pain, the feeling of death, is the privilege of great poets, particularly in periods of transition ("transition"—a word Leopardi hated!).[54] Here we fully experience the efficacy of this movement of the metaphysical imagination; and this forceful overturning of the unease of time, this equally violent unveiling of mystification, organizes the harsh operation. Here we experience the ethical construction of the true, by means of a contrary metaphysics. At this point we understand better the progression of the first and second stanzas: the unease appeared there in a horizontal, transversal, equivalent form, whereas in the third stanza the horizontal form of the contrast is broken; a positive asymmetry is substituted, one that pierces the equivalence, in the sense that the community reveals an ontological privilege and love reveals a potential that break the rigidity and circularity of the natural limit. This explains the sarcasm of the opening stanzas but also that of the *Palinode* and other poems of this period. For if "men loved darkness rather than light,"[55] it is true that light, the voice, subjectivity, love, and community are ontologically more real. This ontological superiority of the voice that calls to the community is the extraordinary new element of the canto. The true is constructed by the community in the war against nature and history, against fate and slavery.

After the first three stanzas, in which the path is suffused with this force, depth, and intensity of poetic construction and philosophical discovery, the frame widens: the ontology fully unfolds. The immersion in the ontology of practice that the thought of community made possible enables Leopardi to retraverse the fundamental passages of his culture (and his century) and subordinate them to his principle, to arrange them in the new ontological material. It is a broad, peaceful reflection, although it is placed in a dramatic context, one that accumulates experiences and arguments, a sort of *Erlebnis* of the totality understood as Leopardi's concrete cultural experience—such, then, is the reflection that develops in stanzas 4 (ll.158–201), 5 (ll.202–36), and 6 (ll.237–96) of *The Broom*. The ethical foundation of thought, of the true, is clarified by comparison with concepts of the infinite, catastrophe, and time. Throughout this clarification, the true as critical event is continually reaffirmed in the face of nothingness and as ethical constitution of the subject. Thus we see, stanza after stanza, reasoning after reasoning, how this unfolding of ontology is carried out.

First of all, the infinite. This theme is well known to us; it pervades all of Leopardi's thought: from the astronomical infinite to the mathematical one, from the infinitely large to the infinitely small, from the classical metaphysical recollections of the concept to the renewals of the problematic in the

Renaissance, Leopardi proposes a radical critique of a whole chapter of the history of western thought. Since the thought of the infinite leads, as it too often has, to finalistic or anthropocentric conceptions, it falsifies experience and the world. In reality, the infinite only demonstrates humankind's wretchedness in the universe, its microscopic presence, its radical contingency. In the face of philosophical pride, "I cannot say / If pity or derision wins the day" (ll.200–1); so the fourth stanza concludes regarding the infinite. But the catastrophe is not merely thinkable on the web of the infinite and of the radical contingency to which human relationships lead. Catastrophe is something that happens; it is an event. Human contingency is not measured solely against the dimension of the infinite and the tension of being, but also in relation to the immediacy and intensity of the catastrophic event. Very beautiful lines again tell the story of the volcano and the ruin it produces. From Pliny the Younger to Voltaire and beyond—the fact that catastrophe comes not only from nature but from history and from empires—thus from Montesquieu to Gibbon to Niebuhr, and why not, to the catastrophe of the Old Regime: it is in this tableau of images that Leopardi's description of the catastrophe is situated.[56] The conclusion is laid out, as usual, on the ethical terrain, with a general reflection on human contingency.

> Nature has no more care
> For man, and no more love
> Than for the pismire: if she massacre
> Men and women less often,
> That is because our race
> Is simply not so very numerous. (ll.231–36)

Finally, in the sixth stanza, the theme of human contingency is examined within the dimension of time that ineluctably slips away: the anguish of the peasant on the slopes of Vesuvius, which always, century after century, erupts again; the reappearance of Pompeii and its sinister image. Then the reflection springs forth.

> So, unaware of man and of the ages
> Which he calls ancient, and the long succession
> Of mortal generations,
> Nature is always young; she seems indeed—
> Her journey is so long—
> To stand quite still. Kingdoms meanwhile are lost,
> Peoples and languages: she pays no heed.
> And proud man makes eternity his boast. (ll.289–96)

Knowledge [*conoscenza*] is thus taken to the limit that alone allows it to become concrete, territorializes it, restores it to humankind—as a sense of radical contingency. Ontology of an absolute contingency faced with the infinite and its articulations, faced with catastrophe, with the ruin of time. The world is absolute contingency. Reason, strictly understood, can lead only to this conclusion, ceaselessly repeated and confirmed in infinite lines of verse. Thus any reason for existence can be given only by ethical reason, by a reason that makes the radical contingency of being into a motif of freedom.[57]

   This is a desperate freedom but a true one. The conclusion of *The Broom* is an ethical masterpiece.

> And you too, gentle broom,
> Whose sweetly scented thickets
> Adorn this desolated countryside,
> You too, before much longer, will succumb
> To the rough strength of subterranean fire,
> Which will return to where
> It is well-known, and stretch its greedy edge
> Over your tender tufts. And you will bow,
> Quite uncomplainingly, your harmless head
> Beneath the mortal load.
> That head of yours was never bowed before
> In cowardly supplication and in vain
> To the oppressor; never held erect
> Either, in crazy pride towards the stars,
> Out of this desert where
> You have your native seat
> Bestowed on you by chance, not by your choice;
> You wiser, and so much
> Less feeble than mankind, since you do not
> Believe that your frail race
> Is made immortal by yourself or fate. (ll.297–317)

This is neither cowardice nor pride but an ethical comportment of resistance and everyday construction.

   In this conclusion of *The Broom*, a materialist Pascal appears with a vigorous declaration against pride and cowardice, a declaration situated in the ontological fabric of practice, and furthermore enclosed within the historical and cultural dimensions that the poem has defined, criticized, and made new. That last stanza constitutes an apology for himself: Leopardi makes the innocence and dignity that his discourse exhibits the subjective correlative of the ethical-metaphysical proposition expressed in the fourth stanza. Thus is ethicality defined—here Leopardi shows his adherence to that project, a project directed once again against nature, without cowardice or pride. Leopardi's apology is anchored in moral affirmation. Optimism of the will faced with the pessimism of the intellect?[58] Certainly not. On the contrary, it is the optimism of the intellect that grasps the true—not its splendor but a delicate, vivacious, productive capacity. Pessimism of the will, on the other hand, knows that its effort will be vain, able only to help subjectivity build on itself toward the community, but also separate, without obvious linear projections in the reconstruction of the world. Nevertheless this path must be traveled; the true, within its limit, must be observed and continually, slowly, ethically reconstructed once again. Here Leopardi creates, as the last word of his poetry, an ethical heroism of great ontological intensity.

How many metamorphoses has heroism undergone in Leopardi's thought and poetics! There is the heroism of the first canti, a patriotic, classical heroism. Then there is the heroism of Petrarchan love, already present in the tradition of Dante. And now there is the ethical heroism of reason, the heroism of the adherence to the rhythm of being, to the true that is being in all its creative or destructive dimensions, in relation to which, without mystification or ideology, we gauge a practice of the voice, of the recognition of the subject, of the constitution of the community. In separation, in the acceptance of the limit, despair and disenchantment become destiny, one not imposed by external forces but willed. The philosophy of the disenchanted true is translated into a theory of practice. The true is operatively constitutive. It had to pass through all the catastrophes and experience all the crises so that this classical thought could once more become actual and so that Brutus could also be a model for us.

Here Leopardi takes up again and brings to a new synthesis the highest and most significant cultural tendencies of his time: on the one hand, he folds the concept of the true that belongs to the age of Enlightenment into the theoretical catastrophe and limit of a practice of becoming-true [*inveramento*]; on the other hand he refers the Romantic concepts of will and practice back to the true, to reason. All this makes Leopardi's thought increasingly dense and strong. The rhythm of *The Broom* is tragic, but it is also a sublime canto. It plunges into the tragedy of ethics, but it simultaneously expresses ethics as a power [*potenza*] that resolves tragedy. This being that is simultaneously within and against tragedy, this formation of a basis for self-valorization, for the critical event—that is to say, for an ethical gesture, which is always situated in the duality of the metaphysical condition but is autonomous and ontologically emancipated—this being is, without any doubt, the highest moment of Leopardi's thought and one of the most significant moments in the history of nineteenth-century thought. Power [*potenza*] against nature, power against history: ethics heroically proposes it.[59]

Here materialism is made new again. We have often said that materialism, to the extent that it leads the universal back to the name, to the hypothesis, to verification, thereby situates the concept of truth in practice and raises ethics to the foundation of knowledge [*sapere*] and metaphysics. But that is not all it involves. Here the framework within which the new materialist tension develops is dualist, anti-dialectical, and anti-totalitarian in historical and practical terms. In Leopardi, this Leopardi, poetic making thus becomes an extraordinary way of staying in being. Leopardi's poetry, as an eminent metaphysical making, excavates historicity and nature and then opposes to them, at various levels of this operation, a resistance, an eruption of alterity. Leopardi is neither a prophetic poet not a sacerdotal poet. This is, instead, a politics of poetry. He is not seated among the gods and does not make them speak regarding nature or history. On the contrary, he shatters reality and continually seeks a rationality of rupture and reconstruction that follows action and is adapted to it. Leopardi's mediation of the real is an operation that concerns the historicity or naturalness of events, which is situated on the terrain of sensibility or of materialist abstraction. Mediation in and of the empirical immediate is non-mediation, a pure internal articulation of the immediate. Leopardi has nothing to do with pure being. He is preoccupied not with the essence of poetry but with the materiality of poetic making.[60] Thus Leopardi sets the essence of poetry back on its feet. All Platonism is dispelled: poetry is neither a return nor an unveiling but rather a construction, an invention.

Poetry is not ingenuousness but labor; it is not simplicity but a complex figure. Poetry is the language of being, yes, but the language of a contradictory and split being that involves traversing, breaking, constructing levels of signification, opposing the enemy, and ultimately expressing in a new way. In this movement of being, subjects take shape and form a world of opposition and autonomy. The foundation of poetry is thus a making that traverses the critical surface of being, and only the criticizing, selecting, and discriminating of being can confer reality upon it. The constitution of being, in the ontological sense, as the project of human community, is the goal of poetry. Materialism is made new again here—the world is not compact but traversed and reconstructed by subjectivity. The Leopardi who undertakes this operation is, we have said, a lyric Machiavelli—the more fully this allegory grasps and describes the real, the more fully Leopardi's poetics establishes itself on the heights of *The Broom*. For both Leopardi

and Machiavelli, being is a subject, a subject that continually shapes itself
into different figures, on the basis of the dissolution of nature and the perception of its malign disaster. The immediacy of being in Leopardi is not
smooth; it is a critical immediacy, practically devastated and theoretically
disenchanted. In Leopardi there is neither a mythology of primordial being
nor mythology as such; there is a natural and historical being, furrowed by
crisis, in relation to which the truth will be measured, tested, and always
concretely confirmed. Leopardi's concept of the true is on the one hand the
index of the crisis and on the other the indication of a necessary verification,
a practical inscription of the subject in being. Nor does this inscription
bring tragedy to an end: it always repeats and reopens itself. There can be
no repose in this continual movement. There can only be liberation, then
crisis once more—life, then death. But what counts is constructing this
non-dialectical reality that is incapable of overcoming and always open to
the event of innovation. Ethics as foundation is the action that is proposed
by the absolute lack of foundation and that is constructed materially and
simultaneously in this frame of being.[61]

Materialism and Poetry

I would like to demonstrate three theses. First, that as a general rule, only
a materialist conception of the world allows us to give an adequate account
of poetry and its creative force. Second, that from the modern era to the
present, immersed in the crisis of Enlightenment and reason and dazzled
by postmodern indifference, materialism increasingly becomes the only
weapon we have in the attempt to give significance to the world and to
transform it—and poetry above all is implicated in this. Third, I would like
to characterize Leopardi's path in materialist terms: his poetry precisely
accompanies the passage from the modern era to the present, anticipates its
outcome, and experiences its entire dynamic, while constructing a beyond
and alluding to truth.

Poetry is inseparable from materialism. What does this mean? It means
that as production, poetry is conceivable only outside an established,
absolute order of truth, separate from a world of ideas, universals, and pre-
constituted elements to reveal. Indeed, only within a materialist horizon,
shaped by contingency, is it possible to create, to practice *poiesis* and the
ontological imagination. In a materialist universe, truth is a name and the
universal is a convention, while poetry is instead a concretion, a process
of construction, the conclusion of a making within the concrete, within
immediacy. Thus all truth, when it becomes real, has a poetic aspect: in the

sense that, extracted from the horizon of the name, confirmed in being, it happens by means of a practice and is led to a concrete determination. Nevertheless, poetry itself is emancipated from every truth, from every technique of verification, in the sense that it is immediacy. It is more than truth because it ontologically precedes truth, the density of which it immediately unveils. It anticipates truth in sensory images, not as in an aurora but in the light of high noon. The true comes after poetry and must adapt to it, since it anticipates the true. Ethical activity is situated between poetry and the true. It is a making innervated by freedom that is determinant in the constitution of the true. But ethics also comes after the truth and leads it back toward poetry: it is an ether, a perfuse climate, a necessary reflexive return. That is the way ethics attains the status of foundational value for the metaphysics of materialism, for it accomplishes the task of mediating between the immediate and the universal, between expression and communication, in freedom, in the metaphysical void that gives sense to freedom.

Poetry moves in the void, in infinite matter, but it constructs and extracts being from nothingness. This construction of immediacy in the void, this extraction of being from nothingness, this excavation of nature with the aim of infringing its boundaries and restoring it to us as signification—all this is possible only within a materialist horizon from which all presuppositions, all fetishes, all foundations have been eliminated. Poetry anticipates the true because it exceeds the limits of the materiality of existence and propels the immediacy of the image forward. Ethical activity is organized on the fabric of poetry. The true is thereby constructed in the ethical verification. Then it returns to poetry, the ever-renewed search carried out through ethical action, until once again rupture, invention, poetic production proposes an other being. This circulation among poetry, ethical action, and truth characterizes the materialist horizon, defines its harshness and hence the necessity to break it up continually, to construct signification aesthetically, to render universal—gradually, languidly, affectionately, gently as Leopardi wants it in *The Broom*—this rupture by means of ethical action, so long as the true, an other true, has not been constructed. Poetry is the moment of rupture, of liberation, that confers signification on the rest: the gentle weave, the construction of a world. "*Verum ipsum factum*": ethics constructs the true, verifies it, makes it a concrete horizon.

But this terrain of life could never have been constituted if the world had not been anticipated in the poetic rupture, in the ability to affirm immediacy as the principle of weaving of every human construction. As it is given to us, the world is irrational; the historical and natural backdrop is absurd, and we are constrained to live within this irrationality. But life begins only where the full necessity of the world—of nature and history—is refused, and humankind, the subject, constructs itself otherwise. Constructing otherwise is freedom; it is the practice of ethics. In this Epicurean physics defined by the irrational fall of atoms and the empty folding of the real back upon itself, only freedom allows us to live. Freedom as subjective *clinamen*, carried out by subjects in their power [*potenza*]. Poetry is the refusal that founds every power [*potenza*], every possibility of ethically enacting the world and therefore of constructing the true.

Poetry is the construction of the immediacy of freedom, its positioning, the opening of true being. Poetry is excavating in nothingness, emptying the sea; it is the act of excavating and extracting from nothingness, from immensity, the positioning of a being, perhaps only one, but potent and other. Poetry is the immediate labor that pre-shapes every intra-mundane relation. Poetry is language, recognition of itself; it is the turn toward the enterprise of creation. Poetry is the mystery of our beginning to be. It is escaping the underworld after having recognized in the fall the dejected and necessary side of materialism and of life just as it is given to us. Materialism, in accepting the senselessness of the world and defining the possibility of value solely as human production, in violently opposing the world to human constructive activity, simultaneously opens onto freedom and the true as the line of making and verification, of choice and construction. But only after the act of existence, the poietic act, the moment of poetry, the liberating *clinamen* has determined the possibility of a creative essence—it has prefigured that possibility by building a bridge on that edge of being where every existence appears, a bridge that leads over that edge toward the void, in a vertiginous and desperate construction. Without the presupposition and the discovery of this poetic making, ethical action and the true would not be present in our reality. Thus poetry is radical; it founds every possible true existence on nothingness.[62]

The great metaphysical tradition of materialism, from classical antiquity to modernity, has always offered this ontological framework to us—or rather, it has always offered it to poetry. But there is a moment when this process of materialist thought clashes with a new reality—that of the great transformation imposed by triumphant capitalism. Materialism, which has always been and still remains the schema of a dualist thought capable of highlighting dualism on the horizon of the real, must now bow to the effectiveness of the circular functioning of the human universe. Indeed, the relationship between humankind and nature, between subject and society, between production and product, between labor and the commodity has been rendered circular; and the dialectic, in its triumphal figure, seems to have substituted itself for every mechanism that ascribed agency to the subject. Poetry is dead—so declares power [*potere*], speaking through Hegel.

The beautiful days of Greek art, like the golden age of the later middle
ages, are gone . . . the conditions of our present time are not favourable
to art. . . . [A]rt, considered in its highest vocation, is and remains for
us a thing of the past. Thereby it has lost for us genuine truth and life,
and has rather been transferred into our *ideas* instead of maintaining its
earlier necessity in reality and occupying its higher place.[63]

Indeed, the circular horizon and the dialectic want no more rupture—or
rather, all the articulations of being would have to be reabsorbed, restored to
the continuity without resolution of dialectical reason. Materialism becomes
dialectical. But can it? There is no more need for rupture: the true has
been explored to the limits of its possibilities, constructed by humankind;
and now ethics can content itself with the effects of such creation—so we
are told. But these effects are perverse; and wanting materialist dualism,
wanting the criteria of identification of the subject and the principles of
reality to resolve in a dialectic is the result of mystification. Nevertheless,
this mystification is real and effective. 'Production for production's sake'
becomes the law that dictates every development and that strips away all
individual characteristics, all concrete determinations, by absorbing them
into the ambiguous density of a maximum abstraction. Here labor, science,
and invention cease to be sources of innovation, imagination, and wealth.
The subsumption of all nature and every form of society within productive development is thus the given:[64] the dialectic wants to function as the
law of this radical absorption. But this subsumption, far from destroying
the antagonisms, dualisms, and tensions, accentuates them. The material
progression toward a complete circularity of the historical universe instead
spurs the advance of chaos, global irrationality, and the lack of human signification of the real. Everything is exchangeable, but everything is thereby
reduced to the neutrality of value, to equivalence, to indifference.

It is interesting to note how the absoluteness of this world reinforces the
overthrown image of absolute contingency. In the impossibility of supporting itself on its own autonomous value, of insisting on its own foundation,
each moment refers to another: the movement of atoms is now circular, a
strong wind creates cyclones and hence that absolute equality that is the
fruit of destruction and an image of death. Each element is indifferent and
equal. Within this immense absorption of being into indifference, the capacity for ethical action to weave a web of sense and constructive intentionality
between sensibility and truth seems to collapse. Ethical action is sucked
into this centripetal drive, this absolutely mystifying breath of subsumed
being. In the old materialism, it was enough for ethical action to be armed
with a simple generic humanism in order to establish an antagonism. Now

there is no possibility of difference. In the new situation, wherever resistance arises, it is less a reconstructive force than a residual condition, an exhausted and split element: the wind of real subsumption collects and compresses into a compact figure every moral force, individualizes it, and denies it independence. Morality, religion, and prophecy no longer constitute alternatives. They no longer govern or unfold the schemas of being, the transcendental imagination, for new being. Morality, religion, and prophecy follow the useless path of the products of subsumption. They obtain no human basis in production; they are simply the residues of a circulation that is henceforth without origin, continuous and blind. Marx writes:

> It is well known that Greek mythology is not only the arsenal of Greek art but also its foundation. Is the view of nature and of social relations on which the Greek imagination and hence Greek mythology is based possible with self-acting mule spindles and railways and locomotives and electrical telegraphs? . . . All mythology overcomes and dominates and shapes the forces of nature in the imagination and by the imagination; it therefore vanishes with the advent of real mastery over them. What becomes of Fama alongside Printing House Square?[65]

What remains of poetry in real subsumption?

The answer is found in the question. Now, only poetry is left to break out and recast the metaphysical power [*potenza*] of ethics. Poetry is the ability to determine difference, to produce immediacy in the face of indifference and absolute mediation. The dualism of the subject is thus recreated, reconstructed, no longer on the basis of the detachment and promethean elevation of humankind, of the author, of the hero against a tragic horizon, but instead as an act of affirmation, of existence, of alternative power [*potenza*] within the nullifying circularity of significations and their destructive indifference. The subject determines its alternative option by traversing the nothingness of indifference and the totality of mediation and by breaking those material constraints. The dualism of the subject is not recorded here; it is constructed; it does not represent an element of dialectical articulation, but rises up against it. Poetry is the act of rupture. I do not define it as foundational, since poetry has none of the characteristics of foundation. It is simply rupture, rupture of indifference, allusion to an other possibility—which is neither that of the servant nor that of the slave but rather the possibility of freeing oneself. Poetry is not a foundation, for it is presupposed by a process of liberation and only in that process does the rupture become real: in this sense, poetry is entrusted to ethics, since the webs of truth can be woven on the basis of ethics through the openings created by revolt.

Poetic rupture opens up the course of ethical intentionality. It thus anticipates the true, but only in a temporal sense: ontologically, the process is
one. All in one: but the true is distant. In its explosive light, poetry reveals
being and indicates the true from afar, on the edge of the beam of light. The
true is distant, and moreover it is an other true, not the one that appeared
to us in the prison in which we were held, locked in. It is other. To break
out of the prison, to launch its own hope into the world, from an other
perspective: such is the vocation of poetry. It does not resolve or close. It
merely constructs a rupture, merely constructs in immediacy this path of
ethics that presses toward the definition of the true. Poetry is the catastrophe
that makes the perspective of the true bifurcate: the possibility of constructing a horizon of liberation runs along the ethical side of the bifurcation.
Materialist philosophy thus makes a specific and determinate proposition
for our present: in the world in which we live, poetry is an anticipation of
ethics, the opening of its weave and its extension, for it is preeminently a
rupture in the irrational subsumption of the world, and hence a moment of
orientation, a sketch of dynamics, a gentle ontological difference.

Rupture is the situation of an other value; it is the production of alterity faced with the indifference and circularity of mediation. Poetry is an
ontological fact: it immediately attains the power [*potenza*] of being. Ethics
will then develop on the basis of this rupture, this instant of extreme separation. After the poetic rupture, ethical self-valorization begins, with all its
ontological density and relevance. The old materialism stressed the time
of aesthetic rupture by making it into an ethics of immediacy. The new
materialism must instead expand the precipitation and violence of every rupture in a movement that is at once destructive and creative, that raises itself
to the alternative: here, rupture is not merely an act of ontological opening,
it is also the plenitude of an orientation, a constitutive intention, a possible
communication. As Marcuse insists, "Art fights reification by making the
petrified world speak, sing, perhaps dance. . . . The horizon of history is still
open. If the remembrance of things past would become a motive power in the
struggle for changing the world, the struggle would be waged for a revolution
hitherto suppressed in the previous historical revolutions."[66]

Here we must emphasize an element that further distinguishes poetic
rupture in the old materialism from that in the new materialism: I am referring to the collective element, to the universality of ethical value and its
function of communication. In the old materialism, the poetic rupture is
individual. Of course, it touches on the universality of the ontological fabric,
and it grasps the vein springing from constitutive human communication;
but precisely in accordance with the rhythm of the articulations of that
ancient universe, it merely alludes to ethical universality instead of radically

constructing it. In the new materialism and the social and natural situation that it registers and manifests, the moment of poetic rupture, in the density that characterizes it, is invested with the highest power [*potenza*] of universality and expressive force. We have already said it: poetry here and now is not merely rupture but reference point, point of orientation. This positive ambiguity must be grasped and made fruitful. What does universality signify if not the complexity of communicative relations, the immediate deployment of a constitutive potential? The knot that ties sensibility to imagination and poetic rupture to ethical constitution is now very tight: consequently, in reconciling the perspective of the true as well, the constitutive process manifests its communicative immediacy. The directions of communicating subjectivity converge on ontology: that is collectivity. The rupture then comprehends in itself and overthrows this density of circulation, this complexity of the horizon of exchange that the productive subsumption of the world of significations had established.[67] Rupture includes this grandeur, this articulation of motives, this plenitude of relations. The old materialism saw the poetic *clinamen* shatter the irrationality of the framework in individual terms: a cry, an exclamation, an invective. The new materialism sees the poetic rupture constitute itself in terms of community, of collective subjectivity. Here rupture itself is a complex operation that ties together temporal and social elements, alternatives on the terrain of foundation and the historical breath of communitarian self-valorization. In both materialisms, old as well as new, poetic labor is central. But in the old materialism it is above all a technique of artistic production, while in the more recent it is a technique of social communication. In both cases, poetic labor is a rupture, but in ancient materialism it is the expression of an intensive discourse, the tension of the subject, whereas in recent materialism it is a vortex of the broadest cooperation, intersubjective and constitutive. Here the ontological unfolding of rupture toward collective dimensions is extremely strong.[68]

In Leopardi's experience we can confirm the passage, within the metaphysics of materialism, from the first to the second kind of situation and signification of poetry. From this viewpoint, Leopardi appears as a cultural hinge at the highest poetic level and as the theoretical anticipation of a historical passage between two different eras. It is essential to grasp in Leopardi this coincidence of a conscious poetic experience and a historical passage. Indeed, this is where the innovative and exemplary European role of his poetry lies. His is a poetry, as we have seen, that arises within materialism— sensualist materialism, worn out by too long a struggle for emancipation and yet nonetheless an instrument of revolutionary critique. It is a poetry of Enlightenment reason, in certain respects, but mitigated by a sense of the crisis of the revolution.[69] Nevertheless, Leopardi fully experiences the myth of negative and utopian reason. For him as for Hölderlin, poetry breaks with the ideological destination of the world and thereby leaves space for ethics. We are in the old materialism, and all Leopardi's youthful poetry, like that of Hölderlin, measures itself against that universe. The comparison of Leopardi to Hölderlin is useful: both in fact fully experienced the sense of the defeat of the revolution, but while the latter holds onto the essential value of utopia wherein he establishes the nexus between poetry and transformative ethics, for Leopardi that same utopia becomes the consistent figure of negative reason, solid nothingness. Thus he asks himself how to displace the problem, how to focus it on a higher opposition, how to implant it in the new. That is what he tries to discover. He develops critique thoroughly and assumes that level of critique as the basis of poetic innovation. He recuperates ethics, as metaphysics of morals, within the sense of a poetic foundation. Leopardi, in short, seeks all the ways to organize a traditional materialist discourse. He aims to create the illusion that the affirmation of true being can become the web of the real, and therefore that the illusion is true. Like Hölderlin, he explores this possibility, but unlike him, Leopardi understands the discontinuity of a reality constructed in accordance with the rhythm of ethical will and poetic intuition, and feels the materiality of the conditions of life, the sense of pain and death, to be irreducible to any mythology whatsoever.[70]

Here we come to that passage within the metaphysics of materialism that is so characteristic of Leopardi: the passage from mythology to disenchantment, from the constitution of a totalizing web of poetic signification to the opposition of subjectivity and nature, second nature, true illusion. Here what stands out is the ontological preeminence of rupture, anti-dialectical affirmation in the negative purity of its expression, the negative as essence that cannot be recuperated. The poetry of modern materialism, modern poetry *tout court*, finds its birthplace here. Rimbaud and the delirium of the gods—that is what Leopardi comprehends and what his mature poetry prefigures. His mature work is in no way a poetry of serenity, of a vague modern stoicism.[71] It is the poetry of the most profound rupture, unease, and disenchantment. But in this, precisely and only in this, it is a fundamental event, absolute modernity, avant-garde and recasting. Poetry as *poiesis*. Poeticality, pure form, the poetic sense explosively anticipates every content. This potent anticipation is what must be grasped, studied in depth, as the innovative basis of modern poetry, a basis which is so evident in Leopardi.[72]

This passage within Leopardi's poetry corresponds to a real passage that has been taken up by philosophical consciousness in its historical development. From the viewpoint of the history of ideas, the real passage marks not the crisis but the realization of the Enlightenment utopia, or rather the dramatic unveiling of its dialectic. From the viewpoint of political and social history, this passage marks, in continental Europe, the victory of the revolution followed by the definitive defeat of Napoleonic imperialism, the assertion of a right adapted to a new mode of production and the revelation of that mode's terrible consequences. The new phase of struggle and development that opens up in the nineteenth century, the age of *Risorgimenti*, is also traversed by the awareness of that past and its crisis—and within the crisis by the different choices that are proposed: a reactionary choice, a reformist choice, and finally an alternative, unpolitical, and yet radically transformative choice. I cannot hide my clear preference for the alternative option: this seems to me to allow us to interpret both a very high level of political intelligence and an act of the radical and founding material apprehension of being. The act of political intelligence, the conviction that the *Risorgimento* in its development would have given rise to terrible problems of inhumanity, is totally subordinated to the ontological choice in Leopardi. This is a refusal of politics as abstraction and reification of the relations of power [*potere*]. It is a denunciation of that reality (and the economic world that corresponds to it: statistics!). Lastly, in positive terms it is the awareness that only a profound poetic rupture can open up an alternative course of ethical propositions and intentions.

Ethics against politics: is that Leopardi's alternative, is that the passage? Some might charge these questions with heavy irony, and if that were the case they would be able to rage sarcastically against the relativity of the words "ancient" and "modern" applied to that so-called passage. But the content of Leopardi's message is precisely not "ethics against politics." With regard to that passage, the historically effective character of which we have noted, Leopardi only extols ethics as foundation and as alternative projection after having brought two operations to a conclusion. The first is the demystification of moral and political illusions, the discovery of nothingness as formal and actual substance of that universe, the denunciation of the mortal destiny that pervades it. The second operation is poetic: it is the complete abstraction, the radical rupture, the fundamental *épochè* that consciousness carries out with respect to this nothingness. Poetic consciousness constructs an other reality. Here there is little ironizing: it is not the eternal, useless utopia of ethics against politics which we read in the secret web of Leopardi's poetics, but rather the opposition of an other ethics (and thus necessarily an other politics) to the nothingness of the present ethical-political universe. The political rupture thus presents itself as a profound and absolutely alternative ontological act, and it is the radicality of this rupture that best corresponds to the concreteness of the historical passage, to the wealth of its potentialities, and to the alternatives that compose it.[73] On the other hand, situating ourselves at this point of view allows us to understand how it is possible to maintain that in these pages, between poetic rupture and ethical project, a force of truth takes shape, that the true alternative is constructed. But we will return to this later. Here it is enough to emphasize once again that there is no possibility other than poetic denunciation in the face of the headlong transformation of utopia into despair, of hope into a prison for the mind. That is what historical reality shows, thereby signifying a tragedy of thought. It is as if there were no possibility of discriminating and rending this dialectical fabric of tragedy, no possibility of restoring to tragedy its role as foundation of the new, other than by means of a poetic act charged with the weight of the whole world. This promethean gesture, this gesture of revolt is not directed against the gods, but seeks the most intimate human reality in the nothingness of a society and a nature that history has constructed. Ethics and politics will come later; they will follow the moment of foundation. Last comes the true, but we consider this later. When the revolution ended in defeat, leaving behind on the one hand statistical—in other words, capitalist— modern-ization and on the other hand nationalist movements and the formative processes of a narrow society, a national managerial elite, it must have been quite difficult to understand that the defeat of the intellect and of a more or less materialist metaphysics founded on the intellect was not followed by a dialectical process but instead by a radical alternative, and that only poetry and ethics could identify a way that would not be a repetition of the recent tragedy. For those who are familiar with the development of modern thought in the nineteenth century, this consciousness appears all the more recalcitrant the rarer it is. Leopardi lacks even the ambiguities that are typical of those who flirted with the dialectic—I am thinking particularly of the German materialist schools or the epigones of sensualism in France.[74] In Leopardi the determination of this path is absolutely clear—from poetic rupture to ethics and then to a new metaphysical foundation of the true. This path corresponds to a series of historical passages that were confused then but today have been clarified by the tragedies that followed and by the critique that describes and illuminates them. These are the historical pas-sages that Leopardi criticizes from within and thus succeeds in describing, in anticipation of an alternative.[75]

We must now turn to the theme of truth. For Leopardi, the true is first of all a given, a characterization of being that must be attained and confirmed. Thus it must be filtered through a making, an experience, in order to under-stand the sense of that characterization. Here we can also grasp in Leopardi's thought an important passage between the two phases of inquiry and meta-physical conclusion. In the first phase, truth as it is given is attained and constructed as system. Yet as soon as this web of sense is comprehensively given, it is revealed as the system of indifference.[76] In the second phase, and in relation to this first crisis, the verification of the true becomes much more radical. It is no longer exercised on the system of the true but against it, as the alternative foundation of any possibility of the true and therefore as the project of its absolute signifying autonomy. We must always keep in mind that from the materialist point of view, the discourse on truth in Leopardi always tends to be identified with the discourse on nature. The example of nature is important in that it brings to light a linear course of Leopardi's thought: the transcendence of nature is gradually destructured—the process of verification becomes increasingly rigorous, and nature ends up being considered as an immanent, abstract, reified cage that must be broken out of, whether nature or second nature. The true then constitutes an alternative to the natural true of the first epistemological approach, an alternative to the true illusion that characterizes the acme of the critical experience, and lastly an alternative to the entire world—in the sense that the definition of the true corresponds to that of ontological alterity. But the definition of the true is not what permits us to attain ontological alterity; that is attained by means of the poetic rupture and its development within the web of the ethical constitution of the subject.[77]

The true is the logic of this autonomous development, this self-valoriza-tion. It is the result of a dialectic of ethics, thus an anti-dialectic. The true is the ultimate product of a verification that is an act of rupture of the horizon of falsity, of repetitive and sterile effectiveness, and that constructs a new reality. Leopardi's procedure gives us the sense that metaphysical time can withdraw from and oppose the time of the real, that ontology can demystify the real. Materialism is very strong here: the constitutive act shatters the real in order to construct it, and above all it reveals a dualist, antagonistic horizon. The reality of the dualism of subjects is opposed to the nothingness of unity. The world is a tragedy that repeats itself, but one in which poetic and ethical action can discover, through disenchantment, the form of a true positioning—of opposition, hope, and labor, and of renewing constitution. The true is constituted through an ethical process, on the basis of poetic rupture. The true is ontological alterity.

Our current experience of the world allows us to understand Leopardi's anticipation perfectly and to make it our own. How in fact does our world present itself? As a complete and self-sufficient circle of significa-tions. Whatever the processes that gave rise to this circle may have been, it is beyond doubt that the sphere of significations includes subjects and expressions, relationships and references. Subsumption, the new determi-nation of this signifying circle, the absolute autonomy and independence of the circuits of signification—all these phenomena that make our lives unworthy of being lived, or at very least difficult, demand a rupture, one that will draw its strength from the deep strata of ontology and open up the possibility of a recasting due to ethics. This moment of poetic rupture is an orientation, and if poetry has nothing to do with morality, it is certain that in this case it proposes, objectively and subjectively, an ethical horizon. This rupture is necessary: the mystery of its explosion, the lack of a "why" it happens, is complementary to the fact that we know [*sappiamo*] how it emerges and which laws of motion it obeys.[78] The subsumption of the world into a reified and abstract sphere that eliminates rationality in favor of a formal rule constitutes a second nature, a kingdom of the intellect that jubilantly proclaims itself progressive and magnificent. In reality, the void of significations is total: every experience of this world is an immersion in nothingness and an approach to death. This diabolical self-referential circle is based on nothingness and makes nothingness and nothingness alone circulate everywhere, like a poison. It must be broken, but how?

The mystery of this rupture is the same as that of poetry—it is poetry, the construction of new being. It is the recovery of an ontologically signifying language that is deep like the individual and collectively charged like the masses. This great game of rupture is the necessary hypothesis for an overthrow of the current inhuman conditions of the world. Then there will be a long road of ethical construction, construction on the basis of which we may even begin to think that we have made the truth. For the moment, all that remains for us to do is to start down that road with a fundamental rupture that tells us something other, that situates our humanity elsewhere. We are neither reactionaries nor progressives, neither ahead nor behind, but outside. The poetic act is revolutionary in that it constructs new collective matter.

We are all living Leopardi's adventure [*vicenda*] in our present. We are compelled to live it. To feel that Leopardi is the father of our destiny, what a strange, extraordinary sensation! Our world of subsumption repeats the unease of Leopardi's second nature and demands an operation of the same kind that Leopardi proposed to resolve it—but much more radical, because it is immediately charged with a collective density, with an utterly unprecedented vital tragedy. But it is not a more intense one: the poetic anticipation condenses in itself the pain of the future. What fools were Giordani and his other condescending friends to consider Leopardi's melancholy as an illness, or even sometimes as a simple display of ill humor; in other words, as the poet's subjective unhappiness. No, that pain involves all of us; it is almost prophetic; and that irony, that sarcasm reveals a profound affliction, a knowledge [*sapere*], and a far-sighted intuition of what for us will be the senselessness of the relationship between significations and the absurd, empty song of progress. Leopardi is close to us in his prophetic suffering.

Our good poet does not console us; he does not make the adventure ideological. He establishes the problem ontologically and demands that metaphysics, in confronting it, keep fully in mind its dimensions, qualities, and tonalities. Ontology must be recounted through philosophy, but first of all it must be expressed, lived—that is to say constructed, made, by means of poetry and ethical action. The most important moment in Leopardi's theoretical adventure is undoubtedly situated on the path that brings it close to nothingness, in the theoretical process that leads him to recognize the disastrous effects of the "dialectic of Enlightenment"—a discovery that he is not the only one in his era to make, but he is surely the only one who succeeded in transforming it into the basis of a growing ethical engagement. This articulation of pessimism and optimism must be acquitted of the negative judgment and released from the immobilization that philosophical pride tries to impose on the relationship between theory and practice. In Leopardi, the force of the negative is such that, at the limit of the thinkable, it makes the mysterious tension of reconstruction and ontological alterity appear.

They come, all these champions of the intellect, to confront the *Night Song of a Wandering Shepherd of Asia* and *The Broom*. Philosophical pride has little to say in the face of these masterpieces of poetic—and ethical—reason because, and here we reach the highest point, that ethical reason recasts metaphysics. The demand expressed in the first fragment of the "systematic program of German idealism," for a mythology of ethical reason, is realized by Leopardi.[79] Although almost all of nineteenth-century philosophical development betrays the proposition of that very first idealism, Leopardi alone, extraordinarily alone and marginalized, traverses and realizes that program. Alone until the twentieth century when, tutored by the terrible consequences of a historical event gone mad, philosophy finally achieves the anti-dialectical consciousness of the crisis—often only in order to imprison itself within it, with great boredom and terrible exhaustion: the inertia of negative thought.

In contrast, Leopardi traverses the regions of nothingness, suffers the catastrophe of the Enlightenment and the dialectic as only poetry knows how to suffer, but without imprisoning himself in that world. Poetry prevents it, dissuades him from it. He experiences the whole arc of modern and contemporary thought from the viewpoint of poetry; by means of it he penetrates the entrails of the mystification and unease of his time—and of time to come—and criticizes the absurd and violent course of the ethical perversion that follows from that mystification and that unease. He does so from the viewpoint of poetry, the viewpoint of an extraordinary and exceptional experience. Leopardi does not console; he comprehends the crisis—not in its generality but in its specificity, in the perverse effects of the dialectic of Enlightenment and the necessary, analogous conclusion of the dialectic *tout court*: until humankind stops rejecting the necessity of the true and instead conquers radical facticity, the ethics of the true, its revolt will end up in nothingness and death. Whereas the sole way to free itself from nothingness and death is to understand them, but in suffering them to ensure passion, and to construct reality between hope and despair, always exposed to circumstance and knowledge [*conoscenza*], to the true and its simulacra, head held high in passion. The problem is thus established ontologically, analyzed philosophically, and resolved poetically.

Often, and particularly in these last pages, Leopardi's poetic emergence, in its Dionysian power [*potenza*] and its Apollinian clarity, has seemed mysterious to us. Poetry is often a mystery for a materialist. As Marx notes, "the difficulty lies not in understanding that the Greek arts and epic are bound up with certain forms of social development. The difficulty is that they still afford us artistic pleasure and that in a certain respect they count as a norm and as an unattainable model."[80] Materialist poetry seems a prodigy, but our amazement is only a tribute to its greatness. In fact there is nothing mysterious in it, particularly if it is seen from a materialist viewpoint; that is to say, from the standpoint of the human species, its history and its capacity for transformation. Poetry is then revealed for what it is, in its divine being. The divine does not amaze us, for we experience it, we are it—that unhappy god that is our humanity, that continuous search for an absolute becoming-true [*inveramento*], a search that never ends. All this is the continuous line of our humanity: a search that sometimes dazzles us when the adventure explodes into poetry. Poetry is the rupture of existence, the solid existence that encloses us. It is the door that opens onto time to come, and above all an enrichment of our language, our consciousness, our possibility of saying and making.

The final Leopardi is fully aware of all these elements: poetic rupture, ontological innovation, ethical alternative—and the construction of a collective subject of this life of ours, on the road that takes us to truth. The poet constructs a collective subject in compassion and constitutes it in love—once again a conception of humankind as unhappy divinity traveling the path of making truth, an ascesis such as Lessing conceived it.[81] It is divinity for it is revealed in the love of human universality, and it is unhappy, for this universality must be constructed in the harshness of the world, through the nothingness of abstraction and the reification of being. Poetry is this advance to the deepest point, this excavation and discovery of a living treasure, a precious mineral that leaps from the earth to make our production new.

Poetry is the world that becomes ours, for an instant or a little while—in that moment we possess it whole, without that possession turning into a sense of power [*potere*]. On the contrary, it is an awareness that this illumination of being is only a possibility of advancing, of observing, of constructing the fragile resistances of a love that wants to be immense and whose immensity is its proof.

Leopardi teaches us this divine, human, atheist way of liberation. For this purpose he grasps the defining articulations of being in the world, traverses them, and on and within them he establishes the will to beauty and above all the ethical power [*potenza*] of the longing for liberation, so that they become thousands and thousands of silhouettes [*profili*], like the shafts of spotlights crisscrossing the sky. Poetry breaks the crust of being—in order to construct new, more universal being.

Notes

Preface to the First Edition: The European Leopardi

1. F. Venturi. "L'Italia fuori d'Italia," in *Storia d'Italia*, vol. 3, *Dal primo Settecento all'Unita* (Turin: Einaudi, 1973), pp. 1402–3.

2. In *Revue des Deux Mondes*, 15 septembre 1844, pp. 910ff. But see also Charles-Augustin Sainte-Beuve, "Leopardi," in *Portraits contemporains* (Paris: Didier, 1855).

3. Originally published in *Quarterly Review*, March 1850, and reprinted in W.E. Gladstone, *Gleanings of Past Years*, vol. 2 (London: John Murray, 1879), pp. 65ff.

4. In *Atheneum français* IV: 13 (31 mars 1855), pp. 255ff. In general, on Leopardi's reception in France during the nineteenth century, see Paul Hazard, *Giacomo Leopardi* (Paris: Blond, 1913).

5. In general, on Leopardi's reception in Germany, beyond the more extensive references that we provide in the course of this work, here it is enough to recall the pages in which Nietzsche expresses the ideal consonance between the German philosopher and the Italian poet on their common philological terrain: "Leopardi is the modern ideal of a philologist: The German philologists can do nothing" (Friedrich Nietzsche, "We Philologists," in *The Complete Works of Nietzsche*, vol. 8, ed. Oscar Levy, trans. J.M. Kennedy [New York: Macmillan, 1911], p. 115). But philology is a veritable terrain of European consonance. . . . See Enrico Caminati, *Leopardi und die deutsche Kritik* (Freiburg: Muther, 1949).

6. G.W.F. Hegel, *Philosophy of Nature*, vol. 1, trans. M.J. Petry (London: Allen & Unwin, 1970), sec. 258, p. 230. [Translator's note: This citation and the next one are drawn from the 1830 edition of Hegel's *Encyclopedia of the Philosophical Sciences in Outline*, which has been translated into English in three separate publications: *The Encyclopedia Logic*, *The Philosophy of Nature*, and *The Philosophy of Mind*.]

7. G.W.F. Hegel, *Philosophy of Mind*, trans. William Wallace (Oxford: Clarendon Press, 1971), sec. 548, p. 275.

8. E. Garin, *La filosofia come sapere storico* (Bari: Laterza, 1959), pp. 83–84.

9. G.W.F. Hegel, *The Science of Logic*, trans. A.V. Miller (Atlantic Highlands: Humanities Press, 1969), p. 142.

10. This is discussed in Schlegel's fragments, cited by Peter Szondi, *Poésie et poétique de l'idéalisme allemand* (Paris: Minuit, 1975), pp. 99 and 108.

11. Martin Heidegger, *Nietzsche*, vol. 1, trans. David Farrell Krell (New York: Harper & Row, 1979), p. 131.

12. Translator's note: Voltaire, *Candide*, in *Romans et contes* (Paris: Pléiade, 1954), p. 201, my translation.

13. G. Colli, *Per una enciclopedia di autori classici* (Milan: Adelphi, 1983), p. 115.

Chapter One: The Catastrophe of Memory

1. *Canto I*, Peruzzi, pp. 1–22; Nichols, p. 3. Concerning the sources and circumstances of composition of this canto, see Ghidetti in *TO I*, p 1424. See also L. Blasucci, "Sulle due prime canzoni leopardiane," in *Giornale storico della letteratura italiana*, vol. 138 (1961) and M. Ricciardi, *Giacomo Leopardi: La logica dei Canti* (Milan: Franco Angeli, 1984), chap. 2.

2. It is principally to M. Ricciardi (*Giacomo Leopardi: La logica dei Canti*, op. cit.) that we owe a reading of the canto *To Italy* that expressly sets out to make evident the relationship between the theme of glory and that of the public. Ricciardi relies on three classics of historical critique and the sociology of knowledge [*conoscenza*] that likewise constitute direct points of reference for the present work: Reinhart Koselleck's *Critique and Crisis* (Cambridge: MIT Press, 1988), Jürgen Habermas's *The Structural Transformation of the Public Sphere*, trans. Thomas Burger (Cambridge: MIT Press, 1989), and Niklas Luhmann's *Social Structure and Semantics*, trans. William Rasch (Stanford: Stanford University Press, 2003). Ricciardi's volume is of great importance because of the precision with which he confronts the theme of the subject-crisis. A slight reservation can be expressed regarding the too limited relationship established among the canti *To Italy, Brutus*, and *Sappho's Last Song*. We prefer to grasp, in this early work of Leopardi, a larger articulation of the problem.

3. It is not by chance that Paul Hazard, later distinguished for his studies of the European crisis of consciousness in the eighteenth century, dedicated one of his first works to an attentive study of Leopardi's thought (*Giacomo Leopardi*, op. cit.). With great precision he situates Leopardi's thought in the sphere of European thought, emphasizing the importance of his involvement in the crisis of an era, which "having lost the ancient values, had not yet found new ones." The crisis of the French Revolution constitutes the basis of Leopardi's coming to consciousness,

and the claim of happiness (in new forms of patriotism) weaves the fabric of the reconstruction of his revolutionary dream. Paul Hazard's reflection (see pp. 212ff. for his conclusions, which we are summarizing) is motivated by the need to update the reading of Leopardi in response to the latest results of criticism, especially those that deal with the publication of the *Zibaldone*. This updating has the freshness of a first reading, one that is perhaps not exceptional but full of vivacity. The part dedicated to the analysis of Leopardi's European reception during the second half of the nineteenth century is also very important; particularly rich in information, these pages have no need to envy those of Venturi (*Storia d'Italia*, op. cit.) even though they were written more than a half-century earlier. Concerning the European reception, Hazard draws attention to this reflection appearing in the supplement to the *Spectator* of 17 February 1833: "We no more want to nourish the spirits of our fellow citizens with the despairing exaggerations of Leopardi than we want to fill their bodies with hashish." Is this not a striking anticipation of the judgments of the Italian liberals, contemporaries, and epigones of the *Risorgimento*, from Capponi to Croce? More on all this later.

4. Bronislaw Baczko, *Utopian Lights*, trans. Judith Greenburg (New York: Paragon House, 1989), and Jean Starobinski, *1789: The Emblems of Reason*, trans. Barbara Bray (Charlottesville, VA: University of Virginia Press, 1982).

5. In this regard, Friedrich Meinecke's book *Historism*, trans. J.E. Anderson (New York: Herder & Herder, 1972), remains fundamental. As is well known, in this work Meinecke rightly aims to show that German historicism was the product of individualist thought by situating its genesis between the end of the Enlightenment and the restoration, independent of the development of revolutionary thought. The polemic against the historicist tradition engendered by Hegelian and post-Hegelian philosophy is extremely clear.

Today the reprise of analogous themes is on the agenda in the framework of the resumption of moderate thought; see in particular the works of M. Gauchet, "L'illusion lucide du liberalisme," introduction to Benjamin Constant's *De la liberté chez les modernes* (Paris: Livre de poche, 1980); "Tocqueville: sur la genèse des démocraties," in *Libre* 7 (1980). While he is immersed, during those years, in the works of Madame de Staël, Leopardi notes the moderate character of her polemic (and how this tone is appropriate to her immediate tasks in literary criticism), which is positioned between the sensualist tradition of the Enlightenment and the new doctrines and practices of Romanticism—both of which are presented, in one way or another, as revolutionary ideologies. This is valid as much on the literary terrain as on the political terrain. Concerning this period, see *Zibaldone*, pp. 88–99 (*TO II*, pp. 50–56; Caesar/D'Intino, pp. 84–91): in these pages, in comparison to his radical nihilism on the philosophical plane (which we will examine shortly), Leopardi seems to opt, on the terrain of literary criticism, for a sort of aesthetic "inertia." Concerning Madame de Staël, Sebastiano Timpanaro, in *Classicismo e Illuminismo nell'Ottocento* (Pisa: Nistri-Lischi, 1969), writes: "Madame de Staël, for example, was a great popularizer of Rousseau and Herder, and Leopardi borrowed from her (as well as from Chateaubriand) numerous Rousseauist and Herderian elements, without however allowing himself to be seduced by the religious and moderate substance of her thought" (p. 39).

Timpanaro's position, which is close to that of A. Frattini's intervention (in the collective volume *Leopardi e il Settecento* [Florence: Olschki, 1964], pp. 269ff.) and G. Moget's contribution ("En marge du bi-centenaire de Madame de Staël: 'Classiques' et Romantiques à Milan en 1816," in *La Pensée*, fevrier 1967, pp. 40ff.), seems over-optimistic to me. On the vicissitudes of Leopardi's relationship with Madame de Staël, see the balanced assessment proposed by M. Fubini, "Giordani, Madame de Staël, Leopardi," (1952) in *Romanticismo italiano: Saggi di Storia della critica e della letteratura* (Bari: Laterza, 1971). See also F. Venturi, "L'Italia fuori di Italia," op. cit., pp. 1179–81, in which a long analysis dedicated to de Staël's *Corinne* emphasizes, in agreement with Fubini, the influence and wide range of this work. S. Gensini insists upon the implications established by Leopardi in the *Zibaldone* among society, language, and culture, which he considers to be determined on the basis of Madame de Staël's teachings (*Linguistica leopardiana* [Bologna: Il Mulino, 1984], pp. 37–49). Nevertheless he concludes, taking up Timpanaro's analysis, that for Leopardi Madame de Staël's texts are valuable as solicitation, as incitement rather than as a template for philosophizing. The same position can be found in Antonio Prete (*Il pensiero poetante* [Milan: Feltrinelli, 1980], p. 96). In any case see also the observations of S. Ravasi, *Leopardi et Madame de Staël* (Milan: Tip. Sociale, 1910). The only real correction proposed to Timpanaro's widely diffused thesis seems to me to be that of N. Badaloni ("La cultura," in *Storia d'Italia*, op. cit., vol. 3, pp. 894–95). According to Badaloni, Madame de Staël's influence must be evaluated not so much in terms of the literary correspondences between her oeuvre and Leopardi's as in terms of the general framework that was transmitted to him through her. Badaloni considers Madame de Staël to have played a fundamental role in the diffusion of the philosophy of the Ideologues and in particular the concept of second nature. From this perspective, the structural character of Madame de Staël's influence becomes evident, and henceforth terms such as "incitement" and "solicitation" take on a new meaning. See in this regard B. Biral, *La posizione storica di Giacomo Leopardi*, 2nd ed. (Turin: Einaudi, 1978), passim.

An analogous problem regarding the valence of the reception is posed concerning the influence of the new German aesthetics and philosophy. With regard to metaphysics, see the information and reflections offered below, in note 51 to this chapter. On the other hand, with regard to literature, we must remain attentive in order to avoid any exaggeration of the importance of the German influence; on this score see M. Puppo, "La 'scoperta' del romanticismo tedesco," in *Lettere italiane* XX (1968), pp. 307ff. Knowledge [*conoscenza*] of German literature is very limited, often restricted to minor authors who find in Italy a singular and unexpected audience—and this is precisely due to the totally superficial level of knowledge [*conoscenza*] of the development of German literature. For an overview of the discussion, see *I manifesti romantici del 1816*, ed. C. Calcaterra, vol. 71 of *Classici italiani* (Turin: Utet, 1951); and *Discussioni e polemiche sul Romanticismo*, ed. A.M. Mutterle, 2 vol. (Bari: Laterza, 1975). Nevertheless, here too the influence of Madame de Staël's *De l'Allemagne*, which Leopardi appears to have read (in the third edition, Paris, 1815), is far from negligible. M.A. Rigoni (*Saggi sul pensiero leopardiano* [Padua: CLEUP, 1982], p. 33 but already pp. 11ff.) indicates that, in all probability, Leopardi did not know the thought of either Schiller or Schlegel directly, despite the extraordinary affinity that, with regard to poetics, connects him to the youthful essays of the latter: "whatever Leopardi knew about the German Romantics came to him from Madame de Staël; and it is truly surprising that he was in a position, beyond this mediation, to work his way back, by himself, to the sources, arriving thus at impressive agreements on many points with the reflection of the first and greatest German Romantics." See also P. Szondi, *Poésie et poétique de l'idéalisme allemand*, op. cit., particularly pp. 95ff.

6. On this thesis, the general historical studies focused on the period (see G. Candeloro, *Storia dell'Italia moderna*, vols. 1 and 2 [Milan: Feltrinelli, 1956 and 1958]) seem to agree with the studies of Leopardi (in particular, concerning this question, see Timpanaro, *Classicismo e Illuminismo nell'Ottocento italiano*, op. cit., and U. Carpi, *Il poeta e la politica* [Naples: Liguori, 1978]). See also the contributions of S.J. Woolf, A. Caracciolo, N. Badaloni, and F. Venturi, on the political, economic, and cultural history and the foreign imaginary, respectively, in vol. 3 of *Storia d'Italia* (Turin: Einaudi, 1973).

7. On this point, see below for a general consideration of the problem. On the other hand, concerning the references to Petrarch's canzone in the *Zibaldone*, see pp. 23, 24, 29–30, 70 (*TO II*, pp. 16, 17, 21, 45; Caesar/D'Intino, pp. 25, 26, 32–34, 74) for the years that concern us.

8. Nichols, p. 6.

9. Ibid., p.5.

10. *Canto X* (Peruzzi, pp. 249–65; Nichols, p. 46). Concerning the different hypotheses for dating, see Ghidetti (*TO I*, p. 1426), who concludes that December 1817 is most probable. According to Peruzzi (and Porena), the definitive version cannot be earlier than the second half of 1818. In any case, the difficulty of composition of this elegy is well known.

11. Ibid.

12. Aside from *To Italy*, here we consider *Canto II, On the Proposed Monument to Dante in Florence* (Peruzzi, pp. 23–66; Nichols, pp. 7–12), composed in Recanati between September and October 1818 (see Ghidetti, *TO I*, p. 1425). On this canto and related ones, see Walter Binni's extremely negative judgment

in his preface to *TO I*, particularly page xxxiv. From a more general perspective, concerning the promotion of the figure of the writer in European literature and the reconfiguration of the memory-literature, author-public relationship, see P.Benichou, *Le sacre de l'écrivain 1750–1830* (Paris; José Corti, 1873).

13. Nichols, pp. 3–4.

14. Ibid., p. 11.

15. Ibid., p. 10.

16. On the internal references to Leopardi's development between the *Canti* and the *Batracomiomachia*, see L. Cellerino, *Tecniche ed etica del paradosso* (Cosenza: Lerici, 1980).

17. *Canto XXXIX* (Peruzzi, pp. 589–609; Nichols, pp.156–58). It was composed at Recanati between November and December 1816. "It is the re-elaboration of the initial fragment of the juvenile *canto* 'Approach of Death,' which was never published in its entirety by the author" (Ghidetti, *TO I*, p. 1426).

18. *Canto XXXVIII* (Peruzzi, pp. 579–88; Nichols, p.155). It includes fifteen lines extracted from a composition of ninety-one lines entitled *Elegy IV*. It was probably composed in 1818.

19. Nichols, p. 155.

20. Ibid., p. 158.

21. Ibid., p. 156.

22. Ibid., p. 47.

23. Benedetto Croce left two essays on Leopardi: "De Sanctis e Schopenhauer" (1902), included in *Saggi filosofici III (Saggio sullo Hegel et altri scritti)* (Bari: Laterza, 1948, pp. 354–68), and *European Literature in the Nineteenth Century*, trans. Douglas Ainslie (New York: Alfred A. Knopf, 1924), pp. 111–30. Croce's theses have been further developed with elegance and a greater respect for the poet's texts above all by Sergio Solmi, whose *Introduzione alle Operetti morali* (Turin: Einaudi-Ricciardi, 1956 and 1976, pp. 241–62) I well recall. Those theses are easy to outline, and we point them out here as a counterpoint to our own position. First of all, consider the historical conditions that make Leopardi a marginal and pessimistic thinker: the historical and political closure of the revolutionary period; the languishing and corruption of hope; "the projection of this long pause marked by uncertainty over the microcosm of Recanati"; and then, physical infirmity with its "complex of inhibitions, inadaptability and revolt." Furthermore, given "the isolation of his earliest education," Leopardi withdrew from his times, seeking refuge in the "atemporal" dimension of classicality, a "static image of life." Hence Leopardi's refusal of "that intuition of history as a process in becoming [. . .], the concept of which was, during those same years, elaborated by the great Romantic philosophers that he almost completely disregarded while feeling an instinctive aversion for them." Thus Leopardi remains "atemporal," classical. "Seeking pure objectivity, he achieved a sort of crystallization of his visual field. [. . .] He did not aim to institute

a dialectical mediation, and could not. Truth is only a mediation equivalent to a justification, and a justification would be accused of being one of those convenient compromises for which he reproached the philosophy of his contemporaries."

It is thus within this limit that Leopardi's poetry—which remains a great poetry—is set free: it becomes poetry when, forgetting philosophy, it becomes the breath of the soul, the pure lyric of emotion. And that is how Leopardi's thought is eliminated . . . and how his poetry comes to be considered as a recompense for his philosophical weakness. Exception is made, naturally, above all through the analysis of his mature works and his last great lyrics, for the hope of a return to the dialectic and of the possibility of reading in *The Broom* his "conscious acceptance of our tormented human condition." This final judgment of Solmi's is not without its own (dialectical?) convergence with the interpreters of a progressive Leopardi. The development of this critique is quite odd in the end: the accusation of "atemporality" leveled at Leopardi's philosophy reminds me of the accusation of "acosmism" leveled at Spinoza's philosophy by Hegel. In fact, this stereotype recurs every time an idealist finds himself faced with a materialist philosophy; then he does not know what to do other than repeat this short prayer! On Solmi's other Leopardian works, see below.

But let us return to Benedetto Croce. The fact that he wages a veritable ideological war against Leopardi is today a critical commonplace, to the point that G. Bollati's pages (introduction to Leopardi, *Crestomazia italiana* [Turin: Einaudi, 1978], particularly pp. lxxiii–lxxv), where he forcefully attacks the Crocean tradition, are no longer capable of upsetting anyone. In fact Benedetto Croce went quite far in his attempt to empty Leopardi's poetry of all philosophical contents, or rather, to demonstrate how the grandeur of the idyll was indifferent to the emptiness of metaphysical thought, to the point of attributing to the philosophy of the *Operetti Morali* the injurious epithet "Monaldesque" (Croce, *European Literature in the Nineteenth Century*, p. 121). In such philosophical poverty, poetic genius could only emerge as "strangled life" (Croce, op. cit., p. 116). How habitual it is to act this way every time thought and poetry break through the indifference of the real, just as it is patriotic to act this way when faced with Leopardi's rupture of the Italian *Risorgimento*. On all these aspects, see C. Luporini, *Leopardi progressivo* (Rome: Editori Riuniti, 1980), pp. 5, 87, 93; and A. Prete, *Il pensiero poetante*, op. cit., p. 69.

24. See M. Ricciardi, *Giacomo Leopardi: La logica dei Canti*, op. cit., passim: a very good analysis of the centrality of this temporal dimension and the alternatives to the concept of time in Leopardi's poetry.

25. Peruzzi, p. 594, variant of line 4.

26. Alexandre Kojève's reading (*Introduction to the Reading of Hegel* [Ithaca: Cornell University Press, 1969]) has made this interpretation canonical. See in any case A. Negri, *Macchina tempo: Rompicapi liberazione costituzione* (Milan: Feltrinelli, 1982), pp. 253ff.

27. G.W.F. Hegel, *Phenomenology of Spirit*, trans. A.V. Miller (Oxford: Oxford University Press, 1977), p. 27. In general see also V. Verra, "Storia e memoria in Hegel," in *Incidenza di Hegel*, ed. F. Tessitore (Naples: Morano, 1970), pp. 341ff.

28. See the publication of the famous fragment by the three authors, "The Oldest Program toward a System in German Idealism," in David Farrell Krell's *The Tragic Absolute: German Idealism and the Languishing of God* (Bloomington: Indiana University Press, 2005), pp. 22–26.

29. Particularly Jean Hyppolite, *Introduction to Hegel's Philosophy of History*, trans. B. Harris and J. Spurlock (Gainesville: University Press of Florida, 1996) and *Studies on Marx and Hegel*, trans. J. O'Neill (New York: Basic Books, 1969); A. Negri, *Stato e diritto nel giovane Hegel* (Padua: CEDAM, 1958); and concerning the particular form of classicism in these authors, Jacques Taminiaux, *La nostalgie de la Grèce à l'aube de l'idéalisme allemande* (The Hague: Martinus Nijhof, 1967) and *Le Regard et l'Excédent* (The Hague: Martinus Nijhof, 1977).

30. Cesare Luporini (*Leopardi progressivo*, op. cit.) and Walter Binni (*La protesta di Leopardi* [Florence: Sansoni, 1971], but already in *La Nuova poetica leopardiana* [Florence: Sansoni, 1947]) have put a definitive end to this current of interpretation. Whatever value one wishes to grant to the progressive interpretation of Leopardi—as far as I'm concerned my reservations are large—it is nevertheless incontestable that Luporini's and Binni's studies have lifted a series of taboos and opened directions for research that cannot be ignored.

31. Nichols, p. 7.

32. Composed at Recanati in 1815 (cf. *TO I*, pp. 769–868).

33. Composed at Recanati in 1817 (cf. *TO I*, pp. 906–10).

34. It is the same in the Enlightenment authors dear to Leopardi, to whom he refers. In general see the contributions and bibliographic indications contained in *Leopardi e il Settecento*, Atti del Convegno internazional di Studi leopardiani, op. cit., and in particular C. Galimberti's article "Fontanelle e Leopardi." Solmi's judgment of the *Essay on the Popular Errors of the Ancients*, in his *Introduzione alle Operette Morali*, op. cit., p. 245, is opposed to ours. According to Solmi, Leopardi's attitude develops laboriously through the opposition between "an Enlightenment revolt against error" and "the amused taste for the evocation of these extravagances." These aspects of Leopardi's consideration would be irreconcilable and paralyzing . . . yet instead they are a terrain of critical engagement and development.

35. Among the numerous works concerning Leopardi's philology, aside from the acts of the Leopardi colloquia, the fundamental texts are those of L. Scheel, *Leopardi und die Antike* (Munich: M. Hueber, 1959) and Sebastiano Timpanaro, *La filologia di Giacomo Leopardi* (Bari: Laterza, 1978). On the relationship between philology and linguistics, see S. Gensini, *Linguistica leopardiana*, op. cit. The

last work problematizes the link with the tradition of Vico; it contains a vast bibliography.

36. Composed at Recanati in 1814 (now in *TO I*, pp. 585–750).

37. Composed at Recanati in 1814 (now in *TO I*, pp. 754–68).

38. Here, naturally, I don't want to engage in long discussions. I will content myself with referring to that Enlightenment literature on which Leopardi is so reliant; see the texts cited in note 34 and the fundamental work of M. De Poli, "L'Illuminismo nella formazione del Leopardi," in *Belfagor* 5 (30 September 1974), pp. 511–46. This is merely to say that the reminder of the tradition of natural history, as it takes shape in eighteenth-century French culture (Fontanelle, Buffon, etc.; on the latter, see A. Prete, *Il pensiero poetante*, op. cit., pp. 162ff.; on the former, cf. L. Cellerino, *Tecniche ed etica del paradosso*, op. cit., passim), combines here with the resumption of scientific discourse (notably that of Galileo and his school) in the formation of the historical-pedagogical model. Concerning other authors of the Enlightenment and their relation to Leopardi, regarding d'Holbach see S. Gensini, *Linguistica leopardiana*, op. cit., pp. 34–40; on La Mettrie, see M.A. Rigoni, *Saggi sul pensiero leopardiano*, op. cit., pp. 57–66; lastly on Locke as an inspiration for the Enlightenment and the uses to which Leopardi put him, see A. Prete, *Il pensiero poetante*, op. cit., pp. 110ff. (n.b.: These indications are intended to aid only in reconstructing certain problematic citations in Leopardi by relying on the most recent studies.) One remark, which is neither the last nor the least useful, is suggested to us by A. Prete, *Il pensiero poetante*, op. cit., p. 130: the critique of the dialectic of Enlightenment in Leopardi is contemporaneous with his knowledge [*conoscenza*] and use of certain fundamental terms of Enlightenment thought. It may be true (as many academic studies—among the most impressive and independent—emphasize) that any analogy between Leopardi's thought and the positions of the Frankfurt School is unjustified (it must be admitted that this analogy has been advanced, with the best intentions of course, but nevertheless often with ax blows, by many of my friends), and that the circles of philosophical development are *toto coelo* distinct. That said, yielding to the necessities of a discipline appropriate less to the academy than to communication, we add: it is nevertheless incontestable that Leopardi's interpretation of the outcome of the Enlightenment converges with that of the major authors of the Frankfurt School. Objection: admitting this, that is to say, the literal repetition of certain motifs, hence the fact that we cannot maintain that Adorno and Horkheimer plagiarized Leopardi (as indeed it appears difficult to do), we must admit that, in all probability, the angle from which Leopardi's critique develops is different, radically different, from that of the members of the Frankfurt School—while admitting the identity of motifs. I agree completely with this objection: the Frankfurt School's critique concerns the 'real subsumption' of society within capital, while Leopardi's involves 'formal subsumption.' Why this identity of motifs? These are precisely the terms

in which the problem must be posed. On the problem of the continuity between Leopardi's thought and Enlightenment thought in general, F. Brioschi furnishes excellent indications under various rubrics ("Politica e metafisica nel Leopardi," in *ACME, Annali della Facoltà di Lettere e Filosofia dell'Università di Milano*, vol. 25, fasc. II, May–August 1972, pp. 141–212). We return to this article later in our work.

39. On this formative synthesis, all the authors on the history of historicism and historiography more or less agree. See in this regard A. Negri, *Saggi sullo storicismo tedesco* (Milan: Feltrinelli, 1959). Concerning Herder more specifically, see the pages F. Meinecke dedicates to him in *Historism*, op. cit., as well as F. Venturi's introduction to Herder's *Ancora una filosoifa della storia per l'educazione dell'umanità* (Turin: Einaudi, 1951).

40. This refers above all to Theodor Haering's neo-Romantic reading, *Hegel, sein Wollen und sein Werk, eine chronologische Entwicklungsgeschichte*, 2 vols. (Leipzig and Berlin: B.G. Teubner, 1929 and 1936), as well as to the innumerable commentaries and editions by J. Hoffmeister.

41. Composed at Recanati between 19 May and 18 June 1815 (now in *TO I*, pp. 869–75). S. Gensini (*Linguistica leopardiana*, op. cit., p. 186) proposes a reading of it that grasps all the oration's complexity and implicit alternatives.

42. This development is amply documented in contemporary philosophy, essentially on the basis of the anti-Hegelian critique inspired by Husserl and Heidegger. In this regard, the books of Herbert Marcuse (*Hegel's Ontology and the Theory of Historicity*, trans. Seyla Benhabib [Cambridge: MIT Press, 1987]) and Massimo Cacciari (*Krisis: Saggio sulla crisi del pensiero negativo da Nietzsche a Wittgenstein* [Milan: Feltrinelli, 1977]) seem interesting to me insofar as they are situated at the extreme points of a debate that is constantly under way from the thirties to the seventies.

43. See in this regard Giorgio Agamben, *Language and Death*, trans. Karen Pinkus and Michael Hardt (Minneapolis: University of Minnesota Press, 1991). But it is quite obviously to Heidegger's *Elucidations of Hölderlin's Poetry*, trans. Keith Hoeller (Amherst, NY: Humanity Books, 2000) that I principally refer here.

44. It is clearly difficult to provide a univocal definition of Jacobin or Jacobinism in the midst of a polemic that is still raging and shows no signs of coming to an end. See the hypotheses of M. Ozouf, "L'héritage jacobin," in *Le Débat* 13 (June 1981). For my part, I would willingly stick, on the historical terrain, to the definitions elaborated from opposite positions by Jean-Pierre Faye and François Furet. The contradictory character of these definitions, the positive and negative that they bring to light, are of equal importance and make obvious that the historiographical polemic is justified and the matter is dialectical. That said, I must specify what I understand here by Jacobin: a radical comportment linked to an ideology of transformation and based on an ethical conception of the true.

45. As M. Ricciardi demonstrates with his habitual expertise (in *Giacomo Leopardi: La logica dei Canti*, op. cit.). It seems worthwhile, simply because we are making abundant use of his book, to undertake a brief critique of a concept that he tries to construct in the course of his treatment. It involves the concept of privacy, which Ricciardi adopts, at first prudently but increasingly explicitly, from a theoretical proposition by Agnes Heller. Now it seems to me that the concept of individuality that takes shape in Leopardi through the experience of the heroic can in no case fall back on the concept of privacy. Leopardi was not familiar with this concept, which comes from an aristocratic tradition that the concept fails to acknowledge. He did not aim for this concept; on the contrary, his last works seek to develop fully an alternative ontological conception of human community not by means of the experience of individuality as privacy but rather by means of the concept of individuality or singularity as crisis, as a field of structurally situated and collectively signifying forces. We will return to all these points at length.

46. Here it is necessary to recall that the voluminous historiography of Wilhelm Dilthey and his school has accounted for this discrepancy between France and Germany in the reception of the Enlightenment (at least so far as its political and rationalist contents are concerned), the revolution, and counterrevolution. There is no paradox in saying that the Enlightenment and the revolution were known less through direct engagement than through the intermediary of works by the counter-revolutionaries Burke and Rehberg. And why not mention here Novalis's prodigious and paradoxical pamphlet *Christenheit oder Europa*?

47. From Recanati, 7 May 1816 (now in *TO I*, pp. 876–78).

48. From Recanati, 18 July 1816 (now in *TO I*, pp. 879–82).

49. All those who have studied linguistics in Leopardi agree on this point. See S. Gensini's recent *Linguistica leopardiana*, op. cit., as well as T. Bolleli, "Leopardi linguista," in *Studi e saggi linguistici* 16 (supplement to *Italia dialettale*, vol. 39), Rome, 1976 (included in *Leopardi linguista ed altri saggi* [Florence/Messina: D'Anna, 1982]).

50. On Hegel's relationship to the French Revolution, see the works of J. Hyppolite already cited; also, from the philological point of view, J. Ritter, *Hegel und die Französische Revolution* (Cologne: Westdeutscher, 1957). From the viewpoint of merit, we must consider the entirety of Hegel's work, or at least his political thought, which is perpetually confronting the French Revolution, from the first political and juridical essays at the beginning of the century right up to the *Philosophy of Right* (trans. T.M. Knox, [Oxford: Oxford University Press, 1952]) and the late text on the English Reform bill (in *Political Writings*, ed. Laurence Dickey and H.B. Nisbet, trans. H.B. Nisbet [Cambridge: Cambridge University Press, 1999]).

51. In the course of our work we will return to the places, especially in the *Zibaldone*, where Leopardi mentions the confused notion of a new development

of German metaphysics. See also notes 5 and 81 of this chapter as well as note 119 of chapter 3, which comments on the reference to Kant and his "sect" in the *Discourse on the Present State of Italian Morals*. Aside from the studies cited in these notes, the work of F. Brioschi ("Politica e metafisica nel Leopardi," in *ACME*, op. cit., pp. 169–78) provides ample and varied information on the philosophical readings of Leopardi and highlights particularly Leopardi's suspicions regarding the Germans. Many different but relatively homogeneous texts make reference to particular aspects of Kantian thought (such as C. Luporini, *Leopardi progressivo*, op. cit., p. 92; A. Prete, *Il pensiero poetante*, op. cit., p. 93; S. Gensini, *Linguistica leopardiana*, op. cit., p. 263). In my view, only N. Badaloni (*Storia d'Italia*, vol. 3, op.cit., p. 896) grasps the fundamental element of Leopardi's relationship with the critical philosophy by situating it at the level of the problem of the completion of the transcendental aesthetic by means of the schematism of reason. We will return to this point at length, but for the moment we must emphasize the enormous importance that this passage takes on in Leopardi's theoretical experience. In general, aside from those to which we will return, keep in mind *Zibaldone*, pp. 105, 350, 1242, 1351, 1352 (*TO II*, pp. 58, 133, 362, 392); Caesar/D'Intino, pp. 95, 214, 593, 643–44).

52. *Letters 26* and *32*; Shaw, pp. 32–42. We are referring to Binni and Ghidetti's numbering of the letters in *TO I*; henceforth we include the name of the correspondent and the date of the letter in the notes.

53. This Fichtean element of the heroic definition of the passions in the early Leopardi deserves to be considered at greater length, not because direct references between the two authors exist, but because in the history of contemporary taste (if the contemporaneity of Romanticism is granted), the role of Fichte's philosophy, his heroic individualism, his philosophical patriotism, and his ontological prometheanism is immense. The depth of the relationship between the positions of Fichte and those of the young Leopardi were perceived by A. Tilgher (*La filosofia di Leopardi* [1940], Bologna, 1979). C. Luporini (*Leopardi progressivo*, op. cit., pp. 67, 73–74) and A. Prete (*Il pensiero poetante*, op. cit., p. 27) both express appreciation for Tilgher's book: his interpretations are highly regarded, but the general spirit animating his work is reproached as uselessly preoccupied (beyond the particular characteristics of his style) with bringing to light insoluble contradictions in Leopardi's thought, especially the association of an intimist and Pascalian reflection with the Fichtean aspect. However, a correct evaluation of Tilgher's interpretation cannot do without a preliminary critique of the general spirit that inspired the interpretation of Leopardi in the thirties—an anti-philosophical interpretation, even when the philosophical elements of Leopardi's thought were perceived and grasped. "Never did Leopardi feel a true passion for speculation. He studied no great philosophical system." This assertion of Giovanni Gentile in *Manzoni e Leopardi* (Florence: Sansoni, 1937), p. 46 is emblematic of a reading then dominant. Tilgher

(as Gentile perhaps already had partially and paradoxically for the *Operetti Morali*, where his critique reaches further than his reflection) initiated the labor of philosophical analysis of Leopardi. His limits, which are consistent, must not deprive him of the credit for having opened up that path. Luporini's radically innovative interpretation of 1948 owes much to Tilgher. On the place of Tilgher's study in Leopardi criticism during the thirties, see M. Boni's introduction to the 1979 edition.

54. *Letter 5*, to Francesco Cancellieri, Recanati, 15 April 1815.

55. On the historical position of Pietro Giordani and his general environment, aside from Timpanaro's work mentioned in note 6, I refer to N. Badaloni, "La cultura," in *Storia d'Italia* vol. 3, *Dal primo Settecento all'Unità*, op. cit.; U. Carpi, *Letteratura e società nella Toscana del Risorgimento: Gli intellettuali dell'Antologia* (Bari: Donato, 1974); A. Ferraris, *Letteratura e impegno civile nell'"Antologia"* (Padua: Liviana, 1978); and above all M. Fubini, *Giordani, Madame de Staël, Leopardi*, op. cit. Also worth consulting are U. Carpi, *Il poeta e la politica*, op. cit., pp. 135–38, and S. Timpanaro, "Antileopardiani e neomoderati della sinistra italiana," in *Belfagor* 1976: I, pp. 1–32. Despite the objections raised by Timpanaro, Carpi's thesis, suggesting the hypothesis on Giordani's part of a political reform centered on the aristocracy and thus in conflict with Vieusseux's bourgeois project, seems to me substantially admissible. On the whole problem of the relationship between Leopardi and Giordani, see B. Biral, op. cit., chapter 1 and passim, and F. Brioschi, op. cit., passim.

56. *Letter 49*, to Pietro Giordani, Recanati, 10 October 1817.

57. Despite the terrible boredom that it inspires, the attempt to construct, by means of the history of literature and philosophy, his own 'particular,' the ideology of his own party, the 'truth' for his disciples as well as for ordinary people, continues to arise. This is the way the reputation of a progressive Leopardi is gradually consolidated (and then tarnished), a reputation for which we would now like to substitute that of Gramscian *tout court*. And as soon as the poetic terrain lends itself in the slightest way to this objective, the Gramscians on duty (a case in point is Stefano Gentile, and his co-disciples in the school of Tullio De Mauro, according to their claims) plow straight onto the terrain of linguistics. One way is just like the other, more mischievous or, if you prefer, more astute because more ontologically distinct, linking Leopardi to a memory: theirs, that of the Gramscians. Shame! These efforts, without managing to tap the deep and inexhaustible pessimism of Leopardi's will, serve only to weaken the demonstrative force of otherwise impressive works.

58. *Letter 79*, to P. Giordani, Recanati, 27 November 1818; Shaw, p. 68.

59. G.W.F. Hegel, "The German Constitution," in *Political Writings*, op. cit.

60. *Letter 79*, to Pietro Giordani, Recanati, 27 November 1818; Shaw, p. 67.

61. In his introduction to *TO*, Walter Binni insists (pp. 28 and 30–32) on the importance of Alfieri's influence on the young Leopardi, an influence that is

indisputable and largely confirmed by the letters and the *Zibaldone*. But in what sense? On this point, it strikes me as necessary to clarify things, for here nuances become fundamental. Let me explain: Binni, and already Luporini, consider Alfieri's important influence as decisive insofar as it would imply a definition, in progressive terms, of the optimism of Leopardi's will, philosophy, and poetics. This influence, therefore, would be an incitement to a dialectical passage in the poet's mind. This interpretation seems justified, but only if we consider it as transitory: it is not capable of permanently characterizing Leopardi's thought but corresponds only to the phase of dialectical experimentation preceding the composition of *The Infinite*. Timpanaro's analysis, in opposition to those of Binni and Luporini, is essential insofar as the non-dialectical and materialist characteristics of Leopardi's thought are concerned ("Il pensiero di Leopardi," in *Classismo e Illuminismo*, op. cit.). Aside from that of Alfieri, it is equally necessary to consider the influence of Foscolo, which tends in the same direction and in an even more explicit way; in this regard I refer to the excellent work of M. Ricciardi, *Giacomo Leopardi: La logica dei Canti*, op. cit., passim. On this theme one can always consult the balanced commentaries of N. Badaloni, *Storia d'Italia*, vol. 3, op. cit, p. 899: Alfieri as aristocrat and scholar; and p. 908: Foscolo and the Jacobin crisis, the poet faced with the reality of defeat and crisis, the poetry of historical pessimism. But it is precisely here that the problematic, even in the terms of the most measured critical approaches, becomes rather difficult to sustain: in effect, Leopardi seems to frustrate every paradigm with absolute rigor. The (Alfierian) aristocrat and scholar is transformed in Leopardi into an irreducible tension that cancels out all the balance points that Giordani conferred upon the relationship between aristocracy, doctrine, and reform; on the other hand, to the crisis and the determination to live it (associated with Foscolo) is opposed the fact that in Leopardi, reason is never pessimistic and history is irreversible. Reason can be senseless and its horizon indifferent, but it never accepts the crisis, or rather for reason, the crisis doesn't exist. The crisis does not exist as an unacceptable condition; therefore, there is no need to refute or flee it. Platonism and the static sense of myth in Foscolo's final production (*Le grazie*) are quite simply inconceivable in Leopardi. Once again, in contrast, interrogating Leopardi's relationship to the poets who were his immediate predecessors allows us to grasp the analogy between his very singular position and that of Hölderlin. The 'kingdom of purposes': such is the 'infinite' in Hölderlin's very singular interpretation of Kant's proposition and in the genetic crisis of dialectical thought (cf. Lucien Goldmann, *Immanuel Kant* [London: New Left books, 1971]). It is an infinite that is the sign of no purposiveness, no teleology, and that is presented simply as a scientific and cognitive horizon, and consequently as ethical tension. It is an infinite woven by an extremely singular relationship between being and myth, by a prodigious historical continuity conjoined with an ontological discontinuity between memory and utopia—in Hölderlin *and* in Leopardi.

62. *Letter 62*, to Pietro Giordani, Recanati, 2 March 1818; Shaw, p. 62. See also *Letters 60* and *61*, to the same correspondent, 16 January and 13 February 1818; Shaw, pp. 60–61.

63. *Letters 65, 67, 68, 69, 71, 72, 73, 74*, all addressed to Pietro Giordani and sent from Recanati during 1818; Shaw, pp. 63–70.

64. *Letter 77*, to Pietro Giordani, Recanati, 19 October 1818; Shaw, pp. 66–67. *Letters 101, 102, 104*, also to Giordani, dated 15, 19 and 22 March 1819, respectively.

65. *Letters 78* and *79*, to Pietro Giordani, 9 and 27 November 1818; Shaw, pp. 67–68.

66. *Letters 81, 83, 86*, to Pietro Giordani, Recanati, 14 December 1818, Christmas day 1818, and 18 January 1819; Shaw, pp. 69–72.

67. *Letters 89* and *90*, to Vincenzo Monti, Recanati, 12 February 1819.

68. *Letter 94*, to Pietro Giordani, Recanati, 19 February 1819.

69. *Letters 115, 116, 117, 118*, to Pietro Giordani, Recanati, 28 May, 4 and 21 June, 26 July 1818; Shaw, pp. 76–78.

70. *Letters 120* and *121*, the letters of flight, late July (undated), left at Recanati, addressed to Carlo and Monaldo Leopardi, respectively; Shaw, pp. 80–84.

71. See G. Ceronetti, *La vita apparente* (Milan: Adelphi, 1982), in particular pp. 112–16. In my view, the emphasis placed on the metaphysical character of Kafka's intuition with respect to the "great anxieties" of the "great loser" Leopardi perhaps does not allow us to perceive that the difference is not between having or not having a metaphysics, but between two metaphysics with distinct orientations. The fact remains that Leopardi's metaphysics is in no way consolatory (see note 3 to chapter 3).

72. *Letter 123*, addressed to Saverio Broglio d'Ajano, Recanati, 13 August 1819; Shaw, pp. 85–88.

73. *Letters 126* and *130*, to Pietro Giordani, Recanati, 20 August (Shaw, p. 89) and 13 September 1819.

74. *Canto XII*, Peruzzi, pp. 271–74; Nichols, p. 53. This idyll was composed at Recanati from spring to autumn 1819. L. Blasucci proposes a reading of it ("Leopardi e i signali dell'*Infinito*," in *Strumenti critici*, vols. 36–37 [October 1978]) that ends up, on the basis of a rigorous stylistic analysis, with the same results as those of our philosophical analysis: "the foundational value of *The Infinite*," a poetics that reveals permanent structures, the reproduction of this thematic and these problems, etc. See also some of the *Noterelle* in B. Biral, *La posizione storica di Giacomo Leopardi*, op. cit., pp. 217ff., as well as the remarkable approach of A. Prete, *Il pensiero poetante*, op. cit., pp. 48ff.

75. Nichols, p. 53.

76. Ibid.

77. Ibid.

78. Ibid.

79. And since the most interesting are the latest (1820–21), the operation is explicitly carried out *à rebours* and perhaps with a bit too much enthusiasm. Nevertheless, see W. Binni, *TO I*, pp. 17 and 37–40.

80. *Zibaldone*, p. 84 (*TO II*, pp. 49–50; Caesar/D'Intino, pp. 81–82).

81. R. Koffler, "Kant, Leopardi and Gorgon Truth," in *The Journal of Aesthetics and Art Criticism* 30 (1971), pp. 27–33, and Antimo Negri, "Leopardi e la filosifia di Kant," in *Trimestre* 5, no. 4 (1979), pp. 475–491. Koffler emphasizes with great precision the implicit relations between the Kantian poetic theory (the theory of imagination) and Leopardi's poetics. Since the theory of imagination constitutes the crowning achievement, at once anti-phenomenalist and anti-dialectical, of Kant's philosophical work, understanding this comparison is essential. Antimo Negri weakens the relationship: his work is nevertheless important from a philological point of view (status of the question, the spread of Kantianism and of German philosophy more generally in Italy, translations . . .). We return to the question of Leopardi's "Kantianism" (if it is possible to speak of such a thing). In our view, Kant's critical, analytical, and transcendental characteristics are taken up by Leopardi, only to the extent that they are strictly articulated with Enlightenment attitudes—as happens with great vigor in writings like "What is Enlightenment?" For other bibliographic notes and references, see chapter 1, note 51.

82. See M. Theunissen's relatively recent work, *Sein und Schein: Der Kritische Funktion des hegelschen Logik* (Frankfurt: Suhrkamp, 1980), in which this problematic is thoroughly analyzed. The classic readings of Kojève and Hyppolite had already brought to light this fundamental Hegelian ambiguity. The thematic of *Bestimmtheit* and *Bestimmung* is present in Hegel from the earliest writings. But in Hegel's philosophy, the tension to control the passive determination is pushed to the point of paradox of the paradigm: "the real is rational," which is a paradigm capable of handling extreme exemplifications, even inversions of the very sense of the determination—which are frequent in his mature thought and above all in his philosophy of history. By its submission, its will to understand the passive determination at all costs, active determination begins by referring to itself and then is reduced to a pure and simple factual state, an effective "whatever," just as it appears on the stage of being. The determinant is the determined: thus a vicious circle is established. Historicism, and especially the reactionary historicism of the Hegelian right and twentieth-century Italian culture, seems to have fully interpreted this sequence. It is indisputable that Croce's reading of Leopardi, along with that of the historicists and in certain cases that of the Gramscians, shows a great taste for historical effectiveness, to the point of relegating Leopardi's poetics to the marginal sphere of elementary aestheticism, emotionality, and the passions (the other face of the elemental vitalism and economism that constitute, for Croce, the backdrop of the historical and social vicissitudes of humankind). This interpretive direction is completely unacceptable, Leopardi never having accepted historical effectiveness.

83. See Giorgio Agamben, *Language and Death*, op. cit.

84. W. Binni, *TO I*: p. xvii. Paradoxically, this interpretation is common to progressives and theoreticians of "poetry/non-poetry," Luporini and Solmi being cases in point. We return several times to the sensualist variables in Leopardi and their sources. In any case, regarding this point, see L. Derla's important study, "La teoria del piacere nella formazione del pensiero di Giacomo Leopardi," in *Rivista critia di storia della filosofia*, April–June 1972, fasc. 2, pp. 148–69.

Since I am citing it for the first time and his work is useful for my own work, I want to make a general remark here that anticipates certain reflections that will be developed later. Derla's analysis of the theory of pleasure in the initial period of Leopardi's thought aims less to define the sources than to define the nature of Leopardi's innovation: the discovery consists in a "diagnosis of unhappiness," viewed not as a historical deviation from nature but rather as the appearance of the "historical and ontological insubstantiality of humankind." Leopardi's position is the "first objective representation, in our modern culture, of the derealization of humankind in the era of bourgeois rationality" (p. 168). This conclusion, with which I concur, is developed in chapter 2 of this work. Nevertheless, Derla's reading confines Leopardi's theory of pleasure to the single systematic nucleus that has just been indicated. I reject this conclusion, not because Leopardi's theory of pleasure presents multiple variants (and from this point of view, Derla's polemic [p. 148] against the three theories of pleasure that Tilgher claims to be able to define is justified), but because the systematic development of the fundamental nucleus is vaster than he is willing to recognize here. Consequently the reduction to a "deep structure" of which Derla speaks is one thing, but the always open dynamic of Leopardi's principle of pleasure, which is exposed to successive catastrophes, and the theoretical overturnings that it implies, are something else. In short, Leopardi's metaphysics does not conclude with the theory of pleasure elaborated in 1820, neither in its depth nor in a possible surface dimension.

85. We return to this aspect of Leopardi's poetic experience, for it is funda-mental. But for the moment we must emphasize the fact (and I do it in reference to the reading of Georges Bataille's *Inner Experience*, trans. Leslie Anne Boldt [Albany: SUNY Press, 1988]) that in Leopardi, the finite/infinite relation, which is so characteristic of modern poetry, escapes from the negative dialectic. Even though it is born in contrast to the world, Leopardi's inner experience is not merely negation, absolute nakedness, the refusal of community; it is not a mystical experience, even an entirely secular one, but rather it is oriented toward the simultaneously theoretical and poetic exhaustion of the "I." We will see Leopardi pass through the negative dialectic; we will see him experience the tragedy of the relationship between the universe of communication and the annihilation of signification (Bataille operates, in this case, by drawing examples from Nietzsche and Rimbaud), just as we have

seen him live through the torture of flight and its failure, but without ever being reduced to it—recovering, on the contrary, a positive relationship with being.

86. This way of living the poetic adventure "from the inside" is not limited to the terrain of ontology. Later we deal with the hermeneutic relationship that links Leopardi's thought to the history of culture, to the poetic past as well as to the future of ideology and culture. Here we must note that, like every great poet, Leopardi too constructs his own history, his own precursors and successors. Thus it is less a matter of simply posing the problem of the history of Leopardi's critique (in this regard, the chapter dedicated to Leopardi by E. Bigi in *Classici italiani nella storia della critica*, vol. 2 [Florence: La Nuova Italia, 1962] is essential) than of understanding the 'cosmos' that Leopardi's cognitive, poetic, and metaphysical will constitutes—from the inside, from below: in short, by connecting the thread of history to his own singular mode of existing. On this problem in general, see Harold Bloom's observations in *The Anxiety of Influence: A Theory of Poetry* (New York: Oxford University Press, 1973), pp. 14–16.

87. See B. Biral's important chapter "La crisi dell'anno 1821," in *La posizione storica di Leopardi*, op. cit., pp. 52ff. My reference to Descartes is by no means a rhetorical expedient. As I have indicated elsewhere (*Political Descartes: Reason, Ideology and the Bourgeois Project*, trans. Matteo Mandarini and Alberto Toscano [New York: Verso, 2007]), Descartes too sets out from the problem of memory, and it is only within the consciousness of its rupture that his metaphysical genius is liberated. In Descartes's era, the problem of memory was posed by the crisis of the revolution of the Renaissance, just as it is posed here by the crisis of the revolution of the Enlightenment. But the analogies end there, since the Cartesian solution to the problem of memory is a dialectical solution, although imperfectly so.

88. *Canto XIV*, Peruzzi, pp. 287–92; Nichols, p. 58. Idyll composed at Recanati in 1819 ("It was a year ago"). Concerning the rewriting of the last lines, see Peruzzi as well as Binni, "Introduzione" to *TO I*, pp. 37–38.

89. *Canto XXXVII*, Peruzzi, pp. 567–78; Nichols, p.153. The fragment was completed, after several rounds of revision, at Recanati in 1819. The verse, "But there is only/This one moon in the sky," which strongly recalls the theme of the contemporaneous idyll *To the Moon* (*Canto XIV*), remains central through different rounds of rewriting.

90. Nichols, p. 58.

91. Ibid.

92. Ibid.

93. Ibid., p. 153.

94. Ibid.

95. See G. Macchia, *La caduta della luna* (Milan: Mondadori, 1973).

96. Nichols, p. 153.

97. This affirmation of the "I" is situated in the grand line of subjective idealism, the philosophical position that, although idealist, is not necessarily hypostatic.
Indeed, if one considers, for example, the fictive idealism of Bishop Berkeley, the
titanic character of the battle waged by the young Schelling against nature and science, the bitter solipsism in which the later Wittgenstein entrenched himself, each of
these philosophical positions is a version of idealism that is irreducible to the others,
and all of them are also completely irreducible to hypostatic, totalitarian absolute
idealism. From this viewpoint, subjective idealism is less an overall conception of
being than a phenomenological condition, a state of mind; these are the terms in
which it is defined by W. Windelband in *History of Philosophy*, trans. James H. Tufts
(New York: Macmillan, 1901), who quite reasonably adopts the criterion current
among the historians of his day, from Dilthey to Lotze. Nevertheless, I must be
allowed to add a remark on this same question. Between June 1820 and January
1821, Leopardi outlines a philosophical alternative in the pages of the *Zibaldone*.
He opposes a possible "ultra-philosophy," the ideal of a complete philosophy and a
people who are natural philosophers, to an effective "demi-philosophy," the reality
of a semi-philosophy that allows one to live but not to free oneself from error.
To both of these he opposes a true philosophy—that is, the subjective consciousness of illusion. On these concepts, see Timpanaro, *Classicismo e Illuminismo*,
op. cit., pp. 96–99; U. Carpi, *Il poeta e la politica*, op. cit., pp. 103–5. In my view,
this set of distinctions is practicable and explicable only if it can be related to a
subjective matrix and only if it can be interpreted in light of an open conception
of the subject. In short, Leopardi escapes from negative teleology by affirming
the subject as limit—not as ultimate limit but as, so to speak, preventative limit.
The refusal of the utopia of an "ultra-philosophy" can be associated with that of
the vulgar "half-philosophy" only if the determinate destruction of those two negative powers [*potenze*] collides with the prior affirmation of the subject. See in this
regard P. Fasano's contribution, "Leopardi controromantico," in *Il Ponte*, July 1977,
pp. 818ff., which exceeds the limits imposed on it as a consequence of being tied to
the traditional schema of literary schools and in which the rational affirmation of the
subject is viewed as the basis, for Fasano, of Romantic enthusiasm, though I would
prefer to say, of production and poetics.

98. The first part was composed at Recanati on 27 March 1818, and the
second part completed in August (see *TO I*, pp. 914–48). This text is a response by
Leopardi to the "Osservazioni del Cavalier di Breme sulla poesia moderna," which
appeared in the *Spettatore italiano* of 1–15 January 1818. Concerning the context
of this debate, cf. C. Calcaterra, ed., *I manifesti romantici del 1816 e gli scritti
principali del "Conciliatore" sul Romanticismo* (Turin: Utet, 1951; Classici italiani,
no. 71); E. Mazzali's edition of the *Discorso di G. Leopardi*, with an introduction by
F. Flora and a Romantic anthology (Bologna: Capelli, 1957). See also the note in the

Zibaldone, p. 16 (*TO II*, pp. 10ff.; Caesar/D'Intino, pp. 16–23: "I have just finished reading Ludovico di Breme's observations in issue no. 91 of the *Spettatore*."

    99. Jacques Derrida, *Writing and Difference*, trans. Alan Bass (Chicago: University of Chicago Press, 1978).

    100. *Discourse of an Italian on Romantic Poetry*, trans. Gabrielle Sims and Fabio A. Camilletti, in Camilletti, *Classicism and Romanticism in Italian Literature: Leopardi's "Discourse on Romantic Poetry"* (London: Pickering & Chatto, 2013), p. 120.

    101. Ibid., p. 126, trans. modified.

    102. M. Ricciardi, *Giacomo Leopardi: la logica dei Canti*, op. cit., passim. See in this regard his judicious reply to G. Carchia's thesis in *La legittimazione dell'arte: Studi sull'intelligibile estetico* (Naples: Guida, 1982), especially pp. 63ff.

    103. *Discourse of an Italian*, op. cit., p. 167.

    104. It is perhaps worthwhile to attempt to pass judgment on the extensive commentaries inspired by this moment of Leopardi's activity, which involve attempts to situate Leopardi's thought and figure within the traditional classification of literary schools. But in fact the most interesting studies are those that exceed this strict disciplinary reading, which is the case with the majority of contemporary interpretations. The most accurate and complete analyses are those of U. Carpi, *Il poeta e il politica*, op. cit., pp. 83ff., and M.Fubini, *Giordani, Madame de Staël, Leopardi*, op. cit.; but in my view the most judicious viewpoint, and the one most likely to inspire agreement, is indisputably that of B. Biral, *La posizione storica*, op. cit., pp. 3–29. For Biral, Leopardi is a Romantic following the paradigm of the creative interchangeability of the forms and contents of thought (writing thought poetically and philosophizing poetry; see A. Prete, *Il pensiero poetante*, op. cit.). They all join hands in the definition of Leopardi as a Romantic. As we know, Fubini considers Leopardi a pre-romantic, not yet extricated from the classical tradition but able to revive it by means of his poetic primitivism. Binni, on the other hand, selects the eclectic formula "classical-romantic" that Timpanaro extends into "classical-progressive"; finally, Fasano ("Leopardi controromantico", op. cit.), as we have seen, opts for a "reason that produces enthusiasm." In the end, all these controversies appear to me to produce quite few results. If we consider the three terms on the basis of which we are developing our analysis (inversion, dislocation, and innovation in relation to the continuous fabric of Leopardi's contemporary aesthetic thematic), the operations of inversion and dislocation accomplished by Leopardi seem to me well grasped by these interpretations (all these elements are also present in the balanced contribution of A. Tartaro, "Giacomo Leopardi," in *Storia della letteratura italiana*, ed. C. Muscetta, *Il primo Ottocento* [Bari: Laterza, 1978]), although the operation of innovation is absent. Therefore it falls to us to prove the depth of the latter. But for the moment it is enough to recall, as a final comment on the works cited, that the creative moves of poetry too often fall back onto a positivist horizon. This is

why bombastic positions like that of G. Bollati appear important to us not only in a polemical vein but also in an exemplary one, in that they exalt the irreducible character of this poetic emergence (on the other hand, the pages that Carpi dedicates to Bollati's work [op. cit., pp. 94–97] appear to us to have lost all good sense and bear witness to a disproportionate political ferocity).

105. The work of J.G. Robertson, *Studies in the Genesis of Romantic Theory in the Eighteenth Century* (Cambridge: Cambridge University Press, 1923) remains fundamental, for me, on this theme of continuity. Concerning Italy more specifically, see U. Bosco, "Preromanticismo e romanticismo," in *Questioni e correnti di storia letteraria* (Milan: 1949). But the continuity to which we are here alluding is above all that which was brought to light, in a critical manner, by Horkheimer and Adorno's book, *Dialectic of Enlightenment*, trans. Edmund Jephcott (Stanford: Stanford University Press, 2002)—namely, the continuity of an abstract project for the domination of nature and spirit. Cultural transformations are confronted by the persistence of an irresistible process of domination that claims, in a mystified form, to be the development of reason. The long process of the conquest of society by capitalism is thus viewed according to a route that reduces the cultural and scientific superstructures to material passages. We witness, between the end of the Enlightenment and Romanticism, the general rehearsal of this spectacle that will tirelessly repeat itself during the nineteenth and twentieth centuries, to the point that the destructive sense of this process becomes no more evident than those claimed emancipatory faculties.

106. The question of the problematic relationship between materialism and mythology is broached in the second chapter, in the course of a reading of the *Zibaldone*. However, the abundance of irrationalist implications that have developed around this theme, not least within Leopardi interpretation, compels me to list in advance the references that seem to me essential for the general definition of the concept of myth and mythology: *Terror und Spiel: Probleme der Mythenrezeption*, ed. M. Fuhrmann (Munich: Fink, 1971), with contributions by H. Blumenberg, J. Bollack, O. Marquard, R. Warning, H.R. Jauss, H. Weinrich, etc.; Hans Blumenberg, *Work on Myth*, trans. Robert M. Wallace (Cambridge: MIT Press, 1988); M. Frank, *Der Kommende Gott: Vorlesungen über die neue Mythologie* (Frankfurt: Suhrkamp, 1983); K.H. Bohrer, ed. *Mythos und Moderne: Begriff und Bild einer Rekonstruktion*, (Frankfurt: Suhrkamp, 1983).

107. It is well known that we owe to Cassirer the illustration of the connection and internal dialectic among rationalism, sense, and feeling, as they are brought to light in his writings dedicated to the Enlightenment, Scottish philosophy, the English Neoplatonic tradition, and so on, as well as in those on the dynamics of symbolic forms: *The Philosophy of the Enlightenment* (Princeton: Princeton University Press, 2009) and *The Philosophy of Symbolic Forms* (New Haven: Yale University Press, 1965) vol. 1–3. These analyses, which closely link materialist

consequences with the philosophy of feeling and the moral sense, were introduced into Italy, against the grain of the dominant idealist culture, by Manlio M. Rossi and above all by the staunch materialists Galvano Della Volpe and G. Preti, notably through their works on Hume and Smith. With regard to Leopardi, conceptions of this sort, if assimilated, could have been so only by means of a profound study of the sensualist currents of the French Enlightenment. See in this regard the overall contribution (and accompanying bibliography) of P. Casini, *Storia della filosofia*, ed. Mario Dal Pra, vol. 8 (Milan: Vallardi, 1974). Nevertheless, to my knowledge there is no study that would lead from the analysis of the "passions of the soul" in the seventeenth century to the materialist definition of the relation among the senses, the passions, and the rational consolidation of ideas comparable to those that have been developed for the period between the culture of the Enlightenment and that of the beginning of the nineteenth century. But it must be noted that those bear on German culture and notably on the fundamental passage represented by Herder, and not on French culture. In this regard we must emphasize the importance of the studies on the development of linguistic theories in the Enlightenment era, an issue which we take up later.

108. Clearly we are referring here to the theoretical necessity of an internal rupture, a *clinamen*, in the experience of materialism, and our argument thus has no particular philological aim. Thus, from a philological viewpoint, we consider as valid various aspects of Timpanaro's conclusions ("Leopardi e i filosofici antichi," in *Classisismo e Illuminismo*, op. cit.). Concerning Lucretius (pp. 222–23), after having emphasized the profound sentimental and poetic harmony between the two authors, Timpanaro specifies: "But spiritual affinity is one thing, and reading and direct derivation is another. [. . .] It is impossible to establish with certainty whether, in his last years, even though he no longer wrote anything in the *Zibaldone* and he stopped itemizing his reading, Leopardi read Lucretius." Concerning Epicurus (pp. 219–22), Timpanaro comes to the same conclusions: "Leopardi, as we know, was abundantly nourished on the Epicurean philosophy of the seventeenth century, but he seems to have felt little need to deal directly with Epicurus and Lucretius." (Despite the fact that Timpanaro is undoubtedly right, I cannot for all that forget C. Marchesi's introduction to his edition of Lucretius or the pages dedicated to him in *Storia della letteratura latina*.) Regarding the thinkers of antiquity in general, Timpanaro writes on page 228:

> I don't believe that I have underestimated the influence of Greek philosophy on Leopardi's thought. The materialist and sensualist thinkers of the eighteenth century, known first through the intermediary of their Catholic adversaries and then known directly, were always his preferred masters in matters of philosophy. Nevertheless there were at least two points of contact with Greek thought that played an essential role in Leopardi's ideological evolution: the discovery of

ancient pessimism, which overthrew the myth of a happy antiquity made up of action, illusion and poetry, and the reading of the Hellenistic philosophers, who offered him the model of a resigned wisdom to which he was particularly sensitive between 1823 and 1827, but without ever completely adhering to it. To these I would add experiences that were certainly less profound, like the reading of Plato, and—even more limited—that of Aristotle, which exercised an influence on Leopardi's thought, principally of a polemical order, which must be accounted for.

The balance that Timpanaro's critical position demonstrates is exemplary. To draw consequences for Leopardi's theory from ancient philosophers seems to me nonetheless perilous, even if this approach remains measured. The confusion promulgated by De Sanctis apropos of Stoic morality and the *Manual* of Epictetus (a confusion noted by C. Luporini, *Leopardi progressivo*, op. cit., pp. 81–82) is typical in this regard. In short, it would be more worthwhile to confine ourselves to sugges-tion, to the capacity for poetic reelaboration, more worthwhile to dare to refer—to cite only one example, echoing L. Cellerino (*Techniche ed etica del paradosso*, op. cit., p. 159)—to the active subject in *The Broom* as a "Leopardian Epicurus."

109. For the reference to Xenophanes, according to whom "if the horse or the ox knew how to paint, they would paint and imagine their Gods in the form and guise of horses or oxen," see *Zibaldone, TO II*, p. 943; Cesar/D'Intino, p. 689.

110. *To Angelo Mai on the Occasion of his Discovery of some Books of Cicero's De Re Publica, Canto III*, Peruzzi, pp. 67–106; Nichols, pp. 13–18. Composed at Recanati in January–February 1820.

111. Nichols, p. 13.

112. Ibid., p. 14.

113. Ibid.

114. Ibid., pp. 14–15.

115. Ibid., p. 15.

116. Ibid., pp. 17–18.

117. Karl Löwith, *From Hegel to Nietzsche: The Revolution in Nineteenth-Century Thought*, trans. David E. Green (New York: Holt, Rinehart & Winston, 1964).

118. Gilles Deleuze, *Nietzsche and Philosophy*, trans. Hugh Tomlinson (New York: Columbia University Press, 1983).

119. Some singular analogies can be established between Leopardi's thought and that of Jacob Burkhardt, despite the temporal interval separating their respec-tive activities, one occupying the first half of the nineteenth century and the other the second half. G. Colli (*Per un'antologia di autori classici* [Milan: Adelphi, 1983], particularly the articles on pp. 129ff.) suggested this juxtaposition to me. Concerning Burkhardt, I am relying particularly on his work *Reflections on History*

(Indianapolis: Liberty Fund, 1979) as well as the texts assembled by Colli in his collection *Enciclopedia Boringhieri*. Like Leopardi, Burkhardt lives in a provincial milieu (in Switzerland), and like Leopardi he participates in the great construction of contemporary philology; like him, he conceives literary labor in strict connection with an anxious search for the solution to the problem of life, and he places the creative activity of the searcher at the center of scientific activity. Both make the crisis of memory and historical time—in other words, the crisis of the French Revolution and the reflection that unfolds concerning the tragic conclusion of the dialectic of Enlightenment and the unsustainable development of nascent capitalist civilization—the centerpiece of their research. Burkhardt's pessimism, which was the object of discussions with his friend Nietzsche, is from this point of view a weapon in the reconstruction of the world of life, as it will gradually become for Leopardi. Here I will permit myself to cite a text with which I completely concur:

> Burkhardt is closer to us today than Ranke is [. . .]. We have had the experience of the nocturnal side of universal history to a degree that Ranke neither knew nor even suspected. Burkhardt plunged more deeply and incisively into the historical character of his era and by virtue of this fact, he came to a better perception of what must be coming. We have lived through the horrible picture of the future that he ceaselessly sketched in the 1870s and 1880s. (F. Meinecke, "Ranke und Burkhardt," in *Deutsches Akademie der Wissenschaft zu Berlin, Schriften und Vorträge* no. 27 [Berlin, 1948])

120. See notes 105–107. To the acknowledgement of the postromantic reconstruction of the Enlightenment and the reaffirmation of its differences as they were established above all by Cassirer, we would like to add the works of two other founders of the modern interpretation of the eighteenth century: Wilhelm Dilthey, "The Eighteenth Century and the Historical World (1901)," in *Hermeneutics and the Study of History: Selected Works*, ed. R.A. Makkreell and F. Rodi, vol. 4 (Princeton: Princeton University Press, 1996) and P. Hazard, *La crise de la conscience européene* (Paris: Librairie générale française, 1994). These references are intended to state that: (a) Leopardi's judgment on the historical world and in particular on that of the Enlightenment is *complex*; that is, it comprehends the Enlightenment as rationalism but also as the construction of a second nature; (b) the *denunciation* of rationalism does not imply a second nature, the world of feeling, etc. Instead it traverses them; (c) therefore Leopardi's thought never confuses itself with the historicist and idealist *refusal* of the Enlightenment—Leopardi lives the second nature and his exit is in no way a *flight*; and (d) this involves a *displacement* and not a fictive overcoming as in the case of the idealists, who end up repeating the perverse dynamics of the *Aufklärung*. All this leads us to Horkheimer and Adorno's hypothesis, which constitutes a central reference for our research in this regard.

M.A. Rigoni (*La pensée de Leopardi*, op. cit., p. 57) emphasizes the fact that "in Leopardi's entire work, we do not find a single citation of an Enlightenment thinker that does not have a negative sense." But this doesn't mean much, and in any case it does not signify an irrationalist inclination of Leopardi's thought. The relationship is much more complex, being precisely that of the dialectic of Enlightenment.

121. Perhaps the moment has come for some reflections concerning the constellation Leopardi-Nietzsche. First of all, some bibliographic references: on Nietzsche as reader of Leopardi, see A. Prete, *Il pensiero poetante*, op. cit., p. 65 where Nietzsche's texts in which the figure of Leopardi appears are recalled: *Untimely Meditations*, trans. R.J. Hollingdale (Cambridge: Cambridge University Press, 1983), II: sec. 1, p. 66; "We Philologists," in *The Complete Works of Nietzsche*, ed. Oscar Levy and trans. J.M. Kennedy, vol. 8 (New York: Macmillan, 1911), p. 115; *The Gay Science*, trans. Walter Kaufmann (New York: Vintage, 1974), book 2, sec. 92, p. 146. Also noted are S. Solmi, *Studi e nuovi studi di Leopardi* (Milan: Ricciardi, 1975), pp. 158ff.; S. Timpanaro, *La filologia di Leopardi* (Bari: Laterza, 1977), pp. 187–89; M.A. Rigoni, *Saggu sul pensiero leopardiano*, op. cit., pp. 36, 40, 62, 65, 66, 83. Timpanaro's analysis is the most important. Rigoni's should not be neglected, even though it is limited to bringing to light correspondences between the two thinkers.

If we consider some of Nietzsche's pages where references to Leopardi appear (and in particular in *The Gay Science*, pp. 145–49), the tone of his propositions is immediately perceptible. Leopardi is remembered as a master of prose. But if, from an objective point of view, prose is the recording of a metaphysical situation without resolution, from a subjective point of view it is an activity of liberation. Leopardi is an Italian who knows, against the wretchedness of life, how to transform serious things into play and suffering into laughter. It is in the course of the reflections that conclude with the declaration of the death of God that Nietzsche constantly reclaims his relationship with Leopardi. Nietzsche experiences the very same passage that Leopardi experienced, with a half-century's delay. It is a passage that is at once the positioning and the crisis of the dialectic. But in this image of the death of God, and by means of the unresolvable character of the concept of the infinite, perhaps Nietzsche grasps a higher passage of the dialectical drama: the plasticity of his foresight allows him to reach the level of real subsumption, to speak in Marxist terms, whereas the justification of Leopardi's discourse is formal subsumption.

Finally, a last remark that seems worth making: *The Gay Science*, an indubitably Leopardian book, is also the most Spinozian and least Schopenhauerian of Nietzsche's books (pp. 144–56). I mean that the heroic transcending of indifference, the appearance of great passion as good in itself has nothing to do with genius or compassion but rather with innocence and the optimism of reason. I ask myself if Nietzsche could have written about Leopardi what he writes about

Spinoza: "I have a precursor, and *what* a precursor!" (post card to Franz Overbeck, Sils-Maria, 30 July 1881, in Nietzsche, *Selected Letters*, ed. and trans. Christopher Middleton [Indianapolis: Hackett, 1969], p. 177).

122. On the relationship between Leopardi and Montesequieu, cf. passim; indeed we will often have to confront this very intimate relationship in the *Zibaldone* and more generally throughout Leopardi's thought. On the continuity of nature and history, see Louis Althusser, "Montesquieu: Politics and History," in *Montesquieu, Rousseau, Marx*, trans. Ben Brewster (London: Verso, 1972). Leopardi reads *Considerations on the Causes of the Greatness of the Romans and Their Decline* in 1820 (on the fundamental characteristics of this reading, see note 56 to chapter 5). It is to this same year that his reading of Montesequieu's *Essay on Taste* dates (on the specifics of this reading, see note 37 to chapter 2).

123. We are returning again to the positions of Heidegger and Marcuse, already mentioned above in note 42 concerning the central position that the ontology of time occupies in the philosophy of classical idealism. We would like to pose another question, that of the contribution made by the Romantic thinkers contemporaneous with Leopardi to this presence of time within his poetry. This means asking how important the Romantic renewal of the Christian idea of time, the reactionary interpretation of the ecclesiastical concept of time, was in the construction of Leopardi's discourse. (For a general study of the nucleus of philosophical thought on time and history taking shape in France amid the rubble of the Napoleonic defeat, see P. Benichou, *Le temps des prophètes: Doctrines de l'âge romantique* [Paris: Gallimard, 1977]—a rather untraditional yet very important text for the wealth of perspectives it offers.) In my view, the answer to these questions cannot be positive. Of course Leopardi never ceased to be driven, particularly in the familial sphere, to the study of the Romantics and the Catholic reactionaries; but his difference from that approach is radical. If there is influence, it does not follow the lines of Leopardi's consciousness and studies but instead forms part of the coordinates of the era. But then could we not ask ourselves, contrary to what has been done up to now, at what point had secular and revolutionary thought wrested this ontological conception of time from Christianity and put it through the filter of the same reaction?

124. I am put in an awkward position every time I must polemicize with the authors of the progressive interpretation of Leopardi, such as Binni, Luporini, Timpanaro, Biral, and all the others. The first awkwardness arises when it turns out that their very generous interpretive experience is not communicable. We are no longer in a *risorgimentale* battle! Alberto Asor Rosa emphasizes this, and rightly so, in his *Sintesi di storia della letteratura italiana* (Florence: La Nuova Italia, 1972, pp. 339ff.)—even if he does not clearly understand why; and whereas a central role is granted to the European reference in Leopardi's poetic sensibility, at the same time the ethical direction and political charge of his last works are undervalued. The reference to the European level remains nevertheless fundamental, but this reference

cannot be merely formal, which in this case would be equivalent to legitimating the surreptitious return to a form of Croceanism. No, the reference to the European level implies the ethical dimension of the later Leopardi's discourse and its insertion into the European context of the crisis of the dialectic. Beyond the formal reference to Europe, there is an anti-dialectical struggle.

The second awkwardness follows from the observation of the sterility of the progressivist interpretation. In effect, after the first heroic phase, we find ourselves faced with either a generic and insignificant acceptance (which explains how diametrically opposed positions can rest on the same historical positioning; see for example the Rigoni-Cioran hypothesis!) or a political or, shall we say, partisan banalization of progressivism (see, for example, the polemic between C. Salinari and E. Sanguineti in *Critica marxista* 4 [1974], pp. 183–206). There really is no more time for this; it is a matter of recognizing that those proceedings have thrown the baby out with the bathwater.

Chapter Two: The Web of Sense

1. *Letter 153*, to Leandro Trissino, from Recanati, undated but between May and June 1820.

2. *Letter 150*, to Pietro Brighenti, 28 April 1820; Shaw, p. 102.

3. *Letter 133*, to Pietro Giordani, 19 November 1819, from Recanati; Shaw, p. 90.

4. *Letter 135*, to Pietro Giordani, from Recanati, 17 December 1819; Shaw, p. 91.

5. *Letter 143*, to Pietro Giordani, from Recanati, 6 March 1820; Shaw, p. 95.

6. *Letter 146*, to Pietro Giordani, from Recanati, 20 March 1820; Shaw, pp. 96–97.

7. *Letter 156*, to Pietro Giordani, 30 June 1820; Shaw, p.105.

8. *Zibaldone*, p. 8 (*TO II*, p. 6; Caesar/D'Intino, p. 9–10).

9. Here I am alluding to the method developed by Husserl in the *Formal and Transcendental Logic* of 1929 (trans. Dorian Cairns [The Hague: Martinus Nijhoff, 1969]), the *Cartesian Meditations* of 1931 (trans. Dorian Cairns [The Hague: Martinus Nijhoff, 1960]), and *The Crisis of European Sciences and Transcendental Phenomenology* of 1935–37 (not published until the fifties; trans. David Carr [Evanston: Northwestern University Press, 1970]). I have no intention of making Leopardi into a precursor, above all in a domain as specialized as that of phenomenological philosophy. Here I want to highlight another fundamental aspect: the construction of second nature, of the interchangeable relation that thought establishes with its object in the production of the natural milieu of its development. In this regard I could refer to a page by N. Badaloni (*Storia d'Italia*, vol. 3, op.

cit., pp. 891–92) where, taking up Marx's analysis of Destutt de Tracy's work in the *Theories of Surplus Value*, he shows how the concept of second nature is the expression of the capitalist ideology of 'production for production's sake.' If I don't do so, it is not because I consider this intuition to be erroneous or inapt, but simply because it appears incomplete to me. This question is reconsidered in its entirety when we discuss the influence of the Ideologues on Leopardi's thought. For the moment, it is enough to add that Leopardi considers second nature not merely as an ideological horizon but rather as a phenomenological condition. The constitutive laws of structure are thus valid for the description of second nature: laws of implication, laws of production, constitutive laws. Second nature is a mystification, but it is a destructive mystification (it destroyed the first nature, which has ceased to exist for us) and an effective one (we live, and by living reproduce, second nature). Phenomenology helps us to understand some of the mechanisms that preside over this Leopardian reconfiguration of the world (cf. note 29 to chapter 5).

10. Concerning the definition of the concept of public sphere [*Öffentlichkeit*], aside from the references to the work of Habermas already mentioned in chapter 1, see also the fundamental work of O. Negt and A. Kluge, *Public Sphere and Experience*, trans. Peter Labanyi et al. (Minneapolis: University of Minnesota Press, 1993). The assertion that the concepts of the public, publicity, and communication are essential for defining the form that experience takes in the era of the capitalist subsumption of society—that is, in the postmodern, or in other words in any postulation of the worldly universe as second nature—constitutes one of the fundamental assumptions of our present study. During the seventies, German philosophy belabored these issues—from Habermas to Negt, but also Appel, Tugendhat, Luhmann, Theunissen, etc.

11. Nichols, p. 13.

12. For Giovanni Gentile (in *Manzoni e Leopardi*, op. cit.) as for Benedetto Croce (see note 23 to chapter 1), the flattening of Leopardi's thought in provincial and marginal isolation is an established fact. Gentile appears nevertheless to be in the better position to understand Leopardi, first of all because Gentile never ceased paying close attention to the relationship of Italian philosophy with European philosophy. And even though he often allowed this relationship to be sacrificed on the altar of universal history, he was broadly engaged with the sense and determination of the anticipatory and foundational role of Italian thought with regard to European thought (corresponding to the temporal anticipation of material civilization). Furthermore, unlike Croce, Gentile had a feeling, free of formalism, for the *risorgimentale* revolution, and in his work the idea that it liberated Italian thought from the dramatic difficulties that followed the crisis of the Renaissance frequently (and often confusedly) reappears. In the second place, in his "Proemio" to the Zanichelli edition of the *Operette morali* (Bologna, 1918), Gentile perfectly perceives the logical rhythm of Leopardi's poetry, or more precisely the poetic

essence of Leopardi's logic. These two factors could have allowed a more judicious approach to Leopardi's poetry and philosophy on the part of twentieth-century Italian culture. But it did not work out that way. Leopardi was pursued by the anathemas of the moderates and the religious. This interdiction, internalized by Italian culture, still persists, just as it persists against Machiavelli and Ariosto, Bruno and Galileo. It would be quite interesting to add to the history of criticism so admirably elaborated by Bigi a chapter dedicated to the history of the political conditions of interpretations of Leopardi within Italian culture, with the aim of showing how an accentuation of the idyllic reading corresponds to each reactionary turn (see the interpretation of the "gossips [*vociani*]").

13. In his introduction to *TO I*, pp. 44–45, Walter Binni situates Leopardi's labor through the years: "If we consider the expansion of the *Zibaldone* in different phases, it appears that: (a) from the beginning of 1817 to 1819, the *Zibaldone* consisted of roughly 100 pages; (b) from January 1820 to the departure for Rome in November 1822, more than 2,500 pages are added; (c) during the sojourn in Rome, only 40 pages; (d) the return to Recanati in 1823, more than 1,300; (e) in 1824 around 120; (f) between 1825 and 1827 around 180; (g) in 1828 and 1829, in Pisa and Recanati, around 220 pages; (h) from 1830 to 1832, only 2 pages. The two most productive phases in the composition of the *Zibaldone* are thus phase b from 1820 to 1822 and, after the Roman interval, phase d in 1823 preceding the *Operette morali*, which together represent more than three-quarters of the composition" (see also pp. 38–40, 44–53, and 68–69). We return at great length to the internal structure and arguments of the *Zibaldone* as well as to the critical literature concerning it. Citations of the *Zibaldone* refer first to Leopardi's pagination, followed by that of the Italian edition (*TO II*), then the English translation by Michael Caesar, Franco D'Intino, et al.

14. *Zibaldone*, p. 99 (*TO II*, p. 56; Caesar/D'Intino, p. 91).

15. Ibid., p. 31 (*TO II*, p. 22; Caesar/D'Intino, p. 35).

16. Ibid., p. 14–15 (*TO II*, p. 10; Caesar/D'Intino, pp. 15–16).

17. Ibid., p. 23 (*TO II*, p. 16; Caesar/D'Intino, p. 24).

18. Ibid., p. 21–23 (*TO II*, pp. 15–16; Caesar/D'Intino, p. 24).

19. We have already insisted upon this particularly modern aspect of Leopardi's thought—namely, its fierce, harsh and constant polemic against every conception of instrumental reason. It is not by chance that we have already mentioned on this subject Horkheimer and Adorno's *Dialectic of Enlightenment*. It is indeed instrumental reason, in its capitalist definition, which Leopardi opposes, just as Adorno and Horkheimer do at more than a century's distance. Can these positions be related to one another? In no way, if one considers their presuppositions, the culture and language to which they belong. But it could become possible if we conceive instrumental reason as a historical constant of capitalism and its development, whatever its degree of maturity and conceptual formalization. So then, faced with

the same phenomenon, it is possible that the distinct judgments, stated with more than a century of distance between them, retain their value and justify conceptually the analogy they present. In effect, the comparison does not depend upon subjectivity but on the unity of the objective process with which the subject, or subjects in the present case, are confronted. Our problem is in fact that of "explain[ing] why humanity, instead of entering a truly human state, is sinking into a new kind of barbarism" (*Dialectic of Enlightenment*, op. cit., xiv). "Just as myths celebrated the *Aufklärung*, the *Aufklärung* with its whole past hurled itself into the depths of a devastating mythology"—so say our authors. What more intimate analogy with the problematic of Leopardi's thought could there be? And all this where the culture of the Enlightenment could only impose its simultaneously progressive and destructive dream obstinately and in the absence of any problematization, where Romantic culture could only accentuate its mystifying capacity!

20. Ibid., pp. 2, 3, 4, 6, 7, 8, 21, etc. (*TO II*, pp. 4, 5, 6, 15, etc.; Caesar/ D'Intino, pp. 4–7, 8–10, 22–23, etc.).

21. Ibid., p. 6 (*TO II*, p. 6; Caesar/D'Intino, p. 8).

22. Ibid., pp. 14–15, 37, 39, etc. (*TO II*, pp. 10, 26, 27; Caesar/D'Intino, pp. 14–16, 42–45, etc.).

23. Ibid., pp. 37, 40, 44, 51 (*TO II*, pp. 26, 28, 31, 35; Caesar/D'Intino, pp. 42–43, 45–47, 50–51, 57–58).

24. Ibid., passim in the pages covering this period, but above all pp. 21–22, 44–45 (*TO II*, pp. 15, 31; Caesar/D'Intino, pp. 22–24, 50–52).

25. Ibid., p. 51 (*TO II*, p. 61; Caesar/D'Intino, p. 58).

26. Ibid., passim in the pages of this period, but above all pp. 23, 52, 60 (*TO II*, pp. 16, 35, 40; Caesar/D'Intino, pp. 24–26, 58–59, 66–67).

27. Leopardi's sensualism has been the object of a very large number of studies, some of which we have already cited and discussed. If the influence exerted by sensualism upon Leopardi is indisputable, on the other hand the exact nature of this influence is not very clear. We will content ourselves with raising several problematic points. Is Leopardi's sensualism a reprise of sensualism in its primary form, à la Condillac, or does it instead belong to the sophisticated sensualist refinements of the Ideologues? Second, doesn't this influence, like other aspects of Leopardi's thought, come through intermediaries—in this case through Madame de Staël? In that case, isn't Leopardi's sensualism more a trace, an index, a working hypothesis—perhaps already bearing the stamp of the Ideologues—than a system? This last supposition seems to me the most acceptable: in effect, Leopardi's philosophical genius is characterized by "cultivated ingenuousness"; that is to say, it makes original constructions out of elements borrowed from the tradition that it disassembles, combines, and reproduces. This is precisely what happens with sensualism, which is absorbed directly from French sources but also from its Italianized variants by Soave, and lastly from the sensualist recuperations of the traditional gnoseology of

classical metaphysics. That said, let us try to put all these elements into order and provide some precisions that will allow us to better evaluate our interpretive choice:

a. The relationship with Condillac seems certain. In this regard see the texts cited in notes 38, 51, and 84 to chapter 1. See also *Linguistica leopardiana*, op. cit., pp. 25–81, by S. Gensini who, although he applies himself principally to linguistic material, offers a broad and useful view of the sensualist influence. It is indisputable that Leopardi read Condillac, particularly the *Essay on the Origin of Human Knowledge* and the *Course of Study for the Instruction of the Prince of Parma*.

b. Leopardi's relation to the thought of the Ideologues also seems certain. See F. Lo Piparo's study, "Matérialisme et linguistique chez Leopardi," in *Historiographia Linguistica* 9, 1982: 3, pp. 361–87, as well as R. Baum's article, "Die *Ideologen* des 18 Jahrhundert und die Sprachwissenschaft," in the same journal (1975: 1, pp. 61–90). Concerning the Ideologues in general, see the works of S. Moravia to which we return later, and above all N. Badaloni (*Storia d'Italia* vol. 3, op. cit., pp. 890–91 as well as pp. 908–15 on the concept of the 'market' in Gioia), who explicitly links the development of the sense-passion-representation-ideology thematic to the constitution of the concept of second nature. It is precisely with regard to this concept that the link connecting Leopardi with the thought of the Ideologues can be asserted with certainty—setting aside, of course, the intermediary role played here by Madame de Staël.

c. That said, it remains no less true that Leopardi's reprise is characterized by a great originality, with regard to confirmations as well as reelaborations. Furthermore, and this aspect must never be forgotten, Leopardi's sensualism is materialist: that means it is metaphysical and not phenomenalist, post-critical and not Kantian. It is never a theory of appearance, but instead a theory, or rather an apprehension of the object. Lastly, it seems to me extremely important to insist on the fact that materialist sensualism makes possible a metaphysics of the beautiful, an entirely original aesthetics as well as a poetics. We return to this aspect when we deal with the singular encounter between certain pages of Leopardi and the thought of Jacques Derrida (who, we do not forget, is also the editor of Condillac).

28. *Zibaldone*, pp. 53, 55, 56, 57, 76, etc. (*TO II*, pp. 36, 37, 38, 39, 47, etc.; Caesar/D'Intino, pp. 59–60, 61–64, 77).

29. Ibid., pp. 59, 66 (*TO II*, pp. 40, 43; Caesar/D'Intino, pp. 65–66, 70–71). It is useless to repeat that this characterization of the dynamic principles of the sensibility leads back not so much to the thought of the eighteenth century as to that of the seventeenth century: thus this sensualist conception is profoundly interwoven with an atomistic horizon, a rigidly mechanical and immanentist conception

of being. I have analyzed the materialist aspects of the atomist sensualism of the seventeenth century at length in my book *Political Descartes: Reason, Ideology and the Bourgeois Project*, trans. Matteo Mandarini and Alberto Toscano (New York: Verso, 2007).

30. Ibid., p. 69 (*TO II*, p. 44; Caesar/D'Intino, p. 73). In this regard we should perhaps examine the seventeenth-century theory of comic illusion—as everyone knows, *L'illusion comique* is a play by the "sublime Corneille." Indeed, an analysis of Leopardi's theory of illusion that relates it to the theory of theatrical illusion elaborated in the seventeenth century would be worth doing. Theatrical illusion opens up on the one hand onto sensory error and on the other hand onto creative fantasy (see in this regard the works of Jean Rousset). And the deeper our inquiry into Leopardi goes, the more we are convinced that the origins of his sensualist thought go back to the seventeenth century—that is to say, to an immediately metaphysical conception of sensualism, strictly connected with atomism. It is beyond doubt that all seventeenth-century science, above all in France, was imbued with this thought, which at that time established hegemony over the spiritualist theories. We could go even further, following an intuition of Paul Hazard, and consider the continuity of Spinozism as the true materialist conception of the universe during the two centuries that interest us. Thus the materialism of the seventeenth century becomes the true matrix for every position, materialist or sensualist, of the succeeding centuries. That said, it remains no less true that Leopardi knew one thing only about the Spinozists—that they were pantheists, which has little to do with materialism; furthermore, according to Leopardi, only an imbecile would call our wretched existence "divine" (*Zibaldone* p. 4274, *TO II*, p. 1143; Caesar/D'Intino, p. 1902).

31. Ibid., p. 85 (*TO II*, p. 50; Caesar/D'Intino, p. 82). But see also pp. 68–69, 72, 84–85 (*TO II*, pp. 44, 46, 50; Caesar/D'Intino, pp. 72–73, 75, 81–82).

32. Ibid., pp. 88–99 (*TO II*, pp. 50–56; Caesar/D'Intino, pp. 84–91). Let us recall in this regard Gramsci's well-known judgment in *Selections from Cultural Writings*, trans. William Boelhower (Cambridge: Harvard University Press, 1985, p. 118): "Leopardi can be described as the poet of the despair created in certain minds by 18th-century sensualism, which in Italy had no corresponding development of material and political forces and struggles as it did in the countries where it was an organic cultural form." It is obvious that we can only partially agree with such a judgment. See the next note for an ideal Marxist response!

33. This passage is central in Leopardi's thought and needs more attention, so we will return to it. That said, it is worthwhile to recall that Leopardi was able, by means of his attentive readings, to rediscover within the philosophy of Enlightenment a post-Kantian, post-critical passage from the transcendental aesthetic to the transcendental imagination. See in this regard Ernst Cassirer's fundamental analyses in *Philosophy of the Enlightenment*, trans. Fritz Koelin

(Princeton: Princeton University Press, 1951), but more so in *The Problem of Knowledge: Philosophy, Science and History Since Hegel*, trans. William H. Woglom (New Haven: Yale University Press, 1969). See also W. Windelband's *History of Philosophy*, op. cit. This passage constitutes the sphere of communication; that is, it resolves transcendentality into communication. This post-critical version of the transcendental is characteristic of a certain sensualism and of the Ideologues, but refers above all, in Germany, to Herder's thought, which exercised a tremendous influence. However, we must add that the consciousness of this passage's central importance is, for the majority of authors whom we mention, rather weak, and (with the possible exception of Herder) it represents the 'substitution' of immediacy, the modification of the reality principle, rather than the 'constitution' of the critical principle. It is quite interesting to note that the Enlightenment thinkers—from Berkeley to the skepticism of Schultze, from the eighteenth-century sensualists to the work of Cabanis—constitute the Enlightenment sources of the discovery, in Schopenhauer's *The World as Will and Representation*, of the passage of the substitution of the real. Schopenhauer thus makes the problem explicit. So does Leopardi. However, the results of this theoretical development are extremely different in the two thinkers: the exaltation of the constitutive function of the critical principle by Leopardi opposing itself to the illusionism of the German philosopher. The fact that certain ambiguities were able to arise from their comparison is nevertheless understandable. We will return to this question later. Our immediate concern is simply to emphasize the importance and consistency of a critical passage that underwent diverse developments at several moments in Enlightenment philosophy. Lastly, let us emphasize that we can find in Marx's *Grundrisse* one of a number of conceptualizations of this post-critical passage within the development of Enlightenment thought.

> Universally developed individuals, whose social relations, as their own communal relations, are hence also subordinated to their own communal control, are no product of nature, but of history. The degree and the universality of the development of wealth where this individuality becomes possible supposes production on the basis of exchange values as a prior condition, whose universality produces not only the alienation of the individual from himself and from others, but also the universality and the comprehensiveness of his relations and capacities. In earlier stages of development the single individual seems to be developed more fully, because he has not yet worked out his relationships in their fullness, or erected them as independent social powers and relations opposite himself. It is as ridiculous to yearn for a return to that original fullness as it is to believe that with this complete emptiness history has come to a standstill. (Marx, *Grundrisse: Introduction to the Critique of Political Economy (Rough Draft)*, trans. Martin Nicolaus [New York: Penguin, 1973] p. 162)

34. On the multiple definitions of nature and in particular on the materialist and idealist variants of its concept, see J. Ehrard, *L'idée de nature en France dans la première moitié du XVIIIe siècle* (Paris: A. Michel, 1994); see also R. Mauzi, *L'idée du Bonheur dans la literature et la pensée française au XVIIIe siècle* (Paris: A. Michel, 1994), to which we return later. Furthermore, see note 36 to chapter 5. The determination of the concept of nature in the Enlightenment era, as in other philosophical eras, far surpasses its stereotypical definition: in particular, the struggle between materialism and idealism here becomes much more acute than it was in the sixteenth and seventeenth centuries. This is due, above all in France and partially in Germany (the English case is a separate matter), to the complete disappearance, the result of profound discrediting, of traditional neo-Platonic mediations. Nature thus presents itself within a multiplicity of determinations, which is traversed by a double direction, toward materialism or toward idealism. Never as in the epoch of the Enlightenment has the implicit adversary of the official philosophy and ideology of existing power [*potere*], the adversary of triumphant idealism, that unspoken and unrecognized adversary in a constant, mute polemic against power [*potere*]—namely materialism, ceasing to be a silent subject—been such an active actor in the metaphysical struggle of the modern age. See in this regard, with all its limitations and yet with all the importance of a unique and singular work, F.A. Lange, *History of Materialism and Criticism of Its Present Importance*, trans. Ernest Chester Thomas (London: Trübner and Co., 1881) in three volumes.

35. *Zibaldone*, p. 38 (*TO II*, p. 26; Caesar/D'Intino, pp. 43–44).

36. Now is not the time to linger over the classics of Rousseau interpretation (E. Cassirer, B. Groethuysen, J. Starobinski, I. Fetscher); it is enough to recall that the guiding thread of these great interpretations is based on the recognition of the transcendentalist conditions of his philosophy—a philosophy of feeling, a transcription of sensualism into spiritual terms, which permits the transformation of the movements of the will into the representation of the will, of the individual will into a participation in the transcendental of the will. This process, this extraordinary singularity of Rousseau's thought, has constantly been brought to light throughout the history of the philosophy of right (see in this regard the works of G. del Vecchio, which remain exemplary despite their great age). Thus it is not surprising that Kant as well as Hegel, to speak only of the greatest, could call themselves Rousseauists. From R. Fester (*Rousseau und die deutsche Geschichtsphilosophie: Ein Beitrag zue Geschichte des deutschen Idealismus* [Geneva: Slatkine, 1972]) to F. Rosenzweig (*Hegel und der Staat* [Berlin: R. Oldenbourg, 1920], 2 vols.) and J. Ritter (*Hegel and the French Revolution*, trans. R.D. Winfield [Cambridge: MIT Press, 1982]), the documentation concerning this question is extensive. There is thus a line that leads from sensualism to the dialectic: it is an aspect that we have emphasized time and again, and this broad transcendental variant of sensualism (see in this regard

T. Todorov, *Frail Happiness: An Essay on Rousseau*, trans. John T. Scott and Robert Zaretsky [University Park: Penn State University Press, 2001]) must be kept in mind whenever one speaks of the relation between Leopardi's thought and the Rousseauist tradition. This relationship is thus extremely complex (see especially our conclusions in note 157 to chapter 4) and certainly cannot be resolved by means of the collation of external resemblances as N. Serban generously tries to do in his work *Leopardi et la France* (Paris: Champion, 1913).

37. The work of Montesquieu contains an immediately materialist operation, as Louis Althusser demonstrates ("Montesquieu: Politics and History," in *Montesquieu, Rousseau, Marx*, trans. Ben Brewster [London: Verso, 1972]). On the quantitative importance of Montesquieu's influence on Leopardi, cf. *Zibaldone*, pp. 113–17, 119–24, 135, 142, 154, 161, 162–63, 170, 178, 186, 189, 191, 198, 204, 213, 222, 262, 274, 331 (*TO II*, pp. 61–65, 68, 71, 75, 78–79, 82, 84, 87, 89, 91, 93, 96, 99, 111, 114; Caesar/D'Intino, pp. 100–106, 111–12, 115, 122–23, 127–28, 132, 136, 140–41, 142, 144, 147–48, 150, 155–56, 160, 178, 183–84, 206). These references are concentrated in the year 1820, during which Leopardi read the *Considerations on the Causes of the Greatness of the Romans and their Decadence* and the *Essay on Taste*. The references to Montesquieu are also frequent later in the *Zibaldone* (pp. 359, 457–58, 883, 915–16, 1043, 1366, 1552, 1601, 3214 (*TO II*, pp. 136, 162, 255, 264, 303, 396, 439, 450, 804; Caesar/D'Intino, pp. 218, 259, 416, 431–32, 495, 649–650, 721, 740, 1320). As for the reception of the discourse on climate and the forms of government, see passim and note 122 of chapter 1. On the theme of historical catastrophe, see note 56 to chapter 5. But the materialist nexus appears most clearly in the usage Leopardi makes of the problematic of taste as it had been elaborated by Montesquieu. On Montesquieu's *Essay* and the problem of taste in general, see Giorgio Agamben (in the *Enciclopedia Einaudi* vol. 6 [Turin, 1979], pp. 1019–38), who insists on the synthetic character of taste and equally on the ambiguity of its concept, two aspects that according to him make up one of the creative themes of western metaphysics. In short, here we have another one of the materialist themes offering an alternative to the dialectic. Furthermore, on other Italian receptions of the Enlightenment problematic of taste, see S. Gensini, *Linguistica leopardiana*, op. cit., pp. 39ff. and the intelligent remarks of Antonio Prete, *Il pensiero poetante*, op. cit., pp. 45–47.

38. For this period, see *Zibaldone*, pp. 100–2316 (*TO II*, pp. 56–600; Caesar/ D'Intino, pp. 91–984).

39. Concerning the year 1820, see *Zibaldone*, pp.100–463 (*TO II*, pp. 56–163; Caesar/D'Intino, pp. 91–261).

40. *Zibaldone*, p. 256 (*TO II*, p. 109; Caesar/D'Intino, p. 176).

41. Ibid.

42. Ibid., p. 107 (*TO II*, p. 59; Caesar/D'Intino, p. 96, emphasis in original).

43. Ibid., pp. 116, 147–49, 155, 160–61, 210, 252, 274–75, 299–300, 302, 311–12, 314–15 (*TO II*, pp. 62, 73, 78, 95, 108, 114, 120–21, 123, 124; Caesar/D'Intino, pp. 102, 118–19, 123, 126–27, 154, 174, 183–84, 192–94, 197–99).

44. See J.S. Spink, *French Free-Thought from Gassendi to Voltaire* (London: Athlone Press, 1960); *Les Libertines au XVIIe siècle* (Paris: Buchet-Castel, 1964), texts selected and presented by A. Adam.

45. *Zibaldone*, p. 356 (*TO II*, p. 135; Caesar/D'Intino, p. 217).

46. Ibid., p. 337 (*TO II*, p. 130; Caesar/D'Intino, p. 208).

47. Ibid., pp. 105, 112, 125, 132–33, 150, 334–38, etc. (*TO II*, pp. 58, 61, 65, 67–68, 74, 129–30, etc.; Caesar/D'Intino, pp. 95, 99–100, 107, 110–11, 120, 207–09, etc.).

48. Ibid., pp. 392–451 (*TO II*, pp. 146–60; Caesar/D'Intino, pp. 233–56).

49. Ibid., p. 341 (*TO II*, p. 131; Caesar/D'Intino, p. 210).

50. C. Luporini (*Leopardi progressivo*, op. cit., pp. 5–7) refers appropriately to a fragment by the young Hegel on the "unhappy consciousness" (which he provides in part there, in advance of translating and publishing it in its entirety in *Società* 1945: 3, pp. 63ff.). In the Lasson edition of Hegel's works, the note to which Luporini refers appears under the title "Freiheit und Schicksal" (in *Hegels Schriften zur Politik und Rechtsphilosophie* vol. 7 [Lipsia, 1923], pp. 138–41; also in J. Hoffmeister, *Dokumente zu Hegels Entwicklung* [Stuttgart: F. Fromann, 1936], pp. 469–70). Luporini's reading of the young Hegel is strongly tinged with existentialism and the citation he makes is a hint of the spirit in which he undertakes the study of Leopardi. I do not believe I am wrong to identify in the persistence of this element, denounced by Timpanaro as strident, a characteristic motif of the singularity of Luporini's interpretation.

51. *Zibaldone*, pp. 108–9 (*TO II*, p. 59; Caesar/D'Intino, p. 97).

52. Ibid., pp.100–4 (*TO II*, pp. 56-57; Caesar/D'Intino, pp. 91–95).

53. Ibid., pp. 138–41, 172–83 (*TO II*, pp. 69–71, 82–86; Caesar/D'Intino, pp. 113–15, 133–39).

54. Ibid., pp. 143–44, 165–72, 185, 194–96, 246–48 (*TO II*, pp. 71–72, 79–82, 87, 90–91, 106–7; Caesar/D'Intino, pp. 115–17, 129–33, 140, 145–46, 171–72).

55. On the possible formation of this sensibility, cf. Giacomo Leopardi, *Fragmenta patrum graecorum*, ed. C. Moreschini (Florence: Le Monnier, 1976).

56. This places us at the center of one of the strongest and liveliest contemporary problematics. The problem of pain, or rather the cognition of pain, constitutes one of the most explicit critical points in Wittgenstein's *Philosophical Investigations* (see Saul Kripke, *Wittgenstein on Rules and Private Language* [Oxford: Blackwell, 1995]). Placed by Wittgenstein at the center of the philosophical problematic through the paradox of linguistic choice, this problem of pain in Kant and in transcendental criticism generally is decentered, so to speak. In Leopardi, it is clear that pain instead reveals the corporeality of consciousness and transforms the transcendental

ego into a universal concrete ego. His interpretation of pain is thus detached from the sensualist tradition in the strict sense and refuses to consider pain merely as one of the forces that determine the dynamic of sense (not that this approach is absent from Leopardi's thought, as we have seen, but it is subordinated to the critical operation). In his work pain is the moment of the positioning of the subject: it is cognition and production. This distinguishes him once again from Schopenhauer, for whom the critical dimension of the perception of pain exhausts itself in a process of successive negations.

57. *Zibaldone*, pp. 213–17 (*TO II*, pp. 97–98; Caesar/D'Intino, pp. 156–57).

58. Ibid., pp. 261, 266, 270–72, 280, 292–94, 298, 305, 309, 325–26, 329–33, 356, etc. (*TO II*, pp. 110, 112, 113, 116, 119, 120, 122–23, 127, 128–29, 135, etc.; Caesar/D'Intino, pp. 177–78, 180–82, 186, 190–92, 195, 197, 203–204, 205–207, 217, etc.).

59. Ibid., pp. 360–62, 364–65, 371–72, 375, 378 (*TO II*, pp. 137, 138, 140, 141, 142; Caesar/D'Intino, pp. 219–20, 221, 224, 225–26, 227).

60. Ibid., pp. 472–73 (*TO II*, p. 166; Caesar/D'Intino, p. 266).

61. Ibid., pp. 491–94, 503–07 (*TO II*, pp. 170, 173; Caesar/D'Intino, pp. 273–74, 278–79).

62. Ibid., passim, but notably pp. 481–84, 514–16 (*TO II*, pp. 168, 175–76; Caesar/D'Intino, pp. 269–270, 283–84).

63. Notice in these pages the fierce reprise of the polemic directed against instrumental knowledge [*sapere*] (*Zibaldone*, pp. 520–22 [*TO II*, pp. 303–4; Caesar/D'Intino, pp. 285–86]): against the half-philosophy that does not get to the foundation of the real. . . . On the other hand, an ambiguous new reference to Rousseau is made here (*Zibaldone*, p. 912 [*TO II*, p. 263; Caesar/D'Intino, p. 430]).

64. *Zibaldone*, pp. 543–85, 587–90 (*TO II*, pp. 182–92; Caesar/D'Intino, pp. 294–311).

65. Concerning this problem of the mediation between ontology and history, which in political matters is collected under the term "multitude"; in other words, concerning the problem of democracy interpreted no longer in terms of the "general will" but in terms of material constitution, permit me to refer to my book *The Savage Anomaly: The Power of Spinoza's Metaphysics and Politics*, trans. Michael Hardt (Minneapolis: University of Minnesota Press, 1990). Referral to this text obviously includes a complex series of cultural references and underlying questions. One of them is not without importance for our present claim: in what terms does democratic thought, however it is posited, incorporate elements drawn from the extraordinary suggestion of Spinoza? It is in any case absolutely essential to get beneath the surface of things whenever we find ourselves faced with the word "multitude," one of the few terms in the history of western thought whose mystification proves difficult—even if Rousseau attempted it.

66. On the "mystical nonsense" of the German students, one of whom assassinated Kotzebue, see *Zibaldone*, pp. 105–6 (*TO II*, p. 58; Caesar/D'Intino, p. 95); for a positive judgment on the Congress of Vienna, see p. 907 (*TO II*, p. 262; Caesar/D'Intino, p. 427); as for the equation French Revolution = philosophy = Enlightenment = depravity of nature = vice = mortal enmity among men and faced with virtue, it is one of the nursery rhymes often repeated by Leopardi, cf. p. 911 (*TO II*, p. 263; Caesar/D'Intino, p. 429–30). It is unbelievable to have to note that in their imperturbable moderation, the progressivist interpreters are in complete agreement with the reactionary and Catholic interpreters, both considering these sinister assertions of the young provincial Leopardi as realistic.

67. *Zibaldone*, pp. 911–25, 1037 (*TO II*, pp. 263–67, 301; Caesar/D'Intino, pp. 429–36, 492).

68. Ibid., pp. 866–911 (*TO II*, pp. 251–63; Caesar/D'Intino, pp. 409–29).

69. Ibid., p. 905 (*TO II*, p. 261; Caesar/D'Intino, pp. 426–27).

70. Ibid., pp. 1026–28 (*TO II*, pp. 298–99; Caesar/D'Intino, pp. 487–88).

71. Ibid., p. 975 (*TO II*, p. 283; Caesar/D'Intino, pp. 460–61).

72. Ibid., p.1077–78 (*TO II*, p. 313; Caesar/D'Intino, p. 511). On the weak *Risorgimento*, aside from the following notes, see notes 192 and 193 of this chapter.

73. Ibid., p. 1101 (*TO II*, p. 379; Caesar/D'Intino, p. 521). See also pages 866–67 (*TO II*, p. 251; Caesar/D'Intino, pp. 409–10), where a cyclical theory of historical-political development is considered as applicable to a present and/or future regeneration of civilization.

74. Ibid., pp. 532–36 (*TO II*, pp. 179–80; Caesar/D'Intino, pp. 290–91).

75. Ibid., pp. 610–11, 618, 629–32, 638, 676, 703, 829–30 (*TO II*, pp. 197, 198, 201, 203, 211, 216, 243; Caesar/D'Intino, pp. 319–20, 322, 326–28, 330, 344, 354, 397–98).

76. Ibid., p. 649 (*TO II*, p. 205; Caesar/D'Intino, p. 334). This reference to Pascal and all the rest that figure in the *Zibaldone* (see the indexes to it) are linked to a fundamental motif of his thought: the theme of the thinking reed, its fragility and grandeur. Leopardi takes up this theme and develops it in materialist terms: the relationship between fragility and grandeur becomes the relationship between first and second nature, or rather it aims to describe the point of their intersection. On the other hand, this intersection, we know, is the fundamental support of the imagination. It is the imagination that, fragilely but potently, determines the passage from first to second nature, develops sensibility to the point of constructing a new world. The way Leopardi comes to understand the intimate dialectical mechanism of the most sophisticated sensualism can be confirmed (as A. Prete indicates, *Il pensiero poetante*, op. cit., p. 86) by comparing it with Jacques Derrida's "Introduction" to Condillac's *Essay on the Origin* (now in *The Archaeology of the Frivolous*, trans. John P. Leavey [Pittsburgh: Duquesne University Press, 1980]), where precisely this double function, simultaneously reproductive and productive,

of the sensualist imagination is thoroughly reconstructed. Leopardi-Pascal represents, from this point of view, metaphysical innovation within the sensualist thematic.

77. Ibid., p. 1044 (*TO II*, p. 303; Caesar/D'Intino, p. 495).

78. Ibid., pp. 646–50 (*TO II*, pp. 204–205; Caesar/D'Intino, pp. 333–34).

79. Ibid., pp. 601–6 (*TO II*, pp. 195–96; Caesar/D'Intino, pp. 316–18).

80. Ibid., pp. 945–49, 950, 960, 1017 (*TO II*, pp. 274–75, 278, 296; Caesar/D'Intino, pp. 446–49, 454, 482–83).

81. Ibid., pp. 1079–82 (*TO II*, pp. 313–14; Caesar/D'Intino, pp. 512–13). But already p. 366 (*TO II*, p. 138; Caesar/D'Intino, p. 222).

82. Ibid., pp. 1087–91 (*TO II*, pp. 316–17; Caesar/D'Intino, pp. 515–17). This idea of an "overturned theodicy" was developed (certainly not starting with Leopardi) by means of a series of successive "sub-juridifications [*subtribunalizzazioni*]" by one of the most acute contemporary critics of the history of ideas. According to him, history is emptied of its theological content through successive degradations of values and judgment: a sort of neo-Platonism of history (see O. Marquard, "L'homme accusé, l'homme disculpé, dans la philosophie du XVIIIe siècle," *Critique* 413 [October 1981], *Vingt ans de pensée allemande*), p. 37.

83. See note 49 to chapter 1, where Bolelli's works on linguistic problems in Leopardi are prominently mentioned. The 1984 publication of S. Gensini's book (*Linguistica leopardiana*, op. cit.) allows me to pass over in silence numerous problems raised by Leopardi's linguistics that Gensini treats in a remarkable way. In particular, his attempt to reassemble the whole poetic and speculative figure of Leopardi around linguistics is of great importance, not because linguistics represents an element more fundamental than any other, but rather insofar as it demonstrates the circularity and continual recomposition of the poet's entire activity. In this way, the analysis is directly opposed to the thesis of the fragmentation and nonsystematic nature of Leopardi's thought proposed, along the lines of Crocean interpretations, by M. Fubini in his essay "L'estetica e la critica letteraria nel pensiero di Giacomo Leopardi" (in *Giornale storico della letteratura italiana* 291 [1931], pp. 241–81). Gensini puts to good use the most fruitful of the new currents of linguistic thinking, in particular those issuing from its new philosophical problematization: K.O. Appel, *L'idea della lingua nella tradition dell'Umanesimo da Dante a Vico* (Bologna: Il Mulino, 1975). In my view, one must be much more prudent regarding the judgment on the Gramscianism of Leopardi's linguistics, which Gensini takes, to my mind in an unconvincing and rather timid fashion, from F. Lo Piparo (*Lingua, intelletuale, egemonia in Gramsci* [Bari: De Donati, 1979]). However, on this last aspect, see note 57 to chapter 1 and note 83 to chapter 3.

84. *Zibaldone*, pp. 685–707 (*TO II*, pp. 213–17; Caesar/D'Intino, pp. 348–55).

85. Ibid., pp. 690–702 (*TO II*, p. 215; Caesar/D'Intino, pp. 349–53).

86. Ibid., pp. 707–8 (*TO II*, p. 217; Caesar/D'Intino, p. 355).

87. Ibid., pp. 838–66 (*TO II*, pp. 245–51; Caesar/D'Intino, pp. 400–9).

88. Ibid., pp. 735–826 (*TO II*, pp. 223–42; Caesar/D'Intino, pp. 364–96).

89. Ibid., pp. 932–40, 964–65, 1022–23, 1024–25, 1037, etc. (*TO II*, pp. 269–72, 280, 297, 298, 301, etc.; Caesar/D'Intino, pp. 440–44, 456, 485–87, 492, etc.).

90. As we noted earlier, S. Gensini (*Linguistica leopardiana*, op. cit.) has thoroughly brought to light the relationship of Leopardi's linguistics (and more generally his whole gnoseological position) to the tradition of Locke and Condillac. He also broaches, in an extremely prudent way, the problem of the relationship with the Ideologues (p. 65ff.), insisting upon the difficulty of establishing a direct filiation between their works and Leopardi's. But if a direct link cannot be demonstrated philologically—or only in an extremely partial manner—the possibility of defining an indirect relation is indisputable, as we have seen. The linguistic datum as it is conceived by the Ideologues (language conceived as an actual and consolidated set of knowledge [*conoscenza*], as the synthesis of the form of communication and the material contents of civilization) is certainly present in Leopardi. It is useless to recall what the fortunes of this conception of language in the development of secular and pedagogical thought in the nineteenth century were: it was the basis of the literary trend in bourgeois pedagogy and scholastic organization in that century. It is more important to emphasize the metaphysical innovation that is confirmed in the conception of language proposed by the Ideologues and taken up by Leopardi. This is a critical passage, not 'synthetic a priori' (as in Kant) but rather 'analytic a posteriori.' In other words, the form of communication is materially articulated around the empirical nature and historicity of linguistic data. This critical innovation is central to the process elaborated by contemporary metaphysics as an alternative to dialectical theory.

91. Wittgenstein's *Philosophical Investigations*, which insists upon language as an exclusive horizon and as the sphere of communication and the ontology of knowledge [*conoscenza*], marks the advent of what contemporary philosophy calls the "linguistic turn." This is not the place to follow the formation of this conception of communication, to analyze its development after Wittgenstein and the determining role it played in the development of linguistic theory, or the way it was applied in the social sciences; all that would constitute a whole chapter in the history of metaphysics in our time. We content ourselves with emphasizing once more our astonishment in the face of Leopardi's extraordinary anticipation. Roberta De Monticelli's work, *Dottrine dell'intelligenza: Saggio su Frege e Wittgenstein* (Bari: De Donato, 1982), constitutes a useful introduction to these themes.

92. *Zibaldone*, pp. 1332–36, 1470–1507 (*TO II*, pp. 387–88, 420–29; Caesar/D'Intino, pp. 635–37, 690–703). Translator's note: The specific citations in the *Zibaldone* to which Negri refers here have not been located.

93. Ibid., for example, pp. 1259–60, 1262, 1303–4, 1305–7, etc. (*TO II*, pp. 366, 367, 380–81, etc.; Caesar/D'Intino, pp. 601–2, 622–25, etc.).

94. Ibid., pp. 1339–61 (*TO II*, pp. 389–94; Caesar/D'Intino, pp. 638–47) and p. 1383 (*TO II*, p. 400; Caesar/D'Intino, pp. 656–57).

95. Ibid., pp. 426–27, 1438–44, 1460–61 (*TO II*: 410, 412–14, 417–18; Caesar/D'Intino, 673–74, 678–80, 686).

96. Ibid., pp. 1597–1623 (*TO II*, pp. 449–56; Caesar/D'Intino, pp. 738–47). But see also pp. 2073–75, 2178–80 (*TO II*, pp. 552, 572; Caesar/D'Intino, pp. 905–6, 939–40).

97. Concerning Condillac and his sensualism, see notes 27 and 90 of the present chapter. His conception is particularly dynamic from the start. Indeed, the development from the senses to reason is progressive; the cognitive faculties are constructed one after another; in short, a certain evolutionism is fundamental for the constitution of the sensualist framework. Next, Condillac's sensualism shapes and transforms the physical image of the world not only on the basis of the naturalistic dynamism of the vital *conatus* but above all by identifying in language a constructive machine for the universe of faculties. In short, language is established as a mediation between the senses, the faculties and representations: if the dynamism of the *conatus* is the systole, the universe of communication is the diastole of the circulation of sense. In this way the sensualist philosophy thus avoids the threat of idealism and solipsism. This surmounting is integrated by means of a pragmatic-realist perspective, by a spirit of experimentation and verification that considerably broadens the constructive mechanism of sense: thus for example the abstract character of the *fictio* of the statue, to which all the senses are gradually attributed, dissipates: in Buffon and Diderot, the *fictio* of the statue is already presented in the form of a constructive hypothesis and in an indisputably vitalist manner. When Leopardi broaches the constructive thematic of sensualism, he has these dynamics in mind. It is also necessary to emphasize the historical-anthropological repercussions of Condillac's discourse: in effect, through sensualist habituation, not only social morals but also the character of peoples are constructed in a progressive dynamic This attempt to ontologically deepen the constitutive thematic of sense is rather interesting and, as we have seen, runs parallel to Leopardi's labor. On Condillac, aside from the works of Jacques Derrida and P. Casini, see the important book by I.F. Knight, *The Geometric Spirit: The Abbé de Condillac and the French Enlightenment* (New Haven: Yale University Press, 1968).

98. *Zibaldone*, pp. 1370–72 (*TO II*, pp. 396–97; Caesar/D'Intino, pp. 65–52).

99. Ibid., p. 1377 (*TO II*, p. 398; Caesar/D'Intino, p. 654).

100. Ibid., pp. 1382, 1383, 1388–91, 1394–99, 1421, 1432–33, 1437–38, 1450–56, 1461–64, 1508–9, 1510–13, 1523–25, 1527–28, 1540–41, 1554–55, 1589–90, and passim (*TO II*, pp. 399, 400–4, 409, 411, 412, 415–16, 418, 428–29, 432, 433, 436, 439, 447, and passim; Caesar/D'Intino, pp. 656–63, 671, 675–76, 677–78, 682–84, 686–87, 704–6, 709–12, 716, 722, 735, and passim).

101. Ibid., pp. 1628–29, 1708 (*TO II*, pp. 457, 475; Caesar/D'Intino, pp. 750, 780).

102. Ibid., pp. 2046–47 (*TO II*, pp. 546, 547; Caesar/D'Intino, pp. 896–97).

103. Ibid., pp. 2039–41, 2047–49, 2110–12 (*TO II*, pp. 545–46, 547, 559; Caesar/D'Intino, pp. 894–95, 897, 917–18).

104. Ibid., pp. 1513–18, 1571–72 (*TO II*, pp. 431–32, 443; Caesar/D'Intino, pp. 706–7, 728).

105. Ibid., pp. 1767, 1923–25 (*TO II*, pp. 488, 521–22; Caesar/D'Intino, pp. 801, 856).

106. For example, *Zibaldone*, pp. 1907–11, 2232–33 (*TO II*, pp. 518–19, 583; Caesar/D'Intino, pp. 850–852, 956).

107. As we have already noted, this aspect is probably the essential point of convergence between Leopardi's materialism/sensualism and ancient philosophy. Aside from the references already made to works by Timpanaro (above all concerning the relationship with ancient philosophy and the most strictly materialist currents), here we must mention the contemporary rediscovery of atomism, Epicureanism, and ancient materialism more generally carried out by the school of J. Bollack. See in particular the summary article by A. Renaut, "Philologie, philosophie: À propos d'Épicure," in *Le Temps de la réflexion* (Paris: Gallimard, 1980), pp. 393–415. Leopardi's materialist/sensualist attempt to grasp the laws of the finite corresponds exactly to what Epicurus and the Epicureans were doing, according to Bollack's illuminating reconstruction: "Epicurus' method tends toward the intellectual reconstruction of the object" and aims to "take possession of the conditions of its genesis." Above all, however, see the discussion by these formidable restorers of the Epicurean texts on the conception of the sensory imagination in Epicurus and the schools of ancient materialism. Secondarily, we should not forget the ingenuity and strength of Paul Nizan's reconstruction of ancient materialism in *Démocrite, Épicure, Lucrèce: Les materialists de l'Antiquité* (Paris: Maspero, 1979).

108. Marx spoke of the sensualism of the seventeenth century, that of Bacon but primarily that of the Italian philosophers of the Renaissance, as a living, sensual, philosophical conception that was physically and naturally strong. In my view, this conception lost its vigor in the seventeenth century: its tradition is embattled, and the pyres on which Vanini and Bruno burn, like the condemnation of Galileo, are not unrelated to the explanation for this weakening. Nevertheless, as we have written, sensualism persists, but it is divided into a genuinely materialist tendency and an idealist one. These two lines develop in tandem throughout the whole course of Enlightenment philosophy, not only in France but also in England and Italy (see note 34). We find in Leopardi a spontaneous reappearance of the most materialist, indeed rigorously materialist thread of sensualist philosophy and of this whole tradition. Leopardi's materialism is linked to the ontological and epistemological tendencies of sensualism/materialism and refuses the gnoseological and idealist currents.

It is vital, sensual, Baconian, in the Renaissance tradition. It is not surprising that productivity and illusion, science and idols exist together within it.

109. *Zibaldone*, pp.1545–48 (*TO II*, pp. 437–38; Caesar/D'Intino, pp. 718–19).

110. Ibid., pp. 1554–55 (*TO II*, p. 439; Caesar/D'Intino, pp. 721–22).

111. Ibid., pp. 1791–92 (*TO II*, p. 494; Caesar/D'Intino, p. 810).

112. Ibid., pp. 1828–65 (*TO II*, pp. 501–9; Caesar/D'Intino, pp. 823–36).

113. Ibid., pp. 1961–62 (*TO II*, p. 530; Caesar/D'Intino, pp. 869–70).

114. Ibid., pp. 1974–78 (*TO II*, pp. 532–33; Caesar/D'Intino, pp. 874–75).

115. Ibid., pp. 1988–90, 2017–18 (*TO II*, pp. 535–41; Caesar/D'Intino, pp. 878–79, 887–88).

116. Ibid., pp. 1957–61, 2032–33, 2114–17 (*TO II*, pp. 529–30, 544, 560; Caesar/D'Intino, pp. 868–69).

117. Ibid., pp. 2132–34 (*TO II*, pp. 563–64; Caesar/D'Intino, pp. 924–25).

118. Ibid., pp. 2028–31 (*TO II*, pp. 543–44; Caesar/D'Intino, pp. 891–92). S. Gensini (*Linguistica leopardiana*, op. cit., pp.107–12 and 258–60) has recently noted the absence of specialized works dedicated to the concept of imagination in Leopardi, while at the same time indicating several viable lines of research. On the one hand he refers to the concept of imagination as it was defined by Aristotle and the Aristotelian tradition, and Bruno and the Renaissance thinkers; on the other, he denounces the absence of any discourse on imaginative innovation in Locke and Condillac—discourse that conversely constitutes the specificity of Leopardi's conception of the imagination. It seems to me (and Derrida and Casini would concur) that in reality, the concept of imagination in Condillac is not actually devoid of power [*potenza*], as I emphasized in note 97; but this is not relevant for the moment. Indeed, in this matter the essential references are neither the empiricists nor the sensualists: Leopardi is here confronted with the thematic of criticism and classical idealism, breathes it in through the Romantic polemic and discriminates it theoretically. This does not mean that Leopardi was unfamiliar with Aristotle, notably *De Anima*, Book 3, paragraphs 8–11, 431b20–434a20, which elaborates a heightened, radical conception of the imagination that many think blows apart all of Aristotelian metaphysics. On Leopardi's generic awareness of Aristotelian thought, see what Timpanaro says, noted above (*La filologia di Giacomo Leopardi*, op. cit.).

But let us turn back to Leopardi's encounter with the thematic of imagination in criticism and classical idealism. In contrast to the Aristotelian tradition that conceives the imagination as movement engendered by actual sensation (*Basic Works of Aristotle*, ed. Richard McKeon [New York: Random House, 1941], pp. 595–600) and the imaginative phantasm as an ontological means, in Kant the imagination, although it can open up into a constitutive function in the schematism of reason, nevertheless is subject to the perverse riposte of phenomenalism and the inaccessibility of the "thing in itself." As Castoriadis has shown ("La découverte de l'imagination," in *Libre* 3 [1978], pp. 151–89), the Kantian problem, or more precisely the ambiguity of the theme, is taken up by Hegel and resolved in negative terms. In Hegel, the imagination becomes the "selective combination of empirical data guided by the Idea," resulting in the "relegation of the imagination to 'psychology' the fixation of its place between sensation and intellect, the merely reproductive and combinatory character of its activity, the deficient, illusory, deceptive or suspect status of its work" (p. 154). See also Martin Heidegger, *Kant and the Problem of Metaphysics*, trans. James S. Churchill (Bloomington: Indiana University Press, 1962), which rediscovers the problem, after the drying up of the neo-Kantian tradition and the idealist betrayal, while reproaching Kant for having opened up a bottomless abyss without exploring it.

Leopardi's conception of imagination is situated at this knot: it anticipates every innovation produced regarding this problematic by contemporary philosophy, and it seems that one can almost read in it the phantasms of the two traditions that are dear to me: on the one hand, the psychological line of Castoriadis, which grasps the collective character of the imaginative function, and on the other hand the humanist line of Bataille, which sees in imagination a power [*potenza*] capable of resolving the intimate existential chaos of interiorized social exchange by means of a decisive ontological displacement. The synthesis of these two tensions in the definition of the imagination and the feeling of prodigious displacement that this intersection demands are frequently noted in the work of Emmanuel Levinas.

119. Let us recall, for this period, only *Zibaldone*, pp. 1952–53, 2271–73, 2292–96 (*TO II*, pp. 528, 591–92, 595–96; Caesar/D'Intino, pp. 866–67, 969–70, 976–78). But already pp. 1563–68 and 1571–72 (*TO II*, pp. 441–42, 443; Caesar/D'Intino, pp. 725–27 and 728).

120. Ibid., pp. 2250–51 (*TO II*, p. 587; Caesar/D'Intino, pp. 962–63). In this regard see G. Lonardi's contribution, *Classicismo ed utopia nella lirica leopardiana* (Florence: Olschki, 1969), which is viewed by U. Carpi (*Il poeta e la politica*, op. cit., p. 248) as a provocation in the style of the Frankfurt School. We advise him to read V. Gazzola Stecchina's *Leopardi politico* (Bari: De Donato, 1974).

121. See note 106 to chapter 1. According to C. Galimberti in "Messagio e forma nella *Ginestra*," in *Poetica e stile*, *Quaderni del circolo filologico linguistico* 8 (Padua: Liviana, 1976), pp. 47–73, the conception of myth in Leopardi is articulated between a plastic and predominantly literary symbolic function and a religious-utopian conception (transformed in the last phase, that is the *Broom* phase, into an ethical projection, though this is not what interest us here). Gallimberti's definition seems to miss the point that in Leopardi the proposition of myth is never dialectical, unlike every religious-utopian function that is rooted in the evaluation of the contingency of the world. Leopardian myth is never predetermined or pre-constituted; it is not a negativity that develops and resolves itself into positivity. All these homologies are excluded from the cognitive and poetic process. The specificity of Leopardi's conception of myth is the "alterity" of the imaginative noema, which

functions as a light that serves to illuminate the system that produced it. From this point of view, the concept of myth in Leopardi is sharply distinguished from the tradition that takes shape in the nineteen-thirties among Rosenzweig, Benjamin, and Bloch, in which the dialectical dimension is absolutely present even when the overcoming tends towards mystical dimensions. The relationship between negative philosophy and mythic production is of course quite strict. Nevertheless, the solutions on the idealist and dialectical terrain are quite different from those on the terrain of materialism and ethics. In Leopardi, myth has a structural and operational function.

122. The reflections of 1822 (from January to November, up to the departure for Rome) cover pages 2316–644 of the *Zibaldone* (*TO II*, pp. 600–73; Caesar/D'Intino, pp. 984–1099). It is difficult to determine the internal order of these thoughts. Indeed, they extend over a long period of time and their design is strongly linked to the circumstances of their drafting. Furthermore, those that interest us the most—that is to say, those that concern philosophy and politics—are scattered amidst numerous extensive philological and linguistic analyses. Certain important characteristics common to the set of these reflections can nevertheless be brought to light.

123. Note that the correspondence we are examining, letters written between October and November 1820, is totally dominated by the expectation of departure. The tone is relatively balanced and serene: personal references are accompanied by an erudite dialogue. The relationship with Giordani is exhausted.

124. *Zibaldone*, pp. 2112–14, 2212–15 (*TO II*, pp. 559, 579–80; Caesar/D'Intino, pp. 918–19, 949–50).

125. Ibid., pp. 2122–32 (*TO II*, pp. 561–63; Caesar/D'Intino, pp. 921–24).

126. This is precisely the case of the concept of the infinite: see *Zibaldone*, pp. 1429–31, 1927–30, 2053–54 (*TO II*, pp. 410–11, 522–23, 548; Caesar/D'Intino, pp. 674–75, 857–58, 899).

127. Ibid., p. 2610 (*TO II*, pp. 665–66; Caesar/D'Intino, p. 1088).

128. Ibid., pp. 2410–14, 2419–20, 2488–92, 2493–96 (*TO II*, pp. 623–24, 625, 641–43; Caesar/D'Intino, pp. 1022–23, 1025, 1049–52).

129. Ibid., pp. 2433–34, 2599–2602 (*TO II*, pp. 628, 662–64; Caesar/D'Intino, pp. 1030, 1084–85).

130. Ibid., pp. 2429–42 (*TO II*, pp. 627–30; Caesar/D'Intino, pp. 1028–33).

131. Ibid., pp. 2602–7 (*TO II*, pp. 664–65; Caesar/D'Intino, pp. 1085–87). But already pp. 1737–40 (*TO II*, pp. 482–83; Caesar/D'Intino, pp. 791–92).

132. *Letter 179*, to Pietro Giordani, Recanati, 20 November 1820; Shaw, p. 108.

133. *Letter 185*, to Pietro Giordani, Recanati, 5 January 1821; Shaw, p. 108.

134. *Letter 194*, to Giulio Perticari, Recanati, 9 April 1821; Shaw, p. 113.

135. *Zibaldone*, pp. 2392–95, 2563–64 (*TO II*, pp. 619, 656; Caesar/D'Intino, pp. 1015–16, 1073).

136. Ibid., pp. 2381, 2456–58, 2463, 2574–77 (*TO II*, pp. 616–17, 634, 635–36, 658; Caesar/D'Intino, pp. 1010–11, 1038–39, 1041, 1076).

137. Ibid., pp. 2402–4, 2492, 2549–55, 2566–67 (*TO II*, pp. 621–22, 642, 653–54, 656; Caesar/D'Intino, pp. 1019–20, 1051, 1069–70, 1073–74).

138. *Canto XIII*, Peruzzi, pp. 275–85 Composed at Recanati in the spring or during the summer and fall of 1820. Walter Binni (introduction to *TO I*: xlii–xliv) sees this canto, which he associates with *The Dream* and *The Solitary Life*, as a failure marked by the return to the private life that is expressed in it. On the concept of privacy, see also M. Ricciardi (*Giacomo Leopardi: la logica dei Canti*, op. cit., passim). Binni nevertheless considers this canto the best of the three from the poetic point of view. How should we interpret this return to privacy? As a poetic, personal correlative, too insistently blunt, to the personal and theoretical crisis expressed in the *Zibaldone*? As poetic compensation? Such are the rhetorical questions that Binni offers to his reader.

139. Nichols, p. 55–56.

140. Ibid., p. 55.

141. Ibid.

142. *Canto XV*, Peruzzi, pp. 293–313. Composed in all probability at Recanati in December 1820, or according to a different hypothesis in October 1821 (see *TO I*, p. 1427).

143. Nichols, pp. 59–61.

144. Ibid., p. 61.

145. *Canto XVI*, Peruzzi, pp. 315–35. Composed at Recanati during summer and fall 1821.

146. Nichols, pp. 62–63.

147. This aspect is understood perfectly by G. De Robertis ("Dalle note dello *Zibaldone* alla poesia dei *Canti*," in Leopardi, *Zibaldone* vol. 1 [Milan: Mondadori, 1972], pp. il–lxvii but already demonstrated in his previous work *Saggio sul Leopardi* [Florence, 1952]). The great importance of De Robertis's discussion results from its methodical ability to unite, from the inside, the diverse articulations of Leopardi's thought. "The music" of the *Canti* is liberated through the *Zibaldone*, "the growth of consciousness therein becoming vast." As for the *Operette morali*, they are in a "very intimate" relation with the *Zibaldone*. Of course De Robertis's grasp of a profound inherence of all the aspects of Leopardi's thought within a stylistic unity is undermined by his interpretation of Leopardi's poetry as being "estranged from the present, its ancient flavor hardly likely to incite a new reflection in studies of aesthetics." Nevertheless, this judgment ends up so abstract in its methodical entirety that it must be ascribed above all to De Robertis's aesthetic mood rather than to his method. Concerning the great force of the stylistic readings of Leopardi, see the works of C. Galimberti, in particular *Linguaggio del vero in Leopardi* (Florence: Olschki, 1959). We can add that such stylistic interpretation

is, for better or for worse, probably directly attributable to De Sanctis, to whom we must give credit for a unitary perception of Leopardi's work (under the aegis of style) and at the same time for the aristocratic refusal of his anti-*Risorgimento* and revolutionary choice; in this regard, see C. Muscetta, op. cit., pp. 149–55.

148. It is extremely important to emphasize the circular characteristics of Leopardi's thought and poetry. See L. Spitzer, who effectively develops the methodology of the *"ganzheitliche Betrachtung"* in his *Studi italiani*, ed. C. Scarpati (Milan: Vita e Pensiero, 1976). Spitzer's stylistic reading dives deeply into the entirety, even into the ontology of Leopardi's discourse. Once again I would like to recall here the critical interpretations that never separated stylistic determinations from the materiality of construction, form from content, idea from matter. The fundamental text from this point of view is indisputably *Idea: A Concept in Art Theory* by Erwin Panofsky, trans. Joseph J.S. Peake (San Francisco: Harper Collins, 1968). This reading is essential, indispensable, whenever we are confronted with problems of innovation, stylistic variation, and expressive transformation. The dynamic conception of style and the circular conceptions of the aesthetic *Gestalt* (that contains and is bound by an indisputable nexus to the cultural contents that it expresses) permit the development of universal functions—and thus it is not by chance that these conceptions had an enormous influence on the analytic models of the history of science and the theories of scientific innovation. In this regard, we must mention the themes and sensibility of Thomas Kuhn, *The Structure of Scientific Revolutions* (Chicago: University of Chicago Press, 1962), but above all the models proposed by Paul Feyerabend.

149. *Letter 199*, to Pietro Giordani, Recanati, 18 June 1821; Shaw, p. 114 (see also *Letter 204*, Shaw, pp. 117–18). *Letter 200*, to Pietro Brighenti, Recanati, 22 June 1821; Shaw, p. 115 (as well as *Letters 197* and *198*, dated May 1821).

150. *Letter 201*, to Pietro Giordani, Recanati, 13 July 1821; Shaw, pp. 116–17.

151. On the "national-popular," see Alberto Asor Rosa, *Scrittori e popolo* (Florence: La Nuova Italia, 1966), as well as the reviews and contributions to a critical deepening of this concept by Timpanaro and Luporini.

152. *Letter 202*, to Pietro Giordani, Recanati, 6 August 1821.

153. Some remarks regarding Hegel's *Aesthetics: Lectures on Fine Art*, trans. T.M. Knox (Oxford: Clarendon Press, 1975) help us to dig deeper into this question. The comparison of the two thinkers, precisely on the theme of the poetic *Darstellung*, reveals the extent to which Leopardi is as a veritable anti-Hegel. For Hegel, art can be discussed only from the most elevated viewpoint of philosophy—in other words not "within" art but "facing" it; whereas Leopardi posits poetry and philosophy within a common metaphysical circulation. For Hegel, then, philosophy is superior to art: philosophical knowing [*conoscere*] is superior to poetic knowing, and art is necessarily dead in our era as a consequence of the triumph of philosophy. Conversely, for Leopardi, art is alive: it nourishes

philosophy, it interprets the world, and it can eliminate its own traditional forms only by shifting its representational power [*potere*] onto the horizon of a higher understanding. In Hegel, the superiority of philosophy and the "death of art" constitute the most radical premises of a universal and historical reconstruction of "the unity of the empirical and ideal viewpoints." This means that Hegel distinguishes artistic genres that function as the representations of spirit in different eras. The history of literary genres corresponds to the progressive stages of the history of the world. For Leopardi, the circulation of philosophy and poetry into one another is an absolute truth; and the diversity of literary genres and historical eras has no other necessity than that that which derives from the vitality of being: the privilege accorded to the classical has no dialectical consequences. Hegel renews Enlightenment thought; Leopardi invents and develops modern thought. In this regard see (despite its very specialized point of view) K. Maurer's work *Leopardis "Canti" und die Auflösung der lyrischen Genera* (Frankfurt: Klostermann, 1957), and its not entirely justified demolition by L. Spitzer, *Studi italiani*, op. cit., pp. 287ff. On the other hand, concerning the late-Enlightenment character of Hegel's *Aesthetic*, see H. Kühn, "Die Vollendung des Klassichen Aesthetik durch Hegel," in *Schriften zur Aesthetik* (Munich: Kösel Verlag, 1966). But let us return to the problem of literary genres: perhaps now we can identify what distinguishes and opposes the Hegelian and Leopardian *Darstellungen* and at the same time make evident the distance that separates Hegel from contemporary Romantic aesthetics. In Hegel, literary genres are the dialectical appearances of the development of poetic reason, up to the point when the latter, having exhausted its ontological grip, has nothing more to say. In Leopardi, Hölderlin, and Schlegel, literary genres are instead particular historical moments that in different ways break with all doctrinal fixity, all structural rigidity, and tend towards a single surmounting: not that of art, but that of the literary genres themselves, toward a universal conception of the aesthetic expression of humanity. On the theme of literary genres in Schlegel's work and early German Romanticism, see Peter Szondi, *Poésie et poétique de l'idéalisme allemand*, op. cit., pp. 117ff., which constantly refers to Georg Lukács's *Theory of the Novel*, trans. Anna Bostock (Cambridge: MIT Press, 1971), (and to Benjamin's writings of the 1920s) as the legacy of and complement to the program of early German Romanticism.

154. Among others, see *Zibaldone*, pp. 1313, 1317, 1531–33, 1708, 2013 (*TO II*, pp. 382, 383, 434, 475, 540; Caesar/D'Intino, pp. 627, 629, 713, 780, 886). On the central presence of Galileo in Leopardi's work, see G. Bollati, introduction to Leopardi, *Crestomazia Italiana, la prosa*, op. cit., pp. xciii–xcv; S. Gensini, in *Linguistica leopardiana*, op. cit., pp. 202–3, notes the progressive character of Galileo's presence, which is increasingly emphasized from the *Zibaldone* of 1821 to the *Pensieri*. Bollati, on the other hand, shows how Galileo is the true hero not only of the *Crestomazia in prosa* but of Leopardi's universe.

155. *Zibaldone*, pp. 2316–17 (*TO II*, p. 600; Caesar/D'Intino, p. 984).

156. Ibid., pp. 2159–60 (*TO II*, p. 569; Caesar/D'Intino, p. 933).

157. Ibid., pp. 143–44 (*TO II*, p. 71; Caesar/D'Intino, p. 116).

158. See note 138. Regarding this entire period, however, Walter Binni (*TO I*, pp. 44ff.) proposes a generally satisfactory interpretation for this new phase, one that defines a kind of internal dialectic among the different canti composed at the time. *Canto IV* (*For the Wedding of his Sister Paolina*) and V (*To a Victor in the Games*) are considered to be tightly linked and constitute an example of active pedagogy. The pair would constitute the basis for unfolding the problematic of the period in question. *Canto VI* (*Brutus*) is a moment of classical and heroic pedagogy—a cry, a blasphemy, the grandeur of the negative. *Canto VII* (*To Spring*) represents a meditative and poetic moment, a reflective pause, a first—but still detached—moment of reconstruction. *Canto IX* (*Sappho's Last Song*) is the masterpiece, the synthesis of *Canti VI* and *VII*, the moment of pure innovation. Then we enter into crisis: *Canto VIII* (*Hymn to the Patriarchs*) is tired and uncertain. We see, in the pursuit of our analysis, if Binni's proposition for reading is admissible. It is in any case important by virtue of its sensitivity to the expressive contents.

159. *Canto IV*, Peruzzi, pp. 107–23. Composed at Recanati in October to November 1821.

160. *Canto V*, Peruzzi, pp. 125–38. Recanati, "completed the last day of November 1821." Doubts remain about the exact date of its composition, but it was composed during autumn 1821.

161. *Canto VI*, Peruzzi, pp. 139–64. Composed at Recanati "in 20 days, December 1821." On this very important canto, see M. Marcazzan, "Leopardi e l'ombra di Bruto," in *Nostro Ottocento* (Brescia: La Scuola, 1955); Walter Binni, introduction (*TO I*, pp. lvi–lviii); M. Ricciardi, *Giacomo Leopardi: La logica dei Canti*, op. cit., passim.

162. Nichols, p. 30.

163. Ibid.

164. Ibid., p. 32.

165. *Canto VII*, Peruzzi, pp. 165–87. Composed at Recanati "in twelve days, January 1822."

166. Nichols, p. 33.

167. Ibid., p. 35.

168. This canto is indisputably the most Hölderlinian of Leopardi's canti. In this regard see Peter Szondi's remarks (in *Poésie et poétique de l'idéalisme allemand*, op. cit., pp. 226ff.) apropos of a particularly significant Hölderlinian thematic: the one Szondi calls "the surmounting of classicism by means of classicism." We noted earlier that this constitutes one of the keys to reading Leopardi's thought and poetics, above all in regard to Leopardi's conception of myth. But something more is here. Classicism reveals itself gradually, and in those years definitively, as one of

the images in which second nature is consolidated. The passage through classicism is an indication of the metaphysical condition to which we are ordained: the passage through second nature is a necessary one. Classicism is a tangle of images: first conceived as the form of representation of the originary myth, it is now the highest form of representation in terms of style and, according to credible interpreters, simultaneously primitivism and the height of style, but with different functions. What can we add? In Leopardi, classicism also marks a transition: it is the symbol of the acceptance of the new world, its necessity, and consequently it corresponds to an advance, to the rediscovery of the truth of the subject.

169. *Canto IX*, Peruzzi, pp. 225–48. Composed at Recanati "in seven days, May 1822." See C. Muscetta, *Leopardi: Schizzi, studi e letture* (Rome: Bonacci, 1976).

170. Nichols, p. 42.

171. Ibid.

172. Ibid.

173. Ibid.

174. *Canto VIII*, Peruzzi, pp. 189–223. Composed at Recanati "in seventeen days, July 1822." This canto has given rise to discussions concerning the religious inspiration of Leopardi's discourse: see G. Getto, "Gli inni cristiani," in *Saggi leopardiani* (Florence: Vallecchi, 1966).

175. Nichols, pp. 37–38.

176. Ibid., p. 38.

177. Ibid.

178. Ibid., pp. 39–40.

179. Here we are referring to the readings of Binni, Muscetta, and Ricciardi. There is effectively a stylistic caesura to the extent that the problem of experiencing the web of sense completely absorbs Leopardi's imagination, sucks up, so to speak, the poetic force. The exclusive character of this experience and the variations it introduces into the lyric in fact mark a caesura in relation to the other phases of Leopardi's poetic labor—a caesura that will be surmounted in both poetry and metaphysics.

180. See *Letters 217–71* (*TO I*), but above all those addressed to the family (*Letters 217–31*). Concerning this trip to Rome, N. Jonard's notes in *Giacomo Leopardi: Essai de biographie intellectuelle* (Paris: Les Belles Lettres, 1977), pp. 195ff. are good.

181. *Letter 219*, to Carlo Leopardi, Rome, 25 November 1822; Shaw, p. 120.

182. *Letter 221*, to Paolina Leopardi, Rome, 3 December 1822; Shaw, pp. 122–23.

183. *Letters 223* and *225*, to Monaldo and Carlo Leopardi, respectively, Rome, 9 and 16 December 1822; Shaw, pp. 126–30.

184. *Letter 222*, to Carlo Leopardi, Rome, 6 December 1822; Shaw, p. 124.

185. *Letter 241*, to Carlo Leopardi, Rome, 22 January 1823; Shaw, pp. 130–32.

186. *Letter 260*, to Carlo Leopardi, Rome, 22 March 1823; Shaw, p. 141.

187. *Letter 252*, to Carlo Leopardi, Rome, 20 February 1823; Shaw, p. 139.

188. Ibid.

189. Ibid.

190. *Zibaldone*, pp. 2656–57 (*TO II*, p. 675; Caesar/D'Intino, pp. 1103–4).

191. Ibid., pp. 2684–85 (*TO II*, p. 682; Caesar/D'Intino, p. 1118).

192. Ibid., pp. 2668–69 (*TO II*, p. 678; Caesar/D'Intino, pp. 1109–10). I do not know if we should see this vindication of the freedom of nature (and the market) against any state constraint as one of the first echoes of liberal political thought which, around 1820, began to prove itself even in Italy. From a certain point of view, this vindication is clearly sufficient to eliminate the hypothesis of the young Leopardi's membership in currents of absolutist thought, despite some scattered emphases in the *Zibaldone* on the need for an "absolute government." In this regard, I consider L. Salvatorelli's work (*Il pensiero politico italiano dal 1700 al 1870* [Turin: Einaudi, 1949]) to have been refuted by C. Luporini (*Leopardi progressivo*, op. cit., pp. 105ff.); that said, the value of Salvatorelli's book is not limited to this unfortunate reduction of Leopardi to absolutism, and we return to some of his analyses, which in some ways anticipate our own, when we examine the Leopardi of *The Broom*. But allow me one last note here. As everyone knows, alongside the first auroral appearances of liberal thought in the 1820s there is a heavy influence of restorationist thought, notably through the wide circulation of Lamennais's *Essai sur l'indifférence en matière de religion*, the first volume of which appeared in 1817 (see G. Candeloro, *Storia dell'Italia moderna*, vol. 2, op. cit., pp. 135ff.). We know that Leopardi was quite well acquainted with Lamennais and heavily criticized the content of that work. But this is not a problem of content. The struggle against indifference undertaken by Leopardi is thus situated at the opposite pole from that prescribed by the Catholic philosopher of restoration. For Leopardi, breaking out of indifference is breaking out of the indifference of the web of sense in order to find, not God, but an ethical direction of being. "Indifference" here is thus a decoy word.

193. Ibid., pp. 1170–74 (*TO II*, pp. 340–41; Caesar/D'Intino, pp. 559–61). Referring to repeated observations Leopardi makes on money (up to *Pensiero XLIV*), U. Carpi (*Il poeta e la politica*, op. cit., pp. 115–18) waxes ironic over the fact that authors like Luporini, faced with the oft-proclaimed ethical-cultural externality of Leopardi with regard to capitalist society (particularly manifest when he speaks of money), have taken this for anti-capitalism. In my view, this irony is off the mark. When Leopardi writes of money, he really describes it as the "form of the market," that market that now invests our whole life and thus corresponds to the form of communication and to second nature. N. Badaloni (*Storia d'Italia*, vol. 3, op. cit.) has clearly seen the continuity of this passage. Leopardi's critique of money concerns not only the capitalism of his own time but also its future tendencies.

Regarding the concept of a "weak *Risorgimento*," see notes 72 and 73 in reference to the *Zibaldone*, pp. 1077–78, 1101 (*TO II*, pp. 313–19; Caesar/D'Intino, pp. 511, 521).

194. Ibid., pp. 1422–23 (*TO II*, p. 409; Caesar/D'Intino, p. 672).

195. *Letter 273*, to Peppino Melchiorri, Recanati, 4 May 1823.

196. *Letter 280*, to Pietro Giordani, Recanati, 4 August 1823; Shaw, pp. 143–45.

197. *Zibaldone*, pp. 2646–47 (*TO II*, p. 673; Caesar/D'Intino, p. 1100).

198. *Letter 290*, to Peppino Melchiorri, Recanati, 19 December 1823; Shaw, pp. 145–47.

199. See the passages in the *Zibaldone* already mentioned (pp. 392–451; *TO II*, pp. 145–60; Caesar/D'Intino, pp. 233–56) as well as the remarks concerning them in the main text and in notes 48, 49, and 50 of the present chapter. The Catholic and more generally Christian interpretations of Leopardi err above all in their attempt to map specific determinations of an impossible religiosity. From this viewpoint, they are clerical interpretations. I say this having before me a text that in other respects will be useful to me: P. Claudel's "Préface" to an edition of Arthur Rimbaud's works (collected in *Oeuvres en prose* [Paris: Gallimard, 1965], pp. 514–21). What does Catholic apologetics do here? Is it perhaps seeking an impossible Catholicism in Rimbaud? By no means. It is seeking the analogy of the mystical act and poetic experience—nothing else.

200. On all these themes, see Karl Löwith, *From Hegel to Nietzsche*, trans. David E. Green (New York: Holt, Rinehart & Winson, 1964): "The road which leads via the Young Hegelians from Hegel to Nietzsche can be characterized most plainly with reference to the idea of the death of God" (p. 188). Leopardi seems to me to be situated entirely within this conceptual schema that can also be explained in these terms: against redemption-*Aufhebung*, post-Hegelian philosophy posits the requirement of a 'real redemption' that pervades the new fabric of being. Against the Hegelian fulfillment of Christian philosophy, it recognizes the immediacy of a 'new nature.' The theme of the 'recognition' of second nature, of capitalist development and the liberal revolution in the process of realization, is accompanied by a 'refusal' to accede to any transcendent perspective whatsoever. Christianity is thus completely overwhelmed in this mechanism: see note 199 to this chapter; Löwith, *From Hegel to Nietzsche*, op. cit., pp. 358ff.: the only possibility of regaining transcendence consists in making paradox and despair the supports of faith—as in Kierkegaard, and so on. But this second process has nothing to do with Leopardi: for him, the death of God is a constructive act. Luporini has correctly perceived the homology between these aspects of Leopardi's thought and the Hegelian Left.

201. Concerning the relationship between the historical-social construction of the web of sense and the problems of communication, see the works of Niklas Luhmann, which we discuss in notes 100 and 101 to chapter 4. For the moment we can note the importance of the studies that bear on the communicative relation,

including its processes of genesis and the dynamics of cultural consolidation. This kind of study, having become fashionable in analyses of the media society, is more difficult to use when it is applied to the past, even though in this case it leads to often surprising results.

202. F. De Sanctis (in *Studio su Giacomo Leopardi* [Naples, 1885], but see also "Schopenhauer e Leopardi: Dialogo fra A e D," in *Saggi critici*, ed. L. Russo [Bari: Laterza, 1952]) mistakenly considers this Leopardian period to be mystical-Platonic, hence an unfocused judgment regarding a fundamental lyric poem, *To His Lady*.

203. *Canto XVIII*, Peruzzi, pp. 359–75, "a work done in six days, September 1823." See C. Luporini's interpretive line (*Leopardi progressivo*, op. cit.) as well as Walter Binni's ("Introduzione" in *TO I*: pp. lxv–lxvi and lxviii–lxxv), which I take up for my own purposes.

204. Nichols, p. 72.

205. Ibid.

206. Ibid., p. 73.

207. Ibid.

208. Giuseppe De Robertis perfectly grasps this passage from metaphysics to practical determination carried out in the canzone *To His Lady* (in his introduction to the Mondadori edition of *Zibaldone*, op. cit., p. lx): "He then composes the *canzone To His Lady*, so intimate and free of all emphasis, an excellent meditation and almost a preface to the *Operette morali*."

209. It is often difficult to get one's bearings when one speaks of a materialist aesthetic. Indeed, on the basis of the contemporary recasting of materialism, in other words once the neo-Kantian definition has been superseded following the publication of F.A. Lange's *History of Materialism* (op. cit.) (and this corresponds to the polemics in Russia against empirio-criticism), materialism becomes a directly political weapon—and consequently its aesthetic is often confused with the necessities of political action and the conquest of hegemony. Many examples of this could be given, notably concerning the manner in which Leopardi's thought was received and utilized by Marxist thought. Nevertheless we believe that the situation today is modified, that such attitudes, whether defensive or offensive, intrusive or reductive, can henceforth be avoided, and constructive elements can be recovered from those authors, even if some of them took part in this aesthetic struggle. Perhaps the time has come to write a history of materialist aesthetics, to extract from Lukács, Bakhtin, Della Volpe, Marcuse, and Bataille a hypothesis that moves from extrinsic determinations toward ontology as the central moment of a materialist consideration of aesthetics. From this point of view, the road that Lukács travels from his *Theory of the Novel* (op. cit.) to his grand ontology is fundamentally important. And in following his tracks, which cover a half-century of (highly dramatic) European cultural and political life, it would probably become possible to outline a contemporary history of Marxist aesthetics.

210. Concerning the contemporary phenomenology of the imaginary, see note 118. What follows in the text, namely the construction of a world in which the conceptual phantasms of the imagination intertwine with the material deposits of the imaginary—as is well known, all that was experienced by twentieth-century philosophy, particularly in France, along two essential lines. On the one hand is the subjective line, phenomenological in the strict sense, which develops between Sartre and Merleau-Ponty (see Vincent Descombes, *Modern French Philosophy*, op. cit.); and on the other hand is the structural line of which Gaston Bachelard is, with regard to the study of aesthetics, the best representative (see especially *Poetics of Space*, trans. Maria Jolas [Boston: Beacon Press, 1964] and *Poetics of Reverie*, trans. Daniel Russell [Boston: Beacon Press, 1971]).

211. Despite what the progressive interpreters say and despite some of my own forcings of Leopardi's texts, the concept of materialism appears explicitly and consciously in Leopardi only in the second half of the 1820s, and more so toward the end of that period than at the beginning. The indexes to the *Zibaldone* are enough to demonstrate this. That said, we must add that during this phase of Leopardi's reflection, this concept is present beyond what is thought or said of it. Materialism manifests itself with an ancient, classical feel in the definition of the dimensions of being, in the indefinite spatio-temporal measure that is attributed to it, as well as in the ethical characterizations, both pessimistic and realist, lodged in this conception of being.

212. See in this regard the indexes to the *Zibaldone*. Here too we find ourselves faced simultaneously with an apparent affirmation of suicide and with its substantial negation. In other words, during this phase, unlike what happens later (the idea of suicide is firmly and decisively banished), the idea of suicide is continually related to that of second nature: if we live in second nature, there is no reason to assert that natural (primary) reason is opposed to suicide! But one can see right away how the argument is actually turned against suicide: this loss of power of its very idea [*sua idea depotenziata*] deprives it of efficacy as a solution to pain, or at least diminishes it. In any case, see our commentaries on *Canti XL* and *XLI* in notes 215 and 216 in the main text.

213. On Marx's references to the freshness and creativity of Renaissance philosophy, see note 108. Concerning the relationship of Leopardi to Galileo, see note 154. On the other hand, there is no explicit reference, at least in the *Zibaldone*, to Giordano Bruno. However, the exaltation that the sixteenth century arouses in Leopardi does not exclude the presence of this author (who represents one of the most active moments of that century and its tragedy). Here it is a matter of understanding at what point Leopardi perceived the rupture that traverses Italian literary, civil, and political history since 1500. Indeed, as we have already seen, one of the fundamental elements of Leopardi's project, which is implicit but continually emerging, is the desire to reinsert Italian thought into the European

family. But it is precisely in the sixteenth century, at the end of that mature period when its tremendous vitality is exhausted, that the isolation and degradation of Italian culture begin. There is an analogy between Leopardi's appreciation of the sixteenth century and Jacob Burckhardt's book *The Civilization of the Renaissance in Italy*, trans. S. Middlemore (Oxford: Phaidon Press, 1945). In Burckhardt, nostalgia becomes philosophy and breaks potently [*potentemente*] with historical pessimism. One last remark: philology is born of the nostalgia for a happier era, but it emerges above all, in Leopardi's project, as a political program aimed at a recomposition of Italian culture that raises it to the highest level of European culture.

214. See note 65 to this chapter and notes 77 and 78 to chapter 4.

215. *Canto XL*, Peruzzi, pp. 611–18, composed at Recanati between 1823 and 1824.

216. *Canto XLI*, Peruzzi, pp. 619–26, composed at Recanati between 1823 and 1824.

217. Nichols, p.159.

218. Nichols, p.162.

219. See Peruzzi, p. 626, the variant of line 24 of *Canto XLI*: *"dubbia"* and/ or *"breve."* Youth?

220. See S. Timpanaro, *La filologia di Giacomo Leopardi*, op. cit. (see also note 35 to chapter 1) for documentation. Clearly philology does not play a neutral role in the progress of Leopardi's metaphysics. Even those authors who follow the formation and developments of Leopardi's philology in the most casual (but attentive) way are compelled to note its constitutive tension. See Leopardi's *Scritti filologici* (Florence: Le Monnier, 1969), assembled by G. Pacella and S. Timpanaro. Leopardi's philology, and above all that which leads to the knowledge [*conoscenza*] of ancient philosophy, is first of all the ability to constitute an object and not simply a means for apprehending a truth. This essential characteristic has been emphasized by V. Di Benedetto ("Giacomo Leopardi e i filosofici antichi," in *Critica storica* VI [1967], pp. 289ff.), who insists on the fact that Leopardi considers ancient philosophy, which he applies so often, as a unitary paradigm. Nevertheless I am not entirely in agreement with him when he attributes to the mature Leopardi an interpretation of ancient thought as a desperately pessimistic thought; nor do I agree with those who accept this conclusion, at least up to the reading of *The Broom*, but we return to all these points later. What is essential here is to emphasize the modality of Leopardi's approach, the use he made of philology to construct truth. In this regard, Timpanaro's judgment is well articulated but remains nonetheless vague. In effect, while emphasizing the constructive spirit of Leopardi's philology (which he thus connects to Herderian sources and makes contemporaneous with the new German foundation of the discipline), at the same time he claims that Leopardi's anti-Romanticism prevents him from fully joining that movement. (See chapter 6,

"Considerazioni sull filologia leopardiana," and chapter 7, "La rinunzia del Leopardi alla filologia," in *La filologia di Giacomo Leopardi*, op. cit., pp. 141ff. and 171ff.)

221. I am not about to repeat here what the dialogue of the past few decades between philosophy and philology has compelled us to restore to the center of discussion—through the rereading of Nietzsche the philologist, his appreciation for the tragic age, and not least through Giorgio Colli's incitements to take up the study of Greek wisdom (in *Filosofia dell'espressione* [Milan, 1969] and *La nascita della filosofia* [Milan, 1975]). See also, summarily, the precise and informative pages that Antimo Negri devotes to these arguments in his *Nietzsche e/o l'innocenza del divenire* (Naples: Liguori, 1985), pp. 26ff., pp. 86–89ff., and p. 118ff. What interests me is the fact that in Leopardi just like today, that is to say before and after the phase of the hegemony of philological positivism, philology is not presented only as knowledge [*conoscenza*] but as an expansion of knowledge, not only as the reconstruction of the text and the figure of the author but as the reproduction of a culture, a living organism.

222. The index to the *Zibaldone* bears witness to the continuity of Leopardi's references to Homer throughout the duration of its composition. See also *Saggio di traduzione dell'Odissea* in *TO I*, pp. 421ff., and note 71 to chapter 3.

223. The list of Leopardi's readings of Plato (begun in 1823) is in Timpanaro's *La filologia di Giacomo Leopardi*, op. cit., p. 103. Beyond this see the *Discorso in proposito di un'orazione greca di Giorgio Gemistio Pletone e volgarizzamento della medesima* in *TO I*, pp. 507ff. The numerous references to neo-Platonic thought do not in any way lead us to consider Leopardi a neo-Platonist; see V. Cilento, "Leopardi e l'antico," in *Studi in onore di F. Flora* (Milan, 1963), pp. 610ff. I realize that the inequality in Leopardi's appreciation of Homer and Plato that I highlight in the main text can appear particularly inappropriate if one sticks to the letter and only to the letter of Leopardi's text: indeed,

> the profoundest of all philosophers, the most penetrating investigators of the truth, and those most capable of taking things in at a glance, were expressly remarkable and singular also for their imaginative faculty and heart, were distinguished by a decidedly poetic bent and genius, and gave egregious proof of this either in their writings or through the actions or sufferings of life that proceed from imagination and sensibility, or by all these things together. Of the ancients, Plato, the profoundest, most wide-ranging and sublime of all ancient philosophers, who ardently desired to conceive of a system that would embrace all existence and make sense of all nature, was, in his style, inventions, etc., a poet in this sense, as everyone knows. (*Zibaldone*, p. 3245, *TO II*, p. 812; Caesar/D'Intino, p. 1332)

(See also the following: "Pascal, who at the end of his life almost went mad as a result of the force of his imagination" [*Zibaldone,* p. 3245, *TO II*, p. 812; Caesar/D'Intino, p. 1332]).

224. The paradigmatic essence of the classical world is a fundamental element of European culture at the end of the eighteenth and the beginning of the nineteenth century. From Winckelmann to Schiller and Schlegel, to say nothing of Hegel, the theme is central and inexhaustible: the classical is the live motor of intellectual production and an index of absolute values. It does not escape Hegel (*Aesthetics*, op. cit., p. 63) that in the classical model, art is "rescued . . . from ways of regarding it as . . . merely imitating nature, and . . . powerfully encouraged to discover the Idea of art in works of art and the history of art." Thus art opens up "for the spirit a new organ and totally new modes of treatment."

225. The deeper we go into the theme of the classical in this phase of European cultural history, the more important this passage, this becoming-ontological of the world of sense by means of the classical prefiguration seems to me. Certainly the true problem, which now opens up, is that of breaking with this prefiguration, this horizon of second nature. The problem of the dialectic is to a great degree confused with this formation of second nature and with the necessity of articulating its movement. Above all, the genesis of the dialectic comes to a head in this veritable phenomenology of the classical, the oppositions of which we have already emphasized many times: Hegel and Hölderlin, Hegel and Leopardi. On the one hand, second nature is made spirit and the classical becomes the fundamental figure of the dialectic; on the other, second nature is subjected to critique, and the web of sense is subjected to the search for sense. The classical is thus reduced to a background, to nostalgia, sometimes perhaps (though not in Leopardi) to utopia; in any case it dissolves into the discovery of the different, the irreconcilable. Tragedy is resolved in Hegel. It remains unresolved in Hölderlin and Leopardi. In this regard see Jacques Taminiaux, *Le regard et l'excédent*, op. cit., and *La nostalgie de la Grèce à l'aube de l'idéalisme allemand*, op. cit.; P. Szondi, *Poésie et poétique de l'idéalisme allemand*, op. cit. I permit myself to refer also to my work *Stato e diritto nel giovane Hegel: Studio sulla genesi illuministica della filosofia giuridica e politica di Hegel* (Padua: CEDAM, 1958), especially chapter 1 and the extensive bibliography.

226. The problem of the "schematism of the pure concepts of the understanding" is posed, as everyone knows, by Kant in the *Critique of Pure Reason*, second part, "Transcendental Logic," first division, "Transcendental Analytic," Book 2, "Analytic of Principles" (Kant, *Critique of Pure Reason*, trans. Norman Kemp Smith [New York: St. Martin's, 1929], pp. 176–296). Concerning the problem of schematism, aside from Martin Heidegger, *Kant and the Problem of Metaphysics*, op. cit., see his *Phenomenological Interpretation of Kant's "Critique of Pure Reason,"* trans. Parvis Emad and Kenneth Maly (Bloomington: Indiana University Press, 1997); Edmund Husserl, *Ideas Pertaining to a Pure Phenomenology and a Phenomenological Philosophy (Ideas II)*, trans. Richard Rojcewicz and André Schuwer (Dordrecht: Kluwer, 1989); H.J. de Vleeschauwer, *La deduction transcendentale dans l'oeuvre de Kant* (New York: Garland, 1976); as well as my work *Alle origini del formalismo*

giuridico: Studio sul problema della forma in Kant (Padua: CEDAM, 1962), especially chapter 2. It seems to me that the problem of schematism, which is a strictly philosophical problem but also a singularly human one (as Kant tells us, it answers Leopardi's question "what is nature?"), is, within the perspective of Leopardi's materialism, posed outside Kantian phenomenalism. The theme is certainly not broached in technically adequate terms. But if we do not want the pleasure of reading Leopardi to be purely musical, if we also want to entertain our intelligence with this game, why not confront these issues? Even more so if they are—and they are—utterly central to cultural life, as they certainly were in the era that manifests the development of Romantic aesthetics on the basis of the *Critique of Judgment*, and as they perhaps are today: indeed, the problem of rejoining the horizon of signification from the sphere of sense appears just as central in the period that some describe as "postmodern" and that others have identified as "the era of real subsumption," all recognizing it as a situation characterized by the hegemony of communication. How do we break with this horizon whose circulation we understand, we know only insofar as, in its lack of signification, it dominates us? How do we restore sense to the web of communication, a signification for the sense of the web? Kantian schematism experiences the same problematic. The concept, which is an integral part of the web of sense, projects itself toward the world of signification. The difficulties are many, and in schematism the concept tests us. The *Critique of Judgment* is in reality only an application of schematism. Kant does not reach matter, the thing in itself. We must see that Leopardi traverses that same reality, and we must understand what he wants, how he goes about it, and what he risks. It is worthwhile to emphasize once again that these problems are still central today. For example, we can recognize in René Thom's catastrophe theory (see his *Structural Stability and Morphogenesis*, trans. D.H. Fowler [Redwood City, CA: Addison-Wesley, 1989]) a forceful attempt to confront the themes of schematism "from below," so to speak, and to resolve them in materialist terms. Concerning the philosophical context of this theory, see J. Petitot, "À propos de Logos et théorie des catastrophes," in *Bablyone* 2/3 (Winter 1983–84), pp. 221–61, as well as my critical intervention in the next issue of the same journal.

Chapter Three: Poetics of True Being

1. *Letter 331*, to Pietro Giordani, Recanati, 6 May 1825; Shaw, p. 154.

2. Summarizing what we recalled earlier concerning Schopenhauer (on the basis of a bibliography including De Sanctis, Nietzsche, Croce, but also R. Bacchelli, *Leopardi e Manzoni. Commenti letterari* [Milan: Mondadori, 1950] and C. Vossler, *Nel centenario di Giacomo Leopardi* [Padua: CEDAM, 1937]), we can establish several things. In the first place, a precise conceptual relationship exists between the development of Leopardi's thought and that of Schopenhauer,

a relationship which consists in making the critical problem the central problem of philosophy, in considering humankind insofar as it is a subject as the revelation of the "thing in itself," in considering the problem of nature as the theme of second nature. Secondly, the distinction between the two authors' philosophies consists in the fact that Schopenhauer gives way to irrationalism while Leopardi experiences the rational dimension of western philosophy with great coherence (on Schopenhauer's irrationalism, see G. Lukács, *The Destruction of Reason*, trans. Peter Palmer [London: Merlin Press, 1980]). S. Timpanaro generally takes up an analogous position, despite an insistence on Leopardi's pessimism, which seems suspiciously extreme to me, compared to the positions adopted by Luporini and Binni. In Timpanaro, in other words, the fascination with a Schopenhauerian interpretation of Leopardi, although dominated by philology, implicitly reappears when the ethical inversion of Leopardi's thought is exclusively attributed to the very last period of his lyrical and vital experience. Thirdly, this relationship has clearly become an obligatory passage in the interpretation of Leopardi, an issue that arouses passions given the centrality of the problem. It seems to me fundamental to take up the study of this relationship once again by emphasizing the fact that in nineteenth-century philosophy, Schopenhauer represents a line that is antithetical to the Hegelian dialectic. Indeed, Leopardi himself could have subscribed to the following radical, philosophically fertile assertion:

> Therefore, working in this spirit, and meanwhile constantly seeing the false and the bad held in general acceptance, indeed humbug and charlatanism in the highest admiration, I long ago renounced the approbation of my contemporaries. It is impossible that an age which for twenty years has extolled a Hegel, that intellectual Caliban, as the greatest of philosophers so loudly that the echo was heard throughout Europe, could make the man who looked at this eager for its approbation. No longer has it any crowns of honor to bestow; its applause is prostituted, its censure signifies nothing. I mean what I say here, as is obvious from the fact that, if I had in any way aspired to the approbation of my contemporaries, I should have had to strike out some twenty passages that wholly contradict all their views, and indeed must in part be offensive to them. But I should reckon it a crime on my part to sacrifice even a single syllable to that approbation. My guiding star has in all seriousness been truth. Following it, I could first aspire only to my own approval, entirely averted from an age that has sunk low as regards all higher intellectual efforts, and from a national literature demoralized but for the exceptions, a literature in which the art of combining lofty words with low sentiments has reached a zenith. Of course, I can never escape the errors and weaknesses necessarily inherent in my nature as in that of everyone else, but I shall not increase them by unworthy accommodations. (Schopenhauer, *The World as Will and Representation*, trans. E.F.J. Payne [New York: Dover, 1969], p. xxi)

3. See note 71 to chapter 1. To sum up:

    a. Concerning the conceptual relationship between Leopardi's thought and that of Kafka, it is indisputable that some of the determinations of their discourses coincide—such as the idea of crisis, the multiplicity of its scenarios, the plurality of aspects of modern rationality, the determination of pain, etc.

    b. Nevertheless, a fundamental difference exists between these two thoughts and this consists in the fact that Kafka fully shares the phenomenalist dimensions of neo-Kantian philosophy and sensibility, as his thesis on the thought of Mach shows.

    c. It seems clear that the judgment concerning this relationship is of a purely sentimental order here.

4. Schopenhauer, *World as Will and Representation*, op. cit., paragraph 68, pp. 379–80.

5. See Massimo Cacciari, *Iconi della legge* (Milan: Adelphi, 1985).

6. *Letters 293* and *296*, to Giampiero Vieusseux, Recanati, 5 January and 2 February 1824; Shaw, pp. 147–50. Concerning the political climate of the era and in particular the evolution of the *Antologia*, see the texts of Candeloro, Badaloni, Carpi (*Antologia*), Ferraris, and Timpanaro, cited in note 55 to chapter 1. See also B. Biral, *La posizione storica di Giacomo Leopardi*, op. cit., passim and U. Carpi, *Il poeta e la politica*, op. cit., pp. 126ff., which provide a good clarification of the general situation to which the political thought of the *Antologia* attests: liberal, progressivist, reformist eclecticism. The successive definitions that Carpi applies to Leopardi's political thought in order to distinguish it (negatively) from that of the other authors of the *Antologia*, according to which he would be doubly marginal as an aristocrat and as an unemployed man of letters, hold little interest; and it is easy to imagine an answer to them. Indeed, in the capitalist world, what else is an unintegrated, non-organic intellectual, and what else can he or she be? Has not the whole history of the centuries of capitalist civilization demonstrated that the only possible position for the intellectual is that of marginalization, of critical freedom? The element that eludes Carpi consists in the fact that Leopardi's situation does not prevent him as a poet from criticizing capitalist development from the inside. He is not linked to positions of aristocratic reformism; he is not prior to capitalism; he is within it. We must also emphasize another aspect that distinguishes Leopardi from Vieusseux and his friends. This is the fact that the Florentine circle of the *Antologia* constitutes one of the crucibles for the transfer of the critical and dialectical thematic from Europe to Italy (see in this regard G. Gentile, *Storia della filosofia italiana da Genovesi al Galluppi* [Milan, 1932]; M.F. Sciacca, *Il pensiero italiano nell'età del Risorgimento* [Milan, 1963]). In reality, the Florentine circle is not merely a point of passage; it is potentially predisposed to accept dialectical discourse. The

contradictory relationship that Leopardi has with the circle is explained by the fact that he accepts the positioning of the critical problem but rejects the dialectical solution to it.

7. Kant's *Groundwork of the Metaphysics of Morals* was published in 1785 at Riga. The two volumes *Metaphysical Elements of Justice* and *Metaphysical Elements of Virtue* appeared separately at Königsberg in January and August 1797. Concerning the critical influence on Leopardi, see note 81 to chapter 1. The well-known paradox contained in the Kantian 'metaphysics of morals,' in other words the continual passage from a priori argument to a posteriori argument, the difficulties facing the deduction of the concrete that are resolved by means of a precise evaluation and a tenacious recuperation of the particular, has as a consequence the fact that, by preserving the general premises, Kant here shifts from synthetic a priori judgment to an analytic a posteriori hypothesis. Whatever the definitions may be, it is indisputable that this critical limit confirms an unresolved tension that while it pervades the originary dualism of Kantian thought, consumes it in the attempt to grasp the great figures of the social and historical order. It is indisputable that, on this terrain, the differences between Kant's thought and Leopardi's can be enormous. But it is also true that, in Kant's metaphysics of morals, the search for an ideal point that would link ethical ideality and institutional concreteness is quite strong, and as Antimo Negri notes, at this point of intersection the differences between the two thoughts are obscured (see "Leopardi e la filosofia di Kant," op. cit., pp. 485ff.): the critical fables, poems, and novels then become legible for Leopardi. Concerning the other aspects of the Kant-Leopardi relationship, see note 105 of this chapter.

8. The *Zibaldone* of 1823 begins upon Leopardi's return from Rome to Recanati, thus in May. From May to December, pages 2686 to 4006 of his great and inspired notebook are composed (*TO II*, pp. 683–1027; Caesar/D'Intino, pp. 1119–1688). This period is of great importance: the various strands of research attain a level of maximum concentration, coming together in the philosophical labor. Beginning in 1824, the decline in work on the *Zibaldone* corresponds to the writing of the *Operette morali*, and then other preoccupations arise. On the importance of the *Zibaldone* of 1823, see Binni and Biral.

9. For a balance sheet of the linguistic pages in the *Zibaldone* from this period, see S. Gensini, *Linguistica leopardiana*, op. cit., passim. This labor of 1823 must naturally be connected to that of 1821 (see paragraph 6 of chapter 2). It is between 1821 and 1823 that Leopardi's linguistics takes shape.

10. *Zibaldone*, pp. 2721–25 (*TO II*, pp. 690–91; Caesar/D'Intino, pp.1130–32); S. Gensini, *Linguistica leopardiana*, op. cit., p. 103ff.

11. *Zibaldone*, pp. 2694–2700 (*TO II*, pp. 684–86; Caesar/D'Intino, pp. 1121–23); S. Gensini, *Linguistica leopardiana*, op. cit., pp. 125ff.

12. See K.O. Appel, *L'idea della lingua nella tradizione dell'Umanesimo da Dante a Vico*, op. cit.; G. Devoto, *Profilo di storia linguistica italiana* (Florence: La

Nuova Italia, 1976); L. Rosiello, *Linguistica illuminista* (Bologna: Il Mulino, 1967). Concerning the modernity of Leopardi's linguistics, I refer to two positions that are widely separated from one another but closely related by the elements of a common sensibility: Leo Spitzer and Mikhail Bakhtin. For both, as linguists, the fundamental problem is to identify the process of integration of linguistic creation and literary creation and to observe the forms of relation that are established between the general linguistic horizon and individual productions. Thus the idealist Spitzer and the materialist Bakhtin (who both work, doubtless without any contact, on Rabelais) arrive at analogous results, for it is in fact the productive centrality of language that characterizes its modern and scientific comprehension, as in Leopardi.

13. On these themes in general, see the indexes to the *Zibaldone*. I myself have focused above all on pages 2845–61 and 2906–17 (*TO II*, pp. 718–22, 733–36; Caesar/D'Intino, pp. 1178–84, 1203–7); see also S. Gensini, *Linguistica leopardiana*, op. cit., pp. 179ff.

14. S. Gensini (*Linguistica leopardiana*, op. cit.) has emphasized the necessity of confronting the problem of imagination in Leopardi. Nevertheless, I doubt that the historicist, Gramscian perspective that he adopts can suffice to resolve such a problem. In my view, as emphasized above, it is from a different, decisively materialist and phenomenological starting point that a deepening of this theme can be undertaken (see note 49 to chapter 1 and note 83 to chapter 2).

15. *Zibaldone*, pp. 2948–60 (*TO II*, pp. 743–46; Caesar/D'Intino, pp. 1219–24).

16. Despite numerous reservations expressed in this regard by many authors, it seems to me legitimate to refer, if not to the positions, in any case to the spirit of the generative analyses of language by Noam Chomsky (*Cartesian Linguistics* [New York: Harper & Row, 1966]). The critiques that L. Rosiello (*Linguistica illuminista*, op. cit.) and H. Aarsleff (*From Locke to Saussure* [London: Athlone, 1982]) address to Chomsky do not seem pertinent to me. But it is clear that the question of a possible influence of Giambattista Vico's thought upon Leopardi must inevitably be posed in this linguistic situation. S. Gensini (*Linguistica leopardiana*, op. cit.) addresses the problem broadly and insists that if it is difficult to demonstrate this influence philologically, the analogies, particularly in linguistic material, are many. To my mind, we must be extremely careful when establishing a Viconian ancestry for Leopardi's thought, for if this influence operates on Leopardi, it does so with a very particular coloring. In effect, the Viconianism of the beginning of the nineteenth century is closely linked with the crisis of Jacobin reason (see N. Badaloni, in *Storia d'Italia*, vol. 3, op. cit., p. 889). Yet we do not find this reactionary or moderate coloring of Viconianism (if its influence is real) in Leopardi. Shouldn't these remarks lead us to conclude that this hypothesis is quite thin? Regarding this argument, see the positions, which are more or less contradictory and often fail to grasp the critical moment of the hypothesis, of A. Tilgher (*La filosofia di Leopardi*,

op. cit., p. 25), A. Frattini (*Letteratura e scienza in Leopardi* [Milan: Marzorati, 1978], p. 42ff.), V. Pacella ("Leopardi e Vico," in *Leopardi e la letteratura Italian dal Duecento al Seicento*, Atti del IV Convegno internazionale di studi leopardiani [Florence: Olschki, 1978], pp. 731–57). In short, if Vico's influence on Leopardi exists, it is extremely generic, representing a second or third level of tradition, and it is in no way direct.

17. As is well known, modern hermeneutics is born in the same philosophical and intellectual atmosphere as critical philosophy and idealism. The fundamental text in this regard is F.D.E. Schleiermacher's *Hermeneutik* (see the edition by H. Kimmerle, Heidelberg: C. Winter, 1974; the text appeared in 1829). There are great currents in the history of thought that, although they don't intersect, are driven by the same forces and follow a similar course in different countries and on different horizons: thus Leopardi's materialism of philology goes back to and draws upon linguistics in order to go deeper into a general hermeneutics of historical knowledge [*sapere*]. Can we speak of the construction of a transcendental hermeneutic on Leopardi's part? I do not know if we can attribute to him an awareness of the fundamental philosophical passages that he carries out. On the other hand, I know that when I read the fundamental texts of H.G. Gadamer (*Truth and Method*, trans. Garrett Barden and John Cumming [New York: Crossroad, 1975]) or P. Szondi (*Poésie et poétique de l'idéalisme allemand*, op. cit., pp. 291ff.) on Schleiermacher and I confront the spirit that guides these authors' analyses with the Leopardi of this era, I get a feeling of déjà vu. On the great currents of contemporary hermeneutics, aside from the texts already cited, see W. Dilthey, "Die Entstehung der Hermeneutik," in *Gesammelte Schriften*, vol. 4 (Leipzig, 1924), pp. 317, 338; Paul Ricoeur, *The Conflict of Interpretations*, trans. Willis Domingo (Evanston: Northwestern University Press, 1974); Manfred Frank, *Das individuelle Allgemeine* (Frankfurt: Suhrkamp, 1977); H.R. Jauss, *Toward an Aesthetic of Reception*, trans. Timothy Bahti (Minneapolis: University of Minnesota Press, 1982). All of this is included, coherently, I think, in our interpretation of Leopardi, for in his thought there is a move that is fundamental for all non-dialectical thought of the nineteenth century: the passage from the concrete to the abstract, not by means of a process of mediation, but through the faithful analysis and reproduction of the abstraction of the real. Then we witness a descent from the abstract to the concrete—a hermeneutic descent, in other words a reconstructive one, which is coherent and homologous with the general channels (of language, of formal sensibility, etc.) that have been constructed. Leopardi experiences all this, and whatever choices of values he makes, he experiences it within these general theoretical dimensions. On this point and no other could we perhaps establish a red thread of continuity linking Leopardi's thought with that of De Sanctis. On the general developments of hermeneutics and hermeneutic historicism between 1880 and 1900, see my book *Saggi sullo storicismo tedesco: Dilthy e Meinecke* (Milan: Feltrinelli, 1959).

18. See paragraph 9 of chapter 2.

19. *Zibaldone*, p. 2702 (*TO II*, p. 686; Caesar/D'Intino, p. 1124).

20. Ibid., p. 3622 (*TO II*, p. 905; Caesar/D'Intino, p. 1483).

21. Ibid., pp. 3682–83 (*TO II*, pp. 919–20; Caesar/D'Intino, p. 1507).

22. Ibid., pp. 3835–36 (*TO II*, p. 965; Caesar/D'Intino, pp. 1582–83).

23. Ibid., p. 3894 (*TO II*, p. 986; Caesar/D'Intino, pp. 1616–17).

24. Ibid., pp. 2736–37, 2752–55, 2926–28, 2960–72, 3078–79, 3837–42 (*TO II*, pp. 693–94, 696–97, 738, 746–48, 774, 965–67; Caesar/D'Intino, pp. 1136, 1141–42, 1211–12, 1224–28, 1270–71, 1583–86).

25. Ibid., pp. 3247–53 (*TO II*, pp. 812–14; Caesar/D'Intino, pp. 1333–35).

26. Ibid., pp. 3271–82, 3291–98, 3361–62, 3480–82 (*TO II*, pp. 818–21, 823–25, 840, 868; Caesar/D'Intino, pp. 1342–46, 1350–53, 1377–78, 1423).

27. Ibid., pp. 2883–84 (*TO II*, pp. 727–28; Caesar/D'Intino, pp. 1193–94).

28. Ibid., p. 3745–46 (*TO II*, p. 936; Caesar/D'Intino, p. 1535).

29. Ibid., pp. 3821–24 (*TO II*, pp. 960–61; Caesar/D'Intino, pp. 1574–76).

30. Ibid., p. 2800 (*TO II*, p. 707, Caesar/D'Intino, pp. 1159).

31. Ibid., p. 2861 (*TO II*, p. 722; Caesar/D'Intino, pp. 1184).

32. Ibid., pp. 2883–84 (*TO II*, pp. 727–28; Caesar/D'Intino, pp. 1193–94).

33. Ibid., pp. 3179–82, 3568 (*TO II*, pp. 795–96, 891; Caesar/D'Intino, pp. 1306–7, 1459–60).

34. Ibid., pp. 3171–72 (*TO II*, pp. 793–94; Caesar/D'Intino, pp. 1302–3).

35. Ibid., pp. 3183–91 (*TO II*, pp. 796–99; Caesar/D'Intino, pp. 1307–11).

36. Ibid., pp. 3265–69 (*TO II*, pp. 816–17; Caesar/D'Intino, pp. 1340–41).

37. Ibid., pp. 3813–15 (*TO II*, pp. 956–57; Caesar/D'Intino, p. 1569).

38. Ibid., pp. 3842–43 (*TO II*, 967; Caesar/D'Intino, 1586–87).

39. Ibid., pp. 3876–78 (*TO II*, 979–80; Caesar/D'Intino, 1606–8).

40. Ibid., pp. 3921–27 (*TO II*, pp. 995–97; Caesar/D'Intino, pp. 1632–36).

41. Ibid., pp. 3941–42, 3950–51 (*TO II*, pp. 1002, 1005–6; Caesar/D'Intino, pp. 1645, 1650–51).

42. Ibid., pp. 3090–94 (*TO II*, pp. 776–77; Caesar/D'Intino, pp. 1274–76).

43. Ibid., pp. 3197–3206, 3314–17 (*TO II*, pp. 800–2, 828–29; Caesar/D'Intino, pp. 1313–17, 1359–60).

44. Ibid., pp. 3518–20 (*TO II*, p. 878; Caesar/D'Intino, pp. 1438–39).

45. Ibid., p. 3525 (*TO II*, p. 879; Caesar/D'Intino, p. 1441).

46. Ibid., pp. 3344–47, 3374–82 (*TO II*, pp. 836, 843–45; Caesar/D'Intino, pp. 1370–71, 1383–86).

47. Ibid., p. 3341 (*TO II*, p. 835; Caesar/D'Intino, p. 1368).

48. See paragraph 9 of chapter 2.

49. *Zibaldone*, pp. 2944–46 (*TO II*, pp. 742–43; Caesar/D'Intino, pp. 1218–19).

50. Ibid., pp. 2759, 2831–35 (*TO II*, pp. 697–98, 715; Caesar/D'Intino, pp. 1143, 1172–74).

51. Ibid., pp. 2936 –44 (*TO II*, pp. 740–42; Caesar/D'Intino, pp. 1215–18).

52. In this regard, among many passages in the *Zibaldone*, see pp. 3638–43, 3878–79 (*TO II*, pp. 909–10, 980; Caesar/D'Intino, pp. 1490–93, 1608). And the "essay on fire," on historical innovation, on pp. 3643–72 (*TO II*, pp. 910–17; Caesar/D'Intino, pp. 1493–1503), and passim.

53. *Zibaldone*, pp. 2895–903 (*TO II*, pp. 731–32; Caesar/D'Intino, pp. 1199–201).

54. Ibid., p. 2712 (*TO II*, p. 688; Caesar/D'Intino, pp. 1127–28).

55. Ibid., p. 3304 (*TO II*, p. 826; Caesar/D'Intino, p. 1355).

56. Ibid., pp. 3237–38 (*TO II*, p. 810; Caesar/D'Intino, pp. 1329–30).

57. Ibid., pp. 3237–45 (*TO II*, pp. 810–12; Caesar/D'Intino, pp. 1329–32).

58. Ibid., pp. 3713–15, 3824–25, 3846–48, 3879–80, 3902–3, 3909–20, 3928–30, etc. (*TO II*, pp. 928, 961, 969–70, 980–81, 988, 991–95, 997–98, etc.; Caesar/D'Intino, pp. 1522, 1576, 1589–90, 1608–9, 1622, 1626–32, 1637–38, etc.).

59. Ibid., p. 3760 (*TO II*, p. 927; Caesar/D'Intino, p. 1542).

60. Ibid., pp. 3854–55 (*TO II*, p. 972; Caesar/D'Intino, pp. 1594–95).

61. Ibid., pp. 3269–71, 3382–86, 3388–89, 3479–80 (*TO II*, pp. 817–18, 845–46, 868; Caesar/D'Intino, pp. 1341–42, 1386–87, 1388, 1422–23).

62. Ibid., pp. 3482–88 (*TO II*, pp. 868–70; Caesar/D'Intino, pp. 1423–26). On the general importance of the chorus in tragedy, particularly in classical tragedy, see pp. 2804–9, 2905–6 (*TO II*, pp. 707–8, 733; Caesar/D'Intino, pp. 1160–62, 1202–3).

63. Ibid., pp. 3254–62 (*TO II*, pp. 814–16; Caesar/D'Intino, pp. 1336–38).

64. Ibid., pp. 3430–34, 3526–40, 3545–46, 3552–57 (*TO II*, pp. 856–57, 880–83, 886–88; Caesar/D'Intino, pp. 1404–6, 1442–47, 1449–50, 1452–54).

65. Ibid., pp. 3434–41, 3447–60 (*TO II*, pp. 857–59, 860–63; Caesar/D'Intino, pp. 1405–8, 1410–15).

66. Ibid., pp. 3410–11 (*TO II*, p. 852; Caesar/D'Intino, pp. 1396–97).

67. Ibid., pp. 3717–20 (*TO II*, p. 929; Caesar/D'Intino, pp. 1523–24).

68. On the concept of poetic activity as productive development of aesthetic experience, as attempt to define poetics in terms of operative and ontological innovation, see H.R. Jauss, "Poiesis: The Productive Side of Aesthetic Experience," in *Aesthetic Experience and Literary Hermeneutics*, trans. Michael Shaw (Minneapolis: University of Minnesota Press, 1982), pp. 46–61. Jauss has worked extensively on the theme of formal innovation as creativity: modern poetry is born on this articulation, appears as "this" liberation. Constructing goes beyond the given knowing; it expresses a specific power [*potere*]: "*constructing* and *knowing* are antinomian, and . . . man's artificial and artistic work is based on an act of a renunciation: he can only act and create because he can 'disregard'" (endnote 44, p. 307, citing Hans Blumenberg). See also W. Conze, "Arbeit," in *Geschichteliche Grundbegriffe: Historisches Lexicon zur politisch-sozialen Sprache in Deutschland*, eds. O. Brunner, W. Conze, R.Koselleck (Stoccarda, 1954), Coll. 154–215; Hugo

Friedrich, *The Structure of Modern Poetry*, trans. Joachim Neugroschel (Evanston: Northwestern University Press, 1974); H. Blumenberg, "Nachahmung der Natur. Zur Vorgeschichte des schopferischen Menchen," in *Studium Generale* 10 (1957), pp. 266–83; J. Mittelstrass, *Neuzeit und Aufklärung* (Berlin: de Gruyter, 1970); F. Fellmann, *Das Vico-Axiom. Der Mensch macht die Geschichte* (Freiburg: K.Alber, 1976). This bibliography clarifies the modern passage between the theory of poïesis and constructive hermeneutics. From another perspective, but always with regard to the poïetic nature of artistic activity, see E.H. Kantorowicz, "La souveraineté de l'artiste. Note sur quelques maximes juridiques et les théories de l'art à la Renaissance," in *Mourir pour la patrie* (Paris: PUF, 1984), pp. 31ff. Kantorowicz shows to what extent artistic consciousness was, at the origin of the modern age, consciousness of creating—a veritable theology of production which, in order to acquire theoretical transparency, makes use of the terminology of juridical and political "making." The reference to these authors and to the tradition that they represent, whether it involves the Renaissance or the Viconian tradition, does not in the case of Leopardi involve a simple assonance but a deepening on a common terrain.

69. *Zibaldone*, p. 3509 (*TO II*, p. 825). See also pp. 3504–14 (*TO II*, pp. 872–77; Caesar/D'Intino, p. 1434).

70. Ibid., pp. 3084–90, 3177–79, 3427–28, 3443–46, 3461–66, etc. (*TO II*, pp. 775–76, 795, 855–56, 859–60, 863–64, etc.; Caesar/D'Intino, pp. 1273–74, 1305, 1402–3, 1409–10, 1415–17, etc.).

71. On the general theme of the *Iliad*, see the indexes to the *Zibaldone*. Here we will limit ourselves to drawing attention to pages 3095–167, 3167–69, 3289–91, 3342–43 (*TO II*, pp. 777–93, 793, 794–95, 822–23, 835; Caesar/D'Intino, pp. 1276–1301, 1349–50, 1369–70). It is also important to note the reflections that develop around the theme and comparison of the *Iliad* and *Jerusalem Delivered* (see pp. 3590–3617, 3768–71 [*TO II*, pp. 896–903, 942–43; Caesar/D'Intino, pp. 1470–81, 1546–47]). In these pages one witnesses a certain diminishment in the enthusiastic judgment passed on Tasso—this will also appear, in a more precise and discursive way, in the *Operette*—who is here considered, despite the grandeur of his lyric, as an author of crisis who is faced with the prodigious, incommensurable epic model that Homer's *Iliad* constitutes. At this point the reflection on the constitutive capacity of the imagination must be opened up once again: the Greek epic model takes on great importance and represents a model of culture as such for the *Risorgimento* generation, but not only that: it is also an ethical-political impulse and reference for all those who experienced and still live in a humanist culture. I am interested in knowing how the *Altertumwissenschaft* was affirmed in Italy, not only under the influence of German culture but precisely through reflections like Leopardi's, and how these contributed to the formation of a poetic influence and the construction of a future for culture. Work on this issue would be useful.

72. *Zibaldone*, pp. 3338–40 (*TO II*, p. 834; Caesar/D'Intino, pp. 1367–68).

73. Ibid., pp. 3318–38 (*TO II*, pp. 829–34; Caesar/D'Intino, pp. 1360–67).

74. The *Discourse* (*TO I*: 966–83) is composed in March 1824. On it, see above all U. Carpi, *Il poeta e la politica*, op. cit., pp. 141–45, who rightly deplores the lack of intensive studies of this work. As for the interpretation that he advances in his book ("an obvious kinship with Giordani's theses" concerning the pedagogical and reformist mission allotted to "the rich aristocratic intellectual"), at this stage of the discourse it seems to me that it can in no way be justified, especially since Leopardi was already trying to move into the circle of Vieusseux, who proposed "professionalism" for the intellectual, and had contact with the political hypotheses elaborated therein. B. Biral (*La posizione storica di Giacomo Leopardi*, op. cit., pp. 98ff.) grasps and intelligently resolves the apparent disagreement between the *Discourse* and the *Operette*: despite the operative tension of the *Discourse* and the metaphysical pessimism of the *Operette*, both works can be situated within the analysis of humankind in nascent capitalist society. Lastly, it appears to me equally useful to study what F. Venturi (*Storia d'Italia*, vol. 3, op. cit., pp. 1179–81) observes concerning the political program underlying Madame de Staël's intervention (*Corinne ou l'Italie*) and already present in Sismondi's work: constructing society so as to surmount political divisions and choosing the social terrain so as to dismantle the degraded tradition of politics and produce a new revival.

75. *Zibaldone*, pp. 3082–84, 3411–12, 3469–71, 3517–18 (*TO II*, pp. 774–75, 852–53, 865–66, 877–78; Caesar/D'Intino, pp. 1272–73, 1397, 1418–19, 1438).

76. Ibid., pp. 3347–49 (*TO II*, pp. 836–37; Caesar/D'Intino, pp. 1371–73). On the theory of climates, see the indexes to the *Zibaldone*.

77. Pages 3773 to 3810 of the *Zibaldone* (*TO II*, pp. 943–55; Caesar/D'Intino, pp. 1547–67) constitute a truly remarkable example of this slackening of the moral tension in Leopardi's political discourse. But also see, during this same period, pp. 3882–84, 3889–90, 3894, 3896, 3942–44 (*TO II*, pp. 981–82, 984, 985, 986, 999–1001, 1003; Caesar/D'Intino, pp. 1610–11, 1614, 1616–17, 1618, 1646–47).

78. *Discourse on the Present State of Italian Morals*, *TO I*, p. 41. [Translator's note: All translations from this work are mine.]

79. Ibid.

80. Ibid., p. 42.

81. Ibid.

82. Ibid., p. 43.

83. It is worthwhile to pause a moment over a proposition for reading that has been advanced above all on the basis of the *Discourse*. It involves Leopardi's so-called Gramscianism. This thesis rests on Leopardi's linguistics but more on the general framing of Leopardi's political thought, and has been asserted by U. Carpi (*Il poeta e la politica*, op. cit., pp. 261–68), F. Lo Piparo (*Lingua, intelletuali, egemonia in Gramsci* [Bari: Laterza, 1979]), S. Gensini (*Linguistica leopardiana*, op.

cit., pp. 139–41, 187–89, 245–48), and also with some frequency by T. de Mauro. But in my view, the sociological formulation of the *Discourse* cannot in any way be compared with Gramsci's political discourse. Even if a concept of hegemony took shape in Leopardi, it would certainly not be the product of the pessimism of the intellect (that is, the reflection on the failure of Jacobinism) but, on the contrary, the product of a firm and impertinent rational will (the continuity of Jacobin memory and the metamorphosis of its project). See the interesting and unconscious objection *avant la lettre* made by Luporini (*Leopardi progressif,* op. cit., appendix I) in the first years following the Second World War to Leopardi's Gramscianism and the considerations that follow for the concept of nation in Leopardi. But at base it is paradoxically possible to speak of an analogy between the political thought of the *Discourse* and Gramsci's thought: it concerns that point in both authors where civil society rises up against the state and poetry rises up against politics. But this clearly offers an interpretation of Gramsci that has nothing to do with Gramscianism; see note 57 to chapter 1.

84. *TO I,* p. 48.

85. A transversal reading allows us to distinguish the themes of the *Discourse* that are subjected to critique and potentially eliminated from those that are capable of serving as a basis for further development. The theme of the Enlightenment and the theory of climates undoubtedly belong to the first group: these paradigms are now completely absorbed into the perspective of second nature, the world of illusion, the horizon of communication. Consequently two perspectives merge here, one that centers on the theme of narrow society and one that comes to a head in a civil theory of literature. From a sociological point of view, the first is doubtless the more important: it brings together the best of the Machiavellian tradition of interpretation of the state, identifying that active social nucleus which, in the *Decades* and *The Art of War,* constitutes the legitimation of power [*potere*]. Furthermore, the constitutive principle is accompanied by an interesting and innovative (though in some respects traditional) analysis of political virtue, in other words the forms of ethical communication in which the tension toward the political horizon can be organized. It is obvious that when the sociological theme is transferred onto the linguistic terrain and refined into a political theory of literature, the *Discourse* reaches one of the highest points of pre-*risorgimentale* political analysis. The incitement to develop this reading is no doubt strong, on the basis of its methodological anticipations of the thought of Simmel and the young Lukács. The analysis R. Tessari proposes for this passage ("Il *Risorgimento* e la crisi di metà secolo," in *Letteratura italiana* vol. I, *Il letterato e le istituzioni* [Turin: Einaudi, 1982], pp. 433ff.) is extremely vague; see note 41 to chapter 4.

86. *TO I,* pp. 48–49.

87. Ibid., p. 50.

88. Ibid.

89. Ibid., p. 49.

90. Ibid., p. 51.

91. Ibid., p. 53.

92. Ibid., p. 58.

93. Ibid., p. 60.

94. Ibid., p. 61.

95. Ibid.

96. Ibid., p. 64.

97. Ibid., p. 66.

98. Ibid., p. 68.

99. Ibid., p. 71.

100. Ibid., p. 79.

101. Ibid., p. 79.

102. Ibid., p. 84.

103. Ibid., pp. 76–77.

104. Ibid., p. 82.

105. Whereas we had, at the beginning of this chapter (note 7), indicated the minimal aspects that suggest a reconciliation and intersection between Kant's metaphysics of morals and this moment of Leopardi's thought, now we are going to proceed in the opposite way, aiming to emphasize how much the differences of formulation separate them. Indeed, Kant's metaphysics of morals never manages to become what it becomes in Leopardi: a physics of morals. In the absence of this internal transformation, of an intimate, profound apprehension of the real movement, the ethical dimension in Kant once again takes on the abstract characteristics of projection and control. Transcendentalism dissolves the inspiration that pressed it toward the hermeneutics of the real, in this case ethics, in order to become once again the mediation of the ideal and the concrete. Nothing could please the philosophy of absolute idealism more, but this is completely foreign to the development of Leopardi's thought.

106. Contrary [eversivo] and not progressive. In the system of Cartesian coordinates, this pair of characterizations for Leopardi's thought corresponds to the abscissa. If we take up the grand lines of the debate that is unfolding, another pair can be taken into account, the pair rationalism-irrationalism. The Cartesian framework, in my view, can thus be filled in (retaining only the most exemplary points): (1) Leopardi as contrary and rationalist according to Timpanaro's interpretation, (2) Leopardi as progressive and rationalist according to Luporini's interpretation, (3) Leopardi as contrary and irrationalist according to the interpretation of Rigoni (and in general for all formalist interpretations), and (4) Leopardi as progressive and irrationalist in Prete (as in all readings based on negative thought). All this is only a game, but one that really brings to light how unusable all these alternatives now are. If interpretation can no longer be brought onto the terrain of ontology and the

major choices that European thought experienced in the nineteenth century, on the poetic terrain as well as on the philosophical one, then every classification ends up deceptive and derisory. The terms of the debate laid out in 1945 are exhausted. The anti-fascist struggle that underpinned the progessivist interpretation of Leopardi is outdated, much too outdated for its terms, the oppositions and articulations that it requires to still be used. The contrarian definition associated with 1968 is just as outdated. In adopting the formula "contrary and not progressive," therefore, I myself acknowledge the tradition while trying to escape from it. Indeed, in my view Leopardi's ontological dimension has absolute priority and prevails over every other extrinsic connotation. "The European Leopardi" is also an attempt to tear his thought (the lyric will do this all by itself) loose from obsolete categories.

107. *Operette morali*, *TO I*, text established by Moroncini. Concerning the different Italian editions of this work, see *TO I*, pp. 1431–36, which includes notes that are useful for understanding the text. I also consulted S. Solmi's edition for the *Classici Ricciardi* (1956), reprinted by Einaudi (Turin, 1976).

108. See De Sanctis, *Studio su G. Leopardi*, ed. Walter Binni (Bari: Laterza, 1953); B. Croce, *European Literature in the Nineteenth Century*, op. cit.; S. Solmi, introduction to the edition cited in the previous note.

109. G. Gentile, introduction to *Operette morali* (Bologna: Zanichelli, 1918); *Poesia e filosofia di Giacomo Leopardi* (Florence: Sansoni, 1939). Antimo Negri offers us the best illustration of Gentile's position in "Il concetto di critica e gli studi leopardiani di Giovanni Gentile," in *Giovanni Gentile: La vita e il pensiero*, vol. 9 (Florence: Sansoni, 1961), pp. 191–218.

110. M. Fubini, "Prosa e poesia nelle *Operette morali* e nei *Pensieri* di Giacomo Leopardi," introduction to the commentary on the *Operette morali* (Florence: Vallecchi, 1933).

111. See above all K. Vossler, *Leopardi* (Naples: Ricciardi, 1925); M. Porena, *Il pessimism di Giacomo Leopardi* (Genoa: Perrella, 1923); A. Tilgher, *La filosofia di Leopardi* (Rome: Religio, 1940/Bologna: Boni, 1987).

112. C. Luporini, *Leopardi progressif*, op. cit., passim.

113. W. Binni, introduction to *TO I*, pp. lxxv, lxxxii, and lxxxviii–xciii.

114. *Letter 297*, to Giuseppe Melchiorri, Recanati, 5 March 1824; Shaw, pp.150–51. This is the way Leopardi describes his own lyrical work.

115. Nietzsche, *The Gay Science*, trans. Walter Kaufmann (New York: Vintage, 1974), sec. 92, pp. 145–46.

116. See in particular E. Bigi, *Dal Petrarca al Leopardi* (Naples: Ricciardi, 1954), pp. 86ff.

117. *Zibaldone*, p. 31 (*TO II*, p. 22; Caesar/D'Intino, pp. 35–36), and passim.

118. Ibid., p. 4111 (*TO II*, p. 1069; Caesar/D'Intino, p. 1764). Dated 11 July 1824, this reflection is therefore written just when Leopardi is composing *Parini*. See below.

119. See the penultimate note to the *Discourse on the Present State of Italian Morals* (*TO I*, p. 982). The reference to Kant and "his sect" corresponds to a positive evaluation of the critical spirit. The Germans, as a result of their predilection for observation and for the constructive spirit in metaphysics, are what the Ancients were in literature, philosophy, and the sciences: systematizers, novelists, ideologues, imaginers, visionaries. This series of terms clearly displays the favorable appreciation and at the same time the reservation contained in Leopardi's judgment. But this reservation, tinged with light irony, does not prevent him from concluding, several lines further on, "It seems that the time of the North has come." With regard to Kant, see notes 7, 105, and 121 of this chapter and notes 51, 81, and passim of chapter 1.

120. G. Ceronetti, *La vita apparente* (Milan: Adelphi, 1982), p. 134.

121. Here I am referring to Kant's "An Answer to the Question: What is Enlightenment?" (in Kant, *Perpetual Peace and Other Essays*, trans. Ted Humphrey [Indianapolis: Hackett, 1983], pp. 41–48), originally published in 1784. The great importance of this Kantian text—and for us the possibility of relating it to the ontological progression of Leopardi's metaphysics of morals—consists in the fact that, contrary to what happens in the *Groundwork* and in the two *Metaphysical Elements* (see notes 7 and 105 of this chapter), here the analytic of reason immediately "declare[s] revolutionary enthusiasm to be an historical indicator that reveals an intelligible arrangement of mankind in the world of phenomena" (J. Habermas, "Taking Aim at the Heart of the Present," in *Foucault: A Critical Reader*, ed. David Cousins Hoy, trans. Sigrid Brauner and Robert Brown (Oxford: Basil Blackwell, 1986), p. 108). According to Foucault's formula, "Kant seems to me to be situated at the origin of two great critical traditions that divide modern philosophy. His critical work founded the tradition that asks what conditions allow true knowledge [*conoscenza*]. On that basis, we could say, an entire field of modern philosophy has developed that I would define as the analytic of truth. But modern and contemporary philosophy contains another kind of question, another type of critical interrogation, and this is precisely the one that we see born in the questioning of the Enlightenment and in the text on revolution. This other tradition poses the following question: what is our actuality? What is the actual field of possible experiences? Here it is not a matter of an analytic of truth, but rather of a sort of ontology of the present, an ontology of ourselves" (Foucault, "Che cos'è l'Illuminismo? Che cos'è la rivoluzione?" in *Il Centauro* no. 11/12, May–December 1984, p. 236).

122. Concerning the philological reconstruction of the project of the *Operette*, see the commentaries cited earlier. It is interesting to note how the genesis of the *Operette* is accompanied by frequent reflections on laughter or irony. See particularly the letters of June 1821 addressed from Recanati to Pietro Giordani and Brighenti (*Letters 199, 200*, and *204*; Shaw, pp. 114–15), in which this connection is very strong. But throughout the epistolary colloquy with these correspondents, the other fundamental element of this period appears: the need to found a "civil

philosophy" for Italians (*Letters 197, 198, 201*; Shaw, pp. 116–17). These letters also refer to the project of the *Operette*. In my view, then, the *Discourse on the Present State of Italian Morals* must thus be considered inseparable from the composition, or rather the very conceptualization of the *Operette*.

123. They appear in *TO I*, pp. 189–211. These are very interesting fragments both as a result of their contents (materials for the "Machiavelli" and the "Fragment on Suicide", to which we return) and because they allow us to follow, through the compositional variants of some dialogues, Leopardi's work method. Faced with these materials, which were excluded from publication either before or after their first appearance and which are all ethical-political arguments, we might ask the reason for Leopardi's rejection. I think the answer is simple—worry about censorship.

124. *TO I*, pp. 79–86. This *operetta* was composed at Recanati from 19 January to 7 February 1824.

125. Ibid., pp. 86–88. Composed from 10 to 13 February 1824.

126. Ibid., pp. 88–89. Composed from 15 to 18 February 1824.

127. Ibid., p. 90; Creagh, pp. 52–53.

128. Ibid., p. 83; Creagh, p. 40.

129. Ibid., p. 87; Creagh, p. 47.

130. Ibid., pp. 90–92. Composed from 22 to 25 February 1824.

131. Ibid., pp. 92–94. Composed at Recanati from 2 to 6 March 1824.

132. Ibid., pp. 95–96. Composed at Recanati from 1 to 3 April 1824.

133. Ibid., pp. 98–101. Composed at Recanati from 24 to 28 April 1824.

134. Ibid., p. 95; Creagh, p. 63.

135. Ibid., p. 101; Creagh, p. 75.

136. Ibid., p. 96; Creagh, p. 64.

137. Ibid., pp. 96–98. Composed at Recanati from 9 to 14 April 1824. See the correspondences between this dialogue and pages 4079–81 (*TO II*, p. 1058; Caesar/D'Intino, pp. 501–2) of the *Zibaldone*. Obviously it is always useful to refer to the correspondences between the *Operette* and the stages of the *Zibaldone*; editions of the *Operette* generally include tables of such correspondences, as does *TO*, the one we are using.

138. Ibid., p. 96; Creagh, p. 65.

139. Ibid., p. 98; Creagh, p. 69.

140. Ibid.

141. Ibid., pp. 102–7. Composed at Recanati from 30 April to 8 May 1824.

142. Ibid., p. 105; Creagh, p. 82.

143. Ibid., pp. 106, 110. Composed at Recanati from 10 to 19 May 1824. See the important correspondences with page 4092 (*TO II*, p. 1062; Caesar/D'Intino, pp. 1751–52) of the *Zibaldone*.

144. Ibid., pp. 114–17. Composed at Recanati from 21 to 30 May 1824. See also *Zibaldone*, pp. 4099–4101 (*TO II*, pp. 1064–65; Caesar/D'Intino, pp. 504–5).

145. Ibid., pp. 10–14. Composed at Recanati from 1 to 10 June 1824. In the notes to *TO I*, see the references to the *Zibaldone* and to the correspondence regarding this most important dialogue.

146. Ibid., pp. 161–65. Composed at Recanati from 14 to 24 June 1824.

147. Ibid., p. 110; Creagh, pp. 89–90.

148. Ibid., p. 109; Creagh, p. 88.

149. Ibid., Creagh, p. 89.

150. Ibid., p. 17; Creagh, p. 104.

151. Ibid.

152. Ibid.

153. Ibid., p. 112; Creagh, p. 92.

154. Ibid., p. 113; Creagh, pp. 94–95.

155. Ibid., Creagh, p. 96.

156. Ibid., Creagh, p. 97.

157. Ibid.

158. "The Dialogue of Timander and Eleander" was written after "Tasso" and before "Parini." It occupies this median position in the *Operette* because it had been composed to serve as a conclusion to the Stella edition of 1827. But in reading it, we understand how this dialogue constitutes a polemical introduction in response to all those who had attacked the *Operette*, rather than a conclusion.

159. *TO I*, p. 161; Creagh, p. 181.

160. Ibid., pp. 117–33. Composed at Recanati from 6 July to 30 August 1824. For the many cross-references to the *Zibaldone*, see the notes in *TO*.

161. Ibid., pp. 134–37. Composed at Recanati from 16 to 23 August 1824.

162. Ibid., pp. 137–49. Composed at Recanati from 29 August to 26 September 1824. This long episode of the *Operette*, treated in the manner of *excerpta*, is in reality a summary of the central points of the moral theory developed in the *Zibaldone*. There are countless interpreters' references to the *Zibaldone* with respect to this text. The list appears in the notes to *TO*.

163. Ibid., p. 118; Creagh, p. 106.

164. Ibid., p. 33; Creagh, p. 130.

165. Ibid., p. 36; Creagh, p. 136.

166. Ibid.

167. Ibid., Creagh, p. 137.

168. Ibid.

169. *Zibaldone*, pp. 4074–75 (*TO II*, pp. 1055–56; Caesar/D'Intino, p. 1740).

170. Let us recall, however, that in Recanati during 1824, Leopardi added only a hundred or so pages to the *Zibaldone* (pp. 4006–123; *TO II*, pp. 1027–74; Caesar/D'Intino, pp. 1688–1776). These pages do not contain any particularly innovative elements. A consolidated philosophical thematic now matures and is formally defined. The materials of the *Zibaldone* thus serve above all to support the *Operette*.

171. *TO I*, p. 139; Creagh, p. 140.

172. From 29 August to 26 September, as we have already noted.

173. *TO I*, pp. 149–51. Composed from 19 to 25 October 1824 at Recanati.

174. Ibid., 150; Creagh, p. 160.

175. Ibid., 151; Creagh, p. 161.

176. Ibid.

177. Ibid., 152–55. Composed at Recanati from 29 October to 5 November1824.

178. Ibid., 158–60. Probably composed at Bologna during the autumn of 1825. Nevertheless it fits perfectly into the ideal framework of the *Operette* of 1824.

179. Ibid., 156–58. Composed at Recanati from 10 to 16 November 1824.

180. Ibid., 152; Creagh, p. 163.

181. Ibid., Creagh, p. 164.

182. Ibid., Creagh, pp. 64–65.

183. Ibid., 153; Creagh, p. 65.

184. Ibid., 154; Creagh, p. 166.

185. Ibid., 155; Creagh, p. 168.

186. Ibid., Creagh, p. 169.

187. Concerning hints of laughter and irony in the correspondence of this period, see note 122 of this chapter. Furthermore, see below the references to Baudelaire's work on the comic and E. Raimondi's commentary in note 99 to chapter 4. Of course Bergson's *Laughter* (in Wylie Sypher, ed., *Comedy* [Baltimore: Johns Hopkins University Press, 1956], pp. 60–190) and the various determinations it establishes should be kept in mind for a deepening of the philosophical discourse on laughter: laughter as social gesture, the unconscious nature of laughter, and his famous definition of laughter as "something mechanical encrusted on the living" (p. 84), etc. For an interesting summary and current discussion of the theme, see J. Duvignaud, *Le proper de l'homme: Histoires du comique et de la dérision* (Paris: Hachette, 1985), which contains an excellent bibliography. Note that the importance that the theme of laughter, the comic, and sarcasm assumes in Leopardi's thought runs contrary to its sense in Hegel's thought. The latter, as a general rule, considers the comic, humor, and irony as elements that break apart the ideal process that leads from art to religion, from "beautiful art" to "true religion" (*Philosophy of Mind*, op. cit., sec. 563, p. 297). Comedy expresses the opposition of the autonomy of spirit to effective historical development—and can go so far as to interpret the degeneration of this relationship. Here we are fully within the kingdom of inessentiality: "the comic [. . .] is a subject who makes his own actions contradictory and so brings them to nothing, while remaining tranquil and self-assured in the process" (Hegel, *Aesthetics*, vol. 2, op. cit., p. 1220). In Leopardi, irony and all its variants instead constitute the sign of truth and of the insurmountable character of the contradiction and therefore of the crisis in which the dialectical rhythm is dissolved. Hegel considers this dissolution to be negative, whereas Leopardi considers it positive. Lastly, see

Nietzsche, fragments from the *Ecce Homo* period, pp. 82–84: "to see tragic natures founder and to be able to laugh about it despite the profound understanding, emotion and sympathy one may feel for them, that is divine." The vicissitudes of Brutus, Leopardi's symbol *par excellence*, also have a potently ironic and divine side.

188. *TO I*, p. 160; Creagh, p. 178.

189. Ibid., 157; Creagh, p. 172.

190. Ibid., Creagh, p. 173.

191. Ibid.

192. Ibid., 158; Creagh, p. 173.

193. See above all the correspondence from Recanati from 1824 until the departure in July 1825; then the start of the wandering, with its poetic returns to Recanati from November 1826 to April 1827 and from November 1828 to September 1829. In that period of preparations for departure, during the composition of the *Operette* of 1824, the correspondence displays Leopardi's great Erasmian serenity. The great worldly adventure follows and the explosion of poetic genius. But the latter rests on a strictly metaphysical, theoretical, philosophical basis consolidated during the years of solitary meditation and with the strength that the confrontation granted: when he learns that he is really one of the first . . .

194. *Zibaldone*, p. 4149 (*TO II*, p. 1086; Caesar/D'Intino, p. 1797).

195. *Letter 560*, to Antonio Papadopoli, Pisa, 14 November 1827.

196. *Letter 670*, to Pietro Colletta, Recanati, March 1829; Shaw, p. 234.

197. *Zibaldone*, pp. 4197–98, 4417–18, 4477–78, 4484, 4518 (*TO II*, pp. 1195–96, 1236, 1219, 1221–22; Caesar/D'Intino, pp. 1838, 1991, 2032, 2037, 2065), and passim for the years 1828–1829.

198. What we said in note 170 about the *Zibaldone* of 1824–1825 could be said with even more justification about the weary and increasingly rare pages composed in the following years, up to 1829. It is well known that between 1830 and 1832, Leopardi composed only two or three pages, which constitute the definitive conclusion of the *Zibaldone*. Here we are analyzing how the *Operette* of 1824 and 1827 and the contemporary pages of the *Zibaldone* intersect on the path of the search for truth that Leopardi follows.

199. *Zibaldone*, pp. 4133–34 (*TO II*, p. 1079; Caesar/D'Intino, pp. 1784–85).

200. Ibid., pp. 4257–59, 4265–66 (*TO II*, pp. 1135, 1139; Caesar/D'Intino, pp. 1888–90, 1895–96).

201. Ibid., pp. 4137, 4168–69 (*TO II*, pp. 1080–81, 1095; Caesar/D'Intino, pp. 1787, 1816–17).

202. This poses a huge problem that we have already broached repeatedly without bringing to a conclusion. However, in order to move forward, let us make some distinctions: (a) seventeenth-century materialism is certainly less teleological than eighteenth-century sensualism. Leopardi often seems to us closer to the first of these traditions; (b) eighteenth-century sensualism and the materialist tendencies

348   Notes

that coexist with it are rather teleological, and it is easy to think about the continuity between rationalism and Cartesian finalism in them (a point emphasized by many commentators, notably Vartanian); (c) although pervaded by teleological instances, eighteenth-century sensualism cannot be reduced to them, as J. Derrida above all has demonstrated; (d) some ambiguities persist in Leopardi; these follow above all, and in a paradoxical manner, from the reception of sensualism, that is from the fact that in Italy sensualism frequently appears (and this is how it appears in Leopardi's education) as a particular figure of scholastic gnoseology. Given all this, it seems obvious how much strength Leopardi's materialism had to develop in order to free itself from that ambiguous tradition.

203. *Zibaldone*, pp. 4127–32 (*TO II*, pp. 1077–79; Caesar/D'Intino, pp. 1781–84).

204. Ibid., pp. 4248, 4283–84 (*TO II*, pp. 1130, 1147; Caesar/D'Intino, pp. 1881–82, 1909–10).

205. Ibid., pp. 4228, 4229–31 (*TO II*, pp. 1120, 1121; Caesar/D'Intino, pp. 1864–67).

206. Ibid., pp. 4413, 4421, 4461–62, 4467–69, 4485–86, 4510, 4517 (*TO II*, pp. 1194, 1197, 1212, 1214–15, 1222, 1233, 1236; Caesar/D'Intino, pp. 1988, 1993, 2019–20, 2024–25, 2038–39, 2058, 2064–65).

207. Ibid., pp. 4135–36, 4194–96, 4227, 4261–63, 4268–71, 4367, 4368 (*TO II*, pp. 1080, 1105–6, 1130, 1136–37, 1140–41, 1178, 1179; Caesar/D'Intino, pp. 1786–87, 1835–37, 1864, 1891–93, 1897–1900, 1961–62).

208. Above all by Luporini and Binni, but also by Prete, Rigoni, etc.

209. *Zibaldone*, pp. 4141–43, 4274–75 (*TO II*, pp. 1083, 1143; Caesar/D'Intino, pp. 1790–92, 1902–3).

210. Ibid., p. 4178 (*TO II*, 1099; Caesar/D'Intino, p. 1824).

211. Ibid., p. 4174 (*TO II*, 1097–98; Caesar/D'Intino, p. 1822).

212. Ibid., pp. 4204–5, 4292 (*TO II*, 1110, 1151; Caesar/D'Intino, pp. 1844–45, 1915–16).

213. Ibid., pp. 4181–82, 4233, etc. (*TO II*, pp. 1100, 1122–23; Caesar/D'Intino, pp. 1826–27, 1868–69).

214. Ibid., p. 4233 (*TO II*, p. 1122; Caesar/D'Intino, pp. 1868–69).

215. Ibid., pp. 4206–8, 4251–53, 4256 (*TO II*, pp. 1111, 1132–33, 1134; Caesar/D'Intino, pp. 1845–47, 1884–86, 1888).

216. Ibid., p. 4288 (*TO II*, p. 1149; Caesar/D'Intino, pp. 1912–13).

217. Ibid., p. 4275 (*TO II*, p. 1143; Caesar/D'Intino, p. 1902).

218. Ibid., pp. 4243–45 (*TO II*, p. 1128; Caesar/D'Intino, pp. 1876–78).

219. Ibid., pp. 4418–19 (*TO II*, 1196; Caesar/D'Intino, pp. 1991–92).

220. Ibid., pp. 4238–39 (*TO II*, pp. 1125–26; Caesar/D'Intino, pp. 1872–73).

221. Ibid., p. 4160–61 (*TO II*, p. 1091; Caesar/D'Intino, pp. 1807–8).

222. Ibid., pp. 4185–88 (*TO II*, pp. 1102–3; Caesar/D'Intino, pp. 1829–30).

223. Ibid., p. 4299 (*TO II*, p. 1154; Caesar/D'Intino, pp. 1920–21).

224. Ibid., p. 4428 (*TO II*, p. 1199; Caesar/D'Intino, pp. 1997–98).

225. Ibid., pp. 4145–46 (*TO II*, p. 1084; Caesar/D'Intino, pp. 1793–94).

226. Ibid., pp. 4426, 4492–93 (*TO II*, pp. 1199, 1225; Caesar/D'Intino, pp. 1996, 2043–44).

227. "Der echte Schmerz begeistert": this line by Hölderlin could serve as a motto for this fundamental passage of Leopardi's thought—inspiration feeds on pain, the "becoming divine [*indivinamento*]" of passion. But see G. Vigolo's introduction to the Einaudi edition of Hölderlin's poems (Turin, 1958) and particularly to the thematization that he makes of the idea of *Begeisterung* [inspiration], which refers to a virtue that extends across the ontological horizon, which constructs being, and which brings consciousness to plenitude. This passage from reason to myth is not a flight from the real but an attempt at poetic (ontological) construction of the real in its entirety. The connection of all the aspects of reality is not merely synchronic: it is also implicated in a constructive mechanism, in the diachronic processes that constitute being. It is indisputable that there are great differences between Hölderlin's poetic perspective and that of Leopardi—differences of tone, of inspiration, of metaphysical background. Nevertheless, in both of them (as later in Rimbaud) there is a common tension: *Begeisterung* and the poetic construction of being.

228. *TO I*, pp. 166–71. Composed in 1827.

229. Ibid., pp. 171–79. Probably composed in Florence in 1827. Concerning the many cross-references to the *Zibaldone*, see the notes in *TO*.

230. Ibid., p. 167; Creagh, p. 192.

231. Ibid., p. 170; Creagh, pp. 196–97.

232. Ibid., p. 176; Creagh, p. 209.

233. Ibid. Creagh, p. 208.

234. Ibid., p. 178; Creagh, p. 210.

235. C. Rosset has well brought to light the existence of at least two materialisms. One is close to ancient materialism and of a rather pessimistic inspiration, and the other is rationalist and revolutionary (see "L'autre materialisme," in *Critique* 371 [April 1978], pp. 347–51). See also M. Abensour, "La théorie critique: une pensée de l'exil?" in *Archives de philosophie* 45 (1982), pp. 179–200. Interrogating the thought of the Frankfurt School in which he sees "materialism dancing," Abensour insists upon the doubling of the traditions of materialism and clarifies how, to the extreme objectivism of ancient materialism, modern materialism opposes a subjective dimension, or at very least a conflictual relationship between subject and object. This is what we are calling "post-critical materialism." This double tradition can quite obviously be distinguished and seen operating in the field of Leopardi studies.

236. This is really not the place to dig deeper into the variants of post-critical materialism. All are present in contemporary French thought, where they contribute to determining a complex but extremely rich figure of philosophical method. I am

thinking of Foucault, in whose work the extreme tension between subjectivity and objectivity instituted by post-critical materialism gives rise to an idea of ontological constitution; I am thinking of Lyotard, in whose work second nature is offered as a veritable "multiverse," and above all of Deleuze, who describes the original keys of production and the difference that animates the surface of this multiverse.

237. *Letter 297*, to Giuseppe Melchiorri, Recanati, 5 March 1824; Shaw, p. 150.

238. *Zibaldone*, p. 58 (*TO II*, p. 39; Caesar/D'Intino, p. 64).

239. Concerning poetic making in the classical tradition and the complementarity of the structural moment and the innovative moment, we refer once again to E.H. Kantorowicz ("La souveraineté de l'artiste: Note sur quelques maximes juridiques et les théories de l'art à la Renaissance," in *Mourir pour la patrie*, op. cit.), keeping in mind the fact that his source and inspiration is Panofsky (*Idea*, op. cit.). On these themes, see note 68 of this chapter. As always in the domain of these studies of the tradition, with reference to the materialism of the Renaissance, see F. Yates, *Giordano Bruno and the Hermetic Tradition* (Chicago: University of Chicago Press, 1964).

240. P. Claudel offers a critical description of this poetic condition in his preface to the edition (op. cit.) of Rimbaud's *Oeuvres*. There he accomplishes a kind of inspired synthesis, in close symbiosis with Rimbaud's poetic process, between a Dionysiac moment of inspiration and an Apollinian moment of stylistic systematization. Claudel reads Nietzsche's critical hypothesis through Rimbaud, so to speak, and anticipates the most modern interpretations in the style of Kristeva:

Here Rimbaud, having arrived at the full mastery of his art, will make us hear that marvelous prose, deeply imbued to its last fibers with intelligible sound, like the dry mellow wood of a Stradivarius. After Chateaubriand, after Maurice de Guérin, our French prose, whose labor and history are so full and so different from our poetry, has never known interruption or gap, and has come to this. All the resources of parenthesis, all the harmony of endings, the richest and most subtle that any human language could prepare, are at last fully utilized. The principle of "internal rhyme," of dominant harmony, posited by Pascal, is developed with a wealth of incomparable modulations and resolutions. Whoever has once submitted to Rimbaud's sorcery is as powerless henceforth to evade it as he would be a phrase by Wagner. The march of thought too, which proceeds no longer by logical development but as a musician does, by melodic designs and the relationship of juxtaposed notes, lends itself to important remarks.

241. The terminology that we are employing is that of Heidegger (*Elucidations of Hölderlin's Poetry*, op. cit.). "These elucidations belong within the dialogue of thinking (*Denken*) with a form of poetry (*Dichten*) whose historical singularity can

never be proved by the history of literature, but which can be pointed out by the dialogue with thinking" (p. 7). See note 271 to this chapter.

242. This is what Vieusseux called Leopardi. See *Letter 422*, to Giampietro Vieusseux, Bologna, 4 March 1826; Shaw, p. 181. This is probably proposed as a pseudonym for a rubric in the *Antologia*.

243. *Canto XIX*, Peruzzi, pp. 377–98. Composed in March and recited by Leopardi to the Accademia dei Felsinei in Bologna on Easter Monday evening.

244. See Binni's very harsh judgment in his introduction to *TO I*, pp. lxxxii–lxxxvii, which is accompanied by a particularly lively polemic against E. Bigi's reading (*Le genesi del Canto notturno ed altri studi su Leopardi* [Palermo: Manfredi, 1967]).

245. Nichols, p. 75.

246. Ibid.

247. Nichols, p. 77.

248. Ibid., p. 78.

249. *Letter 452*, to Carlo Leopardi, Bologna, 30 May 1826; Shaw, p. 185.

250. *Zibaldone*, p. 4301 (*TO II*, p. 1154; Caesar/D'Intino, p. 1922).

251. *Canto XXXVI*, Peruzzi, pp. 563–66. "Pisa, 15 February, last Friday of Carnival, 1828."

252. Nichols, p. 151.

253. Ibid.

254. Ibid.

255. As both Bigi and Binni suggest, despite divergent, even opposed points of departure. The unity and logical linkage of the canti from this period seem total to both of them, although Binni emphasizes the fact that in this period Leopardi's highest materialist and progressive conception takes shape (with the exception of the epistle *To Count Carlo Pepoli*, which he consequently considers a failure and an occasional work), whereas Bigi insists upon the formation of a mature stylistic conception. But in my view, as argued in the main text, the problem does not consist in considering this set of canti as a moment organized by a single poetic inspiration, but as the multiform apparition of a grip on being, the expression of a now mature metaphysical conception.

256. *Canto XX*, Peruzzi, pp. 399–420. Composed at Pisa between 7 and 14 April 1828.

257. Nichols, p. 82.

258. Ibid., p. 81.

259. Ibid., p. 84.

260. Ibid.

261. *Canto XXI*, Peruzzi, pp. 423–33. Composed at Pisa 19 and 20 April 1828. See N. Borsellino, "À Silvia: variazioni su un sonetto pastorale," in *Paragone* 28 (1977), pp. 45–55.

262. It would be very important to compile an inventory of the different styles and meters used in the canti, while relating this inquiry to the internal history of Leopardi's inspiration. Nevertheless such research turns out to be quite arduous since Leopardi's reference to the poetic tradition is so broad and governed by choices that are difficult to define. See in this regard L. Cellerino (*Tecniche ed etica del paradosso*, op. cit., p. 148), who speaks of a "Leopardi of omnivorous memory." Concerning Leopardi's knowledge [*conoscenza*] of the poetic tradition, see the *Crestomazia italiana. La poesia*, ed. G. Savoca (Turin: Einaudi, 1968). In *Studi italiani* (op. cit.), L. Spitzer notes the reappearance of some formal elements from the seventeenth and eighteenth centuries in *The Revival, Aspasia*, etc. For a more general perspective, see M. Fubini, *Metrica e poesia* (Milan: Feltrinelli, 1962).

263. Nichols, p. 86. Regarding the physicality of the canto and the image, see the variant in Peruzzi, vol. 3 bis., p. 427.

264. Ibid., p. 87.

265. *Letter 555*, to Paolina Leopardi, Pisa, 12 November 1827; Shaw, p. 203.

266. *Letter 676*, to Giampietro Vieusseux, Recanati, 12 April 1829; Shaw, p. 234.

267. *Canto XI*, Peruzzi, pp. 267–69. Probably composed at Recanati in 1829. For the polemic, see *TO I*: 1426. B. Biral (*La posizione storica di Giacomo Leopardi*, op. cit.) discusses with great finesse the positions of Monteverdi. On the overall polemic over the dating, see L. Cellerino, *Tecniche ed etica del paradosso*, op. cit., pp. 45, 76, 82.

268. Nichols, p. 52.

269. *Canto XXII*, Peruzzi, pp. 435–60. Composed at Recanati from 26 August to 12 September 1829.

270. Nichols, p. 91.

271. Our reference to Heidegger (see note 241 of this chapter) needs justification. It aims to show that Heidegger's reasoning on Hölderlin represents a useful key for interpreting the European Leopardi while precisely indicating the limits of the "philosophy of crisis" for understanding of Leopardi's poetry. It is indisputable that Heidegger's five fundamental interpretive assertions are also valid for Leopardi: (1) the innocence of writing poetry, (2) the ontological language of writing poetry, (3) "we—human beings—are a conversation" (p. 56), (4) poetic foundation and its autonomy, and (5) poietics as human constitution. See "Hölderlin and the Essence of Poetry," in *Elucidations of Hölderlin's Poetry*, op. cit., pp. 51–65. We must make one further emphasis: the ontological dimension in Leopardi constitutes a central point, a subjective emergence that is possibly even more effective than that in the mature Hölderlin. Between writing poetry and thinking, in the conversation that the two powers [*potenze*] undertake, Leopardi posits being as protagonist. It remains nonetheless obvious that it is precisely in this regard that Heidegger's contradiction, which tends to define poetry, whether for Hölderlin or for Leopardi, as residue or resistance on

a transcendental horizon, explodes—here is where poetry is set on its feet and where ontology is even more radical that any transcendental horizon. There is another critical element in Heidegger's interpretation that is difficult to accept: he is conscious of the historical situation of Hölderlin and Leopardi (within the formal subsumption of capitalist society) just as he is conscious of his own historical situation (within real subsumption), yet he tends to translate "subsumed being" into a mythology of primordial being. But subsumed being is an articulated being; its immediacy is a set of rich, ample, multidirectional relations. It escapes the impotence of the transcendental proposition because it has no need for cognitive articulations, since those articulations are inherent and immediately obvious in the ontological dimension. Heidegger refuses to make this dimension of being operative, a fact of which he is nevertheless aware, hence the failure of his approach: subsumed being has no need to be projected toward any originariness [*originarietà*] whatever. Concerning the Heidegger/Hölderlin relationship, see note 60 to chapter 5.

272. See A. Prete (*Il pensiero poetante*, op. cit., pp. 80, 88, 97), who rightly refers in this regard to F. Schlegel's aesthetic formulation. (In this regard see also P. Szondi, *Poésie et poétique de l'idéalisme allemand*, op. cit., passim.)

273. Once again the reference is to the reconstruction of the great theses on Romantic poetry by P. Szondi, *Poésie et poétique de l'idéalisme allemand*, op. cit. Let us be clear here: I have endorsed the thesis of a Romantic Leopardi solely in the sense of a European Leopardi. In other words, Leopardi's thought and poetry are metaphysically Romantic in the sense that they adhere perfectly to the theoretical and operative hypotheses of German early Romanticism. Its non-dialectical and constitutive line is taken up by Leopardi, although he is unaware of it. He participates in the anti-Hegelian aspects of Romantic aesthetics. From this viewpoint, Leopardi is a Romantic poet, but if one compares his poetry and his thought with the Italian tradition of genres and schools, things look very different. From that viewpoint, paradoxically, he is instead perceived as a classicist. But this is not the aspect that interests us here. Instead, we want to show how Leopardi refuses every idea of art as "reconciliation," as "surmounting" of contradictions and direct "manifestation of God." The confrontation with Hegel emerges again here. Now as the latter says, it is true that in certain aspects "the work of art therefore is just as much a work due to free will, and the artist is the master of the God" (*Philosophy of Mind*, op. cit., sec. 560, p. 294), just as it is true that "in such single shapes the 'absolute' spirit cannot be made explicit" (ibid., sec. 559, p. 294)—however, "in work so inspired the reconciliation appears so obvious in its initial stage that it is without more ado accomplished in the subjective self-consciousness, which is thus self-confident and of good cheer, without the depth and without the sense of its antithesis to the absolute essence" (ibid., sec. 561, pp. 294–95). On the basis of this definition, Hegel denounces Romantic art in terms that Leopardi himself could have taken as his own

program: "Romantic art gives up the task of showing him as such in external form and by means of beauty: it presents him as only condescending to appearance, and the divine as the heart of hearts in an externality from which it always disengages itself. Thus the external can here appear as contingent towards its significance" (ibid., sec. 562, p. 295).

274. The internal continuity, or rather, the construction of a line that leads from early Romanticism to the work of Lukács and Benjamin is developed by P. Szondi. However, the intermediary space between the poetic constructivism of early Romanticism and the critical consciousness of the more contemporary authors deserves to be surveyed more accurately. It is indisputable that, on the plane of critique, the contribution of the Hegelian left, not so much to the solution to properly aesthetic problems as to a deepening of the phenomenology of production in general, is highly relevant. See in this regard G. Lukács, *Contributi alla storia dell'estetica* (Milan: Feltrinelli, 1957) and *Marxismo e la critica letteraria* (Turin: Einaudi, 1957). Nevertheless this reference itself runs the risk of remaining incomplete and, in any case, of not contributing to the reconstruction of the continuous thread of a materialist aesthetic for our present. We would have to repose the problem on a new historical level, on the level required for the critical elaboration of a materialist aesthetic. In other words, the problem is that of constructing a poetic alternative at the level of development of contemporary capitalism, in the present case between the formal subsumption and the real subsumption of society within capital. The great poetic ruptures carried out in the nineteenth century (from Hölderlin to Rimbaud) must, from this point of view, be compared with the consciousness of development and of the historical crisis as they were intuited, described, and represented above all by the novel. But today, in the desolate reality of mature capitalism and its crisis, in the weariness of the revolutionary process and the ontological mutation that it nevertheless produced, we need a synthesis of all these elements, in all probability a subjective synthesis in which poetry and the novel would constitute a *Bildungsroman* for the future (of course, this project also entails the definition of a social practice adapted to the level of development). See in this regard F. Guattari and A. Negri, *New Lines of Alliance, New Spaces of Liberty*, trans. M. Ryan et al. (Brooklyn: Autonomedia, 2010).

275. *Canto XXIV*, Peruzzi, pp. 483–91. Composed at Recanati, 17 and 20 September 1829.

276. *Canto XXV*, Peruzzi, pp. 493–501. Composed at Recanati, 29 September 1829.

277. Nichols, p. 104.

278. Ibid., p. 106.

279. Ibid., p. 105.

280. Ibid., p. 107.

281. It is here that the enormous distance that separates Hegel's *Aesthetics* from the Romantics can be measured: in the latter, the 'third term' that is aesthetically posited between concrete and abstract constitutes a constructive limit, whereas in Hegel it is instead the givenness of a representation of the absolute and as such dialectically recuperable. In this regard, see the following passage in Hölderlin, where the comparison with Hegel's aesthetics seems to me particularly interesting because a common terminology leads to opposite results.

> Thus the poetic spirit cannot content itself with the operation to which it adheres during its transaction, in a harmoniously opposed life, nor with conceiving of and holding fast the same by way of hyperbolical opposition; once it is so advanced, once its transactions lack neither harmonious unity nor significance and energy, neither harmonious spirit in general nor harmonious alternation, then it is necessary—if the unified (to the extent that it can be considered by itself) shall not cancel itself as something undifferentiable and become an empty infinity, or if it shall not lose its identity in an alternation of opposites, however harmonious they may be, thus be no longer anything integral and unified, but shall disintegrate into an infinity of isolated moments (a sequence of atoms, as it were)—I say: then it is necessary that the poetic spirit in its unity and harmonious progress also provide for itself an infinite perspective for its transaction, a unity where in the harmonious progress and alternation everything move forward and backward and, through its sustained characteristic relation to that unity, not only gain objective coherence for the observer [but] also gain [a] felt and tangible coherence and identity in the alternation of oppositions; and it is its last task, to have a thread, to have a recollection so that the spirit remain present to itself never in the individual moment and again in an individual moment, but continue in one moment as in another and in the different moods, just as it is entirely present to itself *in the infinite unity* which is once the point of separation for the unified as such, but then again also point of union for the unified as the opposed, finally is also both at once, so that what is harmoniously opposed within it is neither opposed as something unified nor unified as something opposed but as both in One, is felt as opposed in unified manner as inseparable and is invented as something felt. This sense is veritably poetical character, neither genius nor art, put poetic individuality, and it alone is given the identity of enthusiasm, the perfection of genius and art, the actualization of the infinite, the divine moment. (Hölderlin, *Essays and Letters on Theory*, trans. and ed. Thomas Pfau [Albany: SUNY Press, 1988], pp. 70–71)

282. Nichols, p.105.
283. Ibid., p. 107.

284. Ibid., p. 104.

285. Ibid., p. 150. *Canto XXV, Imitation.* See Peruzzi, p. 561. Regarding the dating ("not before 1828 and perhaps contemporaneous with the *Night Song*"), see *TO I*, p. 1429.

286. See note 274 of this chapter. Let us once again recall the theoretical characteristics of Leopardi's aesthetic materialism: a materialism that is constituted through the deepening of ontological analysis (a veritable hermeneutic of being), by means of the creativity of the intention of truth that is expressed in and through the ontological density, and through the ethical dimension that completes and crowns the entire dynamic of intentionality and project. Leopardi's imagination is directly metaphysical. It is so in post-critical, materialist terms, it pervades the surface as well as the depths of being, the void as well as the fluctuations or solidity of the world.

287. *Canto XXIII*, Peruzzi, pp. 461–81. Composed at Recanati from 22 October 1829 to 9 April 1830. Concerning this canto in general, see C. Muscetta, *Leopardi. Schizzi, studi e letture* (Rome: Bonacci, 1976).

288. *Zibaldone*, pp. 4399–4400 (*TO II*, pp. 1189–90; Caesar/D'Intino, p. 1980).

289. Nichols, p. 94.

290. Ibid., pp. 95–96. We know that this canto initially consisted only of stanzas I, II, and IV. It was enlarged with the addition of stanza III, and then V and VI were later added. See in this regard Peruzzi's edition (pp. 461–81) and above all A. Monteverdi, "La composizione del *Canto notturno*," (1960) in *Frammenti critici leopardiani* (Naples: Vita e pensiero, 1967).

291. Ibid., p. 96.

292. Ibid.

293. Ibid., p. 97.

294. See Peruzzi, p. 481.

Chapter Four: Dialects of Illusion

1. The relationship established in Leopardi between psychology and the constructive foundation of poetics recalls the one instituted in Wilhelm Dilthey's thought between psychology and the phenomenological foundation of knowledge [*sapere*]. Dilthey's reflection on these themes takes shape on the basis of the great German literary tradition (see *Deutsche Dichtung und Musik*, H. Noel and G. Misch, eds. [Leipzig: Teubner, 1933] and *Das Erlebnis und die Dichtung: Lessing, Goethe, Novalis, Hölderlin* [Göttingen: Vandenhoek & Ruprecht, 1985]). On both these texts see my *Saggi sullo storicismo tedesco*, op. cit., pp. 121ff. In this passage from psychology to a theory of expression, which is the basis of a positive hermeneutic, the point that must above all be emphasized consists in the

increasingly obvious configuration of a corporeal horizon, a concept of concrete individuality, and the definitive critique of every transcendental dimension. This reference to Dilthey, which is also a reference to a hermeneutic tradition that runs from Schleiermacher to Gadamer, is essential for it reveals an alternative line to that of the dialectic that is active throughout the twentieth century. In his study of the currents of historicism in the eighteenth and nineteenth centuries, Raymond Aron writes that "in the whole of this study Dilthey thus occupies an exceptional place. He is at the point of departure, but he is at also the conclusion" (*Philosophy critique de l'histoire* [Paris: Vrin, 1950], p. 23). We can certainly expand this assertion to the whole period of the Romantic and postromantic constitution of hermeneutics. If Leopardi moves in unison—but not in contact—with the problematics that issue from German Romantic thought, on the other hand it is necessary to emphasize (in order to complete the reference) the more philologically well-established relationship (although it is philosophically less productive) with the philosophy of the French Ideologues—in which case the problem of the construction not of a psychological but of a structural conception of individuality and the body would come to the forefront.

2. Concerning this period, which runs—for the canti that we are analyzing in this section—from summer 1832 to spring 1834, see Walter Binni's introduction to *TO I*, notably pages c–cv. According to the interpretation summed up in the progressive Leopardi stereotype, we find ourselves faced with the conclusion of our poet's lyric development: the sensualism and voluntarism of the first phase are followed by a period of nihilist materialism, and now a realist philosophy of practice takes shape, which comes to maturity and explodes in the Neapolitan period. Although this progressive interpretation is plausible (and it is indisputably hegemonic in the field of Leopardi studies), it is not without weak points. In this regard see the remarks of N. Jonard, B. Biral, G. Petronio, and L. Cellerino in the volume *Il caso Leopardi* (Palermo: Palombo, 1974), as well as L. Cellerino's commentary in *Tecniche ed etica del paradosso*, op. cit., pp. 70ff. To sum up: the discourse developed by the progressive interpretation is one of discontinuity. Where it is most strict from a philological viewpoint, it is most discontinuous (see Timpanaro, who exalts the detachment of Leopardi's last period). Where it is most diluted, this interpretation, on the contrary, reveals at once the great sensitivity of the interpreter and the difficulties of the thesis (as in Binni's case). In reality Leopardi must be read in continuity, of course a dynamic and articulated continuity, the construction of which encompasses his philosophy and his poetry.

3. Canto *XXVI*, Peruzzi, pp. 503–7. Composed in Florence during summer 1832.

4. Nichols, p. 108.

5. Ibid., pp. 109–10.

6. Ibid., p. 110.

7. Ibid. p. 109.

8. Ibid.

9. Ibid., p. 110–11.

10. Ibid.

11. Ibid., p. 111.

12. Here once again we must emphasize the particular nature of Leopardi's Romanticism, which has been analyzed in the foundational studies of Peter Szondi and the entire tradition (in particular Wilhelm Dilthey) that inspires him. But aesthetic references are not enough. The link between writing poetry and action—an action that constitutes poetics, a poetics that can act—is not the sole point common to Romanticism and Leopardi. There is something more: the determination to act, the specificity of its inherence in being, its ethically and ontologically determined practicality in language as in the universe of historical objects. Since Rimbaud and Joyce, this attitude is purely and simply what defines poetry. Poetry is a universal language that transforms the world. Ontological universality and ethical revolution constitute poetry in language: here, and only here, can the artist appear as the "divine master artist." Poetry, linguistic universality, determines the sole possibility of being. That is the "something more" that Leopardi, our close contemporary, adds to Romantic consciousness. Reality is language stretched across the void, hope hurled across nothingness. The forceful materiality of poetry is the only possible reality.

13. *Canto XXVII*, Peruzzi, pp. 509–12. Composed in Florence toward the middle of 1833.

14. Nichols, p. 113.

15. Ibid.

16. Binni (introduction to *TO I*) considers this canto as the first of the masterpieces of this period. He compares it with the later *Operette* of 1831 to 1832 and concludes that it represents their lyrical side. As I argue, it seems to me that this canto does not fulfill Leopardi's promise to investigate the regions of being, in the present case that of the psyche; what we witness on the contrary is a notable backing down in the face of an encroaching psychologism.

17. Nichols, p. 115.

18. Ibid., p. 113.

19. Ibid., p. 115.

20. Regarding this problem, let us repeat once again that Dilthey clearly perceived the ambiguous relationship that, from Romanticism onward, links psychology and the dialectic. On all this see my *Saggi sullo storicismo tedesco*, op. cit., pp. 72ff., where the great difficulty of detaching philosophical anthropology from psychology is made evident. This knot will give rise to debates straddling two centuries that are among the most interesting in the history of contemporary philosophy: in particular, the polemic between Husserl and Dilthey and the ontological reading of the work of York

von Wartenburg by Heidegger. Modern hermeneutics, which cannot exist if it is not radically separate from the dialectic, is founded in the course of this many-voiced debate: through Husserl's denunciation of psychology and Dilthey's affirmation of a structural expressionism; through York's particular version of historicism and Heidegger's ontological sense. Nevertheless, see all the notes above that we have already dedicated to this problem. These vistas of contemporary philosophy, which Leopardi's thought opens up and through which we can better read Leopardi's labor, will nevertheless end up definitively clarified when they are referred to a materialist horizon.

21. *Canto XVII*, Peruzzi, pp. 337–58. Composed in Florence between autumn 1832 and spring 1833. See B. Biral, *La posizione storica di Giacomo Leopardi*, op. cit., which is accompanied by a bibliography.

22. Nichols, p. 68.

23. Ibid., p. 69.

24. Ibid., p. 70.

25. See Binni's introduction to *TO I*, p. cvii. Binni speaks particularly of the "extensive poetic friction" that will be produced every time the theme of recollection intersects with the experience of the present. He says this above all with regard to *To Silvia* and *The Solitary Thrush*, but the feeling of conflict and difficulty can certainly be generalized to analogous poetic situations. Whatever remarks we make in this regard within the text, it is important to keep in mind the profoundly antagonistic and dramatic character that the most decisively idyllic pages also have in Leopardi.

26. The interpretations of Leopardi derived from so-called negative thought rely on the presupposition of a traversable line, of a homology between the negative place of critical thought's foundation and the analysis of regions of being. A. Prete's reading (*Il pensiero poetante*, op. cit.) is exemplary from this point of view. Nevertheless we must recognize that his work holds up, beyond an oversimplified slippage of the interpretive connections, because his methodical sensibility—as in Barthes, as in Derrida—allows him an adherence to the text that is implicitly contradictory with its point of departure. The remarks that we are making concerning the impossibility of establishing a Heideggerian nexus of continuity between foundation and projection of being are generally valid in the face of the philosophy of crisis.

27. The reference is to the vast metaphysical horizons of a Husserl or a Wittgenstein. Here the transcendental horizon is fully developed or completely transvalued: Wittgenstein's mysticism corresponds to Husserl's asceticism. The schematism of reason coils up on itself and recognizes that either its path is unrealizable or its identity is unrecognizable. But the most striking aspect is the fact that, within this linearity, philosophy is still conceived as a mediation: the ladder, having been climbed, is never thrown away. Thus the dialectical path emerges again among those who seem, and in any case wish, to radically surmount it: it reappears as a constitutive element in the definition of the concept of philosophy. But precisely this point of departure and this path are the negative objects of Leopardi's critique.

28. *Canto XXVIII*, Peruzzi, p. 513; Nichols, p. 118. Composed in Florence during summer 1833. Let us recall that the draft *To Ahriman* was composed in spring 1833, thus in close proximity to *To Himself.* Regarding this canto, see B. Croce, "Leopardi II: Il canto 'A se stesso,'" in *Poesia antica e moderna* (Bari: Laterza, 1943), and A. Monteverdi, "Scomposizione del canto 'A se stesso,'" in *Frammenti critici leopardiani*, op. cit.

29. Ibid.

30. Ibid.

31. Ibid.

32. *Canto XXIX*, Peruzzi, pp. 515–18. Composed in Naples during spring 1834 or perhaps in 1835. See above all L. Spitzer, "L'*Aspasia* di Leopardi," in *Studi italiani*, op. cit., pp. 251–92.

33. Nichols, p. 119.

34. Ibid.

35. In this regard, it is interesting to note that the opposition between Platonism and materialism, traced with great vigor in this canto by L. Spitzer (*Studi italiani*, op. cit.), yields Hölderlinian traits. In other words, the opposition is radicalized from the start of the exposition, and the ideal representation here plays not a role of recomposition but rather a tragic role. The presence in the following stanzas of a protesting or ironic tension that modifies or at least limits the effects of the initial dualism is of little import. In reality, the opposition runs through the whole canto. This 'Diotima effect' seems to me to be an extremely relevant element for the evaluation, not merely of this canto, but of the whole poetic phase that we are analyzing. We find ourselves faced with a complete overturning of the determination of the poetic functions of myth—the abstract idea, taken up in its separation, produces effects of etrangement, constructs an icy horizon, or rather proceeds like a logical scalpel to dissect and arrest the vital chaos. As we see shortly, a direct path links these canti to the poetics of the *Pensieri*. Here again it is worthwhile to emphasize the singular continuity of Leopardi's path, which is all the more linear and all the more continuous the more negative the foundation of the philosophical consideration of the world becomes. It is precisely this immediate positivity of the negative, this non-dialectical and constitutive positivity, that makes Leopardi's thought so important in the contemporary philosophical horizon: thus our critical exposition must also stay within this metaphysical pattern.

36. Nichols, pp. 119–20.

37. Ibid., p. 120.

38. Ibid., p. 121.

39. In Leopardi, the concept of irony is founded on an immediately ethical matrix, unlike the Romantic concept that is oriented in decisively cognitive terms. See I. Strohschneider-Kohrs, *Die Romantische Ironie in Theorie und Gestaltung* (Tübingen: M. Niemeyer, 1960). According to P. Szondi (*Poésie et poétique de*

l'idéalisme allemande, op. cit., pp. 95–113), the Romantic concept of irony, despite being strictly cognitive, includes something like a sense of practical impotence, or at least a reflection on the limits of action. "By preserving negativity, irony, although conceived as its surmounting, itself becomes negativity. It accepts the completion of action only in the past or in the future; everything that the present offers it, it measures by the standard of infinity and thus destroys" (p. 109). Szondi's interpretation is particularly interesting to the extent that, by wresting the concept of irony (as he reads it in Schlegel and Tieck) away from an exclusively cognitive matrix, he thereby wrests it away from any possibility of reinsertion into a dialectical process. This is contrary to what Hegel does throughout his *Aesthetics* (a move which is already present and has more importance in the *Phenomenology*). In Leopardi therefore the concept of irony gravitates toward the side of ethics, as we have seen; it appears immediately as a positivity. Contrary to what happens among the Romantics, Leopardi's irony is the tension that the positivity of the present pits against the inexhaustible character, the negativity, of the past and the future. Ethics is always presence, action, concrete determination. From this point of view, the inexhaustible character of life and its temporal dimensions, and thus its negativity, is commensurate with the insistence of the present: faced with it, the other dimensions are reduced and vanish—and the smile becomes possible.

40. Two *Operette morali* were certainly written in 1832: "Dialogue of an Almanac-Pedlar and a Passerby," composed in Rome or in Florence, and the "Dialogue of Tristan and a Friend," composed in Florence beginning in May. The "Fragment on Suicide," which we consider as dating to 1832, sometimes appears in an appendix to the *Operette*. Concerning its dating and the debates regarding it, see below.

41. The hypothesis of an immanent exhaustion of the poetic vein that had supported the *Operette* at the start, in the compositions of 1832, more or less corresponds to the general interpretive line to be found in Binni as well as Solmi, to mention the most exemplary representatives of interpretations that are at once canonical and opposed. Naturally this immanent exhaustion is the basis for a passage forward: toward the poetic summit of *The Broom*. I ask myself, how one can undertake a history of thought, not just Leopardi's but any author's, that would be the accumulation of things that die—that surmount themselves—that "dissolve in order to resolve themselves at a higher stage"? In any case, when applied to Leopardi, this method is rough going: indeed, in substance it comes down to demonstrating that Leopardi's path leads to resignation. This is true of Solmi and of the stereotypical interpreters we are considering here. In the other current, represented by Binni, resignation is attached to a more or less progressive thread of utopianism. But the fact that this moment of resignation is fundamental in the definition of the thought of the *Operette*, even in examinations coming from the left, so to speak, is ultimately confirmed by R. Tessari's book, *Il Risorgimento e la crisi di metà secolo*,

op. cit., in which the only corrective to resignation that can be found in the *Operette* is cynicism. The hopes of the Resistance that resound in the pages of Luporini and Binni shrink, the pinch of utopia dissolves, and all that remains to the interpreters of a now realist left is resignation and cynicism.

42. *TO I*, pp. 198–199. [Translator's note: All translations from this text are mine.]

43. Ibid., p. 199.

44. Ibid.

45. Ibid.

46. See G. Scarpa, notes to R. Bachelli's edition of the *Opere di Leopardi* (Milan, 1935), p. 1291. The editors of the *TO* themselves seem to accept this dating.

47. *TO I*, pp. 179–80; Creagh, p. 214.

48. Ibid., p. 180; Creagh, p. 215.

49. Ibid., Creagh, pp. 215–16.

50. Ibid., p. 182; Creagh, p. 220.

51. Ibid., p. 183; Creagh, pp. 221–22.

52. Ibid., p. 182; Creagh, pp. 220–21.

53. Ibid., Creagh, p. 221.

54. Ibid., p. 183; Creagh, p. 222.

55. Ibid.

56. Ibid., p. 184; Creagh, p. 223.

57. Ibid. Creagh, pp. 223–24.

58. Ibid., p. 181; Creagh, p. 219.

59. Ibid., p. 184; Creagh, pp. 224–25.

60. Ibid., p. 185; Creagh, p. 225.

61. *Zibaldone*, 4526–27 (*TO II*, p. 1239; Caesar/D'Intino, p. 2071), written in Florence, 4 December 1832.

62. The *Pensieri* were composed in Naples after the interruption of the *Zibaldone* that dates from December 1832. For a general analysis of the *Pensieri*, see A. Diamantini, "CXI *Pensieri* di Giacomo Leopardi," in *Rassegna della letteratura italiana* 1 (1970), pp. 16–34. For an interpretation of the *Pensieri*, see U. Carpi (*Il poeta e la politica*, op. cit., pp. 173–77), who rightly laments the lack of systematic studies of this work. In his judgment, the *Pensieri* represent "the total condemnation of modern civilization": Leopardi "does not ascribe historical evils to *a certain kind* of politics, to *a certain kind of* economy, but rather to *the one and only* economy and to *the one and only* politics." A debatable interpretation, obviously. I consider it important to note the work of L. Cellerino (*Tecniche ed etica del paradosso*, op. cit., pp. 76ff.) on the correspondences, assonances, and general extent of the relationship between the *Pensieri* and the *Canti*. Here, in all probability, we can speak of a complete and unitary flow of prose and poetry—is this not precisely one of the founding acts of modern poetry? See in this regard P. Claudel, "Réflexions

et propositions sur le vers français," in *Réflexions sur la poésie* (Paris: Gallimard, 1960), pp. 7–90.

63. See in *TO I*, p. 1438 a table of correspondences between the *Pensieri* and the pages of the *Zibaldone*. On the *Pensieri* in general, see also A. Momigliano, *Studi di poesia* (Bari: Laterza, 1937).

64. Concerning the polemic that followed Ranieri's publication of the *Pensieri*, see the notes in *TO* and the bibliography dedicated to this work.

65. *Letter 925*, to Luigi De Sinner, Naples, 2 March 1837.

66. In this regard, the reference by L. Cellerino (*Tecniche ed etica del paradosso*, op. cit.) to Roland Barthes ("Literature and Discontinuity," in *Critical Essays*, trans. Richard Howard [Evanston: Northwestern University Press, 1972], pp. 171–83) is excellent. "All the techniques of estrangement, to the point of the interruption of the 'continuity of literary discourse,' that is to say to the point of the subversion of all the rules of the *dispositio*, are only found in the *Pensieri*." We must also refer here to the rupture of context as a specific poetic moment: see J. Derrida, *Of Grammatology*, trans. Gayatri C. Spivak (Baltimore: Johns Hopkins University Press, 1976). A systematic study of the *Pensieri* that on the one hand takes into account the articulations of poetic content (see note 62) and on the other carries out out the analysis of the subversive method, once again, appears extremely important to me.

67. *Pensiero I, TO I*, 216; Di Piero, 29.

68. *Pensiero I, TO I*, 216; Di Piero, 33.

69. *Pensiero XXVIII, TO I*, p. 224; Di Piero, p. 69.

70. *Pensiero LXXV, TO I*, p. 236; Di Piero, p. 121.

71. *Pensiero LXXXIII, TO I*, p. 239; Di Piero, p. 133.

72. *Pensiero C, TO I*, p. 243 Di Piero, p. 151

73. *Pensiero CI, TO I*, p. 244; Di Piero, p. 155.

74. *Pensiero LI, TO I*, p. 231; Di Piero, p. 99.

75. *Pensiero XVI, TO I*, p. 220; Di Piero, p. 51.

76. *Pensiero LXXXII, TO I*, p. 239; Di Piero, p. 131.

77. See the Postulates and Definitions of Part III of Spinoza's *Ethics* and pp. 144ff. of my book *The Savage Anomaly: The Power of Spinoza's Ethics and Politics*, trans. Michael Hardt (Minneapolis: University of Minnesota Press, 1991).

78. On the enormous subterranean influence exercised by Spinoza's thought throughout the centuries of the Enlightenment, see P. Vernière's fundamental work *Spinoza et la pensée française avant la Révolution*, vol. 2 (Paris: PUF, 1954). Nothing even remotely comparable exists concerning Italian culture either before or after the revolution and the revolutionary expansion. This is a gap that must be filled. For my part I am sure that, beyond the places noted, there are many more points that philological study could trace to both the general and the particular influence of Spinoza's thought on Leopardi's work. Nevertheless, from this point

of view, we must recognize that the indexes to Leopardi's works, and notably to the *Zibaldone*, are not much help to us. See nevertheless C. Santinelli, *Spinoza in Italia, Bibliografia delli scritti italiani su Spinoza da 1675 al 1982* (Urbino: Quattro Venti, 1983), a bibliography that must be followed up by a study of the Spinozian tradition in Italy.

79. We must note once again the extraordinary analogy between Leopardi's historical judgment and that of Burckhardt (see note 119 to chapter 1) as well as the references to Nietzsche's thought (see note 121 to chapter 1). It is well known that Burckhardt's pessimistic discourse is linked by a profound relationship to the German philosopher. As for Burckhardt and Leopardi, in both the modernity of judgment passed on present time is accompanied by a quasi-Enlightenment historiographical methodology, in the sense that the large dimensions of the historical time of civilizations and the usage of 'ideal types' for historical judgment constitute the soul of their labor. So that in Burckhardt as in Leopardi, we witness the setting to work of a sort of negative dialectic of Enlightenment, a reprise of long-term analysis and its pessimistic overturning. See G. Colli, *Pour une encyclopédie des auteurs classiques*, op. cit.

80. Despite everything, I believe that L. Bulferetti's essay, "La Restaurazione," in *Questioni di Storia del Risorgimento e dell'Unità d'Italia*, ed. E. Rota (Milan: Marzorati, 1951) remains fundamental for retracing the continuity between the ideology of the Enlightenment, that of the restoration and the *Risorgimento*, at the very least as that continuity presents itself in Italy. Indeed, the specificity of Italian ideological development straddling the French Revolution and the Napoleonic era must never be forgotten.

81. *Pensiero XI, TO I*, p. 219; Di Piero, p. 45.

82. *Pensiero XXVII, TO I*, p. 224; Di Piero, p. 69.

83. *Pensiero XLIV, TO I*, p. 229; Di Piero, p. 89.

84. *Pensiero XLIV, TO I*, p. 229; Di Piero, p. 91.

85. *Pensiero LXXXIV, TO I*, p. 239; Di Piero, p. 133.

86. *Pensiero LXXXV, TO I*, p. 239; Di Piero, p. 135.

87. *Pensiero CIV, TO I*, p. 244; Di Piero, p. 157.

88. *Pensiero CIV, TO I*, pp. 244-245; Di Piero, pp. 157–59.

89. *Pensiero LIX, TO I*, p. 233; Di Piero, p. 107.

90. *Pensiero VI, TO I*, p. 218; Di Piero, p. 41.

91. *Pensiero XXIX, TO I*, p. 224; Di Piero, p. 71.

92. *Pensiero LXVI, TO I*, p. 234; Di Piero, p. 111.

93. *Pensiero LXVIII, TO I*, p. 234; Di Piero, p. 113.

94. *Pensiero LXXVIII, TO I*, p. 237; Di Piero, p. 125.

95. *Pensiero LXIV, TO I*, p. 233; Di Piero, p. 109.

96. *Pensiero XXXVII, TO I*, p. 226; Di Piero, p. 77.

97. *Pensiero LXXXIX, TO I*, p. 240; Di Piero, p.139.

98. Our reference to Nietzsche is in the spirit of G. Deleuze, *Nietzsche and Philosophy*, trans. Hugh Tomlinson (New York: Columbia University Press, 1984), and *Nietzsche* in *Pure Immanence: Essays on a Life*, trans. Anne Boyman (New York: Zone, 2001). Leopardi's poetry is truly the result of a theory of expression, a hermeneutic effort that traverses reality and reconfigures it violently. This theory of expression constitutes the point of convergence of different strands of thought, among them not only Nietzsche's thought of the surface and the will but also the hermeneutic, historicist philological traditions from Romanticism to the modern theories of negative thought by way of Dilthey. This complex process which, in Italian culture, is taken up again only after the Second World War (paradoxically through Marxist culture) is fully experienced, anticipated, and promoted by Leopardi.

99. See E. Raimondi's preface to Charles Baudelaire, *Scritti sull'arte* (Turin: Einaudi, 1981), pp. xxiv–xxvi. See above all Baudelaire's "De l'essence du Rire et généralement du comique dans les arts plastiques," (in *Oeuvres completes*, ed. C. Pichois [Paris: Gallimard/Pléiade, 1976]), which proposes a first-rate categorization of the definitions of the ironic, the comic, the sarcastic, the grotesque, etc. From a general point of view, see on this question the sometimes-opposed conclusions of Wolfgang Kayser (*Das Groteske in Maleri und Dichtung* [Oldenburg: G. Stalling, 1957) and Bahktin. We return to these themes that were already evoked in notes 122 and 187 to chapter 3.

100. See Niklas Luhmann, "I fondamenti sociali dela morale," in Luhmann et al., *Etica e politica: Riflessioni sulla crisi del rapporto fra societa e morale* (Milan: Franco Angeli, 1984). "The idea that double contingency constitutes an unavoidable and sterile self-referential circle" is the basis of this work's analyses that take as examples the values that constitute the genesis of bourgeois sensibility, notably "esteem" and "honor." "Whoever seeks to win the esteem of others, who makes it his objective, deserves discredit. From the 17th century onward, moral theory is the prisoner of this paradox," and "once led to this paradox, morality withdraws from communication." What Luhmann writes seems to correspond to Leopardi's situation, but obviously solely in phenomenological terms, which thus leaves entirely open the metaphysical evaluation of this paradox. Concerning its later developments, for example in regard to *The Broom*, what Luhmann adds in concluding his essay must be kept in mind: "In the framework of Christian tradition, what we are saying could perhaps be expressed by the intuition that 'charity' constitutes the foundation of the conditions of 'esteem.'"

101. Luhmann's analyses of the morality in the centuries of the bourgeoisie's genetic evolution are, in this regard, essential. Aside from *Social Structure and Semantics* (op. cit.), see *Love as Passion: The Codification of Intimacy*, trans. Jeremy Gaines and Doris Jones (Stanford: Stanford University Press, 1998). The central concept that we ourselves take up is the fact that the fabric of morality is intrinsically conflictual, that there is no morality without conflictuality.

102. *Letter 621*, to Pietro Giordani, 24 July 1828; Shaw, p. 222.

103. For example *Zibaldone*, pp. 4135–36, 4138–39, 4261–63, 4268–71 (*TO II*, pp. 1080, 1081, 1130, 1136–37, 1140–41; Caesar/D'Intino, pp. 1786–87, 1788, 1891–93, 1898–1900).

104. We linger for a while over this question in chapter 5, always keeping centrally in mind Karl Löwith's work *From Hegel to Nietzsche* (op. cit.). But it is above all to the history of art and poetry in the nineteenth century that we must refer here. For it is there, particularly in the lyric, that the critical experience of the ontological and metaphysical rupture matures, with the force of anticipation that is proper to poetry. "It can be said of reading a piece of true contemporary poetry, in verse or in prose (but verse gives a more effective impression), and perhaps more aptly (even in such prosaic times as these), what Sterne said about a smile; that it adds 'a thread to the very fabric of our life.' It refreshes us, so to speak; and it increases our vitality. But pieces of this sort are extremely rare today" (*Zibaldone*, 4450, *TO II*, p. 1208; Caesar/D'Intino, p. 2012). We cite this text in order to show how aware Leopardi was of the ontological power [*potenza*] of writing poetry. And it is precisely through the rupture of the dialectical tradition that poetic theory has been able to discover this new constructive terrain, hence the importance of the methodological critique and the construction of a new ontological fabric. To restrict ourselves to our authors, or rather our poets, the radicality of this anti-dialectical passage can be verified in both Hölderlin and Rimbaud just as in Leopardi. But here it is not so much this problem that interests us as it is the need to emphasize that only a revolution in poetic language (and the underlying revolution in metaphysical perspective), only a rupture in the traditional continuity of classical metaphysics and in its idealist renewal could permit this passage. See J. Kristeva, *Revolution in Poetic Language*, trans. Margaret Waller (New York: Columbia University Press, 1984).

105. *Letter 407*, to Monaldo Leopardi, Bologna, 25 January 1826; Shaw, 175.

106. *Letter 454*, to Francesco Puccinotti, Bologna, 5 June 1826; Shaw, 186. It is well known that, unlike Leopardi, Hegel approaches the theme of prose with great ambiguity. As Lukács broadly showed, and then Benjamin and Szondi confirmed, in Hegel prose (the novel) is the literary genre adapted to the everyday life of the bourgeois world. Leftist criticism develops in this direction (and this is already manifest in Marx, at least in his aesthetic thought; see K. Marx and F. Engels, *Scritti sull'arte* [Bari: Laterza, 1978], notably the text on Balzac, pp. 179ff.), preoccupied with making the bourgeois description of the truth of everyday life into a denunciation of that life and that world (*in re ipsa*). Sartre's reflections in *The Family Idiot* are one of the extremely subtle derivations of this starting point. However, we must not forget the negative characterization that is attributed, in spite of its profound ambiguity, to the prose/novel category in Hegel: for him bourgeois everyday life is also the banality of real life and art, to the extent that

this inessentiality yields (must yield), loses that privileged relationship with the real that other centuries, other sensibilities, and other civilizations had attributed to it, and renounces that capacity to weave the internal sense of consciousness to which the poetic function, in the life of the absolute, was destined (see Hegel, *Aesthetic*, op. cit., pp. 1005–7, 1009–10).

107. Concerning the general situation of the author/public relationship and the campaigns in favor of republishing the classics, see the essays by E. Passerin d'Entreves and V. Spinazzola in *Storia della letteratura Italiani, l'Ottocento* (Milan: Garzanti, 1969) as well as the works bearing on Milan in that era by M. Berengo (in particular, *Intelletuali e librai nella Milano della Restaurazione* [Turin: Einaudi, 1980]). Furthermore, in regard to the movement of translations and also to Leopardi as popularizer, see S. Timpanaro, *La filologia di Giacomo Leopardi*, op. cit., pp. 37ff.; E. Bigi, "Leopardi traduttore dei Classici," in *La genesi del Canto notturno*, op. cit., pp. 35ff.; G. Lonardi, *Classicismo e utopia*, op. cit.; in general these analyses are well-documented and balanced. U. Carpi's approach (in *Il poeta e la politica*, op. cit.) is not entirely satisfactory; despite correct motives, he falls into habitual contradictions as a result of overstating his thesis: "Possession of the most disciplined philological tools . . . Realization, through this practice, of a different cultural politics . . . [but], in a certain sense, literature, the *means* of restoring a happy condition, becomes *the only* possible happiness." The excellent analysis by De Robertis ("Dalle note dello Zibaldone alla poesia dei *Canti*," op. cit., pp. lx–lxi) insists on the importance of Leopardi's translations for the construction of his stylistics. But for a general perspective on this question, see G. Bollati's preface to the Einaudi edition of the *Crestomazia in prosa* (op. cit.).

108. *Letter 669*, to Giampiero Vieusseux, Recanati, 16 February 1829.

109. *Letter 691*, to Carlo Bunsen, Recanati, 5 September 1829; Shaw, 239. Leopardi makes frequent references to Niebuhr's work, particularly in his correspondence.

110. *TO I*, p. 1459.

111. Leopardi expresses this concept at different moments of his life, above all, not surprisingly, in his correspondence with foreign friends. For example in *Letter 409* to Bunsen (Bologna, 1 February 1826) in which he polemicizes poetically against the barbarism of the "gothic government" of "our unfortunate Italy" (Shaw, 176), and in *Letter 911* to De Sinner (Naples, 3 October 1835), in which he makes a humoral attack on Italian Jesuitism, the destroyer of philosophy (Shaw, 281). We return to the latter letter.

112. *TO I*, pp. 984–85. These texts date from 1825 to 1826. See once again G. Bollati's preface to the *Crestomazia in prosa*, op. cit., especially concerning Leopardi's preferences in the choice of authors included in both the *Crestomazia in prosa* and the *Crestomazia italiana di poeti*, pp. lx–lxx: an absolute preference, in philosophically and culturally significant terms, is granted to authors of the

fourteenth century and, to a lesser extent and above all with respect to prose, to those of the sixteenth century (see above, the note on Galileo).

113. *TO I*, pp. 985–87.

114. *TO I*, pp. 987–90.

115. *Letter 478*, to Antonio Fortunato Stella, Bologna, 13 September 1826; Shaw, 189.

116. In this sense Leopardi follows the line of Foscolo, whereas Foscolo nevertheless fundamentally exalts Petrarch's poetic loftiness. See Foscolo's presentation of Petrarch's *Canzoniere* (presently in the collection Universale Economia, I Classici, from Feltrinelli) in order to measure the distance that separates him from Leopardi in this regard. Here we obviously cannot reconstruct Leopardi's difficult, ambiguous, weighty relationship with Petrarchan poetry and tradition; we can emphasize only, keeping in mind this difficult communication, the great political importance and significance of Leopardi's work involving the canti.

117. *TO I*, p. 991. See G. Bollati's preface to the *Crestomazia in prosa*, op. cit. Concerning the *Crestomazia*'s preparation, see the letters to Giordani of 13 July 1821, 5 June 1826, 25 February 1828, 5 May 1828, as well as the letters to Stella of 13 September 1826, 19 September 1826, 5 October 1826, and 18 October 1826. Bollati rightly insists on the fact that the *Crestomazia* is born and develops in relation to the prose fervor of 1826 to 1827, in other words with the return to work on the *Operette*.

118. *TO I*, pp. 991–92. See also the Einaudi edition established by G. Savoca, op. cit.

119. For example *Letter 563*, to Antonio Fortunato Stella, Pisa, 23 November 1827. Bollati (preface to the *Crestomazia in prosa*, op. cit., pp. xxiff.) notes how forceful Leopardi's undertaking is in terms of its attack on the purist tradition. He also emphasizes, correctly I think, the implicit polemic in relation to Giordani that this detachment from the purist tradition includes. See in this regard the posthumous attack (1841, though the text seems to have been written in 1833) by N. Tommaseo on the *Crestomazia* (Bollati, pp. xxviiiff.).

120. *Letter 422*, to Giampiero Vieusseux, Bologna, 4 March 1826.

121. For example *Letters 556, 653, 658*, and *693*.

122. *Letter 690*, to Giampiero Vieusseux, Recanati, 28 August 1829; Shaw, 238. These assertions of Leopardi's correspond to the moment at which the fortunes of the *Antologia* were at their height. Concerning the political, economic and cultural situation in the 1830s, see in *Storia d'Italia*, vol. 3, op. cit. the interventions of S.J. Woolf (pp. 323ff.), A. Caracciolo (pp. 587ff.), N. Badaloni (pp. 912ff.). All these authors insist upon the fact that this period saw the constitution of a moderate axis, corresponding politically to a middle way between the Catholics and the secular, and economically to a situation of balance between liberal demands and the continuity of princely reformism—which the *Antologia* advocated. This balance will be upset only at the start of the 1830s following Mazzini's insurrection and the violent repression

that resulted from it. See also, regarding the *Antologia*, above passim and note 139 of this chapter.

123. *Letter 470*, to Paolina Leopardi, Bologna, 16 August 1826.

124. *Letter 706*, to Paolina Leopardi, Florence, 18 May 1830; Shaw, 245.

125. *Letter 734*, to Paolina Leopardi, Florence, 15 November 1830; Shaw, 246.

126. *Letter 530*, to Paolina Leopardi, Florence, 7 July 1827; Shaw, 199. But see also *Letter 736*.

127. *Letters 543, 576, 676*.

128. *Letters 665, 676, 677, 690*.

129. *Letters 543, 576, 676*. Concerning the improper character of some scholarly comparisons and/or oppositions between Leopardi and Manzoni (for example those that appear in the polemic between Salinari and Sanguineti), see the balanced intervention of U. Carpi, *Il poeta e la politica*, op. cit., pp. 226–27 and 249. In any case, to complete what, beyond the diatribe, seems to me to stand out in these pages, see G. Bollati, op. cit., p. xi: "It is a spectacle not without grandeur, men endeavoring to create a new language, the most gifted among them having a clear consciousness that whatever linguistic proposal (and related literary model) ends up prevailing will define the nation. The ancient question of language reemerges from the academic underground, and any intervention into it or any activity that involves its sphere is exposed to an immediate verification of the general scope of the contents involved."

130. *Letter 700*, Recanati, 21 March 1820; Shaw, 241.

131. *Letter 722*, to Paolina Leopardi, from Florence, 28 August 1830.

132. *Letter 745*, to the Provisional Governing Committee, from Florence, 29 March 1831; Shaw, pp. 247–48.

133. *Letter 749*, to Monaldo Leopardi, from Florence, 19 May 1831.

134. *Letter 782*, to Fanny Tozzetti, Rome, 5 December 1831; Shaw, 252.

135. *Letter 788*, to Luigi De Sinner, from Rome, 24 December 1831; Shaw, 255.

136. *Letter 904* to Monaldo Leopardi, from Naples, 27 November 1834.

137. *Letter 905* to Monaldo Leopardi, from Naples, 3 February 1835; Shaw, 278.

138. *Letter 898* to Luigi De Sinner, from Naples, 20 March 1834; Shaw, 275.

139. See note 122 of this chapter in which we emphasize the formation of a centrist line at the end of the 1820s and the complicated situation that it confronts at the start of the 1830s when it is caught in the crossfire between Mazzini's insurrection and the state's repression. During those years, the moderate line, the Catholic-liberal compromise, is winning. De Sanctis insists heavily on this aspect, as a result of his own experience in those years, in his *Manzoni*. On this question see also L. Salvatorelli, *Il pensiero politico italiano*, op. cit., and the polemical commentaries of C. Luporini (*Leopardi progressif*, op. cit.). Leopardi totally rejects the centrist line, not only from the philosophical viewpoint (even though that aspect is strengthened during this phase; see L. Derla, "La teoria del piacere

nella formazione del pensiero di Leopardi," op. cit.), but also from an expressly political point of view.

Leopardi's position in relation to Gioberti is more ambiguous but also more open. Nevertheless, B. Biral (*La posizione storica di Giacomo Leopardi*, op. cit.) properly draws attention to Leopardi's implicit polemic against Gioberti's *Primato*, especially when he asserts there that "any plan for Italian revival that is not based on the cornerstone of Catholicism is nothing." Concerning Leopardi's judgments of Gioberti, see passim. He also notes the frequent—if not constant—irritations caused by the judgments and reactions of the very diverse people who visit Leopardi at the end of his life (see the judgments of Gioberti and Pisacane in B. Biral, *La posizione storica di Giacomo Leopardi*, op. cit., p. 115: the first denounces in Leopardi the curse of philosophy and science, the "principal enemies of humankind"; the second sees in Leopardi a "generous writer, but without depth, for whom the cause of isolation and egotism is not the evils that torment mankind, but the faculty that allows them to be discerned").

As for De Sanctis, he admits that he did not manage to digest the *Paralipomeni*. All this demonstrates the extent of the detachment that separates Leopardi from the centrist ideology that was triumphing then not only in Italy but at the European level (of course with great differences determined by either the absence or on the contrary the different behavior of the aggressive Catholic currents). All this was largely brought to light by F. Meinecke (*Cosmopolitanism and the National State*, trans. Robert B. Kimber [Princeton: Princeton University Press, 1970]). Yet Leopardi not only grasps the depth and extent of the problem, he also opposes it at the level demanded by the problem itself.

Leopardi is the only Italian thinker of the nineteenth century whose thought attains the heights of the German and Parisian *Vormärz*: "In truth, the aristocratic Leopardi was not a liberal but a pure democrat, and he remained faithful to the principles of revolutionary democracy, even the most advanced. One finds in him no hint of reconciliation with the theory of the moderates or the positions of the upper bourgeoisie that were being consolidated then in the most advanced European countries" (see Luporini, *Leopardi progressif*, op. cit., p. 88).

One final remark: in rereading the pages that Luporini dedicates to these problems, I am struck, so to speak, by a feeling of unreality provoked not by Luporini's words but by the fact that today, in an era of generalized penitence, I know very few people disposed to repeat them without blushing. Clearly my book is addressed to the impenitent.

140. *Letters 911* and *924*, to Luigi De Sinner, Naples, 3 October 1835 and 22 December 1836.

141. *Epigramma, TO I*, p. 326. Composed in Naples in August 1836. Leopardi is described in an article by Tommaseo, which appeared in Paris (in *L'Italiano*),

as a poet "in elegant despair, in prolix pain, learnedly bored with the wretchedness of life." *Epigramma* is Leopardi's response.

142. *Potenze intellettuali: Niccolò Tommaseo, TO I*, pp. 994–95. Composed in Naples, perhaps in August 1836. It is a fierce attack on Tommaseo, carried along by a polemic exacerbated by a series of unresolved encounters and clashes that now reemerge at the level of reciprocal vulgarity.

143. *Il Gesuita Moderno*, vol. 3 (Losanna: Bonamici, 1846–1847), p. 484.

144. Concerning Monaldo Leopardi's *Dialoghetti*, see *TO I*, p. 1457; F. Zarella, *Monaldo Leopardi giornalista* (Rome: Opere Nuove, 1967); M. Leopardi, *Autobiografia e dialoghetti*, ed. G. Mariani (Bologna: Capelli, 1972). Regarding the reception of the *Dialoghetti* and the misunderstanding they would inspire, see *Letters 795, 802*, and *810*, as well as those cited next.

145. *Letter 797*, to Paolina Leopardi, Rome, 14 Feburary 1832.

146. *Letter 813*, to Giuseppe Melchiori, Florence, 15 May 1832; Shaw, 261–62. See the other denials in *Letters 812, 816*, and *817*, to Vieusseux, De Sinner, and Cesare Galvani, respectively.

147. *Letter 818*, to Monaldo Leopardi, Florence, 28 May 1832; Shaw, 263–64.

148. *Letter 930*, to Fernando Maestri, Naples, 15 May 1837.

149. *Letter 816*, to Luigi De Sinner, Florence, 24 May 1832; Shaw, 262. The relationship between political contingency and metaphysical discourse appears here in an obvious way. Here we will try to describe Leopardi's political horizon. Never, even when it is fully defined, does it attain a proper autonomy; never is it isolated from the metaphysical context that continually nourishes it. Whether political polemic is transformed into irony and makes use of the typology of the grotesque (regarding the interchange between play and ethics, see the fundamental pages of J. Huizinga, *Homo Ludens* [Boston: Beacon Press, 1955]) or politics appears as the dramatization of all the conditions of ethical definition (see C. Schmitt, *Hamlet or Hecuba: The Intrusion of the Time into the Play*, trans. David Pan and Jennifer R. Rust [Candor, NY: Telos Press, 2009]), politics is revealed to be a section of the ontological continuum.

150. *TO I*, pp. 324–26. Probably composed after September 1835. Concerning the persons at whom the polemic is directed (identifications, general characteristics of the political and polemical climate), see *TO I*, p. 1443. U. Carpi's particularly unfocused interpretation (*Il poeta e la politica*, op. cit., pp. 191–92) is as follows:

> regarding the *Nouvi Credenti*, I note once and for all that these polemical verses, which are brilliant and fastidiously personalized, have nothing to do with the *Palinode* and its wide political inspiration. . . . The *Nuovi Credenti* constitutes a moment, so to speak, of local and occasional usage of an ideo- logical perspective that is articulated differently elsewhere: to exploit the

contemptuous title so as to apply Leopardi's judgment to liberal intellectuality
in its entirety appears to me worse than forced, erroneous.

See also Luporini's analysis, which on the contrary seems to be perfectly
acceptable (*Leopardi progressif*, op. cit., pp. 85–86). On the general Neapolitan
climate of this period, see G. Oldrini, *La cultura filosofica napoletana dell'Ottocento*
(Bari: Laterza, 1973). See also, for other aspects of the question, N. Jonard, *Giacomo
Leopardi: Essai de biographie intellectuelle*, op. cit., pp. 353ff. and 367ff. Concerning
all the canti and the political compositions of this period, see the extremely rigorous
historical compilation and the balanced judgment provided by F. Brioschi, "Politica e
metafisica nel Leopardi," op. cit., pp. 174ff. K. Maurer's judgment (*Leopardi's Canti
und die Auflösung Genera*, op. cit., passim) is excessive in this case: the political
canti are considered as products of the poet's wish to extend the lyrical scale and
rhythmic toolbox by adding to them different rhyme schemes and satiric, grotesque,
and didactic arguments.

151. *Canto XXXII*, Peruzzi, pp. 525–34. Composed in Naples between spring
and September 1835. Concerning the reception of the poetry and Capponi's reaction,
as well as a bibliography, see *TO I*, pp. 1428–29. See U. Carpi (*Il poeta e la politica*,
op. cit., pp. 190ff.), who laments the lack of specific studies of the *Palinode* and
points out, in the accompanying critical commentary, the most useful texts for
understanding this work. L. Cellerino's analysis (*Tecniche ed etica del paradosso*,
op. cit., pp. 56–57) is excellent.

152. Nichols, p.130.

153. Ibid.

154. Ibid.

155. Ibid., p. 131.

156. Ibid., p. 134.

157. The time has come to review the Leopardi-Rousseau relationship. For a
general approach to the question, see S. Battaglia, *L'ideologia letteraria di Leopardi*
(Naples: Liguori, 1968). Up to this point we have noted and criticized the line that
leads from sensualism to transcendentalism, a line we consider fundamental to
Rousseau's thought and the reception it found in German critical philosophy: see
notes 36 and 65 to chapter 2. We have quite naturally refuted the possibility of
translating this line into Leopardi's thought, which precisely adopts an opposed
position. But it seems worthwhile to follow up and analyze the Rousseau-Leopardi
relationship from another viewpoint—that is to say, in relation to the presumed
naturalism common to both authors.

Given that for both thinkers, the state of nature is a pure hypothesis,
a logical fiction, the discourse must immediately come to bear on the concept of
second nature. Second nature is once again, for both, the seat of despotism and the
sign of alienation; but whereas in Leopardi second nature is criticized in itself, in

Rousseau, it is paradoxically criticized in the name of first nature (thereby entailing an insoluble contradiction, if one keeps in mind that the state of nature is a pure hypothesis). Luporini (*Leopardi progressif,* op. cit., pp. 38ff. and 45ff.), reflecting on all these aspects, and notably on the contradiction between Rousseau's *Discourse on the Origins of Inequality* and *The Social Contract*—that is to say, the contradiction between a naturalistic hypothesis that is merely a logical fiction and a concept of nature that brings about positive effects—makes some interesting though general remarks.

Thus it is necessary to specify, in other words to make explicit the fact that if, from a strictly philosophical standpoint (sensualism, transcendentalism), Leopardi in no way approximates the development of Rousseau's thought, this is even more true concerning the concept of nature: the nature-civilization opposition, in Rousseau's terms, can at most be maintained during the very first period of Leopardi's thought, and any concept of a redemption of nature is always absent. For Leopardi, Rousseau thus remains a modern philosopher, an author of rationalism and its destructive dialectic. Leopardi's undoubted sympathy for Rousseau the sentimental philosopher, which criticism has sometimes noted, does not reconcile the two over basic questions. And the pages (like those in the *Zibaldone* dated 8 July 1820) containing the Rousseauist polemic against the geometric spirit and its excesses, pages written in the period of the great readings of Rousseau, wax ironic nevertheless on the Prometheanism of modern philosophy, on its definitive impotence, and against the legislators of Enlightenment—these legislators were incapable of acting, of persisting in practical intents and thus unfit to promote the true revolution:

> even if philosophy paved the way for the French Revolution, it did not bring it about, because philosophy, especially modern philosophy, is incapable by itself of achieving anything. And even if philosophy itself had the power to start a revolution, it could not sustain it. It is really moving to see how the French republican legislators thought that they could keep up the revolution, decide its length, and influence its progress, nature, and scope by reducing everything to pure reason, and expected for the first time *ab orbe condito* [since the earth was formed] to geometricize every aspect of life. Something not only deplorable had it succeeded, and therefore foolish to desire, but something that could not succeed even in this mathematical age because it is directly contrary to the nature of man and the world. (*Zibaldone,* 160, *TO II,* p. 78; Caesar/D'Intino, p. 126)

Leopardi includes Rousseau in the defeat of the revolution.

In conclusion, Leopardi's thought in no way intersects with Rousseau's. Every possibility of reconciliation is merely occasional. The philosophical webs of these two thinkers are divergent—and even if this were not the case, the differences in their historical positions would make it so. For an analysis of the bibliography concerning the Rousseau-Leopardi relationship, see L. Cellerino (*Tecniche ed etica del paradosso*, op. cit., pp. 134–35), whose conclusions are fundamentally different from mine. Nevertheless this work (pp. 149ff.) proposes a good identification of Rousseauist sources for Leopardi's concepts of virtue, love of country, and the heroic; but the human *potentia* at the base of this virtue is not developed by Rousseau in a linear way, just as it is not received and worked up by Leopardi in a linear way. It is quite the contrary: in both, between the genesis and the development of this virtuality different signs and dimensions, forms and contents will be interpolated, so that, paradoxically, instead of demonstrating a conceptual homology and a homogeneity of development, this genetic coincidence emphasizes an effective theoretical separation. Lastly: the collection published by Seuil, *La pensée de Jean-Jacques Rousseau* (Paris, 1984) brings together contributions by the greatest interpreters of Rousseau, among them E. Weil, E. Cassirer, L. Strauss, C. Eisenmann, R. Dérathé, P. Bénichou, and V. Goldschmidt.

158. Leo Strauss, *Thoughts on Machiavelli* (Glenco, IL: The Free Press, 1958): "If it is true that every complete society necessarily recognizes something about which it is absolutely forbidden to laugh, we may say that the determination to transgress that prohibition *sanza alcuno rispetto*, is of the essence of Machiavelli's intention" (p. 40). And of Leopardi's.

159. *Zibaldone*, 4439, *TO II*, p. 1204, Caesar/D'Intino, p. 2005.

160. On utopia as dialectical form, see Ernst Bloch, *The Principle of Hope*, trans. Neville Plaice, Stephen Plaice, and Paul Knight (Cambridge: MIT Press, 1986), and *Subjekt-Objekt: Erläuterungen zu Hegels Philosophie*. On the hermeneutic use of the dialectic, see B. Baczko, *Utopian Lights*, op. cit.

161. See in this regard G. Lonardi, *Classicismo e utopia nella lirica leopardiana*, op. cit., and above all A. Dolfi, *Leopardi tra negazione e utopia. Indagini e ricerche sui Canti* (Padua: Liviana, 1973).

162. *TO I*, pp. 247–92. The *Paralipomeni* were begun around 1831, taken up again in Naples, and took on their definitive (but incomplete) form in the final days of the poet's life. For the dating, see L. Cellerino, *Tecniche ed etica del paradosso*, op. cit., p. 79. For information, remarks, and polemics involving this text, etc., see *TO I*, pp. 1483ff. L. Cellerino's work, which was her last and which is important in several ways, also contains a complete bibliography (p. 41). For contemporary readings, see W. Binni's chapter (in *La nuova poetica leopardiana* [Florence: Sansoni, 1947]); M. Cappucci, "I *Paralipomeni* e la poesia leopardiana," and "La poesia dei *Paralipomeni* leopardiani," in *Convivium* no. 6 (1954), pp. 581ff. and no. 7 (1954), pp. 695ff.; G. Savarese, *Saggio sui "Paralipomeni" di Giacomo Leopardi* (Florence: La Nuova Italia, 1967); A. Brilli, *Satira e mito nei "Paralipomeni" di Leopardi* (Urbino: Argalia, 1968); U. Carpi, *Il poeta e la politica*, op. cit., pp. 193ff.; F. Brioschi, "Politica e metafisica nel Leopardi," op. cit., pp. 199ff.

163. See *TO I*, in 1815, pp. 389ff.; in 1820, pp. 394ff.; in 1826, pp. 400ff.: three draft translations from the original Greek.

164. *TO I*, pp. 382ff.

165. See note 139 to this chapter and the works and notes to which it refers. See also, for the period 1815–1821, G. Candeloro, *Storia dell'Italia moderna*, op. cit., particularly concerning the Mezzogiorno, pp. 64ff. and 75ff. Lastly, specifically regarding Naples in that era, see A. Lepre, *La rivoluzione napolatana dal 1820 al 1821* (Rome: Editori Riuniti, 1967); G. Cingari, *Mezzogiorno e Risorgimento. La restaurazione a Napoli dal 1821 al 1830* (Bari: Laterza, 1970).

166. On the unity of the text, see L. Cellerino, "Romantic Narrative Poetry," in *Tecniche ed etica del paradosso*, op. cit., chap. I, pp. 11–39. Concerning the extraordinary reception of this text starting in the years that followed the Second World War, see the bibliography mentioned above. Regarding the layering of the text, this is undoubtedly relatively difficult to determine; as L. Cellerino indicates (pp. 54–55), "the text presents itself to us as a posthumous work marked by the disastrous loss of all documentary material related to its elaboration and to the historical, biographical and literary circumstances that inspired its conception."

167. The reference is surely to the Neapolitan revolution of 1820 and the occupation of the kingdom by the Austrians (see note 165 to this chapter). However, Leopardi's references are in no way specific but refer to a complex of experiences and to the baffling developments and events of those years of war and revolution. For example, to what precisely does the theme of flight, so central in the *Paralipomeni*, refer? The flight from Tolentino in 1815, the one from Antrodoco in 1821, or that of the Belgians in 1831?

168. Caserta, pp. 47–48.

169. Ibid., p. 69.

170. Ibid., pp. 71–72.

171. See *Letter 806* to Carlo Bunsen (from Rome, 16 March 1832); in this letter Leopardi requests the Prussian consul in Rome to intervene with his Neapolitan counterpart on behalf of Ranieri, a political refugee who is about to reenter Naples, his homeland. The letter is certainly very diplomatic and intends to arouse no political suspicion, which goes without saying when one requests a favor of this sort. But on the basis of this to present Leopardi as a reactionary, or if not a reactionary an apolitical, indifferent person, a *flâneur*, that is too much. In this regard, it is always necessary to recall that in the immediately preceding years, in Florence, although admitted into the circle of the *Antologia*, Leopardi seemed to promote, in any case joked about, the project of a "useless review," a sort of anti-*Antologia*, that he indeed wanted to call *Le flâneur* (see U. Carpi, *Il poeta e la politica*, op. cit., pp. 154ff.). However, it does not seem to me that this element can/must give rise to an indifferent or apolitical reading of Leopardi's thought for at least two reasons: the first is the fact that Leopardi's political attitude cannot be considered

more important, from the viewpoint of his conception of the world and of action, than the other aspects of his philosophical-poetic activity, so that, paradoxically, even if Leopardi adopted an explicitly reactionary position (which he did not), this would not be enough to justify qualifying him as a reactionary, but it would on the contrary appear contradictory to the rest of his thought; in the second place, the concept of the *flâneur* is not necessarily a concept of indifference and reaction; it can be, conversely, that of difference and resistance, or represent a superior critical point of view, as the unforgettable pages of Walter Benjamin have taught us ("The *Flâneur*," in *Charles Baudelaire: A Lyric Poet in the Era of High Capitalism*, trans. Harry Zohn [New York: Verso, 1973], pp. 35–66).

172. *Letter 915*, to Monaldo Leopardi, Naples, 19 February 1836; Shaw, 282. See also *Letter 906*.

173. Caserta, p. 59.

174. Ibid., p. 66.

175. Ibid., pp. 76–79.

176. Ibid., pp. 75–76.

177. Ibid., pp. 81–83.

178. Ibid., pp. 71–73.

179. Ibid., pp. 83–84.

180. Ibid., pp. 36–37.

181. Ibid., pp. 53–54.

182. Ibid., pp. 71–73.

183. Ibid., p. 74.

184. Ibid., pp. 75, 76–78.

185. Ibid., p. 79.

186. Ibid., pp. 79–80.

187. Ibid., pp. 55–58.

188. Ibid., p. 80.

189. The definition of a temporal caesura is at this point a critical common-place; see the comments by Savarese, Brilli, and Cellerino.

190. Caserta, pp. 38–39.

191. Ibid., p. 85.

192. G. Savarese and L. Cellerino have rightly emphasized Dedalus's Leopardian character. See also G. Boffito, "Il *Dedalo modern* nei *Paralipomeni* del Leopardi," in *Giornale storico della letteratura italiana* no. 112 (1938). The reference here is to a hypothesis of Rousseau's, which is taken up by Brilli and Cellerino.

193. Caserta, pp. 92–93. For the correspondences between the *Paralipomeni*, the canti, and other works by Leopardi, see L. Cellerino, *Tecniche ed etica del paradosso*, op. cit., p. 42.

194. Ibid., p .95.

195. Ibid., pp. 97–99.

196. Ibid., pp. 101–4.

197. Ibid., p. 104.

198. Ibid.

199. Ibid., p.105–9.

200. In this regard, Walter Binni calls Leopardi the "evil-thinker," an epithet that perfectly defines the spirit that underpins and orients the composition of this work. It is the choice of critical marginality, or rather of an ideal alternative that Leopardi adopts in the face of an optimistic, spiritualist, and progressivist century. His objection to the political universe is coherent: this objection is addressed not only to all the political variants of reaction but also and above all to the liberal program and to the constitutional monarchy—in other words, to the program of the *Risorgimento*. For a political reading of the *Paralipomeni*, see L. Cellerino, *Tecniche ed etica del paradosso*, op. cit., pp. 87–100. Pages 121–22 of this study propose a conclusive interpretation of Leopardi's thought such as it appears in this work and that clearly shows how "the vindication of Enlightenment thought here in no way sends pessimism into crisis." On the contrary, it illuminates "a coherent thought that is self-sufficient, assuming responsibility for its own negative content: the denunciation of the evils that the historical dialectic is powerless [*impotente*] to confront." I completely share this viewpoint, which bears witness to the importance and singularity of the approach of L. Cellerino, whose book offers unquestionably the best, most lucid analysis of the *Paralipomeni* (aside from the reservations we expressed in note 157 of this chapter concerning the exaggerated presence and disproportionate influence that she grants to Rousseau).

201. R. Tessari (*Il Risorgimento e la crisi di metà secolo*, op. cit.) describes Leopardi's years after 1830 as a period in which the lyric imagination no longer spans the "morals of his country" but only the "laughter of one who knows that he leads a life that resembles death" and hears in the *Paralipomeni* and above all in the *Palinode* "a ferocious and reactionary cry." This interpretation, the imprecision of which we have already emphasized, is nevertheless indicative of the reemergence, in reaction to the progressivist interpretation, of a subtle and malicious interpretive operation in the context of the crisis of communist thought. The progressives have often protested against those who polemicize against their reading, insinuating that this polemic supplied grist for the mill of the idyllic interpretation and the Crocean tradition. These slightly Zdanovian replies do not seem to have attained their objective: the more so if one keeps in mind the fact that readings like Tessari's bear witness to an undeniable respect for the letter of Leopardi's texts and that they add nothing more to the discrediting of the progressivist interpretation than the denunciation of its exaggerations. That said, the problem is not solved, for this progressivist exaggeration was not merely able to propose themes adequate to the development of the interpretation of Leopardi's thought but also to establish analogies and grasp correspondences with what was then happening at the European level.

202. See above the pages we dedicated to the *Discourse* of 1824 that bring to light, always in opposition to the position adopted by Tessari and others, how Leopardi's metaphysics of morals comes to completion here.

203. See Walter Binni, introduction to *TO I*, pp. 111–14.

Chapter Five: A Lyric Machiavelli

1. Concerning Baumgarten's aesthetics and its consequences for the conception of the beautiful, see the always-valuable work of W. Windelband, *History of Philosophy*, op. cit., pp. 484ff.; A. Prete (*Il pensiero poetante*, op. cit., passim. But pp. 79–82 specifically analyze Baumgarten's aesthetic position, its intellectualist direction, the homologies that it has with the position of the Ideologues) adds: "If there is, in Leopardi's writing, the tracing of an aesthetic, it does not go in the direction indicated by Baumgarten and then taken up by the Hegelian system, but follows the paths of the Enlightenment question regarding the place of beauty in the interpretation of nature. A variant of the other question: what is there of the imagination in this process of interpretation?"

It is indisputable that Hegel's aesthetic moves along the line of Baumgarten's, according to which the beautiful is the younger son of the true and aesthetics is the younger daughter of logic. More on this later. What is particularly dangerous in the development of Romantic aesthetics is the fact that the Hegelian hegemony denies, or brings to order after having authorized some escapades, every aesthetic alternative. One witnesses here a highly interesting phenomenon: logicism is arrogantly imposed once again where at least two great alternatives had been proposed, one by Schelling, who conceives the true as a function of the beautiful, and the other by Schlegel, who makes irony, detachment, catastrophe the central elements of aesthetic intuition. For the fundamental aspects of this debate, see P. Szondi, *Poésie et poétique de l'idéalisme allemand*, op. cit. As we have often repeated, this philosophical closure, in logical terms, of the aesthetic debate is surmounted in the course of the nineteenth century by direct poetic experience, and solely by it. Thus, on the terrain of universal history, through Rimbaud's poetic experiments and those of others, and through the great poetry of the figurative arts of the eighteenth and nineteenth centuries, that equal union of the beautiful and the true that Romanticism had broken apart is recomposed. Leopardi is situated in this combination of elements: he indicates, in anticipatory fashion, its resolving tendency. In this regard, see note 104 to chapter 4 and the references it provides.

2. Paradoxically (and to complete what was said in note 1 of this chapter), it seems to me that the rediscovery, against the arrogant domination of idealist logic, of the practical matrix of the true, of poetry as experimentation with the dimensions of life, that imposes itself between the end of the nineteenth century and the beginning

of the twentieth—that this rediscovery and reevaluation of the practical element are accomplished by sacrificing the properly ethical dimensions, that is to say through the expulsion of the dimension of love from the aesthetic debate—which means the expulsion of the collective dimension. With the exception of a few great authors, the aesthetic of socialist realism that is opposed to this new mystifying position interprets the demand to reintroduce the dimensions of love into the aesthetic debate only in a caricatural way. The great exceptions, in the definition of an aesthetic of love, must be sought above all in the schools that attempted to pair expressionism with communism in Germany (Brecht) and, in France, to pair surrealism with communism (Breton). Leopardi constitutes a privileged object of study for whoever has followed this debate. On the other hand, concerning the way that the philosophy and aesthetics as well as the common life of the bourgeoisie have gradually taken control of love in order finally to eliminate it from the set of social passions, see N. Luhmann's forceful observations in *Love As Passion*, op. cit., passim.

3. Here once again we find ourselves faced with an innovative element of Leopardi's aesthetic (after having emphasized his constructive conception of poetics, the collective and amorous dimension that he confers upon it). It can be formulated as follows: critique is an integral part, an internal element of poetics. Rather than insisting on its Romantic origin (in the present case, by referring to Schleiermacher's thought, which this hermeneutic conception includes: we have already amply discussed this when we confronted the problem of hermeneutics in Leopardi), we prefer to emphasize the extreme modernity, or better, the contemporaneity of this formulation. This reflection was inspired by Harold Bloom's book *The Anxiety of Influence: A Theory of Poetry* (op. cit.), which is an attempt to construct a history of poetry in the form of a continuous intersection between influence/interpretation and poetic production. In these modern theories, of which Bloom is a distinguished representative, the moment of critical rupture is fundamental: influence is indeed anxiety, and its content is that of the experience of poetic, ethical, and cognitive values. To say that critique is constructive is thus to identify a fundamental element of poetic making: in effect, only critique brings to poetry the complexity of human making—and the antagonisms of the world. Bloom refers his conception of influence to Kierkegaard's experiment. To my mind, in a well-constructed hermeneutic (and the interpretive traditions of modern philosophy such as they have been synthesized, for example, in Spinoza's *Theological-Political Treatise* are not extraneous to this formation), the reference to Leopardi could be just as if not more foundational.

4. *Canto XXX*, Peruzzi, pp. 519–22. Composed between April 1831 and September 1835. Many commentators, I think correctly, restrict the period of composition to 1834 to 1835, in which case it would have been written in Naples. See in this regard A. Dolfi, *Leopardi tra negazione ed utopia. Indagini e ricerche sui Canti*, op. cit., pp. 81ff.

5. Nichols, p.123.

6. Ibid.

7. Ibid., pp. 123–24.

8. Ibid.

9. Ibid., p. 124.

10. Ibid., p. 125.

11. Ibid.

12. Ibid.

13. *Canto XXXI*, Peruzzi, pp. 523–24. This canto is contemporaneous with the preceding canto (see note 4 of this chapter).

14. Nichols, p. 128.

15. Ibid., pp. 128–29.

16. Ibid., p. 129.

17. Ibid.

18. It is clear that here Leopardi understands the rational true as Hegel understands it, as the relationship between the real and the rational and the reduction of one to the other, of the rational to effectiveness. The dialectic thus becomes a "realist" acceptance of the negative—with all the capers one wants and the function of *Aufhebung* amply permits. See in this regard T.W. Adorno, *Negative Dialectics*, trans. E.B. Ashton (New York: Continuum, 1973). The dialectic becomes the realist acceptance of death, or rather its comprehension. This is what, on the extreme margin of a philosophy that is a meditation on death, Leopardi refuses to concede. He refuses it in an apodictic, absolute manner. That we must die is a fact, or rather a destiny, which one must oppose.

From this viewpoint, Leopardi implicitly rejects not only the Hegelian dialectic—though he did not know it—as a possible solution to the problem that he had experienced, but also the dialectical positions, above all on the terrain of morality, that he knew from Greek thought. I mean in particular the Stoic-Cynic positions on which Leopardi worked extensively (see in particularly his translation of Epictetus's *Manual*, which occupied him from November to December 1825—*TO I*, pp. 492–502). From this viewpoint, the conclusions that S. Timpanaro reaches in his essay *Leopardi e i filosofi antich* (op. cit.) do not seem acceptable. After having noted that the sensualist thinkers of the Enlightenment are no doubt the fundamental philosophical references for Leopardi, Timpanaro asserts that at least two points of contact with Greek thought are essential to the development of his philosophy: "the discovery of ancient pessimism that throws the myth of a happy antiquity, all action, illusion and poetry, into crisis; and the reading of the Hellenistic philosophers, who offered him the model of a resigned wisdom to which he was particularly sensitive between 1823 and 1827, but without ever adhering to it completely."

W. Binni is situated on the same line. It only remains for us to repeat that never in Leopardi does the moral tension retreat to the point of resignation; that this necessary consequence of the Hellenistic dialectic is understood and rejected by Leopardi with great clarity; that the deepening of the analyses and the adherence to the conception of death as destiny never obliterate, in Leopardi, the parallel conception of a conscious and heroic rebellion of the subject against destiny. Brutus, that insignia of Leopardi's, is in no case and at no moment cynical, stoic, or resigned. On the other hand, it is well known that Leopardi's knowledge [*conoscenza*] of the Stoics does not come solely from the reading of Greek texts, but also along the very common side road of contact with the neo-Stoic tradition that dominates European moral thought since the Renaissance. There is no point here in referring to the very abundant work that deals with this question, from Zanta to Oestreich. But in that tradition too, the continuity of pessimistic motives is often accompanied by the refusal of any consolatory or resigned dialectic of death. See what Luporini (*Leopardi progressif,* op. cit., p. 82) writes on this subject: Stoic morality (such as De Sanctis, for example, perceives in Leopardi) "must not be considered as Leopardi's authentic morality, his private morality in contrast with his rhetorical public or even journalistic morality, but rather as an auxiliary morality of Leopardi the man, whom physical weakness and social isolation constrained to attitudes of pure resistance, as, last but certainly not least, did his infinite modesty regarding his own person."

19. Let us return to Leopardi's conception of love. We have already insisted on the extreme modernity of this concept in Leopardi: love is the dynamic of the collective. From this viewpoint, it is clear that this conception is completely materialist and atheist. Love is a power [*potenza*] of nature, a function regained by the construction humankind makes of the world through the collective links of poetry, true illusion. That said, it is indisputable that Christian echoes are present in Leopardi, the philosopher of love. An assertion like Augustine's that "time never stands still, nor does it idly pass without effect upon our feelings or fail to work its wonders on the mind" (*Confessions,* trans. R.S. Pine-Coffin [New York: Penguin, 1961], book IV, chap. 8, p. 78), for example, is capable of clarifying the ontological importance of love during this phase of Leopardi's thought. But his ontology is materialism. Thus it seems to me that the Christian influence on Leopardi's thought (which is difficult to deny, given the environment of his education) is translated, reelaborated and finally taken up again in a supremely atheist and materialist conception of love, which for me sometimes recalls the concept, which is so materialist, so capillary and constructive of the social, that Michel Foucault aims to describe as belonging to the interpretation of the classical philosophers (see *The Use of Pleasure,* trans. Robert Hurley [New York: Vintage, 1984]). Concerning Leopardi as a Christian poet or, in any case, a religious one, see among others G. Getto, *Saggi leopardiani* (Florence: Vallecchi, 1966).

20. Another aspect of the conception of love that emerges so potently in the later Leopardi bears witness to the importance of the Christian influence (which in our view is essentially Augustinian): love considered as experience that leads directly to a fundamental alternative. In Augustine, such is the discovery, through

the analysis of time, of the theological dimension of love. In Leopardi, such is the tension, through the analysis of time and love, toward the foundation of a new horizon, a new vital proposition. Whereas in Christianity and in Augustine, the movement of alterity is projected onto the foundation of transcendence, in Leopardi that movement takes a wholly worldly, intra-mundane direction. Leopardi follows Augustine's intuition and tradition when they lead the conception of time and love to an underlying ontological foundation, and he rejects them when that ontological conception is translated into a theological perspective.

21. De Sanctis, *Schopenhauer e Leopardi*, op. cit., pp. 115–60. B. Croce, *De Sanctis e Schopenhauer*, op. cit. Schopenhauer is known to have been familiar with Leopardi's poetry and De Sanctis's essay: see G. De Lorenzo, *Leopardi e Schopenhauer* (Naples: Ricciardi, 1923).

22. Concerning Schopenhauer, G. Simmel's contribution (*Schopenhauer and Nietzsche*, trans. Helmut Lioskandl, Deena Weinstein, and Michael Weinstein [Urbana: University of Illinois Press, 1991]) remains fundamental, as is the interpretation proposed by G. Lukács (*The Destruction of Reason*, op. cit.), which goes in the same direction as our own interpretion. See also I. Knox, *The Aesthetic Theories of Kant, Hegel and Schopenhauer* (New York: Humanities Press, 1958).

23. K. Löwith's reading of this period, this tendency, and the fundamental authors who belong to it (Feuerbach, Ruge, Marx, Stirner, Bauer, etc.) remains essential: see *From Hegel to Nietzsche* (op. cit.). The original subtitle of his work is "The Revolutionary Break in Nineteenth-Century Thought." See also *Die Hegelsche Linke* (Stuttgart: Frommann, 1962), which Löwith edited.

24. See once again the work of K. Löwith, to which must be added the fundamental work of H. Höffding, *Sören Kierkegaard als Philosoph* (Stuttgart: Frommann, 1896) as well as T.W. Adorno's book *Kierkegaard: Construction of the Aesthetic*, trans. Robert Hullot-Kentor (Minneapolis: University of Minnesota Press, 1989). Furthermore see the *Studi kierkegaardiani*, ed. C. Fabro, published in 1957 in Brescia, which contains numerous essays that were useful to us.

25. Luporini's initial sensitivity to Leopardi's thought doubtless derives from his existentialist engagement during the years preceding the Second World War; see his *Filosofi vecchi e nuovi* (Florence: Sansoni, 1947).

26. Regarding Nietzsche as reader of Leopardi, see the note on this subject by A. Prete (*Il pensiero poetante*, op. cit., p. 65). Furthermore, see the essays of G. Gabetti in the issues of *Il Convegno* for 1923 and 1924; S. Solmi, *Studi e nuovi studi leopardiani*, op. cit., pp. 158ff. Concerning Nietzsche's judgment on the Hegelian left, I refer to my endnotes on the historical conceptions of Nietzsche and Burkhardt. In general, A. Prete's contribution on this Nietzschean juncture in the interpretation of Leopardi is particularly apt.

27. The index of the *Zibaldone* testifies to Leopardi's intense and continual reference to the reform of philosophy and language (the one being intimately linked

to the other) produced by Galileo. Regarding Galileo, see S. Gensini, *Linguistica leopardiana*, op. cit., p. 202. See also above, passim.

28. See in this regard the articles by M. Foucault and J. Habermas on Kant's text "What is Enlightenment?" cited in note 121 to chapter 3.

29. The interchangeability of terms such as "constitutive phenomenology" and "transcendental aesthetic" was gradually established once transcendental phenomenology was interpreted in dynamic terms, thus in terms not of a descriptive eidetic but of intentionality, whereas Kant's aesthetic was always oriented more toward the problems and functions of transcendental schematism. To propose an adequate bibliography on these processes would mean summing up all of twentieth-century philosophical thought and history—at least that which is unrelated to analytic tendencies. Here it is enough to keep in mind M. Heidegger's fundamental work, *Phenomenological Interpretation of Kant's Critique of Pure Reason*, op. cit. Concerning Husserl, see G. Brand, *Welt, Ich und Zeit* (The Hague: Nijhoff, 1955), and concerning Kant, see H. De Vleeschauwer, *La deduction transcendentale dans l'oeuvre de Kant* (Paris: Leroux, 1936). See also note 9 to chapter 2 and passim. On the other hand, by reason of the attention it pays to the above-mentioned interchangeability, not so much from the viewpoint of the dynamic of processes as from that of the corporeality of their intersection (the aesthetic as theory of sensibility), the work of Michel Foucault must be taken into account, above all the early Foucault who translates Kant's *Anthropology* and studies the Ideologues precisely insofar as they reconstruct sensualism into a constitutive philosophy of the transcendental horizon. On certain aspects of this problematic, see my "Sul metodo della critica della politica," in *Macchina tempo: Rompicapi, costituzione, liberazione*, op. cit., pp. 70ff., and "À propos de *Logos et théorie des catastrophes* de Jean Petitot," in *Bablyone* 4 (1985), pp. 219–27.

30. See Walter Benjamin, *Angelus Novus* (Frankfurt: Suhrkamp Verlag, 1966). Leopardi experienced in an absolutely fundamental way this anti-Platonic inversion of the principle of knowledge [*conoscenza*] and reality. His materialism essentially consists in this. This is the reason I find it hard to understand the attempt, most recently renewed by M.A. Rigoni (*Saggi sul pensiero leopardiano*, op. cit.), to relate the formally idealist moments of some of Leopardi's canti to a Platonic discipline. Rigoni refers to the canti *To His Lady, The Dominant Thought* and *Aspasia* as well as some passages in the *Paralipomeni* (like the famous "lovely virtue," V, 47–48). See above, our reading of those canti and the bibliographical references concerning them. In any case, taking up the terms of the polemic regarding a supposed Leopardian Platonism, we can state the following: nothing is further from Leopardi than the ontological fixation of a horizon of universal ideas, and nothing is further from his sensibility than a reading of the world as the apparition of an ideal ontological positivity. The only alternative that remains within this framework of interpretation would be to consider Leopardi's 'theory of ideas' in Schopenhauer's

terms—in other words, as a theory of the ideal appearance and material evanescence of metaphysical nothingness. We have already made clear the difficulties, indeed the impossibility, of such a reading. What then is the apparition of this ideal light within the wretchedness of life? How does Leopardi establish it? This light is the moment of critique, the moment of intelligence, to which the greatest critical tension applies. This aspect was clearly seen (on the basis of De Sanctis's analyses) by G. Savarese ("La canzone leopardiana 'Alla sua donna' tra consapevolezza ed illusione," in *Rassegna della litteratura italiana* 1 [1970], pp. 4ff.) and F. Bandini (introduction to the *Canti del Leopardi*, [Milan: Garzanti, 1975], pp. 159–60), who both insist on the ethical character of this appeal to the essence of poetry, to its eternal scintillation as truth; for her part, L. Cellerino, commenting on stanzas 47 and 48 of canto V of the *Paralipomeni*, brilliantly relates this position to Enlightenment materialism and reveals all the complexity of its ethical insistence (*Tecniche ed etica del paradosso*, op. cit., pp. 149, 157–58).

31. *Canto XXXIII*, Peruzzi, pp. 535–44. Composed at Torre del Greco in spring 1836. See A. Dolfi, op. cit., pp. 107ff.

32. Nichols, p. 138.

33. Ibid.

34. Ibid., pp. 138–39.

35. W. Binni, introduction to *TO I*, pp. cxv-cxvi.

36. An interesting hypothesis has been proposed in this regard—one that more or less exactly concerns this poetic and philosophical passage—according to which the very first elaboration of the conception of nature that appears in these last canti took shape in the draft of the hymn *To Ahriman* (*TO I*: 350; English version in Leopardi, *Canti*, trans. Jonathan Galassi [New York: Farrar Straus Giroux, 2010, pp. 357–59), perhaps composed during the spring of 1833 or in any case at the beginning of the 1830s. The draft was directly inspired by Voltaire's *Poem on the Lisbon Disaster* ("Are we condemned to weep by tyrant law/Of . . . barbarous Ahriman?"); and this reprise contains the ideological translation of a pessimistic concept of nature, certainly characteristic of Voltaire and of the radical currents of Enlightenment materialism. This hypothesis, first suggested by Antognoni and Fubini, was largely developed by U. Carpi (*Il poeta e il politica*, op. cit., pp. 180–213). Now according to Berti, this radically pessimistic conception of Ahriman-nature characterizes all of the mature Leopardi's thought, whether poetic or political. Some aspects of this thesis are certainly admissible: for example, when it stresses the fact that some materialist characteristics that the Enlightenment attributes to the concept of nature reappear here in all their harshness (see in this regard J. Ehrard, *L'idée de Nature en France dans la première moitié du XVIIIe siècle*, op. cit.); when it insists on the non-dialectical or perhaps even anti-dialectical nature of Leopardi's materialism that the conception of Ahriman precisely demonstrates; when it is finally constrained to recognize that the political polemics of the later

Leopardi include an implicit reference to the "other," to a different ontological foundation. But on the other hand it is clear that what escapes it completely is not so much the antagonistic content of Leopardi's later thought as the ethical, ontological, and political determinateness that it implies. In philosophical terms (and partly in response to Carpi's provocation when he maintains that in his final period Leopardi is "philosophically but not politically progressive," a thesis that he does not entirely demonstrate, giving us instead an Ahrimanesque Leopardi), we must conclude that Leopardi's materialism and consequently his idea of nature, if they are anti-dialectical, are in any case post-critical. The problem of knowledge [*conoscenza*] and that of a transformative ethics are therefore central, or rather they concern the very definition of Leopardi's thought. Furthermore, if Carpi is right when he attacks a too narrow definition of materialism such as appears for example in Timpanaro (*Classicismo e illuminismo nell'Ottocento italiano,* op. cit., pp. 182–83), he errs profoundly in not understanding the polemical, ethically overdetermined intensity, the force of Leopardi's hope despite its complete disenchantment—the disutopia of his thought. From this viewpoint, despite his wandering interpretation and the fact that he adheres to materialist parameters that are too old, oddly, Timpanaro gives us a livelier, truer framework. On all these arguments and particularly on Enlightenment pessimism, the thesis of R. Mauzi, *L'idée du Bonheur dans la literature et la pensée française au XVIIIe siècle* (Paris: A. Colin, 1960) has a lot to offer, notably chapters 3, 10, and 11 (pp. 109ff., 386ff., 432ff.), as well as an abundant bibliography.

37. *Canto XXXIV*, Peruzzi, pp. 545–59. Composed at Torre del Greco in spring 1836.

38. See A. Bufano, *Concordanze dei Canti del Leopardi* (Florence: Le Monnier, 1969); the concordances established by L. Lovera and C. Colli for the canti, the *Paralipomeni, poesie varie,* and *traduzioni poetiche,* in the volume of Leopardi's verse edited by C. Muscetta and G. Savoca (Turin, 1968), pp. 966–1570.

39. Nichols, p. 141.

40. Ibid.

41. Ibid., pp. 141–42.

42. Ibid., pp. 142–43.

43. Nichols, p. 141.

44. Ibid., pp. 141–42.

45. Ibid., p. 142. The lines *"The impressive destiny/And fated progress"* figure in the dedication of the *Inni sacri* by Terenzio Mamiani, published in 1832. On Mamiani, philosopher and politician as well as Leopardi's cousin, whose quest to combine spiritualism with experimentalism as a "natural method" led to "temperate idealism," see L. Ferri, *Essai sur l'histoire de la philosophie en Italie au XIXe siècle* (Paris, 1869), vol. 2, pp. 3–140. The annoyance that Leopardi would have felt at the temperates, idealists as well as materialists, is evident to whoever has followed us this far. Thus it is very difficult to accept U. Carpi's evaluations (*Il poeta e la*

politica, op. cit., passim), which insist on the non-political character of Leopardi's polemic, regarding which he concludes, bizarrely, that *I Nuovi credenti* has nothing to do with the *Palinode*, the *Paralipomeni*, and *The Broom*. This is totally false, and nothing better demonstrates it than the insertion into the sublime poetry of *The Broom* of an anti-moderate polemic. That said, it would be just as erroneous to consider that the polemic inspires Leopardi's poetry. This would only repeat in different form the ontological undervaluing of Leopardi's poetry that, from an opposite point of view, Benedetto Croce and the moderate authors in general developed.

46. Ibid.

47. Ibid., p. 142–43.

48. Ibid., pp. 143–44.

49. Ibid., p. 144.

50. The concepts of 'common war' and 'strife' are obviously borrowed from the culture of the Enlightenment, or rather from the pessimist strands, which, from the seventeenth century on, characterized Enlightenment materialism. In this regard it is known that Leopardi had access to Thomas Hobbes's thought and to a certain Spinozist atheist and pessimist tradition, probably through Bayle and his *Dictionary*; and those influences reshaped his recollection of ancient materialism. But the essential point (aside from the Spinozian tradition, to which we will return in later notes) lies in the fact that this concept of war and strife is connected to the construction of solidarity and love: this dialectic—which is already the basis of the extremely singular aesthetic solution to the problem of universal strife in Hobbes (see C. Thorpe, *The Aesthetic Theory of Thomas Hobbes* [Ann Arbor: University of Michigan Press, 1940]), and also present in prodigious form in Spinoza's philosophy, and which constitutes one of the fundamental elements of the post-critical materialist perspective—excludes any hasty resolution of the difficulties and perspectives of Leopardi's ultimate philosophy. In particular it excludes the possibility of accepting an Ahrimanesque interpretation such as Carpi's.

N. Badaloni intervenes concisely but with much intelligence and discretion regarding this question ("La cultura," in *Storia d'Italia,* vol. 3, op. cit., in particular pp. 915–26). His argument is as follows: during the first phase of his thought, Leopardi perceives the contradiction between first and second nature, just as the Enlightenment hands it down to us. Then, through a series of fruitless attempts, he seeks to redeem that dialectic. Not succeeding in that, he finds himself constrained to "Stratonism," to the dramatic absorption of first nature into the nullity, artificiality, and vacuity of the second. The awareness of this impasse becomes a critique of the processes that led to this nullification of the world: knowledge [*conoscenza*] of the true, the anxiety of community, and solidarity with social rebellion constitute the route of liberation. The brevity of Badaloni's reading does not permit us to confront it with a complete critique: instead, its importance lies in the positive results it provides. Thus it seems to me that only in the margins could a brief critique be suggested: I think that, in Leopardi, the absorption of first nature into second nature does not correspond to a process of annihilation but rather one of subsumption. In other words, Leopardi accepts the nothingness of second nature as the necessary terrain within which love and solidarity will have to constitute themselves in new forms. The philosophy and poetics of the later Leopardi reveal a progressive dynamic of the collective, as C. Luporini has well demonstrated (*Leopardi progressif*, op. cit., pp. 16, 17–30, then in appendix I and passim) by insisting on the collective dimension, or rather on the conquest of the collective dimension in Leopardi. This collective dimension seems to me more important than the progressive dimension in Luporini.

51. As a complement to the preceding note, it seems pointless here to go back over the religious and particularly the Catholic interpretations of Leopardi's thought; we have sufficiently demonstrated their total inadequacy. Concerning those years, see U. Bosco, *Titanismo e pièta in Leopardi* (Rome: Bonacci, 1980). All that remains is to emphasize a danger inherent in the progressive interpretation, above all in its intermediary and now-canonical form. Let me explain: if the dialectic between first and second nature is interpreted not as a dialectic aimed at less reality but as one aimed at more collectivity or, more precisely, an increase in human wretchedness but also an increase in the force of human imagination, and if this paradox is not fully experienced, then I do not see how it is possible to oppose the reduction of Leopardi's solidarity and love to Christian *caritas*. That is to say that the difference between the two lies in a completely distinct ontological dimension: the theological perspective empties Christian love of the human, while Leopardi's love is filled with human passion and the collective project. The extraordinary modernity of Leopardi's thought lies in having put us face to face with this leap in the structure of being, which Marx elswhere identified in real subsumption: nature is entirely absorbed into history, and a second nature is miserably but potently consolidated. *Hic Rhodus, hic salta!*

52. Let us return to Spinoza. Beyond the remarks concerning the possible Leopardi-Spinoza relationship through the Spinoza entry in Bayle's *Dictionary* (see A. Prete, *Il pensiero poetante*, op. cit., pp. 28–29, 42, 53) and the too-often repeated considerations on Leopardi's "Stratonian" pessimism and Spinozism (again, see Badaloni), here we must recall that the Spinozism that thrives in the centuries of the Enlightenment is not merely negative thought but also appears as positive thought, as a thought of constitution within the development of modern materialism. Aside from my *Savage Anomaly: The Power of Spinoza's Ethics and Politics*, op. cit., see the clues to Leopardi's lively awareness of this tradition in Luporini, *Leopardi progressive*, op. cit. We can only repeat our urgent wish for a history of Spinozism in Italy comparable to what Vernière has provided for France (see note 78 to chapter 4).

53. Obviously the various shades of the progressivist interpretation have tended to focus on these concluding lines, notably the ambiguity regarding

Leopardi's rationalism. The question is evident: to what extent is Leopardi's progressivism a rationalism? For Badaloni, the problem cannot even be posed, and the implicit response is positive—in his measured presentation he avoids confronting this problem, which is no less crucial for him. Nor is this theme posed in problematic terms by Luporini; nevertheless, to my mind the insistence on the collective dimension of Leopardi's thought somewhat modifies the appreciation of his rationalism. Timpanaro, who for his part clearly broaches the problem, introduces a further distinction: pessimism is for him a permanent and constitutive value of Leopardi's thought; hence he tends to undervalue the solidarity perspective of political progressivism in the final canto, thus entering into a polemic with Luporini—but none of this affects Leopardi's scientific rationalism and progressivism (see "Alcune osservazioni sul pensiero di Leopardi," in *Classicismo e illuminismo*, op. cit., pp. 133ff.). B. Biral (*La posizione storica di Giacomo Leopardi*, op. cit., p. 105) speaks explicitly of the ambivalence of the relationship between materialism and the principle of rationality in Leopardi's thought. M.A. Rigoni, whose aim is not progressive but rather, in imitation of his poet, sincerely regressive (*Saggi sul pensiero leopardiano*, op. cit., pp. 36–37), confronts the problem in a manner that is hardly acceptable. Nevertheless it has the merit of explicitly posing the problem and proclaiming, in opposition to the relative hypocrisy that surrounds this question, its centrality.

54. On this theme, see the very important remarks by Renato Pastore ("Aggiunte leopardiane," in *Nuovi argomenti* 2 [1979], pp. 221–36), who, while admitting the ambivalence of Leopardi's definition of the reason-nature relationship noted by Timpanaro and Biral, vindicates its positive value against their claims—that is, he denies that this ambivalence can be negatively understood. There is in Leopardi a hedonist vindication of the body and instinct; this vindication is in no way irrational, but it is simply a function of human nature and the historical condition. Hence "we can assert that the outcome of *The Broom* can be read as an invitation to the conquest of nature against nature, by means of critical reason and against institutional reason."

55. John 3:19. The citation, in Greek and Italian, serves as an epigraph to *The Broom*.

56. Leopardi's sense of the catastrophe naturally remains to be problematized. To my mind, Montesquieu's *Considerations on the Causes of the Greatness of the Romans and their Decline* constitutes Leopardi's fundamental reference, as a result of its emblematic significance in eighteenth-century European culture. He reads this work in 1820. Concerning the general significance of this work that sums up central elements of Enlightenment ideology, see the introduction by Jean Ehrard to the Garnier-Flammarion edition (Paris, 1968), as well as C. Rosso's work, *Montesquieu moralista. Dalle legge al "Bonheur"* (Pisa: Goliardica, 1965). Of course it is a matter not only of this but also of a (totally Romantic) attention to the sense of historical innovation. Now this sense of historical innovation by means of catastrophe exists

in two variants: the first is a pessimist version to which Leopardi obviously adheres in part (and which must be related to the idea of the 'eternal return'); but the idea of catastrophe also comes to Leopardi after having undergone a double modification: as sociological model, for the analysis of political dynamics, and therefore as a practical model of intervention on the one hand; and on the other hand, as natural, materialist model or, in other words, as model of creative articulation, of innovative destruction, in the kingdom of nature to which humankind belongs. Second nature transforms first nature, but without suppressing the laws of its functioning. See note 122 to chapter 1.

57. An idea of the eternal return is perhaps expressed and affirmed in lines 289 to 296. What significance this idea assumes in the complex argument of the canto is discussed in the main text, but what the sources of this philosophical position are is difficult to identify precisely. There do not seem to be philologically verifiable references to this idea; instead it seems to be constructed almost spontaneously in the course of the philosophical and poetic development of Leopardi's thought.

58. The adage "optimism of the will and pessimism of the intellect" appears to me to constitute the ethics corresponding to the relationship constructed by the progressivist interpretation among reason, nature, and history—a relationship, as we have seen, that is totally devoid of foundation. I take the liberty of referring to the article I dedicated to the critique of this aphorism, "Pessimisme de la raison, optimisme de la volonté: Sur l'opportunité raisonnable de renverser cet aphorisme," in *Chemins de ronde*, Nov. 1985.

59. We will never allow ourselves to assert that this position of Leopardi's is either unpolitical or atemporal, but rather directly implicated in the nineteenth-century historical-social thematic, in Italy and in Europe. We consider all the positions that insist upon the unpolitical character of Leopardi's thought to be not so much reactionary positions as false and unrealistic ones. Let us not forget that the era is that of Romanticism. And it matters little to decide if Leopardi can be considered a Romantic in this regard, for what is certain is that he experiences that era, he is subjected to its mental schemas, he reads its great authors, and enjoys some influence. To my mind, Leopardi's Romanticism is debatable: the influences of Enlightenment culture on his thought are too strong; and his adherence to the philosophical problematic of Romanticism, insofar as it is constructed from a particular, marginal, specific viewpoint, is nevertheless a singular adherence. That said, it is beyond doubt that Leopardi has a relationship with the culture of his time that is certainly not partial or defensive; on the contrary, he considers it as a circulation embracing everything. In short, he experiences that "time of the prophets" (according to Paul Bénichou's titular formula, *Temps des prophètes* [Paris: Gallimard, 1977]) in which the "doctrines of the Romantic age" are being globally elaborated. It is primarily the characteristic of totality that makes up the body of Romantic theory,

sensibility, and ideology. Leopardi, whether he is a Romantic or not, is not free of the spirit of the era. Let us turn to politics. It is a fundamental element of Leopardi's positioning with regard to life. Leopardi is not unpolitical—if he is neither liberal nor Mazzinian, neither centrist Catholic nor moderate, and least of all a reactionary or cleric, then what is he? The question cannot be evaded.

60. In "Hölderlin and the Essence of Poetry," (in *Elucidations of Hölderlin's Poetry*, op. cit.), as we have already seen (in note 271 to chapter 3), Heidegger lays out five fundamental assertions concerning Hölderlin and his "poetizing" (which obviously constitute the fundamental reference for Heidegger's aesthetic theory). Rather than repeating them here, we will simply note that they could be applied equally well to Leopardi. But within those common dimensions, a decisive element distinguishes the thought and "poetizing" of these two authors: Leopardi's materialism. Leopardi sets poetry on its feet. In other words, he overturns the order of propositions prescribed by Heidegger for the good writing of poetry. Criticism is undoubtedly the great discriminator of poetry: Hölderlin and Leopardi both experience the theoretical determinations of criticism, but Hölderlin undergoes them as tragedy, experiences the dialectic as an insurmountable condition, as the production of madness, whereas Leopardi experiences criticism as possibility. Leopardi refuses the dialectic while recognizing the necessity of the conditions and the theoretical framework it proposes. In the form of a myth or in the form of second nature, the world appears to both of them as a remade world: but for Hölderlin, it is the gods who remake the world, while for Leopardi it is humankind. We are wretched, unhappy, despairing—nevertheless, the world is there and illusion is a subject; whereas in Hölderlin/Heidegger the subject is prophecy and myth, and its essence clashes with, and upsets, the immediate projection of being. To the metaphysical essence of poetry Leopardi opposes poetic making. In him, poetic making is the accumulation of a long, tragic, painful experience that unfolds in poetry, but also in history and in nature, while in Heidegger (Hölderlin having been sent away and the philosopher remaining alone), poetic making is a shortcut to the apprehension of being. For the Italian, poietics is the highest point of the lived experience of ethical tragedy, while for the German, it is an opaque immersion in being. For Leopardi, it is a construction of the world (of language, of second nature, of history . . .), a step forward; for Heidegger, it is a return.

61. We have called Leopardi a lyric Machiavelli: precisely this passage allows us to grasp once more the truth of this approach, this sign. It is not solely a matter of the will to put artifice in the service of truth (see *Pensiero XXIX*, Di Piero, pp. 69–71); nor is it a matter of seeking virtue everywhere it can be found, always with the suspicion that it is not a matter of virtue and that only practice could demonstrate or redeem it; nor is it a matter finally of having a sense of the proportions and dimensions of the historical clash (as Hegel remarks, emphasizing the absence of triviality from Machiavelli's discourse, "gangrenous limbs cannot be cured by

lavender-water" [*Political Writings*, ed. Laurence Dickey and H.B. Nisbet (Cambridge: Cambridge University Press, 1999), p. 80]); it also involves the fact that Leopardi, like Machiavelli, seeks the origin of the new, the useful, the positive in immediacy.

Machiavelli's thought is a practice of the schematism of reason, a schematism that wants no analytic sorting of the real to help express it, just as Leopardi's thought is a practice of the schematism of reason that seeks to reconstruct a true being, a new being, through poetic passion. Nothing is more dangerous to the identity of both these authors than oblique readings such as those that have been made of Machiavelli by Alfieri, Foscolo, and Hegel. Let us pause a moment over the last, over the democratic Hegel of 1797: the section of "The German Constitution" on Machiavelli's *Prince* and Italy in *Political Writings*, op. cit., pp. 79–83. Here Machiavelli appears as a nationalist politician who struggles rigorously and effectively for his ideal of the state, for his country, against the corruption and delirious blindness of his time, etc., etc. Morality or truth is sometimes sacrificed to this objective, an objective that is in no way unclean but rather praiseworthy.

We find the same reading in Alfieri, in Foscolo (who does not recall the *Sepolcri*?), and perhaps also in Leopardi, when he directly considers Machiavelli's thought (aside from the disfavor with which he looks upon the latter's language, which is too dissimilar and insufficiently accurate), grasping it more in patriotic terms than theoretical ones. But these meager evaluations (and the emphatic rejection of Machiavellianism expressed in the *Zibaldone*, p. 4198, *TO II*, p. 1107; Caesar/D'Intino, p. 1838) must be recognized as the cipher of a paradox. In effect, Leopardi, like Machiavelli, is irreducible to any oblique reading and never himself gives an oblique reading of the real. So-called oblique reading is a crafty reading, a quasi-dialectical one, a hand-crafted dialectic of the real. There is nothing at all of this in Leopardi. The translation of immediacy into truth through the imagination is a rule that he foregrounds and to which he constantly sticks. The apology for immediacy and the discovery of the wealth of its significations give Leopardi's poetry the happiness and joy of ontological power [*potenze*]. This is also valid for Machiavelli.

62. Here it is difficult to construct a bibliography concerning the founding role of poetry in materialist philosophy. Nevertheless, it appears to me worthwhile at least to explain from a subjective viewpoint the references on which I have founded my reflection, a reflection that unites the creative and radically innovative element of ethical experience with the ontological-materialist element. Contact with the Vienna school (Riegl, Wölfflin, Dvorak, etc.) has been fundamental for me and for many authors of my generation. Thanks to those German and central-European authors, the discovery of artistic innovation succeeds in traversing an immense cultural heritage and a dense methodological tradition in order to show, from a formalist perspective, the specificity of the ontological development that the work of art bears within itself.

Concerning this school and the contribution these authors have made to the construction of a materialist (in any case ontological) historiography of art, see W. Warringer, *Künstlerische Zeitfragen* (Munich: Bruckmann, 1921) and K. Mannheim, "On the Interpretation of *Weltanshauung*" (1922), in *Essays on the Sociology of Knowledge* (Oxford: Oxford University Press, 1952), pp. 33–82. The work of Georg Lukács marks a further passage in this materialist and ontological perspective, which coincides with a fundamental transformation of his own thought, from the critique of reification that characterizes the youthful writings, to the rigorously ontological perspective that follows the ambiguous phase of socialist realism. Here the element of innovation that formally characterizes the work of art as such is not only related to ontology but is also identified in the material, social, and constructive activity that constitutes social ontology. The passage between formalism (with the constructivity that is proper to it), expressionism (with the subjective and ontological rooting that is proper to it), and the mature conception of social ontology is absolutely precise and determinate.

The works of Vygodsky and Bakhtin constitute the third fundamental element of this set. In both, within a general framework that is indisputably materialist, creativity is grasped as the basis and problem of all aesthetic discourse— therefore praxis constitutes art. How can this be analyzed productively? Vygodsky responds to this question in physiological terms (this is not the place to examine his proposals, which are nonetheless fundamental for materialist ontology). Bakhtin, for his part, responds by bringing to light the multiple dimensions and reconnecting the plural voices and forms that, in social history, give rise to the demand for poetry and produce it. Contemporary criticism and great avant-garde poetry have studied, reconstructed, and pressed toward a creative repetition the foundational making of poetry that Leopardi as a materialist wanted.

63. G.W.F. Hegel, *Aesthetics*, op. cit., pp. 10–11.

64. K. Marx, *Grundrisse: Introduction to the Critique of Political Economy (Rough Draft)*, trans. Martin Nicolaus (New York: Penguin, 1973), pp. 702ff.; *Capital*, vol. I, trans. Ben Fowkes (New York: Penguin, 1976), appendix "Results of the Immediate Process of Production," pp. 1023–25, 1034–38. Concerning the concept of real subsumption in Marxist theory, see Antonio Negri, *Marx Beyond Marx: Lessons on the Grundrisse*, trans. Harry Cleaver et al. (Brooklyn: Autonomedia, 1991).

65. Marx, *Grundrisse*, op. cit., p. 110.

66. Herbert Marcuse, *The Aesthetic Dimension: Toward a Critique of Marxist Aesthetics* (Boston: Beacon Press, 1978), p. 73.

67. Once again, as in note 62 above, it is extremely difficult to furnish a bibliography that shows how the materialist ontology of aesthetics, of aesthetic making, includes within itself the dimension of collectivity. Here again we will simply list some of the elements that have been important in our understanding of the problem. They consist once again of three groups of authors. The first includes those who study the

consequences of the resolute and definitive linguistic turn stamped upon contemporary philosophy by Wittgenstein, showing how the linguistic phenomenology he describes has at least two determinations: the first is the communicative determination, according to which no language can exist that is not collectively communicative; the second concerns the aesthetic dimension that, at this level of reflection on the constructive character of language, immediately appears. See in this regard De Monticelli, *Dottrine dell'intelligenza. Saggio su Frege e Wittgenstein* (Bari: De Donato, 1982).

A second group of authors develops a transcendental theory of communication around positions expressed most notably by J. Habermas. See in this regard the works of K.O. Appel, N. Luhmann, O. Marquard, E. Tugendhat, as well as Habermas's essay in *Critique* 413 (October 1981), "Vingt ans de pensée allemande." Of course the problem of the transcendentality of language is not, in itself, immediately a problem of the definition of the status of the collective, but the German debate has increasingly unfolded in that direction, fruitfully absorbing the critique of language into the sociological critique of the social.

The third group of authors who seem to us essential for clarifying the collective dimension of materialist ontology are those who follow the lead of Gilles Deleuze. Here the ontological level itself is immediately characterized in collective terms, and the surface that is to be deciphered appears as a set of structures composed equally of subjects and of languages. See Vincent Descombes, *Modern French Philosophy*, trans. L. Scott-Fox and J.M. Harding (Cambridge: Cambridge University Press, 1980), op. cit. Thus three strands of thought that, in different cultural areas and on the basis of distinct problematic horizons and diverse scientific traditions, grasp the complete socialization of the ontological problem.

68. We owe the definition of the relationship between historical evolution and the moment of rupture, between historicism, collectivism and *Jetzt-Zeit* above all to Walter Benjamin's theses "On the Concept of History," in Benjamin, *Selected Writings*, vol. 4, 1938–1940, ed. Howard Eiland and Michael W. Jennings (Cambridge: Harvard University Press, 2003), pp. 389–400.

69. On this question Luporini's approach (in *Leopardi progressivo*, op. cit., pp. 49ff.) seems highly important and particularly apt to me. He shows how strong the influence of revolutionary thought was on Leopardi, and how "historical disillusion" constituted a decisive element, not of a reactionary conversion, but rather of self-control, reflection, verification: historical disillusion contributes to sustaining Leopardi's positive evaluation of the revolution. Consequently, on another—directly metaphysical—level, the historical crisis is not transposed into the ontological crisis. Luporini judiciously compares Leopardi's thought with that of certain nineteenth-century existentialists, notably Kierkegaard. Whereas the latter shifts the historical crisis into the metaphysical crisis, thus attaining, if not consolation, at least the repose that religious feelings confer, Leopardi maintains his humanist conception

and preserves its constructive project. "Leopardi dissolved his vitalism into nihilism in the most consistent way possible. But it is precisely here that the decisive point for an overall judgment on Leopardi is situated: unlike modern existentialism, his nihilism is never accompanied by any complacency whatsoever, just as his materialism was free of all perplexity" (p. 69). "Materialism, having vanquished all resistance, thus becomes the dominant theoretical motive" (p. 75). Whatever our evaluation of the nihilism-materialism relationship in Leopardi may be (and for us it is more articulated than Luporini conceives), it is nonetheless essential to emphasize the persistence of the revolutionary theoretical intuition in Leopardi's philosophy.

70. A. Prete, *Il pensiero poetante*, op. cit., p. 88.

> If in Hölderlin, as in other German Romantic poets, this dialogue is spoken on the threshold of a relationship with the sacred and traces the contours of Dionysian territory which is then traversed again and "completed" by Nietzsche, in Leopardi, whose gaze is fixed on the tumultuous reasoning of the French Enlightenment, this dialogue is first of all a disarticulation of the power [*potere*] of a *ratio* that, by dispossessing the passions and illusions, claims to pursue the perfection of civilization in the name of a "perfecting" of humankind.

We certainly agree with this reflection and others, although we regret that A. Prete does not historicize this difference, does not grasp its historical determination, the bifurcation in the crisis of dialectical thought.

71. Such an interpretation is laid out above all in the work of F.P. Botti, which is also essential in other ways; see his *La nobiltà del poeta* (Naples: Liguori, 1979). In agreement with Botti, U. Carpi (*Il poeta e la politica*, op. cit.) insists upon the "absence à la Epictetus" for which Leopardi opts during the period that extends from the *Operette morali* to the great *Idylls*. By extension, this stoicism remains a constant of Leopardi's thought, the more so the more it is confronted with the power [*potenza*] of Ahriman. Consequently, on the basis of this assumption, what will Leopardi's political position be? "Leopardi seeks to found a *philosophical* fraternity among men, a sort of democracy of pain" (p. 167, but already on pp. 148 and passim). *Sic!*

72. On this score we seem to be in agreement with H.R. Jauss, *Aesthetic Experience and Literary Hermeneutics*, op. cit.

73. Some interpreters who grasp this force of rupture in Leopardi nevertheless insist upon denying it any historical substrate, on making its dimension solely philosophical and not historical-political—from Croce's "idyllic poet" we pass to the "marginalized philosopher." Carpi's reading (*Il poeta e la politica*, op. cit.) is a particularly lively representative of this type of interpretation; see pp. 120–25 on Leopardi's marginality; pp. 139–56 on the uprooted poet; pp. 172ff. on the deep, consubstantial disharmony between Leopardi's thought and the history of his time. Just one example:

We see how for Leopardi philosophy will one day become a positive tool and
nature a negative principle; but behind the screen of these radical "philosophical" variations, the authentic root of Leopardi's entire ideology will remain
immutable, that is, the need to justify and at the same time hide his own social
marginalization by means of a judgment of guilt turned against the "world" and
its pathologically distorted structure. (p. 124)

Here not even the force of philosophical rupture is ultimately preserved—
so that this interpretation seems to undermine, in a merely journalistic way, the
lively polemic launched by Carpi against the interpretations of the Frankfurt School
(pp. 97, 248, 249, and passim).

74. The reference is to the arguments developed earlier regarding the thought
of the Ideologues in France and the Hegelian left in Germany. I just want to add
one further remark in order to prevent my claim about "those who flirted with the
dialectic" from being misinterpreted with regard to the Ideologues. In his works
which are so valuable and important for clarifying the philosophical turn at the end
of the eighteenth century (*Il tramonto dell'illuminismo* [Bari: Laterza, 1968] and
Il pensiero degli ideologues. Scienza e filosofia in Francia 1780–1815 [Florence:
La Nuova Italia, 1974]), S. Moravia has shown how, despite a remarkable thematic
continuity (that of sensualism), the Ideologues also confronted a dialectical thematic
in the broad sense with a surreptitiously dialectical method. The thought of Victor
Cousin and his school that concludes the Ideological episode represents in my view
the appearance of a Hegelian right, *more gallico*, that reveals the oneness of the
deep fabric of the philosophical transformation occurring during those years all
over Europe.

75. G. Bollati (preface to the *Chrestomathia in prosa*, op. cit., pp. xciii–xcv)
insists with great clarity and efficacy on the correspondences between Leopardi's
theory and the historical problematic to which it is subject. The fact that Leopardi,
as Luporini notes, was on a "longer wavelength [*un'onda più lunga*]" than the politicians of the *Risorgimento* merely means that he considers the *Risorgimento* from a
higher viewpoint. We know how he was thanked for this: by continual falsifications
of his thought, by an incomprehension and a refusal that made him into "an accursed
poet of the bourgeois era." Nevertheless, "his vital force resides in the irreducibly
Cassandra-like obstinacy of his admonitions in posing the final choice: either the
advent of the human kingdom or a demented *Endlösung*."

76. To supplement what was extensively developed in the first chapters of this
book and the references mentioned there, here let us recall, concerning the theme
of the indifference of contradictions (whether from the theoretical viewpoint or the
historical one, whether between rationalism and Romanticism or between egoism
and heroism, among restoration, revolution, and revival, etc.), what C. Luporini
writes (*Leopardi progressif*, op. cit., pp. 8ff., 79ff., and passim): clearly this in no

way involves what today is called "indifferentism [*qualunquismo*]." Indifference constitutes at once a plague and a horizon, a malady and its terrible propagation. It sketches a universe: Luporini calls that universe one of "historical disillusion," whereas I would describe it as postmodern—but isn't that too the fruit of historical disillusion?

77. E. De Angelis ("La riconstruzione della realtà nell'opera di Giacomo Leopardi," in *Studi sull'illuminismo* 4 [Siena: University of Siena, 1976]) seems to me to have perceived with great acuity the negative dialectic that traverses the relationship between nature and reason in Leopardi's work, by retracing the sense of the ontological alternative as the solution to this dualism. But in De Angelis this ontological tension is not deployed in the sense of ethical, metaphysical rupture. The analysis remains at the dialectical level instead of unfolding to follow the structural travail of ontology—in other words, the subjective dimension.

78. I permit myself to refer to reflections that I developed at some length concerning the theme of ethical-political dualism, rupture, and the surmounting of the dialectic in *Macchina tempo. Rompicapi costituzione liberazione*, op. cit., and in *Il comunismo e la guerra* (Milan: Feltrinelli, 1980).

79. Such are the principal determinations of the "oldest systematic program" of German idealism:

> . . . *an ethics*. Inasmuch as the whole of metaphysics will in the future be subsumed under *moral philosophy*—a matter in which Kant, with his two practical postulates, has merely provided an *example*, and has exhausted nothing—this ethics will [contain] be nothing other than a complete system of all ideas, or, which comes to the same, of all practical postulates. The first idea is of course the representation *of me myself* as an absolutely free creature. At the same time, along with the free, self-conscious creature, a whole *world* comes to the fore—out of nothing—the sole true and conceivable *creation out of nothing*.—Here I shall alight on the field of physics. . . . From nature I shall advance to the *works of mankind*. First of all, the idea of humanity—I want to show that there is no idea of the *state*, because the state is something *mechanical*; just as little is there an idea of a *machine*. Only that which is an object of *freedom* is called an *idea*. Thus we must also proceed beyond the state!—For every state has to to treat free human beings like mechanical cogwheels; and it should not be so; hence it should *cease*. [. . .] And at the very end, the idea that unifies all, the idea of *beauty*. (*The Oldest Program toward a System in German Idealism*, op. cit., pp. 22–24.)

80. Marx, *Grundrisse*, op. cit., p. 111.

81. In this regard, in the conclusion of his work (*Leopardi progressif*, op. cit.) Luporini justifiably speaks of "anthropodicy"; the very term takes us back to the

heroic Enlightenment thought of Lessing, but clearly tempered in the new Romantic sensibility. From this viewpoint, we must emphasize that the numerous analogies, sometimes literal ones, which exist between Leopardi the theoretician of modern poetics and ancient poetry and the Schiller of the aesthetic essays (regarding them, see P. Szondi, *La poésie et la poétique de l'idéalisme allemand*, op. cit., pp. 47ff.: "Sur la dialectique des concepts dans l'essai *De la poésie naïve et de la poésie sentimentale* de Schiller") do not touch on the substance of Leopardi's treatment, which remains creatively linked to the theoretical revolution and the individual ascesis of Enlightenment thought—precisely that of Lessing.

Index of Leopardi's Works

✤

Index of Names and Terms